**LANGENSCHEIDT'S
POCKET
DICTIONARIES**

LANGENSCHEIDT'S POCKET GREEK DICTIONARY

CLASSICAL GREEK-ENGLISH

By
DR. KARL FEYERABEND

LANGENSCHEIDT

PREFACE

This Pocket Dictionary is not intended to compete with any of the larger Lexicons, but as it contains all the words which occur in the selections commonly read in schools, and also those of the Greek New Testament, it will perhaps prove useful to beginners, and may also lend occasional service to more advanced students.

Those who use the book should observe that, as a rule, the quantity of doubtful vowels (α, ι, υ) is only indicated when these are long (ᾱ, ῑ, ῡ); when they are short, the mark of quantity is omitted, except in some special cases. Where no mark is found, it is to be assumed that they are short.

As the Substantives ending in -εύς regularly form Genitive in -έως, this termination has been omitted. This applies also to the words ending in -ις with the Genitive in -εως. Unless some other form, such as -ιδος, -ιος, is given, the form in -εως is to be taken for granted.

Some Remarks
on the History of Greek Sounds

As the Greek language, though its tradition is unbroken from Homer and Hesiod down to its present form of Romaic or Modern Greek, has gone through marked changes in grammar and vocabulary, its pronunciation as a living tongue has, in the course of so many centuries, suffered no less considerable alterations.

When in the 15th century, after a long eclipse, the knowledge and study of Greek was once more brought within the intellectual horizon of the western nations of Europe by Byzantine scholars driven from their country, the bearers of the new learning brought with them the mode of pronunciation to which they were accustomed. But soon the observation forced itself on western students that the Byzantine pronunciation was at a wide distance from the written tradition of the language, and did not correspond to the sounds which people were accustomed to give to Greek words in their Latin form, such as *ecclesia* or *alphabetum*. And when it was found out that many passages in ancient authors pointed to another pronunciation, there arose strong doubts as to the authority of Byzantine tradition. Already in 1512, Aldus Manutius the Elder published a small treatise on the faulty pronunciation of some vowels and diphthongs; but the chief champion for a more correct rendering of Greek sounds was the famous Desiderius Erasmus. Though in his own practice he still adhered to the traditional method, yet his (Latin) Dialogue on the right pronunciation of the Latin and Greek languages, 1528, furnished for the first time scientific arguments for the fact that the phonetic system of the period of Plato must have been widely different from that of the Byzantines.

In England, the views of Erasmus, who was a reformer only in word, not in deed, were carried into practical effect by John Cheke and Thos. Smith. Sir J. Cheke, professor of Greek at Cambridge and one of the tutors of the prince, afterwards Edward VI, is chiefly distinguished for his exertions in introducing the study of Greek language and literature into his country. But having dictated to his pupils a certain mode of pronouncing, he was violently assailed on that account by Stephen Gardiner, bishop of Winchester, then Chancellor of the University. Yet, notwithstanding the veto of this arbitrary prelate, the system of Cheke prevailed, and still prevails. Gardiner had strictly forbidden the distinction between αι and ε; ει, οι and ι in pronouncing under penalty of expulsion from the University (1542).

On the Continent, at the close of the 16th century, the Erasmians had made good their case at all the chief seats of classical learning, led by such men as Theodore Beza and Henry Estienne (Stephanus). In all the schools and universities of Europe the so-called Erasmian pronunciation is in use, only modified by the peculiar phonetic systems of the different languages; and at present the modern Greeks are the only nation that apply the sounds of their vernacular speech to the language of their forefathers.

Specimen of modern Greek pronunciation
(the opening lines of Homer's Iliad):

Μῆνιν ἄειδε, θεά, Πηληιάδεω Ἀχιλῆος
mī'nin ai'dhę thęá' pilī'iadhᵉǫ'   aφili'ǫs

οὐλομένην, ἣ μυρί' Ἀχαιοῖς ἄλγε' ἔθηκεν,
ū'lǫmęnī'n   i   mī'rī   aφi'is   a'lyę   ᶕthī'kᶕn

πολλὰς δ' ἰφθίμους ψυχὰς Ἄιδι προΐαψεν
pǫ'las   dh i'fthimū's psiφa's aidhi' prǫia'psęn

ἡρώων, αὐτοὺς δὲ ἑλώρια τεῦχε κύνεσσιν
i'rǫǫ'n   aftū's dhę ᶕlǫ'ria   tᶕ'fφᶕ   kinᶕ'sin

οἰωνοῖσί τε πᾶσι. Διὸς δ' ἐτελείετο βουλή
i'ǫni'sī   tᶕ pa'si dhiǫ's dh ᶕtᶕli'ǝtǫ   vū'lī

ἐξ οὗ δὴ τὰ πρῶτα διαστήτην ἐρίσαντε
ᶕ'ks ū dhī' tᶕ   prǫ'tᶕ   dhia'stītī'n ᶕrisa'ntᶕ

Ἀτρεΐδης τε ἄναξ ἀνδρῶν καὶ δῖος Ἀχιλλεύς.
a'trᶕidhī's tᶕ ana'ks andhrǫ'n kᶕ dhi'ǫs   aφi'lᶕfs.

Specimen of the usual pronunciation of Greek in England.

Μῆνιν ἄειδε, θεά, Πηληιάδεω Ἀχιλῆος
mī'nin āäī'dġ̣ theō' pīlī'iādyō' akil[jōs

οὐλομένην, ἣ μυρί' Ἀχαιοῖς ἄλγε' ἔθηκεν,
aūlŏmĕnī'n hī mjū'ri akaiŏis a'lgĕ ĕthī'kĕn

πολλὰς δ' ἰφθίμους ψυχὰς Ἄιδι προΐαψεν
pŏ'llās d ifthaīmaūs psjükā's eidāi prŏia'psĕ̱̄ɛ

ἡρώων, αὐτοὺς δὲ ἑλώρια τεῦχε κύνεσσιν
hī'rŏō'n ataū's dġ̣ hĕlō'riä tjū'kġ̣ kjünĕ̱̄'sin

οἰωνοῖσί τε πᾶσι. Διὸς δ' ἐτελείετο βουλή
ŏī'ŏnŏī'si tġ̣ pä'si dalŏ's d ĕtĕlaī'ġ̣tŏ bäū'lī

ἐξ οὗ δὴ τὰ πρῶτα διαστήτην ἐρίσαντε
ɛ'ks haū dī' tä prŏ'tä diastītī'n ġ̣risä'ntŏ

Ἀτρεΐδης τε ἄναξ ἀνδρῶν καὶ δῖος Ἀχιλλεύς.
a'traīdī's tġ̣ anä'ks andrŏ'n kaī daī'ŏs aki'ljūs.

(*Hom. Il. I, 1—7.*)

Key to the Transcription.

ạ deep a, half-long, French *bas*.	ǫ open o, half-long, as in French *homme*.
ā = aw in *law*.	
a = a in *can*.	ŏ open o, short, French *poste*.
a = a in *far*.	ū close u, long, as in *true, fool*.
ē = a in *fate*.	jū = u in *music*.
ẹ open e, half-long ⎫ as in ⎬ *bet, chess*.	aī = i in *mine*.
ĕ „ „ short ⎭	aū = ow in *how*.
I = ee in *keen*.	ŏī = oi in *coin*.
i = i in *mint*.	dh = th in *this*.
ị close i, half-long, as in French *dit*.	g as in *get*.
ĭ close i, short, as in French *histoire*.	th = th in *think*.
	v = v in *very*.
ō = o in *note*.	y = y in *year*.
ŏ = o in *not*.	ḥ = ch in Germ. *ach*.
	ç = ch in Germ. *ich*.

A

Α, α (ἄλφα) first letter of the alphabet; as a numeral α' = 1, ‚α = 1000.

ᾱ́ Dor. = ἡ; ᾱ̓ Dor. = ῆ.

ἅ, ἇᾶ int. ah, alas, woe.

ἀ-άᾱτος 2 invulnerable, inviolated; infallible.

ἀ-αγής 2 unbroken; infrangible.

ἄ-απτος 2 untouched; unapproachable.

ἀ-άσχετος 2 = ἄσχετος.

ἀάω, ἀάζω to hurt, infatuate, befool.

ἀ-βᾰκέω to be unknowing or insuspicious.

ἀ-βᾰρής 2 not burdensome.

ἀ-βᾰσάνιστος 2 unexamined, untested. [ent.

ἀ-βᾰσίλευτος 2 independ-

ἄ-βᾰτος 2 impassible; inaccessible; consecrated.

ἀ-βέβαιος 2 unsure, unsteady, precarious.

ἀ-βελτερίᾱ, ἡ silliness; awkwardness. [stupid.

ἀ-βέλτερος 3 and 2 silly,

ἀ-βίωτος 2 not worth living, intolerable.

ἀ-βλᾰβής 2 innoxious, harmless; unhurt. [unused.

ἀ-βλής, ῆτος not yet shot,

ἄ-βλητος 2 unwounded.

ἀ-βληχρός 3 weak, delicate; slow.

ἀ-βουλέω to be unwilling.

ἀ-βούλητος 2 involuntary; undesired.

ἀ-βουλίᾱ, ἡ thoughtlessness; helplessness.

ἄ-βουλος 2 unadvised; careless. [voluptuary.

ἁβρο-δίαιτος 2 weakling,

ἄ-βρομος 2 roaring, noisy.

ἁβρός 3 luxurious; delicate, weak; elegant.

ἁβροσύνη, ἁβρότης, ἡ luxuriousness; elegance.

ἀ-βροτάζω to miss, fail.

ἄ-βροτος 3 and 2 immortal; divine; holy.

ἁβρύνω to spoil; to adorn; M. to boast.

ἀ-βυσσος 2 unfathomable; abyss, nether world.

ἀγάζομαι see ἄγαμαι.

ἀγαθο-εργίᾱ, ἡ deserving deed.

ἀγαθο-εργός, ὁ benefactor.

ἀγαθός 3 good, proper; apt; useful; brave, strong; noble, well-born; wise; honest, righteous; patriotic. — τὸ ἀγαθόν the good, good fortune; welfare; benefit, interest. [bounty.

ἀγαθωσύνη, ἡ goodness,

ἀγαίομαι = ἄγαμαι.

ἀγά-κλεής 2, ἀγα-κλειτός 3, ἀγα-κλῠτός 3 highly renowned, glorious, illustrious.

ἀγαλλιάω and *M.* to rejoice. shout.

ἀγάλλω to adorn, glorify; *P.* to glory, exult.

ἄγαλμα, τό ornament; splendid work; statue.

ἀγαλματο-ποιός, ὁ sculptor.

ἄγαμαι *P.* to wonder, stare; to admire, praise; to annoy; to be jealous; to be indignant or angry. [ingly.]

ἀγαμένως *adv.* approv-

ἄ-γαμος 2 unmarried; ill-fated. [too much.]

ἄγᾶν *adv.* much; entirely;

ἀγανακτέω to be uneasy, vexed, or discontented.

ἀγανακτητός 3 irritating.

ἀγάν-νιφος 2 covered with snow. [cheering.]

ἀγανός 3 friendly, gentle;

ἀγᾶνο-φροσύνη, ἡ gentleness, meekness.

ἀ, ἀνό - φρων 2 tender-hearted, meek.

ἀγάομαι = ἄγαμαι.

ἀγαπάζω (and *M.*), ἀγᾶπάω to welcome; to treat kindly; to love, esteem; to be contented, to acquiesce.

ἀγάπη, ἡ love, charity; agape.

ἀγαπ-ήνωρ, ορος manly.

ἀγαπητός 3 beloved; amiable; welcome; sufficient;

ἀγαπητῶς sufficiently; scarcely.

ἀγά-ρροος (-ρους) 2 gushing vigorously.

ἀγά-στονος 2 rushing vehemently.

ἀγαστός 3 admirable.

ἀ-γαυός 3 illustrious; high, noble. [proud.]

ἀ-γαυρός 3 admirable;

ἀγγᾶρεύω to send as courier. [mail-service.]

ἀγγάρ ιον, τό Persian

ἄγγαρος, ἀγγαρήιος, ὁ courier, riding postman.

ἀγγεῖον, τό vessel, receptacle. urn. [order.]

ἀγγελίᾶ, ἡ message, news;

ἀγγελίης, ὁ messenger.

ἀγγελιη-φόρος, ὁ message-bearer; chamberlain.

ἀγγέλλω to announce, report; to tell, order.

ἄγγελμα, τό = ἀγγελία.

ἄγγελος, ὁ, ἡ messenger; envoy; angel.

ἀγγήιον, τό and ἄγγος, τό = ἀγγεῖον. [come!]

ἄγε, ἄγετε well then! up!

ἀγείρω to gather, collect; to ask alms.

ἀγελαῖος 3 gregarious, forming a flock.

ἀγε-λείη, ἡ driver or dispenser of booty. [band.]

ἀγέλη, ἡ herd. flock; troop,

ἀγεληδόν *adv.* in herds.

ἀ-γενεᾶ-λόγητος 2 without pedigree.

ἀ-γένειος 2 beardless.

ἀ-γενής, ἀ-γεννής 2 unborn; not noble, plebeian, mean, unmanly.

ἀ-γένητος, ἀ-γέννητος 2 unborn, uncreated; ignoble, mean.

ἀ-γέραστος 2 without a gift of honour, disregarded.

ἄγερσις, ἡ collection, gathering.

ἀγέρωχος 2 valiant, gallant; impetuous.

ἄ-γευστος 2 untasted; inexperienced.

ἄγη, ἡ astonishment; envy.

ἀγ-ηλατέω to banish.

ἀγ-ηνορίη, ἡ manliness; haughtiness.

ἀγ-ήνωρ, ορος manly, magnanimous; haughty.

ἀ-γήραος 2, ἀγήρᾱτος 2. ἀγήρως, ων not ageing. imperishable.

ἀγητός 3 = ἀγαστός.

ἁγιάζω, ἁγίζω to consecrate.

ἁγιασμός, ὁ sanctification.

ἁγῑνέω to lead; to carry, convey. [rable.]

ἅγιος 3 holy, sacred. vene-

ἁγιότης, ἡ, ἁγιωσύνη, ἡ holiness, sanctity.

ἀγκάζομαι M. to lift up (in the arms), to embrace.

ἀγ-καλέω = ἀνακαλέω.

ἀγκάλη, ἡ, ἀγκαλίς, ίδος, ἡ, ἀγκοίνη, ἡ elbow, bent arm.

ἀγκάς adv. in the arms.

ἄγκιστρον, τό fishing-hook.

ἀγ-κλίνω = ἀνακλίνω.

ἄγκος, τό ravine, glen.

ἀγ-κρεμάννῡμι = ἀνακρεμάννῡμι. [thong.]

ἀγκύλη, ἡ bend, loop, noose;

ἀγκυλο-μήτης, ου cunning, deceitful, artful.

ἀγκύλος 3 crooked, curved.

ἀγκυλό-τοξος 2 with curved bow. [crooked beak.]

ἀγκυλο-χείλης, ου with

ἄγκῡρα, ἡ anchor; support.

ἀγκών, ῶνος, ὁ curve, bend; elbow; projection; glen.

ἀγλαΐα, ἡ splendour, pomp, magnificence; delight; pride. [make a show.]

ἀγλαΐζομαι to shine, to

ἀγλάϊσμα, τό ornament.

ἀγλαό-καρπος 2 bearing splendid fruit.

ἀγλαός 3 splendid, shining; magnificent.

ἀγλα-ώψ, ῶπος bright, beaming.

ἄ-γλωσσος 2 barbarous, foreign. [not fulled.]

ἄ-γναφος 2 not carded,

ἁγνεία, ἡ purity, chastity.

ἁγνεύω to be pure or chaste; to abhor.

ἁγνίζω to purify, expiate.

ἁγνισμός, ὁ purification, expiation.

ἀ-γνοέω to ignore, not to know; to mistake; to overlook, to wink at; to doubt; to err unconsciously-

ἀ-γνόημα, τό, ἀ-γνοια, ἡ ignorance; indiscernible-ness; mistake.

ἁγνός 3 pure, chaste; holy, sacred; purifying.

ἁγνότης, ἡ purity.

ἄγνῡμι to break (in pieces).

ἀ-γνωμονέω to act thoughtlessly.

ἀ-γνωμοσύνη, ἡ want of judgment, imprudence; misunderstanding; obstinacy; regardlessness.

ἀ-γνώμων 2 imprudent; regardless, unfair; obstinate; not knowing, mistaking.

ἀ-γνώ...ῶτος unknown,

1 *

strange; not knowing, ignorant.

ἀ-γνωσίᾱ, ἡ ignorance; [obscurity.]

ἄ-γνωστος, ἄγνωτος 2 unknown; unrecognisable, unintelligible.

ἄ-γονος 2 unborn; childless; barren.

ἀγορά, ἡ meeting, congregation, assembly; council; speech; eloquence; market-place, market; victuals; commerce, trade.

ἀγοράζω to frequent a market-place; to buy or sell (in the market).

ἀγοραῖος 2 belonging to a public assembly or a market; street-lounger.

ἀγορά-νόμος, ὁ surveyor of the market.

ἀγοράομαι to speak in an assembly or publicly; to tell, order. [purveyor.]

ἀγοραστής, οῦ, ὁ buyer,

ἀγορεύω = ἀγοράομαι.

ἀγορῆθεν adv. from an assembly.

ἀγορήνδε adv. into an assembly.

ἀγορητής, οῦ, ὁ public speaker, orator.

ἀγορητύς, ύος, ἡ gift of speaking.

ἀγός, ὁ leader, captain.

ἄγος[1], τό abomination, blood-guiltiness, crime; expiation. capital

ἄγος[2], τό reverence, awe.

ἀγοστός, ὁ palm of the hand. [capture, game.]

ἄγρα, ἡ chase, hunting;

ἀ-γράμματος 2 unlettered

ἄ-γραπτος 2 unwritten.

ἀγρ-αυλέω to dwell in the open air.

ἀγρ-αυλος 2 dwelling in the fields, rural. [neutral.]

ἄ-γραφος 2 unwritten;

ἀγρευτής, οῦ, ὁ hunter.

ἀγρεύω, ἀγρέω to hunt, catch; ἄγρει, ἀγρεῖτε up! come on!

ἀγριαίνω to grow angry.

ἀγρι-έλαιος, ἡ wild olive, oleaster.

ἄγριος 3 rural; wild; brutal, cruel; malignant; furious, passionate.

ἀγριότης, ητος, ἡ wildness, rudeness.

ἀγριό-φωνος 2 with a harsh voice.

ἀγριόω to infuriate; P. to grow angry, enraged, or cruel. [in the fields.]

ἀγρο-βότης, ου, ὁ feeding

ἀγρόθεν adv. from the field or country.

ἀγρ-οικίᾱ, ἡ rusticity, boorishness.

ἄγρ-οικος or ἀγρ-οῖκος 2 rustic, boorish, churlish: untilled.

ἀγροιώτης = ἀγρότης.

ἀγρόνδε adv. to the country.

ἀγρο-νόμος 2 living in the country; agriculturist.

ἀγρό-νομος 2 used for pasture. [estate, farm.]

ἀγρός, ὁ field, arable land;

ἀγρότερος 3 wild; country-loving.

ἀγρότης, ου, ὁ countryman, rustic. [or awake.]

ἀγρ-υπνέω to be sleepless

ἀγρ-υπνίᾱ, ἡ sleeplessness.

ἄγρ-υπνος 2 sleepless, wakeful.

ἀγρώσσω to hunt, catch.

ἄγρωστις, ἡ field-grass, green provender. [street.]

ἀγυιά, ἡ way, road, path,

ἀγυιεύς, ὁ protector of the roads (Apollo).

ἀ-γύμναστος 2 untrained, unskilled; unplagued.

ἄγυρις, ἡ congregation, meeting; troop.

ἀγυρτάζω to beg, collect.

ἀγύρτης, ου, ὁ beggar, tramp; buffoon.

ἀγχέ-μαχος 2 fighting hand to hand.

ἄγχι adv. and prp. near, at hand, close by; comp. ἆσσον, ἀσσοτέρω, sup. ἄγχιστα. [sea-girt.]

ἀγχί-αλος 2 near the sea;

ἀγχι-βαθής 2 deep near the shore. [to the gods.]

ἀγχί-θεος 2 godlike, akin

ἀγχι-μαχητής, οῦ = ἀγχέμαχος. [close to.]

ἀγχί-μολον adv. near,

ἀγχί-νοια, ἡ presence of mind, sagacity.

ἀγχί-νοος 2 ready of mind, ingenious. [bouring.]

ἀγχί-πτολις, ὁ, ἡ neigh-

ἀγχιστεία (-στεία), ἡ near relationship; succession.

ἀγχιστεύς, ὁ next of kin; heir apparent.

ἀγχιστήρ, ῆρος, ὁ accomplice. [gether.]

ἀγχιστῖνος 3 close to-

ἀγχί-στροφος 2 quick-changing.

ἀγχόθεν adv. from near.

ἀγχόθι adv. = ἄγχι.

ἀγχόνη, ἡ throttling, strangulation; rope.

ἀγχοῦ adv. near; comp. ἀγχότερος; sup., adv. ἀγχότατα, ἀγχοτάτω nearest.

ἄγχω to throttle, strangle.

ἀγχ-ώμαλος 2 nearly equal, undecided.

ἄγω trans. to lead away, off, on, towards, to conduct, drive, bring, convey, fetch, to take along: to estimate; to direct, command, rule, instruct, guide; to keep (a festival), to spend. — intr. to march, move, pass. — M. to lead or take (on, along) with one or for oneself.

ἀγωγεύς, ὁ conveyer, forwarder.

ἀγωγή, ἡ abduction, transport, the leading away; departure, march; a leading, direction; education, discipline; manner of life.

ἀγώγιμος 2 transportable (τὰ ἀ-α cargo); outlawed.

ἀγωγός, ὁ, ἡ leader, guide.

ἀγών, ῶνος, ὁ assembly; meeting-place, place of combat, arena, lists; prize-combat, contest; lawsuit; exertion, labour, struggle, danger. [ϑέτης.]

ἀγων-άρχης, ου = ἀγωνο-

ἀγωνία, ἡ struggle, contention, labour; fear, agony.

ἀγωνιάω to vie, compete, cope; to be irritated or harassed.

ἀγωνίζομαι to fight, contend; to carry on a law-suit; to speak publicly; to strive, to exert oneself.

ἀγώνιος 2 belonging to a (prize-)combat.

ἀγώνισις, ἡ combat.

ἀγώνισμα, τό contest; law-suit; prize, splendid or showy thing; exploit, bravery.   [competition.]

ἀγωνισμός, ὁ contention.

ἀγωνιστής, οῦ, ὁ prize-fighter, rival, champion; advocate, defender.

ἀγωνο-θετέω to arrange a prize-combat; to (act as) umpire.

ἀγωνο-θέτης, ὁ arranger of combat, umpire.

ἀδαγμός, ὁ an itching, biting.

ἀ-δαημονίη, ἡ ignorance, inexperience.   [norant.]

ἀ-δαήμων, ἀδαής 2 ig-

ἀ-δάκρῦτος 2 tearless; unwept; adv. ἀδακρυτί.

ἀδαμάντινος 2 and 3 of steel, steely.

ἀ-δάμας, αντος, ὁ steel.

ἀ-δάμαστος, ἀ-δάματος 2 untamed; invincible, inexorable; unwedded.

ἀ-δάπανος 2 gratuitous.

ἄ-δαστος 2 not yet distributed.

ἀδδεής = ἀδεής.

ἀδδέω = ἀλέω.

ἄδδην = ἄδην.

ἀ-δεής 2 fearless, undaunted; impudent; safe, dangerless; unpunished.

ἄδεια, ἡ fearlessness, secu-

rity; impunity, safe-conduct; permission, liberty; latitude.

ἀ-δειής = ἀδεής.

ἀ-δείμαντος 2 intrepid.

ἄ-δειπνος 2 dinnerless, unfed.   [cide.]

ἀδελφεο-κτόνος, ὁ fratri-

ἀδελφή, ἡ sister.

ἀδελφιδέος, ἀδελφιδοῦς, ὁ nephew.

ἀδελφιδῆ, ἡ niece.

ἀδελφός 3 brotherly, fellow-like; coupled; ὁ brother.

ἀδελφότης, ητος, ἡ brotherhood.

ἄ-δερκτος 2 not seeing.

ἄ-δεσμος 2 unfettered.

ἀ-δευκής 2 bitter, unkind; ignominious.

ἀ-δέψητος 2 untanned.

ἀδέω to be satiated; to surfeit.   [or at a loss.]

ἀ-δηλέω to be uncertain

ἄ-δηλος 2 unseen, invisible, secret, obscure, dark; unknown; uncertain.

ἀ-δηλότης, ητος, ἡ uncertainty.

ἀδημονέω to be uneasy, distressed, or haunted.

ἄδην, ἄδην (ἄδδην) adv enough, sufficiently, abundantly, to the fill.

ἀ-δῆος 2 uninfested.

ἀ-δήριτος 2 unfought, undisputed.

Ἅιδης, ου, ὁ Hades; the nether world.

ἀδη-φάγος 2 voracious, devouring.

ἀ-δῄωτος 2 unwasted.

ἀ-διάβατος 2 impassable.

ἀ-διάκρῐτος 2 indiscernible.

ἀ-διάλειπτος 2 incessant, continuous.   [cilable.]

ἀ-διάλλακτος 2 irrecon-]

ἀ-διάλῠτος 2 indissoluble.

ἀ-διάφθαρτος 2, ἰδιάφθορος 2 incorruptible; unbribable; imperishable.

ἀ-διήγητος 2 indescribable.

ἀδῐκέω to act unjustly or lawlessly; to sin; to be wrong; to injure, wrong, maltreat; to offend. — P. to be wronged.

ἀδίκημα, τό, ἀδικίᾱ, ἡ, ἀδίκιον, τό wrong, injury; offenc ; undue gain.

ἄ-δῐκος 2 unjust, unlawful; dishonest; wrong, foul; unserviceable.

ἀδῑνός, ἀδῐνός 3 agitated, vehement, loud, sonorous, restless, palpitating; copious, crowded.   [lated.]

ἀ-διόρθωτος 2 not regu-]

ἀ-δμής, ῆτος and ἄ-δμητος uncurbed; unmarried.

ἀ-δόκητος 2 unexpected.

ἀ-δοκίμαστος 2 untried; under age.

ἀ-δόκιμος 2 untried, unfit; insignificant. [tattle.]

ἀδολεσχέω to prat(tl)e,]

ἀδολέσχης, ου, ὁ prattler.

ἀδολεσχίᾱ, ἡ prating. gossip.   [nuine, pure.]

ἄ-δολος 2 guileless; ge-]

ἀ-δόξαστος 2 certain, unquestionable.

ἀ-δοξέω to be ill-famed.

ἀ-δοξίᾱ, ἡ ill repute, disrepute.

ἄ-δοξος 2 inglorious.

ἄδος, ἄδος, τό satiety.

ἄ-δρηστος 2 not running away.   [growth, stout.]

ἀδρός 3 grown up, in full]

ἀδροτής, ῆτος, ἡ full vigour, ripeness; rich gift.

ἀδρύνω to make ripe.

ἀ-δῠνᾰμίᾱ, ἡ and ἀ-δῠνᾰσίᾱ, ἡ impotence, weakness.

ἀ-δῠνᾰτέω to be unable.

ἀ-δῠνᾰτος 2 unable; inefficient; feeble, weak; frail; invalid, cripple; poor, needy; impossible.

ἄ-δῠτον, τό holy place, sanctuary.

ᾄδω = ἀείδω.

ἄ-δωρος 2 without gifts; not giving, unyielding; unbribed.

ἀεθλεύω etc. = ἀθλ.

ἀεί, αἰεί adv. always, ever, for ever; every time.

ἀει-γενέτης 2, ἀει-γενής 2 ever-existing, immortal.

ἀ-ειδής 2 shapeless; invisible. [praise, announce.]

ἀείδω to sing, sound; to]

ἀ-εικείη, ἡ ill-treatment.

ἀ-εικέλιος 3 and 2, ἀ-εικής 2 improper; impertinent, unmannerly, shameful; ugly; wretched.

ἀεικίζω to maltreat, dishonour; to deface.

ἀεί-μνηστος 2 not to be forgotten, memorable.

ἀεί-ναος = ἀέναος.

ἀεί-ρῠτος 2 ever-flowing.

ἀείρω = αἴρω.

ἄεισμα = ᾆσμα.

ἀεί-φρουρος 2 keeping in perpetual imprisonment.

ἀεκαζόμενος 3 unwilling.

ἀεκήλιος = ἀεικέλιος.

ἀ-έκητι adv. against the will.

ἀ-έκων = ἄκων.

ἀέλιος = ἥλιος.

ἄελλα, ἡ storm, whirlwind, eddy.

ἀελλαῖος 3, ἀελλάς, άδος, ἡ swift as a storm, stormy.

ἀελλής 2 crowded (eddying).

ἀελλό-πος, ἀελλό-πους, ποδος = ἀελλαῖος.

ἀ-ελπής = ἄελπτος.

ἀ-ελπτέω not to hope.

ἄ-ελπτος 2 unhoped for.

ἀε-νάος 2 and ἀε-ναων 3 ever-flowing.

ἀέξω = αὔξω.

ἀ-εργία, ἀ-εργός see ἀργ.

ἄ-ερκτος 2 unfenced.

ἀερο-βατέω to walk in the air. [trotting, fleet.]

ἀερσί-πους, ποδος swift-

ἄεσα, ἄσα (aor.) to sleep, to rest at night.

ἀεσι-φροσύνη, ἡ silliness.

ἀεσί-φρων 2 silly, foolish.

ἀετός, ὁ eagle. [leather.]

ἀζαλέος 3 dry; of dry

ἄζη, ἡ mould, dirt.

ἄ-ζηλος 2 unenvied; miserable, wretched.

ἀ-ζήλωτος 2 unenviable.

ἀ-ζήμιος 2 unpunished; blameless; not punishing.

ἀ-ζηχής 2 unceasing.

ἄ-ζῦμος 2 unleavened.

ἄζω to dry up. — P. to be parched.

ἄζω and P. ἄζομαι to stand in awe (of), to dread, revere, worship. [less.]

ἀ-ηδής 2 unpleasant, cheer-

ἀ-ηδία, ἡ displeasure; disgust, odiousness. [gale.]

ἀηδών, όνος, ἡ nightin-

ἀ-ήθεια, ἡ unwontedness.

ἀ-ηθέσσω to be unaccustomed. [common.]

ἀ-ήθης 2 unwonted; un-

ἄημα, τό a blast, wind.

ἄημι to blow, to breathe. — P. to be agitated.

ἀήρ, έρος, ὁ, ἡ air; mist, cloud.

ἀήσυλος 2 = αἴσυλος.

ἀήτης, ου, ὁ a blast, wind.

ἄητος 2 stormy, raging; panting. [invincible.]

ἀ-ήττητος 2 unconquered,

ἀ-θανασία, ἡ immortality.

ἀ-θανατίζω to make immortal; to believe in immortality. [everlasting.]

ἀ-θάνατος 2 immortal,

ἄ-θαπτος 2 unburied.

ἀ-θέατος 2 not seeing; unseen.

ἀ-θεεί adv. without God.

ἀ-θέμιστος 2, ἀ-θεμίστιος 2, ἀ-θέμιτος 2 lawless, illegal; criminal, wicked; illicit.

ἄ-θεος 2 godless, infidel, atheist; god-forgotten.

ἀ-θεράπευτος 2 untended, neglected.

ἀθερίζω to despise, disdain. [warmth.]

ἄ-θερμος 2 without

ἄ-θεσμος 2 = ἀθέμιστος.

ἀ-θέσφατος 2 unspeakably huge, enormous.

ἀ-θετέω to do away with, reject. [moval.]

ἀ-θέτησις, ἡ abolition, removal.

ἀθηρη-λοιγός, ὁ winnowing-fan. [or game.]

ἄ-θηρος 2 without beasts]

ἄ-θικτος 2 untouched.

ἀθλεύω and ἀθλέω to contend, fight (for a prize); to toil, struggle; to suffer.

ἄθλησις, εως, ἡ combat.

ἀθλητήρ, ῆρος, ὁ and ἀθλητής, οῦ, ὁ prize-fighter, pugilist, athlete; champion. [ched, distressed.]

ἄθλιος 3 miserable, wretched.

ἀθλιότης, ητος, ἡ wretchedness, drudgery.

ἀθλο-θέτης, ου, ὁ arranger of a contest, umpire.

ἆθλον, τό prize; = ἄθλος.

ἆθλος, ὁ contest, combat; labour, toil; distress.

ἀθλο-φόρος 2 prize-bearer.

ἀθρέω to look at, observe, view; to consider.

ἀθροίζω, ἁθροίζω to gather, collect, assemble.

ἄθροισις, εως, ἡ and ἄθροισμα, τό collection, a compiling, amassing.

ἁ-θρόος, ἁ-θρόος 3 gathered, crowded; in one body, all at once.

ἀ-θῡμέω to despond, to be discouraged; to be fretful.

ἀ-θῡμία, ἡ dejection, despondency; fretfulness.

ἄ-θῡμος 2 desponding, faint-hearted; fretful, without spirit.

ἄθυρμα, τό toy, plaything.

ἀθυρμάτιον, τό little toy.

ἀθυρο-στομέω to speak freely. [lous.]

ἀ-θυρό-στομος 2 garrulous.

ἀθύρω to play, to amuse oneself.

ἄ-θῡτος 2 unsacrificed; not having sacrificed.

ἄ-θῷος 2 unpunished; unhurt, spared; innocent, guiltless.

ἀ-θωράκιστος 2 unmailed.

αἰ, αἴ conj. if, oh that.

αἴ, αἰαῖ int. woe! alas!

αἶα, ἡ earth, land.

αἰάζω to lament, wail.

αἰανής 2 everlasting; painful, afflicting; dismal, gloomy.

αἰγανέη, ἡ javelin.

αἴγειος, αἴγεος 3 of goats.

αἴγειρος, ἡ black poplar.

αἰγι-ἁλός ὁ beach, shore.

αἰγί-βοτος 2 browsed or grazed by goats.

αἰγι-κορεύς, ὁ goat-herd.

αἰγι-λιψ, ῑπος, ὁ, ἡ steep, precipitous; storm-beaten.

αἰγί-οχος 2 aegis-bearing.

αἰγί-πους, πουν, gen. ποδος goat-footed.

αἰγίς, ῑδος, ἡ shield of Jupiter or Minerva; breastplate of leather; storm.

αἴγλη, ἡ brightness, lustre; daylight; torch.

αἰγλήεις 3 bright, brilliant. [faced.]

αἰγο-πρόσωπος 2 goatfaced.

αἰγυπιός, ὁ vulture.

αἰδέομαι P. M. to be ashamed (of); to shun, fear; to revere, respect; to pardon; to reconcile.

ἀ-ΐδηλος 2 absconding, undoing, destroying; invisible, dark; ugly.

αἰδήμων = αἰδοῖος.

ἀΐδιος 2 everlasting.

αἰδοῖον, τό pudenda.

αἰδοῖος 3 shame-faced, bashful; modest; chaste; venerable, respectable.

αἴδομαι = αἰδέομαι.

αἰδό-φρων 2 merciful.

ἀ-ϊδρείη, ἡ ignorance, silliness.

ἄ-ϊδρις 2 ignorant, silly.

αἰδώς, οῦς, ἡ shame; modesty; decency; respect, awe; reverence, veneration; ignominy, disgrace; pudenda.

αἰεί = ἀεί.   [νῆς.]

αἰει-γενέτης, ου = ἀει-γε-

αἰέλ-ουρος, ὁ, ἡ cat.

αἰέν = ἀεί.

αἰε-νάων = ἀέναος.

αἰέν-υπνος 2 lulling in eternal sleep.

αἰετός = ἀετός.

αἰζήϊος, αἰζηός 2 vigorous, robust, young; young man.   [distinct.]

αἴζηλος 2 conspicuous,

αἴητος = ἄητος.

αἰθαλόεις 3 sooty; smoky, blackened.

αἶθε int. oh that!

αἰθέριος 2 and 3 ethereal, aerial.

αἰθήρ, έρος, ἡ or ὁ the upper air, clear sky.

αἴθουσα, ἡ vestibule, colonnade, hall.

αἴθ-οψ, οπος sparkling, shining; fiery, ardent.

αἴθρη, ἡ, αἰθρίᾱ, ἡ brightness of the sky; bright, blue sky.

αἰθρη-γενέτης, ου, αἰθρη-γενής 2 ether-born; clearing up; chilling.

αἶθρος, ὁ chill, hoar-frost.

αἴθυια, ἡ diver, water-hen.

αἴθω trans. to kindle, fire, burn; intr. and P. to flame, burn, shine.

αἴθων 2 burning; sparkling, shining, ruddy; tawny; fiery, hot.

αἴκ’, αἴκε = εἰ ἄν (ἐάν).

αἰκάλλω to flatter.

αἰκή, ἡ rush, impact, press.

αἰκής 2 = ἀεικής.

αἰκίᾱ, ἡ ill-treatment.

αἰκίζω = ἀεικίζω. [=αἰκία.]

αἴκισμα, τό and αἰκισμός, ὁ

αἰκῶς = ἀεικῶς shamefully.

αἴλινος, ὁ plaintive cry, wailing.

αἷμα, τό blood; bloodshed, murder; murderous weapon; life, vigour, strength; kindred, blood-relationship.

αἱμάς, άδος, ἡ effusion of blood.   [fence.]

αἱμασιά, ἡ thornbush;

αἱμάσσω to make bloody, to sprinkle or stain with blood.   [shed.]

αἱματ-εκχυσίᾱ, ἡ blood-

αἱματηρός 3, αἱμάτόεις 3 bloody, bleeding; blood-red.

αἱματόω = αἱμάσσω.

αἱμάτώδης 2 bloodlike; blood-red.   [blood.]

αἱμο-βαφής 2 steeped in

αἱμο-ρροέω to be affected with a flux of blood.

αἱμο-φόρυκτος 2 bloody, raw.

αἱμὅλιος 2, αἱμὅλος 3 flattering, charming; artful, wily. [pert.

αἵμων, ονος knowing, ex-

αἱν-αρέτης, ου, ὁ mischievously brave.

αἴνεσις, εως, ἡ = αἴνη.

αἰνέω to praise, laud; to approve, assent, agree (to); promise; persuade.

αἴνη, ἡ praise, renown.

αἴνιγμα, τό riddle.

αἰνίζομαι M. = αἰνέω.

αἰνίσσομαι M. to speak in riddles, to hint.

αἰνόθεν αἰνῶς adv. more than horrid, most horribly.

αἰνό-μορος 2 ill-fated.

αἰνο-παθής 2 hard-suffering.

αἶνος, ὁ ingenious speech; saying, by-word; praise, encomium.

αἰνός 3 horrible, dreadful; destructive, pernicious; miserable.

αἴνὔμαι M. to take; to lay hold of, seize.

αἴξ or αἶξ, αἰγός. ὁ, ἡ goat. [to and fro.

αἰόλλω to move quickly

αἰολο-θώρηξ, ηκος with a shining breast-plate.

αἰόλος 3 swift, movable; wriggling; flitting; shining, glittering, bright; party-coloured; stained.

αἰολό-στομος 2 ambiguous in speech. [αἰπύς.

αἰπεινός 3, αἰπήεις 3 =

αἰπόλιον, τό herd of goats.

αἰπόλος 2 feeding goats; goatherd, shepherd.

αἰπός 3, αἰπύς 3 high, steep, precipitous; sudden, past help; troublesome.

αἵρεσις, εως, ἡ a taking, capture; option, choice, election; inclination; cast of mind; sect, party; heresy.

αἱρετίζω to choose.

αἱρετικός 3 heretical.

αἱρετός 3 takable, conquerable, superable; intelligible, comprehensible; chosen; eligible, acceptable; desirable.

αἱρέω Act. to take, seize; to overtake, catch, join; to take away; to capture, conquer, subdue; to kill; to convict; to understand. — M. to take or seize for oneself; to get, win, receive, enjoy; to choose, prefer; to wish.

αἴρω trans. to raise, lift, elevate, erect; to render prominent, to extol, enhance, heighten, praise; to take away, remove, carry away; to take, seize, fetch, get; to show, to manifest. — intr. to set out, put to sea, set sail. — P. to rise, mount, soar; to set out; to grow, increase; to grow excited. — M. to lift up, carry away, seize; to get, win, gain, obtain; to take in hand, undertake, undergo.

αἶσα, ἡ due portion, share; the due; fate, destiny,

lot; duration of life, lifetime.

αἰσθάνομαι *M.* to feel, perceive; to notice, observe, to become sensible; to know, understand.

αἴσθησις, εως, ἡ sensation, perception, feeling; sense; knowledge, consciousness.

αἰσθητήριον, τό organ of sense.

αἰσθητός 3 perceptible.

αἴσθομαι = αἰσθάνομαι.

ἄϊσθω to breathe, expire.

αἴσιμος 2 and 3 fatal; due, fit, just, convenient.

αἴσιος 2 and 3 auspicious, lucky.

ἀΐσσω *intr.* to move quickly; to run, rush, dash; to fly away, to hurry up; to rise, soar up; to pounce. — *trans.* to wave.

ἄ-ϊστος 2 unseen, invisible.   [hilate]

ἀ-ϊστόω to destroy, anni-]

αἴσυλος 2 mischievous.

αἰσυ-μνητήρ, ῆρος and **αἰσυ-μνήτης, ου, ὁ** judge, umpire; ruler.

αἶσχος, τό disgrace, shame, ignominy; ugliness.

αἰσχρο-κέρδεια and **-ίᾱ, ἡ** love of gain, greediness.

αἰσχρο-κερδής 2 greedy of gain, covetous.

αἰσχρο-λογίᾱ, ἡ foul talk.

αἰσχρός 3 disgracing; ugly; shameful, base, ignominious, lewd; reviling; unfit.

αἰσχρότης, ητος, ἡ ugliness; infamy.

αἰσχύνη, ἡ shame, disgrace; violation; sense of shame or honour, reverence.

αἰσχυντηρός 3 bashful.

αἰσχύνω to disfigure, deform; to ravish, disgrace, defame; to confound, to put to the blush. — *P.* to be ashamed, to get ashamed.

αἰτέω to ask, demand, desire; to beg. — *M.* to ask, demand for oneself.

αἴτημα, τό and **αἴτησις, εως, ἡ** demand, request, entreaty.

αἰτητός 3 asked for, wanted.

αἰτίᾱ, ἡ cause, reason, motive, occasion, inducement; guilt, imputation, charge, reproach; αἰτίαν ἔχειν to have a cause or reason; to be in fault; to be charged with.   [charge.]

αἰτίᾱμα, τό imputation,]

αἰτιάομαι *M.* to accuse, impeach; to blame; to pretend, allege, feign.

αἰτίζω to ask, beg.

αἴτιος 3 causing, chargeable, guilty; ὁ **αἴτιος** doer, author; culprit; τὸ **αἴτιον** = αἰτία.

αἰτίωμα, τό = αἰτίαμα.

αἰφνίδιος 2 sudden.

αἰχμάζω to throw a lance.

αἰχμ-αλωσίᾱ, ἡ captivity.

αἰχμ-αλωτεύω, -ίζω to make prisoner of war.

αἰχμ-αλωτίς, ίδος, ἡ female captive, slave.

αἰχμ-άλωτος 2 prisoner of war, captive, captured; slave.   [war, battle.]

αἰχμή, ἡ point, edge; lance;]

αἰχμητής, οῦ, ὁ spearman, warrior.

αἰχμο-φόρος, ὁ lance-bearer. [denly.

αἶφα *adv.* quickly, sud-

αἰψηρός 3 quick, swift.

ἀίω to perceive, observe, see, hear, feel; to know.

αἰών, ῶνος, ὁ, ἡ space of time, duration, period; age, lifetime; eternity; spirit of the age.

αἰώνιος 2 and 3 eternal.

αἰώρᾱ, ἡ suspension, swing.

αἰωρέω to lift up, swing. — *P.* to be suspended, to hover, hang, soar (aloft), float; to be anxious or in suspense; to rise.

ἀ-καθαρσίᾱ, ἡ impurity

ἀ-κάθαρτος 2 uncleaned; unatoned; unclean.

ἀ-καιρέομαι to find no opportunity.

ἀ-καιρίᾱ, ἡ wrong or un-seasonable time; importunity.

ἄ-καιρος 2 unseasonable, inopportune, importunate.

ἀ-κάκητα, ὁ helper, redeemer.

ἄ-κακος 2 guileless; harmless, innocent. [flowing.

ἀκάλα-ρρείτης, ου soft-

ἀ-κάλυπτος 2 uncovered.

ἀ-κάμᾱς, αντος and ἀκάμᾱτος 2 and 3 untired, indefatigable.

ἄκανθα, ἡ thorn(-bush); thistle; acacia; spine, backbone.

ἀκανθώδης 2 thorny.

ἀ-καρπίᾱ, ἡ unfruitfulness.

ἄ-καρπος 2 fruitless, barren. [unrequited.

ἀ-κάρπωτος 2 fruitless,

ἀ-κατάγνωστος 2 blameless. [veiled.

ἀ-κατακάλυπτος 2 un-

ἀ-κατάκρῐτος 2 undoomed.

ἀ-κατάλὕτος 2 imperishable.

ἀ-κατάπαστος 2 insatiable.

ἀ-κατάπαυστος 2 restless, incessant.

ἀ-καταστᾰσίᾱ, ἡ unrest, confusion. [unsteady.

ἀ-κατάστᾰτος 2 unstable,

ἀ-κατάσχετος 2 indomitable, unruly. [tious.

ἀ-κατάψευστος 2 not ficti-

ἄκᾰτος, ἡ and ἄκᾰτιον, τό light boat or ship, pirate's vessel; sail.

ἄ-καυστος 2 unburnt.

ἀκαχίζω to trouble, afflict, grieve. [pointed.

ἀκαχμένος 3 sharpened,

ἀκείομαι = ἀκέομαι.

ἀ-κέλευστος 2 unbidden.

ἀκέομαι *M.* to heal, cure; to amend; to reconcile.

ἀ-κέραιος 2 unmixed, pure; uninjured, entire, untouched, fresh.

ἀ-κερδής 2 gainless, unprofitable; bad.

ἀ-κερσε-κόμης, ου with unshorn hair. [ing.

ἄκεσις, εως, ἡ cure, heal-

ἄκεσμα, τό remedy, medicine. [appeaser.

ἀκεστήρ, ῆρος, ὁ healer,

ἀκεστός 3 curable; placable. [head.

ἀ-κέφαλος 2 without a

ἀκέων, ουσα, ον silent, still.

ἀ-κήδεστος 2, ἀ-κηδής 2 uncared for, neglected; unburied; careless, secure; unfeeling.

ἀ-κηδέω to neglect.

ἀ-κήλητος 2 inflexible; incurable.

ἀκήν adv. silently.

ἀ-κηράσιος 2, ἀ-κήρᾱτος 2, ἀ-κήριος[1] = ἀκέραιος.

ἀ-κήριος[2] 2 lifeless; heartless, cowardly.

ἀ-κήρυκτος 2 unannounced, unknown; without a herald's conduct; without mediation, irreconcilable.

ἀ-κίβδηλος 2 unadulterated, sincere.

ἀκιδνός 3 tiny, weak.

ἄ-κῑκυς, υος 2 powerless, feeble.

ἀκῑνάκης, ου dagger.

ἀ-κίνδῡνος 2 without danger, safe; unfailing.

ἀ-κίνητος 2 unmoved; immovable, firm, steady; inflexible; not to be touched, not to be divulged.

ἀ-κίχητος 2 unattainable.

ἀκκίζομαι to behave affectedly.

ἄ-κλαυ(σ)τος 2 unwept, tearless, unpunished.

ἀ-κλεής, ἀ-κλειής 2 inglorious, obscure.

ἄ-κλειστος 2, ἄ-κλῃστος 2 not shut, unlocked.

ἄ-κληρος 2 shareless; needy.   [drawing lots.]

ἀ-κληρωτί adv. without

ἄ-κλητος 2 uncalled.

ἀ-κλῑνής 2 unswerving.

ἀκμάζω to bloom, flourish, to be in vigour or in the prime of life; to abound(in).

ἀκμαῖος 3 full-grown, ripe; vigorous, at the prime; in time.

ἄ-κμᾱτος 2 = ἀκάματος.

ἀκμή, ἡ point, edge; highest point, prime, bloom, climax, pitch, vigour, maturity.

ἀκμήν adv. even now.

ἀκμηνός 3 full-grown.

ἀ-κμής, ῆτος untiring.

ἀκμό-θετον, τό anvil-block.

ἄκμων, ονος, ὁ anvil.

ἄκνηστις, ιος, ἡ spine, back-bone.

ἀκοή, ἡ sense of hearing; listening; ear; hearsay, report, rumour; sermon, preaching.

ἀ-κοινώνητος 2 unsocial.

ἀ-κοίτης, ου, ὁ consort, husband.   [wife.]

ἄ-κοιτις, ιος, ἡ consort.

ἀ-κολάκευτος 2 not flattered.   [ness, debauch.]

ἀ-κολᾱσίᾱ, ἡ licentious-

ἀ-κολασταίνω to be licentious.

ἀ-κόλαστος 2 unrestrained, licentious, dissolute.

ἄκολος, ἡ bit, morsel.

ἀ-κολουθέω to follow, attend; to join; to obey.

ἀ-κόλουθος 2 following, attending; follower, attendant; convenient, agreeing.

ἀ-κομιστίη, ἡ want of tending or nursing.

ἀκονάω to sharpen.

ἀκόνη, ἡ whetstone.

ἀ-κονῑτί *adv.* without dust; without pains.

ἀκοντίζω to throw a (spear), to dart; to hit, wound.

ἀκόντιον, τό javelin, spear.

ἀκόντισις, ἡ, ἀκόντισμα, τό throwing spears.

ἀκοντιστής, οῦ, ὁ darter, spearman.

ἄ-κοπος 2 without pains; unwearied, not wearying.

ἀ-κόρεστος 2, ἀ-κόρητος 2 insatiable, unsated; greedy; insolent.

ἄκος, τό remedy; healing.

ἀ-κοσμέω to be disorderly, to offend.

ἀ-κόσμητος 2 without order, disorderly, confused; unprovided.

ἀ-κοσμίᾱ, ἡ disorder, confusion; unruliness.

ἄ-κοσμος 2 disorderly; refractory.

ἀκουάζομαι to be invited.

ἀκουή = ἀκοή. [or heir.]

ἄ-κουρος 2 without a son

ἀκούσιος 2 = ἄκων.

ἄκουσμα, τό anything heard; report; treat or feast for the ears; instruction.

ἀκουστός 3 audible.

ἀκούω to hear, know; to listen to; to obey; to be called or reputed.

ἄκρᾱ, ἡ end, point, top, height; castle; headland.

ἀκρ-αής 2 blowing strongly.

ἀκραιφνής 2 pure, fresh, vigorous. [unfinished: vain.]

ἄ-κραντος 2 unfulfilled,

ἀ-κρᾱσίᾱ and ἀ-κράτεια, ἡ incontinence, intemperance. [moderate.]

ἀ-κρατής 2 impotent; im-

ἀκρᾱτο-ποσίᾱ, ἡ drinking of unmixed wine.

ἀκρᾱτο-πότης, ου, ὁ drinker of unmixed wine.

ἄ-κρᾱτος 2 unmixed, pure; purified; strong, vigorous; perfect. [τῆς.]

ἀ-κράτωρ, ορος = ἀκρα-

ἄκρητο- see ἀκρατο-.

ἀκρῑβεια, ἡ accuracy, exactness, precision; strictness, severity, discipline; parsimony; perfection.

ἀκρῑβής 2 exact, accurate, careful; severe: adequate, proper; tight(ly fitting); parsimonious, frugal, scanty; perfect.

ἀκρῑβο-λογέομαι *M.* to be precise in language.

ἀκρῑβόω to know or examine thoroughly.

ἄκρις, ιος, ἡ = ἄκρα.

ἀκρίς, ίδος, ἡ locust.

ἀ-κρισίᾱ, ἡ disorder.

ἀκρῑτό-μῡθος 2 talking immoderately.

ἄ-κρῑτος 2 without judgment, arbitrary; unsevered, confused; untried, unjudged; undecided; immoderate, countless. [dense foliage.]

ἀκρῑτό-φυλλος 2 with

ἀκρόᾱμα, τό anything heard; treat or feast for the ears.

ἀκροάομαι *M.* to hear; listen; obey. [obedience.]

ἀκρόᾱσις, εως, ἡ a hearing;

ἀκροατήριον, τό audience; lecture-room.

ἀκροᾱτής, οῦ, ὁ hearer. listener. [mish.]

ἀκρο-βολίζομαι M. to skir-

ἀκρο-βόλισις, εως, ἡ and

ἀκρο-βολισμός, ὁ a skir-mish(ing). [misher.]

ἀκρο-βολιστής, οῦ, ὁ skir-

ἀκρο-βυστίᾱ, ἡ foreskin; the gentiles. [ner-stone.]

ἀκρο-γωνιαῖος(λίθος)cor-

ἀκρό-δρυον, τό fruit-tree.

ἀκρο-θίνιον, τό firstling, first-fruit; votive gift; booty.

ἀκρο-κελαινιάω to be (-come)black on the surface.

ἀκρό-κομος 2 shock-headed, high-tufted.

ἀκρο-μάνής 2 stark raging, madcap.

ἀκρό-πολις, εως, ἡ upper city, castle, citadel.

ἀκρο-πόλος 2 high, lofty.

ἀκρο-πόρος 2 piercing through.

ἄκρος 3 pointed; extreme, upper, topmost; egregious, excellent. — τὸ ἄκρον height, top, summit, ex-tremity, border, skirt, sur-face; castle. [inclined.]

ἀκρο-σφαλής 2 tottering;)

ἀκρο-τελεύτιον, τό ex-treme end (of a verse).

ἀκρο-φύσιον, τό spout of a pair of bellows. [ice.]

ἀ-κρύσταλλος 2 clear of)

ἀκρ-ωνυχίᾱ, ἡ tip of the nail; top. [mountain.]

ἀκρ-ώρεια, ἡ top of a)

ἀκρωτηριάζω and M. to

take off the fore part or extremities; to mutilate.

ἀκρωτήριον, τό point, height, top, peak; projec-tion; promontory; beak; gable; extremity.

ἀ-κτένιστος 2 uncombed.

ἀ-κτέριστος 2 unburied; unconsecrated.

ἀκτή, ἡ coast, shore, beach; neck of land; elevation.

ἀκτή, ἡ groats, meal.

ἀ-κτήμων 2 without pro-perty, poor.

ἀκτίς, ῖνος, ἡ ray, beam; light, splendour; heat.

ἄκῡλος, ἡ esculent acorn.

ἄ-κῡρος 2 without autho-rity, annulled; invalid, powerless.

ἀ-κῡρόω to abolish, cancel.

ἀκωκή, ἡ point, edge.

ἀ-κώλῡτος 2 unhindered.

ἄκων, οντος, ὁ javelin.

ἄκων, ουσα, ον against one's will, involuntary, un-willing; undesigning; un-welcome.

ἆλα, τό = ἅλς.

ἀλάβαστρος, ὁ and ἀλά-βαστρον, τό onyx, ala-baster; salve-box.

ἅλαδε adv. to the sea, sea-ward(s).

ἀλαζονείᾱ, ἡ boasting, swaggering, brag.

ἀλαζονικός 3 and ἀλαζών, όνος, ὁ, ἡ braggart, swag-gerer, impostor; vagabond.

ἀλαλά, ἡ, ἀλαλαγμός, ὁ and ἀλαλητός, ὁ war-cry; shout. [the war-cry.]

ἀλαλάζω and M. to raise)

ἀ-λάλητος 2 unspeakable.

ἄ-λαλος 2 speechless, dumb.

ἀλαλύκτημαι (from ἀλυκτέω) to be in fear or anguish.

ἀ-λάμπετος 2 and ἀ-λαμπής 2 lustreless.

ἀλάομαι to wander, stray, err, rove, ramble about; to doubt.

ἀλᾶός 2 blind; blinding.

ἀλαο-σκοπίη, ἡ vain watch.

ἀλᾶόω to make blind.

ἀ-λάπαδνός 3 weak, feeble.

ἀ-λαπάζω to empty, exhaust; to overwhelm, destroy, kill.

ἄλας, ατος, τό = ἅλς.

ἀλαστέω to be angry, to hate, resent.

ἀ-λάστορος 2 and ἀ-λάστωρ, ορος, ὁ avenger, tormenter; fiend, villain, rascal.

ἄ-λαστος 2 unbearable; unceasing, lasting; memorable; wicked, hateful.

ἀλᾱτᾱς = ἀλήτης.

ἀλαωτύς, ύος, ἡ act of blinding.

ἀλγεινός 3 painful, afflicting, grievous; evil; unpleasant; vehement; difficult; suffering.

ἀλγέω to feel pain, to suffer; to be afflicted, grieved, or sad.

ἀλγηδών, όνος, ἡ, ἄλγημα, τό. ἄλγησις, εως, ἡ, ἄλγος, τό pain, grief, sorrow.

ἀλγύνω to grieve, cause pain; P. = ἀλγέω.

ἀλδαίνω to strengthen, invigorate.

ἀλδήσκω to grow, thrive.

ἀλέᾱ[1], ἡ heat (of the sun).

ἀλέᾱ[2], ἡ avoidance, escape.

ἀλεγεινός = ἀλγεινός.

ἀ-λέγω, ἀλεγίζω, ἀλεγύνω, to care for, mind, attend (to); to heed. [ing.]

ἀλεεινός 3 warm, warm-

ἀλεείνω = ἀλέομαι.

ἀλεής 2 in the noontide heat. [= ἄλευρον.]

ἀλείατα from ἄλειαρ, τό]

ἄλειμμα, τό salve.

ἄλεισον, τό cup, bowl.

ἀλείτης, ου, ὁ offender, sinner.

ἄλειφαρ, ατος, τό salve oil.

ἀ-λείφω to anoint; besmear.

ἄλειψις, εως, ἡ unction, anointing.

ἀλεκτορο-φωνίᾱ, ἡ cockcrow.

ἄ-λεκτρος 2 unwedded; illicit, illegitimate.

ἀλεκτρυών, όνος and ἀλέκτωρ, ορος, ὁ cock.

ἀλέκω = ἀλέξω.

ἀλεξ-άνεμος 2 keeping off the wind.

ἀλέξησις, εως, ἡ a keeping off, defence.

ἀλεξητήρ, ῆρος and ἀλεξήτωρ, ορος, ὁ protector, guardian, helper.

ἀλεξί-κᾰκος 2 keeping off evil. [from death.]

ἀλεξί-μορος 2 defending]

ἀλέξω to keep off; to guard, protect, defend, help. — M. to defend oneself; to assist; to requite.

ἀλέομαι *M.* to turn aside; to avoid, shun, escape.

ἀλέτης, ου, ὁ, ἀλετρίς, ίδος. ἡ grinding.

ἀλετρεύω = ἀλέω.

ἀλεύομαι = ἀλέομαι.

ἄλευρον, τό meal, flour.

ἀλέω to grind, pound.

ἀλεωρή, ἡ escape; protection.   [madness.]

ἄλη, ἡ a wandering about;

ἀλήθεια, ἡ truth; veracity, uprightness; reality; propriety.

ἀληθεύω to speak the truth.

ἀ-ληθής 2 true; sincere, frank; real, genuine, proper; actual. — *adv.* ἀληθῶς, ἀληθές truly, really, indeed.   [θεύω.]

ἀληθίζομαι *M.* = ἀλη-

ἀληθινός 3 = ἀληθής.

ἀλήθω = ἀλέω.

ἀ-λήιος 2 not wealthy.

ἄλημα, τό and ἀλήμων 2 arrant knave; vagabond, fugitive.   [inconceivable.]

ἄ-ληπτος 2 unattainable;

ἀλής 2 crowded, in a mass; altogether.

ἀλητεύω = ἀλάομαι.

ἀλήτης, ου, ὁ = ἄλημα.

ἄλθομαι *P.* to get cured or healed.

ἀλίᾱ, ἡ assembly.

ἀλιάδης, ου, ὁ = ἀλιεύς.

ἀλι-αής 2 blowing seaward.   [incessant.]

ἀ-λίαστος 2 unyielding;

ἀ-λίγκιος 2 like, equal.

ἁλιεύς, ὁ fisherman; mariner, sailor.   [fishermen.]

ἁλιευτικός 3 belonging to

ἁλιεύω to fish.

ἁλίζω to assemble.

ἁλίζω to salt.

ἄ-λιθος 2 without stones.

ἁλί-κλυστος 2 sea-girt.

ἁλί-κτυπος 2 sea-beaten.

ἀ-λίμενος 2 harbourless.

ἀ-λιμενότης, ητος, ἡ harbourlessness.   [the sea.]

ἁλι-μῡρήεις 3 flowing into

ἅλινος 3 (made) of salt.

ἅλιος = ἥλιος.

ἅλιος¹ 3 vain, fruitless.

ἅλιος² 3 belonging to the sea, sea-.   [tured.]

ἁλιο-τρεφής 2 sea-nur-

ἁλιόω to frustrate, make fruitless.   [adorned.]

ἁ-λῑπᾰρής 2 plain, un-

ἁλί-πλαγκτος 2 wandering over the sea.

ἁλί-πλακτος 2 sea-beaten.

ἁλί-πλοος 2 floating in the sea.   [purple.]

ἁλι-πόρφυρος 2 of sea-

ἁλί-ρροθος 2 in the roaring sea.   [fully; amply, enough.]

ἅλις *adv.* in crowds, plenti-

ἁλίσγημα, τό pollution.

ἁλίσκομαι to be taken, caught, captured, conquered, or subdued; to be found (out), apprehended, or convicted.   [offend.]

ἀλῑταίνω and *M.* to sin;

ἀλῑτήμων 2. ἀλιτήριος 2, ἀλιτηρός 2, ἀλιτρός 2 trespassing, offending, sinning, wicked; offender; rascal.

ἀλῑτρίᾱ, ἡ wickedness.

ἄλκαρ, τό defence, protection.

ἀλκή, ἡ defensive power, force, prowess; guard, defence, delivery.

ἄλκιμος 2 fit for battle, warlike, martial; valiant.

ἀλκτήρ, ῆρος, ὁ defender, protector.

ἀλκυών, όνος, ὁ kingfisher.

ἀλλά conj. but, yet, however; notwithstanding; at least; but, except; why, well, certainly, well then.

ἀλλαγή, ἡ change, alteration.

ἀλλάσσω to change, alter, transmute; requite. — M. to take in exchange.

ἀλλαχῇ, ἀλλαχόθι, ἀλλαχοῦ adv. elsewhere; to another place.

ἀλλαχόθεν adv. from another place. [place.]

ἀλλαχόσε adv. to another

ἀλ-λέγω = ἀναλέγω.

ἄλλη adv. = ἀλλαχῇ; otherwise.

ἀλλ-ηγορέω to speak metaphorically, to allegorize.

ἀλληλο-φᾰγία, ἡ the eating one another.

ἀλληλο-φθορίᾱ, ἡ mutual destruction. [other.]

ἀλλήλων one another, each

ἄλλην adv. to another place. [reign.]

ἀλλο-γενής 2 alien, foreign.

ἀλλό-γλωσσος 2 of a foreign language, foreign.

ἀλλο-γνοέω to mistake, not to know. [unknown.]

ἀλλό-γνωτος 2 strange.

ἀλλο-δᾰπός 3 strange, foreign, outlandish.

ἀλλο-ειδής 2 looking differently. [ther place.]

ἄλλοθεν adv. from another

ἄλλοθι adv. elsewhere; far from; else.

ἀλλό-θροος 2 speaking another language; foreign.

ἀλλοῖος 3 different, heterogeneous; changed.

ἀλλοιόω to change, alter.

ἀλλοίωσις, εως, ἡ permutation, change.

ἀλλό-κοτος 2 different; uncommon, strange; unnatural.

ἄλλομαι M. to spring, jump, leap; to fly, run.

ἀλλο-πρόσ-αλλος, ὁ changeable, fickle.

ἄλλος, η, ο another, the other; different, strange, foreign; inconvenient, false. — adv. ἄλλως otherwise (better or worse); in vain, at random; merely, simply; else, besides, already; ἄλλως τε καί especially, above all. [place.]

ἄλλοσε adv. to another

ἄλλοτε adv. at another time.

ἀλλοτριο-ἐπίσκοπος, ὁ meddler, busy-body.

ἀλλότριος 3 belonging to others; foreign, alien, not related; hostile, adverse; changed, strange; inconvenient. [trangement.]

ἀλλοτριότης, ητος, ἡ es-

ἀλλοτριόω to estrange, alienate; to transfer; to rob.

ἀλλοτρίωσις, εως, ἡ rejection.

ἀλ-λοφος 2 crestless.

2*

ἀλλο-φρονέω to think otherwise or wrongly; to be absent in mind.

ἀλλό-φῦλος 2 of another tribe, foreign.

ἄλλῦδις adv. elsewhither.

ἀλλύεσκε see ἀναλύω.

ἄλλως see ἄλλος.

ἅλμα, τό jump, leap, bound.

ἅλμη, ἡ sea-water; brine; saltness.

ἁλμῠρός 3 salt, bitter, sea-.

ἀλοάω to thrash. [liver.]

ἄ-λοβος 2 without lobe of the

ἀ-λογέω to take no heed or notice of, to neglect.

ἀ-λογίᾱ, ἡ disregard; want of reason.

ἀ-λόγιστος 2 unreasonable, absurd; unfathomable.

ἄ-λογος 2 without reason, silly; unexpected; speechless.

ἀλόη, ἡ aloe.

ἁλόθεν adv. from the sea.

ἀλοιάω = ἀλοάω.

ἀλοιφή, ἡ fat, grease; salve.

ἄλοξ, οκος, ἡ furrow; cornland.

ἁλοσ-ύδνη, ἡ sea-born.

ἁλουργής 2 dyed with purple. [dirt.]

ἀ-λουσίᾱ, ἡ unwashedness,

ἄ-λουτος 2 unwashed, dirty.

ἄ-λοχος, ἡ wife, spouse.

ἅλς, ἁλός, ὁ salt; ἡ saltwater, sea. [forest.]

ἄλσος, τό (sacred) grove,

ἁλῠκός 2 salt, briny.

ἁλυκτάζω = ἀλύω.

ἄ-λῡπος and ἀ-λύπητος 2 without pain or grief, easy; not grieving.

ἄ-λῠρος 2 without a lyre, songless.

ἅλῠσις, εως, ἡ chain.

ἀ-λῠσιτελής 2 useless; injurious.

ἀλύσκω, ἀλυσκάζω, ἀ-λυσκάνω to turn aside, escape.

ἀλύσσω = ἀλύω.

ἄ-λῠτος 2 inseparable; infinite.

ἀλύω to be unsteady, beside oneself, troubled, excited.

ἄλφα, τό first letter of the alphabet. [quire.]

ἀλφάνω to earn, gain, ac-

ἀλφεσί-βοιος 3 bringing in cattle; much-wooed.

ἀλφηστής, οῦ, ὁ laborious, industrious; eating bread.

ἄλφιτον, τό barley-meal; bread. [of barley-meal.]

ἀλφῑτο-ποιΐα, ἡ making

ἁλωή, ἡ thrashing-floor; orchard, cornfield.

ἅλων, ωνος, ἡ = ἅλως.

ἀλωπεκῆ and ἀλωπεκίς, ίδος, ἡ foxskin.

ἀλώπηξ, εκος, ἡ fox.

ἅλως, ω and ωος, ἡ thrashing-floor; corn.

ἁλώσῐμος 2, ἁλωτός 3 easily won or conquered or understood.

ἅλωσις, εως, ἡ a taking, capture; conquest.

ἄμ = ἀνά.

ἅμα adv. and prp. together, at the same time, at once, jointly, with.

ἀ-μαθής 2 ignorant, unlearned, unlettered; inexperienced; incalculable.

ἀ-μᾰθίᾱ, ἡ ignorance; in-experience.

ἄμᾰθος, ἡ sand.

ἀμᾰθύνω to reduce to dust.

ἀ-μαιμάκετος 3 huge; raging.

ἀ-μαλδύνω to destroy.

ἀμαλλο-δετήρ, ῆρος, ὁ binder of sheaves.

ἀ-μᾰλός 3 soft, feeble, delicate. [carriage.]

ἅμαξα, ἄμαξα, ἡ waggon,)

ἁμαξεύω to drive (a cart). — P. to be frequented by waggons. [gon.]

ἁμαξιαῖος 3 filling a wag-)

ἁμαξίς, ίδος, ἡ a little waggon. [waggons; road.]

ἁμαξ-ῑτός practicable for)

ἆμαρ = ἦμαρ.

ἀ-μάραντος 2, ἀ-μαράντινος 2 unfading.

ἀ-μάρη, ἡ trench, ditch.

ἁμαρτάνω to miss the mark, err, fail, mistake, lose; to offend, trespass, sin.

ἁμαρτάς, άδος, ἡ, ἁμάρτημα, τό, ἁμαρτίᾱ, ἡ transgression, sin, offence, error.

ἁμαρτέω = ὁμαρτέω.

ἅμ-αρτῇ adv at the same time, at once.

ἁμαρτο-επής 2 speaking falsehood or at random.

ἀ-μάρτῠρος 2 unattested.

ἁμαρτωλός 2 sinful; sinner. [with.]

ἁμα-τροχάω to run along)

ἁμα-τροχίη, ἡ collision of waggons.

ἀ-μαυρός 3 dark, dim; blind; feeble; gloomy; indifferent.

ἀμαυρόω to darken, weaken.

ἀ-μάχητος 2, ἄ-μαχος 2 (adv. ἀμαχεί, ἀμαχητί) without fighting; peaceful; unconquerable. [gather.]

ἀμάω to mow, reap; to)

ἄμ-βᾰσις = ἀνάβασις.

ἀμ-βᾰτός 2 = ἀναβατός.

ἀμ-βλήδην adv. bubbling up.

ἀμβλόνω to blunt, dull; to lessen, disencourage.

ἀμβλύς 3 blunt, dull; slack, feeble, weak. [sighted.]

ἀμβλυώττω to be dim-)

ἀμ-βολάδην = ἀμβλήδην.

ἀμβροσίᾱ, ἡ food of the gods. [immortal, divine.]

ἀμβρόσιος 3, ἄμβροτος 2)

ἀμ-βώσας see ἀναβοάω.

ἀ-μέγαρτος 2 unenvied; unhappy, miserable.

ἀ-μέθυστος, ἡ amethyst.

ἀμείβω and M. to change, alter; to exchange; to pass, cross; to reply, answer; to requite. [(of a roof).]

ἀμείβων, οντος, ὁ rafter)

ἀ-μείλικτος 2, ἀ-μείλιχος 2 harsh, severe; relentless.

ἀμείνων 2 (comp. of ἀγαθός) better, abler, nobler; stronger, more valiant.

ἀ-μειξίᾱ, ἡ = ἀμιξίᾱ.

ἀμέλγω to milk, drain.

ἀμέλει adv. never mind; of course. [negligence.]

ἀ-μέλεια, ἡ carelessness.)

ἀ-μελέτητος 2 unpractised, unskilled.

ἀ-μελέω to be careless, heedless; to neglect, overlook, omit.

ἀ-μελής 2 careless, negligent; neglected.

ἄ-μεμπτος 2 blameless; contented.

ἄμεναι for ἀέμεναι, see ἄω.

ἀ-μενηνός 2 feeble, weak, powerless, swooning; unsteady.

ἀμενηνόω to make weak.

ἀμέρᾱ, ἡ = ἡμέρα.

ἀ-μέρδω to rob, deprive; to blind. — P. to get or become deprived (of).

ἀ-μερής 2 indivisible.

ἀ-μέριμνος 2 free from care; neglected.

ἀμέριος = ἡμέριος.

ἀ-μετάθετος 2 unalterable.

ἀ-μετακίνητος 2 immovable.

ἀ-μεταμέλητος 2, ἀ-μετανόητος 2 impenitent.

ἀμέτερος = ἡμέτερος.

ἀ-μέτρητος, ἄ-μετρος 2 unmeasured, immense; boundless.

ἀ-μετρίᾱ, ἡ want of measure or moderation.

ἀμετρο-επής 2 immoderate talker. [anyhow.]

ἀμῇ, ἀμῆ adv. somehow,

ἀ-μήνῑτος 2 not angry.

ἀμητήρ, ῆρος, ὁ reaper.

ἄμητος, ὁ reaping, harvest, crop. [unmotherly.]

ἀ-μήτωρ, ορος motherless;

ἀ-μηχανέω to be at a loss, helpless, or embarrassed.

ἀ-μηχανίᾱ, ὁ embarrassment, helplessness.

ἀ-μήχανος 2 helpless, embarrassed, puzzled; impossible, unattainable; incredible; indescribable; unco querable; inflexible; irreversible, inevitable.

ἀ-μίαντος 2 undefiled.

ἀ-μιγής, ἄ-μικτος 2 unmixed; unsociable; incompatible.

ἄμιλλα, ἡ rivalry, contest; combat; striving, desire.

ἀμιλλάομαι M. and P. to contend, rival, strive.

ἀμίλλημα, τό = ἄμιλλα.

ἀμιλλητήρ, ῆρος, ὁ competitor, rival.

ἀ-μῖξίᾱ, ἡ want of traffic; unsociableness.

ἄμ-ιππος 2 fleet as a horse; companion of a horse-soldier.

ἄ-μισθος 2 unpaid.

ἀ-μιτρο-χίτων, ωνος in a girdless coat. [smoking.]

ἀμιχθάλόεις 3 reeking,

ἄμμα, τό knot, noose.

ἄμμε = ἡμᾶς; ἄμμες = ἡμεῖς.

ἄμ-μιγα = ἀναμίξ.

ἀμ-μίγνῡμι = ἀναμίγνυμι.

ἀμ-μορίη, ἡ a having no share; misfortune.

ἄμ-μορος 2 without lot, unfortunate. [ground.]

ἄμμος, ἡ sand; riding-

ἀ-μναστέω = ἀμνηστέω.

ἀ-μνημονέω to be forgetful; to pardon.

ἀ-μνηστέω = ἀμνημονέω. P. to fall into oblivion.

ἀμνίον, τό offering-bowl.

ἀμνός, ὁ, ἡ lamb.

ἀ-μογητί adv. without toil or trouble.

ἀμοθεί adv. unanimously

ἀμόθεν (ἀμ.) *adv.* from anywhere.

ἀμοιβαῖος 3 and 2, ἀμοιβάς, άδος alternate.

ἀμοιβή, ἡ change, exchange; reply, answer; recompense, return.

ἀμοιβηδίς *adv.* alternately.

ἀμοιβός 2 substitute, equivalent.

ἄ-μοιρος 2 shareless, free from; unfortunate. [light.]

ἀμολγός, ὁ darkness; twi-]

ἄμορος = ἄμμορος.

ἄ-μορφος 2 deformed, ugly.

ἀμός, ἁμός 3 our, ours; my, mine.

ἄ-μοτον, *adv.* incessantly.

ἀμοῦ *adv.* anywhere.

ἄ-μουσος 2 destitute of the Muses, illiterate, rude.

ἄ-μοχθος 2 without pains or trouble; lazy.

ἀμπαυ- see ἀναπαυ-.

ἀμπείρω see ἀναπείρω.

ἀμπέλινος 3 of the vine.

ἀμπελόεις 3 rich in vines.

ἄμπελος, ἡ vine.

ἀμπελ-ουργός, ὁ vine-dresser.

ἀμπελών, ῶνος, ὁ vineyard.

ἀμπεπαλών see ἀναπάλλω.

ἀμ-περές = διαμπερές.

ἀμπ-εχόνη, ἡ clothing, upper garment.

ἀμπ-έχω to enclose, surround; to clothe. — *P.* to be clothed.

ἀμ-πηδάω = ἀναπηδάω.

ἀμπ-ίσχω = ἀμπέχω.

ἀμπλάκημα, τό offence.

ἀμπλακίσκω to offend; to fail, miss.

ἀμ-πνέω = ἀναπνέω.

ἀμ-πνοή, ἡ breath.

ἀμπν- see ἀναπν-.

ἀμπυκτήριον, τό bridle.

ἄμπυξ, ὕκος, ὁ wheel; circlet; diadem. [tide.]

ἄμπωτις, εως, ἡ ebb, low]

ἀμυγδάλινος 3 of almonds.

ἄμυγμα, τό a tearing, rending. [once.]

ἀμῦδις *adv.* together, at]

ἀμυδρός 3 dim, indistinct.

ἀ-μύητος 2 uninitiated; gaping.

ἀ-μύθητος 2 unspeakable.

ἀ-μύμων 2 blameless.

ἀμῦνάθω = ἀμύνω.

ἀμύντωρ, ορος, ὁ defender; avenger.

ἀμύνω to keep off, ward off, defend; to aid; to requite and *M* to defend oneself; to resist; to requite. [rate.]

ἀμύσσω to scratch, lace-]

ἀμφ-ἀγαπάζω to cherish, foster, befriend.

ἀμφ-ἀγείρομαι *M.* to assemble around one.

ἀμφ-άδιος 3 manifest, public, known; *adv.* ἀμφαδά, ἀμφαδόν, ἀμφαδίην.

ἀμφ-αΐσσομαι *M.* to rush on or charge from all sides.

ἀμφ-άκης = ἀμφήκης.

ἀμφ-αλείφω to anoint all over. [rattle about.]

ἀμφ-αραβέω to clink or]

ἀμφ-ασίη, ἡ speechlessness. [round.]

ἀμφ-αϋτέω to sound all]

ἀμφ-αφάω and *M.* to touch all round; to handle.

ἀμφ-έπω = ἀμφιέπω.

ἀμφ-έρχομαι to surround.

ἀμφ-ηγερέθομαι = ἀμφαγείρομαι.

ἀμφ-ήκης 2 double-edged.

ἄμφ-ημαι to sit all round.

ἀμφ-ηρεφής 2 covered all round, shut. [oars.]

ἀμφ-ηρικός 2 with double

ἀμφ-ήριστος 2 disputed, controverted; undecided.

ἀμφί adv. on both or all sides, around; about. — prp. with gen. near, round, about; concerning, for; with dat. at, about, round; because of; by means of; with acc. round, about, along, at, near; concerning; during.

ἀμφί-αλος 2 sea-girt; between two seas. [sides.]

ἀμφ-ιάχω to sound on all

ἀμφι-βαίνω to walk around, to encompass; to bestride; to protect.

ἀμφι-βάλλω to throw or put round; to embrace; to ensnare. — M. to put on.

ἀμφί-βασις, εως, ἡ protection. [net.]

ἀμφι-βληστρον, τό fishing-

ἀμφι-βολία, ἡ doubt.

ἀμφί-βολος 2 shot upon on all sides; ambiguous, doubtful; undecided, helpless. [whole man.]

ἀμφί-βροτος 3 covering the

ἀμφι-γνοέω to be uncertain or doubtful. [both sides.]

ἀμφι-γυήεις 3 strong on

ἀμφί-γυος 2 double-pointed: = ἀμφιγυήεις.

ἀμφι-δαίω intr. to burn around.

ἀμφί-δασυς 3 tasselled all round.

ἀμφι-δέαι, αἱ ligatures, clasps, bracelets.

ἀμφι-δέξιος 2 skilled with both hands, very dexterous; ambiguous.

ἀμφι-δήριτος 2 disputed, doubtful. [round.]

ἀμφι-δῑνέω to roll all

ἀμφί-δρομος 2 running round.

ἀμφι-δρυφής 2 and ἀμφί-δρυφος 2 scratched on all sides.

ἀμφί-δυμος 2 double.

ἀμφι-δύομαι M. to put on oneself.

ἀμφι-έζω, ἀμφι-έννῡμι and M. to put on, to dress oneself. [rounded.]

ἀμφι-έλισσα, ἡ double-

ἀμφι-έπω to be busy about; take care of; to tend, protect. [ment.]

ἀμφί-εσμα, τό dress, rai-

ἀμφι-εύω to singe all round.

ἀμφ-ιζάνω to sit around, to stick to.

ἀμφι-θαλής 2 with both parents living. [dled.]

ἀμφί-θετος 2 double-han-

ἀμφι-θέω to run round.

ἀμφί-θηκτος 2 double-edged.

ἀμφί-θρεπτος 2 congealed around. [doors.]

ἀμφί-θυρος 2 with double

ἀμφι-καλύπτω to cover, wrap; to veil up, hide; to enclose, envelop, shelter.

ἀμφι-κεάζω to cleave off around.

ἀμφί-κειμαι to lie around, to embrace, to lean on.

ἀμφι-κίων 2 with pillars all round.

ἀμφί-κλυστος 2 washed around by waves.

ἀμφί-κομος 2 with dense foliage.

ἀμφι-κτίονες, οἱ confiners, neighbours. [handled.]

ἀμφι-κύπελλος 2 double-]

ἀμφι-λᾰφής 2 wide, large, huge; copious.

ἀμφι-λᾰχαίνω to dig or hoe round. [tercate.]

ἀμφι-λέγω to dispute, al-]

ἀμφί-λογος 2 disputed, doubtful; altercating.

ἀμφί-λοφος 2 enclosing the nape. [light.]

ἀμφι-λύκη, ἡ dawn, twi-]

ἀμφι-μαίομαι to wipe all round. [round.]

ἀμφι-μάχομαι to fight]

ἀμφι-μέλᾱς, αινα, αν wrapped in darkness.

ἀμφι-μῠκάομαι to roar, low around.

ἀμφι-νεικής, ἀμφι-νείκη-τος 2 courted by warriors.

ἀμφι-νέμομαι to dwell around.

ἀμφι-νοέω = ἀμφιγνοέω.

ἀμφι-ξέω to smooth all round. [hover around.]

ἀμφι-πέλομαι to surround,]

ἀμφι-πένομαι = ἀμφιέπω.

ἀμφι-περι-στέφω to surround on all sides.

ἀμφι-περι-στρωφάω to manage (a horse) round about.

ἀμφι-πίπτω to fall upon.

ἀμφί-πλεκτος 2 entwined, entangled. [around.]

ἀμφί-πληκτος surging]

ἀμφι-πλήξ, ῆγος double-hitting.

ἀμφι-πολεύω = ἀμφιέπω.

ἀμφι-πολέω to move about with.

ἀμφί-πολος 2 attending, serving; servant. [ἕπω.]

ἀμφι-πονέομαι M. = ἀμφι-]

ἀμφι-ποτάομαι M. to flit around. [by a blaze.]

ἀμφί-πῠρος 2 surrounded]

ἀμφί-ρρῠτος flowed around.

ἀμφίς adv. on both sides, round about, on all sides; asunder, apart; far, remote; in two, twofold, differently. — prp. with gen. around; far from, side-ways; with acc. and dat. round about.

ἀμφισ-βᾰσίη, ἡ = ἀμφισ-βήτησις.

ἀμφισ-βητέω (-βᾰτέω) to altercate; to contradict, dispute, doubt; to assert, claim.

ἀμφισ-βητήσῐμος 2, ἀμ-φισ-βήτητος 2 controverted, disputed, doubtful.

ἀμφισ-βήτησις, εως, ἡ controversy, dispute, doubt.

ἀμφ-ίσταμαι M. to stand around, enclose.

ἀμφί-στομος 2 double-mouthed; double.

ἀμφι-στατάομαι M. to besiege, beleaguer.

ἀμφι-στρεφής 2 turning or twisting to all sides.

ἀμφι-τάμνω to cut off all round. [or on.]

ἀμφι-τίθημι to put round]

ἀμφι-τρέμω to tremble all over. [openings or outlets.]

ἀμφι-τρής, ῆτος with two

ἀμφι-τρομέω to tremble for. [crest.]

ἀμφί-φαλος 2 with double]

ἀμφι-φοβέομαι P. to flee on all parts or sides.

ἀμφι-φορεύς, ὁ two-handled pitcher; urn; pail; measure (for fluids).

ἀμφι-φράζομαι M. to consider carefully.

ἀμφι-χάσκω to yawn round.

ἀμφι-χέω to pour or spread around. — P. to flow out, to surround, embrace.

ἀμφί-χῠτος 2 heaped up on both sides.

ἀμφόδιον, τό, ἄμφ-οδον, τό street; quarter of a town.

ἀμφορεύς, ὁ = ἀμφιφορεύς.

ἀμφότερος 3 both, either.

ἀμφοτέρωθεν adv. from or on both sides.

ἀμφοτέρωθι adv. on both sides. [way.]

ἀμφοτέρως adv. in either]

ἀμφοτέρωσε adv. to both sides. [the ground.]

ἀμφ-ουδίς adv. up from]

ἄμφω, ἀμφοῖν both.

ἄμφ-ωτος 2 two-eared, two-handled. [blameless.]

ἀ-μώμητος 2, ἄ-μωμος 2]

ἄμωμον, τό amomum.

ἀμῶς adv. anyhow.

ἄν particle denoting possibility.

ἄν = ἐάν.

ἀνά adv. upwards, above, on high, on the top, thereon. — prp. with dat. on, upon;

with acc. up, upwards; through, throughout, along, about; during; up to, according to, with. [up!]

ἄνα for ἀνάστηθι up! get]

ἀνα-βχθμός, ὁ step, stairs.

ἀνα-βαίνω intr. to go up, mount, ascend; to go up the country; to embark, set off; to land; to mount a horse; to enter, appear; to increase to; to pass, end. — trans. to ascend, mount; to step through, bestride; to bring up; to cause to ascend.

ἀνα-βάλλω to throw up; to put back, defer, delay. — M. to put on; to take upon oneself, to undergo, incur; to begin, lift up one's voice.

ἀνά-βασις, εως, ἡ a going up, ascent; inland expedition; ascending steps, stairs; cavalry.

ἀνα-βάτης, ου, ὁ horseman. [swiftly.]

ἀνα-βᾰτικός 3 mounting]

ἀνα-βῐβάζω to cause to go up or ascend, to lead up; to produce. — M. to cause to appear in court; to take up.

ἀνα-βιόω and ἀνα-βιώσκομαι M. to return to life; to call back to life.

ἀνα-βλαστάνω to shoot or blossom up again.

ἀνα-βλέπω to look up or back (upon); to regain sight.

ἀνά-βλεψις, εως, ἡ recovery of sight.

ἀνά-βλησις, εως, ἡ delay.
ἀνα-βοάω to cry out, shout, scream. call. [delay.]
ἀνα-βολή, ἡ mound; cloak;)
ἀνα-βράχεῖν to clink; to fly open with a clink.
ἀνα-βρόχω to swallow back. — P. to flow back.
ἀνα-βρῡχάομαι M. to raise a roaring. [ment.]
ἀνά-γαιον, τό upper apart-)
ἀν-αγγέλλω to report, give information (about).
ἀνα-γεννάομαι to be born anew.
ἀνα-γιγνώσκω to know again, recognize; to understand thoroughly; to read, recite; to persuade.
ἀναγκάζω to compel, force, urge, ask; to persuade; to prove, demonstrate.
ἀναγκαίη, ἡ = ἀνάγκη.
ἀναγκαῖος 3 and 2 necessary, requisite, wanted, indispensable; inevitable, urgent, violent, compulsory; scanty; related, friendly, allied; forced; bondsman. [forced.]
ἀναγκαστός 3 compelled,)
ἀνάγκη, ἡ necessity, constraint, compulsion; fate, law of nature; means of coercion, violence, torture, confinement; need, distress.
ἀνα-γνάμπτω to bend back or round. [guilt.]
ἀν-αγνος 2 stained with)
ἀνα-γνωρίζω to recognize, acknowledge.
ἀνα-γνωρισμός, ὁ recognition; recital.

ἀν-αγόρευσις, εως, ἡ publication, proclamation.
ἀν-αγορεύω to proclaim publicly. [down.]
ἀνά-γραπτος 2 written)
ἀνα-γραφεύς, ὁ secretary.
ἀνα-γράφή, ἡ record, document.
ἀνα-γράφω to write down, record, enter; inscribe.
ἀν-άγω to lead or bring up (the country, to the high sea); to lift up, raise, exalt; to lead or bring back; intr. to set sail; to retire. — M. and P. to put to sea, to depart; to set about a thing.
ἀν-άγωγή, ἡ departure, putting to sea.
ἀν-άγωγος 2 uneducated, untrained. [contention.]
ἀν-αγώνιστος 2 refusing)
ἀνα-δαίω to divide anew.
ἀνα-δασμός, ὁ distribution.
ἀνα-δείκνῡμι, or -ύω to show forth; to reveal, make public; to appoint.
ἀνά-δειξις, εως, ἡ publication; appointment.
ἀνα-δέχομαι = ἀναδέχομαι. [ther or sister.]
ἀν-άδελφος 2 without bro-)
ἀνα-δέρκομαι to look up.
ἀνα-δέσμη, ἡ headband.
ἀνα-δέχομαι M. to take up, snatch up; to undergo, bear, endure; to promise; to warrant: to accept, receive.
ἀνα-δέω to tie to, to fasten; to tie round, wreath. — M. also to take (a ship) in tow.

ἀνα-διδάσκω to teach better or thoroughly.

ἀνα-δίδωμι to give forth, to yield; to deliver, distribute; *intr.* to burst forth, bubble up.

ἀνα-διπλόω to make double.

ἀνά-δοτος 2 given back.

ἀνα-δύομαι to rise, emerge; to retire, recede, retreat; to hesitate; to shun, to avoid doing.   [wooer's gifts.]

ἀν-άεδνος 2 without a]

ἀν-αείρω to lift up, draw up; to carry off, obtain.

ἀνα-ζάω to revive, return to life.   [again; to start.]

ἀνα-ζεύγνῡμι to harness]

ἀνα-ζέω to boil up.

ἀνα-ζητέω to search; to inquire after.

ἀνα-ζώννῡμι to gird up.

ἀνα-ζωπῠρέω to refresh, revive.

ἀνα-θάλλω to cause to sprout, to renew.

ἀνα-θαρρέω to regain one's courage.   [anew.]

ἀνα-θαρρύνω to encourage]

ἀνά-θεμα, τό execration; an execrated one.

ἀναθεματίζω to execrate.

ἀνά-θεσις, εως, ἡ dedication.   [ly.]

ἀνα-θεωρέω to view close-]

ἀνα-θηλέω to become green again.

ἀνά-θημα, τό consecrated gift, monument; addition.

ἀνα-θορῠβέω to make a noise, to applaud.

ἀν-αθρέω to observe exactly, to examine.

ἀνα-θρώσκω to spring or jump up.   [ness.]

ἀν-αίδεια, ἡ shameless-]

ἀν-αιδής 2 shameless, regardless, impudent.

ἀν-αίμων 2 bloodless.

ἀν-αιμωτί *adv.* without bloodshed.

ἀν-αίνομαι *M.* to refuse, decline; to deny.

ἀν-αίρεσις, εως, ἡ a lifting up, gathering; burial; destruction, murder.

ἀν-αιρέω to take or lift up; to bury; to give an oracle, to prophesy; to take away, abrogate, abolish, remove; to destroy, kill. — *M.* to lift up for oneself; to bury; to accept, receive, obtain, take away; to undergo, undertake.

ἀν-αισθησίᾱ, ἡ insensibility, dulness.

ἀν-αισθητέω to be dull.

ἀν-αίσθητος 2 unfeeling, dull; painless.   [use.]

ἀν-αισῑμόω to consume,]

ἀν-αισῑμωμα, τό expense for maintenance.

ἀν-αΐσσω to start up.

ἀν-αισχυντέω to be shameless or impudent.

ἀν-αισχυντίᾱ, ἡ impudence.   [shameless.]

ἀν-αίσχυντος 2 impudent,]

ἀν-αίτιος 2 guiltless, innocent.   [upright.]

ἀνα-καθίζω and *M.* to sit]

ἀνα-καινίζω, ἀνα-καινόω to renew.   [newal.]

ἀνα-καίνωσις, εως, ἡ re-]

ἀνα-καίω to kindle.

ἀνα-καλέω to call up, to summon; to call back; to cry. — *M.* to call to assistance; to summon; to sound the retreat.   [unveil.]

ἀνα-καλύπτω to uncover,

ἀνα-κάμπτω *intr.* to bend back; to return.

ἀν-άκανθος 2 boneless.

ἀνα-κάπτω to snap up, wallow.

ἀνά-κειμαι *M.* to be laid up, offered, *or* dedicated; to be erected; to belong to, to depend on.

ἀνακεῖον, τό upper story, upper apartment.

ἀνάκειον, τό prison.

ἀνα-κεράννῡμι to mix up.

ἀνα-κεφαλαιόω to comprehend.

ἀνα-κηκίω to spout up.

ἀνα-κηρύσσω to proclaim.

ἀνα-κινδῡνεύω to risk again.

ἀνα-κῑνέω to move *or* swing upwards; to stir.

ἀνα-κίνησις, εως, ἡ commotion.

ἀνα-κλαίω to weep aloud, burst into tears.

ἀνα-κλάω to bend *or* break back.   [cation.]

ἀνά-κλησις, εως, ἡ invo-]

ἀνα-κλίνω *trans.* to lean against; to open; to cause to recline. — *P.* to lie or lean back.

ἀνα-κογχυλιάζω to gargle.

ἀνα-κοινόω to communicate, impart; to consult, take counsel (with).

ἀνα-κομῑδή, ἡ restitution.

ἀνα-κομίζω to carry up *or* back; to bring back. — *M.* to carry up for oneself; to recover. [(a spear).]

ἀν-ακοντίζω to throw up]

ἀνα-κόπτω to thrust *or* push back, to check.

ἀνα-κουφίζω to lift up; to relieve.   [alleviation.]

ἀνα-κούφισις, εως, ἡ relief,]

ἀνα-κράζω to cry out, shout.   [up.]

ἀνα-κρεμάννῡμι to hang]

ἀνα-κρίνω to question, examine; to judge. — *M.* to litigate.

ἀνά-κρισις, εως, ἡ questioning, examination; remonstrance.

ἀνά-κρουσις, εως, ἡ the pushing back.

ἀνα-κρούω to thrust back. — *M.* to row back slowly.

ἀνα-κτάομαι *M.* to acquire *or* obtain again, to regain.

ἀνακτόριος 3 lordly.

ἀνάκτορον, τό sanctuary.

ἀνα-κυκλέω to revolve.

ἀνα-κυμβάλιάζω to tumble rattling.   [to emerge.]

ἀνα-κύπτω to rise out of,]

ἀνα-κωκύω to wail aloud.

ἀνακῶς *adv.* carefully.

ἀνακωχεύω to hold back, stop, check; to anchor on the high sea; to preserve, retain; to keep quiet.

ἀνακωχή, ἡ cessation; armistice.   [war-cry.]

ἀν-αλαλάζω to raise the]

ἀνα-λαμβάνω to take *or* lift up; to seize; to take along with *or* upon one *or*

into one's service; to undergo, take in hand; to
take again, regain; to
restore, encourage; to re-
trieve, retract. — M. to
undergo, incur; to recover.

ἀνα-λάμπω to flame up.

ἀν-αλγησίᾰ, ἡ unfeeling-
ness, dulness.

ἀν-άλγητος 2 unfeeling;
painless.

ἀνα-λέγω to pick up, ga-
ther, collect; to recount.
— M. to pick up for one-
self; to read.

ἀνα-λείχω to lick up.

ἀνά-ληψις, εως, ἡ a taking
up, regaining, repairing;
ascension.

ἀν-ᾱλίσκω to spend, con-
sume, use up, waste; to
kill.

ἀν-αλκείη, ἡ cowardice.

ἄν-αλκις, ιδος weak, cow-
ardly.   [conformity.]

ἀνα-λογίᾱ, ἡ proportion.

ἀνα-λογίζομαι to count
up, calculate; to consider.

ἀνα-λογισμός, ὁ delibera-
tion, reasoning; = ἀνα-
λογία.   [proportionate.]

ἀνά-λογος 2 answering,

ἄν-αλος 2 unsalted.

ἀν-ᾱλόω = ἀναλίσκω.

ἄν-αλτος 2 insatiable.

ἀνά-λῠσις, εως, ἡ disso-
lution, end; start.

ἀνα-λύω to dissolve, de-
tach, unloose; to deliver;
to set out; to return; to
die. — M. to compensate.

ἀν-άλωμα, τό, ἀν-άλωσις,
εως, ἡ expense, cost.

ἀν-άλωτος 2 unconquer-
able.

ἀνα-μαιμάω to rage
through.   [out.]

ἀνα-μανθάνω to search

ἀν-ἀμάξευτος impassable
for waggons.

ἀν-ᾱμάρτητος 2 faultless,
unfailing; unswerving.

ἀνα-μάσσω to wipe off on.

ἀνα-μάχομαι to renew
battle; to begin anew.

ἀνα-μένω to await; to wait,
stay; to delay; to endure.

ἀνά-μεσος 2 midland.

ἀνα-μετρέω to measure
back; to measure out.

ἀνά-μῑγδα adv. = ἀναμίξ.

ἀνα-μίγνῡμι to mix up to-
gether, to intermix.

ἀνα-μιμνήσκω to remind,
mention. — P. to remem-
ber.

ἀνα-μίμνω = ἀναμένω.

ἀνα-μίξ adv. mixed up,
promiscuously.

ἀνα-μίσγω = ἀναμίγνυμι.

ἀνά-μνησις, εως, ἡ remem-
brance.

ἀνα-μορμύρω to rush or
foam up.   [able.]

ἀν-αμπλάκητος 2 inevit-

ἀν-αμφί-λογος 2, ἀν-
αμφισ-βήτητος 2 undis-
puted.

ἀν-ανδρίᾱ, ἡ unmanliness.

ἄν-ανδρος 2 unmanly, cow-
ardly; without men.

ἀνα-νέμομαι to count up,
enumerate.   [anew.]

ἀνα-νέομαι M. to rise

ἀνα-νεόω and M. to renew.

ἀνα-νεύω to deny, refuse.

ἀνα-νήφω to become sober again.

ἄν-αντα *adv.* up-hill.

ἀν-ανταγώνιστος without a rival. [difficult.

ἀν-άντης 2 up-hill, steep;

ἀν-αντίρρητος 2 indisputable.

ἄναξ, ἄνακτος, ὁ lord, nobleman, king, prince, ruler, master.

ἀνα-ξηραίνω to dry up.

ἀν-άξιος 2 and 3 unworthy, not deserving; vile, contemptible.

ἀνα-ξῡνόω = ἀνακοινόω.

ἀναξῠρίδες, αἱ Persian trousers.

ἀνα-οίγω = ἀνοίγω.

ἀνά-πάλιν *adv.* invertedly; back again.

ἀνα-πάλλω to swing up. — *P.* to spring up.

ἀνά-παυλα and ἀνά-παυσις, εως, ἡ rest, recreation, pause.

ἀνα-παυ(σ)τήριος 2 fit for resting.

ἀνα-παύω to cause to cease or leave off, to stop, finish; to bring to rest. — *M.* to leave off, cease, repose; to come to rest. [seduce.

ἀνα-πείθω to persuade,

ἀνα-πειράομαι *M.* to try, to exercise, train (soldiers).

ἀνα-πείρω to spit, broach.

ἀνα-πεμπάζομαι *M.* to think over. [back.

ἀνα-πέμπω to send up or

ἀνα-˜στάννῡμι to spread out, to open. [away.

ἀνα-πέτομαι to fly up or

ἀνα-πηδάω to jump up or forth. [pled.

ἀνά-πηρος 2 maimed, crip-

ἀνα-πίμπλημι to fill up, fulfil, perform; to suffer; to infect.

ἀνα-πίπτω to fall back, to recede, retire; to lie down to table; to lack courage.

ἀν-απλάκητος = ἀναπλά-

ἀνα-πλάσσω to shape, reshape, restore. [back.

ἀνα-πλέω to sail up or

ἀνά-πλεως, ων filled up, full; infected.

ἀνα-πληρόω to fill up, complete.

ἀνά-πλοος, ὁ a sailing upwards, ascent up stream; landing-place.

ἀνα-πλώω = ἀναπλέω.

ἀνά-πνευσις, εως, ἡ a breathing again; recovery.

ἀνα-πνέω to breathe again; to recover.

ἀνα-πνοή, ἡ breathing: recovery, rest. [back.

ἀνα-ποδίζω to call or bring

ἀν-άποινος 2 without ransom, gratis.

ἀνα-πολέω to repeat.

ἀν-απολόγητος 2 inexcusable.

ἀνα-πράσσω to exact, levy.

ἀνα-πρήθω to let burst forth.

ἀνα-πτερόω to lend wings; to incite, instigate.

ἀνα-πτύσσω to unfold, develop; to disclose, unveil.

ἀνα-πτύω to spit or spout up.

ἀν-άπτω to hang up, fasten, attach; to kindle.

ἀνα-πυνθάνομαι *M.* to inquire, search, learn.

ἀνά-πυστος 2 known, notorious.

ἄν-αρθρος 2 enfeebled.

ἀν-αρίθμητος and ἀν-άριθμος 2 numberless, countless; immense.

ἀν-άριστος 2 without breakfast.

ἄν-αρχος 2 not governed, independent. [harmony.]

ἀν-αρμοστέω to be in disᴶ

ἀν-αρμοστίᾱ, ἡ disharmony. [unfit.]

ἀν-άρμοστος 2 discordant,ᴶ

ἀν-αρπάζω to tear or snatch up, to draw up or out; to sweep away, take by force; to rob, destroy. [torn away.]

ἀν-άρπαστος 2 snatched orᴶ

ἀνα-ρρήγνῡμι to rend, break, tear open; to tear in pieces; to break forth.

ἀνά-ρρησις, εως, ἡ publication.

ἀνα-ρριπτέω, ἀναρρίπτω to throw up, to whirl up; to dice; to risk. [back.]

ἀνα-ρροιβδέω to swallowᴶ

ἀνα-ρρώννῡμι to strengthen or encourage again.

ἀν-άρσιος 2 and 3 reluctant, hostile; repulsive.

ἀν-αρτάω to hang up; to suspend; to make dependent upon; to delay. — *M.* to be prepared to do.

ἀν-άρτιος 2 uneven, odd.

ἀν-αρχίᾱ, ἡ anarchy, licentiousness, disobedience.

ἄν-αρχος 2 without a leader. [stir to rebellion.]

ἀνα-σείω to shake up; toᴶ

ἀνα-σεύομαι *M.* to spout up. [πέω.]

ἀνα-σκέπτομαι = ἀνασκο-ᴶ

ἀνα-σκευάζω to pack up; to transport, convey, to clear away. — *M.* to remove, escape. [σταυρόω.]

ἀνα-σκολοπίζω = ἀνα-ᴶ

ἀνα-σκοπέω to consider exactly.

ἀνά-σπαστος and ἀνά-σπαστός 2 drawn back or opened (door); dragged along, exile.

ἀνα-σπάω to draw up or back, to tear up, to open; λόγους to boast; to drag away. [queen.]

ἄνασσα, ἡ mistress, lady,ᴶ

ἀνάσσω and *M.* to rule, reign, sway, to be lord or master.

ἀν-ἄσσω = ἀναΐσσω.

ἀνα-στᾰδόν *adv.* upright, standing.

ἀνά-στᾰσις, εως, ἡ a setting up; resurrection; expulsion, evacuation, ruin; the getting up; departure.

ἀνά-στᾰτος 2 expelled, exiled; destroyed, wasted; submissive; rebelling.

ἀνα-στᾰτόω to raise up, to seduce. [crucify.]

ἀνα-σταυρόω to impale,ᴶ

ἀνα-στέλλω to drive or keep back.

ἀνα-στενάζω, ἀνα-στενᾰχίζω, ἀνα-στενάχω, ἀνα-στένω to groan, heave sighs, bewail.

ἀνα-στρέφω to turn over, up, back, or about; to upset, throw down; to lead back; *intr.* to return, to face. — *M.* and *P.* = *Act. intr.*; to wander, rove; to dwell, sojourn; to behave.

ἀνα-στροφή, ἡ a turning back, return; a dwelling in; mode of life. [and fro.]

ἀνα-στρωφάω to turn to/

ἀνα-σύρομαι to pull up one's clothes, to bare oneself.

ἀνα-σχετός 2 tolerable.

ἀνα-σχίζω to rip up, slit.

ἀνα-σώζω and *M.* to save; to recover, restore; to recall to memory.

ἀνα-ταράσσω to stir up, disturb. [again.]

ἀνα-τάσσομαι to arrange/

ἀν-ατεί *adv.* see ἄνατος.

ἀνα-τείνω to stretch or hold up, to raise; to extend, spread; *intr.* and *M.* to stretch out or up, to expand. [wall).]

ἀνα-τειχίζω to rebuild (a/

ἀνα-τειχισμός, ὁ a rebuilding.

ἀνα-τέλλω to raise, bring forth, produce; *intr.* to rise, grow, issue.

ἀνα-τέμνω to cut up, dissect.

ἀν-ατί *adv.* see ἄνατος.

ἀνα-τίθημι to set up, erect, consecrate, dedicate; to put or lay on, load with; to ascribe, impute, charge; to put back, remove. — *M.* to shift, transpose, al-

ter; to retract; to expose, narrate. [price).]

ἀνα-τιμάω to enhance (the/

ἀνα-τλῆναι to bear, suffer.

ἀνα-τολή, ἡ sunrise, east.

ἄν-ατος 2 unhurt, uninjured.

ἀνα-τρέπω to upset, overthrow, destroy, ruin; to stir up. — *M.* and *P.* to fall down backwards; to perish.

ἀνα-τρέφω to bring up, nourish; to feed again.

ἀνα-τρέχω to run up or back, to ascend, rise; to sprout, shoot up.

ἀνα-τρίβω to rub well.

ἀνα-τροπή, ἡ subversion, downfall.

ἄν-αυδος, ἀν-αύδητος 2 speechless; unutterable, unheard of.

ἀνα-φαίνω to cause to shine or flash up; to show, to make appear, reveal. — *P.* to appear, to become conspicuous.

ἀνα-φανδά and ἀνα-φανδόν *adv.* openly, conspicuously.

ἀνα-φέρω to carry, convey, bring up; to offer; to lift up, raise, heave; to carry or bring back; to refer, ascribe, propose; to bear, suffer; *intr.* to rise, recover; to refer to; to give an account. — *M.* and *P.* to draw a long breath.

ἀνα-φεύγω to flee up or back; to be absolved.

ἀνα-φλύω to bubble up.

ἀνα-φορέω = ἀναφέρω.

ἀνα-φράζομαι M. to re-cognize. [one's senses.]

ἀνα-φρονέω to recover

ἀνα-φύρω to mix up; to soil. [to puff up.]

ἀνα-φῡσάω to blow out;

ἀνα-φύω to let grow, bring forth; *intr.* and *M.* to grow; to sprout (again).

ἀνα-φωνέω to proclaim, recite. [tire, recede.]

ἀνα-χάζω and *M.* to re-

ἀνα-χαιτίζω to throw off; to overthrow.

ἀνα-χέω to pour upon. — *P.* to flow out, to empty oneself. [wantonness.]

ἀνά-χυσις, εως, ἡ excess,

ἀνα-χωρέω to retire, re-treat, withdraw; to return; to pass over, to be trans-ferred.

ἀνα-χώρησις, εως, ἡ a going back, retreat, depar-ture; recess, refuge.

ἀνα-χωρίζω to lead back.

ἀνα-ψηφίζω to cause to vote again. [recreation.]

ἀνά-ψυξις, ἡ a refreshing,

ἀνα-ψύχω to cool, refresh. — *P.* to recover. [tisfy.]

ἀνδάνω to please; to sa-

ἀν-δίχα *adv.* asunder.

ἀνδρ-αγαθία, ἡ manliness, valour, honesty.

ἀνδρ-αγαθίζομαι to act the gentleman.

ἀνδρ-άγρια, τά spoil. booty.

ἀνδράκάς *adv.* man by man, one by one.

ἀνδρᾱποδίζω to kidnap, enslave.

ἀνδρᾱποδισμός, ὁ kidnap-ping, enslavement.

ἀνδρᾱποδιστής, οῦ, ὁ kid-napper, enslaver.

ἀνδράποδον, τό slave; sla-vish man. [servile, mean.]

ἀνδρᾱποδώδης 2 slavish;

ἀνδρ-αχθής 2 burdening a man. [lour, courage.]

ἀνδρεία, ἡ manliness, va-

ἀνδρεῖος 3 of a man; man-ly, valiant, brave.

ἀνδρειότης, ητος, ἡ = ἀνδρεία. [slaying.]

ἀνδρεϊ-φόντης, ου, ὁ man-

ἀνδρεών = ἀνδρών.

ἀνδρηίη, ἀνδρήιος = ἀν-δρεία. ἀνδρεῖος. [nish.]

ἀνδρηλἄτέω to exile, ba-

ἀνδρία, ἡ = ἀνδρεία.

ἀνδριαντο-ποιέω to make statues. [tor.]

ἀνδριαντο-ποιός, ὁ sculp-

ἀνδριάς, άντος, ὁ statue.

ἀνδρίζομαι to prove a man.

ἀνδρικός 3 = ἀνδρεῖος.

ἀνδρό-γυνος, ὁ man-wo-man, hermaphrodite, eu-nuch. [man, artefact.]

ἀνδρό-κμητος 2 made by

ἀνδρο-κτᾰσία, ἡ men-slaughter.

ἀνδρο-κτόνος 2 man-slay-ing, husband-slaying.

ἀνδρόμεος 3 human.

ἀνδρο-μήκης 2 of a man's height. [man.]

ἀνδρόομαι *P.* to become a

ἀνδρό-σφιγξ, ιγγος. ὁ a man-sphinx. [θρεία.]

ἀνδροτής, ητος. ἡ = ἀν-

ἀνδρο-φάγος 2 eating men, cannibal.

ἀνδρο-φθόρος 2 man-destroying.

ἀνδρό-φθορος 2 slain.

ἀνδρο-φόνος 2 man-killing.

ἀνδρώδης 2 = ἀνδρεῖος.

ἀνδρών, ῶνος, ὁ apartment for males.

ἀν-δύομαι = ἀναδύομαι.

ἀν-εγείρω to awake, rouse. — P. to be roused; to wake up. [reproach.]

ἀν-έγκλητος 2 free from

ἀν-έδην adv. let loose; freely; simply, without ceremony: sluggishly.

ἀν-έεδνος = ἀνάεδνος.

ἀν-εθέλητος 2 unwished for.

ἀν-ειλέω and ἀν-είλλω to keep, press or urge back.

ἀν-ειμένος 3 let loose, licentious, without restraint.

ἄν-ειμι to go up, to rise; to return. [ing.]

ἀν-είμων 2 without cloth-

ἀν-ειπεῖν to proclaim, announce.

ἀν-είργω to keep back.

ἀν-είρομαι to inquire of or about, ask.

ἀν-ειρύω = ἀνερύω.

ἀν-είρω to fasten or tie to.

ἀν-ειρωτάω = ἀνερωτάω.

ἀν-έκαθεν adv. from on high; of old. [let.]

ἀν-έκβατος 2 without out-

ἀν-εκδιήγητος 2 indescribable.

ἀν-έκδοτος 2 unmarried.

ἀν-εκλάλητος unspeakable. [ible.]

ἀν-έκλειπτος inexhaust-

ἀν-εκπίμπλημι to fill anew.

ἀν-έκπληκτος 2 undaunted, intrepid.

ἀν-εκτός 2, ἀνεκτέος 3 bearable.

ἀν-έλεγκτος 2 not examined; irrefutable.

ἀν-ελεήμων 2 and ἀν-έλεος 2 unmerciful.

ἀν-ελευθερία, ἡ slavish mind, meanness, shabbiness.

ἀν-ελεύθερος 2 ignoble, mean.

ἀν-ελίσσω to unroll, open.

ἀν-έλκω, -ύω to draw up, back, or out.

ἀν-έλπιστος 2 unhoped for; hopeless, despairing.

ἀ-νεμέσητος 2 blameless, free from reproach.

ἀνεμίζω to agitate with the wind. [as the wind.]

ἀνεμόεις 3 windy; swift

ἄνεμος, ὁ wind, storm.

ἀνεμο-σκεπής 2 screening from the wind.

ἀνεμο-τρεφής fed by the wind. [tile, vain.]

ἀνεμώλιος 2 windy; fu-

ἀν-ένδεκτος 2 inadmissible.

ἀν-εξέλεγκτος 2 = ἀν-έλεγκτος. [able.]

ἀν-εξερεύνητος 2 inscrut-

ἀν-εξέταστος not examined; not scrutinized; without inquiry.

ἀν-εξεύρετος 2 not to be found out.

ἀνεξί-κακος 2 forbearing.

ἀν-εξιχνίαστος 2 untraceable. [no cause for shame.]

ἀν-επαίσχυντος 2 having

ἀν-επαχθής 2 not molesting, without constraint; indulgent.

ἀν-επιβούλευτον, τό unwariness, harmlessness.

ἀν-επιδεής 2 not needy.

ἀν-επιεικής 2 unyielding, unfair.   [κλητος.]

ἀν-επίκλητος 2 = ἀνέγ-

ἀν-επίληπτος 2 unattacked; blameless.

ἀν-επίσκεπτος 2 unnoticed; inconsiderate.

ἀν-επιστημοσύνη, ἡ ignorance.   [unskilled]

ἀν-επιστήμων 2 ignorant,

ἀν-επίτακτος 2 unconstrained.

ἀν-επιτήδειος 2 unfit, inconvenient; adverse.

ἀν-επιτίμητος 2 not censured.   [reproach.]

ἀν-επίφθονος 2 free from

ἀν-έραμαι P. to fall in love again.

ἀν-ερεθίζω to excite, provoke. — P. to strive anew.

ἀν-ερείπομαι M. to snatch off.

ἀν-ερευνάω to trace out.

ἀν-έρομαι = ἀνείρομαι.

ἀν-ερύω to draw up.

ἀν-έρχομαι to go up, rise; to come; to come back, return, to come home.

ἀν-ερωτάω to question.

ἄν-εσις, εως, ἡ cessation; relaxation.

ἀν-έστιος 2 homeless.

ἀν-ετάζω to search, inquire thoroughly (into).

ἄνευ prp. with gen. without; away from, far from; besides.

ἄνευθεν adv. apart, asunder; = ἄνευ.

ἀν-εύθετος 2 inconvenient.

ἀν-εύθῡνος 2 irresponsible.

ἀν-ευρίσκω to find out.

ἀν-ευφημέω to cry aloud.

ἀ-νέφελος 2 cloudless; uncovered.   [ed.]

ἀν-εχέγγυος 2 unwarrant-

ἀν-έχω to hold or lift up; to support, to exalt, honour; to restrain, stop; intr. to project, reach; to emerge, come up; to stop, stay, persist. — M. to hold up; to rise; to stand upright; to keep one's ground; to hold out; to bear, admit; to keep one's temper.

ἀνεψιά, ἡ female cousin.

ἀνεψιός, ὁ male cousin.

ἄνεω, ἄνεῳ (from ἄνεως) silent, mute.   [again.]

ἀν-ηβάω to grow young

ἀν-ηγέομαι M. to count up, relate.

ἄνηθον, τό anise; dill.

ἀν-ήκεστος 2 incurable, irreparable; inexorable; immoderate. [not knowing.]

ἀν-ήκοος 2 not hearing;

ἀν-ηκουστέω not to listen (to).   [horrible.]

ἀν-ήκουστος 2 unheard of,

ἀν-ήκω to be come; to reach to; to rest or depend on; to become, to beseem.

ἀν-ήλιος 2 sunless.

ἀν-ήμελκτος 2 unmilked.

ἀν-ήμερος 2 untamed, wild.

ἀν-ήνεμος 2 calm.

ἀν-ήνοθα perf. to gush forth, mount up.

ἀν-ήνυ(σ)τος 2 unfeasible; unsuccessful, endless.

ἀν-ήνωρ 2 unmanly.

ἀνήρ, ὁ man, male; husband; warrior, hero: man (as opp. to gods and beasts).

ἀν-ήριθμος 2 = ἀνάριθμος. [untilled.]

ἀν-ήροτος 2 unploughed,]

ἄνησον = ἄνηθον.

ἀνθ-αιρέομαι M. to choose instead of. [tend, rival.]

ἀνθ-αμιλλάομαι P. to con-]

ἀνθ-άπτομαι to lay hold of, to seize in turns; to manage, carry on; to blame.

ἀνθ-έλκω to draw to the other side.

ἀνθέμιον, τό flower.

ἀνθεμόεις 3 flowery.

ἀνθερεών, ῶνος, ὁ chin.

ἀνθέριξ, ικος, ὁ awn; ear of corn; stalk.

ἀνθέω to bloom, blossom, flourish; to shine.

ἀνθ-ήλιος 2 = ἀντήλιος.

ἀνθηρός 3 blooming, fresh; gay; violent. [turn.]

ἀνθ-ησσάομαι to yield in]

ἀνθίζω to deck as with flowers. [able.]

ἀνθινός 3 flowery; veget-]

ἀνθ-ίστημι to set against, oppose; intr. and P. to oppose oneself, resist.

ἀνθ-ομολογέομαι M. to concede or grant in turn; to confess; to praise.

ἀνθ-οπλίζομαι to arm oneself against.

ἀνθ-ορμέω to ride at anchor opposite.

ἄνθος, τό flower, blossom.

ἀνθ-οσμίας, ου sweet-scented, fragrant. [coal.]

ἀνθρακιά, ἡ burning char-]

ἄνθραξ, ακος, ὁ (living) coal. [serving.]

ἀνθρωπ-άρεσκος 2 time-]

ἀνθρώπειος 3 and ἀνθρώπινος 3 human; sublunar. [man; wretch.]

ἀνθρώπιον, τό child of]

ἀνθρωπο-ειδής 2 in the shape of man. [slaying.]

ἀνθρωπο-κτόνος 2 man-]

ἄνθρωπος, ὁ man (as opp. to gods and beasts), human being, anyone; husband; inhabitant; slave; ἡ ἄ. woman, concubine.

ἀνθρωπο-φαγέω to be a man-eater. [man species.]

ἀνθρωπο-φυής 2 of hu-]

ἀνθ-υπάγω to accuse in turn. [consul.]

ἀνθ-υπατεύω to be pro-]

ἀνθ-ύπατος, ὁ proconsul.

ἀνθ-υποπτεύομαι P. to be suspected in turn.

ἀνία, ἡ vexation, annoyance; pain, grief.

ἀνιάζω to vex, annoy, tease; to be ill-humoured or grieved.

ἀν-ιάομαι M. to heal again.

ἀνιαρός 3 distressing, molesting, grieving; adverse; melancholy.

ἀν-ίατος 2 incurable.

ἀνιάω to distress, vex; to grieve, molest, annoy.

ἀν-ίδρυτος 2 restless, unsteady; unsociable.

ἀν-ιδρωτί adv. without sweat.

ἀν-ίερος 2 unholy, wicked.

ἀν-ίημι to send up; to raise, produce; to let loose, relax, dismiss, detach, neglect, omit; to incite; to admit, permit, remit; *intr.* to slacken, cease. — *P.* to be loose, free, or licentious; to be exposed, sacrificed, or abandoned.

ἀνίηρός 3 = ἀνιαρός.

ἀ-νίκητος 2 unconquered; invincible.

ἀν-ίλεως 2 unmerciful.

ἀν-ιμάω to pull up.

ἄν-ιππος 2 unmounted; not fit for horses.

ἀ-νιπτό-πους, ποδος with unwashed feet.

ἄ-νιπτος 2 unwashed.

ἄν-ίσος 2 unequal.

ἀν-ισότης, ητος, ἡ inequality.

ἀν-ισόω to equalize.

ἀν-ίστημι to set up, erect, build; to raise, rouse, stir up; to drive away, dislodge; to raise from the dead; to excite; *intr.* and *P.* to be driven away; to rise, get up; to come forth, appear; to start; to recover oneself. [to), investigate.]

ἀν-ιστορέω to inquire (in-

ἀν-ίσχω = ἀνέχω.

ἀν-ίσωσις, ἡ equilibration.

ἀν-ιχνεύω to trace back, descry.

ἀν-νέομαι = ἀνανέομαι.

ἄν-οδος[1], ἡ way up; march up.

ἄν-οδος[2] 2 impassable.

ἀ-νοήμων 2 unwise.

ἀν-νόητος 2 foolish, silly; inconceivable.

ἄ-νοια, ἡ folly, imprudence.

ἀν-οίγνυμι, ἀν-οίγω to open, uncover, disclose.

ἀν-οιδέω to swell up.

ἀν-οικίζομαι to settle in the up-country; to lie inland.

ἀν-οικοδομέω to rebuild, build.

ἄν-οικος 2 houseless, homeless. [pitied.]

ἄν-οικτος 2 pitiless; un-

ἀν-οιμωκτί *adv.* without wailing, with impunity.

ἄν-οιξις, ἡ an opening.

ἀν-οιστέος 3 to be reported.

ἀν-οιστός 3 reported; pending. [see ἀναφ.]

ἀν-οκωχεύω, ἀν-οκωχή

ἀν-όλβιος and ἄν-ολβος 2 unfortunate, miserable.

ἀν-όλεθρος 2 unhurt.

ἀν-ολκή, ἡ a drawing up.

ἀν-ολολύζω to cry out, scream, shout. [bewail.]

ἀν-ολοφύρομαι *M.* to wail,

ἄν-ομβρος 2 without rain.

ἀ-νομέω to act contrary to law.

ἀ-νομία, ἡ lawlessness.

ἀν-όμματος 2 eyeless.

ἀν-όμοιος 2 unequal, unlike. [equality.]

ἀν-ομοιότης, ητος, ἡ in-

ἀν-ομολογέω and *M.* to agree (again).

ἀν-ομολογούμενος 3 inconsistent, contradictory.

ἄ-νομος 2 lawless, wicked; pagan. [enjoying.]

ἀν-όνητος 2 useless; unἄ-νοος 2 foolish.

ἀν-οπαῖα *adv.* through the smoke-hole (or up in the air, or unnoticed).

ἄν-οπλος 2 unarmed.

ἀν-ορθόω to set up, to set right; to rebuild, restore.

ἄν-ορμος 2 harbourless.

ἀν-όρνῦμαι *M.* to rise.

ἀν-ορούω to start or leap up.

ἀν-όσιος 2 unholy, wicked.

ἀν-οσιότης, ητος, ἡ wickedness.

ἄ-νοσος 2 free from disease.

ἀ-νόστιμος and ἄ-νοστος 2 not returning.

ἀν-ούτᾰτος 2 unwounded, *adv.* ἀνουτητί.   [mistiee.]

ἀν-οχή, ἡ patience; ar-

ἀν-σχετός = ἀνασχετός.

ἄντα *adv.* opposite, over against, to the face; straight on; against, before.

ἀντ-ἀγοράζω to buy in return.

ἀντ-ἀγωνίζομαι *M.* to fight or struggle against; to contend.

ἀντ-αγωνιστής, οῦ, ὁ adversary, rival.   [return.]

ἀντ-ἀδικέω to wrong in

ἀνταῖος 3 opposed, in front.

ἀντ-αίρω (-αείρω) and *M.* to lift in defence; to withstand.   [turn.]

ἀντ-αιτέω to ask in re-

ἀνταχαῖος, ὁ sturgeon.

ἀντ-ἀκούω to hear in turn.

ἀντ-ἀλλάσσω to exchange, to give or take in exchange.

ἀντ-ἀμείβομαι *M.* to answer, reply; = ἀντ-αλλάσσω.

ἀντ-αμῦνομαι *M.* to de-

fend or revenge oneself, to resist, to requite.

ἀντ-αναβιβάζω to bring up or cause to go up against.

ἀντ-ανάγω to lead up against, to lead to the high sea; *intr. M.* and *P.* to sail to meet.

ἀντ-αναιρέω to neutralize.

ἀντ-αναμένω to wait in turn.

ἀντ-αναπίμπλημι, ἀντ-αναπληρόω to fill or complete in turn.

ἀντ-άνειμι to go up against.

ἀντ-ανίσταμαι *M.* to rise up against.

ἀντ-άξιος 3 equivalent.

ἀντ-αξιόω to claim in return.   [in return.]

ἀντ-απαιτέω to demand

ἀντ-αποδίδωμι to give back, requite; to correspond.

ἀντ-απόδοσις, ἡ and ἀντ-απόδομα, τό a giving back in turn, requital.

ἀντ-αποκρίνομαι *M.* to answer against; to litigate.

ἀντ-αποκτείνω to kill in return.   [in return.]

ἀντ-απόλλῦμι to destroy

ἀντ-αποφαίνω to adduce as a counter-evidence.

ἀντ-αρκέω to be a match for.   [come in return.]

ἀντ-ασπάζομαι *M.* to wel-

ἀντ-ατῑμάζω to defame in return.   [accost.]

ἀντ-αυδάω to answer; to

ἀντάω = ἀντιάω.

ἀντ-ειπεῖν see ἀντιλέγω.

ἀντ-είρομαι = ἀντέρομαι.

ἀντ-εισάγω to import in return. [in return.]
ἀντ-εκπέμπω to send out]
ἀντ-εκπλέω to sail out against. [against.]
ἀντ-εκτρέχω to sally out]
ἀντ-ελπίζω to hope in return. [roads against.]
ἀντ-εμβάλλω to make in-]
ἀντ-εμβιβάζω to change the crew. [requital.]
ἀντ-εμπίπλημι to fill in]
ἀντ-εμπίπρημι to set on fire in revenge.
ἀντ-έξειμι, ἀντ-εξέρχομαι to march out against.
ἀντ-εξόρμησις, ἡ a starting against.
ἀντ-επάγω to lead to attack in turn; to march against. [out against.]
ἀντ-επανάγομαι to sail]
ἀντ-έπειμι, ἀντ-επέξειμι, ἀντ-επεξελαύνω, ἀντ-επεξέρχομαι = ἀντέξειμι.
ἀντ-επεξάγω to extend the line of battle likewise.
ἀντ-επιβουλεύω to form counter-designs.
ἀντ-επιθυμέω to desire in turn. [return.]
ἀντ-επικουρέω to help in]
ἀντ-επιμελέομαι P. to make counter-preparations.
ἀντ-επιτάσσω to enjoin in turn. [fortify against.]
ἀντ-επιτειχίζομαι M. to]
ἀντ-επιτίθημι to order in return. [in love.]
ἀντ-εραστής, οῦ, ὁ rival]
ἀντ-ερείδω to stand firm against.
ἀντ-ερεῖν see ἀντιλέγω.

ἀντ-έρομαι to ask in return. [return.]
ἀντ-έρως, ωτος, ὁ love in]
ἀντ-ευεργετέω, ἀντ-ευποιέω to benefit in return.
ἀντ-έχω to hold against, to object; to keep off; to bear, sustain; to suffice; to keep one's ground. — M. to object in defence; to cling to; to aim at; to be attached to; to take care of.
ἀντή, ἡ supplication.
ἀντ-ήλιος 2 eastern.
ἄντην adv. opposite, over against, face to face; in front, openly.
ἀντήρης 2 opposite, adverse. [beam.]
ἀντηρίς, ίδος, ἡ supporting]
ἄντησις, εως, ἡ a meeting.
ἀντί prp. with gen. opposite, over against, before; in return of, for the sake of, instead of, for.
ἀντιάζω = ἀντιάω.
ἀντι-άνειρα, ἡ manlike.
ἀντιάω to go or advance to meet; to approach, meet; to attack; to accept, partake; to experience; to solicit, entreat. — M. to partake. [foot against.]
ἀντι-βαίνω to set one's]
ἀντι-βάλλω to throw in turn; to exchange.
ἀντί-βιος 3 hostile, using force; adv. ἀντιβίην with force, in battle.
ἀντι-βλέπω to look straight at.

ἀντι-βοηθέω to assist in turn; to assist the adversary.

ἀντι-βολέω to go to meet, approach, meet; to partake, join in; to solicit, entreat.

ἀντι-βόλησις, ἡ and ἀντι-βολίᾱ, ἡ entreaty.

ἀντι-γενεηλογέω to devise another pedigree.

ἀντι-γραφή, ἡ counter-writ, accusatory libel, protest, counter-plea.

ἀντί-γραφον, τό copy.

ἀντι-γράφω to write in answer; to remonstrate, protest. [turn.

ἀντι-δάκνω to bite in re-

ἀντι-δέομαι P. to beg in turn.

ἀντι-διατίθεμαι to resist.

ἀντι-δίδωμι to give in return, to give back, repay, requite; to atone for; to offer exchange of property.

ἀντι-δῑκέω to be at law, to litigate.

ἀντί-δῑκος, ὁ opponent, adversary. [property.

ἀντί-δοσις, ἡ exchange of

ἀντι-δράω to requite.

ἀντι-δωρέομαι M. to present with in return.

ἀντί-θεος 3 godlike.

ἀντι-θεραπεύω to honour in return.

ἀντί-θεσις, ἡ opposition, the contrary.

ἀντι-θέω to run to meet; to rival in running.

ἀντί-θυρον, τό vestibule, floor. [against.

ἀντι-κάθημαι to sit over

ἀντι-καθίζομαι to be seated over against.

ἀντι-καθίστημι to oppose, to place in lieu of; to encourage; intr. and P. to resist; to be placed in lieu of.

ἀντι-κακουργέω to injure in turn. [turn.

ἀντι-κᾰλέω to invite in

ἀντι-καταλλάσσομαι M. to exchange for.

ἀντί-κειμαι to be opposed.

ἀντι-κελεύω to request in turn.

ἀντι-κλαίω to weep in turn.

ἀντι-κόπτω, ἀντι-κρούω to resist, struggle against.

ἀντι-κρύ, ἄντι-κρυς over against, against, to the face; straight on; outright, thoroughly, really.

ἀντι-κύρω to meet, to fall in with. [weak part.

ἀντι-λᾰβή, ἡ handle, hold;

ἀντι-λαμβάνω to take or receive in turn; to take part with; to hold fast. — M. to take hold of, to lay claim to, to seize, to take care of.

ἀντι-λέγω to gainsay, deny, dispute; to resist; to reply.

ἀντί-λεκτος 2 disputed, controverted.

ἀντί-ληψις, ἡ a receiving in return; seizure, claim; objection; a falling sick, infection; an aiding.

ἀντι-λογέω = ἀντιλέγω.

ἀντι-λογίᾱ, ἡ gainsaying, rejoinder, contradiction; law-suit; contention, enmity.

ἀντι-λογίζομαι *M.* to consider against.

ἀντι-λογικός 3 controversial, sophistical.   [turn.]

ἀντι-λοιδορέω to revile in

ἀντί-λϋρος lyre-like.

ἀντί-λυτρον, τό ransom.

ἀντι-μάχομαι *M.* to be opposed in battle.   [turn.]

ἀντι-μέλλω to await in

ἀντι-μέμφομαι *M.* to blame in turn.   [out again.]

ἀντι-μετρέω to measure]

ἀντι-μέτωπος 2 with opposed fronts.

ἀντι-μηχανάομαι *M.* to devise counter-practises.

ἀντι-μίμησις, ἡ imitation on the other side.

ἀντι-μισθία, ἡ requital.

ἀντι-ναυπηγέω to build ships against; to take preventive measures in shipbuilding.

ἀντί-ξοος 2 hostile, opposed.

ἀντιόομαι *P.* to resist.

ἀντίος 3 opposite, confronting; opposed, contrary.

ἀντιο-στατέω to resist.

ἀντιόω = ἀντιάω.

ἀντί-πᾰλος 2 wrestling against; rival, contrary, adversary; counterpoising, equivalent, counter-balanced.   [pare.]

ἀντι-παραβάλλω to com-]

ἀντι-παραγγέλλω to command in turn.   [against.]

ἀντι-παρκθέω to run past]

ἀντι-παρακᾰλέω to encourage in turn.

ἀντι-παρακελεύομαι *M.* to exhort in turn.

ἀντι-παρᾰλῡπέω to injure in turn.

ἀντι-παραπλέω to sail along on the other side.

ἀντι-παρασκευάζομαι *M.* to make counter-preparations.   [ter-preparation.]

ἀντι-παρασκευή, ἡ coun-]

ἀντι-παρατάσσω to draw out in array against.

ἀντι-παρατίθημι to oppose, to compare.

ἀντι-πάρειμι to march parallel to.

ἀντι-παρεξάγω to lead to battle against.   [πάρειμι.]

ἀντι-παρέρχομαι = ἀντι-]

ἀντι-παρέχω to offer in turn.   [turn.]

ἀντι-πάσχω to suffer in]

ἀντι-πᾰτᾰγέω to outsound.

ἀντι-πέμπω to send against, in return, back, or in supply.

ἀντι-πέραια, τά the opposite coast.

ἀντι-πέρᾱν, ἀντι-πέρᾱς *adv.* over against, opposite.

ἀντί-πετρος 2 hard as stone.

ἀντι-πίπτω to fall out differently.

ἀντι-πλέω to sail against.

ἀντι-πλήξ, ῆγος wavebeaten.   [turn.]

ἀντι-πληρόω to man in]

ἀντι-ποθέω to long for in turn.

ἀντι-ποιέω to do in turn. — *M.* to claim; to rival; to contend.   [atoning.]

ἀντί-ποινος 2 requiting,]

ἀντι-πολεμέω to make war against.

ἀντι-πόλεμος, ὁ enemy.

ἀντι-πολιορκέω to besiege in turn. [march against.]

ἀντι-πορεύομαι P. to ἀντί-πορος 2 opposite.

ἀντι-πράσσω (-πρήσσω) to counter-act.

ἀντι-πρεσβεύομαι M. to send ambassadors in turn.

ἀντι-πρόειμι, ἀντι-πρόσειμι to advance against.

ἀντι-προσερρήθην (from ἀντιπροσαγορεύω) to requite salutation. [face.]

ἀντι-πρόσωπος 2 face to ἀντι-προτείνω to stretch forth in turn.

ἀντί-πρωρος prow to prow.

ἀντί-πυλος 2 with opposite doors.

ἀντί-ρροπος 2 counterpoising, outweighing.

ἀντι-σήκωσις, ἡ equilibrium. [an equal footing.]

ἀντ-ἰσόομαι P. to be on ἀντί-σπαστος 2 spasmodic.

ἀντι-σταθμος 2 equal in weight. [adverse party.]

ἀντι-στασιάζω to form an ἀντι-στασιώτης, ου, ὁ political adversary.

ἀντι-στατέω to resist.

ἀντι-στοιχέω to stand opposite in array.

ἀντι-στρατεύομαι M. to take the field against.

ἀντι-στράτηγος, ὁ general of the enemies.

ἀντι-στρατοπεδεύομαι M. to encamp over against.

ἀντί-στροφος 2 corresponding. [firm in turn]

ἀντ-ισχυρίζομαι M. to af-

ἀντ-ίσχω = ἀντέχω.

ἀντί-ταξις, ἡ opposite line of battle.

ἀντι-τάσσω to range in battle agai st. [pose.]

ἀντι-τείνω to resist, op-

ἀντι-τείχισμα, τό counter-fortification.

ἀντι-τεχνάομαι M. to form a counter-scheme.

ἀντι-τέχνησις, ἡ counter-practise.

ἀντί-τεχνος, ὁ rival in art.

ἀντι-τίθημι to set against, oppose, compare; to compensate, give for.

ἀντι-τιμάω to honour in return. — M. to make a counter-proposal of a fine.

ἀντι-τιμωρέομαι M. to revenge oneself in turn.

ἀντι-τίνω to atone for, suffer punishment.

ἀντι-τολμάω to act boldly in turn. [rows in return.]

ἀντι-τοξεύω to shoot ar-

ἀντι-τορέω to bore through.

ἄν-τιτος 2 requited.

ἀντι-τυγχάνω to get in return.

ἀντί-τυπος 2 repulsive; echoing; ἀντί-τυπον, τό exact representation, prototype.

ἀντι-τύπτω to beat in turn.

ἀντι-φερίζω to think oneself equal.

ἀντι-φέρω to set against, oppose. — M. to resist, cope with.

ἀντί-φημι to gainsay.

ἀντι-φιλέω to love in return.

ἀντί-φονος 2 murdering in return. [caution.]

ἀντι-φῠλάκή, ἡ mutual

ἀντι-φῠλάττομαι M. to be on one's guard against.

ἀντι-φωνέω to reply, gainsay. [turn.]

ἀντι-χαίρω to be glad in

ἀντι-χᾰρίζομαι M. to oblige or favour in turn.

ἀντι-χειροτονέω to vote against.

ἀντι-χράω to suffice.

ἀντί-χριστος, ὁ antichrist.

ἀντλέω to draw water; to empty.

ἄντλημα, τό bucket.

ἀντλίᾱ, ἡ and ἄντλος, ὁ bilge-water; bottom of a ship. [turn.]

ἀντ-οικτίζω to pity in

ἀν-τολή = ἀνατολή.

ἀντ-όμνῡμι to swear in turn. [anew.]

ἀντ-ονομάζω to name

ἀντ-ορύσσω to dig a countermine. [in turn.]

ἀντ-οφείλω to be indebted

ἀντ-οφθαλμέω to withstand to the face.

ἀν-τρέπω = ἀνατρέπω.

ἄντρον, τό cave, grotto, cavern.

ἀντρώδης 2 cavernous.

ἄντυξ, υγος, ἡ circle, rim, edge; rail of a chariot.

ἀντ-υποκρίνομαι M. to answer in return.

ἀντ-υπουργέω to return kindness.

ἀντ-ωμοσίᾱ, ἡ plaintiff's oath; bill of indictment.

ἀντ-ωνέομαι M. to outbid.

ἀντ-ωφελέω to help in return. [drought.]

ἀν-υδρίᾱ, ἡ want of water,

ἄν-υδρος 2 without water, dry; ἡ ἄ. desert.

ἀν-υμέναιος 2 without nuptial song, unwedded.

ἄνῦμι = ἀνύω.

ἀ-νύμφευτος and ἄ-νυμφος 2 unmarried; ill-married.

ἀν-υπέρβλητος 2 insurpassable, insuperable.

ἀν-υπόδητος 2 unshod, barefoot.

ἀν-υπόκρῐτος 2 guileless.

ἀν-ύποπτος 2 unsuspected; unsuspecting. [ible.]

ἀν-υπόστᾰτος 2 irresist-

ἀν-υπότακτος 2 not subjected; disobedient.

ἄνῠσις, εως, ἡ achievement, success.

ἀνυστός 3 to be accomplished, feasible.

ἄνῠτω and ἄνὔτω = ἀνύω.

ἀν-ῠφαίνω to weave anew.

ἀνύω and ἀνύω to accomplish, complete, achieve, perform, effect; to travel over, advance; to consume, finish.

ἄνω = ἀνύω

ἄνω adv. up, upwards, on high, above, aloft; up country, northwards; beyond; ἀνωτέρω higher up; ἀνωτάτω upmost, highest up.

ἄνωγα and ἀνώγω to command, order, advise.

ἀνώ-γαιον, τό and ἀνώ-γεων, ω, τό upper story or apartment; granary.

ἀν-ώδυνος 2 free from pain, painless; soothing pain.

ἄνωθεν adv. from on high, from above; above; downward; ever since; anew.

ἀν-ωθέω to push up or back. — M. to ward off.

ἀν-ώϊστος 2 unexpected; adv. ἀνωϊστί. [able.]

ἀν-ωλεθρος 2 imperish-]

ἀν-ωμαλία, ἡ unevenness, inequality. [equal.]

ἀν-ώμαλος 2 uneven, un-]

ἀν-ωμοτί adv. unsworn.

ἀν-ώνυμος 2 without name.

ἀν-ωρία, ἡ wrong or unseasonable time.

ἀν-ωρος 2 untimely.

ἀνωτερικός 3 situated higher up.

ἀν-ωφελής and ἀν-ωφέλητος 2 useless, hurtful.

ἄ-ξενος 2 inhospitable.

ἄ-ξεστος 2 unpolished.

ἀξία, ἡ worth, value, price; dignity, honour; merit, desert; the due.

ἀξι-αφήγητος 2 worth relating. [thy.]

ἀξι-έπαινος 2 praisewor-]

ἀξίνη, ἡ axe, hatchet.

ἀξιο-βίωτος 2 worth living for. [able.]

ἀξιο-θαύμαστος 2 admir-]

ἀξιο-θέατος 2 worth seeing.

ἀξιό-λογος 2 worth naming; important; just, proper. [battle.]

ἀξιό-μαχος a match for in]

ἀξιο-μνημόνευτος 2 memorable. [tory.]

ἀξιό-νῑκος 2 deserving vic-]

ἀξιό-πιστος 2 trustworthy.

ἄξιος 3 worth, equivalent, compensating; worthy, precious; due, convenient, deserving; right and proper; cheap. [notice.]

ἀξιό-σκεπτος 2 worthy of]

ἀξιο-στράτηγος 2 worthy of being general.

ἀξιο-τέκμαρτος 2 demonstrative.

ἀξιό-χρεως, ων 2 considerable; sufficient; authentic; proper, convenient, worthy.

ἀξιόω to rate, estimate; to think worthy, esteem; to request, claim; to suppose, take for true.

ἀξίωμα, τό, ἀξίωσις, ἡ valuation, estimation; dignity, rank, credit; consideration; importance; request, will; opinion.

ἄ-ξῦλος 2 not cleared of wood; scantily wooded.

ἄξων, ονος, ὁ axle.

ἀοιδή, ἡ song, myth, legend.

ἀοιδιάω to sing.

ἀοίδιμος 2 celebrated in song; notorious.

ἀοιδός, ὁ, ἡ singer, poet; conjurer.

ἀ-οίκητος 2 uninhabited.

ἄ-οικος 2 houseless, homeless, poor; uninhabitable.

ἄ-οινος 2 without wine; disdaining wine.

ἄ-οκνος 2 unhesitating; eager, willing. [crowds.]

ἀ-ολλής 2 all together, in]

ἀ-ολλίζω to assemble.

ἄορ, ἄορος, τό sword.

ἀ-όρᾱτος 2 unseeing; invisible.

ἀ-όριστος 2 undefined.

ἀορτήρ, ῆρος, ὁ baldrick, shoulder-belt. [protector.]

ἀοσσητήρ, ῆρος, ὁ helper,]

ἄ-ουτος 2 unwounded.

ἀ-οχλησίᾱ, ἡ ease.

ἀπ-αγγελίᾱ, ἡ report.

ἀπ-αγγέλλω to report, announce, relate, declare; to praise.

ἀ-πᾱγής 2 not solid.

ἀπ-αγῑνέω to carry off; to pay.

ἀπ-αγορεύω to forbid, deny, dissuade; to fail, fall short, to be worn out.

ἀπ-αγριόομαι P. to become wild or savage.

ἀπ-άγχω to strangle. — M. to hang oneself.

ἀπ-άγω to lead or carry on or away; to remove; to march off, go away; to lead up, back, or home. — M. to take with one.

ἀπ-ᾰγωγή, ἡ a leading off, taking home; payment; motion of arrest.

ἀπ-ᾰδεῖν see ἀφανδάνω.

ἀπ-ᾴδω to sing out of tune.

ἀπ-ᾰείρω = ἀπαίρω.

ἀπ-ᾰθᾰνᾰτίζω to make immortal.

ἀ-πᾰθής 2 without pain, not suffering; uninjured; unfeeling, dull; impatient; unaccustomed.

ἀ-παιδευσίᾱ, ἡ want of education, coarseness.

ἀ-παίδευτος 2 uneducated, rude.

ἀ-παιδίᾱ, ἡ childlessness.

ἀπ-αίνῠμαι to take from, withdraw.

ἀπ-αίρω to lift away, to take or snatch away; to cause to start; intr. to start, march or sail away. — M. to go away.

ἄ-παις, αιδος childless.

ἀπ-αίσσω = ἀπᾴσσω.

ἀπ-αισχῠνομαι to renounce for shame.

ἀπ-αιτέω, ἀπ-αιτίζω to demand back, reclaim.

ἀπ-αίτησις, ἡ reclamation.

ἀπ-ακρῑβόω to work exactly.

ἀ-πάλαμνος 2 awkward, wavering, inactive. [dull.]

ἀπ-αλγέω to forget; to be]

ἀπ-αλείφω to blot out.

ἀπ-αλέξω to ward off; to defend from. — M. to defend oneself. [thoroughly.]

ἀπ-αλθομαι to be cured]

ἀπ-αλλᾰγή, ἡ separation; retreat; deliverance.

ἀπ-αλλαξείω to wish for deliverance. [λαγή.]

ἀπ-άλλαξις, ἡ = ἀπαλ-]

ἀπ-αλλάσσω to set free, release, deliver, dismiss, remove, separate; intr. to get off, to get clear. — P. to go away, depart; to be delivered or released.

ἀπ-αλλοτριόω to estrange.

ἀπ-αλοιάω to crush.

ἀπᾰλός 3 soft, tender, delicate.

ἀπᾰλότης, ητος, ἡ softness, tenderness; effeminacy.

ἀπᾰλο-τρεφής 2 well-fed.

ἀπ-αμάω to cut off, mow.

ἀπ-αμβλόνω to blunt, weaken. [τάνω.]

ἀπ-αμβροτεῖν see ἀφαμαρ-

ἀπ-ἀμείβομαι to answer.

ἀπ-αμελέω to neglect utterly or altogether.

ἀπ-αμόνω to ward off. — M. to repel; to defend oneself. [to refuse.]

ἀπ-αναίνομαι M. to deny;

ἀπ-αναισχυντέω to do with the utmost impudence.

ἀπ-αναλίσκω to consume, waste; to kill.

ἀπ-άνευθεν adv from afar, far off; aside, apart; without (with gen.).

ἀπ-ανίστημι to cause to rise or depart; intr. and M. to rise, depart, emigrate.

ἀπ-αντάω to come or go to meet, to meet; to advance against; to come to pass, to happen.

ἀπάντη adv. everywhere.

ἀπ-άντησις, ἡ meeting.

ἀπ-αντίκρύ, ἀπ-αντίον adv. right over against.

ἀπ-ανύω to finish.

ἄπαξ adv. once; at once, once for all; for the first time.

ἀπ-αξιόω to think unworthy; to detest, reject.

ἀ-παράβατος 2 imperishable. [ρέω.]

ἀπ-αραιρῆσθαι see ἀφαι-

ἀ-παραίτητος 2 inexorable; inevitable. [for.]

ἀ-παράκλητος 2 uncalled

ἀ-παρασκεύαστος 2 and ἀ-παράσκευος 2 unprepared, unarmed.

ἀπ-ἀράσσω to dash down, to strike or cut off.

ἀπ-αρέσκω to displease. — M. to reconcile fully.

ἀπ-ἀριθμέω to count over.

ἀπ-ἀρίθμησις, ἡ a numbering.

ἀπ-αρκέω to suffice.

ἀπ-αρνέομαι P. and M. to deny; to disown, refuse.

ἀπ-αρνος 2 denying.

ἀπ-αρτάω to hang (up), attach; to put away, remove. [cisely.]

ἀπ-αρτί adv. exactly, pre-

ἀπ-άρτι adv. just now, at once. [amount.]

ἀπαρτι-λογία, ἡ full

ἀπ-αρτισμός, ὁ consummation, completion.

ἀπ-ἀρύω to skim off.

ἀπ-αρχή, ἡ firstlings, firstfruit. [sacred act.]

ἀπ-άρχομαι to begin a

ἅπας, ἅπασα, ἅπαν all, all together; whole, entire; each, every.

ἀπ-ᾁσσω to leap down; to rush away; to digress.

ἄ-παστος 2 not having tasted. [beguile.]

ἀπατάω to cheat, deceive,

ἀπ-ἀτερθεν adv. asunder, apart; far from (with gen.).

ἀπατεών, ῶνος, ὁ cheat.

ἀπάτη, ἡ cheating, deceit, fraud.

ἀπατήλιος 2 and ἀπατηλός 3 and 2 deceitful. [roughly.]

ἀπ-ατιμάω to despise tho-

ἀ-πάτωρ, ορος fatherless.

ἀπ-αύγασμα, τό reflection, image.

ἀπ-αυδάω to forbid.

ἀπ-αυθᾱδίζομαι, ἀπ-αυ-θᾱδιάζομαι *M.* to be overweening. [away, to rob.]

ἀπ-αυράω to take or snatch

ἄ-παυστος 2 incessant.

ἀπ-αυτομολέω to desert, go over.

ἀπᾰφίσκω to beguile.

ἄ-πεδος 2 even, flat.

ἀ-πείθεια, ἡ disobedience.

ἀ-πειθέω to disobey; to be an unbeliever.

ἀ-πειθής 2 disobedient; unbelieving.

ἀπ-εικάζω to copy, portray; to describe; to compare.

ἀπ-εικότως *adv.* unjustly.

ἀπ-ειλέω[1] to press hard.

ἀπειλέω[2] to threaten, menace; to boast; to promise.

ἀπειλή, ἡ and ἀπείλημα, τό menace, threat; boast.

ἀπειλητήρ, ῆρος, ὁ braggart.

ἀπειλητήριος 2 and ἀπειλητικός 3 threatening.

ἄπ-ειμι[1] to be away or absent; to be wanting.

ἄπ-ειμι[2] to go away, to leave; to go over; to return.

ἀπ-εῖπον to tell plainly, pronounce; to forbid, deny, refuse; to renounce, resign; *intr.* to fail, fall short. — *M.* to fail; to refuse; to renounce.

ἀ-πείραστος, ἀ-πείρᾱτος, ἀ-πείρητος 2 untried, unattempted; not having tried; inexperienced.

ἀπ-είργω (ἀπ-ειργαθεῖν) to

keep away, separate, define; to remove; to encompass, confine.

ἀ-πειρέσιος = ἄπειρος.

ἀ-πειρίᾱ, ἡ inexperience, ignorance.

ἀπειρό-κᾰκος 2 wanting bad experience. [nered.]

ἀπειρό-κᾰλος 2 ill-man-

ἄ-πειρος 2, ἀ-πείρων 2 unlimited, boundless, innumerable; unexperienced, ignorant.

ἀπ-εκδέχομαι to await.

ἀπ-εκδύομαι to put off one's clothes; to overcome.

ἀπ-εκλανθάνομαι *M.* to forget entirely.

ἀπ-ελαύνω, -ελάω to drive or turn away; to exclude; *intr.* to march or ride off.

ἀπ-ελεγμός, ὁ ill repute.

ἀ-πέλεθρος 2 immense.

ἀπ-ελεύθερος 2 freedman.

ἀπ-ελπίζω to despair; to hope from.

ἀπ-εμέω to spit out.

ἀπ-εμπολάω to sell.

ἀπ-έναντι, ἀπ-εναντίον *adv.* over against. [arms.]

ἀπ-εναρίζω to deprive of

ἀπ-ενιαυτίζω to be absent for a year.

ἀπ-εννέπω to forbid.

ἀπ-έοικα to be unlike; ἀπεικώς unlikely, unnatural; unfair.

ἄπερ just as.

ἀ-πέραντος 2 infinite, endless; impassable.

ἀπ-εργάζομαι *M.* to work off; to contrive, construct, finish.

ἀπ-εργασίᾱ, ἡ a finish(ing), completing, causing.

ἀπ-έργω = ἀπείργω.

ἀπ-έρδω to complete.

ἄπερ-εί just as, like.

ἀπ-ερείδομαι M. to support oneself upon, to lean on; to turn to; to insist upon.

ἀπειρέσιος 2 = ἀπειρέσιος.

ἀ-περίοπτος 2 reckless.

ἀ-περίσκεπτος 2 inconsiderate.

ἀ-περίσπαστος 2 undistracted, unmoved. [cised.]

ἀ-περίτμητος 2 uncircum-

ἀ-περίτροπος 2 unconcerned.

ἀπ-ερύκω to keep off or away. — M. to abstain.

ἀπ-έρχομαι to go away, depart; to go over; to return.

ἀπ-ερωεύς, ὁ destroyer, thwarter. [recoil.]

ἀπ-ερωέω to withdraw,

ἀπ-εσσούᾱ = ἀπεσσύη (from ἀποσεύω) he is gone (dead).

ἀπ-εστώ, οῦς, ἡ absence.

ἀ-πευθής 2 inscrutable; ignorant.

ἀπ-ευθύνω to straighten; direct; judge; to bind back.

ἀπ-ευνάζω to lull to sleep.

ἀπ-εύχομαι M. to execrate; to avert by praying.

ἄπ-εφθος 2 refined.

ἀπ-εχθαίρω to hate; to make hateful.

ἀπ-εχθάνομαι M. to become hated or odious; to turn enemy. [tred.]

ἀπ-έχθεια, ἡ enmity, ha-

ἀπ-εχθής 2 odious, hateful; hostile.

ἀπ-έχω to hold off; prohibit; to have one's share (ἀπέχει it is enough); to be distant or far. — M. to abstain, desist.

ἀπ-ηλεγέως adv. bluntly.

ἀπ-ῆλιξ, ικος elderly.

ἀπ-ηλιώτης, ου, ὁ east wind.

ἀ-πήμαντος 2 unhurt; without pain; harmless; wholesome.

ἀπήνη, ἡ waggon.

ἀπ-ηνής 2 unfriendly, harsh.

ἄ-πηρος 2 unmaimed.

ἀπ-ήωρος 2 hovering far.

ἀπ-ιάλλω to send away.

ἀ-πίθανος 2 incredible, unlikely.

ἀ-πιθέω = ἀπειθέω.

ἀ-πινύσσω to be unconscious or senseless.

ἄπιος 3 far away, distant.

ἀπ-ιπόω to squeeze out.

ἀπ-ισόω to make equal.

ἀ-πιστέω not to believe; to doubt; to mistrust; to disobey.

ἀ-πιστίᾱ, ἡ disbelief; doubt; mistrust; perfidy.

ἄ-πιστος 2 unreliable, perfidious; incredible; doubtful; unbelieving, distrustful; disobedient.

ἀπ-ισχυρίζομαι M. to reject strongly.

ἀπ-ίσχω = ἀπέχω.

ἀ-πλάτος 2 unapproachable; horrible.

ἄ-πλετος 2 immense.

ἀ-πληστίᾱ, ἡ insatiability.

ἄ-πληστος 2 insatiate; infinite.

ἄ-πλοια, ἡ no sailing, calm.

ἁπλοΐζομαι M. to act honestly.

ἁπλοῦς, ίδος, ἡ onefold.

ἁπλόος, ἁπλοῦς 3 onefold, single; simple, plain; sincere, honest; sound; ἁπλῶς plainly, simply; decidedly, without ceremony, in a word.

ἄ-πλοος, ἄπλους 2 unnavigable; unfit for sea, unseaworthy.

ἁπλότης, ητος, ἡ simplicity; honesty.

ἄ-πνευστος 2 breathless.

ἀπό adv. off, away; back. — prep. (with gen.) from, away from; from above; far from; asunder from; since, immediately after; on the part of, by means of, because of, with; after.

ἀπο-βάθρα, ἡ gangway; ladder.

ἀπο-βαίνω to step off, alight, dismount, descend, land; to turn out, end, come to pass, happen, succeed; to prove, become; trans. to disembark.

ἀπο-βάλλω to throw off, to drop; to get clear of the shore; to drive away; to lose.

ἀπο-βάπτω to dip in.

ἀπό-βασις, ἡ a landing, disembarking.   [embark.]

ἀπο-βιβάζω trans. to dis-]

ἀπο-βλάπτω to injure. — P. to be robbed of.

ἀπο-βλαστάνω to sprout forth.

ἀπο-βλάστημα, τό descendant.   [gard.]

ἀπο-βλέπω to look at, re-]

ἀπό-βλητος 2 rejectable.

ἀπο-βλύζω to spirt out.

ἀπο-βολή, ἡ a casting away; loss.

ἀπο-βρίζω to sleep.

ἀπο-γειόω to provide with a sheltering roof.

ἀπο-γεύομαι M. to taste; to try.   [by dikes.]

ἀπο-γεφυρόω to dam up]

ἀπο-γίγνομαι M. to be absent or away; to get lost; to depart this life.

ἀπο-γιγνώσκω to absolve; to give up, resign; to despair; to reject, acquit.

ἀπό-γνοια, ἡ despair.

ἀπό-γονος 2 descendant.

ἀπο-γραφή, ἡ list, catalogue, register; census; indictment of fraud in taxpaying.

ἀπο-γράφω to write down, register, enlist; to depose, give evidence; to bring an action against. — M. to get enlisted or registered; to sign; to note down; to cause to be recorded; to bring in a law-suit.   [feeble.]

ἀπο-γυιόω to lame, en-]

ἀπο-γυμνόω to make bare, to strip of (clothes).

ἀπο-δαίομαι M. to assign; to portion off, single out.

ἀπο-δάσμιος 2 parted off.

ἀπο-δειδίσσομαι to frighten from.

ἀπο-δείκνῡμι, -ύω to show forth, exhibit, set forth; to manifest; to prove, demonstrate; to appoint, designate. [age.]

ἀπο-δειλιάω to lose cour-]

ἀπό-δειξις, ἡ a showing forth, statement, proof.

ἀπο-δειροτομέω to behead; butcher.

ἀπο-δείρω = ἀποδέρω.

ἀπο-δεκατόω to tithe.

ἀπό-δεκτος 2 welcome.

ἀπό-δερμα, τό stripped-off skin.

ἀπο-δέρω to flay, skin (off).

ἀπο-δέχομαι M. to accept, receive; to perceive, understand; to approve of, acknowledge, believe; to be attached to.

ἀπο-δέω[1] to tie to.

ἀπο-δέω[2] to want, lack; to be behind.

ἀπο-δημέω to be absent or abroad; to depart, emigrate.

ἀπο-δημητής, οῦ, ὁ inclined to or fond of travelling.

ἀπο-δημίᾱ, ἡ absence from home, travel abroad.

ἀπό-δημος 2 abroad, travelling.

ἀπο-διδράσκω to run away; to shun, avoid; to be lost (out of sight).

ἀπο-δίδωμι to give away or back, to return, requite, pay off; to perform, accomplish; to surrender, deliver; to concede; to abandon. — M. to sell, let out.

ἀπο-δίεμαι to frighten away.

ἀπο-δικέω to defend oneself in court.

ἀπο-δῑνέω to thrash out.

ἀπο-διο-πομπέομαι M. to expiate. [guish.]

ἀπο-διορίζω to distin-]

ἀπο-διώκω to chase, expel.

ἀπο-δοκέω to displease.

ἀπο-δοκιμάζω to disapprove, reject; abrogate; turn out; to ostracize.

ἀπό-δοσις, ἡ return, payment.

ἀπο-δοχή, ἡ a receiving back; approbation.

ἀπο-δοχμόω to bend sideways. [flight.]

ἀπό-δρᾱσις, ἡ escape,]

ἀπο-δρύφω to rub off, gall.

ἀπο-δύνω = ἀποδύω M.

ἀπ-οδύρομαι to lament, bewail. [ing-room.]

ἀπο-δυτήριον, τό undress-]

ἀπο-δύω to undress, strip off. — M. and ἀπο-δύνω to undress oneself. [from.]

ἀπο-είκω to withdraw]

ἀπο-εργάθω, ἀπο-έργω = ἀπείργω.

ἀπο-ζάω to eke out existence, to earn a scanty livelihood.

ἀπ-όζω to give odour.

ἀπο-θαρρέω to gain courage. [at, marvel.]

ἀπο-θαυμάζω to wonder]

ἄποθεν = ἄπωθεν.

ἀπό-θεσις, ἡ a laying aside, keeping.

ἀπό-θετος 2 despised.

ἀπό-θετος 2 hidden; precious.

ἀπο-θέω to run away.

ἀπο-θήκη, ἡ granary, receptacle, magazine. [up.

ἀπο-θησαυρίζω to store

ἀπο-θλίβω to press hard.

ἀπο-θνήσκω to die; to be killed. [or down.

ἀπο-θρῴσκω to leap up

ἀπό-θῡμιος 2 disagreeable.

ἀπο-θύω to sacrifice.

ἀπ-οικέω to dwell afar (off); emigrate. [ment.

ἀπ-οικία, ἡ colony, settle-

ἀπ-οικίζω to transplant; send away; colonize.

ἀπ-οικίς, ίδος, ἡ = ἀποικία.

ἀπ-οικοδομέω to wall up, block up.

ἄπ-οικος 2 emigrant, colonist, settler; ἡ ἄ. colony.

ἀπ-οικτίζομαι M. to lament.

ἀπ-οιμώζω to bewail.

ἄ-ποινα, τό ransom, fine for homicide; compensation.

ἀπ-οίχομαι M. to be gone; to be far from; to go away.

ἀπο-καθαίρω to wipe off, to clean(se).

ἀπο-κάθαρσις, ἡ lustration; secretion.

ἀπο-κάθημαι to sit apart.

ἀπο-καθίστημι (-καθιστάνω) to restore, reestablish; intr. and P. to be restored.

ἀπο-καίνυμαι to surpass.

ἀπο-καίριος 2 = ἄκαιρος.

ἀπο-καίω to burn off or out; to cause to freeze.

ἀπο-καλέω to call away, aside or back; to name, give names. [uncover.

ἀπο-καλύπτω to unveil,

ἀπο-κάλυψις, ἡ revelation.

ἀπο-κάμνω to grow tired; to abandon from weariness.

ἀπο-κάπω to breathe out.

ἀπο-καρα-δοκία, ἡ a yearning, expectation.

ἀπο-καταλλάσσω to reconcile anew. [ration.

ἀπο-κατάστασις, ἡ resto-

ἀπο-καυλίζω to break off.

ἀπο-κάω = ἀποκαίω.

ἀπό-κειμαι to lie apart or in store, to be ready.

ἀπο-κείρω to shear off; to cut in pieces.

ἀπο-κεφαλίζω to behead.

ἀπο-κηδεύω to mourn the due time. [being careful.

ἀπο-κηδέω to relent in

ἀπο-κινδύνευσις, ἡ risk, dangerous attempt.

ἀπο-κινδυνεύω to venture, attempt, try. [drive away.

ἀπο-κῑνέω to remove; to

ἀπο-κλαίω to burst into tears, to weep oneself out.

ἀπό-κλεισις, ἡ a shutting off, exclusion.

ἀπο-κλείω to shut or lock up, in, or out; to exclude, refrain; to cut off, intercept [lot(s).

ἀπο-κληρόω to draw by

ἀπό-κλησις = ἀπόκλεισις.

ἀπό-κλῑνω to turn as de, divert; intr. and P. to deviate; to stoop, fall; to incline to.

ἀπο-κλύζω to wash away.

ἀπο-κναίω to rub off, to torment.

ἀπ-οκνέω to hesitate; to give up from fear.

ἀπ-όκνησις, ἡ a shrinking from, aversion. [enough.]

ἀπο-κοιμάομαι P. to sleep]

ἀπο-κοιτέω to be absent at night. [by swimming.]

ἀπο-κολυμβάω to escape]

ἀπο-κομιδή, ἡ retreat.

ἀπο-κομίζω to carry away or back. — M. to fetch back. — P. to depart.

ἀπο-κοπή, ἡ abolition.

ἀπο-κόπτω to cut off.

ἀπο-κορυφόω to answer concisely or briefly.

ἀπο-κοσμέω to clear away.

ἀπο-κοτταβίζω to fling the last drops of wine from a cup.

ἀπο-κρατέω to surpass.

ἀπο-κρεμάννῦμι to let hang down. [precipitous.]

ἀπό-κρημνος 2 sloping,]

ἀπό-κριμα, τό answer; sentence.

ἀπο-κρίνω to separate; to select; to vary, distinguish. — P. and M. to part, separate (oneself). — M. to answer, return sentence; to take up the word.

ἀπό-κρισις, ἡ answer.

ἀπό-κροτος 2 hard.

ἀπο-κρούω to strike off or back, to ward off.

ἀπο-κρύπτω to hide from; conceal; to lose from sight. — M. to hide oneself; conceal. [cret.]

ἀπό-κρυφος 2 hidden, se-]

ἀπο-κτείνω, -κτιννύω, -κτίννῦμι to kill, slay.

ἀπο-κυέω, -κύω to bring forth, give birth.

ἀπο-κυλίω to roll off.

ἀπο-κωλύω to hinder, prevent. [lot.]

ἀπο-λαγχάνω to get by]

ἀπο-λαμβάνω to take away or apart; to separate; to cut off; to retain, hinder; to accept, receive; to regain.

ἀπο-λαμπρύνομαι P. to become famous.

ἀπο-λάμπω to shine far, reflect (light).

ἀπό-λαυσις, ἡ enjoyment, advantage. [profit.]

ἀπο-λαύω to enjoy, to]

ἀπο-λέγω to pick out, select. [down.]

ἀπο-λείβομαι P. to drip]

ἀπο-λείπω to leave, lose, relinquish; to leave behind; to leave a distance; to omit; to go away, to leave off; to fail, fall short, to be wanting. — P. to remain, to be left, to remain behind; to miss; to stay away; to be severed.

ἀπο-λείχω to lick off.

ἀπό-λειφις, ἡ a leaving, retreat, depart. [choice.]

ἀπό-λεκτος 2 chosen out,]

ἀ-πόλεμος 2 unwarlike.

ἀπο-λέπω to peel or cut off.

ἀπο-λήγω to leave off, cease, end.

ἀπό-ληφις, ἡ an intercepting, a cutting off.

ἄ-πολις 2 townless; homeless. [to slip.]

ἀπ-ολισθάνω to glide off,]

ἀπο-λιχμάω to lick off.

ἀπ-όλλῦμι (-ύω) to ruin, destroy, undo; to kill; to

lose. — M. (and perf. ἀπόλωλα) to be ruined, undone, destroyed or lost, to perish, die.

ἀπο-λογέομαι M. to defend or justify oneself; to defend.

ἀπο-λογία, ἡ defence.

ἀπο-λογίζομαι M. to give an account (of); to discuss; to calculate, enumerate.

ἀπό-λογος, ὁ tale; fable.

ἀπο-λούω to wash off.

ἀπ-ολοφύρομαι M. to bewail enough.

ἀπο-λῦμαίνομαι M. to clean(se) oneself.

ἀπο-λῦμαντήρ, ῆρος, ὁ one who clears tables, consumer, destroyer.

ἀπό-λῦσις, ἡ release, absolution.   [release.)

ἀπο-λῦτικός 3 disposed to)

ἀπο-λύτρωσις, ἡ a ransoming, redemption.

ἀπο-λύω to loosen, set free, deliver; to dismiss, acquit; to absolve. — M. to free or justify oneself; to redeem, ransom. — M. and P. to depart.

ἀπο-λωβάω to insult.

ἀπο-μανθάνω to unlearn.

ἀπο-μᾰραίνομαι P. to wither, dry up.

ἀπο-μάσσω to scrape or wipe off.

ἀπο-μαστῑγόω to scourge.

ἀπο-μᾰτάϊζω to behave indecently.

ἀπο-μάχομαι M. to fight from; to ward off; to repudiate.

ἀπό-μᾰχος 2 unfit for battle.

ἀπο-μετρέω to measure out.

ἀπο-μηκύνω to lengthen or draw out.   [wrath.)

ἀπο-μηνύω to prolong)

ἀπο-μῑμέομαι M. to copy, counterfeit.

ἀπο-μιμνήσκομαι P. to remember, bear in mind.

ἀπό-μισθος 2 without pay; paid off.   [for hire.)

ἀπο-μισθόω to put out)

ἀπο-μνημονεύμᾰτα, τὰ memoirs, memorable things.

ἀπο-μνημονεύω to keep in memory; to recount.

ἀπο-μνησῐκᾰκέω to resent an evil.

ἀπ-όμνῡμι to swear; to disclaim upon oath.

ἀπο-μονόω to leave alone; to exclude.   [or clean.)

ἀπ-ομόργνῡμι to wipe off)

ἀπο-μῡθέομαι M. to dissuade (from).

ἀπο-ναίω to transplant; to send home. — M. to emigrate.

ἀπο-νέμω to allot, assign.

ἀπο-νέομαι to go away; to return.

ἀ-πόνητος 2 without pains, easy; unpunished. — adv. ἀπονητί.   [bathe.)

ἀπο-νίζω to wash off; to)

ἀπ-ονίναμαι M. to enjoy.

ἀπο-νίπτω = ἀπονίζω.

ἀπο-νοσέομαι P. to be desperate.   [foolhardiness.)

ἀπό-νοια, ἡ folly; despair;)

ἄ-πονος 2 inactive, lazy; easy.

ἀπο-νοστέω to return home.

ἀπο-νόσφιν asunder, apart; far from.

ἀπο-νοσφίζω to put asunder; to deprive; to shun.

ἀπό-ξενος 2 inhospitable.

ἀπο-ξενόω to estrange. — P. to live abroad.

ἀπο-ξέω to smooth, polish; to cut off.

ἀπο-ξηραίνω to dry up.

ἀπ-οξύνω to sharpen, point.

ἀπο-ξυρέω to shear off.

ἀπο-ξύω to shave off.

ἀπο-παπταίνω to look about timidly.

ἀπο-παύω to cause to leave off, to stop. — M. to leave off, cease.

ἀπό-πειρα, ἡ proof, trial, experiment. [prove.

ἀπο-πειράω and P. to try,]

ἀπο-πέμπω to send away or back, to dismiss. — M. to get rid of.

ἀπό-πεμψις, ἡ dismissal.

ἀπο-πέτομαι M. to fly away or back.

ἀπο-πήγνῡμι to cause to freeze. — P. to congeal, curdle.

ἀπο-πηδάω to leap off or away; to desert.

ἀπο-πίμπλημι to fill up, complete; to supply; to satisfy.

ἀπο-πίνω to drink of.

ἀπο-πίπτω to fall down.

ἀπο-πλάζω, ἀπο-πλανάω to lead astray. — P. to go astray, to be cast away.

ἀπο-πλέω to sail off or home.

ἀπό-πληκτος 2 struck by apoplexy; benumbed.

ἀπο-πληρόω = ἀποπίμπλη-μι. [benumbed.

ἀπο-πλήσσομαι P. to be]

ἀπό-πλοος, -πλους, ὁ a sailing away.

ἀπο-πλύνω to rinse off.

ἀπο-πλώω = ἀποπλέω.

ἀπο-πνέω (-πνείω) to breathe forth, exhale; to blow from. [strangle.

ἀπο-πνίγω to choke,]

ἀπό-πολις 2 banished.

ἀπο-πορεύομαι P. to depart, go away.

ἀπο-πρίω to saw off.

ἀπο-πρό adv. far away; far from.

ἀπο-προαιρέω to take away from before.

ἀπό-προθεν adv. from afar.

ἀπό-προθι adv. far off.

ἀπο-προΐημι to send far (away); to shoot forth; to let drop.

ἀπό-πτολις = ἀπόπολις.

ἀπ-οπτος 2 seen from afar; invisible.

ἀπό-πτυστος 2 detested.

ἀπο-πτύω to spit out.

ἀπο-πυνθάνομαι to question, inquire after.

ἀπορέω to be embarrassed, perplexed, at a loss or helpless; to be distressed or needy. [or indestructible.

ἀ-πόρθητος 2 not sacked]

ἀπ-ορθόω to make straight; to direct.

ἀπορίᾱ, ἡ embarrassment, perplexity; doubt; need; difficulty, impassableness.

ἀπ-όρνῠμαι *M.* to start, depart.

ἄ-πορος 2 impassable; difficult; irresistible; impossible; extravagant; helpless; needy, poor; unable.

ἀπ-ορούω to leap off, rebound.

ἀπο-ρρᾳθῡμέω to leave off from timidity.

ἀπο-ρραίνω to spirt about.

ἀπο-ρραίω to tear from.

ἀπο-ρράπτω to sew up.

ἀπο-ρρέω to flow off or down; to vanish.

ἀπο-ρρήγνῡμι to break off, to sever.

ἀπό-ρρητος 2 forbidden; unspeakable; secret; abominable. [from, recoil.]

ἀπο-ρρῑγέω to shrink

ἀπο-ρρῑπτω, -τέω to throw away, reject; to despise.

ἀπο-ρροή and ἀπό-ρροια, ἡ a flowing off or out.

ἀπο-ρροιβδέω to shriek out.

ἀπο-ρρώξ, ῶγος, ὁ, ἡ steep, abrupt; a flowing out; wine of the first press.

ἀπ-ορφανίζομαι *P.* to become an orphan.

ἀπ-ορχέομαι *M.* to lose in dancing.

ἀπο-σᾰλεύω to anchor in the open sea. [lustrate.]

ἀπο-σᾰφέω to explain, il-

ἀπο-σβέννῡμι to extinguish; *intr.* and *P.* to be extinguished, to expire.

ἀπο-σείω to shake off.

ἀπο-σεύομαι *M.* and *P.* to run away.

ἀπο-σημαίνω to announce by signs, to signal. — *M.* to perceive; to seal; to confiscate. [to freeze off.]

ἀπο-σήπομαι *P.* to rot off;

ἀπο-σῑμόω to turn aside.

ἀπο-σῑωπάω to grow speechless. [by trenches.]

ἀπο-σκάπτω to bar (off)

ἀπο-σκεδάννῡμι to scatter, chase; to remove, dismiss.

ἀπο-σκευάζω to clear away. — *M.* to pack up.

ἀπο-σκηνόω to be encamped apart.

ἀπο-σκήπτω to fling on; *intr.* to burst forth; to end.

ἀπο-σκίασμα, τό adumbration; trace. [δάννῡμι.]

ἀπο-σκίδνημι = ἀποσκε-

ἀπο-σκοπέω to look at away from; to regard.

ἀπο-σκυδμαίνω to be wroth or angry.

ἀπο-σκώπτω to scoff.

ἀπό-σπασμα, τό morsel.

ἀπο-σπάω to tear or pull off, to sever; *intr.* and *P.* to go away, part.

ἀπο-σπένδω to pour out (a libation).

ἀπο-σπεύδω to dissuade; to prevent; to frustrate.

ἀπο-στᾰδά, -δόν *adv.* from afar.

ἀπο-στάζω to let drip.

ἀπο-στᾰσίᾱ, ἡ, ἀπόστᾰσις, ἡ a standing away; rebellion, apostasy.

ἀπο-στάσιον, τό (bill of) divorce.

ἀπο-στᾰτέω to stand away; to differ; to apostatize

ἀπο-σταυρόω to palisade.

ἀπο-στεγάζω to unroof.

ἀπο-στείχω to step away, back.

ἀπο-στέλλω to send away or out; to forward; to send back; to chase.

ἀπο-στερέω to deprive; to withhold; to rob, snatch away.

ἀπο-στέρησις, ἡ deprivation. [ρέω.]

ἀπο-στερίσκω = ἀποστε-

ἀπο-στίλβω to shine.

ἀπο-στολεύς, ὁ commissary of the fleet.

ἀπο-στολή, ἡ a sending; apostle's office.

ἀπό-στολος, ὁ messenger; traveller; apostle; naval expedition. [to question.]

ἀπο-στοματίζω to recite;

ἀπο-στρατοπεδεύομαι M. to encamp at a distance.

ἀπο-στρέφω to turn away or back; to tie to the back; to bring back; to cause to return; to drive away or back; to turn to. — intr. and P. to turn away or round; to return; to abhor; to apostatize.

ἀπο-στροφή, ἡ turning away, averting; flight, escape; help; refuge.

ἀπό-στροφος 2 averted.

ἀπο-στῡγέω to abhor, detest. [back.]

ἀπο-στῠφελίζω to push

ἀπο-σῡλάω to rob, spoil.

ἀπο-συνάγωγος 2 ejected from the synagogue.

ἀπο-σύρω to tear off.

ἀπο-σφακελίζω to die of mortification.

ἀπο-σφάλλω to mislead; to frustrate. — P. to miss, fail.

ἀπο-σφάττω to slay, slaughter. [sever.]

ἀπο-σχίζω to split off; to

ἀπο-σῴζω to save, shelter.

ἀπο-τακτός 2 appropriated

ἀπο-τάμνω = ἀποτέμνω.

ἀπο-τάσσω to range apart; to assign specially. — M. to depart from. [a ditch.]

ἀπο-τάφρεύω to fortify by

ἀπο-τείνω to stretch out, lengthen; to reach to; to aim at. — P. to be extended.

ἀπο-τειχίζω to separate or surround by a wall; to wall round or in; to fortify.

ἀπο-τείχισις, ἡ, ἀπο-τεί-χισμα, τό a blockading; circumvallation. [(intr.).]

ἀπο-τελευτάω to end

ἀπο-τελέω to finish, achieve, satisfy, effect, pay, fulfil.

ἀπο-τέμνω to cut off; to tear off; to separate; to make one's own.

ἀπο-τήκομαι to melt away; to vanish.

ἀπο-τηλοῦ adv. far.

ἀ-πότιβατος = ἀπρόσβατος.

ἀπο-τίθημι to put away, aside, or down. — M. to put away, remove; to omit; to defer.

ἀπο-τίλλω to pluck out.

ἀπο-τῑμάω to value, tax.
— M. to get payment.

ἀπο-τῐνάσσω to shake off.

ἀπο-τίνω (-τίνῡμι) to pay off, atone, requite. — M. to exact, punish; to avenge.

ἀπο-τμήγω = ἀποτέμνω.

ἄ-ποτμος 2 unhappy.

ἀπο-τολμάω to venture, dare; to tell freely.

ἀπο-τομή, ἡ a cutting off.

ἀπο-τομίᾱ, ἡ steepness.

ἀπό-τομος 2 steep, precipitous; severe.

ἄ-ποτος 2 not drinking; undrinkable.

ἀπο-τρέπω to turn away or back; to restrain, dissuade; to prevent. — P. and M. intr. to turn away or back; to return, fly; to desist, shun.

ἀπο-τρέχω to run away.

ἀπο-τρῐβω to rub or scour off. — M. to efface. [evil.\

ἀπο-τρόπαιος 2 averting/

ἀπο-τροπή, ἡ an averting, deterring, prevention; aversion.

ἀπό-τροπος 2 averted, banished; averting, horrible.

ἀπό-τροφος 2 brought up abroad.

ἀπο-τρύω to undo, vex.

ἀπο-τρωπάω = ἀποτρέπω.

ἀπο-τυγχάνω to miss, lose, fail. [death.\

ἀπο-τυμπᾰνίζω to beat to/

ἀπο-τύπτομαι M. to cease mourning.

ἀπ-ούρας see ἀπαυράω.

ἀπ-ουρίζω to alter boundary-stones; to lessen.

ἀπ-ουρος 2 distant.

ἄ-πους, ἄπουν, -ποδος footless; lame.

ἀπ-ουσίᾱ, ἡ absence.

ἀπο-φαίνω to show forth, point out, to bring to light; to prove, explain; to describe; to appoint. — P. to appear.

ἀπο-φάσκω = ἀπόφημι.

ἀπο-φέρω to carry off or away; to carry, lead, take, bring back or up; to transmit; to indicate.

ἀπο-φεύγω to flee from, escape; to avoid; to be acquitted.

ἀπό-φημι to speak out, declare; to deny; to refuse.

ἀπο-φθέγγομαι M.to speak plainly. [sentence.\

ἀπό-φθεγμα, τό a saying,/

ἀπο-φθείρω to destroy, undo, ruin.

ἀπο-φθῐνύθω to perish; to lose.

ἀπο-φθίνω, -φθίω to destroy; to perish. [slight.\

ἀπο-φλαυρίζω to despise,/

ἀπο-φοιτάω to go away.

ἀπο-φορά, ἡ tribute, tax.

ἀπο-φορτίζομαι M. to unburden oneself.

ἀπο-φράγνῡμι to bar, block up, stop, intrench. [up.\

ἀπό-φραξις, ἡ a blocking/

ἀπο-φυγή, ἡ escape, flight; refuge.

ἀπο-φώλιος 2 void, vain, useless. [draw.\

ἀπο-χάζομαι M. to with-/

ἀπο-χειρο-βίωτος 2 living by manual labour.

ἀπο-χέω to pour out; to throw down.

ἀπο-χόω to dam up.

ἀπο-χράω to suffice. — P. to be contented. — M. to use out; to misuse; to kill.

ἀπό-χρησις, ἡ misuse; consumption.

ἀπο-χρώντως adv. sufficiently.   [lame.]

ἀπο-χωλόω to make quite] lame.

ἀπο-χώννῡμι = ἀποχόω.

ἀπο-χωρέω to go away; to retreat.   [retreat.]

ἀπο-χώρησις, ἡ return,]

ἀπο-χωρίζω to part, separate. — P. to part.

ἀπο-ψάω to wipe off.

ἀπο-ψηφίζομαι M. to countervote, reject; to acquit. — P. to be rejected.

ἀπο-ψῑλόω to make bald; to deprive.

ἄπ-οψις, ἡ view, prospect.

ἀπο-ψύχω to breathe out, swoon; to cool, refresh; to dry up.

ἀ-πρᾱγμοσύνη, ἡ inactivity; non-intervention.

ἀ-πράγμων 2 inactive; peace-loving; without pains, easy.

ἀ-πρᾱκτος, ἄπρηκτος 2 effecting nothing, useless; inactive; not done, untried; impossible; unconquerable, incurable.

ἀ-πρᾱξίᾱ, ἡ inaction.

ἀ-πρεπής 2 unbecoming.

ἀ-πρίᾱτος 2 and 3, adv. ἀπριάτην, unbought, gratuitous.   [incessantly.]

ἀπρίξ adv. holding fast;]

ἀ-πρόθῡμος 2 disinclined.

ἄ-προικος 2 dowerless.

ἀ-προμήθεια, ἡ imprudence.

ἀ-προνόητος 2 heedless.

ἀ-προσδόκητος 2 unexpected; not expecting.

ἀ-προσήγορος 2 not to be accosted; unkind.

ἀ-πρόσῑτος 2 inaccessible.

ἀ-πρόσκοπος 2 innocent; blameless.

ἀ-πρόσμαχος 2 invincible.

ἀ-πρόσμικτος 2 without intercourse.

ἀ-προσόμῑλος 2 unsociable.

ἀ-προσωπο-λήπτως adv. without respect of persons.

ἀ-προτί-μαστος 2 untouched.

ἀ-προφάσιστος 2 unevasive; unreserved.   [able.]

ἀ-προφύλακτος 2 inevit-]

ἄ-πταιστος 2 without stumbling.

ἄ-πτερος 2, ἀ-πτήν, ῆνος unwinged; not flying away.

ἀ-πτο-επής 2 prattling boldly.

ἀ-πτόλεμος 2 = ἀπόλεμος.

ἅπτω to fasten, attach, fix; to kindle. — M. to touch, grasp, seize, lay hold of; to try; to perceive; to mention; to undertake. — P. to be kindled, to take fire.

ἀ-πύλωτος 2 not closed by a gate.

ἀ-πύργωτος 2 not fortified (by towers).

ἄ-πυρος 2, ἀ-πύρωτος 2 not touched by fire, uncooked, new.

ἄ-πυστος 2 not remembered or known, inaudible; not knowing.

ἀπύω = ἠπύω. [far away.]

ἄπωθεν adv. from afar;

ἀπ-ωθέω to thrust away. — M. to drive away or back; to ward off, repel; to despise. [ruin, loss.]

ἀπ-ώλεια, ἡ destruction,

ἀπ-ώμοτος 2 abjured, abjurable; who abjures.

ἄπ-ωσις, ἡ a driving away.

ἄπ-ωστός 3 expelled, driven away.

ἀπωτάτω adv. farthest off.

ἀπωτέρω adv. farther off.

ἄρᾰ part. of affirmation: then; farther; moreover.

ἆρᾰ part. of interrogation = lat. num or -ne; ἆρ' οὐ = nonne.

ἀρά, ἡ prayer; curse; destruction, revenge.

ἀράβέω to rattle, clatter.

ἄράβος, ὁ and ἀραγμός, ὁ a rattling, clashing, din.

ἀραιός 3 thin, narrow, slender; weak.

ἀραῖος 3 and 2 cursing, dire; accursed.

ἀραίρηκα see αἱρέω.

ἀράομαι M. to pray, implore; to wish; to curse.

ἀραρίσκω to join, put together, fit with; to fix; to build, fit out; intr. to be joined, fastened, or fitted, to suit; to be equipped; to please.

ἀράσσω to strike, knock, hammer, dash. [cursed.]

ἀρᾱτός 3 prayed for; ac-

ἀράχνη, ἡ spider. [cobweb.]

ἀράχνιον, τό spider's web,

ἀργᾰλέος 3 heavy, troublesome, grievous.

ἀργεϊ-φόντης, ου, ὁ epithet of Hermes; swift messenger or killer of Argus.

ἀργεννός 3 = ἀργής.

ἀργεστής, οῦ white; clearing up.

ἀργέω to be idle or inactive.

ἀργής, ῆτος or έτος white, shining, bright.

ἀργίᾱ, ἡ laziness, leisure.

ἀργι-κέραυνος 2 with bright flashes of lightning.

ἀργῑλώδης 2 clayish.

ἀργῑνόεις 3 = ἀργής.

ἀργι-όδους, όδοντος with white teeth.

ἀργί-πους, ποδος with white feet, fleet.

ἄργμα, τό firstlings of an offering. [Argives.]

ἀργολίζω to side with the

ἀργός[1] 3 bright, white; swift.

ἀργός[2] 2 lazy, idle; useless; not done; untilled. [silver.]

ἀργύρεος, ἀργύρεος 3 of

ἀργύριον, τό silver; silver coin; money; silver-mine.

ἀργυρό-δῑνης, ου eddying like silver. [nails.]

ἀργυρό-ηλος 2 with silver

ἀργυρο-κόπος, ὁ silversmith. [money.]

ἀργυρο-λογέω to exact

ἀργυρο-λογίᾱ, ἡ the levying of money. [money.]

ἀργυρο-λόγος 2 exacting

ἀργυρο-πεζα, ἡ, ἀργυρό-πους, ποδος silver-footed.

ἀργυρος, ὁ silver; money.

ἀργῠρό-τοξος 2 with silver bow. [with money.]

ἀργυρ-ώνητος 2 bought]

ἀργῠφεος 3, ἀργῠφος 2 silver-white.

ἄρδην adv. on high, upwards; from on high; utterly, entirely.

ἄρδις, ἡ arrow-head.

ἀρδμός, ὁ watering-place.

ἄρδω to water, irrigate.

ἀρειή, ἡ = ἀρά.

ἀρείων 2 better; braver.

ἄ-ρεκτος 2 unfinished.

ἀρέομαι = ἀράομαι.

ἀρεσκείᾱ, ἡ pleasing disposition.

ἀρέσκω and M. to please, amend, compensate, satisfy. — P. to be agreeable or pleasant; to be pleased or satisfied.

ἀρεστός 3 agreeable, acceptable. [thrive.]

ἀρετάω to be good, to]

ἀρετή, ἡ goodness, excellence, perfection, merit, fitness; bravery, valour; virtue.

ἀρήγω to help, aid.

ἀρηγών, όνος, ὁ, ἡ helper.

ἀρηί-θοος 2 swift in war.

ἀρηι-κτάμενος 3, ἀρηί-φατος 2 killed in battle.

ἀρηί-φιλος 2 loved by Ares. [whelmed.]

ἀρημένος 3 damaged, over-]

ἀρήν, ἀρνός, ὁ, ἡ lamb, sheep.

ἄρηξις, ἡ help, defence.

ἀρητήρ, ῆρος, ὁ one praying, priest.

ἄ-ρητος 2 unspeakable.

ἀρητός = ἀρατός.

ἀρθμέω to be joined together.

ἄρθμιος 3 united, joined; friend; concordant.

ἄρθρον, τό joint; limb.

ἀρθρόω to articulate.

ἀρί-γνωτος 2 and 3 easy to be known; well-known.

ἀρί-δείκετος 2 excellent.

ἀρί-δηλος 2, ἀρίζηλος 2 and 3 most distinct, conspicuous, clear, excellent.

ἀριθμέω to number, count up; to class. [cal.]

ἀριθμητικός 3 arithmeti-]

ἀριθμός, ὁ number; amount, quantity; a counting, muster. [splendid.]

ἀρι-πρεπής 2 eminent,]

ἀριστάω to breakfast.

ἀριστείᾱ, ἡ heroic deed; heroism. [ward, prize.]

ἀριστεῖον, τό victor's re-]

ἀριστερός 3 left, to the left; ἡ ἀ. the left hand; sinister, ominous; clumsy.

ἀριστεύς, ὁ the best or noblest one; prince, hero.

ἀριστεύω to be the best (one), to excel.

ἀριστίνδην adv. according to noble birth.

ἀριστο-κρατέομαι P. to live in an aristocracy.

ἀριστο-κρατίᾱ, [cratical.]
aristo-cracy.]

ἀριστο-κρατικός 3 aristo-]

ἀριστό-μαντις, ὁ the best of the seers.

ἄριστον, τό breakfast.

ἀριστο-ποιέομαι M. to (get one's) breakfast.

ἄριστος 3 the best, bravest or noblest; aristocrat.

ἀριστό-χειρ, ειρος with the bravest hand. [pery.]

ἀρι-σφᾰλής 2 very slip-

ἀρι-φρᾰδής 2 very manifest, easily known.

ἄρκεσις, ἡ help, service.

ἀρκετός 3 sufficient.

ἀρκέω to keep or ward off; to help, assist; to be enough, to suffice; to be able. — P. to be contented or satisfied.

ἄρκιος 3 sufficient, sure.

ἄρκος, τό defence; solace.

ἀρκούντως adv. sufficiently, enough.

ἀρκτέον from ἄρχομαι to begin; to be ruled.

ἄρκτος, ὁ, ἡ bear.

ἀρκτ-οῦρος, ὁ bearherd.

ἄρκυς, υος, ἡ net, snare.

ἀρκύ-στᾰτος 3 and 2 ensnared.

ἅρμα, τό waggon, team.

ἁρμ-άμαξα, ἡ coach, travelling carriage.

ἁρμάτειος 3 belonging to a waggon. [waggon.]

ἁρματ-ηλᾰτέω to drive a

ἁρματ-ηλᾰτης, ὁ charioteer. [wright.]

ἁρμᾰτο-πηγός, ὁ cart-

ἁρμόδιος 3 fitting.

ἁρμόζω = ἁρμόττω.

ἁρμονία, ἡ joint, union; cramp, clasp; treaty, decree; harmony, proportion. [peg.]

ἁρμός, ὁ joint; groove; slit;

ἁρμοστήρ, ῆρος, ὁ and ἁρμοστής, οῦ, ὁ governor, prefect, magistrate.

ἁρμόττω to fit together, join, adjust; to betroth, marry; intr. to fit, suit, become, to be convenient. — M. to be betrothed, married. [sheep.]

ἄρνειος 3 of a lamb or

ἀρνειός, ὁ ram.

ἀρνέομαι to deny, disown, refuse; to despise.

ἀρνευτήρ, ῆρος, ὁ diver.

ἀρνήσιμος 2 to be denied.

ἄρνησις, ἡ denial.

ἀρνίον, τό young lamb.

ἄρνυμαι to gain, earn, obtain, carry off.

ἄροσις, ἡ arable land.

ἀροτήρ, ῆρος, ὁ ploughman.

ἄροτος, ὁ ploughing, husbandry; engendering; produce of the fields.

ἀροτριάω = ἀρόω.

ἄροτρον, τό plough.

ἄρουρα, ἡ plough-land, field, soil; acre.

ἀρουραῖος 3 rustic.

ἀρόω to plough, till; beget, sow.

ἁρπᾰγή, ἡ and ἁρπαγμός, ὁ a robbing, plundering; spoil, plunder.

ἁρπάζω to snatch, seize, rob, plunder; to do in haste.

ἁρπακτήρ, ῆρος, ὁ robber.

ἁρπᾰλέος 3 greedy; pleasant. [robbing.]

ἅρπαξ, αγος rapacious,

ἁρπεδόνη, ἡ lace, rope, string.

ἅρπη, ἡ falcon; sickle.

ἅρπυια, ἡ whirlwind; harpy.

ἀρραβών, ῶνος, ὁ pledge, deposit.

ἄ-ρραφος 2 unsewed, without a seam.

ἄ-ρρηκτος 2 unbreakable, not to be broken or tired.

ἄρρην = ἄρσην.

ἄ-ρρητος 2 unsaid; unknown; unspeakable, secret, holy; abominable.

ἄ-ρρυθμος 2 without rhythm or proportion.

ἀρρωδέω = ὀρρωδέω.

ἄ-ρρώξ, ῶγος untorn.

ἀ-ρρωστέω to be weak, invalid, or sick.

ἀ-ρρώστημα, τό and ἀ-ρρωστίᾱ, ἡ weakness, sickness, depression.

ἄ-ρρωστος 2 weak, sickly, languid. [derast.

ἀρσενο-κοίτης, ου, ὁ pe-

ἄρσην, εν, ενος male; manly, vigorous, strong.

ἀρτάβη, ἡ bushel (a Persian measure).

ἀρτάνη, ἡ rope, sling.

ἀρτάω, -έω to fasten, fix; to hang up. — P. to depend on. — M. to prepare.

ἀρτεμής 2 sound, fresh.

ἀρτέμων, ονος or ωνος, ὁ top-sail. [ear.

ἀρτημα, τό pendant of the

ἀρτηρίᾱ, ἡ artery, vein; air-pipe. [the other day.

ἄρτι adv. just now; lately,

ἀρτι-γέννητος 2 new-born.

ἀρτι-επής 2 ready of speech.

ἀρτί-κολλος 2 close-glued.

ἄρτιος 3 fit; ready; proper, perfect; even (of numbers);

ἀρτίως = ἄρτι.

ἀρτί-πους (-πος), ποδος sound or swift of foot.

ἀρτίσις, ἡ adjustment.

ἀρτί-φρων 2 sensible, intelligent. [spread.

ἀρτί-χριστος 2 newly

ἀρτο-κόπος, ὁ bread-baker.

ἀρτο-ποιΐᾱ, ἡ bread-baking.

ἄρτος, ὁ bread.

ἀρτύνας, ου, ὁ arranger.

ἀρτύνω, ἀρτύω to join; to arrange, prepare; to devise. [for liquids.

ἀρυστήρ, ῆρος, ὁ measure

ἀρύω, ἀρύτω, ἀρύσσω to draw (water).

ἀρχ-άγγελος, ὁ archangel.

ἀρχαιό-γονος 2 ancient, primeval. [stories.

ἀρχαιο-λογέω to tell old

ἀρχαιό-πλουτος 2 rich of old.

ἀρχαῖος 3 ancient, primeval, old, time-honoured, antiquated; former, bygone. [fashioned.

ἀρχαιό-τροπος 2 old-

ἀρχ-αιρεσίᾱ, ἡ election of magistrates.

ἀρχεῖον, τό government-house, town-hall. [making.

ἀρχέ-κακος 2 mischief-

ἀρχέ-λᾱος 2 leading the people. [of wealth.

ἀρχέ-πλουτος 2 founder

ἀρχύω to lead, rule.

ἀρχή, ἡ beginning, commencement, origin; firstling; cause, motive, principle, element; leadership, power, rule, magistrate, office, government; territory, empire.

ἀρχ-ηγετέω, -εύω to begin with; to rule.

ἀρχ-ηγέτης, ου and ἀρχηγός, ὁ ruler, leader, head; author, founder.

ἀρχῆθεν adv. of old, originally.

ἀρχίδιον, τό minor office.

ἀρχ-ιερατικός 3 pontifical.

ἀρχ-ιερεύς, ὁ and ἀρχιέρεως, ω, ὁ high priest, pontiff. [authoritative.]

ἀρχικός 3 commanding,]

ἀρχι-ποιμήν, ένος, ὁ chief shepherd.

ἀρχι-συνάγωγος, ὁ head of the synagogue.

ἀρχι-τέκτων, ονος, ὁ builder, architect, engineer.

ἀρχι-τελώνης, ου, ὁ chief publican. [steward.]

ἀρχι-τρίκλῑνος, ὁ chief]

ἀρχός, ὁ leader, prince.

ἄρχω to be the first, to lead on, guide; to begin; to cause; to be at the head (of), to lead, rule, govern, domineer; to be archon. — P. to be ruled, governed, subject, to obey. — M. to begin, try.

ἄρχων, οντος, ὁ leader, ruler, chief; archon, magistrate.

ἀρωγή, ἡ protection, help.

ἀρωγός 2 helping, aiding; helper.

ἄρωμα, τό spice.

ἀρώσιμος 2 to be sown.

ἀ-σάλευτος 2 unshaken.

ἀ-σάμινθος, ἡ bathing-tub.

ἀ-σάομαι P. to be disgusted.

ἀ-σάφεια, ἡ indistinctness.

ἀ-σαφής 2 indistinct, uncertain, dubious.

ἄ-σβεστος 2 unquenchable; endless.

ἀ-σέβεια, ἡ, ἀσέβημα, τό impiety, wickedness.

ἀ-σεβέω to be godless or wicked.

ἀ-σεβής 2 ungodly, wicked.

ἀσελγαίνω to be licentious.

ἀσέλγεια, ἡ licentiousness, lewdness.

ἀσελγής 2 licentious, lewd.

ἀ-σέληνος 2 moonless.

ἀσεπτέω = ἀσεβέω.

ἄση, ἡ surfeit, woe. [der.]

ἀ-σήμαντος 2 without lea-]

ἄ-σημος 2 and ἀ-σήμων 2 without mark or sign; uncoined; indistinct, unintelligible; obscure.

ἀ-σθένεια, ἡ and ἀ-σθένημα, τό weakness; illness; neediness.

ἀ-σθενής 2 weak, feeble; sick; poor, insignificant.

ἄσθμα, τό shortness of breath, panting.

ἀσθμαίνω to gasp, pant.

ἀ-σινής 2 unhurt; innoxious, harmless.

ἄσις, ἡ mud, mire.

ἀ-σῑτέω to fast, hunger.

ἀ-σῑτίᾱ, ἡ a fasting, hunger. [hungry.]

ἄ-σῑτος 2 without food,]

ἀ-σκελής 2 weak; incessant.

ἀ-σκέπαρνος 2 unhewn.

ἄ-σκεπτος 2 not considered, not examined; inconsiderate.

ἀ-σκευής 2, ἄ-σκευος 2 unprepared; unprotected.

ἀσκέω to work out artificially; to adorn; to practise, exercise, train, drill; to endeavour, strive. [maged.]

ἀ-σκηθής 2 unhurt, undamaged.

ἄσκησις, ἡ practise, training; athletic trade.

ἀσκητής, οῦ, ὁ athlete.

ἀσκητός 3 curiously or artificially wrought; wanting practise; trained.

ἄ-σκοπος 2 inconsiderate; unseen, invisible; unmeasurable; unexpected.

ἀσκός, ὁ hide; leather bag.

ᾆσμα, τό song.

ἄσμενος 3 willing, ready, glad; saved.

ἄ-σοφος 2 unwise, foolish.

ἀσπάζομαι M. to welcome, greet, salute, hail; to visit; to take leave; to hug, caress, love. [kick.]

ἀ-σπαίρω to jerk, struggle,

ἄ-σπαρτος 2 unsown.

ἀσπάσιος, ἀσπαστός 3 welcome, longed for; delighted, glad, willing.

ἀσπασμός, ὁ greeting, embrace.

ἄ-σπερμος 2 without issue.

ἀ-σπερχές adv. eagerly, zealously; incessantly.

ἄ-σπετος 2 unspeakable, incessant, immense.

ἀσπιδιώτης, ου, ὁ shield-bearing.

ἄ-σπιλος 2 unstained.

ἀσπίς, ίδος, ἡ shield; hoplite; adder.

ἀσπιστήρ, ῆρος and ἀσπιστής, οῦ, ὁ shield-bearer, warrior.

ἄ-σπλαγχνος 2 heartless; cowardly.

ἄ-σπονδος 2 without treaty or truce; implacable.

ἄ-σπορος 2 unsown.

ἀ-σπουδεί adv. without zeal or struggle.

ἄσσα = ἅτινα (ὅστις).

ἄσσα = τινά (τὶς).

ἀσσάριον, τό small coin.

ἄσσω = ἀΐσσω.

ἀ-στάθμητος 2 unsteady; unmeasurable.

ἄ-στακτος 2 (adv. ἀστακτί) gushing freely.

ἀ-στασίαστος 2 without party-contests.

ἀ-στατέω to be unstable.

ἀ-σταφίς, ίδος, ἡ raisin.

ἀ-στάχυς, υος, ὁ ear of corn. [shelter.]

ἀ-στέγαστος 2 without

ἀστεῖος 3 of a town, townlike, polite, accomplished.

ἄ-στειπτος 2 untrodden.

ἀ-στεμφής 2 firm, steady.

ἀ-στένακτος 2 without a sigh. [out love.]

ἀ-στεργής 2 unkind, with-

ἀστερόεις 3 starry, starred; sparkling.

ἀστεροπή, ἡ lightning.

ἀστεροπητής, ὁ lightener.

ἀ-στεφάνωτος 2 not wreathed. [male citizen.]

ἀστή, ἡ townswoman, fe-

ἀστήρ, έρος, ὁ star.

ἀ-στήρικτος 2 unsupported, weak.

ἀ-στιβής 2 untrodden; inaccessible. [man.]

ἀστικός 3 of a town; towns-

ἄ-στικτος 2 untatooed.

ἄ-στομος 2 hard-mouthed.

ἄ-στοργος 2 unkind.

ἀστός, ὁ townsman, citizen

ἀ-στοχέω to miss, fail.

ἀστόω = ἀΐστόω.

ἀστραβή, ἡ pack-saddle; saddled mule.

ἀστρᾰγᾰλίζω to dice.

ἀστρᾰγᾰλος, ὁ joint of the spine; ankle-bone; die, dice.

ἀστραπή = ἀστεροπή.

ἀστράπτω to flash, lighten, shine. [from service.]

ἀ-στράτευτος 2 exempt

ἀστρο-λογία, ἡ astronomy.

ἀστρο-λόγος 2 astronomer, astrologer. [tion.]

ἄστρον, τό star, constella-

ἀστρο-νομία, ἡ astronomy.

ἄ-στροφος 2 not turning or looking back.

ἄ-στρωτος 2 without covering, uncovered.

ἄστυ, εως or εος, τό city, capital.

ἀστὔ-βοώτης, ου crying through the city.

ἀστυ-γείτων 2 neighbouring. [tecting, town-ruling.]

ἀστυ-νόμος 2 town-pro-

ἀ-συγ-κρότητος 2 untrained. [able.]

ἀ-σύμβᾰτος 2 irreconcil-

ἀ-σύμβλητος 2 incomprehensible.

ἀ-συμμετρία, ἡ disproportion, deformity. [tionate.]

ἀ-σύμμετρος 2 dispropor-

ἀ-σύμφορος 2 unexpedient; useless; unfit.

ἀ-σύμφωνος 2 discordant.

ἀ-συνεσία, ἡ stupidity.

ἀ-σύνετος 2 stupid.

ἀ-σύνθετος 2 faithless, breaking treaties.

ἀ-σύντακτος 2 not arranged.

ἀ-σύφηλος 2 foolish, disgraceful, mortifying.

ἀσυχαῖος see ἡσυχαῖος.

ἀ-σφάδαστος 2 without convulsion, untrembling.

ἀσφάλεια, ἡ steadiness, safety, security, certainty; truth; safe-conduct; care.

ἀ-σφαλής 2 steadfast, incessant; safe, certain, true; careful.

ἀσφαλίζω to secure.

ἄσφαλτος, ἡ mineral pitch, asphaltum.

ἀ-σφάραγος, ὁ wind-pipe.

ἀσφόδελος, ὁ daffodil.

ἀ-σχαλάω and ἀ-σχάλλω to be grieved, vexed, or indignant.

ἄ-σχετος 2 not to be checked, incontrollable. [seemly.]

ἀ-σχημονέω to behave un-

ἀ-σχημοσύνη, ἡ indecency; deformity. [miserable.]

ἀ-σχήμων 2 indecent; ugly;

ἀ-σχολία ἡ want of leisure, occupation, business; hindrance. [busy.]

ἄ-σχολος 2 without leisure,

ἀ-σώματος 2 incorporeal.

ἀσωτία, ἡ debauch, gluttony. [fligate.]

ἄ-σωτος 2 debauched, pro-

ἀ-τακτέω to be disorderly or undisciplined.

ἄ-τακτος 2 disorderly, undisciplined, dissolute.

ἀ-ταλαίπωρος 2 without pains; indifferent.

ἀ-τάλαντος 2 equivalent.

ἀταλά-φρων 2 harmless, childlike.

ἀ-ταξίᾱ, ἡ want of discipline, disorder; licentiousness.

ἀτάομαι P. to be vexed.

ἀτάρ conj. but. yet, however.

ἀ-τάρακτος 2 intrepid.

ἀ-ταρβής 2, ἀ-τάρβητος 2 fearless, dauntless.

ἀ-ταρπιτός and ἀ-ταρπός, ἡ = ἀτραπιτός. [uncivil.]

ἀταρτηρός 3 mischievous,

ἀτασθαλίᾱ, ἡ recklessness.

ἀτασθάλλω to offend.

ἀτάσθαλος 2 reckless, haughty.

ἄ-ταφος 2 unburied.

ἄτε just as, as if; because, as.

ἄ-τεγκτος 2 unwetted, hard. [away.]

ἀ-τειρής 2 not to be worn

ἀ-τείχιστος 2 unfortified; not blockaded.

ἀ-τέκμαρτος 2 ambiguous, vague, uncertain.

ἄ-τεκνος 2 childless.

ἀ-τέλεια, ἡ exemption, immunity.

ἀ-τέλεστος 2 = ἀτελής; not to be fulfilled; uninitiated. [inexorable.]

ἀ-τελεύτητος 2 unfinished

ἀ-τελής 2 unfinished; not fulfilled; endless; imperfect; unsuccessful; invalid; free from taxes.

ἀτέμβω to hurt, injure; to cheat. — P. to forfeit.

ἀ-τενής 2 strained, tight, intense; firm, persevering, inflexible, steady.

ἀτενίζω to look at intently.

ἄτερ prp. with gen. far from: without, besides; in spite of.

ἀ-τέραμνος 2 hard, inexorable.

ἄτερθεν = ἄτερ.

ἀ-τερπής 2 and ἄ-τερπος unpleasing, sad.

ἀ-τεχνίᾱ, ἡ want of skill.

ἄ-τεχνος 2 without art; ἀτέχνως plainly, without art; ἀτεχνῶς really, of course; quite, utterly.

ἀτέω to be foolhardy.

ἄτη, ἡ infatuation, delusion, stupor; guilt, wickedness, punishment; evil, woe.

ἄ-τηκτος 2 unmelted.

ἀ-τημέλητος 2 not cared for, heedless.

ἀ-τηρίᾱ, ἡ evil, ruin.

ἀτηρός 3 and ἀτήσιμος 2 ruinous; wicked.

ἀ-τίζω not to honour.

ἀ-τῑμάζω, ἀ-τῑμάω to esteem lightly, despise; to defame disgrace, insult.

ἀ-τίμητος 2 despised; not estimated.

ἀ-τῑμίᾱ ἡ dishonour, disgrace; infamy, proscription (loss of civil rights).

ἄ-τῑμος 2 unhonoured. despised; outlaw; not deigned, unworthy; dishonouring, shameful, despicable; unestimated.

ἀ-τῑμόω = ἀτιμάζω.

ἀ-τῑμώρητος 2 unpunished; helpless.

ἀτιτάλλω to bring up.

ἄ-τῑτος 2 unavenged; unpaid.

ἄ-τλᾱτος = ἄτλητος.

5*

ἀ-τλητέω to think unbearable, to be indignant.

ἄ-τλητος 2 unbearable.

ἀτμίζω to steam, reek.

ἀτμίς, ίδος, ἡ and ἀτμός, ὁ steam, vapour, smoke.

ἄ-τοκος 2 barren.

ἀ-τολμίᾱ, ἡ despondency.

ἄ-τολμος 2 cowardly.

ἄ-τομος 2 unmowed; indivisible. [strangeness.]

ἀ-τοπίᾱ, ἡ unusualness,]

ἄ-τοπος 2 unusual, strange; absurd; indecent, wicked.

ἄτος 2 insatiate. [row]

ἄ-τρακτος, ὁ spindle; ar-]

ἀ-τράπῑτός, ἀ-τρᾱπός, ἡ path, road, (foot)way.

ἀ-τρέκεια, ἡ full truth.

ἀ-τρεκής 2 sure, exact, strict, true.

ἀ-τρεμάς adv. without trembling; quietly, silently; circumspectly.

ἀ-τρεμέω to keep quiet.

ἀ-τρεμής 2 unmoved, quiet.

ἀ-τρεμίζω = ἀτρεμέω.

ἄ-τρεστος 2 intrepid.

ἀ-τρῐβής, ἄ-τριπτος 2 unhurt; untrodden; unhardened.

ἄ-τρομος 2 = ἀτρεμής.

ἄ-τροφος 2 underfed.

ἄ-τρύγετος 2 unfruitful, desert; everfluctuating.

ἄ-τρῦτος 2 incessant, unabating.

ἀ-τρῦτώνη, ἡ indomitable.

ἄ-τρωτος 2 unwounded; invulnerable.

ἄττα¹, ὁ father.

ἄττα² = τινά.

ἄττα = ἄτινα.

ἀτταταῖ int. woe! alas!

ἀττέλεβος, ὁ unwinged locust.

ἄττης, ου, ὁ surname of Bacchus.

ἀττικίζω to side with the Athenians.

ἀττικισμός, ὁ inclination towards Athens.

ἀτύζω to alarm, harass, anguish. — P. to be frightened or benumbed; to flee.

ἀ-τύράννευτος 2 not ruled by a tyrant.

ἀ-τῠχέω not to obtain, to miss, fail; to be unlucky or unfortunate.

ἀ-τύχημα, τό and ἀ-τυχίᾱ, ἡ misfortune. [happy.]

ἀ-τῠχής 2 unfortunate, un-]

αὖ adv. back; again, once more; for another time; on the other hand; further.

αὐαίνω, αὐαίνω to dry up, to scorch. — P. to become dry, to wither.

αὐγάζω to illumine; to shine; to perceive. — M. to discern, perceive.

αὐγή, ἡ splendour, brilliancy; ray, beam; eye, glance.

αὐδάζομαι M., αὐδάω and M. to speak, utter, talk, cry, call; to order, advise.

αὐδή, ἡ voice, speech; report, rumour.

αὐδήεις 3 gifted with speech. [back.]

αὖ-ερύω to draw or bend]

αὖθ᾽ = αὖθι, αὖτε.

αὐθ-άδεια αὐθ-αδίᾱ, ἡ self-complacency; arrogance; obstinacy.

αὐθ-άδης 2 self-willed;

arrogant; capricious; arbitrary.

αὐθ-ᾰδίζομαι *M.* to be self-pleasing or arrogant.

αὐθ-αιμος 2 and **αὐθ-αίμων** 2 = αὐθόμαιμος.

αὐθ-αίρετος 2 self-chosen, self-made, voluntary; self-incurred.

αὐθ-έντης, ου, ὁ author, doer; murderer; executioner.

αὐθ-ήμερον *adv.* on the same day; on the spot.

αὖθι *adv.* there, on the spot.

αὐθι-γενής 2 home-born, native, indigenous.

αὖθις = αὖ.

αὐθ-όμαιμος 2 allied by blood; brother, sister.

αὔΐαχος 2 shouting together.

αὖλαξ, ἄκος, ἡ furrow.

αὔλειος 2 belonging to the court.

αὐλέω to play on the flute. — *M.* to be entertained by fluting.

αὐλή, ἡ yard for cattle; farm-yard; court, yard-wall; dwelling, cabin; palace, residence.

αὔλημα, τό and **αὔλησις**, ἡ flute-playing.

αὐλητής, οῦ, ὁ flute-player.

αὐλητικός 3 concerning flute-playing.

αὐλητρίς ίδος, ἡ flute-girl.

αὐλίζομαι *M.* and *P.* to be fenced in; to camp in the open air; to pass the night.

αὔλιον, τό hurdle; farmyard; grotto. [ters; stable.]

αὖλις, ιδος, ἡ night-quar-)

αὐλός, ὁ pipe, tube; nozzle, shank; flash of blood; flute.

αὐλών, ῶνος, ὁ hollow way, ravine, defile; strait; canal, ditch.

αὐλ-ῶπις, ιδος with a tube.

αὐξάνω, αὔξω to increase, augment, enlarge, extol, to let grow. — *P.* to grow, improve, thrive.

αὔξη and **αὔξησις**, ἡ growth, increase, thriving.

ἄ-ὔπνος 2 sleepless.

αὔρᾱ, ἡ air, breath, breeze, draught.

αὔριον *adv.* to-morrow.

αὐσταλέος 3 dry; bristly; dirty.

αὐστηρίᾱ, αὐστηρότης, ητος, ἡ harshness, austerity.

αὐστηρός 3 harsh, sour, austere. [messenger.]

αὐτ-άγγελος 2 one's own)

αὐτ-άγρετος 2 = αὐθαίρ-ετος. [or sister.]

αὐτ-άδελφος 2 full brother)

αὐτάρ *conj.* but, yet, however; further.

αὐτ-άρκεια, ἡ self-sufficiency, independence.

αὐτ-άρκης 2 self-sufficient, independent; secure; contented.

αὖτε = αὖ.

αὐτ-επάγγελτος 2 of one's own accord.

αὐτ-ερέτης, ου, ὁ both rower and soldier.

ἀϋτέω to cry, shout; to roar, ring.

ἀϋτή, ἡ cry; war-cry; battle.

αὐτ-ήκοος 2 ear-witness.

αὐτίκα *adv.* forthwith, instantly, directly; for instance.

αὔτμή, ἡ and αὐτμήν, ένος, ὁ breath, blast, wind; odour; blaze.   [war-cry.]

αὐτο-βοεί adv. at the first)

αὐτο-γέννητος 2 self-engendered.

αὐτο-γνωμονέω to act of one's own will. [solved.]

αὐτό-γνωτος 2 self-re-)

αὐτο-δαής 2 self-taught.

αὐτό-δεκα just ten.

αὐτο-δίδακτος 2 self-taught. [own jurisdiction.]

αὐτό-δίκος 2 with one's)

αὐτόθΐον adv. at once.

αὐτο-έντης, ου, ὁ = αὐθ-έντης.   [same year.]

αὐτό-ετες adv. in the)

αὐτόθεν adv. from the spot, thence, from here; on the spot, at once; from the beginning; therefore; without ceremony.

αὐτόθι adv. on the spot, there, here.   [sister.]

αὐτο-κασιγνήτη, ἡ full)

αὐτο-κασίγνητος, ὁ full brother.   [condemned.]

αὐτο-κατάκρΐτος 2 self-)

αὐτο-κέλευστος 2, αὐτο-κελής 2 self-bidden.

αὐτό-κλητος 2 self-called, of one's own accord.

αὐτο-κρᾰτής 2 and αὐτο-κράτωρ 2 sovereign, absolute, independent; authorized.   [suicide.]

αὐτο-κτονέω to commit)

αὐτό-μᾰτος 2 and 3 self-moved; of one's own will, voluntary; accidental.

αὐτο-μολέω to go over, desert.

αὐτο-μολία, ἡ desertion.

αὐτό-μολος 2 going over, deserter.   [oneself.]

αὐτο-νομέομαι to govern)

αὐτο-νομία, ἡ independence.

αὐτό-νομος 2 independent.

αὐτό-νυχΐ adv. in the same night.

αὐτό-ξυλος 2 quite wooden.

αὐτό-παις, ὁ genuine child.

αὐτό-πετρος 2 of natural stone.

αὐτό-ποιος 2 self-grown.

αὐτό-πολις, ἡ free state.

αὐτο-πολίτης, ὁ citizen of a free state.   [root.]

αὐτό-πρεμνος 2 with the)

αὐτ-όπτης, ου, ὁ eye-witness.

αὐτός, ή, ὁ self, oneself, personal; by oneself, alone; together with; oneself with others; he, she, it; ὁ αὐτός the same.   [same place.]

αὐτόσε adv. just at the)

αὐτο-στᾰδίη, ἡ close fight.

αὐτό-στολος 2 going of oneself.

αὐτο-σφᾰγής 2 self-killed.

αὐτο-σχεδιάζω to improvise, act wantonly or unadvisedly; to judge superficially.

αὐτο-σχεδίη = αὐτοσταδίη.

αὐτο-σχεδόν adv. in close fight.

αὐτο-τελής 2 taxing oneself; arbitrary.

αὐτοῦ adv. in the same place; there, here; at once.

αὐτο-ουργός 2 self-working; workman.

αὐτο-φυής 2 natural.

αὐτό-φωρος 2 caught in the very act; convicted by facts.

αὐτό-χειρ, ρος with one's own hand; doer, murderer.

αὐτο-χειρίᾱ, ἡ one's own deed; murder.

αὐτο-χόωνος 2 solid, massive.

αὔτως, αὕτως adv. just so, quite so; still, only, solely; without ceremony, downright; in vain, uselessly; without reason.

αὐχενίζω to cut one's neck.

αὐχένιος 3 belonging to the nape.

αὐχέω to boast, brag.

αὔχημα, τό pride; boast; ornament.

αὐχήν, ένος, ὁ nape, neck; neck of land; strait; defile; forking.

αὔχησις, ἡ = αὔχημα.

αὐχμέω to be dry, squalid, or rugged.

αὐχμηρός 3 dry, parched; squalid, wild; dark.

αὐχμός, ὁ drought; dirt.

αὐχμώδης = αὐχμηρός.

αὔω[1], αὕω to kindle, to singe.

αὔω[2], ἀΰω to shout, call aloud, roar, sound.

ἀφ-αγνίζω to offer an atonement. [away.]

ἀφ-αίρεσις, ἡ a taking]

ἀφ-αιρέω to take off, away, or from; to remove; to rob, deprive; to free from, to diminish. — M. to take for oneself, to obtain, deprive, rob; to make an end of; to prevent.

ἄ-φαλος 2 without a φάλος.

ἀφ-αμαρτάνω to miss, lose.

ἀφαμαρτο-επής 2 failing in speech.

ἀφ-ανδάνω to displease.

ἀ-φάνεια, ἡ obscurity, insignificance.

ἀ-φανής 2 unseen, invisible; hidden, secret; vanished; uncertain, unknown; insignificant, obscure.

ἀ-φανίζω to make unseen, to cause to vanish, to hide, remove; to destroy, annihilate; to disfigure, deface. — P. to vanish, disappear, cease. [ὁ a vanishing.]

ἀφάνισις, ἡ, ἀφάνισμός,

ἄ-φαντος 2 = ἀφανής.

ἀφ-άπτω to fasten, tie to, hang on. — P. to hang, to be hung on.

ἄφαρ adv. quickly, forthwith, presently.

ἄ-φαρκτος 2 = ἄφρακτος.

ἀφ-αρπάζω to snatch away; to rob.

ἀφάρτερος 3 quicker.

ἀφάσσω = ἀφάω.

ἄ-φατος 2 unutterable; horrible, huge.

ἀφαυρός 3 weak, feeble.

ἀφάω to touch, feel.

ἀ-φεγγής 2 dark, gloomy; terrible.

ἀ-φειδέω not to spare; to overlook, neglect.

ἀ-φειδής 2 unsparing; unmerciful, cruel; plentiful.

ἀ-φειδίᾱ, ἡ profuseness; harshness.

ἀ-φελής 2 simple, plain.

ἀφ-έλκω to draw or drag away; to seduce. [city.]

ἀφελότης, ητος, ἡ simpli-

ἄφενος, τό wealth, stores.

ἀφ-έρπω to steal away.

ἄφ-εσις, ἡ a sending away; a setting free, starting; dimission; remission.

ἄφ-ετος 2 let loose or free; sacred.

ἀφή, ἡ a kindling; a touching, touch; sense of touch; joint.

ἀφ-ηγέομαι M. to lead the way, to lead on or off; to tell, relate.

ἀφ-ήγημα, τό and ἀφ-ήγησις, ἡ tale, narration.

ἀφ-ημαι to sit far off.

ἀφ-ημερεύω to be absent at day.

ἀφήτωρ, ορος, ὁ archer.

ἀ-φθαρσίᾱ, ἡ immortality.

ἄ-φθαρτος 2 incorruptible, immortal. [mute.]

ἄ-φθεγκτος 2 speechless,

ἄ-φθιτος 2 = ἄφθαρτος.

ἄ-φθογγος 2 voiceless, speechless.

ἀ-φθονίᾱ, ἡ freedom from envy, readiness; abundance, plenty.

ἄ-φθονος 2 free from envy; liberal; fertile; abundant, plentiful.

ἀφ-ίημι to send off or away; to throw, shoot; to let loose, set free, acquit; to dissolve, break up; to pronounce, utter; to shed; to give up, neglect; to remit, forgive;

intr. to start; to cease. — M. to free oneself; to escape; to start.

ἀφ-ικάνω = ἀφικνέομαι.

ἀφ-ικνέομαι M. to arrive at, come to; to return; to overcome, befall.

ἀ-φιλ-άγαθος 2 averse to good men. [money.]

ἀ-φιλ-άργυρος 2 not loving

ἀ-φίλητος 2 unloved.

ἄ-φιλος 2 friendless; unfriendly, unkind; ungrateful; disagreeable.

ἄφ-ιξις, ἡ arrival; return; departure. [back.]

ἀφ-ιππεύω to ride off or

ἄφ-ιππος 2 unskilled in riding; not fit for riding.

ἀφ-ίπταμαι = ἀποπέτομαι.

ἀφ-ίστημι to put away, remove, depose; to make fall off or revolt. intr. and P. to go away; to stand aloof; to fall off, revolt; to desist, abstain, omit. — M. to get weighed out, to be paid.

ἄφλαστον, τό ornament of the curved stern of a ship.

ἀφλοισμός, ὁ foam.

ἀφνειός 2 and 3 rich, wealthy.

ἄφνω adv. suddenly.

ἀ-φόβητος, ἄ-φοβος 2 fearless; defenceless.

ἄφ-οδος ἡ departure, retreat; expedient. [to portray.]

ἀφ-ομοιόω to make like,

ἀφ-οπλίζομαι M. to put off one's armour.

ἀφ-οράω and M. to look away from; to look from afar; to behold.

ἀ-φόρητος 2 unbearable.

ἀφ-ορίζω to divide by a boundary-line; to select; to define. [away.]

ἀφ-ορμάω to start, to rush

ἀφ-ορμή, ἡ starting-point; support, means, resources, capital; cause, occasion, chance.

ἄφ-ορμος 2 hastening away.

ἄ-φορος 2 barren.

ἀφ-οσιόω to expiate. — M. to expiate oneself, to perform religious duties.

ἀ-φραδέω to be foolish.

ἀ-φραδής 2 foolish, silly, thoughtless; senseless.

ἀ-φραδία, ἡ thoughtlessness; ignorance.

ἀ-φραίνω = ἀφραδέω.

ἄ-φρακτος 3 unfenced; unguarded; unarmed.

ἄ-φραστος 2 unspeakable; unperceived, secret; inconceivable; unexpected.

ἀφρέω to foam.

ἀ-φρήτωρ 2 without family.

ἀφρίζω = ἀφρέω. [to love.]

ἀφροδῑσιάζω to be given

ἀφροδῑσιος 3 and 2 indulging in love; belonging to Venus.

ἀ-φρονέω to be foolish.

ἀ-φροντιστέω to be heedless or careless.

ἀ-φρόντιστος 2 thoughtless, heedless; out of one's wits.

ἀφρός, ὁ foam. [ness.]

ἀ-φροσύνη, ἡ thoughtless-

ἄ-φρων 2 thoughtless, foolish, senseless; indecent.

ἀ-φυής 2 ungifted, unfit.

ἄ-φυκτος 2 inevitable.

ἀ-φύλακτέω not to be on one's guard.

ἀ-φύλακτος 2 unguarded; careless, heedless.

ἄ-φυλλος 2 leafless.

ἀφ-υπνόω to fall asleep.

ἀφυσγετός, ὁ mud, mire, rubbish.

ἀφύσσω to draw (water); to pour in; to heap up.

ἀφ-υστερέω to come too late; to withhold.

ἀ-φώνητος 2 = ἄφωνος.

ἀ-φωνία, ἡ speechlessness.

ἄ-φωνος 2 speechless, unspeakable. [arms.]

ἄ-χαλκος 2 without brazen

ἄ-χαρις, ιτος 2 without grace or charm, displeasing, ungrateful; unrewarded.

ἀ-χαριστέω to be ungrateful, disobliging.

ἀ-χαριστία, ἡ ingratitude, want of charm.

ἀ-χάριστος 2, ἀ-χάριτος 2 = ἄχαρις.

ἀ-χειροποίητος 2 not made by (human) hands.

ἄ-χειρος 2 without hands; τὰ -α back.

ἀ-χείρωτος 2 unconquered.

ἄχερδος, ἡ wild pear-tree.

ἀχερωΐς, ίδος, ἡ white poplar. [to mourn.]

ἀχεύω, ἀχέω to be sad,

ἀχέω = ἠχέω. [angry.]

ἀχθεινός 3 cumbersome;

ἀχθηδών, όνος, ἡ grief.

ἄχθομαι P. to be burdened, molested, vexed; to be sad, angry, or unwilling.

ἄχθος, τό burden, load; sorrow, grief.

ἀχθο-φόρος 2 carrying burdens. [tunic.

ἄ-χίτων, ωνος 2 without tunic.

ἀχλυόεις 3 dark, gloomy; grieving. [darkness.

ἀχλύς, ύος, ἡ mist, gloom,

ἀχλύω to grow dark.

ἄχνη, ἡ chaff; foam; dew.

ἄχνῦμαι to be sorry, afflicted, or angry.

ἄ-χολος 2 what allays anger.

ἄχομαι = ἄχνυμαι.

ἀ-χόρευτος 2, ἄ-χορος 2 without a dance; joyless.

ἄχος, τό pain, sorrow, grief.

ἄ-χρεῖος 2 useless, unserviceable, weak.

ἀ-χρεόω P. to become useless.

ἀ-χρημᾰτίᾱ, ἡ want of means.

ἀ-χρήμᾰτος 2 without means, poor. [ματία.

ἀ-χρημοσύνη, ἡ = ἀχρη-

ἄ-χρηστος 2 useless, unprofitable; foolish, bad, unfit; not yet employed.

ἄχρι, ἄχρις, adv. wholly, utterly; prp. with gen. and conj. until; as far as.

ἀχυρμίη, ἡ heap of chaff.

ἄχυρον, τό chaff.

ἀχώ, ἡ = ἠχώ.

ἄψ adv. back; again.

ἄ-φαυστος 2 untouched; without touching.

ἀ-φεγγής 2 unblamed.

ἀ-φευδέω not to lie.

ἀ-φευδής 2 truthful, trustworthy; genuine, true.

ἀφίνθιον τό and ἄψινθος, ἡ wormwood.

ἀφό-ρροος 2 flowing backwards.

ἄφορρος 2 going back.

ἄψος, τό joint, limb.

ἀ-ψόφητος and ἄ-ψοφος 2 noiseless.

ἄ-ψυκτος 2 uncooled.

ἄ-ψῦχος 2 without soul, lifeless; spiritless.

ἄω to satiate. — M. to be satisfied.

ἄ-ωρος[1] 2 untimely; unripe; ill-shaped.

ἄωρος[2] 2 invisible; pending.

ἀ-ωτέω to sleep.

ἄωτος, ὁ tuft, lock, wool, fleece.

B

B, β (βῆτα) second letter of the alphabet; as a numeral β´ = 2.

βαβαί int. only look!

βάδην adv. step by step, slowly.

βαδίζω to step, pace, march.

βάδισμα, τό a marching, [pace.

βάζω to talk, say.

βαθμός, ὁ step, stair, degree. [extension.

βάθος, τό depth; height,

βάθρον, τό step, stair; threshold; ladder; bench, seat; base, pedestal; soil; foundation. [soil.

βαθύ-γαιος 2 with deep

βαθυ-δῑνήεις 3, βαθυ-δῑνης 2 deep-eddying.

βαθύ-ζωνος 2 deep-girded.

βαθύ-κολπος 2 deep-bosomed. [grass.

βαθύ-λειμος 2 with high

βαθυ-λήιος 2 with deep corn or crops.

βαθύνω to deepen.

βαθυ-ρρείτης, ου deep-flowing.

βαθύ-ρριζος 2 deep-rooted.

βαθύς 3 deep; high; wide; vehement.

βαθυ-σκαφής 2 deep-dug.

βαθύ-σχοινος 2 with deep rushes.

βαίνω to take strides, to sit astride; to go, step, walk; to mount; to arrive, go away; to depart, die; (perf.) to stand fast, to be settled. — trans. to cause to go, to bring; to cause to descend.

βάϊον, τό palm-branch.

βαιός 3 little, small, short; humble.

βαίτη, ἡ coat of skin.

βακτηρίᾶ, ἡ stick, staff.

βάκχειος and βάκχειος 3 Bacchic, in ecstasy.

βακχεύω to keep the feast of Bacchus; to be frantic, to be in ecstasy.

βάκχη, ἡ and βακχίς, ίδος, ἡ Bacchante.

βάκχιος 3 and βακχιώτης, ου = βακχεῖος. [thusiast.]

βάκχος, ὁ Bacchanal, en-]

βαλαν-άγρᾶ, ἡ key.

βαλανεῖον, τό bath; bathing-house. [eating.]

βαλανη-φάγος 3 acorn-]

βαλανη-φόρος 2 bearing dates.

βάλανος, ἡ acorn; date; chestnut; peg; door-bolt.

βαλάντιον, τό purse.

βαλαντιο-τομέω to cut purses. [battlements.]

βαλβίς, ίδος, ἡ bar, lists;]

βαλιός 3 dappled.

βάλλω to throw, cast, hurl, shoot; to hit, wound, strike; to dash, push; to let fall; to put on; to meet, catch; to put; intr. to fall; to discharge; to rush. — M. to throw around oneself; to take to heart, bear in mind; to deliberate.

βαμβαίνω to shake, totter.

βαναυσίᾶ, ἡ handicraft; vulgar trade. [tisan; vulgar.]

βάναυσος 2 craftsman, ar-]

βάξις, ἡ speech, saying; oracle; report, talk.

βαπτίζω to dip, wash; to baptize.

βάπτισμα, τό and βαπτισμός, ὁ baptism.

βαπτιστής, οῦ, ὁ dyer; baptizer.

βάπτω to dip, wet; to dye; to temper, harden.

βάραθρον, τό gulf, pit (for criminals).

βαρβαρίζω to behave or act like a barbarian; to side with the Persians.

βαρβαρικός 3 and βάρβαρος 2 barbarous, not Greek, foreign, outlandish; rude, uncivilised, cruel.

βαρβαρό-φωνος 2 with a strange voice.

βαρβαρόω to make barbarous. — P. to become barbarous.

βάρδιστος see βραδύς.

βαρέω = βαρύνω.

βᾶρις, ιος or ιδος, ἡ canoe, boat, raft.

βάρος, τό weight, burden, load; grief, sorrow; plenty; dignity.   [sorely.]

βαρυ-άλγητος 2 grieving

βαρυ-ᾰχής 2 groaning heavily.   [thundering.]

βαρυ-βρεμέτης, ου loud-

βαρυ-βρώς, ῶτος greedily eating.

βαρύθω to be burdened.

βαρύνω to burden, load; to vex, torment. — P. to be burdened or tormented; to be vexed, annoyed, or angry.   [unhappy]

βαρύ-ποτμος 2 ill-fated,

βαρύς 3 heavy, burdensome, oppressive; weighty; deep, hollow, loud (voice); grievous, troublesome, painful; unwholesome; hard, cruel; strong, mighty.

βαρύ-στονος 2 groaning heavily, painful.

βαρυ-σύμφορος 2 oppressed by misfortune.

βαρύτης, ητος, ἡ heaviness; load, oppression; bass voice; harshness, pride.

βαρύ-τῑμος 2 precious, costly.   [dejected.]

βαρύ-ψῡχος 2 low-spirited,

βασανίζω to test, try, examine; to (put to the) torture.   [torture.]

βασανισμός, ὁ a torturing,

βασανιστής, οῦ, ὁ torturer, jailer.

βάσᾰνος, ἡ touchstone; test, proof, trial; inquiry; torture.

βασίλεια, ἡ queen, princess.

βασιλεία, ἡ kingdom, monarchy.

βασίλειος 2 and 3 kingly, royal, princely. — τὸ βασίλειον royal palace, court; treasury.

βᾰσῐλεύς, ὁ king, prince, ruler; the king of Persia; lord, nobleman.   [rule.]

βασιλεύω to be king, to

βασιληίς, ίδος, ἡ royal.

βασιλικός 3 kingly, royal, princely.

βασιλίς, ίδος and βασίλισσα, ἡ = βασίλεια.

βάσιμος 2 passable.

βάσις, ἡ step, pace; foot; basis, foundation, pedestal.

βασκαίνω to slander; to fascinate, spell.

βασκανία, ἡ slander; spell.

βάσκᾰνος 2 slanderous, malignant; envious.

βάσκω to go.

βασσάριον, τό Libyan fox.

βαστάζω to touch; to lift up; to bear, hold up; to carry away.

βᾰτός 3 passable, accessible.

βάτος[1], ἡ thorn-bush.

βάτος[2], ὁ a measure for liquids.

βάτρᾰχος, ὁ frog.

βάτταλος, ὁ weakling.

βαττο-λογέω to prattle.

βαφεύς, ὁ dyer.

βᾰφή, ἡ a dipping; dyeing.

βδέλλα, ἡ leech.

βδέλυγμα, τό abomination.

βδελυγμία, ἡ a loathing, disgust.

βδελυκτός 3 abominable.

βδελυρία, ἡ shamelessness.

βδελῠρός 3 disgusting; shameless. [detest, fear.]

βδελύσσομαι P. to abhor,

βέβαιος 2 and 3 firm, steady; trusty; sure, certain.

βεβαιότης, ητος, ἡ firmness, steadiness, safety, certainty.

βεβαιόω to make firm, to confirm, assert; to fulfil. — M. to secure for oneself; to feel confirmed.

βεβαίωσις, ἡ confirmation.

βέβηλος 2 profane; unholy, unclean.

βεβηλόω to profane.

βεβρώθω to devour.

βείομαι = βέομαι.

βέκος, τό bread. [pon.]

βέλεμνον, τό missile weapon,]

βελόνη, ἡ point of an arrow; needle.

βέλος, τό missile weapon, dart, javelin; terror.

βέλτερος 3 = βελτίων.

βέλτιστος 3 the best, noblest, or bravest.

βελτίων 2 better, braver, nobler.

βένθος, τό depth.

βέομαι I shall live.

βέρεθρον, τό = βάραθρον.

βηλός, ὁ threshold.

βῆμα, τό step, stair; raised step, stage, tribune, throne, tribunal.

βήξ, βηχός, ὁ, ἡ cough.

βήρυλλος, ἡ, ὁ beryl.

βῆσσα, ἡ glen, wooded valley.

βήσσω to cough.

βητ-άρμων, ονος, ὁ dancer.

βίᾱ, ἡ strength, force; violence.

βιάζω to force, to use violence; to overpower; to maltreat, oppress, constrain; to defy.

βίαιος 3 and 2 forcible, violent; strong, oppressive; forced. [force.]

βιαστής, οῦ, ὁ one using]

βιάω = βιάζω.

βιβάζω to cause to go; to bring; to lift up.

βιβάσθω, βιβάω, βίβημι to stride, step.

βιβλαρίδιον, βιβλιάριον, βιβλίδιον, τό little book or scroll.

βιβλίον, τό, βίβλος, ἡ bark of the papyrus; paper; book; letter. [sume.]

βιβρώσκω to eat up, con-]

βῖκος or βίκος, ὁ vessel, jug, flagon.

βιό-δωρος 2 life-giving.

βίος, ὁ life; mode of life; livelihood; means.

βιός, ὁ bow. [livelihood.]

βιο-στερής 2 bereft of one's]

βιοτεύω to live. [βίος.]

βιοτή, ἡ and βίοτος, ὁ =]

βιόω to live. — M. to maintain one's life; to preserve life. [endurable.]

βιώσιμος 2 worth living;]

βίωσις, ἡ mode of life.

βιωτικός 3 belonging to life, earthly.

βιωτός 3 = βιώσιμος

βλαβερός 3 noxious, hurtful.

βλάβη, ἡ and βλάβος, τό damage; hurt; loss.

βλάβω = βλάπτω.

βλᾱκείᾱ, ἡ sloth; stupidity.

βλᾱκεύω to be lazy, indolent.

βλάξ, βλᾱκός, ὁ lazy, indolent, careless; stupid.

βλάπτω to hinder; to weaken; to damage, hurt; to deceive, confound.

βλαστάνω to sprout, bud, germinate; to grow up; to be descended from; *trans.* to bring forth.

βλάστη, ἡ, βλάστημα, τό, βλάστος, ὁ sprout, bud; growth; descendant; origin.

βλασ-φημέω to blaspheme, slander.   [slander.\

βλασ-φημίᾱ, ἡ blasphemy,/

βλάσ-φημος 2 blaspheming, slandering.

βλεμεαίνω to exult in.

βλέμμα, τό look, glance.

βλεπτός 3 worth seeing.

βλέπω to look at or on; to see, regard, observe; to have sight; to beware of.

βλεφαρίς, ίδος or ῖδος, ἡ eyelash.

βλέφαρον, τό eyelid; eye.

βλῆμα, τό shot; wound.

βλῆτρον, τό ring, hoop.

βληχή, ἡ a bleating.

βλίττω to cut out honeycombs.

βλοσυρός 3 grim, terrible.

βλοσυρ-ῶπις, ιδος, ἡ grimlooking.

βλωθρός 3 tall, high grown.

βλώσκω to go; to come.

βοάγριον, τό leather shield.

βοάω to cry, shout, roar, howl; to call to; to praise.

— *P.* to be known or famous.

βοεικός 3 and βόειος 3 of or for oxen, of ox-hide (shield).

βοεύς, ὁ thong of ox-leather.

βοή, ἡ cry, shout; war-cry; battle; call; sound; loud speech, voice; prayer.

βοή, ἡ ox-hide.

βοη-δρομιών, ῶνος, ὁ name of a month (September to October).

βοήθεια, ἡ help, aid, rescue, succour; protection; auxiliary force.

βοηθέω to succour, to come to the rescue, to aid, help, assist.   [battle.\

βοη-θόος 2 hasting to the/

βοηθός 2 helping; assistant.

βο-ηλᾰσίᾱ, ἡ a robbing of cattle.

βο-ηλάτης, ου, ὁ driver.

βοητύς, ύος, ἡ a crying, shouting.   [hole, pit.\

βόθρος, ὁ, βόθῠνος, ὁ/

βοιωτ-αρχέω to be a magistrate with the Bœotians.

βοιωτ-άρχης, ου, βοιώταρχος, ὁ magistrate in Bœotia.

βοιωτιάζω to speak Bœotian; to side with the Bœotians.   [ray.\

βολή, ἡ throw, shot; glance;/

βολίζω to throw the sounding-lead.   [plummet.\

βολίς, ίδος, ἡ missile;/

βόλομαι = βούλομαι.

βόλος, ὁ = βολή; fishing-net.

βομβέω to sound deep, hum, huzz, ring.

βόμβος, ὁ hollow sound.

βορά, ἡ food, meat.

βόρβορος, ὁ mud, mire, dirt.

βορβορώδης 2 miry.

βορέας, ου, ὁ north wind; north. [northern.]

βόρειος 2 and βορήιος 3|

βορρᾶς, ᾶ, ὁ = βορέας.

βόρυς, υος, ὁ gazelle.

βόσις, ἡ food. [pasture.]

βόσκημα, τό cattle, herd;|

βόσκω to feed, nourish. — P. and M. to be fed, maintained, to graze.

βόστρῠχος, ὁ lock of hair.

βοτάνη, ἡ fodder, pasture.

βοτήρ, ῆρος, ὁ shepherd.

βοτόν, τό grazing cattle.

βοτρῦδόν adv. in the shape of grapes.

βότρυς, υος, ὁ grape.

βούβαλις, ιος, ἡ antelope

βού-βοτος, ἡ pasture for cattle.

βού-βρωστις, ἡ hungry evil; craving greediness.

βουβών, ῶνος, ὁ groin; abdomen.

βου-γάϊος, ὁ braggart.

βου-θερής 2 feeder of cattle. [cattle.]

βου-θῠτέω to sacrifice|

βού-θῠτος 2 belonging to a sacrifice of cattle

βού-κερως, ων horned like an ox.

βου-κολέω to feed cattle. — P. and M. to be fed, to graze.

βου-κολίη, ἡ and βου-κό-λιον, τό herd of cattle.

βού-κολος, ὁ cowherd, herdsman.

βουλείᾱ, ἡ office of counsellor.

βούλευμα, τό resolution; decree, plan; wish, opinion; counsel.

βουλευτήριον, τό council-house, council-board.

βουλευτής, οῦ, ὁ counsellor, alderman.

βουλευτικός 3 belonging to counsellors.

βουλεύω to be counsellor; and M. to take counsel; to contrive, devise; to consider; to determine, resolve; to give counsel.

βουλή, ἡ will, determination; counsel, advice; project; council, senate.

βούλημα, τό, βούλησις, ἡ will, determination; purpose.

βουλη-φόρος 2 counselling.

βου-λῑμιάω to suffer from canine hunger.

βούλομαι to will, wish, want, like; to be willing or resolved; to prefer, choose; ὁ βουλόμενος anyone.

βου-λῠτός, ὁ evening, time of unyoking oxen.

βου-νόμος 2 cattle-feeding.

βουνός, ὁ hill, height.

βου-πλήξ, ῆγος, ἡ goad.

βου-πόρος 2 piercing through an ox.

βού-πρῳρος 2 with the head of an ox.

βοῦς, βοός, ὁ, ἡ cow, ox, bull; cattle; ox-hide, shield of ox-hide.

βου-φονέω to kill oxen.

βου-φορβός, ὁ cowherd.

βο-ῶπις, ιδος, ἡ ox-eyed.

βραβεῖον, τό prize in a contest.

βραβεύς, ὁ, βραβευτής, οῦ, ὁ judge, umpire.

βραβεύω to be a judge, to (be) umpire; to rule.

βράγχος, ὁ hoarseness, sore-throat.   [loiter.]

βραδύνω to delay; to tarry,]

βραδυ-πλοέω to sail slowly.

βραδύς 3 slow, heavy; lazy.

βραδυτής, ῆτος, ἡ slowness, tardiness.

βράσσων 2 = βραδύτερος.

βραχεῖν to rattle, ring, roar.

βράχιστος 3 = βραχύτατος.

βραχίων, ονος, ὁ arm, shoul-der.

βράχος, τό shallows (spot).

βραχυ-λογία, ἡ brevity in speech.   [speech.]

βραχυ-λόγος 2 short in]

βραχύς 3 short, not far off; little, shallow.

βραχύτης, ἡ shortness.

βρέμω and M. to roar, sound, clash.

βρέφος, τό unborn child; newborn child; young one, colt.   [head.]

βρεχμός, ὁ forepart of the]

βρέχω to wet, sprinkle; to let rain; P. to be wetted.

βρῐαρός 3 weighty, strong.

βρίζω to sleep, slumber.

βρι-ήπυος 2 loud shouting.

βρῐθοσύνη, ἡ weight, hea-viness.

βρῐθύς 3 weighty, heavy.

βρίθω and M. to be weighty

or loaded, to be bent down to teem, abound; to out weigh, prevail.

βρομέω to hum, huzz.

βρόμος, ὁ noise, huzzing, roar.

βροντάω to thunder.

βροντή, ἡ thunder; stupe-faction.

βρότειος 3 and 2 = βροτός.

βροτόεις 3 bloody.   [ing.]

βροτο-λοιγός 2 man-slay-]

βρότος, ὁ gore.

βροτός, ὁ, ἡ mortal, man.

βροτόω to stain with blood.

βροχή, ἡ rain.

βρόχος, ὁ rope, noose.

βρυγμός, ὁ a gnashing.

βρύκω to bite; to devour.

βρυχάομαι M. and P. to roar, shout aloud.

βρύχω to gnash the teeth.

βρύω to sprout, bud, swell; to cause to come forth.

βρῶμα, τό and βρώμη, ἡ, βρῶσις, ἡ, βρωτύς, ὔος, ἡ food, meat; an eating.

βύβλινος 3 made of byblus.

βύβλος, ἡ papyrus plant; bark of papyrus.

βύζην adv. closely, thickly.

βυθίζω to let sink; to sink.

βυθός, ὁ depth, abyss.

βύκτης, ου howling.

βύνέω = βύω.

βύρσα, ἡ skin, hide.

βυρσεύς, ὁ and βυρσο-δέψης, ου, ὁ tanner.

βύσσινος 3 of fine linen.

βυσσο-δομεύω to contrive secretly.   [depth.]

βυσσόθεν adv. from the]

βυσσός, ὁ = βυθός.

βύσσος, ἡ fine linen.
βύω to cram, to stuff full.
βωθέω = βοηθέω.
βῶλος, ἡ clod of earth.
βώμιος 3 belonging to an altar.

βωμίς, ίδος, ἡ step, stair.
βωμός, ὁ raised place, step, stand, pedestal, altar.
βωστρέω to call to. [ing.]
βωτι-άνειρα, ἡ man-feed-
βώτωρ, ορος, ὁ herdsman.

Γ

Γ, γ (γάμμα) third letter of the alphabet; as a numeral γ' = 3.
γάγγραινα, ἡ gangrene, cancer.
γάζα, ἡ, γαζο-φυλάκιον, τό treasury.
γαῖα, ἡ = γῆ.
γαιά-οχος = γαιήοχος.
γαιήτος sprung from Gæa.
γαιή-οχος 2 earth-compassing; land-protecting.
γαίω to exult.
γάλα, ακτος, τό milk.
γαλα-θηνός 2 milk-suck-
ing. [drinker.]
γαλακτο-πότης, ου, ὁ milk-
γαλέη and γαλῆ, ἡ weasel; cat.
γαλήνη, ἡ calm, stillness of wind; tranquillity.
γαλόως, ω, ἡ sister-in-law.
γαμβρός, ὁ son-in-law; brother-in-law.
γαμετή, ἡ wife.
γαμέτης, ου, ὁ husband.
γαμέω to marry, take to wife. — M. to be given to wife; to give in marriage.
γαμηλιών, ῶνος, ὁ an Attic month (January to February).
γαμίζω to give in marriage. — P. to be wed.
γαμικός 3 bridal.
γαμίσκω = γαμίζω.

γάμμα the letter Gamma.
γᾱ-μόρος = γεωμόρος.
γάμος, ὁ a wedding, marriage, wedding-feast.
γαμφηλή, ἡ jaw.
γαμφ-ῶνυξ, υχος with curved talons. [bright.]
γανάω to shine, to be
γάνυμαι M. to be delighted.
γάρ conj. for; since, as; why, what; o that!
γαργαλισμός, ὁ a tickling.
γαστήρ, στρός, ἡ belly; womb; kind of sausage.
γάστρᾱ, ἡ belly. [tony.]
γαστρι-μαργία, ἡ glut-
γαυλικός, γαυλιτικός 3 belonging to a merchant-ship. [merchant-vessel.]
γαυλός, ὁ milk-pail, bucket;
γαυριάω to pride oneself.
γδουπέω = δουπέω.
γέ conj. at least, at any rate, even, just, of course, indeed.
γέγωνα perf. to make oneself heard, to cry, shout; to proclaim.
γέεννα, ἡ hell.
γείνομαι M. to be begotten or born; to beget. [bour.]
γειτνιάω to be a neigh-
γείτων, ονος, ὁ. ἡ neighbouring; neighbour.

γελασείω to be inclined to laughing.   [mocker.]

γελαστής, οῦ, ὁ laugher,

γελαστός 3 laughable.

γελάω, γελοιάω to laugh, smile, shine; to sneer at.

γελοῖος and γέλοιος 3 laughable; facetious, jesting.

γέλως, ωτος, ὁ and γέλος, ὁ laughter, laughing; joke, mocking.   [laughter.]

γελωτο-ποιέω to cause

γελωτο-ποιός, ὁ jester, buffoon.

γεμίζω to fill, load.

γέμω to be full.

γενεά, ἡ birth, descent; race, family, tribe; home; generation.

γενεά-λογέω to trace a pedigree. — P. to derive one's pedigree. [pedigree.]

γενεᾱ-λογία, ἡ genealogy;

γενέθλη, ἡ = γενεά.

γενέθλιος 2 belonging to one's birth; τὰ γενέθλια birthday or funeral festival; belonging to a family.   [descent.]

γένεθλον, τό descendant;

γενειάς, άδος, ἡ beard; chin; cheek.

γενειά(σκ)ω to get a beard.

γένειον, τό chin; beard.

γενέσιος 2 = γενέθλιος.

γένεσις, ἡ origin, birth, engendering; a being, creature; race.

γενετή, ἡ birth.

γενέτης, ου, ὁ, γενέτωρ, ορος, ὁ, father; ancestor; son.

γενηΐς, ίδος, ἡ axe; shovel.

γεννάδᾱς, ου noble.

γενναῖος 3 innate; high-born, noble, generous, high-minded; genuine, sincere.

γενναιότης, ητος, ἡ noble-ness, magnanimity.

γεννάω to engender, beget.

γέννημα, τό product, fruit; child; nature.

γέννησις, ἡ a begetting.

γεννητής, οῦ, ὁ begetter, parent.

γεννητός 3 begotten, born.

γεννήτωρ, ορος, ὁ = γεν-νητής.

γένος, τό birth, descent; race, family, kindred; descendant, child; sex, gender; one's own country; kind, species; generation.

γέντο he seized or grasped.

γένυς, υος, ἡ jaw; pl. mouth; chin; axe.

γεραιός 3 old, aged; old man; οἱ γεραίτεροι the elders, senators.

γεραίρω to honour, reward.

γέρανος, ἡ crane.

γεραός 3 = γεραιός.

γεραρός 3 reverend; stately.

γέρας, αος and ως, τό gift of honour; honour; privilege; gift, reward.

γεροντ-αγωγέω to guide an old man.

γερόντιον, τό old man.

γερουσίᾱ, ἡ council of elders, senate. [the elders.]

γερούσιος 3 belonging to

γέρρον, τό wicker-work; wicker-shield.

γερρο-φόρος, ὁ bearer of a wicker-shield.

γέρων, οντος, ὁ old; old man: pl. aldermen, elders, senators.

γεύω to give to taste. — M. to taste, to eat of; to try.

γέφϋρα, ἡ mound; bridge; battle-field.

γεφῡρόω to dam, embank; to bridge over.

γεω-γράφος, ὁ geographer.

γεώδης 2 earthy.

γεω-μέτρης, ου, ὁ surveyor, geometer.

γεω-μετρίᾱ, ἡ land-surveying, geometry. [cal.]

γεω-μετρικός 3 geometri-

γεω-μόρος, ὁ land-owner; peasant; landed proprietor.

γεω-πέδιον, γεώ-πεδον, τό piece of land.

γεω-πείνης, ου poor in land.

γεωργέω to till, cultivate.

γεωργίᾱ, ἡ agriculture; arable land.

γεωργικός 3 belonging to agriculture; farmer, skilled in farming.

γεωργός 2 tilling; husbandman; vine-dresser.

γεωρῠχέω to dig mines.

γῆ, ἡ earth, land; soil, ground, field; empire; home.

γη-γενής 2 earthborn.

γῆθεν adv. from the earth.

γηθέω to be glad, to rejoice.

γηθοσύνη, ἡ joy, delight.

γηθόσυνος 2 gay, glad.

γήϊνος 3 of earth.

γή-λοφος, ὁ hill.

γη-οχέω to possess land.

γηραιός 3 old, aged.

γῆρας, αος, ως, τό old age.

γηράσκω, γηράω to become old; to ripen.

γηρο-βοσκός 2 feeding one's old parents.

γηρο-τροφέω to feed in old age.

γηρο-τρόφος 2 = γηροβοσκός. [speech.]

γῆρυς, υος, ἡ voice; sound;

γήτης, ου, ὁ husbandman.

γίγνομαι to become, grow; to be born; to come in (revenue); to result, amount to; to happen, occur.

γιγνώσκω to perceive, to gain knowledge (of), to know, learn, understand; to judge, determine, decide; to think; to resolve.

γίνομαι = γίγνομαι.

γῑνώσκω = γιγνώσκω.

γλάγος, τό milk. [eating.]

γλακτο-φάγος 2 milk-

γλαυκιάων 3 with sparkling eyes.

γλαυκ-όμματος 2, γλαυκῶπις, ιδος, ἡ bright-eyed; owl-eyed.

γλαυκός, 3 clear, bright, gleaming; bluish.

γλαῦξ, γλαύξ, κός, ἡ owl.

γλαφϋρός 3 hollow, convex; smoothed.

γλεῦκος, τό sweet wine.

γλήνη, ἡ eye-ball; puppet.

γλῆνος, τό ornament.

γλίσχρος 2 slippery; scanty, scarce, petty.

γλίχομαι M. to be fond of, to strive after.

γλοιός, ὁ resin, gum.

γλουτός, ὁ buttock.

γλυκερός 3 = γλυκύς.

γλυκύ - θῡμος 2 sweet-minded. [lovely; kind.]

γλυκύς 3 sweet, delightful,

γλυκύτης, ητος, ἡ sweetness. [arrow.]

γλῠφίς, ἰδος, ἡ notch of an]

γλῠφω to carve, engrave.

γλῶσσα, γλῶττα, ἡ tongue; mouth; speech; dialect.

γλωσσό-κομον, τό case for money.

γλωχίς, ῑνος, ἡ point of a nail or of an arrow.

γναθμός, ὁ and γνάθος, ἡ jaw, mouth. [flexible.]

γναμπτός 3 curved, bent;]

γνάμπτω to curve, bend.

γναφεῖον, γναφεύς see κναφεῖον. [nuine, true.]

γνήσιος 3 legitimate; ge-]

γνόφος, ὁ darkness.

γνύξ adv. with bent knees.

γνύφη, ἡ hollow, cave.

γνῶμα, τό mark, token; knowledge.

γνώμη, ἡ mind, understanding, reason, judgment; opinion, persuasion; discretion; resolution, purpose; wish, intention; sentence, truism; advice, proposal.

γνώμων, ονος, ὁ one that knows, judge, umpire, arbiter; overseer; sun-dial.

γνωρίζω to perceive, make out, discover; to know, to become acquainted with; to declare.

γνώρῐμος 2 known, familiar; perceptible, knowable; noble, aristocrat. [mind.]

γνωσι-μάχέω to alter one's]

γνῶσις, ἡ knowledge, wis-

dom, understanding; judicial sentence. [knows.]

γνώστης, ου, ὁ one that]

γνωστός 3 = γνώριμος.

γνωτός 3 known; knowable; kinsman, brother, sister.

γοάω and M. to wail; to bewail.

γογγύζω to murmur, mutter.

γογγυσμός, ὁ a muttering.

γογγυστής, οῦ, ὁ mutterer.

γοή, ἡ = γόος.

γόης, ητος, ὁ enchanter, wizzard; juggler, cheater.

γοητεία, ἡ sorcery, witchcraft, delusion. [delude.]

γοητεύω to bewitch, cheat,]

γόμος, ὁ cargo, freight.

γομφίος, ὁ cheek-tooth, molar (tooth).

γόμφος, ὁ peg, nail.

γονεύς, ὁ parent, ancestor.

γονή, ἡ a begetting; birth, origin; descendant, offspring; seed. [ductive.]

γόνῐμος 2 vigorous, pro-]

γόνυ, γόνατος, τό knee.

γονυ-πετέω to fall or go down on one's knees.

γόος ὁ a wailing, lament, dirge, incantation. [fierce.]

γοργός 3 terrible, wild,]

γοργύρη, ἡ underground dungeon. [looking.]

γοργ-ῶπις, ῐδος fierce-]

γοῦν (γὲ οὖν) at least, at any rate; of course; for instance; yet, indeed.

γουνάζομαι, γουνόομαι M. to be prostrate, to entreat, supplicate.

γουνός, ὁ angle of fruit-land; promontory; hill.

γράδιον, γραΐδιον, τό old woman. [old, knowing.]

γραῖα, ἡ old woman; adj.

γράμμα, τό letter of the alphabet; writing, writ; note-book, letter, document, catalogue; inscription; picture; pl. letters, learning.

γραμματεῖον, τό tablet, note-book; document; account-book.

γραμματεύς, ὁ scribe, writer, secretary. [tary.]

γραμματεύω to be secre-]

γραμματικός 3 knowing to write and read; belonging to grammar.

γραμματιστής, οῦ, ὁ secretary; school-master.

γραμμή, ἡ stroke, line in writing.

γραπτός 3 written.

γραπτύς, ύος, ἡ a scratching, wound. [hag.]

γραῦς, γραός, ἡ old woman,]

γραφεύς, ὁ writer; painter.

γραφή, ἡ picture, drawing; writing, document; bill of indictment, public prosecution.

γραφικός 3 belonging to writing or painting. [style.]

γραφίς, ίδος, ἡ writing-]

γράφω to scratch, engrave; to write, draw, paint; to write down, to register; to describe; to inscribe. — M. to write for oneself, to note down; to have something painted; to indict.

γραώδης 2 like an old woman. [live.]

γρηγορέω to be awake; to]

γρηῦς, γρῆυς = γραῦς.

γρύψ, γρῦπός, ὁ griffin.

γύαλον, τό a hollow, curvature, bow; armour-plate; cave, grotto, den.

γύης, ου, ὁ corn-field.

γυῖον, τό joint, limb; knee, leg, arm.

γυιόω to lame.

γυμνάζω to train, exercise, accustom. [ercise.]

γυμνασία, ἡ training, ex-]

γυμνασί-αρχος, ὁ training-master.

γυμνάσιον, τό exercise; place of exercise, training-school. [master.]

γυμναστής, οῦ, ὁ training-]

γυμναστικός 3 belonging to training, gymnastic.

γυμνής, ῆτος and γυμνήτης, ου ὁ light-armed foot-soldier.

γυμνητεία, ἡ light infantry.

γυμνητεύω to be naked, light-armed.

γυμνητικός 3 belonging to one lightly armed.

γυμνικός 3 = γυμναστικός.

γυμνο-παιδίαι, αἱ gymnastic festival.

γυμνός 3 naked; unarmed, lightly clad or armed; bare, destitute.

γυμνότης, ητος, ἡ, γύμνωσις, ἡ nakedness, denudation.

γυμνόω to bare, denudate.

γυναικάριον, τό = γύναιον.

γυναικεῖος 3 womanly, feminine.

γυναικωνῖτις, ιδος ἡ women's apartment.

γυναι-μανής 2 devoted to women.   [wench.]

γύναιον, τό little woman;

γύναιος 3 = γυναικεῖος.

γυνή, γυναικός, ἡ woman, lady; wife; mistress; widow; servant.

γυρός 3 round, curved.

γύψ, γυπός, ὁ vulture.

γύψος, ἡ chalk, gypsum.

γυψόω to besmear with gypsum.

γῶν = γοῦν.

γωνίᾱ, ἡ angle, corner; joiner's square; corner-stone.

γωνιώδης 2 angular.

γωρυτός, ὁ bow-case.

Δ

Δ, δ (δέλτα) fourth letter of the alphabet; as a numeral δ' = 4.

δαδοῦχος, ὁ torch-bearer.

δαήμων 2 knowing, experienced.   [to know.]

δαῆναι to teach; to learn;

δαήρ, έρος. ὁ brother-in-law.

δαί; τί δαί what then? πῶς δαί how then?

δαιδάλεος 3 cunningly or curiously wrought.

δαιδάλλω to work or adorn curiously.

δαίδαλον, τό work of art.

δαΐζω to divide, tear, pierce; to kill.   [battle.]

δαϊ-κτάμενος 3 killed in

δαιμονάω, δαιμονίζομαι P. to be mad or raving.

δαιμόνιος 3 divine, god-like; possessed by a demon, unfortunate; supernatural, wonderful; poor, odd, or infatuated man.' — τὸ δαιμόνιον divine being, inferior deity, evil spirit, demon, devil; guardian spirit; divine operation, fate; genius (with Socrates).

δαιμονιώδης 2 devilish.

δαίμων, ονος, ὁ, ἡ divine being, (inferior) deity, guardian spirit; evil spirit, demon, devil, spectre; fate, evil, death.

δαίνῡμι to portion out; to give a feast. — M. to eat, feast.

δάϊος 3 burning, hot; pernicious, hostile; unhappy.

δαΐς, ίδος, ἡ pine-wood; torch; battle.

δαίς, δαιτός, ἡ banquet, feast; portion.

δαίτη, ἡ meal, feast.

δαιτρεύω to portion out; to carve.

δαιτρόν, τό portion.

δαιτρός, ὁ carver.   [ing.]

δαιτροσύνη, ἡ art of carv-

δαιτυμών, όνος, ὁ guest, companion at table.

δαιτύς, ύος, ἡ meal.

δαΐ-φρων 2 knowing, intelligent; warlike.

δαίω[1] to kindle, set on fire. — P. to burn, blaze.

δαίω[2] and M. to divide, part out; to tear.

δακέ-θῡμος 2 heart-biting.

δάκνω to bite, sting; to hurt, vex.

δάκρυ, υος, δάκρῡμα, τό and δάκρυον, τό tear.

δακρύόεις 3 tearful; weeping. [in tears.]

δακρυ-πλώω to be bathed/

δακρυ-ρροέω to shed tears.

δακρύω to weep; to shed tears; to weep for.

δακτύλιος, ὁ finger-ring.

δάκτυλος, ὁ finger; toe; finger's breadth; short space. [of wood.]

δᾱλός, ὁ firebrand; billet/

δᾰμάζω see δαμάω.

δάμᾰλις, ἡ young cow, calf.

δάμᾱρ, δάμαρτος, ἡ wife, spouse.

δᾰμάω to tame, break; to subdue, overpower; to slay; to give in marriage.

δᾰνείζω to lend, to put out at usury. — M. to borrow.

δάνειον and δάνεισμα, τό loan. [ing, usury.]

δᾰνεισμός, ὁ money-lend-/

δᾰνειστής, δᾰνιστής, οῦ, ὁ money-lender, usurer.

δᾰνός 3 dry, parched.

δάος, τό torch.

δᾰπᾰνάω to spend; to spend on; to consume, waste.

δᾰπάνη, ἡ, δᾰπάνημα, τό a spending, expense, cost; extravagance; tribute.

δᾰπᾰνηρός 3 and δάπᾰνος 2 expensive; extravagant.

δά-πεδον, τό soil, flat country; floor. [to devour.]

δάπτω to tear in pieces;/

δαρδάπτω to pluck in pieces; to devour.

δαρεικός, ὁ Persian gold-coin.

δαρθάνω to sleep.

δᾱρός 3 = δηρός.

δάς, δᾳδός, ἡ = δαίς.

δά-σκιος 2 thick-shaded.

δάσμευσις, ἡ distribution.

δασμο-λογέω to exact tribute.

δασμός, ὁ division; tax, tribute. [bute.]

δασμο-φόρος 2 paying tri-/

δασ-πλῆτις, ἡ hard-striking. [fleeced.]

δασύ-μαλλος 2 thickly/

δασύς 3 hairy, bushy, thick grown; densely wooded; rough. [gy breast.]

δασύ-στερνος 2 with shag-/

δατέομαι M. to divide, portion out; to carve; to crush.

δάφνη, ἡ laurel. [laurel.]

δαφνη-φόρος 2 bearing/

δα-φοινός 2 blood-red.

δαψιλής 2 liberal, profuse; abundant.

δέ conj. but, on the other hand; further; thus; then.

δέᾱται he seems, δέᾱτο he seemed. [come.]

δεδίσκομαι to greet, wel-/

δεδίσσομαι M. to frighten, alarm; to get frightened; to wait.

δεδοκημένος 3 lying in wait.

δέελος 3 = δῆλος.

δέησις, ἡ prayer, entreating.

δεῖ one must, one ought; τὸ δέον, τὰ δέοντα the needful, the necessary or proper thing, the thing required. — δεῖ τινος there is need of.

δεῖγμα, τό proof, sample, specimen; show, bazaar.

δειγματίζω to expose to shame.

δειδήμων 2 timorous, cowardly.

δείδια see δείδω.

δειδίσκομαι = δεδίσκομαι.

δειδίσσομαι = δεδίσσομαι.

δείδω to be afraid, fear, apprehend. [ing meal.]

δειελιάω to take an evening meal.

δείελος 2 belonging to the evening; evening.

δειχανάομαι to welcome.

δείχηλον, τό representation.

δείχνῡμι, -ύω to show, point out, exhibit, display; to prove, demonstrate, explain; to tell; to teach. — M. to welcome, to pledge with.

δείλη, ἡ afternoon; evening.

δειλίᾱ, ἡ cowardice.

δειλιάω to be dismayed or afraid. [evening).]

δείλομαι M. to set (towards

δειλός 3 timid, cowardly; vile, mean; unhappy.

δεῖμα, τό fear, terror, horror.

δειμαίνω to fear, to be afraid or alarmed.

δειματόω to frighten.

δεῖνα, ὁ, ἡ, τό any one, a certain one.

δεινο-λογέομαι M. to complain vehemently.

δεινό-πους, ποδος striding fearfully.

δεινός 3 venerable; fearful, terrible, frightful, awful, dangerous; τὸ δεινόν danger, terror, distress; extraordinary; mighty, powerful; clever, skilful; unheard of, shocking, strange, wonderful, marvellous.

δεινότης, ητος, ἡ terribleness, sternness; power, ability.

δεινόω to exaggerate.

δειν-ώφ, ῶπος horrible-looking.

δεῖος, τό = δέος.

δειπνέω to take the chief meal, to dine.

δείπνηστος, ὁ meal-time.

δειπνίζω to treat at table.

δεῖπνον, τό meal, chief meal; banquet; food.

δειπνο-ποιέομαι M. to prepare a meal; to dine.

δειράς, άδος, ἡ ridge of a hill; rock.

δειρή, ἡ neck, nape.

δειρο-τομέω to cut the throat of a person; to behead.

δείρω = δέρω.

δεισι-δαιμονίᾱ, ἡ fear of the gods; religion; superstition.

δεισι-δαίμων 2 god-fearing; superstitious.

δέκα ten. [men.]

δεκαδ-αρχίᾱ, ἡ rule of ten

δεκάδ-αρχος, -άρχης, ου, ὁ commander of ten men.

δεκα-δύο twelve.

δεκα-ετής 2 ten years old.

δεκάκις adv. ten times.

δεκά-μηνος 2 ten months old.

δεκα-πέντε fifteen.

δεκά-πηχυς, υ ten cubits long or high.

δεκα-πλάσιος 3 tenfold.

δεκά-πλεθρος 2 ten plethra long. [αρχος.]

δεκ-άρχης, ου, ὁ = δεκάδδεκ-αρχίά, ἡ = δεκαδαρχία.

δεκάς, άδος, ἡ the number ten; a body of ten.

δεκαταῖος 3 on the tenth day.

δεκα-τέσσαρες, α fourteen.

δεκατευτήριον, τό customhouse.

δεκατεύω to tithe, to give or take the tenth; to consecrate.

δέκατος 3 tenth.

δεκατόω to take the tenth. — P. to give the tenth.

δεκά-φῦλος 2 divided into ten tribes.

δεκά-χῑλοι 3 ten thousand.

δεκ-έτης 2 ten years old.

δέκνῡμι = δείκνυμι.

δέκομαι = δέχομαι.

δέκτης, ου, ὁ receiver, beggar.

δεκτός 3 acceptable.

δελεάζω to entice (by a bait), to bait.

δέλεαρ, ατος, τό bait.

δέλτα, τό delta.

δελτίον, τό, δέλτος, ὁ writing-tablet.

δέλφαξ, ακος, ἡ young pig.

δελφῖνο-φόρος 2 bearing a dolphin.

δελφίς, ῖνος, ὁ dolphin.

δέμας, τό body, figure, frame, stature; adv. in the form or shape of.

δέμνιον, τό bedstead, bed.

δέμω to build.

δενδίλλω to glance at.

δένδρεον = δένδρον.

δενδρήεις 3 rich in trees.

δενδρο-κοπέω to cut trees.

δένδρον, ου and δένδρος, τό tree. [κοπέω.]

δενδρο-τομέω = δενδρο-]

δεννάζω to revile.

δέννος, ὁ abuse, reproach.

δεξαμένη, ἡ cistern.

δεξιο-βόλος, ὁ slinger.

δεξιο-λάβος, ὁ lancebearer.

δεξιόομαι M. to give the right hand; to greet.

δεξιός 3 at the right-hand side (ἡ δεξιά the right hand; promise, agreement); prosperous, fortunate; dexterous, ready.

δεξιό-σειρος 2 near or right-hand horse.

δεξιότης, ητος, ἡ dexterity, readiness.

δεξιόφιν adv. to the right.

δεξιτερός 3 = δεξιός.

δεξίωμα, τό offering of the right hand, pledge.

δέομαι see δέω.

δέος, τό fear, awe, reverence; danger. [to look at.]

δέρκομαι P. to look, see;]

δέρμα, τό hide, skin; leather; bag.

δερμάτινος 3 leathern.

δέρρις, ἡ hide, skin.

δέτρον, τό caul.

δέρω to skin, flay; to cudgel.

δέσμα, τό = δεσμός.

δεσμεύω, δεσμέω to fetter; to throw into prison.

δέσμη, δεσμή, ἡ bundle.

δέσμιος 2 fettered, captive.

δεσμός, ὁ band, fillet; fetter, string, thong; cable; imprisonment.

δεσμο-φύλαξ, ακος, ὁ jailer.

δέσμωμα, τό fetter.

δεσμωτήριον, τό prison.

δεσμώτης, ου, δεσμῶτις, ιδος prisoner.

δεσπόζω to be or become master, ruler.

δέσποινα, ἡ mistress, lady.

δεσποσύνη, ἡ absolute power. [owner.]

δεσπότης, ου, ὁ lord, master,

δεσποτικός 3 imperious, despotic. [ποινα.]

δεσπότις, ιδος, ἡ = δέσ-

δετή, ἡ fagot; torch.

δεύομαι = δέομαι.

δεῦρο, δεύρω adv. hither; come hither! up!; till now, hitherto.

δεύτατος 3 the last.

δεῦτε pl. of δεῦρο.

δευτεραῖος 3 on the second or next day.

δευτερεῖα, τά second prize.

δευτερό-πρωτος 2 next to the first. [inferior.]

δεύτερος 3 second, next;

δεύω[1] to wet.

δεύω[2] = δέω.

δεχ-ήμερος 2 for ten days.

δέχομαι M. to take, accept, receive; to approve; to choose; to suffer patiently; to take for; to receive kindly, to treat; to make head against, to stand one's ground; to lie in wait.

δέφω to soften, mould, knead; to tan. [imprison.]

δέω[1] to bind, fasten, fetter,

δέω[2] to be far from; to want, lack, to be in need of.

— M. δέομαι to be behind; to be in need of; to want,

wish, strive after; to ask, to beg for.

δή adv. = ἤδη; now, already, just now; presently, at once; then; of course, indeed, manifestly; even; yet, only, therefore; as said before.

δῆγμα, τό bite, sting.

δηθά adv. long.

δῆθεν adv. manifestly, forsooth; in vain; of course, really; perhaps.

δηθύνω to tarry, loiter.

δήϊος 3 = δάϊος.

δηϊότης, ητος, ἡ enmity; battle.

δηϊόω = δηόω.

δηλαδή adv. plainly, of course. [plainly.]

δηλ-αυγῶς adv. quite

δηλέομαι M. to hurt, damage, destroy.

δήλημα, τό hurt, ruin, destruction. [stroyer.]

δηλήμων 2 pernicious; de-

δήλησις, ἡ a hurting, ruin.

δῆλον-ὅτι adv. plainly, clearly, of course.

δῆλος 3 manifest, visible, evident, plain, clear.

δηλόω to manifest, show, signify; to explain, prove; δηλοῖ it is clear.

δήλωσις, ἡ manifestation, a pointing out, advertisement, order, proof.

δημ-αγωγέω to be a popular leader or d magogue.

δημ-αγωγός, ὁ popular leader, demagogue.

δήμ-αρχος, ὁ chief of a district.

δήμευσις, ἡ confiscation.

δημεύω to confiscate; to make known.

δημ-ηγορέω to be a public orator, to harangue the people. [speech.]

δημ-ηγορία, ἡ public / δημ-ηγορικός 3 qualified for public speaking.

δημ-ηγόρος, ὁ public orator. [ουργός.]

δημιο-εργός 2 = δημι-/ δῆμιος 2 belonging to the whole people, public.

δημιουργέω to carry on a trade; to work.

δημιουργία, ἡ trade; handicraft, work. [to craftsmen.]

δημιουργικός 3 belonging/ δημιουργός 2 working for the common weal; craftsman, workman, artist, master; maker, creator; magistrate.

δημο-βόρος 2 consuming the people's goods.

δημο-γέρων, οντος, ὁ elder of the people. [pense.]

δημόθεν adv. at public ex-/ δημο-κρατέομαι P. to live in a democracy.

δημο-κρατία, ἡ democracy.

δημο-κρατικός 3 democratic. [the people.]

δημό-λευστος 2 stoned by/ δῆμος, ὁ land, country, district; common people, community; popular assembly; democracy.

δημός, ὁ fat.

δημοσιεύω to carry on a public trade, to be in the civil service; to confiscate.

δημόσιος 3 public, of or for the state; public officer or slave. τὸ δημόσιον the commons, state, state affairs, general weal; state treasury; state prison; δημοσίᾳ publicly, in the name of the state.

δημοσιόω to confiscate.

δημο-τελής 2 public, at public expense.

δημοτεύομαι M. to belong to a demos.

δημότης, ου, ὁ man of the people, private man; fellow-citizen.

δημοτικός 3 belonging to the people, common, public, civilian.

δημοῦχος 2 inhabitant of the country; protector of the country. [mon.]

δημώδης 2 popular; com-/ δήν adv. long.

δηναιός 3 long-living.

δηνάριον, τό denarius (a Roman coin).

δῆνος, τό counsel, project.

δῇος 3 = δάϊος.

δηόω to treat as an enemy, to slay, fight; to rend; to destroy, waste.

δή-ποτε adv. ever, once, at some time.

δή-που, δή-πουθεν adv. indeed, certainly; perhaps.

δηριάομαι, M. and δηρίομαι M. to contend, fight.

δῆρις, ἡ strife, fight, contest.

δηρός 3 long.

δῆτα adv. certainly, indeed, of course, plainly; therefore, then.

δήω I shall find.

διά *adv.* asunder; through, throughout. — *prp.* with *gen.* through, right through, through between; during; since; by means of, arising from. with *acc.* through; during; on account of, because of, by reason of; with a view to.

δια-βαδίζω to go over.

δια-βαίνω to stride; to stand firm; to cross, go over, step across.

δια-βάλλω to throw over, carry across; to disunite; to slander, accuse falsely, calumniate, revile; to cheat.

διά-βασις, ἡ a crossing, passage, bridge, ford, pass.

δια-βατήρια, τά offerings for a happy crossing.

δια-βατός 2 passable, fordable. [sert, confirm.]

δια-βεβαιόομαι *M.* to as-

δια-βιβάζω to lead, bring, or carry over.

δια-βιόω to live through; to pass one's life.

δια-βλέπω to look through; to look straight on or round; to consider.

δια-βοάω to cry loud or promiscuously; to cry out, proclaim.

δια-βολή, ἡ slander, calumny, false accusation, reproach; bad fame; suspicion; hatred.

διά-βολος 2 slanderous; ὁ δ. slanderer, fiend, devil.

δια-βόρος 2 eating through, consuming.

διά-βορος 2 eaten through.

δια-βουλεύομαι *M.* to consult well.

διά-βροχος 2 wet; soaked, leaky [push through.]

δια-βῡνέω to thrust or

δι-αγγέλλω to notify, announce, send message, proclaim. — *M.* to inform one another, to pass the word of command.

δι-άγγελος, ὁ negotiator, go-between.

δια-γελάω to laugh at.

δια-γίγνομαι *M.* to continue, live on, survive, remain; to be between, elapse.

δια-γιγνώσκω to discern, distinguish; to perceive well; to resolve, determine, decide.

δι-αγκυλίζομαι, δι-αγκύλόομαι *M.* to hold the javelin in readiness.

δια-γλάφω to hollow out.

δια-γνώμη, ἡ distinction; resolution, decree, judgment, sentence. [known.]

δια-γνωρίζω to make

διά-γνωσις, ἡ = διαγνώμη.

δια-γογγύζω to mutter promiscuously.

δι-αγορεύω to state precisely.

διά-γραμμα, τό a drawing, figure; register; decree.

δια-γράφω to draw out, paint out; to strike out, reject. [awake.]

δια-γρηγορέω to remain

δι-άγω to lead through, over, across, or up; to pass, live, spend; to tarry, delay; to continue, keep; to accomplish.

δι-αγωγή, ἡ a leading across; course of life.

δι-αγωνίζομαι M. to contend, fight; to carry on a lawsuit; to fight to the end.

δια-δαίομαι M. to divide; to destroy.

δια-δάπτω to rend, lacerate. [bute.

δια-δατέομαι M. to distri-

δια-δείκνῡμι to point out exactly, to explain, show.

δια-δέξιος 2 quite auspicious.

δια-δέρκομαι to see or perceive through.

δια-δέχομαι M. to receive in turn; to take up, succeed to; to relieve.

δια-δέω to fasten or bind to; to fetter. [to pieces.

δια-δηλέομαι to tear in or

διά-δηλος 2 quite distinct, manifest.

διά-δημα, τό circlet, diadem.

δια-διδράσκω to run away, escape.

δια-δίδωμι to pass on, give over; to distribute, pay off.

δια-δικάζω to carry on a lawsuit; to pass sentence.

δια-δικαιόω to plead.

δια-δικασία, ἡ decision; action for precedence.

δια-δοχή, ἡ a taking up; succession; relief.

διά-δοχος 2 taking up, alternating; successor.

δια-δρηστεύω to run away.

δια-δύομαι to pass or slip through; to escape.

δια-είδομαι to show clearly; to appear clearly.

δια-ζάω to survive; to maintain life.

δια-ζεύγνῡμι to disjoin.

διά-ζευξις, ἡ a disjoining.

διά-ζωμα, τό girdle; apron.

δια-ζώννῡμι to cut through; to gird round.

δια-ζώω = διαζάω.

δι-άημι to blow through.

δια-θεάομαι M. to view closely.

δια-θειόω to fumigate through with brimstone.

διά-θεσις, ἡ arrangement, disposition, condition; constitution; mind.

δια-θέτης, ου, ὁ arranger.

δια-θέω to run through or about; to spread; to run in contest.

δια-θήκη, ἡ arrangement, disposition; testament; treaty, covenant.

δια-θορυβέω to trouble vehemently.

δια-θροέω to spread a report.

δια-θρῡλέω to spread abroad; to have always in one's mouth.

δια-θρύπτω to break in or to pieces; to spoil, weaken; to make vain.

διαί = διά.

διαίνω to wet, moisten.

δι-αίρεσις, ἡ division; distribution; distinction.

δι-αίρετος 2 divided.

δι-αιρέω to divide, sever, cut in two; to pull down, demolish, destroy; to distribute; to explain, interpret; to define; to decide.

δι-αϊστόω to kill, murder.

δίαιτα, ἡ life; mode of life; diet; intercourse; food; dwelling.

διαιτάω to be umpire. — P. to lead a life, to live, dwell.

διαίτημα, τό = δίαιτα.

διαιτητής, οῦ, ὁ arbiter, umpire.   [thoroughly.]

δια-καθαρίζω to clean(se)

δια-καίω to burn through.

δια-καλύπτω to cover thoroughly.

δια-καρτερέω to last out, persevere.   [fute utterly.]

δια-κατελέγχομαι to con-

δια-κεάζω to split in two.

δια-κειμαι to be in a certain condition or disposition, to be affected or disposed; to be settled.

δια-κείρω to frustrate.

δια-κελεύομαι M. to exhort, encourage, impel.

διά-κενος 2 empty between.

δια-κηρύκευομαι M. to negotiate through a herald.

δια-κινδυνεύω to run a risk, to face danger; to make head against.

δια-κινέω to shake thoroughly; to put in disorder.

δια-κλάω to break in two.

δια-κλέπτω to steal away, to abstract, to remove by stealth; to betray.

δια-κληρόω to assign by lot; to let draw lots.

δια-κομιδή, ἡ a carrying over.

δια-κομίζω to carry over or across; to bring to an end.

διᾱκονέω and M. to render service, to wait on, serve; to provide, attend to.

διᾱκονίᾱ, ἡ service, attendance, business; deacon's office.   [servile.]

διᾱκονικός 3 serviceable,

διάκονος, ὁ servant, attendant; deacon.

δι-ακοντίζομαι M. to contend in spear-throwing.

δια-κόπτω to cut or break through; to beat to pieces.

διά-κορος 2 satiated.

διᾱκόσιοι 3 two hundred.

δια-κοσμέω to dispose, arrange.

δια-κόσμησις, ἡ, διά-κοσμος, ὁ arrangement, battle-array.   [listen to.]

δι-ακούω to hear out; to

δι-ακρῑβόω and M. to do accurately; to examine thoroughly; to know exactly.

δια-κρῐδόν adv. eminently.

δια-κρίνω to discern, separate, divide; to choose; to decide, judge. — P. and M. to be divided; to part; to dispute with one another; to be reconciled; to doubt.

διά-κρῐσις, ἡ separation; distinction; decision.

διά-κρουσις, ἡ delay.

δια-κρούω to hinder. — M. to push off; to deceive, elude; to delay.

διάκτορος, ὁ guide, messenger of the gods.

δια-κυκάω to mix together.

δια-κύπτω to peep through.

δια-κωλῠτής, οῦ, ὁ hinderer.

δια-κωλύω to hinder, prevent, check; to forbid.

δια-κωμῳδέω to ridicule.

δι-ακωχή, ἡ = διοκωχή.

δια-λαγχάνω to assign by lot.

δια-λαλέω to talk over.

δια-λαμβάνω to take asunder, to separate, to take apart; to distinguish; to divide, distribute; to pause; to grasp, seize, hold fast; to deliberate. [through.]

δια-λάμπω to shine or flash.

δια-λανθάνω to be hidden, escape notice.

δια-λέγω to pick out, choose. — P. to consider; to talk with, converse, negotiate; to recite, speak (a dialect).

διά-λειμμα, τό interval, gap.

δια-λείπω to leave an interval or gap; to let pass; to leave off, desist; to lie between.

δια-λεκτικός 3 skilled in discourse; belonging to dialectics.

διά-λεκτος, ἡ conversation; speech; dialect.

δι-αλλᾰγή, ἡ change; reconciliation, agreement. [tor.]

δι-αλλακτής, οῦ, ὁ mediaδι-αλλάσσω to interchange, change; to reconcile; to differ. — P. and M. to exchange between one another; to be reconciled; to be different.

δια-λογίζομαι M. to consider, reflect; to examine together.

δια-λογισμός, ὁ consideration, thought; doubt.

διά-λογος, ὁ conversation, dialogue.

δια-λοιδορέομαι P. to revile grossly. [treat.]

δια-λῡμαίνομαι M. to malδιά-λῠσις, ἡ a loosing, separation, ending; a paying off, settling of accounts; reconciliation, peace.

δια-λῠτής, οῦ, ὁ destroyer.

δια-λῠτός 3 dissoluble.

δια-λύω to dissolve, divide, separate; to destroy; to end, break off; to reconcile; to pay.

δι-αμαρτάνω to miss or fail entirely; not to obtain; to go astray; to err.

δι-αμαρτία, ἡ mistake, failure, error. [witnesses.]

δια-μαρτῠρέω to refute byδια-μαρτῠρομαι M. to give solemn evidence (of), to conjure, to abjure.

δια-μαστῑγόω to whip well.

δια-μάχομαι M. to fight through; to fight, struggle; to endeavour.

δι-αμάω and M. to cut through; to scrape away.

δι-αμείβω to exchange; to change, alter. — M. to exchange for oneself; to change one's mind.

δια-μέλλησις, ἡ a tarrying, delay.

δια-μέλλω to delay continually.

δια-μέμφομαι *M.* to blame severely. [tinue, persevere.]

δια-μένω to remain, con-)
δια-μερίζω to divide. — *P.* and *M.* to be at variance.

δια-μερισμός, ὁ dissension.

δια-μετρέω to measure out or off; to sell. — *M.* to have measured out to one; to portion out among themselves. [out.]

δια-μέτρητος 2 measured)

δια-μηχανάομαι *M.* to contrive, devise. [tend, rival.]

δι-αμιλλάομαι *P.* to con-)
δια-μιμνήσκομαι to remember continually.

δια-μιστύλλω to cut in little pieces.

δια-μνημονεύω to remember well: to mention.

δια-μοιράω to portion out; to rend.

δι-αμπάξ *adv.* quite through.

δι-αμ-περές *adv.* quite through; continually; throughout; altogether.

δια-μυθολογέω to converse. [pel.]

δι-αναγκάζω to force, com-)
δι-αναπαύω to give rest for a moment. — *M.* to cease for a while. [sea.]

δια-ναυμαχέω to fight at)
δι-άνδιχα *adv.* two ways; in either way.

δια-νέμω to distribute, portion out. — *M.* to divide between themselves. [to.]

δια-νεύω to nod or beckon)
δια-νέω to swim through.

δι-ανίσταμαι *M.* to depart from.

δια-νοέομαι *P.* to consider, reflect; to think, intend.

δια-νόημα, τό thought; purpose.

διά-νοια, ἡ thought, intellect, mind; opinion; intention. [plain.]

δι-ανοίγω to open; to ex-)
δια-νομή, ἡ distribution.

δια-νυκτερεύω to pass the night. [finish, accomplish.]

δι-ανύω, δι-ανύτω to)
δια-παιδεύω to educate thoroughly.

δια-παντός *adv.* throughout.

δια-παρα-τρῐβή, ἡ altercation. [flower.]

δια-παρθενεύω to de-)
δια-πασσαλεύω to fasten with nails.

δια-πάσσω to strew about.

δια-παύομαι *P.* to cease. — *M.* to pause.

δι-απειλέω to threaten violently. [trial.]

διά-πειρα, ἡ experiment,)
δια-πειράομαι *P.* to try, to make a proof (of); to know by experience. [through.]

δια-πείρω to pierce or bore)
δια-πέμπω to send over; to send to; to send about.

δια-περαίνω and *M.* to finish, to bring to an end.

δια-περαιόομαι *P.* to go over or across; to be drawn to one another.

δια-περάω to go over or across, to pass; to endure, get through. [tally.]

δια-πέρθω to destroy to-)
δια-πέτομαι *M.* to fly through or away.

δια-πίμπλημι to fill up (completely).

δια-πίνω to vie with one another in drinking.

δια-πίπτω to fall or go to pieces; to escape.

δια-πιστεύω to entrust.

δια-πλέκω to interweave; to weave to the end.

δια-πλέω to sail through or across. [pieces.

δια-πλήσσω to dash to|

διά-πλους, ὁ a sailing across, passage.

δια-πνέω to blow through; to revive. [adorn.

δια-ποικίλλω to variegate,|

δια-πολεμέω to end war; to carry on the war.

δια-πολέμησις, ἡ an ending of the war.

δια-πολιορκέω to carry a siege through. [sage.

δια-πομπή, ἡ legacy; mes-|

δια-πονέω to toil; to work out with labour, to elaborate; to train, make hardy. — M. to endeavour; to get practised; to be vexed.

δια-πόντιος 2 transmarine.

δια-πορεύω to carry over or through. — P. to go or march through.

δι-απορέω and M. to be at a loss, to be undecided.

δια-πορθέω = διαπέρθω.

δια-πορθμεύω to carry over, across; to carry a message.

δια-πραγματεύομαι M. to examine closely; to do a thing diligently.

δια-πράσσω and M. to finish,

accomplish, effect; to procure, get; to make an appointment; to kill.

δια-πρεπής 2 conspicuous, excellent. [to adorn.

δια-πρέπω to be eminent;|

δια-πρεσβεύομαι M. to send embassies about.

δια-πρήσσω = διαπράσσω.

δια-πρηστεύω to betray.

δια-πρίω to saw through. — P. to grow furious.

δια-πρό adv. quite through, thoroughly.

δια-πρύσιος 3 and 2 piercing; far-stretching.

δια-πτοέω, -πτοιέω to frighten or scare away.

δια-πτύσσω to disclose.

διά-πῦρος 2 glowing, firy.

δια-πωλέω to sell.

δι-αράσσω to strike or knock through.

δι-αρθρόω to articulate; to form; to dissect.

δι-αριθμέω to count up. — M. to judge. [dure.

δι-αρκέω to suffice; to en-|

δι-αρκής 2 enduring; sufficient. [ing.

δι-αρπαγή, ἡ a plunder-|

δι-αρπάζω to tear to pieces; to rob, plunder.

δια-ρραίνω M. to drizzle down about.

δια-ρραίω to tear or dash to pieces; to destroy.

δια-ρρέω to flow through; to vanish; to melt away.

δια-ρρήγνῦμι to break through; to break to or in pieces; to destroy; to rend; to pierce. — P. to burst.

διά-ρρήδην adv. expressly.

διά-ρρίπτέω, -ρρίπτω to throw through; to fling about, to distribute.

διά-ρρίψις, ἡ a flinging about.

διά-ρροια, ἡ diarrhœa.

δια-ρροιζέω to whiz through.

δια-σάφέω, δια-σαφηνίζω to make conspicuous, to explain; to report.

δια-σείω to shake or stir violently; to extort.

δια-σεύομαι M. to rush, run, or dart through.

δια-σημαίνω to point out, mark.

διά-σημος 2 quite perceptible. [lent.]

δια-σιωπάω to remain si-]

δια-σκάπτω to dig through.

δια-σκαρίφάομαι M. to scrape up.

δια-σκεδάννῡμι to scatter about; to disband; to destroy. [σκοπέω.]

δια-σκέπτομαι = δια-]

δια-σκευάζομαι M. to prepare for battle.

δια-σκηνέω, -όω to encamp in different quarters; to rise from the table.

δια-σκίδνημι = διασκεδάννυμι.

δια-σκοπέω and M. to view closely, to examine, consider; to look round. [out.]

δια-σκοπιάομαι M. to spy]

δια-σκορπίζω to scatte about; to winnow; to waste.

δια-σμάω, -σμέω to wipe out, to rinse.

δια-σπάω to draw asunder, to tear to pieces; to sever; to scatter; to split.

δια-σπείρω to scatter about; to waste.

δια-σπορά, ἡ dispersion.

δια-σπουδάζω and M. to endeavour, do earnestly.

δι-άσσω to rush through.

διά-στάσις, ἡ distance; interval; dissension, discord, enmity. [lisade.]

δια-σταυρόομαι M. to pa-]

δια-στέλλω and M. to separate; to distinguish; to command. [distance.]

διά-στημα, τό interval,]

δια-στοιβάζω to stuff in between. [difference.]

δια-στολή, ἡ distinction,]

δια-στρέφω to turn aside, pervert; to distort; to incite (to rebellion), to stir up.

διά-στροφος 2 distorted, crippled; perverted.

δια-σύρω to mock.

δια-σφάξ, αγος, ἡ cleft, ravine.

δια-σφενδονάω to fling about from a sling. — P. to burst.

δια-σχίζω to cleave in two, to tear asunder.

δια-σῴζω to save through; to preserve; to keep in memory.

δια-τάγή, ἡ and διά-ταγμα, τό arrangement, order.

δια-τάμνω = διατέμνω.

δια-τάξις, ἡ disposition, order of battle.

δια-ταράσσω to throw into confusion, to confound.

δια-τάσσω to dispose, arrange well; to draw up for battle; to arrange separately; to command.

δια-τείνω t stretch out; and M. to stretch oneself; to exert oneself; to affirm; to get ready for shooting.

δια-τείχισμα, τό (intermediate) fortification.

δια-τελευτάω to finish entirely.

δια-τελέω to finish, complete; to come to; to continue or keep doing.

δια-τελής 2 permanent.

δια-τέμνω to cut through; to divide.

δια-τετραίνω to perforate.

δια-τήκω to melt.

δια-τηρέω to keep, preserve; to watch; to beware (of).

δια-τίθημι to put asunder; to dispose, arrange, manage, treat; to influence. — P. to be disposed, to be in a mind. — M. to dispose of, make a testament; to sell off, to settle; to make use of.

δια-τινάσσω to shake to and fro; to shake to pieces.

δια-τμήγω to cut through; to sever; to scatter. — P. to be dispersed.

διά-τορος 2 pierced.

δια-τρέφω to feed through.

δια-τρέχω to run or sail through. [sides.]

δια-τρέω to flee to all

δια-τρῐβή, ἡ a wasting of time; a lingering, delay, stay; pastime, employment, study, conversation.

δια-τρίβω to rub away; to waste, consume; to prevent; to delay; to stay, live; to converse; to busy or occupy oneself with.

δια-τροφή, ἡ sustenance.

δια-τρύγιος 2 to be gathered in at different times.

δι-αυγάζω to shine through.

δι-αυγής 2 transparent.

δί-αυλος, ὁ double pipe.

δια-φαίνω to make shine through. — M. to shine through, to become visible.

δια-φάνεια, ἡ transparency.

δια-φανής 2 transparent; manifest, evident.

δια-φερόντως adv. differently; excellently, especially.

δια-φέρω to carry across; to bring to an end; to live; to bear; to carry different ways, to throw about; to differ, to be different, to excel; διαφέρει it makes a difference; it is of consequence τὸ διαφέρον interest, point of dispute. — P. to be at variance.

δια-φεύγω to flee through, escape, avoid.

διά-φευξις, ἡ escape.

δια-φημίζω to divulge.

δια-φθείρω to destroy, ruin, corrupt, spoil, waste; to bribe. — P. to be destroyed or lost; to perish.

δια-φθορά, ἡ destruction, ruin; corruption; seduction.

δια-φθορεύς, ὁ destroyer; seducer.

δι-αφίημι to dismiss.

7*

διά-φοιβάζω to drive mad.

διά-φοιτάω to rove about.

διά-φορά, ἡ difference; controversy.

διά-φορέω to carry over; to carry different ways; to disperse; to plunder; to tear to pieces.

διά-φορος 2 different; at variance; excellent. τὸ διάφορον difference; disagreement, dispute, object of controversy; interest, profit.

διά-φραγμα, τό partition-wall; diaphragm. [clearly.]

διά-φράζω to show or tell]

διά-φρέω to let through.

διά-φυγγάνω = διαφεύγω.

διά-φυγή, ἡ an escaping.

διά-φυή, ἡ growth between; joint, knot, partition.

διά-φυλάσσω to watch carefully, to preserve.

διά-φύομαι M. to intervene, elapse.

διά-φῡσάω to blow away.

δι-αφύσσω to draw out; to drink up; to tear out; to rend.

διά-φωνέω to sound discordantly; to disagree.

διά-φώσκω to dawn.

διά-χάζω and M. to retreat separated; to part.

διά-χειμάζω to pass the winter. [M. to slay.]

διά-χειρίζω to manage.—]

διά-χείρισις, ἡ management; direction. [by vote.]

διά-χειροτονέω to decide]

διά-χειροτονίᾱ, ἡ a voting.

διά-χέω to pour out; to

melt; to confound, frustrate; to clear up. — P. to be melted; to fall to pieces.

διά-χόω to heap up a mound.

διά-χράομαι M. to use, employ, have; to kill.

διά-χωρέω to go through (of diarrhœa).

διά-χωρίζω to separate.

διά-ψεύδω and M. to lie; to deceive. — P. to be mistaken. [cide by vote.]

διά-ψηφίζομαι M. to de-]

διά-ψήφισις, ἡ a voting.

διά-ψύχω to cool; to make dry.

δί-γλωσσος 2 speaking two languages. [teaching.]

διδακτικός 3 skilled in]

διδακτός 3 that can be taught; taught, instructed.

διδασκαλεῖον, τό school.

διδασκαλία, ἡ a teaching, instruction; a rehearsing.

διδασκαλικός 3 belonging to teaching; = διδακτικός.

διδασκάλιον, τό science.

διδάσκαλος, ὁ teacher, master.

διδάσκω to teach, instruct, train; to show, prove; to prepare a play. — P. to learn. — M. to devise, contrive; to apprentice to.

διδαχή, ἡ teaching, doctrine.

δίδημι = δέω (to bind).

διδράσκω to run.

δί-δραχμος 2 of two drachms. [brother.]

διδύμάων, ονος, ὁ twin-]

δίδυμος 3 double, twofold.

δίδωμι to give, present,

grant; to afford, pay; to consecrate, devote; to concede, permit, give over; to pardon, release; to allow.

δι-εγγυάω to give bail for; to release on bail.

δι-εγείρω to arouse.

δί-ειμι[1] (-ιέναι) to go or march through; to discuss.

δί-ειμι[2] (-εῖναι) to be continually.

δι-εῖπον to speak through; to explain, tell exactly.

δι-είργω to separate, keep asunder.

δι-είρομαι to question.

δι-ειρύω to draw across.

δι-είρω to put across.

δι-έκ, δι-έξ adv. through.

δι-εκπεράω to go or sail through, across. [through.]

δι-εκπλέω to sail out

δι-έκπλοος, ὁ a sailing through; a breaking the enemy's kill.

δι-εκπλώω = διεκπλέω.

δι-έκροος, ὁ a flowing out, outlet.

δι-ελαύνω to drive through; to pierce through; to ride or march through.

δι-ελέγχω to refute or examine thoroughly.

δι-έλκω, -ύω pull or tear asunder.

δίεμαι M. to chase, frighten away; to flee in awe.

δι-εμπολάω to sell; to betray. [intently.]

δι-ενθυμέομαι P. to think

δι-ενιαυτίζω to live out the year. [parate.]

δι-εξειλίσσω to sift, se-

δι-έξειμι to go out through; to examine, peruse; to describe.

δι-εξελαύνω to drive, ride, or march through.

δι-εξερέομαι to question.

δι-εξέρχομαι to go out through, to pass through, to elapse, to come to; to go through, explain, recount. [plain, recount.]

δι-εξηγέομαι M. to ex-

δι-έξιημι to let out through; to empty itself.

δι-έξοδος, ἡ passage, outlet, issue, event; crossroad; detailed account, recital, statement.

δι-εορτάζω to keep a feast to the end.

δι-έπω to manage, take care of, attend to; to arrange; to pass through.

δι-εργάζομαι M. to ruin, kill.

δι-έργω = διείργω.

δι-ερέσσω to row through; to row well.

δι-ερευνάω and M. to search, examine closely.

δι-ερμηνευτής, οῦ, ὁ interpreter. [translate.]

δι-ερμηνεύω to interpret,

διερός[1] 3 fugitive, quick.

διερός[2] 3 long-lived; fresh.

δι-έρπω to step through.

δι-έρχομαι to go, walk, drive, or pass through; to arrive at; to narrate, explain; to consider.

δι-ερωτάω to question continually. [through.]

δι-εσθίω to eat or bite

δι-ετής 2 of two years.

δι-ετήσιος 2 lasting the whole year. [years.]

δι-ετίᾱ, ἡ space of two

δι-ευλαβέομαι to take heed well. [tinually.]

δι-ευτυχέω to prosper con-

δι-έχω to keep asunder or aloof; to reach through; to be extended to; to stand apart, to be distant; τὸ διέχον interval.

δίζημαι M. to seek out, to aspire to or after; to examine.

δί-ζυξ, υγος doubly-yoked.

δίζω to doubt.

δι-ηγέομαι M. to explain, describe, narrate.

δι-ήγησις, ἡ discussion; narration.

δι-ηθέω to sift, strain through; to cleanse; to filter through.

δι-ηκονέω = διᾱκονέω.

δι-ήκω to come through, pervade. [whole day.]

δι-ημερεύω to pass the

δι-ηνεκής 2 uninterrupted, continual; far-reaching; exact, full.

δι-ήνεμος 2 windy.

δι-θάλασσος 2 between two seas.

διθύραμβος, ὁ dithyramb.

δι-ίημι to send, thrust, or shoot through; to let pass through; to dismiss.

δι-ικνέομαι M. to go through; to reach, meet; to recount.

διί-πετής 2 fallen from heaven, heaven-sent.

δι-ίστημι to set apart or asunder; to divide, to set at variance; intr. and M. to stand apart or at intervals; to part; to differ; to be ajar; to remove; to quarrel.

δι-ισχῡρίζομαι M. to be at ease, to abide; to affirm.

διΐ-φιλος 2 loved by Zeus.

δικάζω to judge, administer jus ice; to decide, determine. M. to plead, speak in court. [ment.]

δικαιο-κρισίᾱ, ἡ just judg-

δίκαιος 3 just; righteous, honest; legal, lawful, right, proper; useful, fit, convenient; regular; entitled to, worthy of, bound to. τὸ δίκαιον and τὰ δίκαια right, justice, privilege, law-question, argument, judicial proceeding.

δικαιοσύνη, ἡ, δικαιότης, ητος, ἡ justice; administration of justice.

δικαιόω to think right, to justify, judge; to condemn; to claim, desire.

δικαίωμα, τό legal axiom, right; argument, justification; legal claim; judgment; legal act.

δικαίωσις, ἡ summons at law; condemnation; legal claim; (good) pleasure, judgment; justification.

δικᾱνικός 3 skilled in law; lawyer; lawyer-like, arrogant.

δικασ-πόλος, ὁ judge.

δικαστήριον, τό court of justice.

δικαστής, οῦ, ὁ judge.

δικαστικός 3 judicial, of a judge; skilled in law.

δίκελλα, ἡ mattock, pick-axe.

δίκη, ἡ custom, usage (δίκην after the manner of); right, law, order, justice; judgment, sentence; judicature, lawsuit, action at law, trial; fine, penalty, satisfaction; δίκην διδόναι to suffer punishment.

δι-κλίς, ίδος double-folding (door).   [ful.

δι-κρατής 2 doubly power-

δί-κροτος 2 vessel with two decks.   [in meshes.

δικτυό-κλωστος 2 woven

δίκτυον, τό fishing-net.

δί-λογος 2 double-tongued.

δί-λοφος 2 with two peaks.

δί-μνεως 2 worth two minæ.

δι-μοιρίᾱ, ἡ double amount.

δῑνεύω, δῑνέω to whirl or spin round (tr. and intr.).

δίνη, ἡ whirlpool, eddy.

δῑνήεις 3 eddying.

δῑνωτός 3 turned on a lathe, elaborated nicely.

διξός 3 = δισσός.   [fore.

διό (δι' ὅ) wherefore; there-

διό-βολος 2 hurled by Zeus.

διο-γενής 2 sprung from Zeus. [to travel through.

δι-οδεύω, δι-οδοιπορέω

δί-οδος, ἡ passage through, thoroughfare; mountain-pass; way.

δι-οίγω to open.

δί-οιδα to know exactly.

δι-οικέω to administer, manage; to direct; to treat.

δι-οίκησις, ἡ house-keeping; management, government; province.

δι-οικίζω to let live apart; to scatter. — M. to settle apart; to change place.

δι-οίκισις, ἡ remove.

δι-οικοδομέω to bar off by a wall.

δι-οϊστέω to shoot an arrow through or across.

δι-οίχομαι to pass away, be gone.   [abating.

δι-οκωχή, ἡ a ceasing, an

δι-όλλῡμι to destroy or ruin utterly; to forget. — P. to perish utterly.

δι-όμνῡμι and P. to swear, take an oath; to affirm solemnly.

δι-ομολογέω and M. to agree (to), grant, accord.

διόπερ = διό.

διο-πετής = διϊπετής.

δι-οπτεύω to spy about; to look about.

δι-οπτήρ, ῆρος, ὁ spy, scout.

δι-οράω to see through.

δι-όργυιος 2 two fathoms long.   [right, amend.

δι-ορθόω and M. to set

δι-όρθωμα, τό and δι-όρθωσις, ἡ correction, amendment.

δι-ορίζω to divide; to distinguish; to define; to ordain; to banish. [canal.

δι-όρυγμα, τό ditch, trench,

δι-ορύσσω to dig through; to rake up; to undermine; to block up.

δῖος 3 shining, brilliant; excellent, noble; divine.

δι-ότι *conj.* for the reason that, since; wherefrom; that. [Zeus.\

διο-τρεφής 2 sprung from/

δι-ουρίζω = διορίζω.

δί-παλτος 2 double, twofold.

δί-πηχυς, υ of two cubits.

διπλάζω to double; to be doubled.

δίπλαξ, ακος, ἡ double-folded garment, cloak.

διπλασιάζω to double.

δι-πλάσιος 3 double, twice as much.

διπλασιόω to double.

δί-πλεθρος 2 of two plethra.

δι-πλόος, -πλοῦς 3 double, twofold: both; alternating; double-minded.

διπλόω to double.

δί-πους, ποδος two-footed.

δί-πτυξ, υχος and δί-πτυχος 2 folded together.

δί-πυλος 2 with two gates.

δίς adv. twice, double.

δισ-θανής twice dying.

δισκεύω, δισκέω to throw the disk or quoit. [quoit.\

δίσκος, ὁ disk, discus,/

δίσκ-ουρα, ων, τά quoit's cast. [number 20 000.\

δισ-μυριάς, άδος, ἡ the/

δισ-μύριοι 3 twenty thousand. [ing.\

δισσ-άρχης, ου doubly rul-/

δισσός 3 double, twofold; ambiguous, doubtful.

διστάζω to doubt. [gether.\

δί-στολος 2 in pairs, to-/

δί-στομος 2 double-mouthed, with two entrances; two-edged.

δισ-χίλιοι 3 two thousand.

δι-τάλαντος 2 weighing two talents.

δι-ϋλίζω to strain, filter.

δι-φάσιος 3 double, twofold.

δīφάω to seek, search, dive after.

διφθέρα, ἡ skin, hide, leather; anything made of leather (coat, bag, coverlet).

διφθέρινος 3 of leather.

διφρευτής, οῦ, ὁ charioteer.

διφρ-ηλατέω to drive in a chariot. [ρευτής.\

διφρ-ηλάτης, ου, ὁ = διφ-/

δίφρος, ὁ chariot-board; chariot; chair.

διφρο-φορέομαι *P.* to be carried in a chair or litter.

δι-φυής 2 of double form.

δίχα adv. in two, at two, twofold; apart, asunder; at variance, different. *Prep.* with *gen.* far from; without.

διχάζω to divide in two; to make disagree, disunite.

διχῇ adv. = δίχα.

διχθά adv. in two.

διχθάδιος 3 double, twofold.

διχο-γνωμονέω to differ in opinion.

διχόθεν adv. from two sides.

διχο-στασία, ἡ division, quarrel.

διχο-στατέω to stand asunder, to disagree.

διχο-τομέω to split in two.

διχοῦ = δίχα.

δίψα, ἡ thirst.

δῑψάω to thirst, to be dry.

δίψιος 3 thirsty, dry.

δί-ψυχος 2 double-minded, doubtful. [δίεμαι.\

δίω to fear, flee. — *M.* =/

δι-ωβελίᾱ, ἡ payment of two obols.

διωγμός, ὁ = δίωξις.

δι-ώδυνος 2 very painful.

δι-ωθέω to push or tear asunder; to pierce or break through. — M. to push away from oneself, to repulse; to refuse; to break through.

διωκάθω = διώκω.

διώκτης, ου, ὁ pursuer.

διώκω to pursue, chase, drive, hunt; to expel, banish; to run after, follow, catch; to strive after; to be attached to; to prosecute, accuse; to drive a chariot; to haste. — M. to chase, drive before oneself.

δι-ώμοτος 2 bound by oath.

δίωξις, ἡ chase, pursuit; persecution; striving after.

δι-ῶρυξ, υχος, ἡ ditch, trench, canal; underground gallery.

δμῆσις, ἡ a taming.

δμήτειρα, ἡ tamer.

δμωή, ἡ female slave.servant.

δμώς, ωός, ὁ slave. [abount.]

δνοπαλίζω to shake, push⌋

δνοφερός 3 dark, dusky.

δοάσσατο it seemed.

δόγμα, τό opinion; decree, resolution; doctrine.

δογματίζομαι P. to be subject to statutes.

δοιή, ἡ doubt.

δοιοί 3 two, both.

δοκάζω, δοκάω, δοκεύω to expect; to watch, lie in wait.

δοκέω to think, suppose, imagine; to resolve; to seem, appear; to appear to be something; δοκῶ μοι I seem to myself; methinks; δοκεῖ it seems; it seems good, it is decreed.

δόκησις, ἡ opinion; suspicion; appearance.

δοκιμάζω to prove, test, examine; to approve, to declare good.

δοκιμασίᾱ, ἡ examination, a proving; a mustering.

δοκιμαστής, οῦ, ὁ examiner.

δοκιμή, ἡ and δοκίμιον, τό examination, proof, test.

δόκιμος 2 tried, approved; esteemed; considerable.

δοκός, ἡ wooden beam.

δολερός 3 cunning, deceitful.

δολιό-μῡθος 2 artful.

δολιό-πους, ποδος of stealthy foot, dodging.

δόλιος 3 = δολερός.

δολιόω to betray, cheat.

δολίχ-αυλος 2 with a long pipe.   [spear.]

δολιχ-εγχής 2 with a long⌋

δολιχ-ήρετμος 2 with long oars.   [runner.]

δολιχο-δρόμος 2 prize-⌋

δολιχός 3 long, far.

δόλιχος, ὁ long course; stadium.

δολιχό-σκιος 2 casting a long shadow.

δολόεις 3 = δολερός.

δολο-μήτης, ου and δολό-μητις, ιος wily, artful.

δολο-ποιός 2 = δολερός.

δόλος, ὁ bait, inducement; cunning, deceit, treachery.

δολο - φρονέω to devise treachery.

δολο - φροσύνη, ἡ deceit, cunning, intrigue.

δολόω to cheat, entice, beguile; to disguise.

δόμα, τό gift.

δόμος, ὁ house, building; dwelling, apartment, room, hall; layer; home; family; household.

δοναχεύς, ὁ thicket of canes or reeds.   [canes.

δονακό - χλοος 2 green with

δόναξ, ακος, ὁ cane, reed; arrow; shepherd's pipe.

δονέω to shake, stir, drive about. — P. to be agitated; to be in commotion.

δόξα, ἡ opinion, notion; expectation; false opinion, delusion, fancy; decree, project; judgment; reputation, report, estimation, honour; glory, splendour.

δοξάζω to think, believe, suppose, presume; to extol.

δοξόομαι P. to bear a reputation.

δορά, ἡ hide, skin.

δοράτιον, τό javelin; pole.

δορί-άλωτος 2, δορί-κτητος 2, δορί-ληπτος 2 taken in war, captive.

δορί-μαργος 2 eager for combat.

δορκάς, άδος, ἡ roe, gazelle.

δορός, ὁ leather bag.

δορπέω to take supper.

δορπηστός, ὁ supper-time, evening.

δορπία, ἡ eve of a feast.

δόρπον, τό supper.

δόρυ, ατος, τό wood, stem of a tree, beam, timber; ship; pole: shaft of a spear; spear; battle, war; spearbearer, warrior; army; booty; ἐπὶ δόρυ to the right hand.   [άλωτος.

δορυ - άλωτος 2 = δορι-

δορυ - δρέπανον, τό handle of a sickle; grappling-hook.

δορύ - ξενος, ὁ companion in arms, comrade.

δορυ - σσόης, ητος and δορυ - σσόος 2 brandishing a spear, warlike.

δορυ - φορέω to be a bodyguard, to attend as a guard.

δορυ - φόρος, ὁ lance-bearer; body-guard; pole-bearer.

δοσί-δικος 2 = δωσίδικος.

δόσις, ἡ act of giving; gift, present; portion.

δοτήρ, ῆρος, ὁ and δότης, ου, ὁ giver, dispenser.

δουλ - αγωγέω to lead into slavery.

δουλεία, ἡ slavery, thraldom, bondage, servility; bondmen, menials.

δούλειος 2 slavish, servile.

δούλευμα, τό slavery; slave.

δουλεύω to be a slave, to serve.

δούλη, ἡ female slave.

δουλία, ἡ = δουλεία.

δουλικός 3 and δούλιος 2 = δούλειος.

δουλιχό - δειρος 2 longnecked.   [a slave.

δουλο - πρεπής 2 befitting

δοῦλος 3 slavish, servile; enslaved, subject; ὁ, ἡ slave.

δουλοσύνη, ἡ = δουλεία.

δουλόω to enslave, subdue; to discourage.

δούλωσις, ἡ an enslaving, subjugation. [to roar.]

δουπέω to sound hollow;]

δοῦπος, ὁ hollow sound, roaring, noise.

δουράτεος 3 wooden.

δουρ-ηνεκές adv. a spear's cast off. [ἄλωτος.]

δουρι-άλωτος 2 = δορι-]

δουρι-κλειτός, -κλυτός 2 famous as a spearman.

δουρί-ληπτος 2 = δορί-ληπτος. [spears.]

δουρο-δόκη, ἡ case for]

δοχή, ἡ banquet.

δόχμιος 3 and δοχμός 3 slanting, sideways.

δράγμα, δράγμα, τό handful; sheaf.

δραγμεύω to collect sheaves.

δραίνω to be about to do.

δράκαινα, ἡ she-dragon.

δράκων, οντος, ὁ dragon; serpent.

δρᾶμα, τό action, deed; play.

δράμημα, τό = δρόμος.

δραπετεύω to run away, escape

δραπέτης, ου, ὁ runaway, fugitive slave; falling to pieces.

δρασείω to be willing to do.

δρασμός, ὁ escape, flight.

δράσσομαι M. to grasp, seize. [enterprising.]

δραστήριος 2 active, busy,]

δρατός 3 flayed.

δραχμή, ἡ drachm.

δράω to be active; to do, perform, accomplish.

δρεπάνη, ἡ = δρέπανον.

δρεπάνη-φόρος 2 bearing a sickle. [shaped.]

δρεπανο-ειδής 2 sickle-]

δρέπανον, τό sickle, scythe; curved sabre.

δρέπω, δρέπτω to pluck.

δρησμός, ὁ = δρασμός.

δρήστειρα, ἡ, δρηστήρ, ῆρος, ὁ worker, servant.

δρηστοσύνη, ἡ service.

δριμύς 3 piercing, biting; violent, sharp, bitter; shrewd. [wood.]

δρίος, τό thicket, brush-]

δρομαῖος 3, δρομάς, άδος 2 running, fleet.

δρομεύς, ὁ runner.

δρομικός 3 running swift; τὰ δρομικά foot-race.

δρόμος, ὁ a running, course, race; δρόμῳ in rapid march, swiftly; place for running, race-course, stadium.

δροσερός 3 dewy. [water.]

δρόσος, ἡ dew, dewdrop;]

δρύϊνος 3 oaken.

δρυμός, ὁ oak-wood; wood.

δρύ-οχος, ὁ rib of a ship.

δρύπτω to peel off, to scratch, tear; to snatch away.

δρῦς, υός, ἡ oak; tree; wood.

δρυ-τόμος 2 wood-cutter.

δρύ-φακτον, τό and δρύφακτος, ὁ fence, railing.

δρύφω = δρύπτω. [two.]

δυάς, άδος, ἡ the number]

δυάω to drive into misery.

δύη, ἡ misery, woe, pain.

δύναμαι P. to be able or capable; to be strong, mighty, or powerful; to be worth; to signify.

δύναμις, ἡ ability; might,

power, strength; military force, army; expedient, implement; talent, faculty; power of speech; miracle; influence, consequence; worth, value; meaning, signification.

δυναμόω to strengthen.

δύνασις, ἡ = δύναμις.

δυναστεία, ἡ sovereignty, lordship, rule. [to sway.)

δυναστεύω to have power,)

δυνάστης, ου, ὁ sovereign, lord, ruler, master; nobleman.

δυνατέω to be powerful.

δυνατός 3 able; strong, mighty, powerful; fit, apt; noble; possible.

δύνω = δύομαι, see δύω.

δύο two, both.

δυο-καί-δεκα = δώδεκα.

δυοκαιδεκά-μηνος 2 of twelve months.

δύρομαι = ὀδύρομαι.

δυσ-αής 2 ill-blowing.

δυσ-άθλιος 2 most miserable.   [miserably.)

δυσ-αίων, ωνος living)

δυσ-άλγητος 2 unfeeling.

δυσ-άλωτος 2 hard to catch.

δυσ-άμμορος 2 most unhappy.

δυσ-ανασχετέω to find unbearable; to be beside oneself.

δυσ-άνεκτος 2 unbearable.

δυσ-άνεμος 2 wind-beaten, stormy.

δυσ-απάλλακτος 2 hard to ward off, stubborn.

δυσ-απότρεπτος 2 hard to turn away

δυσ-άρεστος 2 ill-pleased, morose.

δυσ-αριστο-τόκεια, ἡ unhappy mother of a hero.

δύσ-αυλος 2 uncomfortable for lodging.   [bear.)

δυσ-βάστακτος 2 hard to)

δύσ-βατος 2 impassable.

δυσ-βουλία, ἡ ill counsel, folly.

δυσ-γένεια, ἡ low birth.

δύσ-γνωστος 2 hard to discern or know.

δυσ-γοήτευτος 2 difficult to be charmed. [misery.)

δυσ-δαιμονία, ἡ ill fate,)

δυσ-δαίμων 2 ill-fated.

δυσ-διάβατος 2 hard to cross.   [ugly.)

δυσ-ειδής 2 misshapen,)

δύσ-ελπις, ιδος hopeless.

δυσ-έμβατος 2 difficult of access.

δυσ-έμβολος 2 impregnable, inaccessible.

δυσ-εντερία, ἡ dysentery.

δυσ-εξαπάτητος 2 hard to deceive.   [refute.)

δυσ-εξέλεγκτος hard to)

δύσ-ερις, ιδος quarrelsome, captious.   [able.)

δυσ-έριστος 2 unconquer-)

δυσ-ερμήνευτος 2 hard to be understood.

δύσ-ερως, ωτος crossed in love; passionately loving.

δυσ-έσβολος 2 = δυσέμβολος.

δυσ-εύρετος 2 hard to find.

δύσ-ζηλος 2 irascible.

δυσ-ηλεγής 2 painful.

δυσ-ηχής 2 ill-sounding, raging.

δυσ-θαλπής 2 chilly.

δυσ-θανατέω to suffer dying agonies. [dismal.]

δυσ-θέατος 2 horrible,

δύσ-θεος 2 hated by the gods. [tend.]

δυσ-θεράπευτος 2 hard to

δυσ-θετέομαι P. to be out of humour. [able.]

δυσ-θρήνητος 2 lament-

δυσ-θυμέω to be disheart-ened; to despond.

δυσ-θυμίᾱ, ἡ ill humour; despondency.] desponding.]

δύσ-θυμος 2 ill-humoured]

δυσ-ίᾱτος 2 hard to heal, incurable. [valry.]

δύσ-ιππος 2 unfit for ca-]

δύσις, ἡ sunset; west.

δυσ-κάθαρτος 2 hard to expiate. [check.]

δυσ-κάθεκτος 2 hard to]

δυσ-κατέργαστος 2 hard to obtain by labour.

δυσ-κέλαδος 2 ill-sound-ing, harsh.

δυσ-κηδής 2 sad, sorry.

δυσ-κλεής 2 inglorious, in-famous. [shame.]

δύσ-κλεια, ἡ bad fame,

δυσ-κοινώνητος 2 unsoci-able. [or discontented.]

δυσ-κολαίνω to be peevish]

δυσ-κολίᾱ, ἡ peevishness, discontent; difficulty, per-plexity.

δύσ-κολος 2 peevish, dis-contented, fretful; difficult, perplexing.

δυσ-κόμιστος 2 unbearable.

δύσ-κριτος 2 hard to dis-cern or decide. [able.]

δυσ-λόγιστος 2 inconceiv-]

δυσ-μαθής 2 indocile; dull; difficult to be learnt.

δυσ-μαχέω to fight with ill luck.

δύσ-μαχος 2 hard to fight with; unconquerable.

δυσ-μεναίνω to be peevish; to be hostile. [mity.]

δυσ-μένεια, ἡ ill-will, en-]

δυσ-μενέων 3. δυσ-μενής 2 hostile, malevolent.

δυσ-μεταχείριστος 2 hard to fight with.

δυσμή, ἡ = δύσις. [mother.]

δυσ-μήτηρ, ἡ not a true]

δύσ-μοιρος 2, δύσ-μορος 2 unhappy, miserable.

δυσ-μορφίᾱ, ἡ ugliness.

δύσ-νιπτος 2 not to be washed off.

δυσ-νόητος 2 difficult to be understood.

δύσ-νοια, ἡ dislike, ill-will.

δύσ-νοος, -νους 2 hostile, malign; ill-disposed.

δύσ-νυμφος 2 ill-betrothed.

δυσ-ξύμβολος 2 unsoci-able. [gible, obscure.]

δυσ-ξύνετος 2 unintell-]

δύσ-οδμος 2 ill-smelling.

δύσ-οδος 2 scarcely passable.

δύσ-οιστος 2 unbearable, hard to bear.

δύσ-ομβρος 2 with adverse showers of rain.

δύσ-οργος 2 irascible.

δυσ-οσμίᾱ, ἡ bad smell.

δυσ-ούριστος 2 driven on by bad winds. [querable.]

δυσ-πάλαιστος 2 uncon-]

δυσ-πάρευνος 2 ill-mated.

Δύσ-παρις, ὁ unlucky Paris.

δυσ-πάριτος 2 hard to pass.

δυσ-πειθής 2 disobedient, refractory. [suade.]
δύς-πειστος 2 hard to per-)
δυσ-πέμφελος 2 stormy.
δυσ-πέρᾱτος 2 hard to bring through.
δυσ-πετής 2 difficult.
δυσ-πῐνής 2 very dirty.
δύς-πνοος 2 breathless; adverse (wind).
δυσ-πολέμητος 2 hard to make war upon.
δυσ-πολιόρκητος 2 hard to take by siege.
δυσ-πονής 2, δυσ-πόνητος 2, δύσ-πονος 2 toilsome, hard-earned.
δυσ-πόρευτος 2, δύσ-πορος scarcely passable. [age.]
δυσ-πορία, ἡ difficult pass-)
δύς-ποτμος 2 ill-fated.
δυσ-πρᾱξίᾱ, ἡ misfortune.
δυσ-πρόσβατος 2, δυσ-πρόσοδος 2 hardly accessible. [friendly, gloomy.]
δυσ-πρόσοιστος 2 un-)
δυσ-πρόσοπτος 2, δυσ-πρόσωπος 2 of ill aspect.
δύς-ρῑγος 2 sensible to cold.
δυσ-σέβεια, ἡ impiety.
δυσ-σεβέω to be impious; to act impiously. [less.]
δυσ-σεβής 2 impious, god-)
δυσ-τάλᾱς, αινα, αν most unhappy.
δυσ-τέκμαρτος 2 hard to conclude. [a mother.]
δύς-τεκνος 2 unhappy as)
δύστηνος 2 unhappy; wretched, abominable.
δυστομέω to revile, defame.
δυσ-τράπελος 2, δύσ-τροπος 2 stubborn.

δυσ-τυχέω to be unlucky. — P. to fail. [τυχία.]
δυσ-τύχημα, τό = δυσ-)
δυσ-τυχής 2 unlucky, unhappy, miserable.
δυσ-τυχίᾱ, ἡ ill luck, misfortune, mishap; defeat.
δυσ-φημέω to speak words of an evil omen; to revile, slander.
δυσ-φημίᾱ, ἡ words of ill omen; a reviling; lamentation; bad fame.
δυσ-φιλής 2 hateful; ugly.
δυσ-φορέω to bear with resentment; to do unwillingly.
δύς-φορος 2 hard to bear, heavy, oppressive; misleading.
δύσ-φρων 2 sorrowful, melancholy; hostile, ill-disposed; senseless. [stormy.]
δυσ-χείμερος 2 wintry,)
δυσ-χείρωμα, τό hard work.
δυσ-χείρωτος 2 hard to overcome.
δυσ-χεραίνω to be or become discontented or angry; to disapprove, reject; to make difficulties; to rouse indignation.
δυσ-χέρεια, ἡ incommodity; annoyance.
δυσ-χερής 2 hard to manage, difficult; annoying, unpleasant, vexatious; peevish, ill-affected.
δύσ-χρηστος 2 hard to use; useless.
δυσ-χωρίᾱ, ἡ disadvantageous ground.
δυσ-ώδης 2 ill-smelling.

δυσ-ώνυμος 2 bearing an ill name; ominous, ill-reputed.   [or timid.]
δυσ-ωπέομαι P. to be shy)
δυσ-ωρέω to keep a painful watch.
δύτης, ου, ὁ diver.
δύω and M. intr. to dive, sink; to enter; to perish; trans. to put on.
δύω = δύο.
δυώ-δεκα = δώδεκα.
δυωδεκά-βοιος 2 worth twelve oxen.
δυωδεκά-πολις 2 belonging to a confederation of twelve cities.   [τος.]
δυωδέκατος 3 = δωδέκα-)
δυωκαιεικοσί-μετρος 2 holding 22 measures.
δυωκαιεικοσί-πηχυς, υ 22 cubits long.
δῶ, τό = δῶμα.
δώδεκα twelve.
δωδεκά-σκυτος 2 composed of 12 pieces of leather.
δωδέκατος 3 twelfth.
δωδεκά-φυλον, τό the twelve tribes.

δῶμα, τό dwelling, house; palace, temple; chamber, hall; roof; family, household.   [chamber.]
δωμάτιον, τό room, bed-)
δωρεά, ἡ gift, present; gift of honour; benefit;
δωρεάν adv. freely, gratis.
δωρέω and M. to give, present.
δώρημα, τό = δωρεά.
δωρητός 3 given; open to gifts.
δωριστί adv. in Dorian manner, dialect, or tune.
δωρο-δοκέω to accept presents, to get bribed.
δωρο-δόκημα, τό, δωρο-δοκίᾱ, ἡ bribe; bribery.
δωρο-δόκος 2 taking bribes.
δῶρον, τό gift, present.
δωρο-φορίᾱ, ἡ the bringing of presents.
δωσί-δικος 2 submitting to justice.
δωτήρ, ῆρος, ὁ giver.
δωτῑνάζω to collect gifts.
δωτίνη, ἡ = δῶρον.
δώτωρ, ορος, ὁ = δωτήρ.

E

E, ε (ἒ ψῑλόν) fifth letter of the alphabet; as a numeral ε' = 5.
ἒ, mostly ἒ ἒ int. woe!   [ah!]
ἒ him-, her-, it-self.
ἑᾶ int. denoting wonder: ha!)
ἐάν conj. if, if so be that, in case that; as often as, whenever; if, whether.
ἑᾰνός 3 wrapping up; smooth, pliant.
ἑᾰνός, ὁ a woman's robe.

ἔαρ, ἔαρος, τό spring, prime.
ἐαρίζω to pass the spring.
ἐαρινός 3 belonging to spring.
ἑαυτοῦ, ῆς, οῦ of himself, herself, or itself; of oneself.
ἐάφθη = ἥφθη, see ἅπτω.
ἐάω to let, permit, allow, suffer; to let or leave alone or unnoticed; to omit, give up.

ἑβδομαῖος 3 on the seventh day.

ἑβδόματος 3 = ἕβδομος.

ἑβδομήκοντα seventy.

ἑβδομηκοντάκις seventy times.

ἕβδομος 3 seventh.

ἔβενος, ἡ ebony(-tree,-wood).

ἐγ-γείνομαι to engender in.

ἔγ-γειος 2 within the boundaries of the country; in the earth.   [mock.]

ἐγ-γελάω to laugh at,

ἐγ-γενής 2 blood-related; native; inborn.

ἐγ-γηράσκω to grow old at a place.

ἐγ-γίγνομαι M. to be born in; to happen, take place in, to arise; to be innate or infused; to intervene, pass; to be possible.

ἐγγίζω to approach, draw near.   [ἐγγύς.]

ἔγγιον and ἔγγιστα from

ἐγ-γλύσσω to have a sweetish taste.

ἐγ-γλύφω to engrave, carve, cut in.

ἐγ-γνάμπτω to bend in.

ἔγ-γονος, ὁ, ἡ relation; descendant.

ἐγ-γράφω to engrave; to write, draw, or paint in; to write down.   [to grant.]

ἐγ-γυαλίζω to hand over;

ἐγ-γυάω and M. to stand security; to betroth, engage, promise; to be betrothed.   [pledge.]

ἐγ-γύη, ἡ security, bail,

ἐγ-γυητής, οῦ, ὁ, ἔγγυος, ὁ warranter, surety.

ἐγγύς adv. near, in the neighbourhood, neighbouring; coming near; like, nearly; soon; at last; comp. ἐγγίω, ἐγγύτερος; superl. ἔγγιστος, ἐγγύτατος.

ἐγ-γώνιος 2 forming a (right) angle.

ἐγείρω to awaken, rouse; to stir, excite; to raise.

ἔγερσις, ἡ a rousing, raising.

ἐγερτί adv. in an exciting way.

ἐγ-καθέζομαι M. to sit down in, to encamp in.

ἐγ-κάθετος 2 suborned; watcher.

ἐγ-καθιδρύω to set up in.

ἐγ-καθίζω to set in or upon; to seat oneself on. — M. to sit on; to take one's seat.

ἐγ-καθίστημι to place, put, or set in; to establish, arrange; intr. to be established.

ἐγ-καθορμίζομαι M. to run into the harbour.

ἐγ-καίνια, τά feast of the dedication of the temple.

ἐγ-καινίζω to renew, renovate.   [to relax.]

ἐγ-κακέω to grow weary,

ἐγ-καλέω to call in; to accuse, reproach, blame, to bring a charge (against); to claim (a debt).   [ment.]

ἐγ-καλλώπισμα, τό orna-

ἐγ-καλύπτω to veil in, wrap up, hide.

ἔγ-καρπος 2 fruitful.

ἐγ-κάρσιος 3 and 2 oblique, transverse.

ἐγ-καρτερέω to persevere, persist (in); to control one-self. [trails.]

ἔγκατα, τά bowels, en-

ἐγ-καταδέω to bind fast in.

ἐγ-καταζεύγνῦμι to join with, to unite. [sleep in.]

ἐγ-κατακοιμάομαι P. to

ἐγ-καταλαμβάνω to catch in a place, to seize, take, apprehend, arrest; to cut off.

ἐγ-καταλέγω to gather in; to enlist.

ἐγ-καταλείπω to leave behind in a place or with one. — P. to be left behind.

ἐγ-κατάληψις, ἡ a catching, capture.

ἐγ-καταμ(ε)ίγνῡμι to mix up in; to place between.

ἐγ-καταπήγνῡμι to thrust into, to fix in.

ἐγ-κατασκήπτω to fling down into; to break out; to invade. [pieces.]

ἐγ-κατατέμνω to cut into

ἐγ-κατατίθεμαι M. to lay in or hide for oneself.

ἐγ-κατοικέω to live in or among. [in or aside.]

ἐγ-κατοικοδομέω to build

ἐγ-καυχάομαι to boast.

ἔγ-κειμαι to lie in or on, to be placed in; to press on, urge, importune, attack; to be intent upon.

ἐγ-κέλευστος 2 bidden, ordered; suborned.

ἐγ-κεντρίζω to ingraft.

ἐγ-κεράννῡμι, ἐγ-κεράω to mix in. — M. to suborn, contrive. [row.]

ἐγ-κέφαλος, ὁ brain; mar-

ἐγ-κλείω to shut in, confine; to shut fast or up.

ἔγ-κλημα, τό accusation, charge, reproach, complaint; controversy; fault, guilt.

ἔγ-κληρος 2 sharing, partaking; heir, heiress; destined by lot. [κλείω.]

ἐγ-κλήω, ἐγ-κληΐω = ἐγ-

ἐγ-κλίνω to bend or incline towards. — intr. and P. to be bent; to lean on; to yield; to turn to flight.

ἐγ-κοιλαίνω to hollow out.

ἔγ-κοιλος 2 hollowed out.

ἐγ-κολάπτω to cut in, engrave.

ἐγ-κομβόομαι to make one's own. [busy.]

ἐγ-κονέω to hasten; to be

ἐγ-κοπή, ἡ hindrance.

ἐγ-κόπτω to hinder, trouble; to delay.

ἐγ-κοσμέω to arrange within. [hatred.]

ἔγ-κοτος, ὁ resentment,

ἐγ-κράζω to shriek at.

ἐγ-κράτεια, ἡ self-control, temperance; induration.

ἐγ-κρατεύομαι M. to be frugal or abstemious.

ἐγ-κρατής 2 strong, stout; having mastery over; self-disciplined, sober.

ἐγ-κρίνω to choose among, to admit, adopt; to reckon among.

ἐγ-κροτέω to strike against, to beat time with the feet. — M. to strike one another.

ἐγ-κρύπτω to hide in.

ἐγ-κτάομαι M. to acquire possessions in a place.

ἔγ-κτησις, ἡ landed property in a place.

ἐγ-κυκάω to mix up in.

ἐγ-κυκλόω to move about in a circle.

ἐγ-κυλίομαι P. to wallow in, to be given to. [child.]

ἔγ-κυος 2 pregnant, with

ἐγ-κύπτω to stoop; to peep, to cast a side-glance.

ἐγ-κύρεω, ἐγ-κύρω to meet with; to fall into.

ἐγ-κωμιάζω to praise, extol, laud.

ἐγ-κώμιον, τό song of praise; glory. [battle.]

ἐγρε-μάχης 2 exciting the

ἐγρηγοράω to be awake.

ἐγρηγορτί adv. awake.

ἐγρήσσω to be awake.

ἐγ-χαλινόω to bridle.

ἐγ-χειρέω to take in hand, to undertake, to try; to attack.

ἐγ-χείρημα, τό, ἐγ-χείρησις, ἡ an undertaking, execution. [ing.]

ἐγ-χειρητικός 3 enterpris

ἐγ-χειρίδιον, τό dagger, knife.

ἐγ-χειρίζω to hand over, deliver, entrust. — M. to take upon oneself.

ἐγχειρί-θετος 2 handed over, delivered. [eel.]

ἔγχελυς, υος and εως, ἡ

ἐγχεσί-μωρος 2 famous with the spear.

ἐγχέσ-παλος 2 lancebrandishing.

ἐγ-χέω to pour in.

ἔγχος, τό spear, lance; weapon, sword.

ἐγ-χραύω to dash or push into.

ἐγ-χρίμπτω to cause to strike against; to dash or drive against, to bring near; to approach, to come to land. — P. to touch, verge, reach to.

ἐγ-χρίω to anoint.

ἐγ-χρονίζω to tarry; to become inveterate.

ἐγ-χωρέω to give way or room; ἐγχωρεῖ it is possible.

ἐγ-χώριος 2 and 3, ἐγχωρος 2 native, indigenous; inhabitant; rustic.

ἐγώ I, myself; ἔγωγε I for my part.

ἐδανός 3 lovely, delicious.

ἐδαφίζω to level with the earth. [floor, bottom.]

ἔδαφος, τό ground, soil,

ἔδεσμα, τό food, meat, dish.

ἐδεστής, οῦ, ὁ eater.

ἐδεστός 3 eaten, consumed.

ἐδητύς, ύος, ἡ food.

ἕδνα, τά nuptial gifts; dowry.

ἕδος, τό, ἕδρα, ἡ seat, chair, bench, row; sittingpart; abode, dwelling; temple, altar, statue; foundation; base, station, stand, act of sitting, a sitting still, inaction; session.

ἑδραῖος 3 sitting still, sedentary, unmoved.

ἑδραίωμα, τό foundation, support.

ἕδρανον, τό = ἕδρα.

ἑδριάομαι M. to sit down.

ἔδω to eat, consume.

ἐδωδή, ἡ food, fodder; bait.

ἐδώδιμος 2 eatable.

ἐδώλιον, τό seat, residence; rowing-bench.

ἕε = ἓ him.

ἔεδνα, τά = ἕδνα.

ἐεδνόομαι M. to betroth.

ἐεδνωτής, οῦ, ὁ father of a bride.   [twenty oxen.]

ἐεικοσά - βοιος 2 worth

ἐείκοσι = εἴκοσι.

ἐέλδομαι = ἔλδομαι.

ἐέλδωρ, τό = ἔλδωρ.

ἐέλπομαι = ἔλπομαι.

ἐεργάθω = ἐργάθω.

ἐέρση = ἔρση.

ἕζω to set, place, settle. — M. to sit down; to sit; to settle (down).

ἐθάς, άδος accustomed, wont.

ἔθειρα, ἡ hair; mane; horse-tail; plume of a helmet.

ἐθείρω to till, cultivate.

ἐθελο-θρησκεία, ἡ arbitrary worship.

ἐθελο-κακέω to be bad or cowardly on purpose.

ἐθελοντηδόν, ἐθελοντήν, ἐθελοντί adv. on purpose, willingly.

ἐθελοντήρ, ῆρος, ἐθελοντής, οῦ voluntary, willing.

ἐθελό-πονος 2 willing to work.   [willing proxenus.]

ἐθελο-πρόξενος, ὁ self-

ἐθελούσιος 3 and 2 = ἐθελοντής.

ἐθέλω to be willing, to wish, want, desire, to be resolved or inclined; to be able; to have power; to be wont, to mean.

ἔθεν = ἕο, οὗ.

ἐθίζω to accustom. — P. to be accustomed.

ἐθν-άρχης, ου, ὁ governor, prefect.

ἐθνικός 3 national; gentile.

ἔθνος, τό company, band; people, nation, tribe; class of men; gentiles.

ἔθος, τό custom, manner.

ἔθω to be wont or accustomed; perf. εἴωθα, part. εἰωθώς wont, accustomed, usual.

εἰ conj. if, whether.

εἶα int. up, on, well then.

εἰαμενή, ἡ lowland, meadow(-land).

εἰανός, ὁ = ἑανός.

εἶαρ, τό = ἔαρ.

εἰαρινός 3 = ἐαρινός.

εἴβω and M. to drop. trickle.

εἰδάλιμος 3 shapely, comely.

εἶδαρ, ατος, τό food, fodder; bait.

εἶδος, τό act of seeing; appearance, shape, form; beauty; notion, idea; kind, species, description; nature.

εἴδω and M., aor. εἶδον, ἰδεῖν to see, behold, perceive, know; to have an appearance, to look, seem; to resemble; to feign. — perf. οἶδα, εἰδέναι to know, to be knowing, skilled, or cunning.

εἰδωλεῖον, τό idol's temple.

εἰδωλό-θυτος 2 offered to idols.

εἰδωλο-λατρεία, ἡ idolatry.

εἰδωλο-λάτρης, ου, ὁ idolater.

εἴδωλον, τό image, shape, phantom; vision, idol.

εἶεν *adv.* well (then).

εἶθαρ *adv.* at once, forthwith, immediately.

εἴ-θε *int.* o that.

εἰκάζω to make like to; to portray; to compare: to conjecture, guess, examine. — *P.* to resemble, to be like.

εἰκάθω = εἴκω.

εἰκασία, ἡ image.

εἰκαστής, οῦ, ὁ guesser.

εἴκελος 3 like, resembling.

εἰκῇ, εἰκῆ *adv.* at random, headlessly, in vain.

εἰκός, ότος, τό probable, likely, natural, fair, reasonable.   [years old.]

εἴκοσα - έτης 2 twenty

εἰκοσάκις *adv.* twenty times.

εἴκοσι twenty.

εἰκοσι-νήριτος 2 twenty times immense.

εἰκοσί-πηχυς, υ of twenty cubits.   [oars.]

εἰκόσ-ορος 2 with twenty

εἰκοστός 3 the twentieth.

εἰκότως *adv.* probably, naturally, of course, fairly, reasonably.

εἴκω[1] to yield, give way, retire; to submit, resign; to grant, allow.

εἴκω[2], εἶκε it seemed good.

ἔοικα to be or look like; to seem, to have the appearance (of); to think, believe; to be fit, right, or fair.

εἰκών, όνος, ἡ likeness, image, picture, painting; simile; phantom; notion.

εἰκώς 3 = ἐοικώς.

εἰλαπινάζω to feast, dine.

εἰλαπιναστής, οῦ, ὁ companion at table.

εἰλαπίνη, ἡ feast, banquet.

εἶλαρ, τό protection, shelter.

εἰλάτινος 3 = ἐλάτινος.

εἰλέω, εἴλλω to press hard; to force together; to shut up in; to strike; to check; to drive. — *P.* to be shut up or pressed together; to be crowded, assembled, or drawn together; to go or turn about.

εἴλησις, ἡ heat of the sun.

εἰλι-κρίνεια, ἡ purity.

εἰλι-κρινής 2 sun-bright, manifest; pure, uncorrupted, genuine.

εἰλί-πους, ποδος trailing the feet.

εἴλλω see εἰλέω.

εἶλυμα, τό cover, clothing.

εἰλυφάζω, εἰλυφάω to roll along.

εἰλύω to roll, whirl; to involve, enfold. — *P.* to roll on; to crawl, creep, wind along; to cling to, to couch.

εἴλω = εἰλέω.

εἵλως, ωτος and εἱλώτης, ου, ὁ Helot, Spartan serf.

εἷμα, τό garment, cover.

εἱμαρμένη, ἡ destiny.

εἵμαρται see μείρομαι.

εἰμί to be, exist, live, continue; to take place, to come to pass; to dwell, sojourn; to be in a certain state; to behave; to be real; to mean, signify; to be descended; to belong to.

εἶμι to go, come, wander,

travel, drive, sail, fly; to march, progress, advance; to go away; to retire; to arrive.

εἴν = ἐν.

εἰνα-ετής 2 (neutr. εἰνά-ετες) of nine years.

εἰνάκις = ἐνάκις nine times.

εἰνακόσιοι 3 = ἐνακόσιοι.

εἰν-άλιος 3 = ἐνάλιος.

εἰνά-νυχες adv. nine nights long. [law.]

εἰνατέρες, αἱ sisters-in-}

εἴνατος 3 = ἔνατος ninth.

εἵνεκα = ἕνεκα.

εἰνί = ἐν.

εἰν-όδιος 3 = ἐνόδιος.

εἰν-οσί-γαιος, ὁ = ἐννοσί-γαιος. [the leaves.]

εἰν-οσί-φυλλος 2 shaking}

εἴξασι from ἔοικα.

εἶος = ἕως.

εἶπον aor. II, inf. εἰπεῖν, belongs to ἀγορεύω.

εἰργάθω = εἴργω.

εἰργμός, ὁ prison. [jailer.]

εἰργμο-φύλαξ, ακος, ὁ}

εἴργω, εἴργω, εἵργνῡμι to press, enclose, shut in, confine, include, arrest; to shut out, exclude, separate; to prohibit, hinder, prevent. — M. to abstain from; to spare.

εἴρερος, ὁ slavery.

εἰρεσία, ἡ a rowing.

εἴρη, ἡ place of assembly.

εἰρήν, ένος, ὁ = ἰρήν.

εἰρηναῖος 3 peaceful.

εἰρηνεύω to keep peace, to live in peace.

εἰρήνη, ἡ peace; peace-

making; time of peace, rest; blessing.

εἰρηνικός 3 peaceful.

εἰρηνο - ποιέω to make peace. [maker.]

εἰρηνο-ποιός 2 and 3 peace-}

εἰρίνεος 2 woollen.

εἴριον, τό wool.

εἰρκτή, ἡ enclosure; prison.

εἰρο-κόμος 2 wool-dress-ing. [ἐρέω.]

εἴρομαι M. to ask, see}

εἰρο-πόκος 2 wool-fleeced.

εἶρος, τό wool.

εἰρύω = ἐρύω.

εἴρω[1] to say, speak, tell; to report, order; εἴρομαι = ἐρέω. [join.]

εἴρω[2] to string together, to}

εἴρων, ωνος, ὁ dissembler.

εἰρωνεία, ἡ a dissembling, disguise, mockery; evasion, pretext, irony.

εἰρωνεύομαι M. to dissemble, to feign ignorance.

εἰρωνικός 3 ironical.

εἰρωτάω = ἐρωτάω.

εἰς, ἐς adv. and prp. with acc. into, towards, in; against; until; for; for the purpose of; up to; about.

εἷς, μία, ἕν one, one alone, a single one; the same; each one, any one.

εἶσα see ἕζω. [cer, usher.]

εἰσ-αγγελεύς, ὁ announ-}

εἰσ-αγγελία, ἡ announce-ment; impeachment.

εἰσ-αγγέλλω to announce, report; to denounce, impeach. [place.]

εἰσ-αγείρω to gather in a}

εἰσ-άγω to lead into; to

lead up; to import; to produce; to admit, introduce; to bring before an assembly, to summon before a court. — *M.* to bring into one's house. to marry.

εἰσ-αεί *adv.* for ever.

εἰσ-αθρέω to look at, descry.

εἰσ-ακοντίζω to throw spears into or against.

εἰσ-ακούω to listen or hearken to; to obey, follow.

εἰσ-άλλομαι *M.* to leap into or upon, to assail.

εἰσάμην see ἔζω.

εἰσ-αναβαίνω to go up into.

εἰσ-ανάγω to lead up into.

εἰσ-άνειμι to go up into.

εἰσ-άντα *adv.* to the face.

εἰσ-άπαξ *adv.* at once; for once.   [to drive back.]

εἰσ-αράσσω to drive into;

εἰσ-αῦθις *adv.* for another time, hereafter.

εἰσ-αφικάνω, εἰσ-αφικνέομαι to come or go into, to arrive at.

εἰσ-βαίνω to go or come into; to lead into.

εἰσ-βάλλω to throw into; to drive into; *intr.* to throw oneself into; to fall into; to invade, make an inroad, to enter. — *M.* to put on board.

εἰσ-βασις, ἡ embarkation.

εἰσ-βατός 3 accessible.

εἰσ-βιβάζω to embark.

εἰσ-βλέπω to look at.

εἰσ-βολή, ἡ inroad, attack; entrance; pass; mouth (of a river).

εἰσ-γράφω to inscribe. — *M.* to write down for oneself; to inscribe oneself.

εἰσ-δέρκομαι to look at, behold.   [admit.]

εἰσ-δέχομαι *M.* to receive.]

εἰσ-δρομή, ἡ inroad, attack.

εἰσ-δύνω, εἰσ-δύομαι to enter, to slip into; to come over, seize.

εἰσ-ειμι to come or go into, to enter; to visit; to make one's appearance; to come before the court; to come into one's mind, to seize.

εἰσ-ελαύνω, -ελάω to drive into; to enter, invade.

εἰσ-έπειτα *adv.* henceforth, in future.

εἰσ-έργνῦμι to shut up into.

εἰσ-ερύω to draw into.

εἰσ-έρχομαι = εἴσειμι.

εἰσ-έχω to stretch into, reach; to shine into.

ἔίση see ἴσος.

εἰσ-ηγέομαι *M.* to lead into; to introduce, propose, advise; to instruct.

εἰσ-ήγησις, ἡ a proposing; a contriving.

εἰσ-ηγητής, οῦ, ὁ proposer; contriver.

εἰσ-ηθέω to inject, syringe.

εἰσ-θρῴσκω to leap into.

εἰσ-ιδρύω to build in.

εἰσ-ίζομαι *M.* to lie down in.

εἰσ-ίημι to send into; to put into. — *M.* to admit to oneself; to betake oneself to, to resort to.

εἰσ-ίθμη, ἡ entrance.

εἰσ-ικνέομαι *M.* to come into, arrive at.

εἰσ-καλέω and M. to call into; to summon; to invite.

εἰσ-καταβαίνω to go down into.

εἴσ-κειμαι to lie in to be put in.   [proclaim.]

εἰσ-κηρύσσω to call in; to

εἰσ-κομιδή, ἡ import(ation), supply.

εἰσ-κομίζω to bring into, import, procure. — M. to lay in provisions. — P. to take shelter in a place.

εἴσκω = ἴσκω.

εἰσ-λεύσσω to look into, behold.   [the hand.]

εἰσ-μαίομαι M. to put in

εἰσ-νέω to swim over to.

εἰσ-νοέω to perceive, remark.   [bule; admission.]

εἴσ-οδος, ἡ entrance; vesti-

εἰσ-οικείω to introduce as a friend.

εἰσ-οίκησις, ἡ dwelling.

εἰσ-οικίζομαι P. to settle oneself.   [into.]

εἰσ-οικοδομέω to build

εἰσ-οιχνέω to step into.

εἰσόκε adv. until; as long as.

εἰσ-οπίσω adv. in future.

εἴσ-οπτος 2 visible.

εἰσ-οράω to look into, upon, or at; to view, behold; to descry. perceive; to consider.

εἰσ-ορμάω and P. to force one's way into.

ἔτσος, εἴσος = ἴσος.

εἰσ-παίω to dash in.   [in.]

εἰσ-πέμπω to send or bring

εἰσ-πέτομαι M. to fly into; to arrive at.

εἰσ-πηδάω to jump into.

εἰσ-πίπτω to fall into. rush

into; to invade, attack, fall upon; to be thrown into.

εἰσ-πλέω to sail into.

εἴσ-πλους, ὁ a sailing in; entrance of a harbour.

εἰσ-ποιέω to put in; to add; to give to be adopted.

εἰσ-πορεύομαι P. to go into. to enter.

εἰσ-πρᾶξις, ἡ exaction of money.   [act, collect.]

εἰσ-πράσσω and M. to ex-

εἰσ-ρέω to flow into.

εἰσ-τίθημι to put or place into or upon.

εἰσ-τοξεύω to shoot into.

εἰσ-τρέχω to run into.

εἰσ-φέρω to carry or bring into; to bring in; to contribute, pay (an income-tax); to bring forward, propose. — M. to carry with one, to import. — P. to get into.

εἰσ-φορέω = εἰσφέρω.

εἰσ-φρέω to let in, admit.

εἰσ-χειρίζω to hand over to.

εἰσ-χέω to pour into.

ἔσω, ἔσω adv. in(to a place), inward(s); within; between; within the reach of.

εἰσ-ωθέομαι M. to force one's way into.

εἰσ-ωπός 2 in front of.

εἶτα adv. then; after, further; and then, and yet; therefore.

εἴτε ... εἴτε conj. either ... or; whether ... or.

εἴωθα pf. of ἔθω.

εἰωθότως adv. in the wonted way.

εἴως = ἕως.

ἐκ, ἐξ prp. with gen. out of, from, from among, without, far from; since, immediately after; on the part of, because of, in consequence of; accordingly.

ἑκά-εργος 2 working from afar. [far off.]

ἕκα-θεν adv. from afar;

ἑκάς adv. far off; prp. with gen. far from.

ἑκασταχόθεν adv. from every side.

ἑκασταχόθι, ἑκασταχοῦ, ἑκάστοθι adv.everywhere.

ἑκασταχόσε adv. to all sides.

ἕκαστος 3 every, every one, εἷς ἕκαστος each one.

ἑκάστοτε adv. every time.

ἑκατεράκις adv. (at) both times.

ἑκάτερθεν = ἑκατέρωθεν.

ἑκάτερος 3 each of (the) two, either; pl. both, both parties.

ἑκατέρωθεν adv. from each side. [side.]

ἑκατέρωσε adv. to each

ἑκατη-βελέτης, ου, ὁ, ἑκατη-βόλος 2 far-shooting. never failing.

ἕκᾱτι = ἕκητι.

ἑκατόγ-χειρος 2 with a hundred hands.

ἑκατό-ζυγος 2 with a hundred rowing-benches.

ἑκατόμ-βη, ἡ hecatomb (a sacrifice of a hundred oxen).

ἑκατόμ-βοιος 2 worth a hundred oxen.

ἑκατόμ-πεδος 2, -ποδος 2 a hundred feet long.

ἑκατόμ-πολις 2 with a hundred towns.

ἑκατόμ-πους, ποδος with a hundred feet. [gated.]

ἑκατόμ-πυλος 2 hundred-

ἑκατόν, οἱ, αἱ. τά a hundred.

ἑκατοντα-έτης 2 a hundred years old.

ἑκατοντα-πλασίων 2 hundredfold, centuple.

ἑκατοντ-άρχης, ου, ὁ, ἑκατόντ-αρχος, ου, ὁ centurion.

ἑκατοντάς, άδος, ἡ the number one hundred.

ἕκατος, ὁ = ἑκηβόλος.

ἑκατοστός 3 the hundredth.

ἑκατοστύς, ύος, ἡ = ἑκατοντάς.

ἐκ-βαίνω to step, go, or come out, disembark, leave; to depart from; to turn out, to happen; to digress. trans. to put on shore; to transgress. [tic.]

ἐκ-βακχεύω to make fran-

ἐκ-βάλλω to throw or cast out; to expel, banish; to cast away; to fell; to strike out; to let fall, drop, to lose; to reject; to recant.

ἔκ-βασις, ἡ a disembarking, landing; egress; mountain-pass; ascent.

ἐκ-βάω = ἐκβαίνω.

ἐκ-βιάζομαι P. to be wrested from.

ἐκ-βιβάζω to make step out; to lead away.

ἐκ-βλαστάνω to sprout out.

ἐκ-βοάω to cry out, shout.

ἐκ-βοήθεια, ἡ a marching out to aid; sally.

ἐκ-βοηθέω to march out to aid; to sally out.

ἐκ-βολή, ἡ a throwing out, expulsion, banishment; outlet, defile; digression; loss; what is cast out; a shooting forth; origin.

ἔκ-βολος 2 cast out; ὁ ἔκβολος promontory, beach.

ἐκ-βράσσω to throw up on shore, to cast ashore.

ἐκ-βρῡχάομαι M. to roar out.

ἔκ-βρωμα, τό what is eaten out. [in marriage.]

ἐκ-γαμίζω to give away]

ἐκ-γαμίσκομαι P. to be given in marriage.

ἐκ-γελάω to laugh loud.

ἐκ-γενής 2 without family.

ἐκ-γί(γ)νομαι to be born (of), to spring from, to descend from; to have gone by or elapsed; to be permitted.

ἔκ-γονος 2 descended; descendant, offspring, relation, pl. posterity.

ἐκ-δακρῡω to burst into tears. [oneself up.]

ἐκ-δαπανάω P. to offer]

ἔκ-δεια, ἡ a falling short; being in arrears.

ἐκ-δείκνῡμι to show openly.

ἐκ-δέκομαι = ἐκδέχομαι.

ἔκ-δεξις, ἡ succession.

ἐκ-δέρκομαι to look out from.

ἐκ-δέρω to flay (off).

ἐκ-δέχομαι M. to take or receive from; to take upon oneself; to acquire, learn; to succeed, follow; to wait, expect.

ἐκ-δέω to fasten or bind to; to shut in. — M. to put on.

ἔκ-δηλος 2 quite plain, manifest; excellent.

ἐκ-δημέω to go or be abroad, to travel.

ἔκ-δημος 2 abroad, (away) from home. [through.]

ἐκ-διαβαίνω to step quite]

ἐκ-διαιτάομαι to depart from one's mode of life.

ἐκ-διδάσκω to teach thoroughly. [escape.]

ἐκ-διδράσκω to run away,]

ἐκ-δίδωμι to give out or up, to surrender; to give away in marriage; to lend out, to let out (on hire); intr. to run out (into).

ἐκ-διηγέομαι M. to tell to the end.

ἐκ-δικέω to avenge, punish; to defend, vindicate.

ἐκ-δίκησις, ἡ punishment, revenge. [avenging.]

ἔκ-δικος 2 lawless, unjust;]

ἐκ-διώκω to expel.

ἔκ-δοσις, ἡ a surrendering; giving in marriage.

ἔκ-δοτος 2 surrendered.

ἐκ-δοχή, ἡ expectation; succession.

ἐκ-δρομή, ἡ sally, raid; scouring party.

ἔκ-δρομος 2 skirmisher.

ἐκ-δύνω = ἐκδύομαι.

ἔκ-δυσις, ἡ a slipping out, escape; final event.

ἐκ-δύω to strip off; intr. and M. to strip oneself of, to put off; to escape.

ἐκ-δωριόομαι P. to become quite a Dorian.

ἐκεῖ adv. there; thither; then; in that case.

ἐκεῖθεν adv. thence; from that time; therefore,

ἐκεῖθι, ἐκείνη = ἐκεῖ.

ἐκεῖνος, η, ο (= Lat. ille) that.

ἐκεῖσε, adv. thither; then.

ἐκε-χειρία, ἡ armistice.

ἐκ-ζέω to boil out; to swarm with. [to avenge.]

ἐκ-ζητέω to search eagerly;

ἐκ-ζήτησις, ἡ matter of dispute. [from afar.]

ἐκη-βολίᾱ, ἡ a shooting

ἐκη-βόλος, ὁ shooter, archer.

ἔκηλος 2 quiet, at one's ease; untroubled.

ἕκητι, adv. at the pleasure of; for the sake of.

ἐκ-θαμβέομαι P to be amazed.

ἔκ-θαμβος 2 quite amazed.

ἐκ-θαυμάζω to wonder, be astonished. [the end.]

ἐκ-θεάομαι M. to see to

ἔκ-θεσις, ἡ exposure of a child.

ἔκ-θετος 2 exposed.

ἐκ-θέω to run out; to sally.

ἐκ-θηρεύω to catch.

ἐκ-θλίβω to force away.

ἐκ-θνήσκω to be dying.

ἐκ-θρῴσκω to leap out or down. [passionate.]

ἔκ-θῡμος 2 courageous;

ἐκ-θύω to offer for atonement. — M. to atone for.

ἐκ-καθαίρω to cleanse, purify; to clear away.

ἐκ-καθεύδω to sleep out of doors.

ἐκ-καί-δεκα sixteen.

ἐκκαιδεκά-δωρος sixteen palms long.

ἐκκαιδεκά-πηχυς, υ sixteen cubits long.

ἐκ-καίω to burn out; to kindle, inflame.

ἐκ-κακέω to get tired, to grow weary.

ἐκ-καλέω to call out to oneself; to call forth, exhort, excite.

ἐκ-καλύπτω to uncover.

ἐκ-κάμνω to get tired, grow weary; to fall short.

ἐκ-καρπόομαι M. to enjoy the fruit of. [down.]

ἐκ-καταπάλλομαι to leap

ἔκ-κειμαι to be exposed, to lie there at large.

ἐκ-κενόω to empty; to unpeople, depopulate.

ἐκ-κεντέω to pierce.

ἐκ-κηρύσσω to proclaim by a herald; to banish.

ἐκ-κῑνέω to move out; to stir; to expel.

ἐκ-κίω to go out.

ἐκ-κλάω to break in or to pieces.

ἐκ-κλείω to shut out; to hinder, oppress.

ἐκ-κλέπτω to remove by stealth; to abduct; to deceive.

ἐκκλησίᾱ, ἡ assembly of citizens or soldiers; corporation; church; assembly-room.

ἐκ-κλησιάζω to call together an assembly; to sit in assembly.

ἐκκλησιαστής, οῦ, ὁ partaker of an assembly.

ἔκ-κλητος 2 called forth; member of an assembly.

ἐκ-κλίνω to bend aside. *intr.* to turn away; to give way; to withdraw; to degenerate.

ἐκ-κνάω to rub off.

ἐκ-κολάπτω to chisel off.

ἐκ-κολυμβάω to swim out of.   [out; a saving.)

ἐκ-κομιδή, ἡ a bringing)

ἐκ-κομίζω to carry or bring away; to save.

ἐκ-κομπάζω to boast.

ἐκ-κοπή, ἡ hindrance.

ἐκ-κόπτω to knock out; to cut off or down, to fell; to demolish; to chase; to destroy.

ἐκ-κρέμαμαι *P.* to hang upon.   [upon; cling to.)

ἐκ-κρεμάννυμαι to hang)

ἐκ-κρίνω to single out; to choose, select.

ἔκ-κριτος 2 chosen.

ἐκ-κρούω to beat out; to expel, drive away; to frustrate, thwart.   [merset.)

ἐκ-κυβιστάω to turn a so-)

ἐκ-κυλίνδω, ἐκ-κυλίω to roll out. — *P.* to be rolled out; to tumble out of.

ἐκ-κυμαίνω to undulate; to make the front-line uneven.   [lot).)

ἐκ-λαγχάνω to obtain (by)

ἐκ-λαλέω to speak or let out.

ἐκ-λαμβάνω to take out of; to choose; to receive; to perceive, understand.

ἐκ-λάμπω to shine forth.

ἐκ-λανθάνω to escape notice; to make forget. — *M.* to forget utterly.

ἐκ-λέγω to pick out, choose; to collect; to exact.

ἐκ-λείπω to leave out, omit; to forsake, abandon; to be unmindful (of), neglect; *intr.* to cease, disappear; to run short; to die; to be eclipsed.

ἔκ-λειψις, ἡ a forsaking; a disappearing; loss; eclipse.

ἐκ-λεκτός 3 selected.

ἐκ-λέπω to hatch.

ἐκ-λήγω to cease.

ἔκ-λησις, ἡ forgetfulness.

ἐκ-λιπής 2 wanting, failing, deficient; eclipsed.

ἐκ-λογή, ἡ choice, selection.

ἐκ-λογίζομαι *M.* to calculate, consider.   [ness.)

ἔκ-λυσις, ἡ release; weak-)

ἐκ-λυτήριος 2 releasing.

ἐκ-λύω to loose, set free, release, redeem; to dissolve, weaken, exhaust; to abrogate, put an end to. — *P.* to be exhausted or wearied out, to despond.

ἐκ-λωβάομαι *M.* to treat shamefully.

ἐκ-λωπίζω to uncover.

ἐκ-μαίνω to drive mad, enrage. — *P.* to rave, to be frantic.

ἐκ-μανθάνω to learn thoroughly; to learn by heart; to examine closely

ἐκ-μάσσω to wipe away.

ἐκ-μείρομαι to partake of.

ἐκ-μετρέω to measure out.

ἔκ-μηνος 2 of six months.

ἐκ-μηρύομαι *M.* to file off.

ἐκ-μῑμέομαι *M.* to imitate closely.   [farm out.]

ἐκ-μισθόω to let on hire,

ἐκ-μολεῖν to go out.

ἐκ-μυζάω to suck out.

ἐκ-μυκτηρίζω to mock at.

ἐκ-νέμω and *M.* to go forth.

ἐκ-νευρίζω to unnerve.

ἐκ-νεύω to nod away; *intr.* to turn aside.

ἐκ-νέω to swim out of or away; to escape. [again.]

ἐκ-νήφω to become sober]

ἐκ-νίζω to wash off; to expiate.

ἐκ-νῑκάω to become victorious; to prevail, be in use.

ἐκ-νοστέω to return again.

ἑκούσιος 2 and 3 = ἑκών.

ἐκ-παγλέομαι to be highly amazed, to wonder at.

ἔκ-παγλος 2 astonishing, frightful, terrible.

ἐκ-παιδεύω to educate thoroughly.

ἐκ-παιφάσσω to shine forth.

ἔκ-παλαι *adv.* of old, long since.   [out.]

ἐκ-πάλλομαι *M.* to spirt]

ἐκ-πατάσσω to knock out.

ἐκ-παύομαι *M.* to cease entirely.

ἐκ-πείθω to persuade.

ἐκ-πειράομαι *P.* and ἐκ-πειράζω to try, test.

ἐκ-πέλει = ἔξεστι it is allowed.

ἐκ-πέμπω to send out or away; to export; to convey; to chase, banish; to dismiss; to send for.

ἔκ-πεμψις, ἡ a sending away.

ἐκ-πεπταμένως *adv.* extravagantly. [end.achieve.]

ἐκ-περαίνω to bring to an]

ἐκ-περάω to go or pass through or along. [terly.]

ἐκ-πέρθω to destroy ut-]

ἐκ-πετάννῡμι to spread out.   [forth; to rush on.]

ἐκ-πηδάω to leap out or]

ἐκ-πίμπλημι to fill up; to satiate, satisfy; to spend; to atone for.

ἐκ-πίνω to drink out, to drain; to drink up.

ἐκ-πιπράσκω to sell out.

ἐκ-πίπτω to fall out of or down; to fall from, depart from; to be hissed off; to step short; to turn out, result; to lose; to cease; to be confounded; to be banished, driven out of; to be wrecked or cast on shore; to come or sally forth; to escape; to empty itself.

ἐκ-πλέω to sail out, leave port; to swim out; to outsail.

ἔκ-πλεως, ων filled up, full; complete, abundant.

ἐκ-πλήγνῡμι = ἐκπλήσσω.

ἐκ-πληκτικός 3 terrifying.

ἔκ-πληξις, ἡ fright, terror, perplexity, consternation; awe.

ἐκ-πληρόω = ἐκπίμπλημι.

ἐκ-πλήρωσις, ἡ a filling up, completion.

ἐκ-πλήσσω to strike out, drive away; to frighten, astound. — *P.* to be out of one's senses, to be amazed, frightened or panic-struck.

ἔκ-πλοος, ὁ a sailing out; port of departure.

ἐκ-πλύνω to wash out.

ἐκ-πλώω = ἐκπλέω.

ἐκ-πνέω to breathe out, forth, or away; *intr.* to expire, to be killed; to blow along.

ἐκ-ποδών *adv.* out of the way, away.

ἐκ-ποιέω to complete, finish; to build up.

ἐκ-ποίησις, ἡ emission of seed.

ἐκ-πολεμέω to make war from; to excite to war.

ἐκ-πολιορκέω to take by assault or siege, to overpower.

ἐκ-πομπή, ἡ a sending out.

ἐκ-πονέω to work out, finish, execute; to digest; to bring to perfection; to train; to be eager.

ἐκ-πορεύομαι *P.* to march or go out. [plunder.]

ἐκ-πορθέω to devastate,]

ἐκ-πορίζω to make out; to contrive; to provide.

ἐκ-πορνεύω to be given to lewdness. [from.]

ἐκ-ποτέομαι to fly down]

ἐκ-πράττω to finish, to achieve, effect, kill; to exact punishment; to avenge. — *M.* to avenge.

ἐκ-πρεπής 2 prominent, excellent, extraordinary.

ἐκ-πρίασθαι *aor.* see ἐξωνέομαι.

ἐκ-πρίω to saw off or out.

ἐκ-προκαλέομαι *M.* to call forth to oneself.

ἐκ-προλείπω to forsake.

ἐκ-προτῑμάω to honour above others. [detest.]

ἐκ-πτύω to spit out; to]

ἐκ-πυνθάνομαι *M.* to search out; to hear, of.

ἐκ-πυρόω to set on fire.

ἔκ-πυστος 2 known, notorious.

ἔκ-πωμα, τό drinking-cup.

ἐκ-ραίνω to sputter out.

ἐκ-ρέω to flow out; to vanish.

ἐκ-ρήγνῡμι to break out or off, to tear in or to pieces; *intr.* and *P.* to sally forth, to burst out; to become known.

ἐκ-ριζόω to root out.

ἐκ-ρίπτω to throw out.

ἐκ-ροή, ἡ, **ἔκ-ροος**, ὁ outflow.

ἐκ-σαόω = ἐκ-σῴζω.

ἐκ-σείω to shake out.

ἐκ-σεύομαι *P.* to rush out, to hasten away.

ἐκ-σημαίνω to signify.

ἐκ-σμάω to wipe out or off.

ἐκ-σπάω to draw out.

ἔκ-σπονδος 2 excluded from treaty. [trance.]

ἔκ-στασις, ἡ astonishment,]

ἐκ-στέλλω to equip; to send out. [garlands.]

ἐκ-στέφω to adorn with]

ἐκ-στρατεύω and *M.* to march out to war; to end war. [encamp outside.]

ἐκ-στρατοπεδεύομαι *M.*to]

ἐκ-στρέφω to turn or pull out; to turn inside out; to change, make worse.

ἐκ-σῴζω to save.

ἐκ-τάδιος 3 and 2 far off.

ἐκταῖος 3 on the sixth day.

ἐκ-τανύω = ἐκ-τείνω.

ἐκ-ταράσσω to confound, trouble. [out in order.]

ἐκ-τάσσω to arrange, draw

ἐκ-τείνω to stretch out, extend; to draw out; to strain; to prostrate.

ἐκ-τειχίζω to build or fortify completely.

ἐκ-τελέω to finish, bring to an end, achieve, satisfy; to spend (time).

ἐκ-τέμνω to cut out from, to cut off; to castrate.

ἐκ-τένεια, ἡ zeal.

ἐκ-τενής 2 zealous, earnest, assiduous. [trive, devise.]

ἐκ-τεχνάομαι M. to con-

ἐκ-τίθημι to put out or outside; to explain.

ἐκ-τιμάω to honour much.

ἔκ-τιμος 2 not honouring.

ἐκ-τινάσσω to strike or shake out or off.

ἐκ-τίνω to pay off, requite, make amends (for). — M. to punish.

ἐκ-τιτρώσκω to miscarry.

ἔκτοθεν = ἔκτοσθεν.

ἔκτοθι adv. outside.

ἐκ-τομίας, ου, ὁ eunuch.

ἐκ-τοξεύω to shoot arrows out of; to spend in shooting.

ἐκ-τόπιος 3 and 2, ἔκ-τοπος 2 away from a place, distant; strange, extraordinary.

ἔκτος 3 the sixth.

ἐκτός adv. without, outside; out of, far from; without, except.

ἔκτοσε adv. outwards.

ἔκτοσθε(ν) adv. from without, outside. — prp. with gen. out of, far from.

ἐκ-τραχηλίζω to throw over the head, to throw down.

ἐκ-τρέπω to turn away or aside, divert; to drive away; to sprain; to dissuade from; to lead to. — P. and M. to turn (oneself) aside from; to deviate; to avoid.

ἐκ-τρέφω to feed, rear up.

ἐκ-τρέχω to run out; to sally forth; to degenerate.

ἐκ-τρίβω to rub out of; to destroy by rubbing.

ἐκ-τροπή, ἡ a turning off or aside; digression; sideway.

ἐκ-τρῡχόω to wear out.

ἔκ-τρωμα, τό abortion.

ἐκ-τυφλόω to make blind.

ἐκ-τύφλωσις, ἡ a making blind.

ἑκυρά, ἡ mother-in-law.

ἑκυρός, ὁ father-in-law.

ἐκ-φαίνω to show forth, to bring to light, reveal, betray. — P. to appear, come to light.

ἐκ-φανής 2 manifest.

ἔκ-φασις, ἡ a saying.

ἐκ-φαυλίζω to make bad, depreciate.

ἐκ-φέρω to carry out of or away; to bury; to begin (war); to carry off (a prize); to steal; to lead out or away; to accomplish; to speak out, tell; to produce; to bring to light; to proclaim, publish; to put to sea; to run ahead. — *P.* to come forth; to come to; to be agitated. [escape.]

ἐκ-φεύγω to flee away.

ἔκ-φημι to speak out.

ἐκ-φθίνω to consume, destroy. [*P.* to fear.]

ἐκ-φοβέω to frighten. —

ἔκ-φοβος 2 frightened.

ἐκ-φοιτάω to go out or away.

ἐκ-φορά, ἡ burial.

ἐκ-φορέω = ἐκφέρω,

ἐκ-φόριον, τό produce, crop; rent. [known.]

ἔκ-φορος 2 to be made]

ἐκ-φορτίζω to sell away.

ἐκ-φροντίζω to devise; to deliberate.

ἔκ-φρων 2 senseless, mad.

ἐκ-φυλάσσω to watch carefully.

ἐκ-φύω to cause to grow out of; to produce, beget; *intr.* and *M.* to grow from; to be born from.

ἐκ-χέω to pour out, shed, spill; to lavish, squander, spoil. — *P.* to stream out; to indulge in.

ἐκ-χράω[1] to suffice.

ἐκ-χράω[2] to declare; to give oracle.

ἐκ-χρηματίζομαι *M.* to extort money.

ἐκ-χώννῦμι to heap up earth; to fill with mud.

ἐκ-χωρέω to go away, depart; to make way. [last.]

ἐκ-ψύχω to breathe one's]

ἑκών, οὖσα, όν voluntary, willing; on purpose.

ἐλάα, ἐλαίᾱ, ἡ olive-tree; olive. [olive-wood.]

ἐλάϊνεος, ἐλάϊνος 3 of]

ἔλαιον, τό olive-oil.

ἔλαιος, ὁ wild olive-tree.

ἐλαιών, ῶνος, ὁ olive-garden.

ἔλασις, ἡ a driving, chasing; a riding, march, expedition; attack.

ἐλασσόω to make less, to damage. — *P.* to become smaller, to decrease; to be a loser, to come short of.

ἐλάσσων 2 *comp.* of ἐλαχύς.

ἐλαστρέω to drive, row.

ἐλάτη, ἡ pine, fir; oar; canoe. [waggoner.]

ἐλατήρ, ῆρος, ὁ driver,]

ἐλάτινος 3 of pine-wood.

ἐλαττονέω to be or have less.

ἐλάττωμα, τό loss, want.

ἐλαύνω to drive, drive on, lead; to chase, expel; to vex, press; to strike, beat, hit, hurt, wound; to beat out (metal); to draw out; to build; to produce. — *intr* to drive, ride, row, march, advance.

ἐλάφειος 2 of deer.

ἐλαφη-βολίᾱ, ἡ deer-hunt.

ἐλαφη-βολιών, ῶνος, ὁ ninth month of the Athenian calendar (March-April).

ἐλαφη-βόλος 2 deer-hunter.

ἔλαφος, ἡ and ὁ deer, stag, hind. [ness.]

ἐλαφρίᾱ, ἡ light-minded-]

ἐλαφρός 3 light, swift, nimble; active; light-armed; easy, without trouble.

ἐλαχίστερος 3 smaller, the smallest.

ἐλαχύς 3 little, small; *comp.* ἐλάσσων 2 smaller, less, worse, inferior; *superl.* ἐλάχιστος 3 (the) smallest, least, shortest.

ἐλάω = ἐλαύνω.

ἔλδομαι, ἐέλδομαι to wish, long for; to be wished for.

ἐλεαίρω, ἐλεάω = ἐλεέω.

ἐλεγεῖον, τό distich.

ἐλεγμός, ὁ and ἔλεγξις, ἡ a convincing, refuting; a blaming.

ἐλεγχείη, ἡ = ἔλεγχος, τό.

ἐλεγχής 2 shameful; cowardly; wretched.

ἔλεγχος[1], τό reproach, disgrace; coward.

ἔλεγχος[2], ὁ means of proving, proof, trial; conviction, refutation, reproach; test, examination; account; sentence, judgment.

ἐλέγχω to revile, blame, reproach; to put to shame; to despise, reject; to convince, refute; to prove, show; to examine, search, question.

ἐλεεινός 2 pitiable, pitied, miserable; pitiful.

ἐλεέω to have pity (upon), to pity. [mercy; alms.]

ἐλεημοσύνη, ἡ charity,

ἐλεήμων 2 pitiful.

ἐλεητύς, ύος, ἡ pity, mercy.

ἐλεινός 3 = ἐλεεινός.

ἕλειος 2 living in swamps.

ἐλελίζω[1] to raise the warcry.

ἐλελίζω[2] to cause to shake or tremble; to whirl round, to turn round quickly. — *P.* to tremble, shake; to turn oneself quickly. — *M.* to coil. [ing.]

ἐλελί-χθων 2 earth-shak-

ἐλεό-θρεπτος 2 swamp-bred. [dresser.]

ἐλεός, ὁ kitchen-table;

ἔλεος, ὁ (and τό) pity, mercy.

ἑλετός 3 to be caught.

ἐλευθερίᾱ, ἡ freedom, liberty; generosity.

ἐλευθέριος 3 like a free man, noble-minded, frank, liberal, noble; freeing, delivering; releaser.

ἐλεύθερος 3 free, freeborn, independent; free from, freed; liberal, free-spirited; noble, honest.

ἐλευθερόω to set free, release, acquit.

ἐλευθέρωσις, ἡ a setting free, release. [rival.]

ἔλευσις, ἡ a coming, ar-

ἐλεφαίρομαι *M.* to deceive.

ἐλεφάντινος 3 of ivory.

ἐλέφᾱς, αντος, ὁ ivory; elephant. [medley.]

ἕλιγμα, τό what is rolled;

ἐλιγμός, ὁ a winding; a rolling. [of the ear.]

ἑλικτήρ, ῆρος, ὁ pendant

ἑλικτός 3 rolled, wreathed.

ἑλίκ-ωψ, ωπος and ἑλικ-ῶπις, ιδος with bright eyes.

ἐλῑνύω to rest, repose.

ἕλιξ[1], ικος twisted; with twisted horns.

ἕλιξ[2], ικος, ἡ a winding, torsion, coil, curl; circle;

spiral line; bracelet, earring.

ἑλίσσω to turn about or round; to roll, whirl; swing; to wind, wrap round; to revolve, reflect. — *P.* and *M.* to turn round, coil; to move quickly, to spin round; to reflect.

ἑλκεσί-πεπλος 2, ἑλκε-χίτων, ωνος with trailing robe.

ἑλκέω = ἕλκω.

ἑλκηθμός, ὁ a dragging away.

ἕλκος, τό wound; ulcer; evil. [to ulcerate.]

ἑλκόω to wound. — *P.*]

ἑλκυστάζω to drag along.

ἑλκύω, ἕλκω to draw, drag, pull, tear; to maltreat; to bend or draw (a bow, sail), to draw up or down; to weigh; to tear off (the hair); to draw out, stretch.

ἕλκωσις, ἡ ulceration.

ἐλ-λάμπομαι *M.* to shine forth. [hellebore.]

ἑλλέβορος, ὁ sneezewort,]

ἑλλεδανός, ὁ straw-rope.

ἔλ-λειμμα, τό a short-coming.

ἐλ-λείπω to leave behind; to leave out, omit, neglect *intr.* and *P.* to be left, to remain; to be inferior, to lack, to come short of: to be needed.

ἔλ-λειψις. ἡ deficiency.

ἔλ-λεσχος 2 subject to public talk.

ἑλληνίζω to speak Greek; to make Greek.

ἑλληνικῶς, ἑλληνιστί *adv.* in Greek fashion; in Greek.

ἐλ-λιπής 2 wanting, defective; inferior.

ἐλ-λογάω, -έω to impute.

ἐλ-λόγιμος 2 considerable, notable, excellent.

ἑλλός[1], ὁ young deer, fawn.

ἑλλός[2] 3 mute. [(for).]

ἐλ-λοχάω to lie in wait]

ἐλ-λύχνιον, τό lamp-wick.

ἕλος, τό marsh, swamp; meadow.

ἐλπίζω to hope, expect; to think; to fear.

ἐλπίς, ίδος, ἡ hope, expectation; opinion; fear.

ἔλπω to cause to hope. — *M.* = ἐλπίζω.

ἐλπωρή, ἡ = ἐλπίς.

ἔλυτρον, τό cover, case; cistern, reservoir.

ἐλύω = εἰλύω.

ἐλωΐ, ἐλωεί (Hebr.) my God!

ἔλωρ, ωρος and ἑλώριον, τό booty, prey, spoil; spoliation, murder.

ἐμ-βαδόν *adv.* on foot.

ἐμ-βαίνω to step in or into, to enter; to go on board, embark; to mount; to tread upon; to be fixed upon; to step on; to intervene. — *trans.* to bring into.

ἐμ-βάλλω to throw, put, or lay in: to throw upon; to inject, cause; *intr.* to make an inroad; to attack; to take in hand; to encounter, to rush against; to run out into.

ἐμ-βαμμα, τό sauce, soup.

ἐμ-βάπτω to dip in.

ἐμ-βάς, άδος, ἡ shoe, slipper. [over.]

ἐμ-βασιλεύω to be king.

ἐμ-βατεύω to step along, in, or upon; to enter on possession; to persist in.

ἐμ-βάφιον, τό bowl, vessel.

ἐμ-βιβάζω to bring in; to put on board.

ἐμ-βλέπω to look at.

ἐμ-βοάω to shout aloud, to call to.

ἐμ-βολή, ἡ a throwing in, shot; attack, inroad; stroke (of a ship in battle); leak; head of a battering-ram; entrance, pass; mouth of a river. [tercalary.]

ἐμ-βόλιμος 2 inserted, in-

ἐμ-βολον, τό and ἔμ-βολος, ὁ wedge; tongue of land between two rivers; cuneiform order of battle; beak of a ship.

ἔμ-βραχυ adv. in short.

ἐμ-βρέμομαι M. to roar in.

ἐμ-βρῑθής 2 weighty, heavy, firm; grave.

ἐμ-βρῑμάομαι to snap one short, to be indignant.

ἐμ-βροντάω to thunder at; to stun.

ἐμ-βρόντητος 2 thunderstricken; frightened, stupid.

ἔμ-βρυον, τό little lamb.

ἔμετος, ὁ a vomiting.

ἐμέω to vomit; to spit out.

ἐμ-μαίνομαι P. to rave, to be mad.

ἐμ-μανής 2 raving, mad.

ἐμ-μαπέως adv. at once, quickly.

ἐμ-μάχομαι M. to fight in.

ἐμ-μέλεια, ἡ harmony; tune; dance.

ἐμ-μελής 2 harmonious, in tune; correct, regular, fit, agreeable; elegant, witty.

ἐμ-μεμαώς, υῖα, ός eager, hasty, ardent, impetuous.

ἐμ-μέμονα to be agitated.

ἐμ-μενής 2 steady, unceasing.

ἐμ-μένω to abide in; to remain steadfast, to keep to; to continue.

ἔμ-μετρος 2 in measure, moderate; metrical.

ἔμ-μηνος 2 happening every month. [involve in.]

ἐμ-μίγνῡμι to mix in; to

ἔμ-μισθος 2 in pay, hired; earning money.

ἐμ-μονή, ἡ an abiding in; continuance. [steadfast.]

ἔμ-μονος 2 abiding in,

ἔμ-μορος 2 partaking in.

ἐμός 3 my, mine.

ἐμ-πάζομαι to care for.

ἐμ-παιγμονή, ἡ and ἐμπαιγμός, ὁ a jesting, mocking.

ἐμ-παίζω to mock, jest, trifle with; to deceive.

ἐμ-παίκτης, ου, ὁ mocker.

ἐμ-παιος 2 skilled, practised (in). [entangle.]

ἐμ-παίω to strike in; to

ἔμ-παλιν (τό) adv. backwards, back; contrary to, in the reverse order; on the other side or hand.

ἐμ-παρέχω to offer, to hand over; to abandon.

ἔμ-πας adv. altogether, at

all events, on the whole, throughout; yet, in spite of; although. [embroider.]

ἐμ-πάσσω to strew in; to bind with fetters, to check.

ἐμ-πεδάω to bind with fetters, to check.

ἐμπεδ-ορκέω to abide by one's oath.

ἔμ-πεδος 2 steadfast, unmoved, firm; certain; continuous. [fastly.]

ἐμ-πεδόω to keep stead-]

ἐμ-πειρίᾱ, ἡ experience, knowledge, skill, practise.

ἔμ-πειρος 2 experienced, skilful; proved by experience.

ἐμ-περιπατέω to walk about in. [thrust in.]

ἐμ-πήγνῡμι to fix in; to]

ἔμ-πηρος 2 crippled.

ἔμπης = ἔμπας.

ἐμ-πικραίνομαι P. to be imbittered.

ἐμ-πί(μ)πλημι to fill full or up; to satiate. — P. and M. to fill oneself; to be satisfied or satiated; to get tired of.

ἐμ-πί(μ)πρημι to set on fire, burn; to blow into.

ἐμ-πίνω to drink in.

ἐμ-πίπτω to fall in or upon; to rush into, to throw oneself into; to attack, assault, to invade, burst in; to fall in with; to come over, to seize.

ἐμπίς, ίδος, ἡ gnat.

ἐμ-πίτνω = ἐμπίπτω.

ἐμ-πλάσσω to plaster up.

ἔμ-πλειος 3 = ἔμπλεος.

ἐμ-πλέκω to plait in; to entangle.

ἔμ-πλεος 2 full, filled up.

ἐμ-πλέω to sail in or on.

ἐμ-πλήγδην adv. rashly, at random.

ἔμ-πληκτος 2 out of countenance, perplexed; rash; fickle.

ἔμ-πλην adv. close by.

ἐμ-πλήσσω to fall into.

ἐμ-πλοκή, ἡ a plaiting in.

ἐμ-πνέω to breathe in or on; to breathe, live; to inspire. — P. to recover oneself. [breathing, alive.]

ἔμ-πνοος, ἔμ-πνους 2]

ἐμ-ποδίζω to bind, fetter; to be in the way of, to hinder; to make doubtful; to cause to fall.

ἐμ-πόδιος 2 impeding.

ἐμ-πόδισμα, τό hindrance.

ἐμ-ποδών adv. before the feet, in the way, as a hindrance; what comes in one's way.

ἐμ-ποιέω to make or put in, insert; to cause, inspire, suggest.

ἐμ-πολάω to buy, purchase; to earn, gain by selling. — M. to acquire by trade; to bribe. [in war.]

ἐμ-πολέμιος 2 taking place]

ἐμ-πολή, ἡ traffic; merchandise. [sold.]

ἐμ-πολητός 3 bought and]

ἔμ-πολις, ὁ fellow-citizen.

ἐμ-πολιτεύω to be a citizen.

ἐμ-πορεύομαι P. to travel to. — M. to trade, traffic; to overreach.

ἐμ-πορίᾱ, ἡ traffic, trade. commerce, business.

9*

ἐμ-πορικός 3 commercial.

ἐμ-πόριον, τό trading-place; pack-house.

ἔμ-πορος, ὁ passenger (on a ship); traveller; merchant, trader; furnisher.

ἐμ-πορπάομαι M. to fix on with a brooch.

ἐμ-πρέπω to excel.

ἐμ-πρήθω = ἐμπίπρημι.

ἔμ-πρησις, ἡ a setting on fire, ignition.

ἔμ-προσθεν adv. before, in front of, anterior, earlier.

ἐμ-πτύω to spit upon or at.

ἔμ-πυος 2 purulent.

ἐμ-πῠρι-βήτης, ου standing over the fire.

ἔμ-πῠρος 2 in or on the fire; τὰ -α burnt sacrifice. [low.]

ἐμ-φαγεῖν to eat up, swallow.

ἐμ-φαίνω to show, to make visible or conspicuous. — P. to show oneself, to appear.

ἐμ-φανής 2 conspicuous, visible; manifest, clear; known, public.

ἐμ-φανίζω = ἐμ-φαίνω.

ἐμ-φερής 2 equivalent, similar.

ἐμ-φέρω to hold up to, to object to. [tened.]

ἔμ-φοβος 2 fearful; frightened.

ἐμ-φορέω to bear in; to object to. — P. to be borne about; to enjoy fully; to do to excess. [up.]

ἐμ-φράσσω to stop or block.

ἐμ-φρουρέω to keep guard in. [garrisoned.]

ἔμ-φρουρος on guard in;

ἔμ-φρων 2 sensible; prudent.

ἔμ-φῦλιος 2, ἔμ-φῦλος 2 of the same tribe, native; kindred.

ἐμ-φῦσάω to breathe upon.

ἐμ-φυτεύω to (im)plant.

ἔμ-φῠτος 2 inborn, innate, implanted.

ἐμ-φύω to implant; intr. and M. to grow into; to be rooted in; to cling to; to be inborn or innate, to be in.

ἔμ-ψῠχος 2 souled, alive.

ἐν adv. within; with; upon; besides. — prp. with dat. in, at, on; between, among; during, within; by means of, with, through; from; upon, by dint of.

ἐν-αγής 2 guilty, polluted; bound by an oath. [dead.]

ἐν-αγίζω to sacrifice for the

ἐν-αγκαλίζομαι M. to take in one's arms.

ἐν-αγκυλάω to provide with a leash.

ἔν-αγχος adv. just now, lately, the other day.

ἐν-άγω to lead in, on, or to; to urge, incite, promote.

ἐν-αγωνίζομαι M. to contend in, on, or among. to be one of the prize-fighters.

ἔν-αιμος 2 filled with blood. [undo, destroy.]

ἐν-αίρω and M. to kill; to

ἐν-αίσιμος, ἐν-αίσιος 2 foreboding, auspicious, sent by fate; seemly, proper, fit; favourable.

ἐν-ακούω to listen to.

ἐν-αλείφω to anoint; to whitewash. [like.]

ἐν-αλίγκιος 2 resembling,

ἐν-άλιος 2 (and 3) in or of the sea.

ἐν-αλλάξ adv. alternately.

ἐν-αλλάσσω to exchange; to change, alter. — P. to deal with, to have intercourse with. [rush upon.]

ἐν-άλλομαι M. to leap on,

ἐν-αμέλγω to milk into.

ἐν-άμιλλος 2 a match for, equal to.

ἔν-αντα, ἔν-αντι adv. opposite, over against.

ἐναντί-βιον adv. against.

ἐν-αντίος 3 opposite, over against, facing; opposing, contrary, reverse, discordant, contradictory; hostile, adverse; enemy.

ἐναντιόω to place opposite. — P. to oppose oneself (to), to withstand, to be adverse to; to contradict; to forbid.

ἐναντίωμα, τό hindrance.

ἐναντίωσις, ἡ opposition.

ἐν-αποδείκνυμαι M. to distinguish oneself.

ἐν-αποθνήσκω to die in.

ἐν-αποκλάω to break off in.

ἐν-απόλλυμαι to perish in.

ἐν-απονίζομαι to wash oneself in.

ἐν-άπτω to fasten or bind to; to kindle. — M. to clothe oneself.

ἔναρα, τά armour; spoil.

ἐν-άργεια, ἡ distinctness.

ἐν-αργής 2 visible; distinct, bright, manifest.

ἐν-αρηρώς, υῖα, ός fastened in. [dite.]

ἐνάρης, ους, ὁ hermaphro-

ἐναρίζω to strip of arms; to slay. [among.]

ἐν-αριθμέω to reckon

ἐν-αρίθμιος 2, ἐν-αρίθμος 2 counted among; esteemed.

ἐν-άρχομαι M. to begin.

ἐναταῖος 3 on the ninth day.

ἔνατος 3 ninth.

ἐν-αυλίζω and P., M. to pass the night in; to stop for the night.

ἔν-αυλος[1], ὁ torrent; water-channel. [ears.]

ἔν-αυλος[2] 2 ringing in one's

ἔν-αυλος[3] 2 dwelling in.

ἐν-αύω to kindle.

ἐν-αφίημι to put in.

ἐν-δατέομαι M. to distribute. — P. to be portioned out.

ἐν-δεής 2 needy, wanting, lacking; deficient, incomplete; inferior, worse, less.

ἔνδεια, ἡ want, need.

ἔν-δειγμα, τό proof.

ἐν-δείκνυμι to mark out; to denounce. — M. to display, make known, prove; to declare oneself; to show, to hold out a prospect of.

ἔν-δειξις, ἡ a marking out, proof.

ἔν-δεκα, οἱ, αἱ eleven.

ἐνδεκά-πηχυς, υ eleven cubits long.

ἐνδέκατος 3 eleventh.

ἐν-δέχομαι = ἐνδέχομαι.

ἐνδελεχής 2 continual.

ἐν-δέμω to build in.

ἐν-δέξιος 3 on or to the right hand; propitious, favourable.

ἐν-δέχομαι *M.* to take upon oneself; to believe; to approve of, admit; ἐνδέχεται it is possible *or* allowed.

ἐν-δέω[1] to bind to.

ἐν-δέω[2] to be in want (of); to be wanting; ἐνδεῖ μοι I am in want of. — *M.* to be in want *or* need of.

ἔν-δηλος 2 = δῆλος.

ἐν-δημέω to be at home.

ἔν-δημος 2 at home, native; intestine.

ἐν-διαιτάομαι *P.* to live *or* dwell in; to sojourn.

ἐν-διατάσσω to arrange in.

ἐν-διατρίβω to pass *or* spend in; to dwell on.

ἐν-διδύσκω to put on.

ἐν-δίδωμι to surrender, give up; to betray; to offer; to exhibit, show, prove; to cause; to give way (to); to admit. — *intr.* to surrender oneself; to yield; to empty oneself.

ἐν-δίημι to chase. [just.]

ἔν-δικος 2 legal, right,

ἔνδινα, τά entrails.

ἔν-διος 2 at midday.

ἐν-δίφριος, ὁ companion *or* neighbour at table.

ἔνδοθεν *adv.* from within; within.

ἔνδοθι *adv.* = ἔνδον.

ἐν-δοιάζω to waver, hesitate. — *P.* to be thought possible.

ἐνδοιαστός 3 doubtful.

ἐν-δόμησις, ἡ building, structure.

ἐνδό-μυχος 2 hidden in the inmost part.

ἔνδον *adv.* and *prp.* with *gen.* within, at home, at heart.

ἐνδοξάζω to glorify.

ἔν-δοξος 2 glorious, renowned; honoured.

ἐν-δουπέω to fall with a hollow sound.

ἐν-δυκέως *adv.* carefully, zealously, earnestly.

ἔν-δυμα, τό garment.

ἐν-δυναμόω to strengthen.

ἐν-δυναστεύω to rule in; to prevail (upon) by authority.

ἐν-δύνω, ἐν-δύνέω = ἐν-δύομαι see ἐνδύω.

ἐν-δύω to put on; to clothe. — *intr.* and *M.* to put on; to wear; to enter, go in; to undergo, to engage (oneself) in. [ambush.]

ἐν-έδρᾱ, ἡ a lying in wait;

ἐν-εδρεύω and *M.* to lie in wait *or* ambush.

ἔν-εδρος 2 inhabitant; τὸ ἔνεδρον = ἐνέδρα.

ἐν-ειλέω to press in; to wrap in.

ἐν-ειλίσσω = ἐνελίσσω.

ἐν-είλλω = ἐνειλέω.

ἔν-ειμι to be within, in, on, *or* at; to dwell in; to be present, extant; ἔνεστι *or* ἔνι it is possible.

ἐν-είρω to file on a string; to entwine; to join.

ἕνεκα, ἕνεκεν *prp.* with *gen.* on account of, for the sake of; with respect to, by force of.

ἐν-ελίσσω to wrap up in.

ἐν-εμέω to vomit in.

ἐνενήκοντα ninety.

ἐνενηκοστός 3 ninetieth.

ἐνεός 3 deaf and dumb; speechless.

ἐνέπω to speak, tell, relate; to address, accost.

ἐν-εργάζομαι M. to pursue one's calling at home; to make in; to create; to inject.

ἐν-έργεια, ἡ activity, efficacy, effect. [work.]

ἐν-εργέω to be active, to]

ἐν-έργημα, τό = ἐνέργεια.

ἐν-εργής 2 and ἐν-εργός 2 active, busy, working; fertile; effective, energetic.

ἐν-ερείδω to thrust in.

ἔνερθεν adv. from beneath; beneath, in the nether world. — prp. with gen. beneath.

ἔνεροι, οἱ the dead, those beneath the earth; comp. ἐνέρτερος 3 lower.

ἔν-ερσις, ἡ a putting in.

ἐν-ετή, ἡ pin, brooch.

ἐν-ετός 3 incited. [in.]

ἐν-ευδαιμονέω to be happy]

ἐν-ευδοκιμέω to make the most of for one's glory.

ἐν-εύδω to sleep in or on.

ἐν-εύναιον, τό bed-clothes, bed.

ἐν-έχυρον, τό pledge.

ἐν-έχω to keep within, to entertain, cherish; to be angry. — M. and P. to be held fast, to be caught; to be affected with.

ἐν-ζεύγνυμι to bind together, to fasten.

ἐν-ηβητήριον, τό place of amusement.

ἐνηείη, ἡ kindness.

ἐν-ηής 2 kind, friendly.

ἔν-ημαι to sit in. [up in.]

ἐνήνοθα perf. to mount]

ἔνθα adv. there; thither; where; then; when. [now.]

ἐνθάδε adv. thither; there;]

ἐν-θᾰκέω to sit on or in.

ἐν-θάκησις, ἡ a sitting in or on.

ἔνθαπερ adv. just where.

ἐνθαῦτα = ἐνταῦθα.

ἐν-θεάζω to be inspired.

ἔνθεν adv. thence, from there; whence; after that, since, thereupon.

ἐνθένδε adv. hence, henceforward.

ἔνθενπερ adv. just whence.

ἔν-θεος 2 inspired.

ἐν-θερμαίνω to heat through.

ἐνθεῦτεν = ἐντεῦθεν.

ἔν-θηρος 2 savage, wild.

ἐν-θνῄσκω to die in; to die of.

ἐνθουσιάζω to be inspired.

ἐνθουσιασμός, ὁ inspiration, ecstasy. [upon.]

ἐν-θρῴσκω to leap into or]

ἐν-θῡμέομαι P. to take to heart; to consider, ponder, deliberate; to devise.

ἐν-θῡμημα, τό, ἐν-θῡμησις, ἡ, ἐν-θῡμίᾱ, ἡ thought, consideration; device; advice, warning.

ἐν-θῡμιος 2 perceived; taken to heart, causing scruple or care.

ἐν-θῡμιστός = ἐνθῡμιος.

ἐν-θωρᾱκίζω to arm with a coat of mail.

ἔνι = ἔνεστι.

ἐνί = ἐν.

ἐνιαύσιος 3 and 2 one year old; for a year; year by year, yearly.

ἐνιαυτός, ὁ year.

ἐν-ιαύω to dwell in.

ἐνιαχῇ, ἐνιαχοῦ adv. in several places; sometimes.

ἐν-ιδρύω to set up in.

ἐν-ίζω, -ιζάνω to sit down in or on.

ἐν-ίημι to send, drive, or let into; to incite, cause; to inspire.   [trans.]

ἐνι-κλάω to break, frus-

ἔνιοι 3 some, several.

ἐνί-οτε adv. sometimes.

ἐνῑπή, ἡ a scolding, revile; reproach; threat.

ἐνι-πίμπλημι = ἐμπίπλημι.

ἐνί-πλειος 2 = ἔμπλειος.

ἐνι-πλήσσω = ἐμπλήσσω.

ἐν-ιππεύω to ride in or on.

ἐνι-πρήθω = ἐμπίμπρημι.

ἐνίπτω to rebuke, reprove, upbraid, blame; to tell.

ἐνι-σκίμπτω to stick in; to lower down.

ἐνίσπω = ἐνέπω.

ἐνίσσω = ἐνίπτω.

ἐν-ίστημι to put or place in or on; intr. and M. to undertake, begin; to stand in; to enter; to be present or extant; to be opposed (to), resist.

ἐν-ισχύω to strengthen.

ἐν-ίσχω = ἐνέχω.

ἐνι-χρίμπτω = ἐγχρίμπτω.

ἐννάετες = εἰνάετες.

ἐν-ναίω to dwell in.

ἐννάκις = ἐνάκις.

ἐν-ναυπηγέω to build ships in.

ἐννέα nine.   [oxen.]

ἐννεά-βοιος 2 worth nine

ἐννεα-καί-δεκα nineteen.

ἐννεά-κρουνος 2 with nine springs or water-pipes.

ἐννεά-μηνος 2 of nine months.

ἐννεά-πηχυς, υ nine cubits long.

ἐννεά-χῑλοι nine thousand.

ἐννε-όργυιος 2 nine fathoms long.

ἐννέπω = ἐνέπω.

ἐν-νεύω to nod to, to beckon.

ἐννέ-ωρος 2 nine years old.

ἐννήκοντα = ἐνενήκοντα.

ἐνν-ῆμαρ adv. for nine days.

ἐν-νοέω and M. P. to have in mind, to consider, think of; to contrive, devise; to plan, intend; to think, believe; to fear; to perceive, observe; to understand.

ἔν-νοια, ἡ thought, consideration; notion; intent, mind.

ἔν-νομος 2 legal, lawful; just, right.   [shaker.]

ἐννοσί-γαιος, ὁ earth-

ἔν-νους 2 sensible, prudent.

ἔννῡμι to put on. — P. and M. to clothe oneself; perf. to be clad.

ἐν-νυχεύω to pass the night in, to lurk in secret.

ἐν-νύχιος 3 and 2, ἔν-νυχος 2 at night, nightly.

ἐν-όδιος 3 and 2 by the road, on the road.

ἐν-οικέω to dwell in, to inhabit.

ἐν-οίκησις, ἡ a dwelling in.

ἐν-οικίζω to settle in a

place. — *M.* and *P.* to be settled, to dwell in.

ἐν-οικοδομέω to build in or on; — *M.* to build for oneself.

ἔν-οικος, ὁ inhabitant.

ἐν-οινο-χοέω to pour in wine.

ἐν-οπή, ἡ sound, voice; battle-cry; woeful cry.

ἐν-όπλιος 2, ἔν-οπλος in arms, armed.

ἐν-οράω to look at, see, observe; to understand.

ἔν-ορκος 2 bound by oath; included in a treaty; sworn.

ἐν-όρνῡμι to arouse in. — *M.* to arise. [assail.]

ἐν-ορούω to leap upon, to

ἐν-όρχης, ου, ἔν-ορχις, ιδος, ἔν-ορχος, ου uncastrated. [one year old.]

ἔνος, ἔνος 3 last year's,

ἐνοσί-χθων, ονος, ὁ earthshaker. [cord.]

ἑνότης, ητος, ἡ unity; con-

ἐν-ουρέω to make water in.

ἐν-οχλέω to molest, trouble, to be in one's way.

ἔν-οχος 2 held in, liable to, subject to.

ἐν-ράπτω to sew in.

ἐν-σείω to shake, drive, or hurl into.

ἐν-σημαίνω to show or make known in, at, or through. — *M.* to make oneself known.

ἐν-σκευάζω to fit out, prepare, adorn. [to fall in.]

ἐν-σκήπτω to hurl into;

ἔν-σπονδος 2 allied; ally.

ἐν-στάζω to instil.

ἐν-στάτης, ου, ὁ adversary.

ἐν-στέλλω to clothe, dress in. [in.]

ἐν-στηρίζω *P.* to be fixed

ἐν-στρατοπεδεύω and *M.* to encamp in.

ἐν-στρέφομαι *P.* to turn in.

ἔν-ταλμα, τό = ἐντολή.

ἐν-τάμνω = ἐντέμνω.

ἐν-τανύω = ἐντείνω.

ἐν-τάσσω to range in, to enrol.

ἐνταῦθα *adv.* there; here; thither; hither; then; now; thereupon, in that case.

ἐν-ταυθοῖ *adv.* hither; thither; here. [bury.]

ἐν-ταφιάζω to embalm; to

ἐν-ταφιασμός, ὁ an embalming. [a burial.]

ἐν-τάφιος 2 belonging to

ἔντεα, εων, τά arms, armour; tools, appliances.

ἐν-τείνω to stretch or strain in; to bend; to versify; to set to music; to plait over; to strain, exert; to extend, stretch out.

ἐν-τειχίζω to fortify; to build in; — *M.* to wall in.

ἐν-τελευτάω to die in.

ἐν-τελής 2 complete; perfect, spotless. [command.]

ἐν-τέλλομαι *M.* to enjoin,

ἐν-τέμνω to cut in, engrave; to kill, sacrifice.

ἔντερον, τό gut; *pl.* entrails. [harness.]

ἐντεσι-εργός 2 working in

ἐν-τεταμένως *adv.* intensively, zealously.

ἐντεῦθεν *adv.* thence; hence; henceforward, then; thereupon; therefore.

ἔν-τευξις, ἡ encounter, meeting, visit; conversation; prayer, petition.

ἔν-τεχνος 2 artistical, ingenious.

ἐν-τήκω to melt in; to impress. *intr.* and *P.* to be impressed; to be molten.

ἐν-τίθημι to put in; to inspire; to put or lay over or on.

ἐν-τίκτω to engender in.

ἔν-τιμος 2 honoured, noble, esteemed; costly, precious; honest.   [injunction.)

ἐν-τολή, ἡ commandment.)

ἔν-τομος 2 cut up; τὰ ἔντομα sacrifices, victims.

ἔν-τονος 2 strained; earnest, vehement.

ἐν-τόπιος 2, ἔν-τοπος 2 native; inhabitant.

ἐντός *adv.* and *prp.* with *gen.* within, inside.

ἔντοσθεν = ἐντός.

ἐν-τρέπω to turn about or over; to put to shame. — *P.* to turn oneself round or towards; to give heed (to), to notice; to revere; to feel or be ashamed (of); to hesitate.   [up in.)

ἐν-τρέφω to feed or bring)

ἐν-τρέχω to run in.

ἐν-τριβής 2 skilled, active.

ἔν-τριψις, ἡ a rubbing in.

ἔν-τρομος 2 trembling.

ἐν-τροπαλίζομαι *M.* to turn oneself repeatedly.

ἐν-τροπή, ἡ respect, regard; shame.   [concerned in.)

ἔν-τροφος 2 brought up in;)

ἐν-τρυφάω to revel in; to be delicate; to mock.

ἐν-τυγχάνω to encounter, fall in with; to incur; to get; to meet; to visit; to converse; to entreat, accost.

ἐν-τυλίσσω to wrap up.

ἐντύνω to prepare, equip, make ready; to adorn.

ἐν-τυπάς, *adv.* enveloped tightly.   [grave.)

ἐν-τυπόω to stamp in, en-)

ἐντύω = ἐντύνω.

ἐνυάλιος 2 warlike.

ἐν-υβρίζω to insult (one) in (a thing).

ἔν-υδρις, ἡ otter.

ἔν-υδρος 2 living in water; watery.   [dream.)

ἐν-υπνιάζω and *M.* to)

ἐν-ύπνιον, τό dream, vision.

ἐν-ύπνιος 2 in (one's) sleep, sleeping, in dreams.

ἐν-υφαίνω to weave in.

ἐνωμοτ-άρχης, ου, ὁ leader of an ἐνωμοτία.

ἐν-ωμοτία, ἡ a division of Spartan soldiers (25 or 30 men).   [by oath)

ἐν-ώμοτος 2 sworn, bound)

ἐνωπαδίως *adv.* to one's face.   [openly.)

ἐν-ωπή, ἡ face; ἐνωπῇ)

ἐν-ώπιος 2 to the face; τὰ ἐνώπια the front, outer or side-walls.

ἐν-ωτίζομαι to hear.

ἐξ = ἐκ.

ἕξ six.

ἐξ-αγγέλλω and *M.* to publish, tell, report, send word; to blab out; to promise.

ἐξ-άγγελος, ὁ messenger.

ἐξ-άγγελτος 2 told out.

ἐξ-αγινέω = ἐξάγω.

ἐξ-άγιστος 2 most holy; abominable.

ἐξ-αγνῡμι to break away.

ἐξ-αγοράζω and M. to buy off; to redeem.

ἐξ-αγορεύω to speak out, publish; to betray.

ἐξ-αγριαίνω, ἐξ-αγριόω to make wild; to exasperate.

ἐξ-άγω to lead out or away, to carry out, export; to lead to death; to expel; to bring forth; to lead on, excite, seduce; intr. to march out, go on.

ἐξ-αγωγή, ἡ a leading, carrying, drawing out; expulsion; way out.

ἐξ-ᾴδω to begin a song.

ἐξ-αείρω = ἐξαίρω.

ἑξά-ετες adv. for six years.

ἐξ-αιμάσσω to make bloody.   [to rob.]

ἐξ-αίνυμαι to take away;

ἐξ-αίρεσις, ἡ a taking out; an unbowelling.

ἐξ-αίρετος 2 taken out; picked out; chosen, excellent.   [taken out.]

ἐξ-αιρετός 2 what can be

ἐξ-αιρέω to take out; to unbowel; to disembark; to pick out, choose; to dedicate; to except; to take away, remove; to capture; to destroy; to confound; to drive away. — M. to take out for oneself; to unload; to rob; to set free.

ἐξ-αίρω to lift up; to extol, exalt, praise; to excite; to encourage; to make angry; to lead away, carry off,

remove. — M. to carry off for oneself, to win.

ἐξ-αίσιος 2 and 3 undue; immoderate.   [out.]

ἐξ-αίσσω and P. to rush

ἐξ-αιτέω to demand from, to demand one's surrender. — M. to beg for oneself.

ἐξ-αιτος 2 chosen.

ἐξ-αίφνης adv. suddenly.

ἐξ-ακέομαι M. to heal thoroughly; to make up for; to appease.

ἑξάκις adv. six times.

ἑξακισ-μύριοι 3 six thousand.

ἐξ-ακολουθέω to follow.

ἐξ-ακοντίζω to throw a spear; to shoot.

ἑξακόσιοι 3 six hundred.

ἐξ-ακούω to hear, listen to.

ἐξ-ακρῑβόω to do exactly.

ἐξ-αλαόω to make quite blind. [unpeople, destroy.]

ἐξ-αλαπάζω to sack; to

ἐξ-αλείφω to wipe out or off; to destroy; to besmear.

ἐξ-αλέομαι, -εύομαι M. to shun; to escape.

ἐξ-αλλάσσω to exchange; to alter; to turn away or aside.

ἐξ-άλλομαι M. to spring out of; to spring down or away, to rear (of horses).

ἐξ-αλύσκω = ἐξαλέομαι.

ἐξ-αμαρτάνω to mistake, err; transgress, sin.

ἐξ-αμαρτία, ἡ mistake, error.   [destroy.]

ἐξ-αμάω to mow off; to

ἐξ-αμελέω to neglect utterly or altogether.

ἑξά-μετρος 2 of six metres.

ἑξά-μηνος 2 lasting six months.

ἐξ-αναγκάζω to drive away by force; to compel.

ἐξ-ανάγομαι M. and P. to put to sea, to set sail.

ἐξ-αναδύομαι M. to rise out of, emerge.

ἐξ-ανακρούομαι M. to put to sea again.

ἐξ-αναλίσκω to consume or lavish utterly. [save.]

ἐξ-αναλύω to set free,]

ἐξ-ανασπάω to draw out.

ἐξ-ανάστασις, ἡ resurrection.

ἐξ-ανατέλλω to rise from.

ἐξ-αναφανδόν adv. openly.

ἐξ-αναχωρέω to retreat, withdraw.

ἐξ-ανδραποδίζω and M. to reduce to slavery.

ἐξ-ανδραπόδισις, ἡ a reducing to slavery.

ἐξ-ανδρόομαι P. to grow up to be a man. [devise.]

ἐξ-ανευρίσκω to find out,]

ἐξ-ανέχομαι M. to take upon oneself, to bear.

ἐξ-ανθέω to bloom forth; to burst forth; to fade.

ἐξ-ανίημι to send out, dismiss; intr. to slacken, relax.

ἐξ-ανίστημι to make rise from; to remove, expel; to unpeople, destroy; to lead out. — intr. and M. to rise; to depart, start, emigrate; to be driven out.

ἐξ-ανύ(τ)ω to accomplish, fulfil, perform, manage;

to kill; to finish one's way, to arrive.

ἐξα-πάλαιστος 2 of six handbreadths.

ἐξ-απαλλάσσω to make quite free. — P. to come off.

ἐξ-απατάω to deceive utterly, to cheat.

ἐξ-απάτη, ἡ deception.

ἐξ-απαφίσκω and M. = ἐξαπατάω.

ἐξά-πεδος 3 six feet long.

ἐξ-απεῖδον aor. to see from afar. [long.]

ἑξά-πηχυς, υ six cubits]

ἐξ-απιναῖος 3 and 2 sudden.

ἑξά-πλεθρος 2 six plethra long.

ἐξ-απλήσιος 3 sixfold.

ἐξ-αποβαίνω to step out of.

ἐξ-αποδίεμαι to chase away. [off.]

ἐξ-αποδύνω to put or take]

ἐξ-απόλλῦμι to kill, destroy utterly. — intr. and M. to perish.

ἐξ-απονέομαι to return.

ἐξ-απονίζω to wash off.

ἐξ-απορέω and P. to be utterly at a loss, to despair. [or away.]

ἐξ-αποστέλλω to send out]

ἐξ-αποτίνω to atone fully.

ἐξ-αποφθείρω to destroy utterly.

ἐξ-άπτω to fasten to, attach to; to kindle. — M. to hang from, cling to; to attack.

ἐξ-αραίρημαι see ἐξαιρέω.

ἐξ-αράομαι M. to curse.

ἐξ-αράσσω to knock out of.

ἐξ-αργέω to do carelessly

ἐξ-αργυρίζω, ἐξ-αργυ-ρόω to turn into money.

ἐξ-αριθμέω to count; to number, reckon.

ἐξ-αρκέω to suffice, to be enough; to satisfy; to be able.

ἐξ-αρκής 2 sufficient, enough; in good order.

ἐξ-αρκούντως adv. enough.

ἐξ-αρνέομαι P. to deny; to refuse.

ἔξ-αρνος 2 denying.

ἐξ-αρπάζω to snatch away; to rob; to rescue.

ἐξ-αρτάω to hang on, to attach (to); to make depend. — P. to be fastened or attached to, to be hung upon.

ἐξ-αρτίζω to finish.

ἐξ-αρτύω to prepare, equip, fit out. — M. to fit out for oneself; to get ready.

ἔξ-αρχος 2 beginning; leader of the chorus.

ἐξ-άρχω and M. to begin (a song); to be beginner or author.

ἐξ-ασκέω to adorn.

ἐξ-ατιμάζω not to care for. [up.

ἐξ-αυαίνω to dry or parch

ἐξ-αυδάω to speak out.

ἐξ-αυλίζομαι P. to start from an encampment.

ἐξ-αυτῆς adv. at once.

ἐξ-αῦτις adv. over again; back. [lieve firmly.

ἐξ-αυχέω to boast; to be-

ἐξ-αΰω to cry aloud.

ἐξ-αφαιρέομαι M. to take out; to rob.

ἐξ-αφίημι to set free.

ἐξ-αφίσταμαι M. to step aside; to withdraw, to depart.

ἐξ-αφοράω to see from afar.

ἐξ-αφύω, ἐξ-αφύσσω to draw (water) out of.

ἐξ-εγγυάω to set free on bail, to bail out.

ἐξ-εγείρω to arouse, awake.

ἔξ-εδρος 2 away from home.

ἐξείης = ἑξῆς. [to copy.

ἐξ-εικάζω to make like,

ἔξ-ειμι[1] (-ιέναι) to go out, away, or forward; to march out; to come to an end.

ἔξ-ειμι[2] (-εῖναι) to come from; ἔξεστι it is allowed or possible; ἐξόν it being possible.

ἐξ-εῖπον aor. to speak out.

ἐξ-είργω to shut out, exclude, keep off; to chase, expel; to hinder, prevent; to press, urge, compel.

ἐξ-είρομαί τινα to inquire of a person.

ἐξ-είρω[1] to speak out (openly), publish, tell.

ἐξ-είρω[2] to thrust out.

ἐξ-έλασις, ἡ expulsion; departure; expedition.

ἐξ-ελαύνω, -ελάω to drive out, expel, chase, banish; to beat out, hammer out; intr. to set out, march out or on; to ride out or up.

ἐξ-ελέγχω to test, examine, search out; to convict, confute; to prove. — P. to be wrong.

ἐξ-ελευθερο-στομέω to speak out freely.

ἐξ-ελίσσω to unfold, develop, draw out.

ἐξ-έλκω, -ελκύω to draw out; to drag away; to entice.

ἐξ-εμέω to vomit.

ἐξ-εμπολάω, -έω to sell out; to gain by traffic; to betray. [arms; to slay.]

ἐξ-εναρίζω to strip of]

ἐξ-επάδω to heal by incantation; to appease.

ἐξ-επεύχομαι M. to boast into the bargain.

ἐξ-επίσταμαι P. to know thoroughly, to understand fully. [pose.]

ἐξ-επίτηδες adv. on pur-]

ἐξ-εράμα, τό vomit.

ἐξ-εργάζομαι M. to work out, to execute, finish, accomplish, make, do; to cause; to cultivate; to undo, destroy. [in work.]

ἐξ-εργαστικός 3 skilled]

ἐξ-έργω = ἐξείργω.

ἐξ-ερεείνω and M. = ἐξ-ερέω[1]. [to tumble down.]

ἐξ-ερείπω to fall out of.]

ἐξ-ερεύγω P. to empty oneself. [inquire after.]

ἐξ-ερευνάω to search out,]

ἐξ-ερέω[1] and M. to search out; to examine; to question.

ἐξ-ερέω[2] fut. of ἐξ-είρω.

ἐξ-ερημόω to make empty or desolate. [εἴρομαι.]

ἐξ-έρομαι = ἐξερέω[1].]

ἐξ-έρπω to creep out of; to come out or forth.

ἐξ-ερύκω to tear out.

ἐξ-έρχομαι to go or come out or away, to march out; to sally out; to come to one's turn; to come to an end, to elapse, expire; to come to pass, to come true; to turn out, to become.

ἐξ-ερωέω to shy, bolt.

ἐξ-εσία, ἡ a sending out, mission. [vorce.]

ἐξ-εσις, ἡ dismissal, di-]

ἐξ-ετάζω to search out; to examine, test, question; to review, muster; to judge after, to compare with.

ἐξ-έτασις, ἡ examination, scrutiny, a searching out; review, inspection.

ἐξ-εταστικός 3 skilled in examining.

ἐξ-έτης 2 six years old.

ἐξ-έτι prp. with gen. since, from. [very cautious.]

ἐξ-ευλαβέομαι P. to be]

ἐξ-ευπορίζω to convey to a place plentifully.

ἐξ-εύρεσις, ἡ, ἐξ-εύρημα, τό invention.

ἐξ-ευρίσκω to find out, discover, invent; to devise, decipher; to make possible, to cause. [command.]

ἐξ-εφίεμαι M. to enjoin,]

ἐξ-έφω to boil thoroughly.

ἐξ-ηγέομαι M. to lead out or on; to be leader, to lead the way; to direct, govern, guide, teach; to explain, interpret; to describe, tell, narrate. [tion.]

ἐξ-ήγησις, ἡ interpreta-]

ἐξ-ηγητής, οῦ, ὁ teacher, adviser, guide; interpreter.

ἐξήκοντα sixty.

ἐξηκοστός 3 sixtieth.

ἐξ-ήκω to have come out; to have arrived; to have

expired or elapsed; to come true. to come to pass.

ἐξ-ήλατος 2 beaten out.

ἐξ-ήλυσις, ἡ a going out, way out.

ἐξ-ῆμαρ adv. for six days.

ἐξ-ημερόω to tame, cultivate, civilize.

ἐξ-ημοιβός 2 for change.

ἑξῆς adv. in order, one after the other, successively; next: next to, further.

ἐξ-ηχέω to publish.

ἐξ-ιάομαι to heal thoroughly. [one's own.]

ἐξ-ιδιόομαι to make quite

ἐξ-ιδρύω to let repose.

ἐξ-ίημι to send out, away, or forth; to empty oneself. — M. to send from oneself.

ἐξ-ιθύνω to make quite straight. [earnestly.]

ἐξ-ικετεύω to entreat

ἐξ-ικνέομαι to come to, arrive at, reach; to meet; to obtain, attain; to be sufficient, to suffice.

ἐξ-ιλάσκομαι M. to propitiate.

ἕξις, ἡ condition, state; behaviour, habit, mode of life; faculty, skill.

ἐξ-ισόω to make equal or even. — intr. and P. to be equal, to resemble.

ἐξ-ίστημι to put out or away; to change, alter. — intr. and M. to step or stand aside from, to retire or remove from; to be far from; to be beside oneself, lose one's senses; to give up, abandon, leave; to

lose, forget; to be changed; to degenerate.

ἐξ-ιστορέω to inquire into.

ἐξ-ισχύω to be quite able.

ἐξ-ίσχω to put forth.

ἐξ-ίτηλος 2 destroyed, extinct. [track, trace out.]

ἐξ-ιχνο-σκοπέω and M. to

ἐξ-ογκόω to make swell up. — P. to be over-full, to be puffed (up).

ἐξ-οδεία, ία, ἡ a marching out, expedition.

ἐξ-οδοιπορέω to go out of.

ἐξ-οδος, ἡ way out; gate; mouth; a going or marching out, start, sally, expedition; procession; end. close.

ἐξ-οιδα to know well.

ἐξ-οικέω to make the most of a dwelling.

ἐξ-οικήσιμος 2 habitable.

ἐξ-οικίζω to drive from home; to banish. — M. to go from home, emigrate.

ἐξ-οικοδομέω to build up.

ἐξ-οιμώζω to lament, wail.

ἐξ-οιχνέω to go out.

ἐξ-οίχομαι to have gone out or away.

ἐξ-οκέλλω to run aground; to go astray.

ἐξ-ολισθαίνω to slip off.

ἐξ-ολλῡμι to destroy wholly. — intr. and M. to perish utterly.

ἐξ-ολοθρεύω = ἐξόλλῡμι.

ἐξ-όμνῡμι and M. to deny upon oath.

ἐξ-ομοιόω to make like. — P. to become like.

ἐξ-ομολογέω and M. to

confess, admit; to agree; to thank, praise.

ἐξ-ονειδίζω to revile.

ἐξ-ονομάζω, ἐξ-ονομαίνω to call by name; to speak out, to utter. [name.]

ἐξ-ονομα-κλήδην adv. by)

ἐξ-όπι(σ)θεν adv. and prp. with gen. behind, backward(s); from behind.

ἐξ-οπίσω adv. behind; hereafter. [completely.]

ἐξ-οπλίζω to arm or equip)

ἐξ-οπλισία, ἐξ-όπλισις, ἡ complete equipment; mustering under arms.

ἐξ-οπτάω to bake sufficiently.

ἐξ-οράω see ἐξεῖδον.

ἐξ-οργίζω to make very angry.

ἐξ-ορθόω to set upright.

ἐξ-ορίζω to banish.

ἐξ-ορκίζω, ἐξ-ορκόω to bind by oath; to conjure, exorcise. [exorcist.]

ἐξ-ορκιστής, οῦ.ὁ conjurer,)

ἐξ-όρκωσις, ἡ the binding by an oath.

ἐξ-ορμάω trans. to stir, start; to send out; to impel, excite; intr. and P. to set out, go away.

ἐξ-ορούω to leap out of.

ἐξ-ορύσσω to dig out or up.

ἐξ-οστρακίζω to banish by ostracism.

ἐξ-οτρύνω to excite.

ἐξ-ουδενέω, -όω, ἐξ-ου-θενέω to set at naught, to despise.

ἐξ-ουσίᾱ, ἡ means, fortune; right, power, per-

mission, liberty; free will; authority, rule; magistrate, government; abundance.

ἐξ-ουσιάζω to have power or authority.

ἐξ-οφέλλω to increase abundantly. [minence.]

ἐξ-οχή, ἡ preference, pro-)

ἔξ-οχος 2 prominent; excellent; ἔξοχον adv. with gen. eminent among.

ἐξ-υβρίζω to become insolent; to do mischief; to revolt. [from under.]

ἐξ-υπανίσταμαι to rise)

ἐξ-ύπερθε adv. from above.

ἐξ-υπηρετέω to be quite at one's service. [sleep.]

ἐξ-υπνίζω to rouse from)

ἔξ-υπνος 2 awakened.

ἐξ-υφαίνω to weave to the end. [the way.]

ἐξ-υφηγέομαι M. to lead)

ἔξω adv. and prp. with gen. on the outside, without, outwards, outside of; beyond; far from, except.

ἔξωθεν adv. from without; without.

ἐξ-ωθέω to thrust out, to chase, drive, expel; to delay: to reject.

ἐξ-ώλεια, ἡ utter ruin.

ἐξ-ώλης 2 quite ruined.

ἐξωμιδο-ποιίᾱ, ἡ the making of ἐξωμίδες.

ἐξ-ωμίς, ίδος, ἡ short sleeveless coat.

ἐξ-ωνέομαι M. to buy off, to buy in advance; to ransom, redeem.

ἔξ-ωρος 2 untimely; inconvenient.

ἐξ-ώστης, ου, ὁ adverse.

ἐξωτάτω outermost.

ἐξώτερος 3 outer.

ἔοικα see εἴκω.

ἔολπα see ἔλπω.

ἔοργα see ἔρδω.

ἑορτάζω to keep a festival.

ἑορτή, ἡ feast, festival, holiday; amusement.

ἑός, ἑή, ἑόν his, hers, his or her own. [ult in.]

ἐπ-αγάλλομαι M. to ex-

ἐπ-αγγελίᾱ, ἡ announcement; promise.

ἐπ-αγγέλλω to announce, tell, proclaim, make known; to promise; to enjoin, command; to demand, ask. — M. to promise, offer; to profess (a calling); to claim; to command.

ἐπ-άγγελμα, τό promise; profession, business.

ἐπ-αγείρω to gather together. — M. to assemble in crowds. [thering.]

ἐπ-άγερσις, ιος, ἡ a ga-

ἐπ-αγῑνέω = ἐπάγω. [in.]

ἐπ-αγλαΐζομαι M. to exult

ἐπ-άγω to lead, bring, or drive to or on; to add; to apply; to impel, cause, instigate, seduce; intr. to march up, advance. — M. to bring or draw to oneself; to call to aid; to mention, quote; to procure; to bring on oneself.

ἐπ-αγωγή, ἡ a bringing on; an advancing, attack.

ἐπ-αγωγός 2 seductive.

ἐπ-αγωνίζομαι M. to contend for a thing.

ἐπ-ᾴδω to sing to; to lead the song; to charm by singing; to heal by incantations.

ἐπ-αείρω = ἐπαίρω.

ἐπ-αέξω to make thrive.

ἐπ-αθροίζομαι P. to assemble in crowds.

ἐπ-αιγίζω to rush upon.

ἐπ-αιδέομαι P. to be ashamed of.

ἐπ-αινέτης, ου, ὁ praiser, panegyrist.

ἐπ-αινέω to approve, sanction; to consent (to); to praise, commend; to thank, congratulate; to advise, persuade.

ἐπ-αίνημι = ἐπαινέω.

ἔπ-αινος, ὁ praise, eulogy; panegyric; reward.

ἐπ-αινός 3 awful.

ἐπ-αίρω to lift up, to set up; to excite, rouse, instigate; to seduce, induce; to exalt, to make haughty or wanton; intr. to raise oneself. — P. to be excited, induced, or impelled; to rise, to be roused, to be wanton or haughty; to exult in, to be proud.

ἐπ-αισθάνομαι M. to perceive, feel; to learn, hear.

ἐπ-αΐσσω to rush or dart upon, to assail. — M. to rush upon. [known.]

ἐπ-άϊστος 2 heard of,

ἐπ-αισχύνομαι P. to be ashamed of.

ἐπ-αιτέω to demand in addition; to solicit, beg.

ἐπ-αιτιάομαι M. to state

as a cause; to bring a charge against; to accuse.

ἐπ-αίτιος 2 guilty; blamed for.

ἐπ-αΐω to hear, listen to; to perceive. understand; to be expert (in).

ἐπ-ακολουθέω to follow, attend, join; to be attached (to); to yield; to understand.

ἐπ-ακούω to listen to; to obey.   [ken or listen to.]

ἐπ-ακροάομαι M. to hear-]

ἐπ-ακτήρ, ῆρος, ὁ huntsman.   [shore.]

ἐπ-άκτιος 3 and 2 on the

ἐπ-ακτός 3 imported, foreign, alien.   [canoe.]

ἐπ-ακτρίς, ίδος, ἡ boat,]

ἐπ-αλαλάζω to raise the war-cry.   [about.]

ἐπ-αλάομαι P. to wander]

ἐπ-αλαστέω to be vexed or troubled at.

ἐπ-αλείφω to besmear.

ἐπ-αλέξω to defend; to assist.

ἐπ-αληθεύω to verify.

ἐπ-αλλαγή, ἡ mutual union, exchange.   [interchange.]

ἐπ-αλλάσσω to exchange,]

ἐπ-άλληλος 2 mutual.

ἔπ-αλξις, ἡ parapet; defence.   [together.]

ἐπ-αμάομαι M. to heap up]

ἐπ-αμείβω to change; to exchange.   [see ἐφάπτω.]

ἐπ-αμμένος = ἐφημμένος,

ἐπ-αμοιβαδίς adv. alternately.   [fender, helper.]

ἐπ-αμύντωρ, ορος, ὁ de-]

ἐπ-αμύνω to defend, help.

ἐπ-αμφοτερίζω to doubt,

hesitate, to be inclined to both sides.

ἐπάν, ἐπήν = ἐπειδάν.

ἐπ-αναβαίνω to go up; to mount (on horse-back).

ἐπ-αναβιβάζω to cause to mount.   [thrown over.]

ἐπ-αναβληδόν adv. being]

ἐπ-αναγκάζω to force, compel.

ἐπ-άναγκες adv. necessarily, on compulsion.

ἐπ-ανάγω to lead or bring up; to put to sea; to excite; to lead or bring back; intr. to return. — P. to put to sea; to set sail against; to be carried to.

ἐπ-αναγωγή a sailing out, attack.

ἐπ-αναίρω and M. to lift up against one or one against the other.

ἐπ-αναλαμβάνω to resume, repeat.

ἐπ-αναμένω to stay on.

ἐπ-αναμιμνήσκω to remind one again.

ἐπ-αναπαύομαι to repose upon; to rely on:

ἐπ-αναπλέω, -πλώω to sail up against; to sail back; to overflow.

ἐπ-ανάσεισις, ἡ a brandishing.

ἐπ-ανάστασις, ἡ subversion; a rising up, rebellion.   [or wheel round.]

ἐπ-αναστρέφω to turn]

ἐπ-ανατείνω to hold up to.

ἐπ-ανατέλλω to rise.

ἐπ-ανατίθημι to put upon; to shut again.

ἐπ-αναφέρω to bring back; to refer to; to report; to return.

ἐπ-αναχωρέω to retreat.

ἐπ-αναχώρησις, ἡ retreat.

ἐπ-άνειμι to go up; to return, go back.

ἐπ-ανειπεῖν to proclaim in addition.

ἐπ-ανέρομαι, -είρομαι M. = ἐπανερωτάω.

ἐπ-ανέρχομαι = ἐπάνειμι.

ἐπ-ανερωτάω to question again. [again.]

ἐπ-ανήκω to come back]

ἐπ-ανθέω to bloom; to appear on the surface.

ἐπ-ανίημι to let loose; to incite; to abandon.

ἐπ-ανισόω to make equal.

ἐπ-ανίσταμαι M. to stand upon; to rise, stand up; to revolt.

ἐπ-άνοδος, ἡ return.

ἐπ-ανορθόω and M. to set up, set upright; to re-establish; to amend, improve, correct.

ἐπ-ανόρθωμα, τό, ἐπ-ανόρθωσις, ἡ a correcting, improving.

ἐπ-άντης 2 steep, rugged.

ἐπ-αντλέω to draw (water); to pour over.

ἐπ-άνω adv. above; formerly; superior to.

ἐπ-άνωθεν adv. from above, from the inland.

ἐπ-άξιος 3 worthy, deserving; suitable.

ἐπ-αξιόω to appreciate, to think worthy, right, or meet.

ἐπ-αοιδή = ἐπῳδή.

ἐπ-απειλέω to threaten besides.

ἐπ-αρά, ἡ curse.

ἐπ-αράομαι M. to wish one an evil, to curse.

ἐπ-αραρίσκω to fasten to; to fit upon; intr. to be fit.

ἐπ-αράσσω to dash in(to) pieces.

ἐπ-άρατος 2 accursed.

ἐπ-άργυρος 2 overlaid with silver, silver-mounted.

ἐπ-αρήγω to help, assist.

ἐπ-άρκεια, ἡ, ἐπ-άρκεσις, ἡ help. aid, assistance.

ἐπ-αρκέω to suffice; to remain valid; to help, aid, assist; to supply, furnish; to hinder, prevent. [ciently.]

ἐπ-αρκούντως adv. suffi-]

ἐπ-άρουρος, ὁ rustic serf.

ἐπ-αρτάομαι P. to impend.

ἐπ-αρτής 2 ready.

ἐπ-αρτύω, -ύνω to fix to.

ἐπ-αρχία, ἡ prefecture, province. [vernor.]

ἔπ-αρχος, ὁ prefect, go-]

ἐπ-άρχω to rule, govern. — M. to begin a libation.

ἐπ-αρωγός, ὁ helper.

ἐπ-ασκέω to work carefully, to practice.

ἐπ-ασσύτερος 3 crowded, one upon another.

ἐπ-άσσω = ἐπαίσσω. [upon.]

ἐπ-αυδάω and M. to call]

ἐπ-αυλίζομαι M. and P. to pass the night near.

ἔπ-αυλις, ἡ dwelling, quarters. [dwelling.]

ἔπ-αυλος, ὁ fold, stable;]

ἐπ-αυξάνω, ἐπ-αύξω to increase, enlarge, augment.

ἐπ-αύρεσις, ἡ enjoyment, fruit.

ἐπ-αύριον adv. to-morrow.

ἐπ-αυρίσκω to touch; to reach; to enjoy, taste, share. — M. to obtain; to involve oneself in; to enjoy, reap.

ἐπ-αυχέω to exult in, boast of.

ἐπ-αΰω to shout to.

ἐπ-αφρίζω to foam up.

ἐπ-αφρόδιτος 2 lovely, charming. [in addition.]

ἐπ αφύσσω to pour over

ἐπ-αχθής 2 onerous; troublesome, grievous.

ἐπεάν = ἐπάν. [mock at.]

ἐπ-εγγελάω to laugh at,

ἐπ-εγείρω to arouse, awaken; to excite. — P. to be roused; to awake.

ἐπ-έδρη, ἡ = ἐφέδρα.

ἐπεί conj. when, after that, since; as soon as; as often as; because, seeing that, for that; although; since really.

ἐπείγω to press, urge, pursue, drive, hasten, manage, forward, speed. — P. to be pressed upon; to hurry; to long for. ἐπεί.]

ἐπειδάν, ἐπειδή conj. = ἐπειδήπερ, ἐπειή conj. since really.

ἐπ-εικάζω to conjecture.

ἔπ-ειμι[1] (ἐπεῖναι) to be upon or at, to be fixed upon; to be existing, at hand, or forth-coming; to be set over; to be added; to live after, to be left.

ἔπ-ειμι[2] (ἐπιέναι) to go or come to or upon; to go through; to approach, to advance against, to attack; to befall, to enter one's mind; to impend.

ἐπ-ειπεῖν aor. to say besides, to add.

ἐπείπερ conj. since really.

ἐπ-είρομαι = ἐπέρομαι.

ἐπ-ειρύω = ἐπερύω.

ἐπ-ειρωτάω, -έω = ἐπερωτάω.

ἐπ-εισαγωγή, ἡ introduction, a bringing in besides; entrance.

ἐπ-εισαγώγιμος 2, ἐπ-είσακτος 2 brought in from abroad.

ἐπ-εισβαίνω to step in also. [again.]

ἐπ-εισβάλλω to invade

ἐπ-είσειμι, ἐπεισέρχομαι to enter besides, likewise, or after; to come in or on; to appear. [entrance.]

ἐπ-είσοδος, ἡ intervention;

ἐπ-εισπίπτω to fall in or to invade besides; to fall upon.

ἐπ-εισπλέω to sail in or on besides; to sail in against, to attack.

ἐπ-εισφέρω to bring in besides. — M. to bring in for oneself. — P. to intervene.

ἐπ-εισφρέω to let in after.

ἔπ-ειτα adv. thereupon, thereafter, then, thenceforward; further; therefore; nevertheless.

ἐπεί-τε = ἐπεί τε since, because.

ἔπειτεν = ἔπειτα.

ἐπ - εκβαίνω to disembark besides. [to aid.]

ἐπ - εκβοηθέω to come out]

ἐπ - εκδιδάσκω to teach thoroughly in addition.

ἐπ - εκδιηγέομαι = ἐπεκδιδάσκω.

ἐπ - εκδρομή, ἡ excursion, expedition. [yond.]

ἐπ-έκεινα adv. yonder, be-]

ἐπ - εκθέω = ἐπεκτρέχω.

ἐπ - εκπλέω to sail out against. [out against.]

ἐπ - έκπλους, ὁ a sailing]

ἐπ - εκτρέχω to rush or sally out to attack.

ἐπ - ελαύνω to drive upon or over; to beat out on the surface; to lead on; intr. to come, march, or drive up, to approach.

ἐπ - ελπίζω to lead to hope.

ἐπ - εμβαίνω to step on or in; to stand upon; to tread down, insult.

ἐπ - εμβάλλω to put on besides; to add; to offer; to flow in besides. [man.]

ἐπ - εμβάτης, ου, ὁ horse-]

ἐπ - εμπίπτω to fall in.

ἐπ - εναρίζω to slay besides.

ἐπ - ενδύνω, ἐπ - ενδύομαι to put on besides.

ἐπ - ενδύτης, ου, ὁ upper garment. [grown upon.]

ἐπ - ενήνοθα perf. to have]

ἐπ - ενθρῴσκω to leap or rush upon.

ἐπ - εντανύω, ἐπ - εντείνω to stretch upon. — P. to lean upon. [sides.]

ἐπ - εντέλλω to enjoin be-]

ἐπ - εντύνω, -τύω to pre-

pare, equip. — P. to be ready.

ἐπ - εξάγω to lead out against; to lengthen a front line; intr. to march out. [ing.]

ἐπ - εξαγωγή, ἡ a lengthen-]

ἐπ - έξειμι = ἐπεξέρχομαι.

ἐπ - εξελαύνω to drive on against.

ἐπ - εξεργάζομαι to do besides; to slay once more.

ἐπ - εξέρχομαι to go out against, to advance against; to march out, to sally forth, attack; to punish, proceed against, pursue; to go on, wander through; to go through, inspect; to execute.

ἐπ - εξέτασις, ἡ repeated inspection. [besides.]

ἐπ - εξευρίσκω to invent]

ἐπ - εξῆς = ἐφεξῆς.

ἐπ - εξόδια, τά sacrifice at a departure. [against.]

ἐπ - έξοδος, ἡ a march out]

ἐπ - έοικα perf. to be like; to be likely; to be convenient, fitting, or reasonable.

ἐπ - εργάζομαι M. to cultivate.

ἐπ - εργασίᾱ, ἡ unlawful cultivation of sacred land.

ἐπ - ερείδω to urge on, to apply vast strength to.

ἐπ - ερέφω to roof a building.

ἐπ - έρομαι M. = ἐπερωτάω.

ἐπ - ερύω to draw or pull on or up. — M. to draw on oneself.

ἐπ - έρχομαι to go or come up, towards, forward, or on,

to approach, attack; to occur, befall, come into one's mind; to go over; to visit; to go through, examine; to execute; to be at hand, impend.

ἐπ-ερωτάω to question, ask; to inquire of again; to consult.

ἐπ-ερώτημα, τό, ἐπ-ερώτησις, ἡ question, inquiry; demand.

ἐπεσ-βολία, ἡ forward talk.

ἐπεσ-βόλος 2 talking idly.

ἐπ-εσθίω to eat besides.

ἐπ-έτειος, ἐπ-έτεος 2 and 3 lasting the whole year; yearly.   [servant.

ἐπέτης, ου, ὁ attendant,

ἐπ-ετήσιος 2 = ἐπέτειος,

ἐπ-ευθύνω to direct upon.

ἐπ-ευφημέω to applaud; to demand aloud; to shout assent.

ἐπ-εύχομαι M. to pray at; to invoke; to wish; to accurse; to boast, exult, triumph.

ἐπ-έχω to have or hold upon; to place upon; to hold out, present, offer; to have opposite oneself; to keep shut; to hold fast, retain, hinder; to delay, retard; to reach to, extend; to have in one's power. — intr. to be intent upon, to turn one's mind to; to stop, stay, wait; to desist, hold back. — M. to aim at; to put (to the lips); to offer; to delay.

ἐπήβολος 2 partaking of, master of.

ἐπ-ηγκενίς, ίδος, ἡ plank of a ship.

ἐπ-ηγορεύω, -έω to reproach, upbraid.

ἐπηετανός 2 and 3 lasting; abundant, plentiful.

ἐπ-ήκοος 2 listening to; audible; within hearing.

ἐπ-ηλυγάζομαι M. to overshadow; to hide oneself.

ἐπ-ήλυς, υδος, ἐπ-ηλύτης, ου one coming, immigrant, foreigner.   [changing.

ἐπ-ημοιβός 2 in turn,

ἐπ-ημύω to drop or sink at.

ἐπήν = ἐπάν.   [plaud.

ἐπ-ηπύω to shout to, ap-

ἐπ-ήρατος 2 lovely, charming.

ἐπ-ηρεάζω to mortify; to revile, abuse, insult; to threaten.

ἐπ-ήρεια, ἡ insult, malice.

ἐπ-ήρετμος 2 rowing; furnished with oars.

ἐπ-ηρεφής 2 hanging over, covering; steep.

ἐπητής, οῦ considerate; kind.   [crowds.

ἐπ-ήτριμος 2 close, in

ἐπητύς, ύος, ἡ kindness.

ἐπ-ηχέω to re-echo.

ἐπί adv. on, at, or to it; afterwards, then; on the contrary; besides. — prp. with gen. on, upon, at, by, near, with; towards; in presence of; during, in the time of; over; with regard to, concerning; on the ground of. — with dat. on, in, at, near, beside; upon; after; towards, against;

during, in the time of; immediately after; in addition to; by reason of, on the ground of, for the purpose of, for the sake of, in respect to; in honour of, on condition of; in the power or under the rule of. — with *acc.* extending over, towards, up to; against; until; (with numbers) about, nearly; during; in quest of.

ἔπι = ἔπεστι it is there or at hand.

ἐπ-ιάλλω to send to; to lay on; to cause. [μαι.]

ἐπι-άλμενος see ἐφάλλο-

ἐπι-ανδάνω = ἐφανδάνω.

ἐπ-ιάχω to shout to; to shout aloud. [fare.]

ἐπί-βαθρον, τό passenger's

ἐπι-βαίνω to tread or walk upon; to go up, mount, ascend; to go over, to cross, to arrive at; to set on, attack, fall upon. — *trans.* to cause to mount, to bring, put, or send upon; to make arrive at.

ἐπι-βάλλω to throw, cast, or lay upon; to put on; *intr.* to go towards; to fall upon, to attack; to think of; to fall to, to be due. — *M.* to put upon oneself; to take upon oneself; to desire (earnestly), covet.

ἐπι-βαρέω to burden.

ἐπί-βασις, ἡ attack; approach: occasion, motive.

ἐπι-βάσκω to lead into.

ἐπι-βατεύω to be a sailor or passenger; to tread

upon; to mount; to lean upon.

ἐπι-βάτης, ου, ὁ horseman; sailor; naval soldier; passenger.

ἐπι-βατός 3 accessible.

ἐπι-βήτωρ, ορος, ὁ one who mounts; male animal, boar, bull. [cend.]

ἐπι-βιβάζω to cause to as-

ἐπι-βιόω to live through; to survive; to live to see.

ἐπι-βλέπω to look at or upon, to regard.

ἐπί-βλημα, τό patch.

ἐπι-βλής, ῆτος, ὁ bar, bolt.

ἐπι-βοάω and *M.* to cry out to; to call to aid, invoke; to decry.

ἐπι-βοήθεια, ἡ succour, a coming to aid.

ἐπι-βοηθέω to come to aid.

ἐπι-βόημα, τό a call to.

ἐπι-βόητος 2 decried, ill spoken of.

ἐπι-βολή, ἡ a throwing or putting on; attack; attempt, project; cover; layer; penalty. [herdsman.]

ἐπι-βουκόλος, ὁ cowherd;

ἐπι-βουλευτής, οῦ, ὁ insidious foe.

ἐπι-βουλεύω to plot or plan against, to lay snares; to lie in wait for; to have a mind to, to intend, aim at.

ἐπι-βουλή, ἡ plot, plan against; treachery, deceit; wait, snare.

ἐπί-βουλος 2 plotting against, insidious. [into.]

ἐπι-βρέμω to roar over or

ἐπι-βρίθω to weigh down.

ἐπι-βρόντητος 2 stunned.

ἐπι-βώτωρ, ορος, ὁ shepherd.

ἐπί-γαιος 2 = ἐπίγειος.

ἐπι-γαμβρεύω to marry the brother's widow.

ἐπι-γαμία, ἡ intermarriage.

ἐπί-γαμος 2 marriageable.

ἐπι-γδουπέω to thunder at.

ἐπί-γειος 2 on the earth, earthly.

ἐπι-γελάω to laugh at or about.

ἐπι-γίγνομαι M. to be born, to come or live after; to follow, elapse; to approach, come, happen; to fall upon, attack.

ἐπι-γιγνώσκω to recognize, know exactly, observe; to discover, become conscious of; to contrive; to decide.

ἐπι-γνάμπτω to bend; to make one alter his intentions. [overseer.]

ἐπί-γνωμων 2 arbiter;]

ἐπί-γνωσις, ἡ knowledge.

ἐπί-γονος 3 born after.

ἐπι-γουνίς, ίδος, ἡ thigh.

ἐπι-γράβδην adv. scratching.

ἐπί-γραμμα, τό. ἐπι-γραφή, ἡ inscription, epigram.

ἐπι-γράφω to scratch (the surface), to graze; to write upon, inscribe; to order by letter; to enter in a register. — M. to paint on for oneself.

ἐπί-γρυπος 2 with a crooked beak.

ἐπι-δάμος 2 = ἐπιδήμιος.

ἐπι-δαψιλεύομαι M. to give abundantly in addition. [of; less.]

ἐπι-δεής 2 needy, in want)

ἐπί-δειγμα, τό specimen, example, pattern.

ἐπι-δείκνῡμι, -ύω to show forth, exhibit, to show as a pattern; to represent; to demonstrate, prove. — M. to show oneself, to make oneself seen or heard.

ἐπι-δεικτικός 3 showy, for display.

ἐπί-δειξις, ἡ a showing, exhibition, display; review; specimen, pattern; panegyric; proof.

ἐπι-δέκατος 3 the tenth part; one and one tenth.

ἐπι-δέχομαι = ἐπιδέχομαι.

ἐπι-δέξιος 2 to the right.

ἐπί-δεξις, ἡ = ἐπιδείξις.

ἐπι-δέρχομαι to look at.

ἐπι-δευής 2 = ἐπιδεής.

ἐπι-δεύομαι = ἐπιδέομαι, see ἐπιδέω.

ἐπι-δέχομαι M. to receive or admit in addition.

ἐπι-δέω[1] to bind on; to bandage.

ἐπι-δέω[2] to want, lack. — P. to be in want of, to need; to fall short of, to be inferior (to).

ἐπί-δηλος 2 manifest, plain, conspicuous, known.

ἐπι-δημέω, -εύω to be at home; to return home; to be a stranger in a place.

ἐπι-δήμιος 2 living at home, native; spread among the people; living as a stranger.

ἐπι-δημιουργός, ὁ controller of magistrates.

ἐπί-δημος 2 = ἐπιδήμιος.

ἐπι-διαβαίνω to cross over in addition or one after the other. [sider anew.]

ἐπι-διαγινώσκω to consider anew.

ἐπι-διαιρέω to distribute. — M. to share among themselves. [finally.]

ἐπι-διακρίνω to decide finally.

ἐπι-διατάσσομαι to command besides.

ἐπι-διαφέρω to carry across after. [addition.]

ἐπι-διδάσκω to teach in addition.

ἐπι-δίδωμι to give besides; to give with; to deliver, yield. — intr. to increase, improve, grow. — M. to add; to present.

ἐπι-δίζημαι M. to seek or inquire for besides.

ἐπι-δῑνέω to swing round. — P. to move in a circle. — M. to reflect upon.

ἐπι-διορθόω to set fully in order.

ἐπι-διφριάς, άδος, ἡ chariot-rail. [chariot-seat.]

ἐπι-δίφριος 2 on the chariot-seat.

ἐπι-διώκω to pursue further.

ἐπί-δοξος 2 causing expectation; to be expected, likely.

ἐπί-δοσις, ἡ addition, contribution; increase, progress.

ἐπι-δοχή, ἡ reception after.

ἐπι-δρομή, ἡ inroad, raid.

ἐπί-δρομος 2 to be taken by storm, assailable.

ἐπι-δύω to go down or set upon.

ἐπι-είκεια, ἡ propriety, decency; equity, fairness; clemency.

ἐπι-είκελος 2 like.

ἐπι-εικής 2 fitting, suitable; fair, decent; moderate, kind; proper, fit; likely; ἐπιεικῶς properly, justly; in some respect, in a certain manner.

ἐπι-εικτός 3 yielding; to be conquered.

ἐπι-έλπομαι M. to hope for.

ἐπι-έννῡμι to put on over.

ἐπι-ζάφελος 2 vehement, furious.

ἐπι-ζάω = ἐπιβιόω.

ἐπι-ζεύγνῡμι, -ύω to fasten or join to.

ἐπι-ζεφύριος 2 towards the west, occidental.

ἐπι-ζέω to boil or flash up; to inflame.

ἐπι-ζήμιος 2 hurtful.

ἐπι-ζημιόω to punish.

ἐπι-ζητέω to seek for or after; to long, wish, or crave for, covet.

ἐπι-ζώννῡμι to gird on.

ἐπι-ζώω = ἐπιζάω.

ἐπι-ήρανος 2, ἐπί-ηρος 2 pleasing, pleasant.

ἐπι-θαλασσίδιος 2, ἐπι-θαλάσσιος 2 and 3 lying on the sea. [to death.]

ἐπι-θανάτιος 2 condemned to death.

ἐπι-θαρσύνω to encourage.

ἐπι-θειάζω to invoke the gods; to adjure.

ἐπι-θειασμός, ὁ adjuration.

ἐπι-θεραπεύω to be compliant or courteous; to be intent on.

ἐπί-θεσις, ἡ a laying upon; attack.

ἐπι-θεσπίζω to pronounce oracles. [tack.]

ἐπι-θετικός 3 ready to at-]

ἐπί-θετος 2 added; not natural, affected, studied.

ἐπι-θέω to run at or after.

ἐπί-θημα, τό cover, lid.

ἐπι-θορυβέω to make a noise at; to applaud.

ἐπι-θρῴσκω to leap upon.

ἐπι-θῡμέω to desire, long for, wish, covet.

ἐπι-θῡμητής, οῦ, ὁ desirous; lover, adherent.

ἐπι-θῡμητικός 3 desiring.

ἐπι-θῡμίᾱ, ἡ desire, longing, wish; lust.

ἐπι-θῡμίᾱμα, τό incense.

ἐπ-ῑθΰνω to direct against.

ἐπι-θΰω to sacrifice after.

ἐπ-ῑθΰω to rush at.

ἐπι-θώσσω to ring to; to shout to.

ἐπι-ίστωρ, ορος acquainted with; accomplice.

ἐπι-καθαιρέω to demolish completely.

ἐπι-κάθημαι to sit upon; to weigh upon; to besiege.

ἐπι-καθίζω to set upon; to sit upon.

ἐπι-καθίσταμαι M. to put down for oneself.

ἐπι-καίριος 2 seasonable, fit, convenient; necessary; considerable, important, chief.

ἐπί-καιρος 2 seasonable, convenient, fit, proper.

ἐπι-καίω to kindle or burn at.

ἐπι-καλέω to summon, call in; to invoke; to give a surname; to accuse, reproach. — M. to call to oneself, to call to aid; to challenge.

ἐπι-κάλυμμα, τό covering, cloak. [hide.]

ἐπι-καλύπτω to cover up,]

ἐπι-καμπή, ἡ bend, curve, projection. [wheel round.]

ἐπι-κάμπτω to bend; to]

ἐπι-κάρσιος 2 head foremost; sideways, crosswise; at an angle. [against.]

ἐπι-καταβαίνω to go down]

ἐπι-κατάγομαι P. to come to land afterwards.

ἐπι-καταδαρθάνω to fall asleep at. [flow besides.]

ἐπι-κατακλΰζω to over-]

ἐπι-κατακοιμάομαι P. to lie down to sleep upon.

ἐπι-καταλαμβάνω to overtake, to catch up. [longer.]

ἐπι-καταμένω to stay yet]

ἐπι-κατάρᾱτος 2 accursed.

ἐπι-καταρριπτέω to throw down after.

ἐπι-κατασφάζω, -σφάττω to kill upon or at.

ἐπι-καταψεύδομαι M. to tell lies in addition.

ἐπι-κάτειμι to go down.

ἐπί-καυτος 2 burnt at the end.

ἐπί-κειμαι M. to be laid or to lie upon, in, at, or near; to entreat; to press upon, to attack; to impend; to be imposed.

ἐπι-κείρω to cut, mow off or down; to baffle.

ἐπι-κελαδέω to shout at.

ἐπι-κέλευσις, ἡ exhortation, cheer. [exhort.]

ἐπι-κελεύω and M.to cheer,]

ἐπι-κέλλω to drive to the shore; to come ashore.

ἐπι-κέλομαι M. to call upon or to. [to mix after.]

ἐπι-κεράννῡμι to mix in;]

ἐπι-κερδίᾱ, ἡ profit in trade. [tease.]

ἐπι-κερτομέω to scoff; to]

ἐπι-κεύθω to hide from.

ἐπι-κηρῡκείᾱ, ἡ negotiation through heralds.

ἐπι-κηρῡκεύομαι M. to send message by a herald; to treat, transact.

ἐπι-κηρύσσω to proclaim publicly.

ἐπι-κίδνημι to spread over. — M. to be extended over.

ἐπι-κίνδῡνος 2 dangerous; in danger. [νῡμι.]

ἐπι-κίρνημι = ἐπικεράν-]

ἐπι-κλάω to break, bend, move; to dispirit. [more.]

ἐπι-κλείω to extol the]

ἐπί-κλημα, τό reproach, accusation. [and heiress.]

ἐπί-κληρος, ἡ daughter]

ἐπί-κλησις, ἡ surname, name.

ἐπί-κλητος 2 called, assembled; called to aid.

ἐπι-κλῑνής 2 sloping, steep.

ἐπι-κλίνω to bend towards, to lay upon; intr. to recline, to turn.

ἐπί-κλοπος 2 thievish: wily, cunning.

ἐπι-κλύζω to overflow.

ἐπί-κλυσις, ἡ flood, overflow.

ἐπι-κλύω to listen to.

ἐπι-κλώθω to spin to; to assign, allot.

ἐπί-κοινος 2 common.

ἐπι-κοινόω to communicate. [common with.]

ἐπι-κοινωνέω to have in]

ἐπι-κομπέω to boast.

ἐπι-κόπτω to slay.

ἐπι-κοσμέω to adorn; to celebrate.

ἐπι-κουρέω to help, assist, to serve as a mercenary; to keep off from.

ἐπι-κούρημα, τό protection.

ἐπι-κουρίᾱ, ἡ help, auxiliary forces. [auxiliary.]

ἐπι-κουρικός 3 helping,]

ἐπί-κουρος 2 helping, assisting. [to lift up.]

ἐπι-κουφίζω to relieve;]

ἐπι-κραίνω, -κραταίνω to accomplish, fulfil.

ἐπι-κράτεια, ἡ dominion, supremacy; reach.

ἐπι-κρατέω to prevail over, conquer, overcome; to obtain, achieve; to rule, govern. [torious, violent.]

ἐπι-κρατής 2 superior, vic-]

ἐπι-κράτησις, ἡ an overcoming, overwhelming.

ἐπι-κρεμάννῡμαι, -κρέμαμαι P. to impend over, to threaten.

ἐπι-κρίνω to decide.

ἐπί-κριον, τό sail-yard.

ἐπι-κρύπτω to hide, conceal. — M. to hide oneself.

ἐπι-κτάομαι M. to gain besides; to win; to enlarge.

ἐπι-κτείνω to kill anew.

ἐπί-κτησις, ἡ new gain.

ἐπί-κτητος 2 gained besides, acquired.

ἐπι-κῦδής 2 glorious, splendid; important.

ἐπι-κυΐσκομαι to become doubly pregnant. [upon.)

ἐπι-κυλινδέω to roll(down))

ἐπι-κύπτω to stoop down over. [to meet.)

ἐπι-κῦρέω to fall in with;)

ἐπι-κῦρόω to confirm, ratify; determine.

ἐπι-κωκύω to lament at.

ἐπι-κωμῳδέω to mock at.

ἐπι-λαγχάνω to come last (by lot).

ἐπι-λαμβάνω to take or seize besides; to lay hold of, catch, oppress, attack; to retain; to prevent; to fall in with, to live to see; to reach to. — M. to seize, hold fast; to keep to; to attack; to blame, chide; to object to; to fall in with, get possession of.

ἐπί-λαμπτος 2 = ἐπίληπτος. [to dawn.)

ἐπι-λάμπω to shine again;)

ἐπι-λανθάνομαι M. to cause to forget; to forget; to conceal.

ἐπι-λεαίνω to smooth over; to make plausible.

ἐπι-λέγω to say at or besides, to add; to name; to select, pick out. — M. to collect, choose for one-self; to read; to think over; to care for; to fear.

ἐπι-λείβω to pour upon.

ἐπι-λείπω to leave behind; to omit; intr. to fail, to be gone or wanting; to give out; to be dried up. — P. to be left.

ἐπι-λείχω to lick.

ἐπί-λειψις, ἡ failure.

ἐπί-λεκτος 2 chosen.

ἐπι-λεύσσω to look before one. [forget.)

ἐπί-ληθος 2 causing to)

ἐπι-λήθω = ἐπιλανθάνομαι.

ἐπι-ληΐς, ίδος, ἡ captured.

ἐπι-ληκέω to applaud by measure.

ἐπί-ληπτος 2 caught (at it).

ἐπι-λησμονή, ἡ forgetfulness. [unmindful.)

ἐπι-λήσμων 2 forgetful;)

ἐπι-λίγδην adv. scratching.

ἐπ-ιλλίζω to wink at.

ἐπι-λογίζομαι M. and P. to reflect (upon), consider.

ἐπί-λογος, ὁ consideration; conclusion.

ἐπί-λοιπος 2 still left; future. [sides.)

ἐπι-λῦπέω to grieve be-)

ἐπι-λύω to loose; to decide; to refute. — M. to release, protect.

ἐπι-λωβεύω to mock at.

ἐπι-μαίνομαι P. and M. to be mad after.

ἐπι-μαίομαι M. to touch, feel; to seize; to strive after, aim at.

ἐπι-μανθάνω to learn after.

ἐπι-μαρτῠρέω to bear witness (to).

ἐπι-μαρτῠρίᾱ, ἡ a calling to witness.

ἐπι-μαρτόρομαι *M.* to call to witness; to conjure, implore.

ἐπι-μάρτῠρος 2 witness.

ἐπι-μάσσομαι *fut.* of ἐπιμαίομαι.

ἐπί-μαστος 2 dirty, squalid.

ἐπι-μαχέω to protect in arms. [liance.)

ἐπι-μαχίᾱ, ἡ defensive alliance.

ἐπί-μαχος 2 assailable.

ἐπι-μειδάω, -μειδιάω to smile at.

ἐπι-μέλεια, ἡ care, diligence, attention; training, practice; direction, management; respect.

ἐπι-μελέομαι *P.* to take care of, pay attention to; to manage, superintend; to take pains, to toil; to respect.

ἐπι-μελής 2 caring for, careful, zealous; causing care, object of care.

ἐπι-μελητής, οῦ, ὁ provider, guardian; manager, superintendent.

ἐπι-μέλομαι = ἐπιμελέομαι. [after.)

ἐπι-μέμονα *perf.* to strive.

ἐπι-μέμφομαι *M.* to find fault (with), to blame, grumble at, complain.

ἐπι-μένω to stay on; to adhere to; to tarry, wait; to expect. [send for after.)

ἐπι-μεταπέμπομαι *M.* to.

ἐπι-μετρέω to measure out to. [against.)

ἐπι-μήδομαι *M.* to devise.

ἐπι-μήνιος 2 monthly.

ἐπι-μηνίω to be angry.

ἐπι-μηχανάομαι *M.* to devise against; to devise besides.

ἐπι-μήχανος 2 contriver.

ἐπι-μίγνῡμι (-μείγν.) and *M.* to mix in or with; to converse; to meet.

ἐπι-μιμνήσκομαι *P.* to remember, recall to mind; to mention.

ἐπι-μίμνω = ἐπιμένω.

ἐπι-μίξ *adv.* mixedly.

ἐπι-μιξίᾱ, ἡ intercourse.

ἐπι-μίσγω = ἐπιμίγνυμι.

ἐπι-μονή, ἡ delay.

ἐπι-μύζω to murmur at.

ἐπί-νειον, τό anchorage, dock, port; arsenal.

ἐπι-νέμω to allot, distribute; to lead to pasture. —*M.* to graze; to devastate.

ἐπι-νεύω to nod at or to; to assent; to grant.

ἐπι-νέφελος 2 clouded.

ἐπι-νεφρίδιος 2 upon the kidneys.

ἐπι-νέω[1] to spin to.

ἐπι-νέω[2] to load with; to heap or pile up.

ἐπι-νίκειος 2 victorious.

ἐπι-νίκιος 2 belonging to victory.

ἐπι-νίσσομαι to go or flow over, overflow.

ἐπι-νοέω to think of: to contrive, devise; to observe, perceive.

ἐπί-νοια, ἡ thought, intention, project; a thinking; after-thought.

ἐπι-νύμφειος 2 bridal.

ἐπι-νωμάω to allot, distribute.

ἐπί-ξῡνος 2 = ἐπίκοινος.

ἐπι-ορκέω to swear falsely, to forswear oneself.

ἐπί-ορκος 2 perjured, forsworn; τὸ -ον false oath.

ἐπι-όσσομαι to look at.

ἐπί-ουρος, ὁ guard; ruler.

ἐπ-ιοῦσα, ἡ the coming day.

ἐπ-ιούσιος 2 sufficient for the day, daily.

ἐπι-πᾶν adv. on the whole, generally.   [besides.]

ἐπι-παρανέω to heap up]

ἐπι-παρασκευάζομαι M. to prepare besides.

ἐπι-πάρειμι[1] (-εῖναι) to be present or near.

ἐπι-πάρειμι[2] (-ιέναι) to come on too; to advance against; to march back; to march on the height alongside of.   [upon.]

ἐπι-πάσσω to sprinkle]

ἐπί-πεδος 2 level, flat.

ἐπι-πείθομαι P. to be persuaded; to obey.

ἐπι-πέλομαι M. to come near, approach.

ἐπι-πέμπω to send besides or after; to send to.

ἐπί-πεμψις, ἡ a sending to.

ἐπι-πέτομαι M. to fly to.

ἐπι-πίλναμαι to approach.

ἐπι-πίνω to drink besides.

ἐπι-πίπτω to fall upon or into; to attack; to befall; to put to shore.

ἔπιπλα, τά movables, goods and chattels, furniture.

ἐπι-πλάζομαι P. to be driven or wander over.

ἐπί-πλεος 3 full.

ἐπί-πλευσις, ἡ a sailing against, naval attack.

ἐπι-πλέω to sail upon or with; to sail against.

ἐπι-πληρόω to man (a ship) anew.

ἐπι-πλήσσω to strike at; to blame, revile, reproach.

ἐπίπλοα = ἔπιπλα.

ἐπί-πλοος[1], ὁ caul.

ἐπί-πλοος[2], ὁ a sailing upon or against, attack of a fleet, naval expedition.

ἐπι-πλώω = ἐπιπλέω.

ἐπι-πνέω, -πνείω to breathe or blow upon; to blow at or after.

ἐπι-πόδιος 3 upon the feet.

ἐπι-ποθέω to long or yearn for.   [θίᾱ, ἡ a longing.]

ἐπι-πόθησις, ἡ, ἐπι-πο-)

ἐπι-πόθητος 2 longed for.

ἐπι-ποιμήν, ένος, ὁ, ἡ shepherd, shepherdess.

ἐπι-πολάζω to be on the surface (of); to get to the top, to prevail.

ἐπι-πολή, ἡ surface, top.

ἐπί-πολος, ὁ servant.

ἐπι-πονέω to persevere in work.

ἐπί-πονος 2 toilsome; portending toil.

ἐπι-πορεύομαι P. to march or travel to or against.

ἐπι-πρέπω to be prominent at, to be conspicuous.

ἐπι-προϊάλλω to send out or place before one.

ἐπι-προΐημι to send forth towards; to send out; to steer towards.

ἐπί - προσθεν *adv.* before, near; in the way.

ἐπι - πταίρω to sneeze at.

ἐπι - πωλέομαι *M.* to go about, to inspect.

ἐπι - πώλησις, ἡ review.

ἐπι - ρράπτω to sew on.

ἐπι - ρράσσω = ἐπιρρήσσω.

ἐπι - ρρέζω to sacrifice upon.

ἐπι - ρρέπω to bend towards; to sink down.

ἐπι - ρρέω to flow on the surface (of); to stream to.

ἐπι - ρρήσσω to dash against, to push forward violently; *intr.* to burst forth.

ἐπι - ρρίπτέω, -ρρίπτω to throw upon.

ἐπί - ρροθος[1] 2 reviling, scolding. [tector.]

ἐπί-ρροθος[2] 2 aiding; pro-

ἐπί - ρρυτος 2 watered.

ἐπι - ρρώννῡμι to strengthen, encourage. — *P.* to recover strength, take heart.

ἐπι - ρρώομαι *M.* to be active; to flow down. [den.]

ἐπί - σαγμα, τό load, bur-

ἐπι - σάσσω to heap or load upon; to saddle. [against.]

ἐπι - σείω to shake at or

ἐπι - σεύω to put in motion against, to incite. — *P.* to be stirred; to hurry or hasten towards; to rush at, attack.

ἐπι - σημαίνω to mark; to announce; to give a sign of approval; to appear as a sign or omen. — *M.* to mark with a sign for oneself.

ἐπί - σημον, τό mark, device; symbol, emblem.

ἐπι - σῑμόω to cause to turn sideways.

ἐπι - σῑτίζομαι *M.* to provide oneself with food; to forage.

ἐπι - σῑτισμός, ὁ a victualling, supplying with provisions. [σκοπέω.]

ἐπι - σκέπτομαι *M.* = ἐπι-

ἐπι - σκευάζω to prepare, fit out, get ready; to restore; to pack upon. — *M.* to prepare for oneself.

ἐπι - σκευή, ἡ repair, restoration; a raising up.

ἐπί - σκεψις, ἡ inspection; inquiry. [tent, openly.]

ἐπί - σκηνος 2 before the

ἐπι - σκηνόω to live in, to be immanent or inherent.

ἐπι - σκήπτω to impose on, enjoin; to implore, entreat; to wish one something; to accuse. — *M.* to refuse; to indict, summon.

ἐπι - σκιάζω to overshadow; to hide. [shadowed.]

ἐπί - σκιος 2 shading; over-

ἐπι - σκοπέω to look upon or at; to regard, review, inspect, visit, examine, consider; to pay attention to, to take care of.

ἐπι - σκοπή, ἡ visitation, inspection; office of an overseer or bishop.

ἐπί - σκοπος[1], ὁ overseer, guardian; bishop.

ἐπί - σκοπος[2] 2 hitting the mark; convenient.

ἐπι - σκοτέω to darken, overshade. [furious.]

ἐπι - σκύζομαι *M.* to grow

ἐπι-σκυθίζω to cause to drink in Scythian manner.

ἐπι-σκύνιον, τό skin of the brows. [mock at; to jest.]

ἐπι-σκώπτω to laugh or

ἐπι-σμυγερῶς adv. shamefully, miserably.

ἐπι-σπαστήρ, ῆρος, ὁ handle of the door. [oneself.]

ἐπί-σπαστος 2 drawn upon]

ἐπι-σπάω to draw upon; to drag on; to pull to; to seize; to gain; to draw along. — M. to draw to oneself, to induce, seduce; to obtain.

ἐπι-σπείρω to sow upon.

ἐπί-σπεισις, ἡ a pouring out on, libation.

ἐπι-σπένδω to pour upon, to offer a libation. — M. to make a new treaty.

ἐπι-σπέρχω to incite; intr. to rush on.

ἐπι-σπεύδω to urge, hasten; to hurry on.

ἐπι-σπονδαί, αἱ new treaty.

ἐπι-σσείω etc. see ἐπι-σείω.

ἐπί-σσωτρον, τό metal hoop of a wheel.

ἐπι-σταδόν adv. assistingly; earnestly.

ἐπί-σταθμος, ὁ commandant of a place.

ἐπίσταμαι P. to understand, know, to have insight (in), to be versed, skilled, or experienced (in); to be able; to think, believe.

ἐπι-στασία and ἐπί-στασις, ἡ a stopping, checking. halt; assembly; inspection; attention.

ἐπι-στατέω to be set over, to be prefect or overseer; to command, preside.

ἐπι-στάτης, ου, ὁ one who is present; one who stands upon something; the man behind; commander, overseer, prefect; master.

ἐπι-στείβω to tread on.

ἐπι-στέλλω to send to, to send message; to enjoin, command.

ἐπι-στενάζω, ἐπι-στενάχω, ἐπι-στένω to groan or lament at. [brim.]

ἐπι-στεφής 2 filled to the]

ἐπι-στέφω to offer. — M. to fill to the brim.

ἐπι-στήμη, ἡ knowledge, intelligence, insight; skill; science, art.

ἐπι-στήμων 2 knowing, intelligent, skilful; learned.

ἐπι-στηρίζομαι to lean upon.

ἐπίστιον, τό dock for ships.

ἐπίστιος = ἐφέστιος.

ἐπι-στολεύς, ὁ vice-admiral; letter-carrier.

ἐπι-στολή, ἡ message, order; letter. [στολεύς.]

ἐπι-στολιᾶ-φόρος, ὁ = ἐπι-]

ἐπι-στολιμαῖος 2 existing only in papers.

ἐπι-στομίζω to bridle; to stop one's mouth.

ἐπι-στοναχέω to roar at.

ἐπι-στρατεία, -στράτευσις, ἡ expedition against.

ἐπι-στρατεύω and M. to march against.

ἐπι-στρεφής 2 intense; attentive, careful; anxious.

ἐπι-στρέφω to turn to, direct to; to turn about or back; to force back; to correct. — *intr., M.* and *P.* to turn oneself round, back, or forward(s); to visit; to care for. [about.]

ἐπι-στροφάδην *adv.* round

ἐπι-στροφή, ἡ a turning to; a warning; punishment; care, regard; a turning back, wheeling round, return; change; conversion

ἐπί-στροφος 2 conversant with.

ἐπι-στρωφάω to frequent.

ἐπι-συνάγω to gather together.

ἐπι-συναγωγή, ἡ assembly.

ἐπι-συντρέχω to run together at. [meeting.]

ἐπι-σύστασις, ἡ a riotous

ἐπι-σφάζω, ἐπι-σφάττω to slaughter or kill over.

ἐπι-σφαλής 2 unsteady; dangerous.

ἐπι-σφραγίζομαι *M.* to put a seal or mark upon.

ἐπι-σφύριον, τό clasp over the ankle. [file.]

ἐπι-σχερώ *adv.* in single

ἐπι-σχεσίᾱ, ἡ pretext.

ἐπί-σχεσις, ἡ a stopping, checking; moderation, reluctance. [to insist upon.]

ἐπ-ισχύω to press hard;

ἐπ-ίσχω = ἐπέχω.

ἐπι-σωρεύω to heap up.

ἐπί-ταγμα, τό, ἐπι-ταγή, ἡ order, command.

ἐπί-τακτοι, οἱ reserve, rear-guard. [yet more.]

ἐπι-ταλαιπωρέω to labour

ἐπί-ταξις, ἡ = ἐπίταγμα.

ἐπι-ταράσσω to trouble yet more. [assistant.]

ἐπιτάρροθος, ὁ, ἡ helper,

ἐπι-τάσσω and *M.* to arrange at; to place behind; to put in command; to command, order, enjoin, impose.

ἐπι-τάφιος 2 funeral.

ἐπι-ταχύνω to hasten on or forward.

ἐπι-τείνω to stretch upon or over; to strain, urge, heighten, increase; to excite.

ἐπι-τειχίζω to build a fortress or bulwark, to fortify.

ἐπι-τείχισις, ἡ, ἐπι-τειχισμός, ὁ the building a fortress; fort, bulwark.

ἐπι-τείχισμα, τό fortification, bulwark.

ἐπι-τελέω to finish, complete, accomplish, perform; to sacrifice; to pay. — *M.* to take upon oneself; to end. [complete.]

ἐπι-τελής 2 accomplished,

ἐπι-τέλλω and *M.* to enjoin, command; to rise.

ἐπι-τέμνω to make a cut into, to cut off.

ἐπι-τεξ, εκος, ἡ about to bring forth. [in.]

ἐπι-τέρπομαι *P.* to delight

ἐπι-τεχνάομαι *M.* to contrive besides.

ἐπι-τέχνησις, ἡ contrivance, additional improvement.

ἐπι-τήδειος 3 and 2 fit,

convenient, useful, serviceable; necessary; τὰ ἐπιτήδεια necessaries, victuals; ὁ ἐπ. relation, friend.

ἐπι-τηδές and ἐπίτηδες *adv.* for the purpose, purposely; sufficiently.

ἐπι-τήδευμα, τό and ἐπιτήδευσις, ἡ pursuit, business, practice; study; habits, manner of life.

ἐπι-τηδεύω to do on purpose, to pursue, practice; to invent.

ἐπι-τήκω to melt upon.

ἐπι-τηρέω to watch for, to wait attentively.

ἐπι-τίθημι to put or lay upon; to impose on, enjoin, cause; to grant; to add; to close by putting before. — *intr.* and *M.* to put on oneself or for oneself; to engage oneself in, to undertake; to attack, make an attempt upon.

ἐπι-τιμάω to honour or value after; to pronounce judgment; to punish, fine; to blame, reprove.

ἐπι-τίμησις, ἡ blame, reproach. [ger; protector.]

ἐπι-τιμήτωρ, ορος, ὁ aven-

ἐπι-τιμίᾱ, ἡ enjoyment of civil rights; punishment, reproach. [rights.]

ἐπί-τιμος 2 enjoying civil]

ἐπι-τλῆναι *aor.* to bear patiently.

ἐπι-τολή, ἡ a rising.

ἐπι-τολμάω to endure at.

ἐπί-τονος, ὁ stretched rope; back stay (of the mast).

ἐπι-τοξάζομαι to shoot at.

ἐπι-τραπέω to give over.

ἐπι-τρέπω to turn to or towards; to give over, entrust, to put into one's hand; to leave; to admit, allow, permit; to enjoin, ordain; *intr.* to turn to; to entrust oneself to; to yield, succumb. — *M.* to turn oneself to, to incline to; to entrust oneself to.

ἐπι-τρέφω to feed, bring up. — *P.* to grow (up) after; to grow up.

ἐπι-τρέχω to run at, upon, after, or over; to attack, oppress, overrun.

ἐπι-τρίβω to rub on the surface; to weaken, afflict, destroy. [ning.]

ἐπί-τριπτος 2 crafty, cun-

ἐπι-τροπαῖος 3 tutelar, pupillary.

ἐπι-τροπεύω to be guardian, tutor, trustee, or governor.

ἐπι-τροπή, ἡ an entrusting, charge, trust; decision, arbitration; guardianship.

ἐπί-τροπος, ὁ trustee, guardian, governor.

ἐπι-τροχάδην *adv.* fluently.

ἐπι-τυγχάνω to meet with, fall in with; to reach, attain, obtain, succeed.

ἐπι-τύμβιος 2 belonging to a tomb.

ἐπι-φαίνομαι *P.* and -φαίνω to appear, become conspicuous; to show oneself. [manifestation.]

ἐπι-φάνεια, ἡ appearance,

ἐπι - φανής 2 conspicuous, manifest; excellent, famous, illustrious.

ἐπί-φαντος 2 conspicuous, still living.

ἐπι-φαύσκω to shine upon.

ἐπι-φέρω to bring, carry, or put upon or up; to cause, occasion; to add, increase; to throw or lay upon, to impose, inflict, impute, reproach. — M. to bring with oneself. — P. to rush on, attack, assail, rebuke; to pursue, follow.

ἐπι - φημίζω M. to foretel (bad) omens. [(bad) omen.]

ἐπι - φήμισμα, τό word of

ἐπι-φθέγγομαι M. to call out at; to sound a charge.

ἐπι - φθονέω to envy, grudge; to hate.

ἐπί-φθονος 2 envious, jealous, hostile; envied, hated.

ἐπι-φλέγω to burn; to consume.

ἐπι-φοιτάω, -έω to go or come repeatedly to, to visit frequently; to invade; to come after. [pay.]

ἐπι - φορά, ἡ addition to

ἐπι-φορέω = ἐπιφέρω.

ἐπί-φόρημα, τό dessert.

ἐπί-φορος 2 carrying towards: favourable.

ἐπι-φράζομαι M. to think of, reflect on, consider; to contrive; to discover.

ἐπι-φράσσω to fence in; to stop up.

ἐπι-φρονέω to be prudent.

ἐπι-φροσύνη, ἡ thoughtfulness, presence of mind.

ἐπί-φρων 2 thoughtful, prudent. [upon or at.]

ἐπί-φύομαι M. to grow

ἐπι-φωνέω to call at.

ἐπι-φώσκω to dawn.

ἐπι-χαίρω to rejoice at.

ἐπί - χαλκος 2 of brass or copper.

ἐπί-χαρις, ι pleasing, agreeable, engaging.

ἐπί-χαρτος 2 delightful.

ἐπι-χειμάζω to pass the winter at.

ἐπί - χειρα, τά wages; earnest-money.

ἐπι-χειρέω to put one's hand to; to attack, assail; to undertake, attempt, try, venture, manage.

ἐπι - χείρημα, τό, ἐπι-χείρησις, ἡ an undertaking, a beginning, attempt, project; attack.

ἐπι-χειρητής, οῦ ὁ an enterprising man of action.

ἐπι-χειροτονέω to vote by show of hands.

ἐπι-χέω to pour or shed over, upon, or at. — M. and P. to flood in, befall.

ἐπι-χθόνιος 2 earthy.

ἐπί-χολος 2 producing bile.

ἐπι-χορηγέω to afford, procure in addition.

ἐπι-χορηγίᾱ, ἡ supply.

ἐπι-χράομαι M. to make use of; to converse with.

ἐπι-χράω, -χραύω to rush upon, attack.

ἐπι-χρίω to anoint, besmear. — M. to anoint oneself. [gold.]

ἐπί-χρῡσος 2 overlaid with

11*

ἐπι-χωρέω to come up or on, to advance; to yield, concede.

ἐπι-χωριάζω to visit often.

ἐπι-χώριος 2 native, indigenous, in the fashion of the country. [surface.]

ἐπι-φαύω to touch on the/

ἐπι-ψηλαφάω to grope for.

ἐπι-ψηφίζω to put to the vote. — M. to vote, decree, confirm by vote.

ἐπ-ιωγή, ἡ shelter, anchorage, landing-place.

ἐπ-οικέω to go or live as a settler or colonist; to dwell in: to be a neighbour.

ἐπ-οικοδομέω to build up, repair; to build upon.

ἔπ-οικος, ὁ settler, colonist; foreigner; inhabitant; (near) neighbour.

ἐπ-οικτείρω, ἐπ-οικτίζω to have compassion with.

ἐπ-οίχομαι M. to go or come towards, to approach; to attack; to go over, through, or along; to review, inspect; to set to work.

ἐπ-οκέλλω to run ashore (trans. and intr.), to be wrecked.

ἕπομαι M. to follow; to accompany, escort; to pursue. [upon or by.]

ἐπ-όμνῦμι, -ὒω to swear)

ἐπ-ομφάλιος 2 upon the navel. [to be reproached.]

ἐπ-ονείδιστος 2 shameful,)

ἐπ-ονομάζω to give a name, to surname; to call by name. [with awe.]

ἐπ-οπίζομαι M. to regard)

ἐπο-ποιΐα, ἡ epic poetry.

ἐπο-ποιός, ὁ epic poet.

ἐπ-οπτάω to roast upon.

ἐπ-οπτεύω to look on or at; to inspect, watch over.

ἐπ-όπτης, ου, ὁ watcher, guardian; witness.

ἐπ-ορέγω to hand to. — M. and P. to stretch oneself towards; to desire yet more.

ἐπ-ορθρεύομαι M. to rise early.

ἐπ-όρνῦμι to arouse, stir up, excite; to send to. — P. to rise, rush on.

ἐπ-οροΰω to rush at, to fall upon.

ἐπ-ορχέομαι M. to dance to.

ἔπος, τό word; speech, tale, saying; promise; oracle; maxim; advice, order; legend, report; song, epic poem; thing, story, something. [up, rouse.]

ἐπ-οτρΰνω to incite, stir)

ἐπ-ουράνιος 2 heavenly.

ἔπ-ουρος 2 blowing favourably. [still.]

ἐπ-οφείλω to be indebted)

ἐπ-οχέομαι to ride upon.

ἐπ-οχετεύω to bring water by a channel to a place.

ἔπ-οχος riding or mounted upon; firm in the saddle.

ἔποψ, οπος, ὁ hoopoe.

ἐπ-όψιμος 2 that can be looked on or seen.

ἐπ-όψιος 3 visible, manifest; all-seeing.

ἔπ-οψις, ἡ view; range of vision, sight.

ἑπτά seven.

ἑπτα-βόειος 2, ἑπτά-βοιος
of seven bull's-hides.

ἑπτα-ετής, ἑπτα-έτης 2
seven years old, for seven
years.

ἑπτα-καί-δεκα seventeen.

ἑπτα-καί-δέκατος 3 se-
venteenth.

ἑπτάκις adv. seven times.

ἑπτακισ-μύριοι 3 seventy
thousand.

ἑπτακισ-χίλιοι 3 seven
thousand.   [dred.]

ἑπτακόσιοι 3 seven hun-}

ἑπτά-λογχος 2 of seven
lances, under seven leaders.

ἑπτά-μηνος 2 of seven
months.

ἑπτά-πηχυς, υ seven cu-
bits long.   [long.]

ἑπτα-πόδης, ου seven feet}

ἑπτά-πυλος 2 seven-gated.

ἑπτά-τονος 2 seven-toned.

ἕπταχα adv. in seven parts.

ἑπτ-έτης 2 = ἑπταέτης.

ἕπτω to be busy or engaged
with; to go; to come.

ἐπ-φδή, ἡ incantation, magic song; spell, charm.

ἐπ-φδός 2 acting as a
charm; enchanter, helper;
ἡ ἐ. concluding stanza.

ἐπ-ωμίς, ίδος, ἡ upper
part of the shoulder, arm
and shoulder.

ἐπ-ώμοτος 2 on oath;
sworn witness.   [name.]

ἐπ-ωνυμία, ἡ surname;}

ἐπ-ώνυμος, -ωνύμιος 2
named after, surnamed;
giving one's name to.

ἐπ-ωτίδες, αἱ battering
beams of a ship.

ἐπ-ωφελέω to aid, help.

ἐπ-ωφέλημα, τό help.

ἐπ-ώχατο they were shut
(from ἐπέχω).

ἔραζε adv. to the earth.

ἔραμαι = ἐράω.

ἐραννός 3 lovely.

ἔρανος, ὁ common meal,
picnic; contribution; kindness.   [money, covetous.]

ἐρασι-χρήματος 2 loving}

ἐράσμιος 2, ἐραστός 3
lovely, charming, pleasant,
amiable; welcome.

ἐραστής, οῦ, ὁ lover, friend,
adherent.

ἐρατεινός 3 = ἐράσιμος.

ἐρατίζω to lust after or for.

ἐρᾱτύω = ἐρητύω.

ἐράω and P. to love pas-
sionately, to fall in love
(with); to desire, long for.

ἐργάζομαι M. to work, be
busy; to do, perform, accomplish; to effect, cause; to
earn; to carry on a trade;
to do to, commit upon.

ἐργάθω = εἴργω.

ἐργαλεῖον, τό tool, instrument.   [to do.]

ἐργασείω to have a mind}

ἐργασίᾱ, ἡ work, business,
occupation;   husbandry;
trade; effect; a working at;
workmanship; gain, profit.

ἐργαστήριον, τό workshop,
factory.   [industrious.]

ἐργαστικός 3 laborious,}

ἐργάτης, ου, ὁ worker,
workman; husbandman.

ἐργατικός 3 = ἐργαστικός.

ἐργάτις, ιδος, ἡ fem. of
ἐργάτης.

ἔργμα, τό = ἔργον. [son.)

ἔργμα, τό confinement, pri-)

ἐργο-λαβέω to enter upon work by contract.

ἔργον, τό work, deed, action, enterprise; fact, reality; business, occupation, employment, labour; husbandry; trade; war, combat; great or hard work; product of labour, building, cornfield; thing, matter, piece; circumstance.

ἔργω = εἴργω.   [cult.)

ἐργώδης 2 toilsome, diffi-)

ἔρδω, ἔρδω to do, make, act; to offer, sacrifice.

ἐρεβεννός 3 dark, gloomy.

ἐρέβινθος, ὁ chick-pea.

ἔρεβος, τό the dark nether world.

ἐρείνω and M. to ask.

ἐρεθ.ζω, ἐρέθω to provoke, irritate, tease, excite.

ἐρείδω to prop, stay, support; to press, urge, push; intr. to lean against; to rush on. — P. and M. to prop or support oneself, to lean upon; to be fixed in.

ἐρείκω to tear, break, crush; to pierce; to burst.

ἐρείπια, τά ruins.

ἐρείπω to pull down, dash down; intr. and P. to fall down in ruins.

ἔρεισμα, τό prop, support.

ἐρεμνός 3 dark, gloomy.

ἐρέπτομαι M. to pluck off.

ἐρέσσω to row; to move quickly, to ply.

ἐρέτης, ου, ὁ rower.

ἐρετμόν, τό oar.

ἐρεύγομαι[1] to spit out, vomit; to splash up, surge; to break out.

ἐρεύγομαι[2] to roar.

ἐρευθέδανον, τό madder.

ἐρεύθω to make red.

ἔρευνα, ἡ inquiry.

ἐρευνάω to search after, inquire (into), examine.

ἐρέφω to cover, roof in; to crown.   [shatter.)

ἐρέχθω to rend; to dash,)

ἐρέω[1] fut. I shall say.

ἐρέω[2], ἐρέομαι M. εἴρομαι to ask, inquire, question.

ἐρημίᾱ, ἡ solitude, desert, loneliness; helplessness; absence, want.

ἐρῆμος and ἔρημος 3 and 2 lonely, solitary, desert, desolate, waste; helpless, abandoned, needy, destitute; ἡ ἐρήμη (δίκη) trial in default of appearance.

ἐρημόω to make solitary, to desolate, devastate, evacuate; to deprive, bereave; to abandon. [devastation.)

ἐρήμωσις, ἡ desolation,)

ἐρητύω to keep back, to check, hinder, restrain.

ἐρι-αύχην, ενος with a strong neck. [thundering.)

ἐρι-βρεμέτης, ου loud-)

ἐρι-βῶλαξ, ακος, ἐρι-βῶλος 2 with large clods.

ἐρί-γδουπος 2 thundering, loud-roaring.

ἐριδαίνω = ἐρίζω.

ἐριθμαίνω to provoke, irritate.   [πος.)

ἐρί-δουπος 2 = ἐρίγδου-)

ἐρίζω to quarrel, wrangle, contend, rival; to be a match for, be equal to.

ἐρί-ηρος 2 dear, loving, beloved.

ἐρῑθείᾱ, ἡ = ἔρις. [fertile.]

ἐρι-θηλής 2 luxurious,

ἔρῑθος, ὁ, ἡ day-labourer; reaper. [mous.]

ἐρι-κῡδής 2 glorious, fa-

ἐρί-μυκος 2 loud-bellowing.

ἐρῐνεός, ὁ wild fig-tree.

Ἐρῑνύς, ύος, ἡ Erinys (avenging deity); revenge, punishment; curse; destruction.

ἔριον, τό wool.

ἐρι-ούνης, ἐρι-ούνιος, ὁ helper, bliss-bearer. [wool.]

ἐριουργέω to work in

ἔρις, ιδος, ἡ quarrel, strife, discord, animosity; jealousy; combat; zeal, contention.

ἐρι-σθενής 2 very mighty.

ἔρισμα, τό cause of quarrel.

ἐρι-στάφυλος 2 with large clusters.

ἐριστός 3 to be disputed.

ἐρι-τῑμος 2 most honoured, highly prized.

ἐρίφειος 2 of a kid.

ἔριφος, ὁ, ἡ and ἐρίφιον, τό goat, kid.

ἑρκεῖος, ἕρκειος 2 belonging to a yard or enclosure; house-protecting.

ἑρκίον, τό, ἕρκος, τό fence, enclosure, hedge, wall; farm-yard; defence, protection; snare, net.

ἑρκτή, ἡ = εἱρκτή.

ἕρμα¹, τό prop, support, defence; reef, rock; hill.

ἕρμα², τό pendant of the ear; foundation, cause.

ἕρμαιον, τό godsend, windfall. [pretation.]

ἑρμηνείᾱ, ἡ speech; inter-

ἑρμηνεύς, ὁ, ἑρμηνευτής, οῦ, ὁ herald; interpreter, expounder.

ἑρμηνεύω to expound, interpret, translate, explain.

ἑρμίς, ῖνος, ὁ bed-post.

ἑρμο-γλυφεῖον, τό sculptor's workshop.

ἔρνος, τό shoot, scion, child.

ἑρξίης, ὁ worker.

ἔρομαι M. to ask, inquire.

ἑρπετόν, τό creeping animal, reptile; living being.

ἕρπω, ἑρπύζω to creep, crawl; to go; to come.

ἔρρω to walk slowly, to go away; to perish, be lost.

ἐρρωμένος 3 strong, stout; vigorous. [νυμι.]

ἔρρωσο fare-well; see ῥών-

ἔρση, ἔρσῃ, ἡ dew, dewdrop; new-born or late-born lamb.

ἐρσήεις 3 dewy; fresh.

ἔρσην, ενος = ἄρρην.

ἐρύγμηλος 1 loud-bellowing.

ἐρυθαίνω to make red. — P. to become red, to blush.

ἐρύθημα, τ redness; inflammation. [to blush.]

ἐρυθραίνομαι, ἐρυθριάω

ἐρυθρός 3 red.

ἐρύκω, ἐρυκανάω, ἐρυκάνω to keep back, stop, restrain, check, hinder; to keep asunder. — M. and P. to be detained; to tarry.

ἔρυμα, τό fence, bulwark; fort; castle. [tected.]

ἐρυμνός 3 fortified, pro-

ἐρύομαι *M.* to save, rescue, protect; to watch, observe; to lie in wait (for), to espy; to ward off, check.

ἐρυσ-άρματες, οἱ chariot-drawing.

ἐρυσίβη, ἡ mildew.

ἐρυσί-πτολις town-protecting.

ἐρυστός 3 drawn.

ἐρύω to draw, push; to bend (a bow); to tear off or away, to snatch from; to drag, pull, trail. — *M.* to draw to oneself, to snatch; to outweigh. [up.]

ἐρχατάομαι *P.* to be shut]

ἔρχομαι *M.* to come, go, arrive at; to march, travel, drive; to flow, fly; to go away, march out; to be lost; to come back, return; to be about to do.

ἐρῳδιός, ὁ heron.

ἐρωέω[1] to flow, stream.

ἐρωέω[2] to rest, repose, cease from; to stay behind; *trans.* to drive or push back.

ἐρωή[1], ἡ quick motion, force, impetus.

ἐρωή[2], ἡ rest.

ἔρως, ωτος, ὁ love; desire.

ἐρωτάω to ask, request; to inquire.

ἐρώτημα, τό, ἐρώτησις, ἡ question; questioning.

ἐρωτικός 3 of love; inclined to love, fond.

ἐς = εἰς.

ἐσθέω to clothe.

ἔσθημα, τό, ἐσθής, ῆτος, ἡ, ἔσθησις, ἡ garment, dress, clothing.

ἐσθίω = ἔδω.

ἐσθλός 3 good, kind; generous, noble; brave, valiant; valuable; lucky, favourable.

ἔσθος, τό = ἔσθημα.

ἔσθ' ὅτε sometimes.

ἔσθω = ἔδω, ἐσθίω.

ἑσμός, ὁ swarm, flock; plenty.

ἔσ-οπτρον, τό mirror.

ἑσπέρα, ἡ evening; west.

ἑσπέριος 3 and ἕσπερος 2 in the evening; western.

ἑσπερός, ὁ = ἑσπέρα.

ἔσπετε = εἴπετε see εἶπον.

ἐσσόομαι = ἡσσάομαι.

ἔσσυμαι see σεύω.

ἐσσύμενος 3 eager; hasty.

ἔσσων 2 = ἥσσων.

ἔστε *adv.* and *conj.* till, until; as long as; even to.

ἑστία, ἡ hearth; house, home, family; altar; Hestia = Vesta.

ἑστίαμα, τό, ἑστίασις, ἡ feast, banquet. [tainer.]

ἑστιάτωρ, ορος, ὁ enter-]

ἑστιάω to receive hospitably, to feast, entertain. — *P.* to feast on.

ἑστιοῦχος 2 guarding the house; with holy altars.

ἑστιῶτις, ιδος belonging to the house.

ἕστωρ, ορος, ὁ pole-nail.

ἐσχάρα, ἡ hearth; fireplace; coal-pan; altar.

ἐσχατιά, ἡ extreme part, remotest place, end, border.

ἔσχατος 3 the farthest, remotest, uttermost, extreme; latest; highest; last; worst; lowest.

ἐσχατόων 3 the farthest; lying on the edge or border.

ἔσω = εἴσω.　[within.]

ἔσωθεν adv. from within;

ἐσώτερος 3 inner.

ἑταίρᾱ, ἡ female companion or friend; sweetheart, courtesan.

ἑταιρεία, ἡ companionship, association, brotherhood; political club.

ἑταιρεῖος 3 of comrades or partisans.

ἑταιρίᾱ, ἡ = ἑταιρεία.

ἑταιρίζω to be a companion. — M. to choose for companion.

ἑταιρικός 3 = ἑταιρεῖος.

ἑταιρίς, ίδος, ἡ = ἑταίρα.

ἑταῖρος, ὁ companion, comrade, mate, friend.

ἑταιρίζω = ἑταιρίζω.

ἕταρος, ὁ = ἑταῖρος.

ἐτεός 3 true, real.

ἑτερ-αλκής 2 giving strength to one of two, changing, doubtful.

ἑτερ-ήμερος 2 on alternate days.

ἑτέρηφι adv. with one or the other hand.

ἑτερό-γλωσσος 2 speaking a foreign language.

ἑτερο-διδασκαλέω to teach false doctrine.

ἑτερο-ζυγέω to be put to another yoke.　[kind.]

ἑτεροῖος 3 of a different

ἕτερος 3 the other, one of two, another; the second; different, of another kind; at variance.

ἑτέρωθεν adv. from the other side; on the other side.

ἑτέρωθι adv. on the other side; elsewhere, to another place, sideways.

ἔτης, ου, ὁ kinsman, clansman, friend.

ἐτησίαι, οἱ periodical winds.

ἐτήσιος 2 for a year, yearly.

ἐτήτυμος 2 true, real, genuine.

ἔτι adv. yet, as yet, yet longer, still; besides.

ἑτοιμάζω to make ready, to prepare.

ἑτοιμασία, ἡ readiness.

ἑτοῖμος and ἕτοιμος 2 and 3 extant, ready, at hand, disposable; willing, quick, active, prompt; easy; real, confirmed.

ἔτος, τό year.

ἐτός adv. without reason.

ἔτυμος 2 real, true, actual.

ἐτώσιος 2 idle, useless.

εὖ, ἐΰ adv. well, properly, rightly; luckily.

εὖ = οὖ.　[bring good news.]

εὐ-αγγελίζω and M. to

εὐ-αγγέλιον, τό good news, glad tidings, gospel; reward for good news.

εὐ-αγγελιστής, οῦ, ὁ evangelist.

εὐ-αγής 2 guiltless, pure, pious; purifying; shining, conspicuous.　[ing.]

εὔ-αγρος 2 lucky in hunt-

εὐ-άγωγος 2 easily led.

εὔαδε aor. of ἀνδάνω.

εὐάζω to cry εὐά.

εὐ-αής 2 blowing fair; friendly.

εὐ-αίρετος 2 easy to be taken, chosen, or known.

εὐ-αίων, ωνος happy; making happy.

εὐ-άμερος 2 = εὐήμερος.

εὐ-ανδρία, ἡ plenty of good men.

εὐ-άνεμος 2 well aired.

εὐ-ανθής 2 blooming; flowery, gay. [described.]

εὐ-απήγητος 2 easy to be

εὐ-απόβατος 2 convenient for disembarking.

εὐ-αποτείχιστος 2 easy to be blockaded.

εὐ-αρεστέω to please well.

εὐ-άρεστος 2 well-pleasing; easily satisfied.

εὐ-αρίθμητος 2 easy to be counted. [chariots.]

εὐ-άρματος 2 famous for

εὐ-αρμοστία, ἡ harmony, evenness of temper.

εὐ-άρμοστος 2 well-adapted, harmonious, even.

εὐ-αυγής 2 far-seeing.

εὐ-βάστακτος 2 easy to be carried.

εὔ-βατος 2 accessible.

εὔ-βοτος 2 rich in pastures and cattle.

εὔ-βοτρυς, υ rich in grapes.

εὐ-βουλία, ἡ good counsel, prudence. [prudent.]

εὔ-βουλος 2 well-advised,

εὐ-γάθητος 2 joyous.

εὖγε = εὖ γε well done!

εὐ-γένεια, ἡ noble descent; generosity.

εὐ-γένειος 2 well-bearded.

εὐ-γενής 2 well-born, noble, generous. [vow.]

εὔγμα, τό boast; prayer,

εὐ-γναμπτος 2 well-bent.

εὐ-γνώμων 2 generous; kind; fair; sensible.

εὔ-γνωστος 2 well-known; visible. [or prosperous.]

εὐ-δαιμονέω to be happy

εὐ-δαιμονία, ἡ happiness, prosperity. [happy.]

εὐ-δαιμονίζω to consider

εὐ-δαιμονικός 3 of happiness; happy; making happy.

εὐ-δαίμων 2 happy; fortunate, lucky; prosperous, wealthy.

εὐ-δείελος 2 far-seen.

εὔ-δηλος 2 quite manifest.

εὐ-δία, ἡ fair weather; calm; security. [crossed.]

εὐ-διάβατος 2 easy to be

εὐ-διάβολος 2 exposed to misinterpretation.

εὐ-δικία, ἡ justice.

εὔ-διος 2 fair, clear, calm.

εὔ-δμητος 2 well-built.

εὐ-δοκέω to be pleased with; to consent to.

εὐ-δοκία, ἡ satisfaction, delight; wish.

εὐ-δοκιμέω to be of good repute, to be famous or distinguished.

εὐ-δόκιμος 2 honoured, esteemed, renowned.

εὐ-δοξέω = εὐδοκιμέω.

εὐ-δοξία, ἡ good repute, renown; approval.

εὔ-δοξος 2 = εὐδόκιμος.

εὐ-δρακής 2 sharp-sighted.

εὕδω to sleep; to fall asleep.

εὐ-ειδής 2 well-shaped.
εὐ-έλεγκτος 2 easy to be refuted or to be convinced.
εὔ-ελπις, ι hopeful.
εὐ-εξάλειπτος 2 easy to be blotted out.
εὐ-εξέλεγκτος 2 = εὐέλεγκτος. [being.]
εὐ-εξία, ἡ good state; well-
εὐ-έπεια, ἡ good wish.
εὐ-επής 2 well-speaking; well-spoken.
εὐ-επιβούλευτος 2 open to snares. [attacked.]
εὐ-επίθετος 2 easy to be
εὐ-εργεσία, ἡ well-doing, kindness, good deed.
εὐ-εργετέω to do good, show kindness. — P. to receive a kindness.
εὐ-εργέτημα, τό = εὐεργεσία.
εὐ-εργέτης, ου, ὁ well-doer, benefactor; well-deserving man. [well-done.]
εὐεργής 2 well-wrought;
εὐ-εργός 2 doing good; easy to be wrought.
εὐ-ερκής 2 well-fenced.
εὔ-ερος 2 with good wool.
εὐ-εστώ, οῦς, ἡ well-being, happiness.
εὐ-ετηρία, ἡ good harvest.
εὐ-εύρετος 2 easy to find.
εὐ-έφοδος 2 easily accessible.
εὔ-ζυγος 2 well-joined.
εὔ-ζωνος 2 well-girt, girt up; active.
εὐ-ηγενής 2 = εὐγενής.
εὐ-ηγεσία, ἡ good government. [plicity.]
εὐ-ήθεια, ἡ goodness; sim-

εὐ-ήθης 2 good-natured; simple, silly.
εὐ-ηθικός 3 = εὐήθης.
εὐ-ήκης 2 well-pointed.
εὐ-ήλατος 2 easy to ride over.
εὐ-ημερέω to be happy or successful. [day.]
εὐ-ημερία, ἡ fine or happy
εὐ-ήμερος 2 bringing a fine day.
εὐ-ήνεμος 2 = εὐάνεμος.
εὐ-ήνωρ, ορος manly; giving manly strength.
εὔ-ηρατος 2 lovely.
εὐ-ήρετμος 2 rowing well; well-rowed.
εὐ-ήρης 2 manageable.
εὐ-ηφενής 2 wealthy.
εὐ-θάλασσος 2 of the mighty sea. [manly.]
εὐ-θαρσής 2 courageous,
εὐ-θενέω and P. to thrive, be prosperous. [win.]
εὐ-θεράπευτος 2 easy to
εὔ-θετος 2 convenient.
εὐθέως = εὐθύς.
εὐ-θηνέω = εὐθενέω.
εὔ-θριξ, τριχος having beautiful hair. [ful seat.]
εὔ-θρονος 2 on a beauti-
εὐθύ adv. = εὐθύς.
εὐθυ-δρομέω to run or come straight.
εὐ-θυμέω and M. to be of good cheer. [gladness.]
εὐ-θυμία, ἡ cheerfulness,
εὔ-θυμος 2 well-disposed; cheerful, glad; eager.
εὐθύνη, εὔθυνα, ἡ the giving an account; account, vindication; chastisement.

εὐθύνω and *M.* to make or direct straight, to guide; to correct; to blame; to accuse, call to account; to punish.

εὐθύς, εῖα, ὐ straight, direct; plain, honest. — *adv.* εὐθύς, εὐθύ, εὐθέως straightforward; forthwith, at once; without reserve; for instance.

εὐθύτης, ητος, ἡ straightness; justice.

εὐθύ-ωρον *adv.* = εὐθύς.

εὔιος 2 shouting; rejoicing; Bacchic.

εὔ-ιππος 2 with good horses; well-mounted.

εὐ-καθαίρετος 2 easy to overthrow.

εὐ-καιρέω to have leisure.

εὐ-καιρίᾱ, ἡ opportunity.

εὔ-καιρος 2 in time, seasonable, opportune.

εὐ-καμπής 2 well-bent.

εὐ-κάρδιος 2 stout-hearted.

εὔ-καρπος 2 fruitful.

εὐ-κατάλυτος 2 easy to destroy.   [spicable.]

εὐ-καταφρόνητος 2 despicable.

εὐ-κατέργαστος 2 easy to work or to digest. [accuse.]

εὐ-κατηγόρητος 2 easy to accuse.

εὔ-κέατος 2 well-split.

εὔ-κερως, ων well-horned.

εὔκηλος 2 = ἔκηλος.

εὐ-κλεής 2 famous, glorious, noble.   [renown.]

εὔ-κλεια, ἡ good fame, renown.

εὐ-κλεής = εὐκλεής.

εὐ-κλήϊς, ῖδος well-closed.

εὐ-κνήμις, ῖδος with good greaves.

εὔ-κολος 2 well-disposed; gay; easy; contented.

εὐ-κομιδής 2 well-cared for.

εὔ-κομος = ἠΰκομος.

εὔ-κοπος 2 easy, without pains. [modesty, decency.]

εὐ-κοσμίᾱ, ἡ good order; modesty, decency.

εὔ-κοσμος 2 well-ordered; well-adorned, graceful; easy to arrange.

εὐ-κρινής 2 well-ordered; distinct, clear.

εὐ-κρότητος 2 well-hammered.   [tive.]

εὐκταῖος 3 prayed for, votive.

εὐ-κτίμενος 3, εὔ-κτιτος well-built, well-made.

εὐκτός 3 wished for; desirable.

εὐλάβεια, ἡ caution, circumspection; awe, fear; piety.

εὐλαβέομαι *P.* to be cautious, circumspect, or careful; to fear, beware of; to reverence, worship; to care for.

εὐ-λαβής 2 cautious, circumspect, anxious; conscientious; devout.

εὐλάζω to plough.

εὐλάκα, ἡ ploughshare.

εὐ-λείμων 2 rich in meadows.

εὔ-λεκτρος 2 fit for marriage, bridal, lovely.

εὐλή, ἡ maggot, worm.

εὔ-ληπτος 2 easy to be taken or conquered.

εὔληρα, τά reins.

εὐ-λογέω to praise; to give thanks; to bless.

εὐ-λογητός 3 blessed.

εὐ-λογίᾱ, ἡ praise, eulogy; fair - speaking; blessing; kindness, bounty.

εὔ-λογος 2 sounding well; reasonable; probable.

εὔ-λοφος 2 with a fine plume.   [solve.]

εὔ-λυτος 2 easy to dis-]

εὐ-μάθεια, ἡ docility.

εὐ-μαθής 2 docile; easy to be learned or understood.

εὐ-μάρεια, -ίᾱ, ἡ easiness; convenience; possibility; preventive; abundance; comfort; stool, privy.

εὐ - μαρής 2 easy; convenient.   [or great.]

εὐ-μεγέθης 2 very large]

εὐ-μένεια, ἡ good will, kindness.

εὐ-μενής 2, εὐ-μενέτης, ου well-disposed, kind; favourable; convenient.

εὐ-μετάβολος 2 changeable, fickle.

εὐ-μετάδοτος 2 liberal.

εὐ-μεταχείριστος 2 easy to manage or to conquer.

εὔ-μηλος 2 rich in sheep.

εὐ-μήχανος 2 inventive; ingenious.   [threads.]

εὔ - μιτος 2 with fine]

εὔ-μμελίης, ου skilled in thrusting spears. [bering.]

εὔ-μναστος 2 well-remem-]

εὔ-μορφος 2 well-shaped.

εὐ-μουσίᾱ, ἡ taste for the fine arts.

εὔ-μουσος 2 musical.

εὐνάζω to lay to sleep; to lay in ambush; to lull to sleep; to assuage. — P. and M. to

lie down; to go asleep; to rest.

εὐ-ναιετάων, ουσα, ον and εὐ-ναιόμενος 3 well-inhabited or peopled.

εὐναῖος 3 of a couch; matrimonial; resting.

εὐνά(σ)τήριον, τό, εὐνή, ἡ bed, couch; marriage-bed; bed-chamber; stone used as an anchor.

εὐνῆθεν adv. out of bed.

εὐνήτρια, ἡ. εὔνις[1], ιδος, ἡ wife.   [destitute.]

εὔνις[2], ι(δ)ος, ὁ, ἡ bereft,]

εὔ - ννητος 2 well-woven.

εὐ-νοέω to be well-disposed, favourable, or friendly.

εὔ-νοια, ἡ good will, kindness, favour.   [friendly.]

εὐ-νοϊκός 3 benevolent,]

εὐ-νομέομαι P. to have good laws.

εὐ-νομίᾱ, ἡ the having good laws; order, legal constitution.

εὔ-νοος, εὔ-νους 2 welldisposed, kind, friendly, benevolent.

εὐνουχίζω to unman.

εὐνοῦχος, ὁ eunuch; chamberlain.

εὐ-νώμᾱς, ου quick moving.

εὔ-ξε(ι)νος 2 hospitable.

εὔ-ξεστος, εὔ-ξοος 2 wellpolished.   [συμ-, -συν-.]

εὐ - ξυμ-, εὐ-ξυν- see εὐ-]

εὔ-οδος 2 easy to travel in.

εὐοῖ int. Lat. evoe!

εὔ-οικος 2 convenient for dwelling in; economical.

εὔ-ολβος 2 very wealthy.

εὔ-οπλος 2 well-armed.

εὐ-όργητος 2 even-tempered. [oath.]

εὐ-ορκέω to keep one's/

εὐ-ορκος 2 true to one's oath; according to an oath. [chorage.]

εὐ-ορμος 2 with good an-/

εὐ-πάθεια, ἡ sensual enjoyment, luxury. [things.]

εὐ-παθέω to enjoy good/

εὐ-παιδίᾱ, ἡ the having good children.

εὐ-παις, -παιδος having good children.

εὐ-πάρεδρος 2 persevering.

εὐ-πάτερεια, ἡ daughter of a noble father.

εὐ-πατρίδης, ου, εὐ-πατρις, ιδος of a noble father; noble.

εὐ-πειθής 2, εὐ-πειστος 2 obedient, yielding.

εὐ-πεπλος 2 with a fine robe. [ensnaring.]

εὐ-περίστατος 2 easily/

εὐ-πέτεια, ἡ easiness, an easy getting.

εὐ-πετής 2 easy, convenient, without trouble.

εὐ-πηγής, εὐ-πηκτος 2 well put togéther, stout, compact.

εὐ-πιστος 2 trustworthy.

εὐ-πλαστος 2 plastic.

εὐ-πλειος 2 quite full.

εὐ-πλεκής, εὐ-πλεκτος 2 well-plaited.

εὐ-πλοια, ἡ good sailing.

εὐ-πλόκαμος 2, εὐ-πλοκαμίς, ιδος with fine locks.

εὐ-πλυνής 2 well-washed.

εὐ-ποίητος 2 well-wrought.

εὐ-ποιΐᾱ, ἡ beneficence.

εὐ-πομπος 2 well-conducting.

εὐ-πορέω to have abundance or plenty (of); to be prosperous or successful; to find a way, to be able; trans. to supply abundantly.

εὐ-πορίᾱ, ἡ facility, opportunity; means, supply, resources; plenty, wealth.

εὐ-πορος 2 easy to pass over; convenient, easy; ready, ingenious, inventive; wealthy, rich.

εὐ-πρᾱγέω to be well off.

εὐ-πρᾱγίᾱ, ἡ, εὐ-πρᾱξίᾱ, ἡ well-doing, success, welfare; good action. [done.]

εὐ-πρᾱκτος 2 easy to be/

εὐ-πρέπεια, ἡ comely appearance, beauty; palliation, excuse.

εὐ-πρεπής 2 comely, well-looking, decent; distinguished, conspicuous; specious, shining.

εὐ-πρηστος 2 sparkling.

εὐ-πρόσδεκτος 2 acceptable. [affable.]

εὐ-πρόσοδος 2 accessible;/

εὐ-προσωπέω to please.

εὐ-πρόσωπος 2 with a fine face; cheerful.

εὐ-προφάσιστος 2 convincing, plausible. [stern.]

εὐ-πρυμνος 2 with a fine/

εὐ-πτερος 2 well-winged.

εὐ-πτυκτος 2 easy to be folded. [towers.]

εὐ-πυργος 2 with good/

εὐ-πωλος 2 with fine colts.

εὐρ-ακύλων, ωνος, ὁ northeast-wind.

εὐράξ *adv.* sideways.

εὐ-ραφής 2 well-sewed.

εὕρεσις, ἡ a finding.

εὑρετής, οῦ. ὁ inventor.

εὑρετικός 3 inventive.

εὑρετός 3 found, invented; to be found.

εὕρημα, τό a thing found; windfall, unexpected gain; foundling; invention.

εὔ-ρῑνος 2, εὔ-ρῑς, ῑνος 2 with a scenting nose.

εὔριπος, ὁ strait, narrow sea.

εὑρίσκω to find, find out, discover; to invent, contrive; to procure; to meet; to gain, obtain; to fetch money (of merchandise).

εὔ-ροος 2 fine-flowing.

εὖρος[1], ὁ south-east-wind.

εὖρος[2], τό breadth, width.

ἐΰ-ρραφής = εὐραφής.

ἐΰ-ρρεής 2, ἐΰ-ρρείτης, ου = εὔροος.

εὐρυ-άγυιος 3 with wide streets.

εὐρυ-εδής 2 spacious.

εὐ-ρυθμίᾱ, ἡ good time; proportion.

εὔ-ρυθμος 2 in good time or measure, fitting well; rhythmical; graceful.

εὐρυ-κρείων, οντος wideruling.

εὐρυ-μέτωπος 2 broad-fronted. [broad.]

εὐρύνω to make wide or

εὐρύ-νωτος 2 broad-backed.

εὐρυ-όδειος 3 with broad ways.

εὐρύ-οπα, ὁ far-thundering; others: far-seeing

εὐρύ-πορος 2 with wide passage. [gates.]

εὐρυ-πυλής 2 with wide

εὐρυ-ρέεθρος 2 and εὐρυ-ρέων 3 broad-flowing.

εὐρύς 3 broad, wide; widespread. [ing.]

εὐρυ-σθενής 2 wide-rul-

εὐρυ-φυής 2 growing broad.

εὐρύ-χορος 2 with spacious places for dancing.

εὐρυ-χωρίᾱ, ἡ free space, open country.

εὐρώδης 2 = εὐρύς.

εὐρώεις 3 mouldy; dark.

εὐρώς, ῶτος, ὁ mould, must.

εὔ-ρωστος 2 stout, strong.

ἐΰς, ἐΰ good, brave.

εὐ-σέβεια, ἡ reverence, piety; filial love.

εὐ-σεβής 2 pious, religious, reverent. [deck.]

εὔ-σελμος 2 with good

εὐ-σεπτος 2 most reverend.

εὔ-σημος 2 of good omen; clear, manifest.

εὔ-σκαρθμος 2 swift-springing.

εὐ-σκέπαστος 2 well-covered, protected.

εὐ-σκευέω to be well equipped.

εὐ-σκίαστος 2 well-shaded.

εὔ-σκοπος 2 sharp-glancing; shooting well.

εὔ-σοια, ἡ welfare.

εὔ-σπλαγχνος 2 compassionate.

ἐΰ-σσελμος 2 = εὔσελμος.

ἐΰ-σσωτρος 2 with good wheel-bands. [firmly built.]

εὐ-σταθής 2 steadfast,

εὐ-σταλής 2 well-equipped; happy, easy; decent, simple.

εὐ-στέφανος 2 well-crowned; well-walled.

εὔ-στολος 2 = εὐσταλής.

εὔ-στομος 2 speaking good words; keeping silence.

εὔ-στρεπτος 2, εὐ-στρεφής 2, εὔ-στροφος 2 well-twisted.   [lars.)

εὔ-στῦλος 2 with fine pil-

εὐ-σύμβλητος 2 easy to explain or guess.

εὐ-σύμβολος 2 sociable.

εὐ-σύνετος 2 intelligent.

εὐ-σχημοσύνη, ἡ good grace, decent behaviour.

εὐ-σχήμων 2 graceful, becoming; specious, shining.

εὐ-τακτέω to keep order, to be subordinate.

εὔ-τακτος 2 well-arranged; well-disciplined, orderly; modest.

εὐ-ταξία, ἡ good order, discipline, obedience.

εὖτε adv. at the time when, during that time; as often as; in the case that; just as.

εὐ-τειχής 2 well-walled.

εὐ-τέλεια, ἡ cheapness; frugality, economy.

εὐ-τελής 2 cheap; worthless, vile; frugal, plain.

εὔ-τμητος 2 well-cut.

εὔ-τολμος 2 daring, bold.

εὔ-τονος 2 sinewy, strong.

εὐ-τραπελία 2 versatility in jesting; politeness.

εὐ-τράπελος 2 versatile, witty, clever; cunning.

εὐ-τραφής 2 well-fed, fat.

εὐ-τρεπής 2 ready, prepared.

εὐ-τρεπίζω to make ready, prepare; to repair.

εὐ-τρεφής 2 = εὐτραφής.

εὔ-τρητος 2 well-bored.

εὔ-τριχος 2 = εὔθριξ.

εὐ-τροφία, ἡ good feeding; fatness.   [wheels.)

εὔ-τροχος 2 with good)

εὔ-τυκτος 2 well-wrought, well-made.

εὐ-τυχέω to be lucky, to meet with success; to turn out well.

εὐ-τύχημα, τό piece of good luck; success.

εὐ-τυχής 2 lucky, fortunate, happy; prosperous, successful.

εὐ-τυχία, ἡ = εὐτύχημα.

εὔ-υδρος 2 well-watered.

εὐ-υφής 2 well-woven.

εὐ-φαρέτρης, ου with beautiful quiver.

εὐ-φημέω to speak words of good omen; to observe solemn silence.

εὐ-φημία, ἡ solemn silence; good repute.

εὔ-φημος 2 speaking words of good omen; religiously silent; auspicious; of good sound.

εὐ-φιλής 2 well-beloved.

εὔ-φλεκτος 2 easy to set on fire.   [fruit.)

εὐ-φορέω to bear good)

εὔ-φορος 2 bearing well; patient; easily borne.

εὐ-φραδής 2 eloquent, considerate.

εὐ-φραίνω to cheer, gladden. — *M.* and *P.* to rejoice, to be glad or cheerful.

εὐ-φρονέων 3 well-meaning; sensible.

εὐ-φρόνη, ἡ night.

εὐ-φροσύνη, ἡ mirth, cheerfulness; joy.

εὔ-φρων 2 cheerful, joyous; well-minded, generous; cheering.

εὐ-φυής 2 well-grown, comely; well-gifted, clever; serviceable.   [guard; safe.]

εὐ-φύλακτος 2 easy to

εὐ-φωνίᾰ, ἡ good or loud voice.   [loud-voiced.]

εὔ-φωνος 2 well-voiced,

εὔ-χαλκος 2 finely wrought of brass or copper.

εὔ-χαρις, ι graceful, lovely, pleasing; witty; decent.

εὐ-χαριστέω to be thankful; to return thanks.

εὐ-χαριστίᾱ, ἡ thankfulness; thanksgiving.

εὐ-χάρι(σ)τος 2 thankful; pleasant; witty.

εὔ-χειρ, ειρος dexterous.

εὐ-χείρωτος 2 easy to overcome.

εὐ-χέρεια, ἡ readiness, dexterity; inclination.

εὐ-χερής 2 placid; easy, without trouble; ready, quick; reckless, hasty.

εὐχετάομαι = εὔχομαι.

εὐχή, ἡ prayer; vow; wish; curse.

εὔ-χλοος 2 becoming green; making green.

εὔχομαι to boast; to assert, profess; to pray, beseech; to wish, vow.

εὖχος, τό boast; glory; vow; wish.   [serviceable.]

εὔ-χρηστος 2 fit for use,

εὔ-χροος, εὔ-χρους 2, εὐ-χροής 2 of good complexion.

εὔ-χρῡσος 2 rich in gold.

εὐχωλή, ἡ boast, pride; shout; object of pride; prayer; vow; wish.

εὐχωλιμαῖος 3 bound by a vow.   [courage.]

εὐ-ψῡχέω to be of good

εὐ-ψῡχίᾱ, ἡ courage.

εὔ-ψῡχος 2 courageous.

εὔω to singe.   [fragrant.]

εὐ-ώδης 2 sweet-scented,

εὐ-ωδίᾱ, ἡ fragrance.

εὔ-ωνος 2 cheap.

εὐ-ώνυμος 2 of good name, of good omen; of the left hand.

εὐ-ῶπις, ιδος fair-faced.

εὐ-ωχέω to treat well, feast, entertain. — *P.* to be entertained; to make a hearty meal (of).   [fare.]

εὐ-ωχίᾱ, ἡ a feasting; good

εὐ-ώψ, ῶπος = εὐῶπις.

ἐφ-αγιστεύω, ἐφ-αγνίζω to observe holy rites; to make offerings on a grave.

ἐφ-αιρέω to choose in addition   [upon or towards.]

ἐφ-άλλομαι *M.* to spring

ἔφ-αλος 2 by the sea.

ἐφ-άμιλλος 2 disputed; rivalling; equal.

ἐφ-ανδάνω to please.

ἐφ-άπαξ *adv.* at once, once for all.

ἐφ-άπτω to fasten to, tie to; to decree, to cause. —

M. to touch, grasp; to undertake, partake of; to reach, attain.

ἐφ-αρμόζω to fit on, adapt, put on; to add; *intr.* to be fit.

ἐφ-έδρᾱ, ἡ siege.

ἐφ-εδρεύω to sit at or upon; to lie in wait.

ἔφ-εδρος 2 seated upon; lying in wait; lying in reserve; fresh enemy.

ἐφ-έζω to lay upon; to embark. — *M.* to sit upon, by, or near.

ἐφ-εῖσα *aor.* of ἐφέζω.

ἐφ-ελκύω, ἐφ-έλκω to draw on, attract; to drag, trail after. — *P.* ἐφελκόμενος straggler. — *M.* to draw to or after oneself.

ἐφ-έννῡμι = ἐπιέννυμι.

ἐφ-εξῆς = ἐξῆς.

ἐφ-έπω to follow; to pursue, press on, drive on; to run through; to strive after, to manage. — *M.* to follow, pursue; to yield, obey.

ἐφ-έσπερος 2 western.

ἐφ-έστιος 2 on the hearth, at the fireside; inmate, domestic; suppliant; protector of the household.

ἐφ-ετμή, ἡ order, injunction.

ἐφ-ευρετής, οῦ, ὁ inventor.

ἐφ-ευρίσκω to catch, to detect; to invent.

ἐφ-εφιάομαι *M.* to mock at.

ἐφ-ηβάω to grow to maturity.

ἔφ-ηβος, ὁ grown-up youth.

ἐφ-ηγέομαι *M.* to lead on.

ἐφ-ήδομαι to feel (mischievous) joy. [be present.]

ἐφ-ήκω to arrive at; to)

ἔφ-ημαι to sit at, on, or by.

ἐφ-ημερίᾱ, ἡ daily service; section of priests on duty.

ἐφ-ημέριος 2, **ἐφ-ήμερος** 2 lasting one day, during the day, for one day, ephemeral.

ἐφ-ημοσύνη = ἐφετμή.

ἑφθός 3 boiled.

ἐφ-ιζάνω, ἐφ-ίζω to sit on, at, or by.

ἐφ-ίημι to send to, against, or at; to launch, to let go; to incite; to lay upon, impose, decree; to permit, abandon, yield; *intr.* to abandon oneself to. — *M.* to aim at, long after, desire; to enjoin, to allow.

ἐφ-ικνέομαι *M.* to reach to, arrive at; to hit, touch.

ἐφ-ίμερος 2 longed for.

ἐφ-ιππος 2 mounted, on horseback.

ἐφ-ίστημι to set or place upon, at, or near; to establish, set up, fix, appoint, order; to set over; to check, stop. — *intr.* and *M.* to stand upon, tread on; to stand near; to approach, impend, be at hand; to surprise; to stand against; to assist; to be set over, to be at the head, to direct; to set to, attend; to halt, stop.

ἐφ-οδεύω and *M.* to go the rounds, inspect.

ἐφ-οδιάζω to supply with money or stores for travelling. — *M.* to receive money for travelling.

ἐφ-όδιον, τό money or supplies for travelling.

ἔφ-οδος[1] 2 accessible.

ἔφ-οδος[2], ἡ way to, approach; intercourse, access; attack.

ἐφ-όλκαιον, τό rudder.

ἐφ-ολκός 2 attractive.

ἐφ-ομαρτέω to go along with. [ready, prepare.]

ἐφ-οπλίζω to equip, get]

ἐφ-οράω to look on, oversee, inspect, observe; to visit; to choose; to live to see.

ἐφ-ορεύω to be an ephor.

ἐφ-ορμάω to stir up against, rouse. — *P.* to be stirred up or roused; to set on, assail, attack.

ἐφ-ορμέω to lie at anchor; to blockade.

ἐφ-ορμή, ἡ access; attack.

ἐφ-όρμησις, ἡ anchorage; blockade.

ἐφ-ορμίζομαι *P.* to come to anchor. [chor.]

ἔφ-ορμος[1] 2 lying at an-]

ἔφ-ορμος[2], ὁ = ἐφόρμησις.

ἔφ-ορος, ὁ overseer, guardian; ephor.

ἐφ-υβρίζω to act insolently or wantonly; to insult; to illtreat. [ing rain.]

ἔφ-υδρος 2 watery, bring-]

ἐφ-υμνέω to sing at or over; to sing a funeral song; to wish one something; to curse.

ἐφ-ύπερθεν *adv.* from above, above; over along.

ἐφ-υστερίζω to be later.

ἐχ-έγγυος 2 trustworthy, secure; on security.

ἐχέ-θυμος 2 under self-control. [cing.]

ἐχε-πευκής 2 sharp, pier-]

ἐχέ-φρων 2 sensible, prudent.

ἐχθαίρω to hate.

ἐχθαρτέος 3 to be hated.

ἐχθές *adv.* yesterday, = χθές. [mity with.]

ἐχθοδοπέω to be at en-]

ἐχθοδοπός 3 hostile.

ἔχθος, τό, ἔχθρα, ἡ hatred, enmity.

ἐχθρός 3 hated, hateful; hating, hostile; ὁ ἐ. enemy, adversary.

ἔχθω to hate.

ἔχιδνα, ἡ adder, viper.

ἔχμα, τό hindrance, obstacle, bulwark; support, prop, holdfast. [cure, safe.]

ἐχυρός 3 firm, strong, se-]

ἔχω to have; to hold, to hold fast; to possess, to have wealth; to have to wife; to inhabit; to rule, govern; to suffer; to occupy; to obtain, to seize; to have put on; to contain, compass; to know, be able; to cause, imply, infer; to preserve; to detain; to protect; to retain, restrain, check, hinder; to direct to, to aim at. — *intr.* to behave, to be disposed, to be in a state; to stand fast, to keep one's ground, to hold out, endure; to reach to. — *M.* to have or hold for oneself. — *M.* and *P.* to hold oneself to, to cling to, to depend upon; to hold fast, to continue; to be attached or fixed to; to border on, to be next to; to concern, affect; to abstain, refrain.

ἔφημα, τό what can be boiled.

ἔφησις, ἡ a boiling.

ἐφητός 3 boiled. [oneself.]

ἐφιάομαι *M.* to jest, amuse]

ἔφω to boil.

ἔωθα = εἴωθα.

ἔωθεν *adv.* at dawn.

ἐωθινός 3 early in the morning. [mains.]

ἑωλο-κρασία, ἡ dregs, re-]

ἔωμεν, ἑῶμεν *aor. conj.* we have enough.

ἐῷος 3 in the morning, at dawn; eastern.

ἑώρα, ἡ suspension, string.

ἔως¹, ω, ἡ dawn (of day), day-break, morning; east.

ἔως² *conj.* as long as, while; till; in order that. — *adv.* for some time; till when.

ἔωσ-περ even till. [star.]

ἑωσ-φόρος, ὁ morning-]

Z

Z, ζ (ζῆτα) sixth letter of the alphabet; as a numeral ζ' = 7.

ζόγκλον, τό sickle.

ζαής 2 strong blowing.

ζά-θεος 3 most holy.

ζά-κοτος 2 wrathful.

ζάλη, ἡ surge, spray; storm.

ζα-μενής 2 very violent, raging, angry.

ζά-πλουτος 2 very rich or wealthy.

ζα-τρεφής 2 well-fed.

ζα-φλεγής 2 fiery, vigorous.

ζα-χρηής 2 vehement, impetuous, stormy.

ζά-χρῦσος 2 rich in gold.

ζάω to live, to be alive; to lead a life; to live on, to be strong.

ζειά, ἡ spelt. amel-corn.

ζεί-δωρος 2 corn-producing.

ζειρά, ἡ long cloak.

ζευγ-ηλατέω to drive a team; to plough.

ζευγ-ηλάτης, ου, ὁ driver of a team, ploughman.

ζεύγλη, ἡ collar of the yoke; rudder-band.

ζεῦγμα, τό band, bond; bar, impediment; bridge.

ζεύγνῦμι to join or link together; to yoke, harness, fetter; to marry, unite; to join by a bridge, to throw a bridge over, to close; to calk (ships).

ζεῦγος, τό yoke, team; carriage, vehicle; pair, couple.

ζευκτήριος 3 fit for joining.

ζεῦξις, ἡ a yoking, harnessing; a joining by a bridge.

ζέφυρος, ὁ west wind; west.

ζέω to boil, seethe; to be hot, to rage.

ζηλεύω = ζηλόω.

ζηλήμων 2 jealous.

ζῆλος, ὁ and τό eagerness, emulation, admiration, jealousy, envy, zeal, passion, anger; enviable happiness.

ζηλο-τυπέω to be jealous, to envy.

ζηλόω to rival, vie with; to admire, praise; to envy, to be jealous; to strive after.

ζήλωμα, τό emulation, pursuit; high fortune.

ζήλωσις, ἡ emulation.

ζηλωτής, οῦ, ὁ rival, admirer; zealot.

ζηλωτός 3 admired; envied; enviable.

ζημία, ἡ damage, loss; penalty, punishment; fine.

ζημιόω to damage, to punish, chastise; to fine. — P. to be hurt, to suffer damage.

ζημιώδης injurious.

ζημίωμα, τό punishment.

ζητέω to seek, seek for; to inquire into, examine; to endeavour, desire, demand.

ζήτημα, τό a seeking, inquiry, examination; question, problem.

ζήτησις, ἡ a seeking, seeking for, searching, inquiry, investigation; problem, dispute. [searcher.]

ζητητής, οῦ, ὁ inquirer,]

ζητητός 3 sought for.

ζιζάνιον, τό darnel.

ζόη, ζοή, ἡ = ζωή.

ζορκάς, ἡ = δορκάς.

ζόφος, ὁ darkness, gloom; reign of darkness; west.

ζύγαστρον, τό wooden chest or box. [thong.]

ζυγό-δεσμον, τό yoke-]

ζυγόν, τό, ζυγός, ὁ yoke, cross-bar; team, pair; bridge of a lyre; bank of oars; beam of the balance; balance; row, line. [horses.]

ζυγωτός 3 drawn by good]

ζύμη, ἡ leaven.

ζυμίτης, ου leavened.

ζυμόω to leaven, to cause to ferment. [saving life.]

ζω-άγρια, τά reward for]

ζω-γραφία, ἡ painting.

ζω-γράφος, ὁ painter.

ζωγρέω to catch alive; to give quarter to; to restore to life.

ζωγρία, ἡ a catching alive.

ζῴδιον, τό small animal; figure, image.

ζωή, ἡ life; lifetime; manner or mode of life; subsistence; property, goods.

ζῶμα, τό girdle, belt, apron; part of the armour.

ζώνη, ἡ belt, girdle; waist, loins.

ζώννῡμι, -ύω to gird. — M. to gird oneself (for battle or work).

ζωο-γονέω to produce living beings; to preserve alive.

ζῷον, ζῶον, τό living being, animal, creature, beast; figure, image, picture, painting, ornament ζωο-ποιέω to make alive, quicken.

ζωός, ζωός 3 alive.

ζωρός 2 strong, stout, unmixed.

ζώς, ζών = ζωός. [belt.]

ζωστήρ, ῆρος, ὁ girdle,

ζῶστρον, τό girdle.

ζωτικός 3 full of life, lively, animated.

H

H, η (ἦτα) seventh letter of the alphabet; as a numeral η' = 8.

ἦ adv. truly, verily; as an interr. particle = Lat. num, nonne.

ἤ conj. or, ἤ ... ἤ either ... or; if, whether, ἤ ... ἤ whether ... or; than.

ᾖ adv. where; whither; how, as, as far as; wherefore.

ἦ = ἦν I was (εἶναι); = ἔφη he said (from ἠμί = φημί).

ἦα = ᾖειν (ἰέναι); = ᾖα, τά.

ἡ-βαιός 3 small, little, tiny. [estate.]

ἡβάσκω to come to man's

ἡβάω to be at man's estate, to be in the prime of youth.

ἥβη, ἡ youth, prime of youth; vigour; young men; manhood.

ἡβηδόν adv. in manhood.

ἡβητικός 3, ἡβός 3 youthful.

ἡγά-θεος 3 most holy.

ἡγεμονεύω to guide, lead the way; to be leader, to rule, command.

ἡγεμονία, ἡ the leading the way, leadership, command, chief place; sovereignty, supremacy.

ἡγεμονικός 3 fit for enterprising, for leading or commanding.

ἡγεμόσυνα, τά thank-offerings for safe-conduct.

ἡγεμών, όνος, ὁ, ἡ guide, leader; chief, ruler, commander; prince, governor.

ἡγέομαι M. to lead the way, to go before; to lead the van; to be leader, ruler, or chief; to think, mean, believe. [together.]

ἡγερέθομαι to be gathered

ἡγηλάζω to guide.

ἡγητήρ, ῆρος and ἡγήτωρ, ορος, ὁ = ἡγεμών.

ἠδέ and; ἠμέν ... ἠδέ as well as.

ἤδη adv. already, now; presently, forthwith; besides, further; therefore; even; yet.

ἥδομαι P. to rejoice, to be pleased or glad, to enjoy oneself. to delight.

ἡδονή, ἡ joy, pleasure, delight, enjoyment; lust; comfort; profit, gain; mischievous joy.

ἦδος, τό = ἡδονή.

ἡδυ-επής 2 sweet-speaking.

ἥδυμος 2 sweet, refreshing.

ἡδύ-οσμον, τό mint.

ἡδυ-παθέω to live pleasantly; to be luxurious.

ἡδύ-πνοος 2 sweet-breathing, auspicious.

ἡδύ-πολις, ὁ, ἡ agreeable to the city.

ἡδύ-ποτος 2 sweet to drink.

ἡδύς 3 sweet, pleasant, lovely, agreeable; joyous, amiable; dear; well-minded, kind.

ἥδυσμα, τό spice.

ἠέ or ἦε = ἤ.

ἠέλιος = ἥλιος.

ἠέπερ = ἤπερ.

ἠερέθομαι to float, to hang waving in the air; to be flighty.   [morning.]

ἠέριος 3 early in the

ἠερόεις 3, ἠερο-ειδής 2 aëriform; misty, dark.

ἠερο-φοῖτις, ιδος, ἡ walking in the dark.

ἠερό-φωνος 2 loud-voiced.

ἠήρ, ἠέρος = ἀήρ.

ἠθάς, άδος wont, accustomed; acquainted with.

ἠθεῖος 3 dear, beloved.

ἤθεος, ὁ = ἠΐθεος.

ἠθικός 3 ethical, moral.

ἠθμός, ἠθμός, ὁ sieve, strainer.

ἦθος, τό accustomed place, seat, station, abode, stable; disposition, character, temper; custom; morality.

ἤϊα, τό provisions, food; prey.

ἠΐθεος, ὁ youth, bachelor.

ἤϊκτο he was like (from ἔοικα)

ἠϊόεις 3 with high banks.

ἦϊος, ὁ shooting (or shining).

ἠϊών, όνος, ἡ shore, beach.

ἦκα adv. softly, gently; slowly.

ἤκεστος 3 ungoaded (or unmanageable).

ἥκιστα adv. least, not at all.

ἥκιστος 3 slowest, slackest

ἥκου = ἦπου.

ἥκω to have or be come, to be here; to be back; to have come to, to possess; to arrive, come to pass, occur.   [distaff.]

ἠλάκατα, τά wool on the

ἠλακάτη, ἡ distaff, spindle.

ἠλασκάζω, ἠλάσκω to wander, stray; to shun, flee from.

ἤλεκτρον, τό, ἤλεκτρος, ὁ, ἡ electron, alloy of gold and silver; amber.

ἠλέκτωρ, ορος beaming; the sun.

ἠλεός 3 distracted, befooled; befooling.

ἡλιαία, ἡ law-court, jury.

ἠλίβατος 2 steep, abrupt.

ἦλιθα adv. plentifully.

ἠλίθιος 3 silly; vain, idle.

ἠλιθιότης, ητος, ἡ silliness.

ἡλικία, ἡ time of life, age; prime of life, manhood; those of the same age; fit to bear arms, comrades; age, time, century; stature, bodily growth.

ἡλικιώτης, ου, ὁ of the same age; comrade.

ἡλίκος 3 as big or great as; how great, how old.

ἧλιξ, ικος = ἡλικιώτης.

ἥλιος, ὁ sun; sunlight, daylight, day; east; the sungod.   [from the sun.]

ἡλιο-στεγής 2 protecting

ἠλιτό-μηνος 2 prematurely born. [the sun.]

ἠλιῶτις, ιδος belonging to ἧλος, ὁ nail, stud.

ἧλυσις, ἡ a coming.

ἧμα, τό a throw.

ἠμαθόεις 3 sandy.

ἧμαι to sit; to be at leisure; to lie in wait; to tarry; to be built.

ἧμαρ, ατος, τό = ἡμέρα.

ἡμάτιος 3 by day; daily.

ἡμεῖς we. [ly.]

ἠμελημένως adv. careless-

ἠμέν ... ἠδέ as well as.

ἡμέρᾱ, ἡ day; daylight; time; time of life; fate.

ἡμερεύω to pass the day, to live on.

ἡμερήσιος 2 and 3, ἡμερινός 3, ἡμέριος 2 by day, daily; a day long; short-lived. [vine.]

ἡμερίς, ιδος, ἡ cultivated

ἡμερο-δρόμος, ὁ day-runner, courier. [days.]

ἡμερο-λογέω to count by

ἥμερος 2 tame; improved, cultivated; gentle.

ἡμερο-σκόπος, ὁ day-watcher. [ἡμεροσκόπος.]

ἡμερο-φύλαξ, ακος, ὁ =

ἡμερόω to tame; to cultivate. — M. to subdue.

ἡμέτερος 3 our; ours.

ἠμί I say.

ἡμί-βρωτος 2 half-eaten.

ἡμι-δαής 2 half-burnt.

ἡμι-δᾱρεικόν, τό half-daric.

ἡμι-δεής 2 half-full.

ἡμι-εργος, ὁ half-done.

ἡμι-θανής 2 = ἡμιθνής.

ἡμί-θεος, ὁ demigod.

ἡμι-θνής, ῆτος half-dead.

ἡμι-μναῖον, τό a half-mine.

ἡμι-μόχθηρος 2 half-wretched.

ἡμι-όλιος 3 one and the half; half as large again.

ἡμιόνειος 3, ἡμιονικός 3 of mules.

ἡμί-ονος, ἡ, ὁ mule.

ἡμι-πέλεκκον, τό half-axe.

ἡμί-πλεθρον, τό half-plethron. [brick.]

ἡμι-πλίνθιον, τό half-

ἥμισυς 3 half. [talent.]

ἡμι-τάλαντον, τό half-

ἡμι-τέλεστος 2, ἡμι-τελής 2 half-finished. [through.]

ἡμί-τομος 2 half-cut

ἡμι-ωβολιαῖος 3 as large as a half-obol.

ἡμι-ωβόλιον, τό half-obol.

ἡμι-ώριον, τό, ἡμί-ωρον, τό half-hour. [soon as.]

ἧμος conj. when, while; as

ἡμύω to sink, droop.

ἥμων, ονος spear-throwing.

ἠνεμόεις 3 = ἀνεμόεις.

ἡνίᾱ, ἡ rein, bridle; pl. also τὰ ἡνία.

ἡνίκα conj. when, at the time when.

ἡνίον see ἡνία. [shop.]

ἡνιο-ποιεῖον, τό saddler's

ἡνιο-στρόφος, ὁ = ἡνίοχος.

ἡνι-οχεία, ἡ a driving; a directing.

ἡνι-οχέω, -εύω to hold the reins, drive.

ἡνί-οχος, ἡνι-οχεύς, ὁ driver, charioteer.

ἧνις, ἧνῑς, ιος yearling (shining?) [ness.]

ἠνορέη, ἡ strength, manliἦν-οφ, οπος shining.

ἠνώγεα see ἄνωγα.

ἠοίη, ἡ morning. [eastern.]

ἠοῖος 3 in the morning;

ἦος = ἕως.

ἦπαρ, ατος, τό liver; heart.

ἠπεδανός 3 feeble, infirm.

ἤπειρος, ἡ continent, mainland; inland. [mainland.]

ἠπειρόω to convert into

ἠπειρώτης, ου, ὁ, ἠπειρῶτις, ιδος, ἡ, ἠπειρωτικός 3 of the mainland, continental; Asiatic.

ἤπερ conj. even where; just as.

ἠπεροπεύς, ἠπεροπευτής, οῦ, ὁ deceiver. [cheat.]

ἠπεροπεύω to deceive,

ἠπιό-δωρος 2 kindly giving.

ἤπιος 3 gentle, mild, kind, friendly; soothing. [less.]

ἦπου adv. certainly, doubt-

ἦπου adv. or perhaps.

ἠπύτα, ὁ loud-calling; crier.

ἠπύω to cry aloud, to cry to; to sound, roar.

ἦρ, ἦρος, τό = ἔαρ. [ness]

ἦρα (φέρειν) favour, kind-

ἠρέμα adv. softly, gently, quietly; slowly; slightly.

ἠρεμαῖος 3 gentle, quiet.

ἠρεμέω to be or keep quiet or unchanged.

ἠρεμία, ἡ stillness, rest.

ἤρεμος 2 = ἠρεμαῖος.

ἦρι adv. early, in the morning.

ἠρι-γένεια, ἡ early-born.

ἠρινός 3 = ἐαρινός.

ἠρίον, τό mound, tomb.

ἠρωϊκός 3 heroic, of heroes.

ἡρῷος 3 = ἡρωϊκός; τό ἡρῷον temple of a hero.

ἥρως, ωος, ὁ hero; demigod.

ἧσσα, ἡ defeat.

ἡσσάομαι P. to be less, weaker, or inferior; to be defeated or beaten; to be subject, to be under the control of; to lose one's cause.

ἥσσων 2 less, weaker, inferior; defeated, subject, yielding; adv. ἧσσον less.

ἡσυχάζω to rest, be quiet; to stop, halt; to be silent; to give up resistance; trans. to calm, soothe.

ἡσυχαῖος 3 quiet, still, gentle; slow, cautious; peaceable; placid; untroubled, secure; secret.

ἡσυχῇ adv. = ἡσύχως.

ἡσυχία, ἡ stillness, quiet, silence; loneliness; rest, leisure; ease, content.

ἡσύχιος 2, ἥσυχος 2 = ἡσυχαῖος.

ἦτε adv. truly, verily, surely.

ἦτε conj. or, or also.

ἤτοι conj. surely, verily, indeed; now; therefore.

ἦτορ, ορος, τό heart, mind, soul; life, spirit, vigour.

ἦτρον, τό belly.

ἧττ- see ἧσσ-.

ἠϋ-γένειος 2 = εὐγένειος.

ἠϋ-ζωνος = εὔζωνος.

ἠϋ-κομος 2 = with fine locks.

ἠΰς, ἠΰ = εύς. [locks.]

ἠΰτε conj. as, like as, as if.

ἡφαιστό-τευκτος 2 made or wrought by Vulcane.

ἠχέω to sound, ring; to cause to sound, to utter.

ἠχή, ἡ sound, noise; cries; rumour.

ἠχήεις 3 sounding, roaring.

ἦχι adv. where.

ἦχος, ὁ and τό = ἠχή.

ἠχώ, οῦς, ἡ sound, echo; lament; report, rumour.

ἠῶθεν adv. from morning, at dawn.

ἠῶθι adv. early in the morning.

ἠών, όνος, ἡ = ἠϊών.

ἦφος 3 = ἕφος.

ἠώς, ἠοῦς, ἡ = ἕως[1].

Θ

Θ, ϑ (ϑῆτα) eighth letter of the alphabet; as a numeral ϑ' = 9.

θαάσσω to sit.

θαιρός, ὁ hinge of a door.

θᾱκέω to sit.

θάκημα, τό, θάκησις, ἡ a sitting; seat; residence.

θαλάμη, ἡ = θάλαμος.

θαλαμη-πόλος 2 belonging to the bridal chamber; ὁ ϑ. bridegroom; ἡ ϑ. bridesmaid.

θαλαμίη, ἡ hole for an oar.

θαλάμιος, θαλαμιός, ὁ rower of the lowest bench.

θάλαμος, ὁ couch, chamber, apartment, bedroom; women's apartment; bridal chamber; store-room, treasury; palace.

θάλασσα, ἡ sea, sea-water.

θαλασσεύω to be at sea.

θαλάσσιος 3 of the sea, maritime, seafaring.

θαλασσο-κρατέω to be master of the sea.

θαλασσο-κράτωρ, ορος, ὁ master of the sea.

θάλεα, έων, τά good things, delights. [swelled (up).]

θαλέθω to bloom; to be]

θαλερός 3 blooming, fresh, young, vigorous; copious, abundant.

θαλίᾱ, ἡ bloom, happiness; good cheer, feast.

θαλλός, ὁ sprouting twig; olive-branch; foliage.

θάλλω to sprout, shoot, bloom, flourish; to be abundant, rich, or swelling; to grow; to prosper; to be esteemed.

θάλος, τό = θαλλός.

θαλπιάω to be warm.

θάλπος, τό warmth, heat.

θάλπω to warm, heat; to inflame; to be or become warm, to glow. [comfort.]

θαλπωρή, ἡ a warming,]

θάλυς 3 blooming; θάλεια δαίς delicious feast.

θαλύσια, τά offering of first-fruits. [in crowds.]

θαμά adv. often, frequently;]

θαμβέω to amaze; to be astonished or amazed; to shudder. [horror.]

θάμβος, τό astonishment;]

θαμέες, οἱ, αἱ, θαμειός 3 frequent, thick, in crowds.

θαμίζω to come often, to frequent; to be frequent.

θαμινά adv. = θαμά.

θάμνος, ὁ bush, shrub.

θανάσιμος 2 belonging to death; deadly; mortal, dying; dead.

θανατάω to long for death.

θανατη-φόρος 2 death-bringing.

θανάτόεις 3 = θανάσιμος.

θάνατος, ὁ death; murder; execution.

θανατόω to put to death, to kill, slay, execute.

θάομαι = θεάομαι.

θάπτω to bury, inter.

Θαργηλιών, ῶνος, ὁ the eleventh month of the Athenians (May to June).

θαρσαλέος, θαρραλέος 3 bold, daring, courageous; insolent, presumptious; encouraging, dangerless.

θαρσέω, θαρρέω to be bold, daring, courageous, confident, or presumptious; to believe confidently.

θάρσησις, ἡ confidence.

θάρσος, τό courage, boldness, confidence; daring, presumption.

θαρσῦνος 2 confident, of good cheer. [θρασύνω.]

θαρσύνω, θαρρύνω =

θάσσω to sit.

θάτερον = τὸ ἕτερον.

θαῦμα, τό wonder, marvel, wondrous thing; astonishment, admiration.

θαυμάζω to be astonished or amazed, to wonder; to admire, esteem; to wonder at; to be curious to learn.

θαυμαίνω = θαυμάζω.

θαυμάσιος 3 wondrous, wonderful, extraordinary;

marvellous, strange; admirable, excellent.

θαυμαστός 3 = θαυμάσιος.

θαυματο-ποιός, ὁ juggler, conjurer.

θάω to suckle, feed. — M. to suck; to milk.

θεά, θέαινα, ἡ goddess.

θέα, ἡ a looking at, view; spectacle.

θέαμα, τό sight, spectacle.

θεάομαι M. to view, behold, observe; to reflect, know; to admire, gaze at.

θεαρός, ὁ = θεωρός.

θεᾱτής, οῦ, ὁ looker-on, spectator.

θεᾱτός 3 to be seen.

θεᾱτρίζω to expose to ridicule.

θέᾱτρον, τό theatre, stage; spectators, audience; play.

θέειον, τό = θεῖον.

θεειόω to fumigate with brimstone.

θε-ήλατος 2 sent by god; driven for the gods.

θειάζω to prophesy.

θειασμός, ὁ superstition.

θειλό-πεδον, τό sunny place.

θείνω to beat, strike, hit.

θεῖον, τό brimstone.

θεῖος[1], ὁ uncle.

θεῖος[2] 3 of gods, divine; holy, sacred; godlike, superhuman, sublime, august. τὸ θεῖον deity, divine being; τὰ θεῖα divine things; religion, oracles, worship.

θειότης, ητος, ἡ divinity, divine nature. [(τίθημι).]

θείω = θέω to run; = θύω

θειώδης 2 sulphurous.

θέλγω to charm, enchant; to blind, cheat, seduce; to fascinate, win.

θέλημα, τό, θέλησις, ἡ a willing, will.

θελκτήριος 2 charming, enchanting; τὸ θ. spell, charm; delight.   [ριον.

θέλκτρον, τό = θελκτή-

θέλω = ἐθέλω.

θέμεθλα, τά, θεμείλια, τά see θεμέλιος.

θεμέλιος, ὁ and θεμέλιον, τό foundation-stone; base, bottom, foundation.

θεμελιόω to found; to make firm.

θέμις, ιστος, ἡ divine right, law, custom, pre- rogative, privilege; judi- cial sentence; tax.

θεμιστεύω to give law; to give oracles.

θεμιστός 3, θεμιτός 3 lawful, just.

θεμόω to cause.   [hand.

θέναρ, αρος, τό flat of the

θεο-βλαβής 2 stricken with madness.   [descent.

θεο-γεννής 2 of divine

θεο-γονίᾱ, ἡ genealogy of the gods.   [God.

θεο-δίδακτος 2 taught by

θεό-δμητος 2 god-built.

θεο-ειδής 2, θεο-είκελος 2 godlike.

θεόθεν adv. from the gods.

θεο-λόγος, ὁ theologian.

θεό-μαντις, ὁ soothsayer.

θεο-μαχέω to fight against God.   [gods.

θεο-μαχίᾱ, ἡ battle of the

θεο-μάχος 2 fighting against God.

θεο-προπέω to prophesy.

θεο-προπίᾱ, ἡ, θεο-πρό- πιον, τό prophecy, oracle.

θεο-πρόπος 2 prophetic; prophet, soothsayer.

θεός, ὁ, ἡ god, goddess; deity, divine being.

θεο-σέβεια, ἡ fear of God.

θεο-σεβής 2 God-fearing, religious.

θεο-στυγής 2 hated by God; hating God

θεότης, ητος, ἡ divinity.

θεουδής 2 fearing God.

θεο-φάνια, τά spring-fes- tival at Delphi.

θεο-φιλής 2 beloved by God; blessed.   [vant.

θεράπαινα, ἡ maid-ser-

θεραπείᾱ, ἡ, θεράπευμα, τό service, attendance, a courting, deference, flat- tery; care, worship; a fostering, nurture, medical treatment, nursing, finery; servants, retinue.   [ράπων.

θεραπευτής, οῦ, ὁ = θε-

θεραπευτικός 3 courteous, obedient.   [fostered.

θεραπευτός 3 to be

θεραπεύω to serve, attend, wait on; to court, flatter, honour, win; to take care of, to treat carefully, to tend, nurse, heal; to cul- tivate; to pay attention to.

θεράπων, οντος, ὁ servant, attendant, waiter; com- panion in arms, comrade.

θερείᾱ, ἡ summer-time.

θερίζω to pass the summer; to reap; to cut off; to destroy.

θερινός 3 in summer.

θερισμός, δ a reaping; harvest-time; crop.

θεριστής, οῦ, δ reaper.

θερμαίνω to warm, heat; to burn. — *P.* to become warm or hot.

θερμασία, ἡ warmth, heat.

θέρμη, ἡ warmth; fever; hot spring.

θερμός 3 warm, hot; rash.

θερμότης, ητος, ἡ = θερμασία. [ing, rash.)

θερμουργός 2 hot in act-)

θέρμω = θερμαίνω.

θέρομαι *P.* to become warm or hot; to be burnt.

θέρος, τό summer; harvest.

θέσις, ἡ a setting, placing; condition, situation; proposition.

θέσκελος 2 marvellous.

θέσμιος 2 according to law.

θεσμο-θέτης, ου, δ lawgiver; Athenian magistrate.

θεσμός, δ place; statute, law, rule; institution, custom.

θεσμο-φόρια, τά a festival of the Athenian women.

θεσμο-φοριάζω to keep the Thesmophoria.

θεσμο-φόρος 2 lawgiving.

θεσμο-φύλαξ, ακος, δ guardian of the law.

θεσπέσιος 3 and 2 divinely sounding or singing; divine, august, unspeakable.

θεσπι-δαής 2 blazing prodigiously.

θεσπι-έπεια, ἡ prophetic.

θεσπίζω to prophesy.

θέσπις, ιος, δ, ἡ inspired (by God), divine.

θέσπισμα, τό oracle.

θέσ-φατος 2 announced or decreed by God; made by God.

θετός 3 adopted.

θέω to run, hasten.

θεωρέω to look at, view, behold, observe; to be a spectator; to consider, contemplate, examine; to perceive. [tacle.)

θεώρημα, τό sight, spec-)

θεωρία, ἡ a looking at, beholding, viewing; curiosity, presence at a festival; examination, contemplation, theory; festival, spectacle; sending of ambassadors to an oracle.

θεωρικός 3 belonging to a spectacle or festival; τὰ θεωρικά money for spectacles.

θεωρίς, ίδος, ἡ sacred ship for carrying ambassadors.

θεωρός, δ spectator; ambassador sent to a festival or oracle.

θεώτερος 3 = θειότερος.

θηγάνη, ἡ whetstone.

θήγω to whet, sharpen; to incite, encourage.

θήσομαι = θεάομαι.

θηητήρ, ῆρος, δ = θεατής.

θηκαῖος 3 belonging to a sepulchre.

θήκη, ἡ box, chest; tomb, coffin; sheath. [to suck.)

θηλάζω and *M.* to suckle;)

θηλέω to flourish.

θηλυδρίας, ου, ὁ effeminate man. [prolific.]

θῆλυς 3 female; effeminate;

θημών, ῶνος, ὁ heap.

θήν adv. certainly, surely.

θήρ, θηρός, ὁ wild beast, beast of prey; monster.

θήρα, ἡ a hunting, chase; game. [or won.]

θηρατέος 3 to be hunted

θηρατικός 3 belonging or pertaining to hunting.

θήρατρον, τό hunting-equipage.

θηράω and M. to hunt, chase, pursue; to catch.

θήρειος 2 of wild beasts.

θηρευτής, οῦ, ὁ hunter.

θηρευτικός 3 belonging or pertaining to the chase.

θηρεύω = θηράω.

θηρητήρ, ῆρος and θηρήτωρ, ορος, ὁ = θηρευτής.

θηριο-μαχέω to fight with wild beasts.

θηρίον, τό = θήρ.

θηριώδης 2 full of wild beasts; beastly, brutal.

θηροβολέω to kill wild beasts. [journeyman.]

θής, θητός, ὁ labourer;

θησαυρίζω to treasure up, lay in.

θησαύρισμα, τό store.

θησαυρός, ὁ store-room, treasure-house; store, treasure.

θητεία, ἡ hired service.

θητεύω to work for pay.

θίασος, ὁ band of revellers in honour of Bacchus; procession; dance; company.

θιγγάνω to touch, handle, take hold of; to reach, gain.

θίς, θινός, ὁ, ἡ heap (of sand), sand; beach, strand; sand-bank, sandy desert.

θλάω to crush, bruise.

θλίβω to press; to rub; to oppress, confine.

θλῖψις and θλίψις, ἡ oppression, affliction, distress.

θνήσκω, θνήσκω to die, perish; to be killed.

θνητο-γενής 2 of mortal race. [nature.]

θνητο-ειδής 2 of mortal

θνητός 3 mortal; human.

θοάζω to hurry along; to move quickly; = θάσσω.

θοινάω to feast, entertain; to eat. [enjoyment.]

θοίνη, ἡ banquet, feast;

θολερός 3 muddy, dirty; troubled.

θόλος, ἡ dome-shaped roof; vaulted building.

θοός[1] 3 quick, swift.

θοός[2] 3 sharp, pointed.

θοόω to make pointed.

θορή, ἡ, θορός, ὁ seed of the male, semen.

θόρνυμαι to copulate.

θορυβάζω to trouble.

θορυβέω to make a noise; to applaud; to murmur; to trouble, disturb.

θόρυβος, ὁ noise; uproar, confusion.

θούριος 3 and θοῦρος 2, fem. θοῦρις, ιδος rushing on, impetuous.

θόωκος, ὁ = θῶκος, θᾶκος.

θρᾱνίτης, ου, ὁ rower of the uppermost bench.

θράσος, τό = θάρσος.

θράσσω to trouble.

θρασυ-κάρδιος 2 stout-hearted. [bold.]

θρασυ-μέμνων 2 enduring,

θρασύνω to encourage. — intr., P. and M. to take comfort; to be bold.

θρασύς 3 = θαρσαλέος.

θρασυ-στομέω to speak boldly.

θρασύτης, ητος, ἡ boldness, audaciousness. [crush.]

θραύω to break, shiver,

θρέμμα, τό nursling, child; cattle for breeding; breed.

θρέομαι to cry, lament.

θρεπτήρια, θρέπτρα, τά food; reward for bringing up.

θρηνέω to wail, lament.

θρῆνος, ὁ a wailing, lamenting; dirge.

θρῆνυς, υος, ὁ footstool.

θρησκεία, ἡ worship, religious observance.

θρησκεύω to observe religiously.

θρῆσκος 2 religious.

θριαμβεύω to triumph; to cause to triumph.

θρίαμβος, ὁ hymn; procession, triumph.

θριγκός, ὁ cornice, projection of a wall.

θριγκόω to surround with a cornice, to fence in, to finish.

θρίδαξ, ακος, ἡ lettuce.

θρίξ, τριχός, ἡ hair; wool, bristle.

θροέω to cry aloud, shreak; to utter, tell, speak; to frighten. — P. to be afraid.

θρόμβος, ὁ lump.

θρομβώδης 2 clotty.

θρόνα, τά flowers (in embroidery). [throne.]

θρόνος, ὁ seat, chair;

θρόος, θροῦς, ὁ cry, shout; murmur; report.

θρῡλέω to babble; to discuss. to make a great talk of.

θρῡλίσσω to shiver.

θρύον, τό rush.

θρυπτικός 3 exhausted; effeminate.

θρύπτω to grind, crush. — P. to be or become enfeebled or enervated; to boast. [fly; to assault.]

θρᾠσκω to spring, leap,

θρωσμός, ὁ height; hill.

θυγάτηρ, τρός, ἡ daughter.

θυγατριδέος, ὁ grandson.

θυγατριδῆ, ἡ grand-daughter. [ter.]

θυγάτριον, τό little daughter

θύελλα, ἡ whirlwind, storm.

θυήεις 3 fragrant.

θυηλή, ἡ burnt-offering.

θυΐα, θυΐάς, άδος, ἡ Bacchante. [wood.]

θυΐνος 3 made of cedar

θύλακος, ὁ, θῡλάκιον, τό bag, pouch. [fice.]

θῦμα, τό offering, sacri-

θῡμαίνω to be angry.

θῡμ-αλγής 2 aggrieving.

θῡμ-ἄρής 2 well-pleasing, dear. [one's spirit.]

θῡμ-ηγερέω to collect

θῡμ-ηδής 2 well-pleasing.

θῡμ-ήρης = θυμαρής.

Θῠμίᾰμα, τό incense.

Θῠμιᾱτήριον, τό censer.

Θῠμιάω to burn as incense.

Θῠμο-βόρος 2, Θῠμο-δακής aggrieving, mortifying.

Θῠμο-ειδής 2 courageous; angry, hot, wild. [hearted.]

Θῠμο-λέων, οντος lion-]

Θῠμο-μαχέω to fight with all one's heart.

Θῠμο-ραϊστής, οῦ life-destroying.

Θῠμός, ὁ soul, life; will, desire; appetite; resolution; thought; mind, heart, sense; courage, spirit, passion, anger, wrath.

Θῠμο-φθορέω to fret.

Θῠμο-φθόρος 2 life-destroying; mortifying.

Θῠμόω to make angry. — P. to become angry, wroth, or excited.

Θύννος, ὁ tunny(-fish).

Θύνω = θύω.

Θῠόεις 3 fragrant.

Θύον, τό cypress; cedar or lemon-tree.

Θύος, τό incense; offering.

Θῠο-σκόος, ὁ sacrificer.

Θῠόω to make fragrant.

Θύρᾱ, ἡ fold of a door; door, gate; palace, royal court; entrance, threshold; table, board, raft.

Θύρᾱζε adv. to the door; outside the door, outdoors.

Θύρᾱθεν, θύρηθε adv. from without; outside.

Θῠραῖος 3 outside the door, outdoor(s), abroad; alien, stranger.

Θύρᾱσι adv. outside, out of doors; abroad. [shield.]

Θῠρεός, ὁ door-stone; large]

Θύρετρα, τά = θύρα.

Θῠρίς, ίδος, ἡ small door.

Θῠρόω to furnish with doors. [staff of Bacchantes.]

Θύρσος, ὁ thyrsus (wreathed]

Θύρωμα, τό door with frame, portal. [vestibule.]

Θῠρών, ῶνος, ὁ anteroom.]

Θῠρωρός, ὁ, ἡ door-keeper.

Θῠσᾰνόεις 3 tasselled, fringed.

Θύσᾰνος, ὁ tassel, tuft.

Θῠσᾰνωτός 3 = θυσανόεις.

Θύσθλα, τά sacred implements. [sacrifice.]

Θῠσία, ἡ a sacrificing;]

Θῠσιαστήριον, τό altar.

Θύσιμος 2 fit for sacrifice.

Θῠσσᾰνόεις 3 = θυσανόεις.

Θῠστάς, άδος, ἡ sacrificial.

Θῠτήρ, ῆρος, ὁ sacrificer.

Θύω[1] to move oneself quickly, to rush on or along; to roar, rage.

Θύω[2] to burn (incense), to offer burnt-sacrifice; to slay, kill; intr. to smoke. — M. to sacrifice for oneself.

Θύωμα, τό incense.

Θωή, ἡ penalty [θάκος.]

Θωκέω, θῶκος see θακέω,]

Θῶμα, θωμάζω, θωμάσιος see θαῦμα. [string.]

Θῶμιγξ, ιγγος, ὁ cord,]

Θωπεύω to flatter; to serve.

Θωρᾱκίζω to arm with a breast-plate.

Θωρᾱκο-ποιός, ὁ maker of breast-plates.

ϑωρᾱκο-φόρος 2 wearing a breast-plate.

ϑώρᾱξ, ᾱκος, ὁ breast-plate, cuirass.

ϑωρηκτής, οῦ, ὁ = ϑωρακοφόρος.

ϑωρήσσω to arm with a breast-plate. to equip, arm.

ϑώς, ϑωός, ὁ jackal.

ϑῶμα etc. see ϑαῦμα.

ϑωΰσσω to cry aloud, shout.

ϑώψ, ϑωπός, ὁ flatterer.

I

I, ι (ἰῶτα) ninth letter of the alphabet, as a numeral ι' = 10.

ἰά, ἡ sound, voice, cry.

ἴα, ἰῆς one; see ἴος.

ἰά, τά pl. of ἰός.

ἰαίνω to warm, heat; to refresh, cheer.

ἰακχάζω, ἰακχέω to raise the cry of Bacchus.

ἴακχος, ὁ the cry of Bacchus.

ἰάλλω to send, throw, or put forth; to assail.

ἴᾱμα, τό remedy, healing.

ἰαμβεῖον, τό iambic verse.

ἰαμβο-φάγος, ὁ bad reciter of iambic verses.

ἰάομαι to heal, cure.

ἰάπτω to move, stir; to send, thrust; to hit, wound, hurt.

ἰάσιμος 2 healable.

ἴᾱσις, ἡ a healing.

ἴασπις, ιδος, ἡ jasper.

ἰαστί adv. in Ionic fashion.

ἰᾱτήρ, ῆρος, ὁ = ἰατρός.

ἰᾱτορίᾱ, ἡ art of healing.

ἰᾱτρείᾱ, ἡ = ἴασις.

ἰᾱτρεῖον, τό infirmary.

ἰᾱτρεύω to be a physician, to heal.

ἰᾱτρικός 3 medical.

ἰᾱτρός, ὁ physician, surgeon.

ἰαύω to pass the night, to sleep.

ἰαχέω, ἰάχω to cry aloud, to shout.

ἴβις, ιος, ἡ ibis.   [knee.]

ἰγνύᾱ, ἡ hollow of the

ἰδέ¹, ἴδε lo! behold!

ἰδέ² = ἠδέ and.

ἰδέᾱ, ἡ appearance, form; way, manner, nature; opinion, notion, idea.

ἴδη, ἡ woody mountain; wood, timber.

ἰδιο-βουλέω to act according to one's own will.

ἴδιος 3 one's own, personal, private; peculiar, strange; adv. ἰδίᾳ separately, privately, for oneself.

ἰδιότης, ητος, ἡ peculiarity.

ἰδιο-τρόφος 2 feeding separately.

ἰδίω to sweat.

ἰδιωτεύω to live as a private man; to know nothing of a certain art.

ἰδιώτης, ου, ὁ private man, single citizen; private soldier; bungler.

ἰδιωτικός 3 belonging to a private man or to a single person; common, trivial; ignorant, unlearned.

ἰδνόομαι P. to writhe.

ἰδού lo! behold! there! well, up!

ἰδρείᾱ, ἡ knowledge, skill.

ἴδρις, ι knowing, skilful, experienced.

ἱδρόω to sweat, perspire.

ἵδρῡμα, τό foundation; building; statue, image.

ἱδρύω to make sit down; to fix, settle, establish. — P. to be established, settled, or seated; to sit still; to be placed or situated. — M. to establish, found for oneself, build, erect.

ἱδρώς, ῶτος, ὁ sweat, perspiration.   [sible.]

ἰδυῖα, ἡ knowing, sen-

ἱέρᾱξ, ᾱκος, ὁ hawk, falcon.

ἱεράομαι M. to be a priest or priestess.

ἱερᾱτείᾱ, ἡ, ἱεράτευμα, τό priesthood, body of priests.

ἱερᾱτεύω to be a priest.

ἱέρεια, ἡ priestess.

ἱερεῖον, τό victim; cattle to be killed.

ἱερεύς, ὁ priest.

ἱερεύω to sacrifice; to slaughter.   [flesh.]

ἱερό-θυτον, τό offered

ἱερο-μηνίᾱ, ἡ, ἱερο-μήνιᾱ, τά festive month; festivity.

ἱερο-μνήμων, ονος, ὁ ambassador to the Amphictyons; chief magistrate.

ἱερο-ποιός, ὁ overseer of sacrifices.

ἱερο-πρεπής 2 becoming a sacred matter.

ἱερός 3 vigorous, strong, fresh; holy, sacred; τό

ἱερόν, τὰ ἱερά victim, sacrifice, offering, dedica-

tion; holy place, temple, oracle; omen, auspices, mystery, sacred rite, worship.

ἱερο-σῡλέω to rob a temple.

ἱερο-σῡλίᾱ, ἡ temple-robbery.   [temple.]

ἱερό-σῡλος, ὁ robbing a

ἱερουργέω to perform sacred rites.

ἱερουργίᾱ, ἡ worship.

ἱερο-φάντης, ου, ὁ initiating priest.

ἱερόω to dedicate.

ἱερωσύνη, ἡ office of a priest; priest's living.

ἱζάνω, ἵζω to cause to sit; intr. and M. to sit down, to place oneself; to encamp; to sink in.

ἰή, ἡ = ἰά.

ἰήιος 2 wailing, mournful; helper (in need).

ἴημα, τό = ἴαμα.

ἵημι to send (off), let go; to utter; to cast, throw, shoot; to let down; intr. to flow. — M. to be driven; to hasten, hurry; to long for, desire.

ἴησις etc. see ἴασις.

ἰθᾱ-γενής 2, ἰθαι-γενής 2 of good birth, legitimate; genuine; natural.

ἰθεῖα, ἰθέως see εὐθύς.

ἴθμα, τό gait, step.

ἰθύ-θριξ, τριχος with straight hair.

ἰθυ-μαχίᾱ, ἡ direct battle.

ἰθύντατα adv. most rightly.

ἰθύνω = εὐθύνω.

ἰθυ-πτίων, ωνος flying straight on.

ἰθύς¹ 3 = εὐθύς.

ἰθύς², ύος, ἡ direct course; undertaking; bent of mind, endeavour.

ἰθύω to go straight on, to rush (up)on; to strive after, desire.

ἱκανός 3 sufficient, enough, copious; fit, serviceable, becoming; empowered; considerable, respectable, trustworthy. [ciency; ability.]

ἱκανότης, ητος, ἡ suffi-/ ἱκανόω to make able or sufficient.

ἱκάνω and M. = ἵκω.

ἵκελος 3 like, similar.

ἱκέσιος 3 = ἱκετήριος.

ἱκετείᾱ, ἡ, ἱκέτευμα, τό supplication.

ἱκετεύω to supplicate.

ἱκετήριος 3 suppliant, entreating; ἡ ἱκετηρία olive branch of suppliants; entreaty.

ἱκέτης, ου, ὁ suppliant, entreating; one protected.

ἱκετήσιος 3 = ἱκετήριος.

ἱκέτις, ιδος, ἡ fem. of ἱκέτης.

ἱκμάς, άδος ἡ moisture.

ἵκμενος 2 favourable.

ἱκνέομαι M. = ἵκω.

ἴκρια, τά props of a ship; deck; board; scaffold.

ἱκτήρ, ῆρος ὁ suppliant.

ἱκτήριος 3 = ἱκετήριος.

ἰκτῖνος, ὁ kite.

ἵκω, ἱκάνω, ἱκνέομαι to come; to arrive at, reach; to come upon or over; to come as a suppliant; to implore; to be due.

ἰλαδόν adv. in troops.

ἱλάομαι = ἱλάσκομαι.

ἵλαος 2 gracious; propitious; gentle, cheerful.

ἱλαρός 3 cheerful, gay.

ἱλαρότης, ητος, ἡ gaiety.

ἱλάσκομαι M. to propitiate, reconcile; to appease; to atone for.

ἱλασμός, ὁ atonement.

ἱλαστήριον, τό means of propitiation, mercy-seat.

ἵλεως 2 = ἵλαος.

ἴλη, ἡ troop, band; squadron of horse.

ἵλημι, ἱλήκω to be propitious. [giddy.]

ἰλιγγιάω to be or become/ ἴλιγγος, ὁ giddiness, swoon.

ἱλλάς, άδος, ἡ rope, band, noose.

ἵλλω to roll; to force together, shut up. — P. to turn round.

ἰλύς, ύος, ἡ mud, slime.

ἱμάντινος 3 of leather thongs.

ἱμάς, άντος, ὁ thong, strap; rein; shoe-string; doorlatch: girdle of Venus.

ἱμάσθλη, ἡ whip.

ἱμάσσω to whip, scourge.

ἱματίζω to clothe.

ἱμάτιον, τό garment; upper garment, cloak; piece of cloth.

ἱματισμός, ὁ clothing.

ἱμείρω and M. and P. to long for, desire.

ἱμερόεις 3 exciting desire; lovely, charming; longing.

ἵμερος, ὁ a longing, yearning; love; charm.

ἱμερτός 3 lovely.

ἵνα adv. there; where; to what place, whither. — conj. that, in order that.

ἰνδάλλομαι P. to appear.

ἔνιον, τό neck, nape.

ἴξαλος αἴξ wild goat, stone-buck.

ἰξύς, ύος, ἡ groin, waist.

ἰο-δνεφής 2 violet.

ἰο-δόκος 2 holding arrows.

ἰο-ειδής 2 violet-coloured.

ἰόεις 3 = ἰοειδής.

ἰό-μωρος 2 arrow-shooting; braggart.

ἴον, τό a violet.

ἰονθάς, άδος shaggy.

ἰός¹, ὁ arrow.

ἰός², ὁ poison; rust.

ἴος, ἴα, ἴον one, the same.

ἰότης, ητος, ἡ will, desire.

ἰού oh! woe! hey-day!

ἰουδαΐζω to live in the Jewish fashion.

ἰουδαϊσμός, ὁ Judaism.

ἴουλος, ὁ down of the cheek. [rows.

ἰο-χέαιρα, ἡ shooting ar-

ἰπνός, ὁ oven, furnace.

ἱππ-αγρέτης, ου, ὁ leader of Spartan horse-guards.

ἱππ-αγωγός 2 transporting horses.

ἱππάζομαι M. to guide horses; to drive; to ride.

ἱππ-αρμοστής, οῦ, ὁ = ἵππαρχος.

ἱππ-αρχέω to command the cavalry. [of cavalry.

ἵππ-αρχος, ὁ commander

ἱππάς, άδος, ἡ riding-coat.

ἱππασία, ἡ = ἱππεία.

ἱππάσιμος 2 fit for horses.

ἱππεία, ἡ a riding, driving, horsemanship; cavalry.

ἵππειος 3 = ἱππικός.

ἱππεύς, ὁ horseman, rider, charioteer, knight.

ἱππεύω to ride, to be a horseman.

ἱππ-ηλάσιος 2 fit for riding or driving. [knight.

ἱππ-ηλάτα, ὁ horseman.

ἱππ-ήλατος 2 = ἱππηλάσιος. [milker.

ἱππ-ημολγός, ὁ mare-

ἱππικός 3 of a horse, belonging to horses, for riding or driving; for horsemen; skilled in riding; ἡ ἱππική horsemanship, τὸ ἱππικόν cavalry.

ἵππιος 3 rich in horses; chivalrous.

ἱππιο-χαίτης, ου with horse-hair. [fighter.

ἱππιο-χάρμης, ου chariot-

ἱππο-βότης, ου breeder of horses, knight.

ἱππό-βοτος 2 fed on by horses. [horses.

ἱππό-δαμος 2 tamer of

ἱππό-δασυς 3 thick with horse-hair. [horses.

ἱππο-δέτης, ου bridling

ἱππο-δρομιά, ἡ horse-race.

ἱππό-δρομος, ὁ race-course.

ἱππο-δρόμος, ὁ light horse-man.

ἱππόθεν from the horse.

ἱππο-κέλευθος 2 driving horses. [dier's boy.

ἱππο-κόμος, ὁ groom; sol-

ἱππό-κομος 2 of horse-hair. [teer, knight.

ἱππο-κορυστής, οῦ charioἱππο-κρατέω to be superior in cavalry. — *P.* to be inferior in cavalry.

ἱππο-μανής 2 swarming with horses; what makes horses mad. [horseback.]

ἱππο-μαχέω to fight on

ἱππο-μαχία, ἡ combat of horsemen. [horseback.]

ἱππό-μαχος 2 fighting on

ἱππο-νώμᾱς, ου guiding horses. [horses.]

ἱππο-πόλος 2 breeding

ἵππος, ὁ, ἡ horse; chariot; charioteers; ἡ ἵ. cavalry.

ἱπποσύνη, ἡ horsemanship; cavalry.

ἱππότης, ου, ἱππότα, ὁ on horseback, mounted; horseman, knight. [ed archer.]

ἱππο-τοξότης, ου, ὁ mount-

ἱππο-τροφέω to feed or keep horses. [of horses.]

ἱππο-τροφία, ἡ the feeding

ἱππο-τρόφος 2 feeding or keeping horses.

ἵππ-ουρις = ἱππόκομος.

ἱππο-φόρβιον, τό troop of horses; stable. [to punish.]

ἵπτομαι *M.* to press hard;

ἱράομαι, etc. see ἱεράομαι.

ἱρήϊον, τό = ἱερεῖον.

ἱρήν, ένος, ὁ Spartan young man.

ἵρηξ, ηκος, ὁ = ἱέραξ.

ἶρις, ιδος, ἡ rainbow.

ἱρός, ἱρόν see ἱερός.

ἴς, ἰνός, ἡ sinew, nerve, muscle; strength, force.

ἰσ-άγγελος 2 angel-like.

ἰσάζω to make equal. — *M.* to hold oneself equal.

ἰσ-ηγορίᾱ, ἡ equal free-

dom of speech; equality in rights.

ἴσθμιον, τό necklace.

ἰσθμός, ὁ neck of land.

ἰσθμώδης 2 isthmus-like.

ἔσκε he said.

ἔσκω to make like or equal; to think or hold like; to suppose, think.

ἰσο-δίαιτος 2 equal in mode of life.

ἰσό-θεος 2 godlike.

ἰσο-κίνδῡνος 2 equal to the danger. [power.]

ἰσο-κρατής 2 equal in

ἰσο-κρατίᾱ, ἡ equal right of citizens, democracy.

ἰσο-μέτρητος 2 equal in measure. [front.]

ἰσο-μέτωπος 2 with equal

ἰσο-μοιρέω to have equal share or rights.

ἰσο-μοιρίᾱ, ἡ equal share; partnership.

ἰσό-μοιρος 2, ἰσό-μορος 2 having (an) equal share; enjoying the same right.

ἰσο-νομέομαι *M.* to have equal rights.

ἰσο-νομίᾱ, ἡ equality of rights, democracy.

ἰσο-νομικός 2 democratical.

ἰσο-παλής 2 equal in fight.

ἰσό-πεδος 2 level, even.

ἰσο-πλατής 2 equal in breadth.

ἰσό-πλευρος 2 equilateral.

ἰσο-πληθής 2 equal in number.

ἰσο-ρροπίᾱ, ἡ equipoise.

ἰσό-ρροπος 2 equally balanced; equivalent; equally matched.

ἴσος, ἴσος, εἴσος 3 equal; the same; proportionable, equally distributed, reasonable, due, fair, impartial; ἡ ἴση, τὸ ἴσον, τὰ ἴσα equality, equilibrium, equal share or proportion, right, equity, compensation. — adv. ἴσον, ἴσα equally; ἴσως perhaps, probably; fairly; about.

ἰσο-σκελής 2 with equal legs.   [taxation.]

ἰσο-τέλεια, ἡ equality in/

ἰσο-τέλεστος 2 making all equal at last.

ἰσότης, ητος, ἡ equality.

ἰσό-τιμος 2 equally honoured.

ἰσο-φαρίζω to cope with.

ἰσο-φόρος 2 equal in strength.   [the edge.]

ἰσο-χειλής 2 level with/

ἰσό-ψηφος 2 having an equal vote.   [same mind.]

ἰσό-ψῡχος 2 having the

ἰσόω to make equal. — M. and P. to be equal.

ἰστάω, ἰστάνω = ἴστημι.

ἴστημι to cause to stand; to set, place, establish, fix; to set up, to raise up; to stir, to begin; to stop, check; to balance, weigh; to appoint. — intr. to stand, be placed; to place oneself; to rise, arise, begin; to lie, be situated; to stand firm, be fixed; to be inactive; to continue.

ἰστιάω, ἰστίη, ἡ = ἑστ.

ἰστιητόριον, τό public inn.

ἰστίον, τό sail.

ἰστο-δόκη, ἡ mast-holder.

ἰστο-πέδη, ἡ hole for fixing the mast in.

ἰστορέω and M. to inquire, question, search; to know by inquiry; to narrate.

ἰστορίᾱ, ἡ inquiry, knowledge, information; science; narration: history.

ἰστός, ὁ ship's mast; yarnbeam; loom; warp; web.

ἰστουργέω to weave.

ἴστωρ, ορος knowing; judge.

ἰσχαλέος 3 dry.

ἰσχανάω, ἰσχάνω to hold back, to check; to cling to.

ἰσχίον, τό socket of the hip-bone.

ἰσχναίνω to make dry, withered, or thin.

ἰσχνός 3 dry; thin; lean.

ἰσχνό-φωνος 2 with a weak voice, stammering.

ἰσχῡρίζομαι to exert oneself; to insist strongly (upon); to affirm; to persist in.

ἰσχῡρός 3 strong, mighty, powerful; firm, fortified; safe, lasting; resolute; violent.

ἰσχῡς, ύος, ἡ strength, power, firmness, force; troops.

ἰσχύω to be strong, mighty, powerful.

ἴσχω = ἔχω.

ἰτέα, ἡ willow.

ἰτεΐνος 3 of willows.

ἴτης, ου, ὁ bold, impetuous; insolent, impudent.

ἴττω = ἴστω (οἶδα).

ἴτυς, υος, ἡ rim or felloe of a wheel; edge of a shield.

ἰῡγή, ἡ, ἰυγμός, ὁ cry, howling, shout, yelling.

ἰύζω to yell, shout, shriek.

ἴφθῑμος 3 and 2 strong, stout, stalwart.

ἶφι adv. valiantly.

ἶφιος 3 strong; fat.

ἰχθυάω to fish.

ἰχθύδιον, τό little fish.

ἰχθυο-ειδής 2 fish-like; swarming with fish.

ἰχθυο-φάγος, ὁ fish-eating.

ἰχθύς, ύος, ὁ fish.

ἰχθυώδης 2 = ἰχθυοειδής.

ἰχνευτής, οῦ, ὁ ichneumon.

ἰχνεύω to track, trace out, find out.

ἴχνος, τό, ἴχνιον, τό footstep, track, trace; pl. movement, gait. [gods; lymph.]

ἰχώρ, ῶρος, ὁ blood of the

ἴψ, ἰπός, ὁ worm that bores through wood.

ἰώ oh! woe! hey-day!

ἰωγή, ἡ defence, shelter.

ἰωή, ἡ a roaring, whistling, sounding.

ἰῶκα = ἰωκήν.

ἰωκή, ἡ battle-din.

ἰῶτα, τό iota.

ἰωχμός, ὁ = ἰωκή.

K

K, κ (κάππα) tenth letter of the alphabet; as a numeral κ' = 20.

κά = κέ (see ἄν).

καβ-βάλλω = καταβ.

κάγ = κατά γε.

κάγκανος 2 dry.

καγχάζω, καγχαλάω to laugh aloud; to shout.

κάδ = κατά δέ.

καδίσκος, ὁ balloting-urn.

κάδος, ὁ pitcher, jar, pail.

καθά (καθ' ἅ) according as.

καθ-αγίζω, καθ-αγνίζω to dedicate, devote, offer; to burn; to bury.

καθ-αίρεσις, ἡ a taking down, destruction. [down.]

καθ-αιρετέος 3 to be put

καθ-αιρέω to take or pull down; to close (the eyes of the dead); to demolish, destroy, kill; to overpower; to take away, carry off, seize; to achieve; to con-

demn; to obtain; to catch, surprise.

καθαίρω to clean, cleanse, purify; to atone; to wash off.

καθ-άλλομαι M. to spring down. [μέριος.]

καθ-ᾱμέριος 2 = καθη-

καθ-ανύω = κατανύω.

καθ-άπαξ adv. once for all.

καθά-περ adv. just as.

καθ-άπτω to tie to, fasten on, attach to, to take hold of. — M. to lay hold of, seize, attack, scold; to call to witness.

καθαρεύω to keep oneself clean; to keep clean.

καθαρίζω to make clean, purify.

καθαριότης, ητος, ἡ purity, cleanliness. [μός.]

καθαρισμός, ὁ = καθαρ-

κάθαρμα, τό off-scourings, rubbish, filth; outcast.

καθ-αρμόζω to fit to.

καθαρμός, ὁ a cleansing, purifying; atonement.

καθαρός 3 pure, clean, unsoiled; sound; undisturbed; unmixed, unalloyed, genuine; guiltless, innocent, chaste; honest; perfect.

καθαρότης, ητος, ἡ purity.

καθάρσιος 2 purifying, cleansing, atoning.

κάθαρσις, ἡ = καθαρμός.

καθαρτής, οῦ, ὁ purifier, atoner.

καθ-έδρᾱ, ἡ seat, couch, chair; a sitting still.

καθ-έζω to place, set down, establish. — M. to sit down, sit still, tarry.

καθ-είργνῡμι = κατείργω.

καθεῖς = καθ' εἷς one by one.   [back.]

καθ-εκτός 3 to be held]

καθ-έλκω, -ύω to draw down; to launch.

καθ-εξῆς adv. in succession, one after the other.

κάθ-εξις, ἡ a holding fast.

καθ-εύδω to sleep, be at rest.

καθ-ευρίσκω to find out.

καθ-εψιάομαι to mock at.

καθ-ηγεμών, όνος. ὁ guide.

καθ-ηγέομαι M. to lead the way, to guide, to show the way; to do first.

καθ-ηγητής, οῦ, ὁ leader, guide; teacher.   [der.]

καθ-ηδυπαθέω to squan-]

καθ-ήκω to come down; to reach to; to arrive; to be meet, proper, or sufficient.

κάθ-ημαι to be seated; to sit in court; to sit still or idle; to stop; to be encamped.

καθ-ημερινός 3 daily.

καθ-ημέριος 3 of to-day.

καθ-ιδρύω to make sit down; to set down, establish, settle.

καθ-ιερεύω, -όω to dedicate, vow, offer.

καθ-ίζω, καθ-ιζάνω to make sit down; to set down; to place, establish, appoint, constitute; to place in a certain condition. — intr. and M. to sit down, to be settled or seated.

καθ-ίημι to send down; to let down; to let return. — intr. and M. to come down; to reach to; to move on.

καθ-ικετεύω to implore.

καθ-ικνέομαι M. to come to, arrive at.

καθ-ιππάζομαι M. to ride down, to overrun with horse.

καθ-ίστημι trans. to set down, put down, place; to establish, appoint, constitute, ordain; to place in a certain condition. — intr. to be placed, set down, established, or appointed; to stand; to appear; to come to; to be in a certain condition, to become or have become; to stand still, be fixed, ordained; to exist; to be in value. — M. (also = intr.)

to set down or place for oneself.

καθό = καθ' ὅ in so far as.

κάθ-οδος, ἡ way down or back.

καθ-ολικός 3 universal.

καθ-όλου adv. on the whole, generally.

καθ-ομολογέω to grant, consent (to). [to overcome.]

καθ-οπλίζω to arm, equip;]

καθ-οράω and M. to look down; to see from afar; to behold, view; to perceive, know.

καθ-ορμίζω to bring to anchor. — M. and P. to come into harbour.

καθ-ότι adv. in so far as, in what manner.

καθ-υβρίζω to be insolent, haughty, or wicked; to insult, treat with contempt.

κάθ-υδρος 2 full of water.

καθ-υπάρχω to exist, to fall to one's lot.

καθ-ύπερθεν adv. from above; above, on high; yonder; before.

καθ-υπέρτερος 3 upper, higher, superior; **καθ-υπέρτατος** 3 highest.

καθ-υπνόω and M. to fall asleep; to sleep sound.

καθ-υφίημι and M. to let go, abandon, betray; to yield.

καθ-ώς adv. as.

καθ-ώσπερ adv. just as.

καί conj. and, also, even, though; especially; **καί** ... **καί** as well as, both ... and. [verns or chasms.]

καιετάεις 3 rich in ca-]

καινίζω to make new.

καινο-παθής 2 never before suffered.

καινο-ποιέω to make new.

καινός 3 new; unheard of, strange. [ness.]

καινότης, ητος, ἡ new-]

καινο-τομέω to begin something new, to make innovations. [new way.]

καινουργέω to act in a]

καινόω to make new; to consecrate anew. [pass.]

καίνυμαι to excel; to sur-]

καίνω to kill.

καί-περ conj. although.

καίριος 3 happening at the right time and place, seasonable; vital, deadly.

καιρός, ὁ right proportion, due measure; right place; right time or season, opportunity; time, circumstances; critical moment; embarrassment; importance, influence; profit, success.

καιροσσέων gen. pl. fem. of καιρόεις 3 close-woven.

καί-τοι adv. and yet, and indeed; however; although.

καίω to kindle, set on fire, burn, waste. — P. to be set on fire, to be burnt; to burn. [evil tidings.]

κακ-αγγελέω to bring]

κακ-άγγελος 2 caused by bad news.

κακ-ανδρία, ἡ unmanliness.

κάκη, ἡ = κακία.

κακ-ηγορέω to abuse, revile, slander.

κακία, ἡ badness, wickedness, vice, cowardice, shame; disgrace; reproach.

κακίζω to make bad; to abuse, blame. — *P.* to be reproached or blamed; to play the coward.

κακ-κεῖαι, κακκῆαι see κατακαίω. [κείοντες.]

κακ-κείοντες = κατα-

κακό-βιος 2 living wretchedly. [bour of misery.]

κακο-γείτων, ονος neigh-

κακο-δαιμονάω, -έω to be possessed by an evil spirit.

κακο-δαιμονία, ἡ misfortune; infatuation; raving madness.

κακο-δαίμων 2 unhappy, wretched. [repute.]

κακο-δοξέω to be in ill

κακο-είμων 2 badly clad.

κακο-εργία, ἡ = κακουργία.

κακο-ήθεια, ἡ malignity.

κακο-ήθης 2 malicious.

κακό-θροος, -θρους 2 slanderous. [Ilios.]

κακο-ίλιος ἡ unhappy

κακο-λογέω to abuse, slander, accurse.

κακο-λογία, ἡ slander.

κακο-μήχανος 2 contriving evil, mischievous.

κακό-νοια, ἡ ill will, enmity. [laws.]

κακό-νομος 2 with bad

κακό-νοος 2 ill-disposed, hostile. [guests.]

κακό-ξεινος 2 having ill

κακο-ξύνετος 2 guileful.

κακο-πάθεια, ἡ suffering, distress. [be distressed.]

κακο-παθέω to suffer evil,

κακο-πινής 2 foul.

κακο-ποιέω to do ill; to hurt, spoil.

κακο-ποιός, ὁ wrong-doer.

κακό-πους, ποδος with bad feet.

κακο-πραγέω to be unfortunate, to fail in one's enterprise.

κακο-πραγία, ἡ ill condition; failure. [vous.]

κακο-πράγμων 2 mischie-

κακός 3 bad, ill, evil; useless, unfit; mean, vile; foul, unfair, wicked, mischievous, shameful; injurious, hurtful; miserable, wretched. τὸ κακόν evil, ill, mischief, distress, suffering; damage; vice.

κακο-σκελής 2 with bad legs. [language.]

κακο-στομέω to use bad

κακο-τεχνέω to act maliciously.

κακό-τεχνος 2 artful.

κακότης, ητος, ἡ badness; cowardice; misfortune, distress; defeat.

κακο-τροπία, ἡ bad habits.

κακο-τυχέω to be unfortunate.

κακουργέω to do evil, to act badly; to hurt, damage; to ravage.

κακούργημα, τό, κακ-ουργία, ἡ bad or wicked deed, wickedness.

κακοῦργος, ὁ doing evil, mischievous, artful; damaging; wrong-doer, criminal, knave.

κακουχέω to treat ill.

κακο-φραδής 2 devising ill.

κακό-φρων 2 ill-minded; foolish.

κακόω to treat ill, to maltreat, vex, hurt, destroy; to make angry, exasperate.

κάκτανε see κατακτείνω.

κάκωσις, ἡ ill-treatment; humiliation; suffering, distress. [reed; stubble.]

καλάμη, ἡ stalk of corn,]

καλαμη-φόρος 2 carrying reeds. [cane.]

καλάμινος 3 of reed or]

κάλαμος, ὁ reed, cane; writing-reed.

καλάσῑρις, ἡ long garment of females.

καλαῦροψ, οπος, ἡ shepherd's staff.

καλέω to call, call by name (P. to be called, ὁ καλούμενος the so-called); to summon, to call to aid; to invoke, implore; to summon before the court; to invite.

καλήτωρ, ορος, ὁ crier.

καλινδέομαι P. to roll, wallow; to be busied with.

καλλείπω = καταλείπω.

καλλι-βόᾱς, ου beautiful-sounding.

καλλί-βοτρυς, υος with beautiful grapes.

καλλι-γύναιξ, αικος with beautiful women.

καλλι-έλαιος, ἡ cultivated olive. [speech.]

καλλι-επέω to use flowery]

καλλι-ιερέω to sacrifice with good omens, to give good omens.

καλλί-ζωνος 2 with beautiful girdles.

καλλί-θριξ, τριχος with beautiful hair or mane.

καλλί-κομος 2 with fine hair. [fine hair-bands.]

καλλι-κρήδεμνος 2 with]

κάλλιμος 2 = καλός.

καλλι-πάρῃος 2 with beautiful cheeks.

καλλι-πλόκαμος 2 with beautiful locks or braids.

καλλί-ρέεθρος 2, καλλί-ρροος 2 beautifully flowing.

καλλιστεῖον, τό prize of beauty or valour.

καλλιστεύω and M. to be the most beautiful.

καλλί-σφυρος 2 with beautiful ankles.

καλλί-φθογγος 2 sounding beautifully.

καλλί-χορος 2 with beautiful dancing-places.

καλλονή, ἡ, κάλλος, τό beauty; ornament; excellence; beautiful thing.

καλλύνω to beautify, embellish. — M. to boast, pride oneself (up)on.

καλλ-ωπίζω to beautify, embellish, adorn. — M. to adorn oneself; to boast, pride oneself (up)on; to be affected or coy.

καλλ-ώπισμα, τό, καλλ-ωπισμός, ὁ embellishment, ornament, finery.

καλο-διδάσκαλος, ὁ, ἡ teacher of virtue.

καλοκἀγαθίᾱ, ἡ nobleness and goodness.

κᾶλον, τό wood; ship.

καλο-ποιέω to do good.

καλό-πους, ποδος, ὁ shoe-maker's last.

κᾰλός 3 beautiful, fair, charming, lovely, pretty; honest, noble, good, right, virtuous; agreeable, auspicious, favourable, dear. καλὸς κἀγαθός honest man, gentleman, aristocrat. τὸ καλόν the beautiful, beauty; virtue, honesty, honour; joy, happiness.

κάλος, ὁ = κάλως.

κάλπις, ιδος, ἡ pitcher, urn.

καλύβη, ἡ hut, cabin.

κάλυμμα, τό covering, veil.

κάλυξ, υκος, ἡ husk, shell; cup; bud; pendant of the ear.

καλυπτός 3 enveloping.

καλύπτρᾱ, ἡ covering, cover; veil.   [conceal.]

καλύπτω to cover, envelop,

καλχαίνω to be agitated in mind, to consider deeply.

καλώδιον, τό rope, cord.

κάλως, ω, ὁ rope, cable.

κάμαξ, ακος, ἡ pole for vines.   [coach.]

καμάρα, ἡ chamber, vault;

καματηρός 3 wearisome; sick.   [labour; distress.]

κάματος, ὁ weariness; toil,

κάμηλος, ὁ, ἡ camel.

κάμιλος, ὁ anchor-cable.

κάμινος, ἡ furnace, kiln.

καμῑνώ, οῦς, ἡ furnace-woman.   [victory.]

καμ-μονίη, ἡ endurance,

κάμ-μορος 2 unfortunate.

κάμνω to work hard; to toil, exert oneself; to be

weary, exhausted, or tired; to be sick or ill; to feel trouble. — M. to work out; to gain by toil. [turning.]

καμπή, ἡ a bending, curve,

κάμπτω to bend, bow, turn round; to make one alter his sentiments.

καμπύλος 3 curved, bent.

κἄν = καὶ ἄν, καὶ ἐάν.

καναναῖος, κανανίτης, ου, ὁ zealot.

καναχέω to clash, clang.

καναχή, ἡ ringing sound, clash, gnashing, noise.

καναχίζω = καναχέω.

κάνδυς, υος, ὁ caftan.

κάνεον, κάνειον, τό basket; dish.

κάνθαρος, ὁ beetle.

κανθήλιος, ὁ pack-ass.

κάνναβις, ἡ hemp; hempen garment.

καννεύσας = κατανεύσας.

κανοῦν, τό = κάνεον.

κανών, όνος, ὁ rod, bar; weaving-staff; handle of the shield; rule, ruler, level; precept, law; model, standard; district.

κάπετος, ἡ ditch, trench; hole, grave.

κάπη, ἡ manger.   [vern.]

καπηλεῖον, τό shop; ta-

καπηλεύω to be a retail-dealer, to hawk, sell; to adulterate.

κάπηλος, ὁ retailer, shop-keeper; innkeeper.

καπίθη, ἡ a Persian measure.

καπνίζω to light a fire.

καπνο-δόκη, ἡ smoke-hole.

καπνός, ὁ smoke, steam, vapour.

κάπριος 2 like a wild boar; = κάπρος.

κάπρος, ὁ wild boar.

χ. ρ¹ = κάρα head.

κάρ², καρός, τό chip; ἐν καρὸς αἴσῃ for nothing.

κάρᾱ, τό head; top, summit; mountain-castle.

καρα-δοκέω to watch, expect eagerly.

καρᾱ-δοκίᾱ, ἡ expectation.

κάρᾱνος, ὁ chief, lord.

καρᾱ-τομος 2 cut off from the head. [shoe.]

καρβατίνη, ἡ peasant's]

καρδίᾱ, ἡ heart, mind, soul, interior; stomach.

καρδιο-γνώστης, ου, ὁ knower of hearts.

κάρδοπος, ἡ trough.

κάρη, τό = κάρα.

καρη-κομόωντες, οἱ with hair on the head.

κάρηνον, τό = κάρα.

καρκαίρω to ring; to quake.

καρκίνος, ὁ cancer, crab.

καρπαία, ἡ a mimic dance.

καρπάλιμος 2 swift, quick, hasty.

καρπός¹, ὁ fruit, corn, harvest, produce; profit, success.

καρπός², ὁ wrist.

καρπο-φορέω to bear fruit.

καρπο-φόρος 2 fruit-bearing.

καρπόω to bear fruit. — M. to gather fruit, to reap; to have the usufruct or enjoyment of; to plunder.

καρ-ρέζω = καταρέζω.

κάρτα adv. very, very much.

καρτερέω to be firm, steadfast, or patient; to endure, bear, persist in.

καρτέρησις, καρτερίᾱ, ἡ patience, endurance; abstinence, self-control.

καρτερικός 3 enduring, patient. [hearted.]

καρτερό-θῡμος 2 stout-]

καρτερός 3 strong, firm, staunch; enduring, steadfast; mighty, master, valiant, courageous, brave; violent, obstinate, cruel.

κάρτιστος 3 = κράτιστος.

κάρτος, τό = κράτος.

καρτύνω = κρατύνω.

κάρυον, τό nut. [(sound).]

καρφαλέος 3 dry; hollow]

κάρφη, ἡ, **κάρφος**, τό dry stalk, hay, straw, chaff, dry stick; mote.

κάρφω to make dry or withered. [dry.]

καρχαλέος 3 rough, hoarse,]

καρχαρ-όδους, -όδοντος with sharp teeth.

κασίᾱ, ἡ cassia.

κασι-γνήτη, ἡ sister.

κασί-γνητος 3 brotherly, sisterly; ὁ κ. brother.

κάσις, ὁ, ἡ brother, sister.

κασσίτερος, ὁ tin.

κάστωρ, ορος, ὁ beaver.

κατά adv. downwards, down; entirely. — prp. with gen. from above, down from; down upon; opposite to, against. — with acc. downwards, down; over; among; throughout, along; near, opposite, at; during, about;

because of; in search of; in relation to, concerning. according to, answering to; after; κατὰ τρεῖς three at a time; κατὰ φῦλα by tribes; κατ' ἐνιαυτόν year by year.

κᾶτα = καὶ εἶτα.

κατα-βαίνω to go or come down, to go down to the sea; to go into the arena (as a fighter); to fall down; to condescend; to come to; to enter into.

κατα-βάλλω to throw or cast down, to overthrow; to let fall, drop, lay down; to slay, destroy; to put down, pay off; to bring or carry down, to store up; to throw away, reject, disparage.

κατα-βαρέω, -βαρύνω to weigh down, burden, molest.

κατά-βασις, ἡ a going down, way or march down, descent, return.

κατα-βιβάζω to cause to go down, to lead or bring down.

κατα-βιβρώσκω to eat up.

κατα-βιόω to live through.

κατα-βλᾱκεύω to spoil by carelessness. [through.]

κατα-βλώσκω to go)

κατα-βοάω to cry aloud, to cry out against, to complain of.

κατα-βοή, ἡ outcry against; report; accusation.

κατα-βολή, ἡ attack, payment, foundation.

κατα-βραβεύω to decide against. [down.]

κατα-βρόχω to swallow)

κατα-βυρσόω to cover over with hides.

κατά-γαιος 2 = κατάγειος.

κατ-αγγελεύς, ὁ announcer.

κατ-αγγέλλω to announce, proclaim.

κατ-άγγελτος 2 betrayed.

κατά-γειος 2 underground; on the ground.

κατα-γέλαστος 2 ridiculous. [mock.]

κατα-γελάω to laugh at,)

κατά-γελως, ωτος, ὁ mockery, ridiculousness.

κατα-γηράσκω, -γηράω to grow old.

κατα-γιγνώσκω to observe, discover, perceive; to think ill of; to charge with, to condemn, to give judgment against.

κατ-αγῑνέω = κατάγω.

κάτ-αγμα, τό flock of wool.

κατ-άγνῡμι to break in or to pieces, shatter, shiver. — intr. and P. to be broken, to burst.

κατά-γνωσις, ἡ disregard, contempt; condemnation.

κατα-γοητεύω to bewitch, enchant; to impose upon.

κατ-αγορεύω to denounce.

κατα-γράφω to scratch; to write down.

κατ-άγω to lead, bring, or carry down; to lead to a place; to bring down from the sea to the land; to lead or bring back or home.

— *M.* to come to land, put in; to return.

κατ-αγωγή, ἡ a landing, putting in; harbour, quarters. [abode.]

κατ-αγώγιον, τό quarters,

κατ-αγωνίζομαι *M.* to overpower. [rend asunder.]

κατα-δαίομαι to divide.

κατα-δακρύω to weep, lament. [due.]

κατα-δαμάζομαι to subdue.

κατα-δαπανάω to use up, spend entirely.

κατα-δάπτω to rend to pieces. [asleep.]

κατα-δαρθάνω to fall

κατα-δεής 2 needy; καταδεέστερος inferior, weaker, less.

κατα-δείδω to fear much.

κατα-δείκνῡμι to show, make known; to teach.

κατα-δειλιάω to neglect from fear or cowardice.

κατα-δέομαι *P.* to entreat earnestly. [down upon.]

κατα-δέρχομαι *P.* to look

κατα-δεύω to wet.

κατα-δέχομαι *M.* to admit, receive back.

κατα-δέω[1] to bind to; to fetter, imprison; to tie up, close, shut up; to check; to convict, condemn.

κατα-δέω[2] to want, lack, need.

κατά-δηλος 2 quite manifest or conspicuous.

κατα-δημοβορέω to consume public goods.

κατα-διαιτάω to decide against (as an arbiter).

κατα-δίδωμι to flow into.

κατα-δικάζω to give judgment against, to condemn. — *M.* to obtain judgment against another, to gain one's lawsuit.

κατα-δίκη, ἡ condemnation; fine. [chase.]

κατα-διώκω to pursue,

κατα-δοκέω, κατα-δοξάζω to think ill of one, to suspect; to think, suppose. judge.

κατα-δουλόω to enslave, subdue. [slaving.]

κατα-δούλωσις, ἡ an en-

κατα-δρέπω to pluck off.

κατα-δρομή, ἡ raid, inroad.

κατα-δυναστεύω = καταδουλόω. [μαι *M.*]

κατα-δύνω = καταδύο-

κατα-δύω *trans.* to dive, submerge, dip; to cause to sink. — *intr.* and *M.* to go under water, to sink; to enter; to go down, set; to creep into; to hide oneself; to put on (garments, arms).

κατ-ᾴδω to annoy one by singing; to sing to; to sing a spell; to conjure.

κατα-έννῡμι to clothe, cover.

κατ-αξαίνω to dry up.

κατα-ζεύγνῡμι to yoke together, harness; to bind, tie, fetter, imprison.

κατα-θάπτω to bury, inter.

κατα-θεάομαι *M.* to look down upon, to behold, watch, view.

κατα-θέλγω to subdue by charms.

κατά-θεμα, τό curse; accursed thing.

κατα-θεματίζω to curse.

κατα-θέω to run down; to make an inroad or raid, to overrun, attack.

κατα-θεωρέω = κατα-θεάομαι.

κατα-θνήσκω to die (away).

κατα-θνητός 3 mortal.

κατα-θορυβέω to silence by noise.

κατα-θρώσκω to leap down or over. [heart.)

κατ-αθδμέω to lose all)

κατα-θύμιος 3 being in or upon the mind.

κατα-θύω to slaughter, sacrifice; to dedicate.

καται-βατός 2 accessible.

κατ-αιδέομαι to feel or be ashamed; to reverence.

κατ-αικίζω to disfigure.

κατ-αινέω to agree, assent to, approve of; to grant, promise.

κατ-αίρω to come to land.

κατ-αισθάνομαι M. to perceive or understand fully.

κατ-αισχύνω to disgrace, dishonour; to shame, put to the blush; to deceive. — P. to feel ashamed.

κατα-ίσχω to possess.

κατ-αιτιάομαι M. to accuse, lay to one's charge.

καταῖτυξ, υγος, ἡ steelcap.

κατα-καίνω = κατακτείνω.

κατα-καίριος 2 deadly.

κατα-καίω to burn down.

κατα-καλέω to summon.

κατα-καλύπτω to envelop, cover up.

κατα-καυχάομαι M. to boast against; to treat with contempt.

κατά-κειμαι M. to lie down; to lie at table; to lie hid, still, or sick.

κατα-κείρω to cut down; to consume, waste.

κατα-κείω to go asleep.

κατα-κερτομέω to mock at.

κατα-κηλέω to enchant.

κατα-κηρόω to cover with wax.

κατα-κηρύσσω to proclaim by a herald. [wail.)

κατα-κλαίω and M. to be-)

κατα-κλάω to break off, to break in or to pieces; to move or shake one's heart.

κατα-κλείω to shut up or in, blockade; to decree, stipulate.

κατα-κληροδοτέω to distribute by lot.

κατα-κλήω = κατακλείω.

κατα-κλίνω to lay down; to make lie down (at table). — P. to lie down.

κατά-κλισις, ἡ a making to lie down.

κατα-κλύζω to inundate.

κατα-κλυσμός, ὁ inundation, flood.

κατα-κοιμάω, -κοιμίζω to put to sleep; to lull to sleep; to let fall into oblivion; to sleep through. — P. to fall asleep.

κατ-ακολουθέω to follow.

κατα-κολπίζω to run into a bay.

κατα-κολυμβάω to dive.

κατα-κομιδή, ἡ exportation.

κατα-κομίζω to bring down to the sea; to import. — *P.* to arrive, come into harbour.

κατ-ακοντίζω to strike down with a spear.

κατα-κόπτω to strike down, slay, kill; to coin money; to rend, tear to pieces.

κατά-κορος 2 excessive.

κατα-κοσμέω to arrange, set in order; to adorn.

κατ-ακούω to hear, hearken to; to obey.

κατ-άκρας *adv.* thoroughly.

κατα-κρατέω to prevail, to be superior. [upon.]

κατα-κρεμάννῦμι to hang

κατα-κρεουργέω to cut to pieces, lacerate.

κατά-κρηθεν *adv.* from the head downwards; entirely.

κατα-κρημνίζω to throw down a precipice. [κρίσις.]

κατά-κρῖμα, τό = κατά-

κατα-κρίνω to give judgment against, to condemn.

κατά-κρισις, ἡ judgment, condemnation. [ceal.]

κατα-κρύπτω to hide, con-

κατα-κρυφή, ἡ pretext, evasion. [possess.]

κατα-κτάομαι *M.* to gain,

κατα-κτείνω to kill, destroy, execute.

κατα-κυλίομαι *P.* to roll or fall down.

κατα-κύπτω to bend down, stoop. [mand.]

κατα-κῦριεύω to com-

κατα-κῦρόω to ratify. — *P.* to be fulfilled or realised.

κατα-κωλύω to keep back.

κατα-λαλέω to slander.

κατα-λαλιά, ἡ slander, calumny.

κατά-λαλος, ὁ slanderer.

κατα-λαμβάνω to seize, lay hold of, take possession of, take away, occupy; to catch, overtake, surprise, discover, find out, meet; *intr.* to happen, come to pass, befal; to hold fast or back, to check; to bind by oath; to oblige. — *M.* to seize for oneself, to occupy, conquer; to understand, apprehend.

κατα-λάμπω to shine upon.

κατ-αλγέω to suffer pain.

κατα-λέγω[1] to recite, count up, relate, tell, explain, mention; to pick out, choose; to enlist, enrol.

κατα-λέγω[2] = καταλέχω.

κατα-λείβομαι *P.* to trickle or drop down. [residue.]

κατά-λειμμα, τό remnant,

κατα-λείπω to leave behind, bequeath; to spare one's life; to forsake, abandon; to lose. — *P.* to remain behind; to be impending. — *M.* to leave behind for oneself, to retain, reserve to oneself.

κατα-λεύω to stone to death.

κατα-λέχω to lay down.

— *M.* to lie down, to sleep.

κατ-αλέω to grind down.

κατα-λήθομαι *M.* to forget wholly.

κατα-ληπτός 3 to be seized.

κατά-ληψις, ἡ a seizing, catching, capture; assault.

κατα-λιθόω, **-λιθάζω** to stone to death.   [λείπω.]

κατα-λιμπάνω = κατα-)

κατα-λῖπαρέω to entreat earnestly.   [tion.)

κατ-αλλαγή, ἡ reconcilia-)

κατ-αλλάσσω to change, exchange; to reconcile. — *P.* to become reconciled. — *M.* to exchange for oneself.   [prose.)

κατα-λογάδην *adv* in)

κατ-αλογέω to despise.

κατα-λογίζομαι *M.* to count among; to reckon; to consider.

κατά-λογος, ὁ a counting up; catalogue, list.

κατά-λοιπος 2 remaining.

κατα-λοφάδεια *adv.* on the neck.

κατά-λυμα, τό inn.

κατα-λύσιμος 2 to be repaired.

κατά-λυσις, ἡ a dissolving, disbanding; destruction, end, overthrow, expulsion; resting-place, inn.

κατα-λύω to dissolve; to destroy, end, abolish, depose, dismiss, disband. — *intr.* and *M.* to make peace, become reconciled; to make halt, to repose, to alight; to cease.

κατα-λωφάω to rest, recover.

κατα-μανθάνω to learn exactly; to know well; to search out; to perceive; to consider; to understand.

κατα-μαργέω to turn *or* go mad.   [hold of.)

κατα-μάρπτω to catch)

κατα-μαρτυρέω to bear witness against.

κατ-αμάω to mow down. — *M.* to pile *or* heap up.

κατ-αμβλύνω to make blunt.

κατα-μεθύσκω to make drunk.   [μίγνυμι.)

κατα-μείγνῡμι = κατα-)

κατ-αμελέω to neglect.

κατά-μεμπτος 2 blamable.

κατα-μέμφομαι *M.* to blame, accuse, reproach.

κατά-μεμψις, ἡ a blaming.

κατα-μένω to stay behind, remain; to sojourn.

κατα-μερίζω to distribute.

κατα-μετρέω to measure out to.

κατα-μηνύω to give information; to bear witness against; to convict.

κατα-μιαίνω *P.* to wear mourning-dress.

κατα-μίγνῡμι to mix up. — *M.* to be mixed with, to intrude oneself.

κατα-μόνᾱς *adv.* alone, apart.   [rend.)

κατ-αμύσσω to scratch,)

κατα-μύω to close the eyes.   [velop fully.)

κατ-αμφικαλύπτω to en-)

κατ-αναγκάζω to obtain

by force; to constrain, fetter.

κατ-ανάθεμα, τό curse.

κατ-αναθεματίζω to curse.

κατ-αναλίσκω to consume, spend; to waste.

κατα-ναρκάω to be burdensome to.

κατα-νάσσω to beat down.

κατα-ναυμαχέω to conquer at sea.

κατα-νέμω to distribute; to divide. — *M.* to divide among themselves.

κατα-νεύω to nod assent; to consent, grant.

κατα-νέω[1] to impart by spinning.

κατα-νέω[2] to heap or pile up.

κατ-ανθρακόω to burn to coal.

κατα-νοέω to perceive, observe, watch, to learn (to know); take to heart; to consider. [arrive at.]

κατ-αντάω to come to; to]

κατ-άντης 2 and **κάτ-αντα** *adv.* down-hill, downwards.

κατ-άντησιν *adv.* just opposite.

κατ-αντικρύ,-αντίον,κατ-αντιπέρας *adv.* just opposite; over against; downwards.

κατά-νυξις, ἡ stupefaction.

κατα-νύσσω to prick; to aggrieve.

κατ-ανύω, -ανύτω to finish; to arrive at; to alight; to accomplish, fulfil, grant.

κατα-ξαίνω to scratch; to tear to pieces; to stone to death.

κατ-άξιος 2 quite worthy.

κατ-αξιόω to think worthy, esteem; to desire.

κατα-πακτός 3 fastened downwards. [down.]

κατα-πάλλομαι *M.* to leap]

κατα-πατέω to tread or trample down. [fort.]

κατά-παυμα τό rest, com-]

κατά-παυσις, ἡ a stopping; a deposing.

κατα-παύω to put to rest, stop, finish, assuage; to check, hinder; to depose. — *intr.* to rest.

κατα-πεδάω to fetter.

κατ-απειλέω to threaten.

κατα-πειράζω to try, put to the test.

κατα-πειρητηρίη, ἡ sounding-line.

κατα-πέμπω to send down.

κατα-πέσσω to digest; to swallow, suppress.

κατα-πετάννῦμι to spread out over. [veil.]

κατα-πέτασμα, τό curtain,]

κατα-πέτομαι *M.* to fly down. [death.]

κατα-πετρόω to stone to]

κατα-πεφνεῖν to kill.

κατα-πήγνῦμι to stick fast, to fix. — *intr.* and *P.* to be firmly fixed, stand fast.

κατα-πηδάω to leap down.

κατα-πίμπλημι to fill quite full. [down.]

κατα-πίνω to swallow]

κατα-πίπτω to fall down; to subside, sink.

κατα-πισσόω to cover with pitch.

14*

κατα-πλάσσω to besmear, plaster. [plaster.]

κατα-πλαστύς, ύος, ἡ

κατα-πλέκω to entwine; to unroll, unweave; to finish.

κατα-πλέω to sail down; to put to shore; to sail back. [nation, terror.]

κατά-πληξις, ἡ conster-

κατα-πλήσσω to strike down; to terrify, confound. — P. to be frightened or amazed.

κατά-πλους, ὁ a sailing down; a landing; course, passage, return.

κατα-πλουτίζω to enrich.

κατα-πλώω = καταπλέω.

κατα-πολεμέω to conquer in war, to overcome.

κατα-πολῑτεύομαι M. to ruin by one's policy. [toil.]

κατα-πονέω to vex with

κατα-ποντίζω, κατα-πον-τίεω to throw into the sea; to drown.

κατα-ποντιστής, οῦ, ὁ pirate. [tute.]

κατα-πορνεύω to prosti-

κατα-πράσσω to effect, accomplish, achieve. — M. to achieve for oneself, to obtain.

κατα-πρᾱΰνω to appease.

κατα-πρηνής 2 head fore-most (downwards).

κατα-πρίω to saw to pieces.

κατα-προδίδωμι to betray.

κατα-προΐσσομαι to do with impunity.

κατα-πτήσσω to cower down, creep away; to be timid.

κατά-πτυστος 2 despicable.

κατα-πτύω to spit upon; to abhor. [πτήσσω.]

κατα-πτώσσω = κατα-

κατα-πύθομαι P. to become rotten.

κατ-ᾱρά, ἡ curse.

κατ-ᾱράομαι M. to curse, utter imprecations; to wish one evil.

κατ-ᾱράσσω to dash down, smash; to push back.

κατ-ᾱρᾱτος 2 cursed; abominable.

κατ-αργέω to make inactive or barren; to undo, abolish, remove, release.

κάτ-αργμα, τό introductory offering; firstlings.

κατ-αργυρόω to overlay with silver; to bribe.

κατα-ρέζω to stroke, caress.

κατ-ᾱρέομαι = καταρά-ομαι.

κατ-ρῑγηλός 2 horrible.

κατ-αριθμέω and M. to count up or among.

κατ-αρκέω to be quite sufficient.

κατ-αρνέομαι P. to deny.

κατα-ρρᾳθῡμέω to be careless; to lose by careless-ness. [rags.]

κατα-ρρακόω to tear to

κατα-ρράκτης, ου, ὁ, κατα-ρρακτός 2 precipitous, gushing down; waterfall.

κατα-ρράπτω to stitch up.

κατα-ρρέπω to fall down.

κατα-ρρέω to flow down; to fall down; to collapse.

κατα-ρρήγνῡμι to break or

tear down; to tear to or in pieces. — *intr.* and *P.* to fall down; to burst out.

κατα-ρροφέω to swallow down. [down.

κατα-ρρυής 2 flowing

κατα-ρρυπαίνω to soil, dirty.

κατά-ρρυτος 2 alluvial.

κατ-αρρωδέω to be afraid.

κατα-ρρώξ, ῶγος precipitous, broken.

κάτ-αρσις, ἡ landing-place.

κατ-αρτάω, -αρτίζω to adjust fitly, prepare, restore, repair, equip.

κατ-άρτισις, ἡ, -αρτισμός, ὁ restoration, perfection.

κατ-αρτύω to prepare, adjust, arrange; to train, master.

κατ-άρχω to begin. do first. — *M.* to begin the rites.

κατα-σβέννῡμι to quench, extinguish. — *intr.* and *P.* to be quenched.

κατα-σείω to shake down; to beckon. [down.

κατα-σεύομαι *M.* to rush

κατα-σημαίνω to mark. — *M.* to seal.

κατα-σήπω to let rot. — *intr.* to rot away.

κατα-σῑγάω to keep secret.

κατα-σῑτέομαι *M.* to eat up.

κατα-σιωπάω to keep secret; to silence. — *M.* to impose silence.

κατα-σκάπτω to dig down, demolish. [lishing; tomb]

κατα-σκαφή, ἡ a demo-

κατα-σκαφής 2 underground.

κατα-σκεδάννῡμι to scatter about. [κατασκοπέω.]

κατα-σκέπτομαι *M.* =]

κατα-σκευάζω to prepare, equip, adjust, furnish, adorn; to get ready; to make, build, found; to provide, supply, contrive. — *M.* to prepare oneself or for oneself.

κατα-σκευή, ἡ preparation, equipment, furniture; a building; state, condition; furniture; baggage.

κατα-σκηνάω, -όω to take up one's quarters; to pitch a tent, encamp.

κατα-σκήνωσις, ἡ an encamping, rest(ing place).

κατα-σκήπτω to rush down upon; to be hurled down upon; to assail, attack.

κατα-σκιάζω, -σκιάω to overshadow; to bury.

κατά-σκιος 2 overshadowed.

κατα-σκοπέω to inspect, view, examine; to spy out, explore.

κατά-σκοπος, ὁ spy, scout.

κατα-σκώπτω to mock.

κατα-σμύχω to burn slowly.

κατα-σοφίζομαι *M.* to circumvent, cheat. [down.]

κατα-σπάω to draw or pull]

κατα-σπείρω to sow; to spread out; to cause.

κατα-σπένδω to pour out as a libation; to pour out upon; = σπένδω.

κατα-σπέρχω to press or urge upon.

κατα-σπουδάζομαι to be earnest about.

κατα-στάζω to trickle down, to drop.

κατα-στασιάζω to overthrow by a counter-party.

κατά-στασις, ἡ an establishing, appointing, arragement, presentation, equipment; state, condition; surety; constitution, nature.

κατα-στάτης, ου, ὁ arranger, establisher. [over.)

κατα-στεγάζω to cover)

κατα-στέγασμα, τό a covering, roof. [vered.]

κατά-στεγος 2 roofed, co-)

κατα-στείβω to tread or step on. [to check.)

κατα-στέλλω to arrange;)

κατα-στένω to sigh over.

κατα-στεφής 2 wreathed.

κατα-στημα, τό condition, state, bearing.

κατα-στολή, ἡ dress.

κατα-στόρνῡμι = κατα-στρώννῡμι. [lightning.)

κατ-αστράπτω to flash)

κατα-στρατοπεδεύω to cause to encamp. — intr. and M. to encamp.

κατα-στρέφω to turn over, overturn, bring to an end. — M. to subdue.

κατα-στρηνιάω to behave greedily towards.

κατα-στροφή, ἡ an overturning, overthrowing, sudden turn, end, death, perdition; a subduing.

κατά-στρωμα, τό deck of a ship.

κατα-στρώννῡμι to spread over, to strow to the ground; to kill, overthrow; to cover.

κατα-στυγέω to shudder at.

κατα-σύρω to drag away; to plunder. [kill.)

κατα-σφάζω to slaughter,)

κατα-σφραγίζω to seal up.

κατά-σχεσις, ἡ occupation, possession.

κατά-σχετος 2 held back.

κατα-σχίζω to cleave asunder, to break or burst open.

κατα-σχολάζω to linger, tarry.

κατα-σώχω to rub or grind to powder, to pound, bruise.

κατα-τάσσω to arrange, draw up in order; to classify; to appoint.

κατα-τείνω to stretch out, to strain, force; intr. to exert oneself; to reach to.

κατα-τέμνω to cut into pieces, mutilate; to cut (trenches).

κατα-τήκω to cause to melt, to dissolve. — intr. and P. to melt, to pine away.

κατα-τίθημι to place or put down, to lay down, propose (a prize); to lay in, preserve; to pay. — M. to lay down for oneself, to deposit, lay up in store; to put away, lay aside; to neglect; to put an end to.

κατα-τιτρώσκω to wound.

κατα-τομή, ἡ a cutting into pieces, mutilation.

κατα-τοξεύω to shoot down.

κατα-τραυματίζω to injure, wound; to make leaky.

κατα-τρέχω to run down; to attack, rush on against; to run over, overrun.

κατα-τρίβω to rub down or in pieces; to wear away or out; to waste, exhaust. — P. to be worn out or exhausted; to be weary.

κατα-τρύχω to rub down; to wear out, exhaust.

κατα-τρωματίζω = κατατραυματίζω.

κατα-τυγχάνω to reach, obtain; to be successful.

κατ-αυδάω to declare aloud.

κατ-αυλέω to play on the flute. — M. to listen to flute-playing.

κατ-αυλίζομαι P. to encamp, pass the night.

κατα-φαίνομαι P. to appear, become visible.

κατα-φανής 2 visible; conspicuous, manifest.

κατά-φαρκτος 2 = κατάφρακτος.

κατα-φαρμάσσω to poison, enchant. [protest.]

κατα-φατίζω to assure,

κατα-φερής 2 inclining, inclined, setting.

κατα-φέρω to carry or bring down. — P. to be driven down; to be carried to.

κατα-φεύγω to flee down; to take to flight; to resort to. [fuge; evasion.]

κατά-φευξις, ἡ flight; re-

κατά-φημι to assent to.

κατα-φθείρω to ruin.

κατα-φθίνω to perish.

κατα-φθίω to ruin, destroy, kill. — P. to perish, waste away, be ruined or destroyed.

κατ-αφίημι to let glide down. [derly.]

κατα-φιλέω to kiss ten-

κατα-φλέγω to burn down.

κατα-φοβέω to frighten.

κατα-φοιτάω to use to come down.

κατα-φονεύω to slay, kill.

κατα-φορέω = καταφέρω.

κατα-φράζομαι M. and P. to observe, see.

κατά-φρακτος 2 fenced in; covered, decked.

κατα-φρονέω to despise, disdain, scorn; to think of, suppose.

κατα-φρόνημα, τό, κατα-φρόνησις, ἡ contempt; haughtiness.

κατα-φρονητής, οῦ, ὁ despiser. [scornfully.]

κατα-φρονητικῶς adv.

κατα-φυγγάνω = καταφεύγω.

κατα-φυγή, ἡ = κατάφευξις. [by tribes.]

κατα-φῦλαδόν adv. in or

κατα-φωράω to catch in the act, discover; to betray; to convict.

κατα-χαίρω to feel mischievous joy. [with brass.]

κατα-χαλκόω to cover

κατα-χαρίζομαι M. to do a favour; to flatter; to abandon to. [against.]

κατα-χειροτονέω to vote

κατα-χέω to pour down

upon or over, to shed; to let fall; to throw down; to spread out. — *P.* to fall down; to flow out. — *M.* to cause to be melted down.

κατα-χθόνιος 2 underground, infernal.

κατα-χορδεύω to split up.

κατα-χορηγέω to spend.

κατα-χόω = καταχώννῡμι.

κατα-χράω to suffice, be enough. — *M.* to make use of, to use up, consume; to misuse; to destroy, murder.

κατα-χρῡσόω to overlay with gold, to gild.

κατα-χώννῡμι to cover with earth, to inter.

κατα-χωρίζω to place properly.

κατα-ψάω to stroke.

κατα-ψεύδομαι *M.* to invent, feign.

κατα-ψευδομαρτυρέομαι *P.* to be condemned by false witness. [feigned.]

κατα-ψευστός 2 invented,

κατα-ψηφίζομαι *M.* to vote against.

κατα-ψήχω to rub down. — *P.* to crumble away.

κατα-ψύχω to cool.

κατ-έαται = κάθηνται.

κατ-έδω = κατεσθίω.

κατ-είβω to let flow down, to shed. — *M.* to flow down; to elapse. [idols.]

κατ-είδωλος 2 full of

κατ-εικάζω to make (a)like; to guess. — *P.* to be (a)like.

κατ-ειλέω to force together, enclose.

κατ-ειλίσσω to wrap round, enfold.

κατ-ειλύω to cover up.

κάτ-ειμι (-ιέναι) to go or come down, to fall or flow down; to come back.

κατ-εῖπον to speak against, accuse; to speak out, tell, denounce.

κατ-είργω, -είργνῡμι to press hard; to confine; to force; to hinder.

κατ-ειρύω = κατερύω.

κατ-ελεέω to have pity.

κατ-ελπίζω to hope confidently. [kill, destroy.]

κατ-εναίρω, -εναρίζω to

κατ-εναντίον, κατ-έναντι *adv.* over against, opposite.

κατ-ένωπα, -ενώπιον *adv.* right opposite.

κατ-εξουσιάζω to exercise authority over. [against.]

κατ-επᾴδω to use charms

κατ-επείγω to press hard, oppress, urge, hasten.

κατ-εργάζομαι *M.* to accomplish, achieve, effect; to acquire, gain; to overcome, oppress; to kill.

κατ-έργνῡμι, κατ-έργω = κατείργω.

κατ-ερείκω to tear, rend.

κατ-ερείπω to demolish, destroy, to cast down. — *intr.* to fall down, perish.

κατ-ερητύω, -ερῡκάνω, -ερῡκω to hold back, detain, hinder. [to launch.]

κατ-ερύω to draw down;

κατ-έρχομαι = κάτειμι.

κατ-εσθίω, -έσθω to eat up, consume.

κάτ-ευγμα, τό vow, wish; prayer; votive offering.

κατ-ευθύνω to make straight; to direct.

κατ-ευλογέω to bless.

κατ-ευνάζω, -ευνάω to lull to sleep; to soothe. — P. to lie down to sleep.

κατ-εύχομαι M. to wish, pray, vow; to curse.

κατ-ευωχέομαι to feast, make merry.

κατ-εφάλλομαι M. to spring down upon.

κατ-εφίσταμαι to rise up against.

κατ-έχω to keep down or back; to direct to; to check, restrain, withhold, delay; to occupy, possess, keep; to bear, suffer. — intr. to come to pass, happen, befal; to dwell, sojourn; to continue; to stop, cease. — M. to keep for oneself, retain; to stop, to make a halt.

κατ-ηγορέω to speak against; to accuse, blame, reproach; to assert, state, signify, indicate, prove.

κατ-ηγόρημα, τό, κατ-ηγορίᾱ, ἡ accusation, reproach, charge.

κατ-ήγορος, ὁ, κατ-ήγωρ, ορος accuser.

κατ-ήκοος 2 obedient, subject; listener, spy.

κατ-ηπιάω to assuage.

κατ-ηρεμίζω, -μέω to calm, soothe.

κατ-ηρεφής 2 covered; roofed; overshadowed.

κατ-ήρης 2 well-supplied.

κατ-ηρτημένως adv. most deliberately. [shame.]

κατήφεια, ἡ dejection;

κατηφέω to be dejected or dismayed.

κατηφής 2 dejected, downcast, despised. [reprobate.]

κατηφών, όνος, ὁ knave,

κατ-ηχέω to resound; to teach; to inform.

κατ-ιάπτω to hurt, disfigure. [against.]

κατ-ισθύ adv. just over

κατ-ιόομαι P. to grow rusty. [or lean.]

κατ-ισχναίνω to make thin,

κατ-ισχύω to gather strength; to have power; to prevail over.

κατ-ίσχω = κατέχω.

κάτ-οιδα to know exactly.

κατ-οικέω to inhabit; to regulate by laws. — intr. and M. to settle down; to dwell. [dwelling-place.]

κατ-οίκησις, ἡ a settling;

κατ-οικητήριον, τό, κατ-οικία, ἡ dwelling, habitation.

κατ-οικίζω to remove to a colony, to settle; to colonize, found or establish a colony in. — P. to be or become a colonist, to be colonized. [colonization.]

κατ-οίκισις, ἡ settlement,

κατ-οικτείρω to have compassion; to pity.

κατ-οικτίζω = κατοικτείρω; to excite pity. — M. to lament. [tate.]

κατ-οκνέω to doubt, hesi-

κατ-ολοφύρομαι *M.* to bewail, lament.

κατ-όμνῡμι and *M.* to confirm by oath; to accuse.

κατ-όνομαι *P.* to depreciate, disdain.

κατ-όπιν, **κατ-όπισθεν**
adv. behind, after; afterwards.   [discover.]

κατ-οπτεύω to spy out,]

κατ-όπτης, ου, ὁ spy.

κάτ-οπτος 2 visible.

κάτ-οπτρον, τό mirror.

κατ-ορθόω to set right,
make straight, manage
well; to mend; to erect;
to keep sound. — *intr.* and
P. to be successful, prosperous.   [emendation.]

κατ-όρθωμα, τό success,]

κατ-ορύσσω to bury, inter.

κατ-ορχέομαι *M.* to insult,
mock.   [destination.]

κατ-ουρίζω to reach one's]

κατ-οχή, ἡ a holding fast;
detention.

κάτ-οχος 2 constrained.

κατ-τάδε = κατὰ τάδε.

κάτω *adv.* down, downwards; beneath, below; in
the nether world; down
to the coast.   [below.]

κάτωθεν *adv.* from below;]

κατ-ωθέω to thrust down.

κατ-ωμάδιος down from
the shoulder.   [shoulder.]

κατ-ωμαδόν *adv.* from the]

κατ-ωμοσία, ἡ accusation
on oath.

κατ-ῶρυξ, υχος imbedded
in the earth, underground;
ἡ κ. pit, cavern.

κατώτατος 3 nethermost.

κατώτερος 3 lower.

καυλός, ὁ stalk, stem;
shaft; hilt.

καῦμα, τό heat.   [heat.]

καυματίζω to consume by]

καύσιμος 2 combustible.

καῦσις, ἡ a burning.

καυσόομαι *P.* to perish
from heat.

καύστειρα, ἡ burning, hot.

καύσων, ωνος, ὁ = καῦμα.

καυ(σ)τηριάζω to cast a
brand upon, stigmatize.

καυχάομαι *M.* to boast.

καύχημα, τό, **καύχησις**, ἡ
object of boasting; a boast.

καχ-εξία, ἡ neglected state.

κάχληξ, ηκος, ὁ pebble,
gravel.

κάω, **κάω** = καίω.

κέ, **κέν** = ἄν.

κεάζω to split, shiver.

κέαρ, τό = κῆρ heart.

κέγχρος, ὁ millet; spawn
of fish.

κεδάννῡμι = σκεδάννυμι.

κεδνός 3 careful; able, excellent; dear, valued; respectable; modest.

κεδρία, ἡ cedar-resin.

κέδρινος 2 of cedar-wood.

κέδρος, ἡ cedar-tree.

κεῖθεν, **κεῖθι** = ἐκεῖθεν,
ἐκεῖθι.

κεῖμαι to be laid down, to
lie; to lie inactive, idle,
still, sick, despised, dead,
or unburied; to be situated;
to be ready, present, or extant; to be in value; to
be fixed or proposed.

κειμήλιον, τό treasure, ornament.

κεῖνος 3 = ἐκεῖνος.

κεινός 3 = κενός.

κειρίᾱ, ἡ bandage; bed-girth.

κείρω to cut off, clip, shear; to hew off; to eat off, consume entirely; to waste, ravage. — M. to cut off one's hair.

κεῖσε = ἐκεῖσε.

κείω[1] to split, cleave.

κείω[2] to wish to sleep.

κεκαδών see χάζομαι.

κεκαφηώς 3 weak, gasping.

κέκονα see καίνω.

κεκρύφαλος, ὁ woman's hood; hair-net. [ing.]

κελαδεινός 3 noisy. roar-

κέλαδος, ὁ noise, tumult, sound, clap. [δεινός.]

κελάδων, οντος = κελα-

κελαι-νεφής 2 with dark clouds; dark. [black.]

κελαινός 3 dark, gloomy,

κελαιν-ῶπης 2 black-faced, gloomy. [mur.]

κελαρύζω to ripple, mur-

κέλευθος, ἡ way, road, path; gait; journey.

κέλευ(σ)μα, τό, κελευσ-μοσύνη, ἡ order, command; call. [mander of rowers.]

κελευστής, οῦ, ὁ com-

κελευτιάω to exhort repeatedly.

κελεύω to exhort, command, bid, order; to beseech, desire; to grant, permit.

κέλης, ητος, ὁ courser, race-horse; swift-sailing yacht. [horse.]

κελητίζω to ride a race-

κελήτιον, τό yacht.

κέλλω to drive on, push ashore; to run ashore.

κέλομαι M. = κελεύω and καλέω.

κέλωρ, ὁ son.

κεμάς, άδος, ἡ young deer.

κέν = κέ (ἄν).

κέν-ανδρος 2 empty of men. [ous.]

κενε-αυχής 2 vain-glori-

κενεός 3 = κενός. [groins.]

κενεών, ῶνος, ὁ flank,

κενο-δοξίᾱ, ἡ vain-glory.

κενό-δοξος 2 vain-glorious.

κενός 3 empty, hollow, void; destitute, bereft; vain, idle, fruitless. [tomb.]

κενο-τάφιον, τό empty

κενο-φωνίᾱ, ἡ idle talk.

κενόω to empty; to unpeople; to bereave, bare.

κεντέω, -όω to prick, sting, goad, stab, pierce; to incite; to scourge, beat, torture.

κεντρ-ηνεκής 2 goaded on.

κέντρον, τό sting, prick, goad, spur; pain.

κεντρόω to furnish with stings; to pierce. [turion.]

κεντυρίων, ωνος, ὁ cen-

κέντωρ, ορος, ὁ goader.

κέομαι = κεῖμαι.

κεραίᾱ, ἡ sail-yard; beam, pole; stroke, tittle.

κεραΐζω to destroy, plunder, ravage; to kill, exterminate; to sink (a ship).

κεραίω = κεράννῡμι.

κεραμεία, ἡ pottery.

κεραμεοῦς, ᾶ, οῦν earthen, of clay.

κεραμεύς, ὁ potter.

κεραμεύω to be a potter.

κεραμικός 3, **κεράμι(ν)ος** 3 = κεραμεοῦς.

κεράμιον, τό earthenware vessel.   [tile.]

κεραμίς, ίδος or ῖδος, ή

κέραμος[1], ὁ potter's earth, clay; pot, jar, earthenware; tile.

κέραμος[2], ὁ prison.

κεράννῡμι to mix, mix up; to temper, blend together.

κεραο-ξόος 2 polishing horn.

κεραός 3 horned.

κέρᾱς, ᾱτος and ως, τό horn, antlers; bow; horn for blowing or drinking; mountain-peak, branch of a river; wing of an army or fleet, flank. ἐπὶ κέρως in single file, in column.

κεράστης, ου horned.

κεράτινος 3 of horn.

κεράτιον, τό fruit. of the carob-tree.   [struck.]

κεραύνιος 3 and 2 thunder-]

κεραυνός, ὁ lightning, thunderbolt.

κεραυνόω to strike with the thunderbolt.

κεράω = κεράννῡμι.

κερδαίνω to win, gain, profit, to be benefited (by); to spare. save trouble.

κερδαλέος 3 profitable; crafty, cunning. [of gain.]

κερδαλεό-φρων 2 greedy]

κερδίων 2 more profitable.

κέρδιστος 3 most profitable or useful; most cunning.

κέρδος, τό gain, profit, advantage, wages, pay;

greediness of gain; *pl.* cunning arts, tricks.

κερδοσύνη, ἡ cunning.

κερκίς, ίδος, ἡ weaver's shuttle

κέρκουρος, ὁ cutter.

κέρμα, τό small coin, change. [scoff, mortify.]

κερτομέω to mock, deride,]

κερτόμησις, **κερτομία**, ἡ mockery.

κερτόμιος 2, **κέρτομος** 2 stinging, mocking.

κέσκετο = ἔκειτο (κεῖμαι).

κεστός 3 embroidered.

κευθάνω = κεύθω.

κευθμός, ὁ, **κευθμών**, ῶνος, ὁ, **κεῦθος**, τό hiding-place; hole, den, dwelling; abyss, depth.

κεύθω to hide, conceal, to keep secret. — *intr.* and *P.* to be hidden.

κεφάλαιον, τό chief point, main thing; summary, sum, chief result; capital.

κεφαλαιόω to sum up, to bring under heads; to beat on the head.   [total.]

κεφαλαίωμα, τό sum, the]

κεφαλ-αλγής 2 causing a headache.

κεφαλή, ἡ head; front; end, point; source, top; chief person.

κεφαλίς, ίδος, ἡ little head.

κέω = κείω.

κῇ, **κή** = πῇ, πή.

κηδεία, ἡ affinity, connexion by marriage.

κήδειος 2 dear, beloved; sepulchral.

κηδεμών, όνος, ὁ tutor,

guardian, protector; relation; chief mourner.

κήδεος 2 = κήδειος.

κηδεστής, οῦ, ὁ allied by marriage. [marriage.]

κηδεστίᾱ, ἡ connexion by]

κήδευμα, τό affinity.

κηδεύω to care for, tend; to bury; *intr.* to ally oneself in marriage.

κήδιστος 3 dearest.

κήδος, τό care, concern, mourning; burial; distress, sorrow, misery; affinity; marriage.

κήδω to grieve, distress, mortify; to hurt, damage. — *M.* to be troubled, anxious, or distressed; to care for, favour.

κηκίς, ῖδος, ἡ grease, juice.

κηκίω and *P.* to gush forth.

κήλεος, κήλειος 2 blazing.

κηλέω to charm, fascinate, delight; to beguile, seduce; to soothe.

κηληθμός, ὁ fascination.

κηλητήριον, τό charm.

κηλίς, ῖδος, ἡ burn; stain; blemish.

κῆλον, τό arrow.

κηλώνειον, -ήϊον, τό pump, machine for drawing water.

κημόω to muzzle.

κῆνσος, ὁ capitation-tax.

κήξ, κηκός, ἡ sea-gull.

κηπίον, τό little garden.

κῆπος, ὁ garden, orchard.

κηπ-ουρός, ὁ gardener.

κῆρ, κῆρος, τό heart, breast.

κήρ, κηρός, ἡ fate, death; goddess of death; doom, destruction, mischief, evil.

κηρεσσι-φόρητος 2 driven on by the goddesses of fate.

κηρίον, τό honeycomb.

κηρο-δέτης, ου bound together by wax.

κηρόθι *adv.* heartily.

κηρός, ὁ wax.

κήρυγμα, τό a herald's proclamation, order; sermon, teaching.

κηρύκειον, κηρύκήιον, κηρύκιον, τό herald's staff.

κηρύκηίη, ἡ herald's office.

κῆρυξ, ῦκος, ὁ herald, town-crier; ambassador; preacher.

κηρύσσω to be a herald, to proclaim *or* summon as a herald; to order publicly; to announce; to praise; to preach. [ster.]

κῆτος, τό abyss; sea-mon-]

κητώεις 2 rich in caverns.

κηφήν, ῆνος, ὁ drone.

κηώδης 2, κηώεις 3 fragrant.

κίβδηλος 2 adulterated, spurious, ambiguous, bastard.

κῑβωτός, ἡ, κῑβώτιον, τό chest, box; ark; ark of the covenant.

κιγχάνω = κιχάνω.

κίδναμαι = σκεδάννυμαι.

κιθάρᾱ, κίθαρις, ἡ lyre; lyre-playing.

κιθαρίζω to play the lyre.

κιθάρισις, ἡ lyre-playing.

κιθάρισμα, τό piece for the lyre.

κιθαριστής, οῦ, ὁ player on the lyre. [playing.]

κιθαριστικός 3 for lyre-]

κιθαριστύς, ύος, ἡ art of playing the lyre.

κιθαρ-ῳδέω to sing to the lyre. [lyre.]

κιθαρ-ῳδός player on the

κιθών, ῶνος, ὁ = χιτών.

κίκι, εως, τό castor-oil; castor-plant.

κικλήσκω = καλέω.

κῖκυς, υος, ἡ strength, vigour.

κίναδος, τό fox.

κίναιδος, ὁ voluptuary.

κινάμωμον, τό = κιννάμωμον.

κινδύνευμα, τό = κίνδυνος.

κινδυνευτής, οῦ, ὁ rash, foolhardy man.

κινδυνεύω to get into danger, to run a risk, to be in danger; to be bold, daring; to be likely or possible; to be feared. — P. to be exposed to danger, to be hazarded.

κίνδυνος, ὁ danger, risk, hazard, venture, experiment; law-suit; battle.

κῑνέω to move, set in motion, to urge on, advance; to shake, stir, arouse, trouble, excite; to turn, change. — P. to be put in motion, to be moved; to march on; to be shaken.

κίνησις, ἡ motion; tumult, disturbance.

κιννάμωμον, τό cinnamom.

κίνυμαι P. to be moved, to move. [ing.]

κινυρός 3 whining, wail-

κῑό-κρανον, τό capital of a column.

κίρκος, ὁ hawk. [ράννυμι.]

κιρνάω, κίρνημι = κε-

κισσ-ήρης 2 ivy-clad.

κισσός, ὁ ivy. [with ivy.]

κισσο-φόρος 2 crowned

κισσύβιον, τό bowl, cup.

κίστη, ἡ chest, box.

κιττός, ὁ = κισσός.

κιχάνω and M. to arrive at; to catch, meet, find.

κίχλη, ἡ thrush. [borrow.]

κίχρημι to lend. — M. to

κίω to go (away). [pillar.]

κίων, ονος, ὁ, ἡ column,

κλαγγή, ἡ sound; song; scream, noise. [noise.]

κλαγγηδόν adv. with a

κλάδος, ὁ branch; shoot.

κλάζω to sound, clash, clang; to scream, make a noise.

κλαίω to weep, wail, lament, to have cause to repent; to bewail.

κλάσις, ἡ a breaking.

κλάσμα, τό fragment, morsel.

κλαυθμός, ὁ, κλαῦμα, τό a weeping, wailing; woe.

κλαυσί-γελως, ωτος, ὁ smiles and tears.

κλαυστός 3 to be bewailed.

κλάω¹ to break off; to break to pieces.

κλάω², κλάω = κλαίω.

κληηδών, ἡ = κληδών.

κλεῖθρον, τό bolt, bar, lock. [ous; noble.]

κλεινός 3 renowned, fam-

κλείς, κλειδός, ἡ bar; bolt; key; hook; tongue of a clasp; thole; collar-bone.

κλεισιάς, άδος, ἡ = κλισιάς.

κλείσιον, τό servants' hall.

κλεισίον, τό hut, stable.
κλειστός 3 = κληστός.
κλειτός 3 = κλεινός.
κλείω¹ = κλέω.
κλείω² to shut, close; to confine; to block up.
κλέμμα, τό theft; trick.
κλέος, τό report, fame, rumour; glory, good repute, honour.
κλέπτης, ου, ὁ thief; cheat, rogue.
κλεπτικός 3 thievish.
κλεπτοσύνη, ἡ thievishness; roguery.
κλέπτω to steal, purloin; to do stealthily or secretly; to cheat, deceive; to conceal, hide.
κλεψ-ύδρα, ἡ water-clock.
κλέω to make famous, praise, extol. — P. to become famous.
κλήδην adv. by name.
κληδ-οῦχος, ὁ, ἡ priest, priestess.
κληδών, κληηδών, όνος, ἡ = κλέος; omen, presage; favourable cry.
κλήζω to praise, extol; to call, name. — P. to be called.
κλήθρη, ἡ alder.
κλῆθρον, τό = κλεῖθρον.
κληΐζω = κλήζω.
κληΐς, ῖδος, ἡ = κλείς.
κληϊστός 3 = κληστός.
κληΐω = κλείω².
κλῆμα, τό, κληματίς, ῖδος, ἡ shoot, branch; vine-twig; faggot-wood.
κληρο-νομέω to inherit, to obtain by inheritance.

κληρο-νομία, ἡ inheritance, patrimony, property.
κληρο-νόμος 2 getting a share; heir, heiress.
κλῆρος, ὁ lot, allotment; share, portion, inheritance; estate, piece of land.
κληρ-ουχέω to possess by allotment.
κληρ-οῦχος 2 possessing an allotment, colonist.
κληρόω to choose by lot, to allot, assign. — P. to be allotted to. — M. to draw lots; to obtain by lot.
κλήρωσις, ἡ a choosing by lots.
κλής, κλῇδος = κλείς.
κλῆσις, ἡ a calling, shouting; invitation; summons.
κλῇσις, ἡ a blockading.
κλητεύω to summon into court.   [welcome.]
κλητός 3 called; chosen;
κλήτωρ, ορος, ὁ witness for a legal summons.
κλήω = κλείω².   [oven.]
κλίβανος, ὁ pan, baking
κλίμα, κλῖμα, τό region, district; climate.
κλῖμαξ, ακος, ἡ ladder, staircase; a clasping in one's arms.
κλίνη, ἡ, κλινάριον, τό couch, bed; bier, litter; dining-sopha.
κλινο-πετής 2 bedridden.
κλιντήρ, ῆρος, ὁ arm-chair, couch, bed.
κλίνω to incline, bend; to turn; to put to flight; to make recline; intr. to lean, sink, be sloping; to lie down

at table.— *M.* to lie against, recline. — *P.* to be bent, to lean; to rest, support oneself against; to stoop, sink, fall down; to lie down; to be situated.

κλισίᾱ, ἡ hut, tent, cabin; couch; company of guests.

κλισιάς, άδος, ἡ *pl.* door, gate. [tent.]

κλισίηθεν *adv.* out of the

κλισίηνδε *adv.* to the tent.

κλισίηφι *adv.* in the tent.

κλίσιον, τό = κλείσιον.

κλισμός, ὁ reclining-chair.

κλῑτύς, ύος, ἡ slope, hillside. [lory.]

κλοιός, ὁ iron collar, pil-

κλονέω to press hard, drive on; to confound, agitate. — *P.* to flee in confusion; to be chased wildly.

κλόνος, ὁ press of battle, bustle, throng.

κλοπεύς, ὁ thief; secret wrong-doer.

κλοπή, ἡ theft, fraud; secret flight; trick.

κλόπιος 3 thievish.

κλοτοπεύω to use idle talk.

κλύδων, ωνος. ὁ wave, billow, surge; tempest, throng.

κλυδωνίζομαι *P.* to be tossed (about) by the waves.

κλυδώνιον, τό little wave.

κλύζω to wash, splash; to ripple over; to rinse, wash out *or* away. — *P.* to surge.

κλύσμα, τό clyster, drench.

κλυστήρ, ῆρος, ὁ clysterpipe.

κλυτο-εργός 2 famous for work.

κλυτό-πωλος 2 famous for horses. [loud, noisy.]

κλυτός3 = κλεινός; audible,

κλυτο-τέχνης, ου famous artist. [cher.]

κλυτό-τοξος 2 famous archer.

κλύω to hear, listen to; to learn by hearing; to perceive; to know; to obey; to be spoken of. [ners.]

κλῶθες, αἱ (female) spin-

κλώθω to spin.

κλωμακόεις 3 rocky.

κλών, κλωνός, ὁ shoot, sprout, twig.

κλωπεύω to steal.

κλώψ, κλωπός, ὁ thief, robber.

κνάπτω to scratch; to full.

κναφεῖον, τό fuller's shop.

κναφεύς, ὁ fuller.

κνάφος, ὁ instrument of torture.

κνάω to scrape, grate.

κνέφας, αος, τό darkness, dusk, twilight.

κνήθομαι *P.* to itch.

κνήμη, ἡ shin-bone, leg.

κνημῖδο-φόρος wearing greaves. [legging.]

κνημίς, ῖδος, ἡ greave;

κνημός, ὁ wooded valley.

κνησιάω to itch. [grater.]

κνῆστις, ἡ scraping-knife,

κνίζω to scrape, scratch; to itch; to vex, tease.

κνῖσα, κνίση, ἡ steam of burnt-offerings; fat.

κνῑσήεις 3 steaming with burnt fat.

κνυζέομαι *M.* to gnarl, whine, whimper.

κνυζηθμός, ὁ a whining.

κνύζημα, τό a stammering.

κνυζόω to make dim.

κνώδαλον, τό dangerous animal, monster.

κνώδων, οντος, ὁ sword; sword-hook.

κνώσσω to sleep.

κόγχη, ἡ muscle(-shell).

κογχυλιάτης, ου, ὁ shell-limestone. [cockle, shell.]

κογχύλιον, τό muscle.

κοδράντης, ου, ὁ quarter of a Roman as (halfpenny).

κόθεν = πόθεν.

κόθορνος, ὁ cothurn, buskin (high boot worn by tragic actors).

κοιλαίνω to hollow out.

κοιλίᾱ, ἡ hollow of the belly; belly; womb.

κοῖλος 3 hollow, hollowed; lying in a vale.

κοιμάω, -έω to lull to sleep; to calm, soothe, assuage. — P. and M. to go to bed; to fall asleep; to rest, cease.

κοίμημα, τό sleep; bed-rite.

κοίμησις, ἡ a sleeping, sleep.

κοιμίζω = κοιμάω.

κοινᾱνέω = κοινωνέω.

κοινο-λεχής 2 bedfellow.

κοινο-λογέομαι M. to consult together. [gether.]

κοινό-πλους 2 sailing to-]

κοινό-πους, ποδος walking together.

κοινός 3 common, public, belonging to the state; kindred; affable, popular, impartial; profane; τὸ κοινόν community, state, republic; common weal, pub-

lic affair, administration; state authorities, public treasury; κοινῇ, κοινῶς in common, publicly.

κοινό-τοκος 2 brotherly.

κοινόω to make common; to communicate; to make unclean, to pollute, profane. — M. to have communion; to consult or act in common; to make public.

κοινωνέω to have a share in, partake of.

κοινωνίᾱ, ἡ communion; share; company, society; intercourse; charity.

κοινωνικός 3 communicative, liberal. [ner, fellow.]

κοινωνός 2 common; part-]

κοῖος 3 = ποῖος.

κοιρανέω to be master or lord; to rule, command.

κοιρανίδης, ου, ὁ = κοίρανος. [master.]

κοίρανος, ὁ ruler; lord,]

κοιταῖος 3 lying in bed.

κοίτη, ἡ, κοῖτος, ὁ a going to bed; sleep; couch, bed; marriage-bed; embryo; offspring. [ber.]

κοιτών, ῶνος, ὁ bed-cham-]

κόκκινος 3 scarlet.

κόκκος, ὁ kernel; scarlet-berry.

κολάζω and M. to hold in check, tame; to chastise, punish; to correct.

κολακεία, ἡ flattery.

κολακευτικός 3 flattering.

κολακεύω to flatter, deceive. [τικός.]

κολακικός 3 = κολακευ-]

κόλαξ, ακος, ὁ flatterer.

κόλασις, ἡ a punishing; correction. [ment, prison.]

κολαστήριον, τό punish-

κολαστής, οῦ. ὁ chastiser, punisher. [a p.'s ears.]

κολαφίζω to cuff; to box

κολεός, ὁ sheath of a sword.

κόλλα, ἡ glue.

κολλάω to glue (together), cement. — P. to attach oneself to, cleave to.

κόλλησις 3, κολλητός 3 glued together, cemented; welded. [gether; welding.]

κόλλησις, ἡ a gluing to-

κολλ(o)ύριον, τό eye-salve.

κόλλοφ, οπος, ὁ screw of the lyre. [changer.]

κολλυβιστής, οῦ, ὁ money-

κολοβόω to shorten.

κολοιός, ὁ jackdaw.

κόλος 2 curtailed.

κολοσσός, ὁ gigantic statue.

κολοσυρτός, ὁ noise, up-roar. [lessen, abridge.]

κολούω to curtail, shorten,

κόλπος, ὁ bosom; womb; fold of a garment; bay; hollow, depth.

κολυμβάω to dive.

κολυμβήθρα, ἡ swimming-bath; pond. [swimmer.]

κολυμβητής, οῦ, ὁ diver,

κολῳάω to croak, brawl, scold. [hill; mound, tomb.]

κολώνη, ἡ, κολωνός, ὁ

κολωνία, ἡ colony.

κολῳός, ὁ screaming, noise, altercation.

κομάω, -έω to wear long hair; to be proud or haughty.

κομέω to tend, take care of.

κόμη, ἡ the hair, foliage.

κομήτης, ου, ὁ long-haired; feathered; comet.

κομιδή, ἡ care, attendance; a carrying of supplies, transport, stores; recovery; a going and coming; pas-sage; return.

κομιδῇ adv. with care, wholly, altogether, very much so, just so, indeed.

κομίζω to take care of, tend, mind; to mention; to receive hospitably; to man-age; to carry away, con-vey; to store up; to fetch, bring back. — P. to be carried or conveyed; to tra-vel, betake oneself to; to return. — M. to shelter, entertain; to get, gain, procure; to keep, save, preserve; to bring to, to rescue, recover.

κόμμι, ιδος and εως, τό gum. [finery.]

κομμωτικός 3 given to

κομπάζω, κομπέω to clat-ter, clank; to vaunt, boast.

κόμπος, ὁ noise, rattling; boasting, vaunt.

κομπώδης 2 boastful.

κομφεία, ἡ refinement, subtlety.

κομφεύω and M. to refine; to make a display of wit.

κομφός 3 refined, well-dressed; pretty; elegant; witty, clever, exquisite.

κοναβέω to sound, clash, resound. [ing.]

κόναβος, ὁ noise, a clash-

κονία, ἡ dust; sand; cinders, ashes; limestone; plaster.

κονιᾱτός 3 whitewashed.

κονιάω to whitewash.

κονι-ορτός, ὁ cloud of dust, dust.

κόνις, ἡ = κονία.

κονί-σαλος, ὁ = κονιορτός.

κονίω to cover, fill, or sprinkle with dust; to raise dust; to speed.

κοντός, ὁ pole. [weary.]

κοπάζω to grow tired or

κοπίς, ίδος, ἡ knife, sword; axe.

κόπος, ὁ a striking, beating; wailing; weariness, trouble, pain.

κοπρέω to manure.

κοπρία, ἡ, κόπριον, τό, κόπρος, ὁ dung, manure; filth, dirt; dung-yard, stable.   [dung.]

κοπρο-φόρος 2 carrying

κόπτω to strike, cut, slay, fell; to lay waste, damage, hurt, wound, weary; to hammer, forge, coin; to knock, peck. — M. to beat oneself; to mourn; to get coined.

κόραξ, ακος, ὁ raven.

κοράσιον, τό little girl.

κόρδαξ, ᾱκος, κορδακισ-μός, ὁ an obscene dance.

κορέννῡμι, κορέω[1] to satisfy; to glut, surfeit. — P. and M. to have one's fill; to grow weary of the.

κορέω[2] to sweep, brush.

κόρη, ἡ girl, maid; newly-married woman; daughter; doll; puppet; eye-ball; long sleeve.   [to rise.]

κορθύω to lift up. — P.

κορμός, ὁ trunk of a tree.

κόρος[1], ὁ lad, youth; warrior; boy, son; youthful, noble.   [insolence.]

κόρος[2], ὁ satiety, surfeit;

κόρρη, κόρση, ἡ side of the forehead; temples.

κορυβαντιάω to be in ecstasy like a Corybant.

κορυθ - άιξ, ικος, κορυθ-αίολος 2 helmet-shaking.

κόρυμβος, ὁ top, peak; cluster of flowers.

κορύνη, ἡ club, staff.

κορυνήτης, ου, κορυνη-φόρος, ὁ club-bearer.

κόρυς, υθος, ἡ helmet.

κορύσσω to rear; to stir; to arm, equip, array. — P. to rise, swell; to arm oneself.

κορυστής, οῦ armed.

κορυφαῖος 3 at the head; leader, chief, first man.

κορυφή, ἡ top, summit; crown of the head.

κορυφόω to bring to a head. — P. to rise high.

κορώνη[1], ἡ crow, raven.

κορώνη[2], ἡ handle of a door; tip of a bow.

κορωνίς, ίδος curved.

κόσκινον, τό sieve.

κοσμέω to order, arrange; to equip; to keep in order; to rule, govern; to adorn, deck, embellish; to honour, extol.   [ornament.]

κόσμησις, ἡ an adorning;

κοσμητός 3 well-arranged.

κοσμήτωρ, ορος, ὁ arranger, ruler.   [earthly.]

κοσμικός 3 of the world,

κόσμιος 3 orderly, modest,

chaste, decent, obedient; regular, well-arranged.

κοσμιότης, ητος, ἡ decency.

κοσμο - κράτωρ, ορος, ὁ ruler of the world.

κόσμος, ὁ order, arrangement; decency, good behaviour; regularity, good government, constitution; world, universe; ornament, decoration, finery; glory, honour.

κόσος 3 = πόσος.

κότε, κοτέ = πότε, ποτέ.

κότερος = πότερος.

κοτέω and M. to bear a grudge, to be angry.

κοτήεις 3 angry. [hatred.

κότος, ὁ grudge, anger.

κοτύλη, ὁ small cup; socket of the hip-bone.

κοτυληδών, όνος, ὁ sucker of the ink-fish.

κοτυλ - ήρυτος 2 flowing abundantly.

κουλεός = κολεός. [ping.

κουρά, ἡ a shearing, clip-

κουρεῖον, τό barber's shop.

κουρεύς, ὁ barber.

κούρη, ἡ = κόρη.

κούρητες, ων, οἱ young men. [ded.

κουρίδιος 3 lawfully wed-

κουρίζω to be youthful or vigorous.

κουρίξ adv. by the hair.

κοῦρος, ὁ = κόρος.

κουρο - τρόφος 2 rearing or bringing up boys.

κουφίζω to make light, lift up; to relieve, help, assuage; to bury. — intr.

and P. to be light; to rise; to be relieved. [relief.

κούφισις, ἡ a lightening,

κουφο-λογίᾱ, ἡ light talk.

κουφό-νοος 2 light-minded, silly, gay.

κοῦφος 3 light, unloaded; nimble, dexterous; indifferent, little; soft; digestible; easy, light-minded; vain.

κόφινος, ὁ basket.

κόχλος, ὁ muscle. shell.

κράββατος, ὁ couch, bed.

κραγγάνομαι M. to cry aloud. [swing, brandish.

κραδαίνω, κραδάω to

κραδίᾱ, ἡ = καρδίᾱ.

κράζω to croak; to scream.

κραίνω, κραιαίνω to accomplish, fulfil, execute; to rule, command. [debauch.

κραιπάλη, ἡ intoxication;

κραιπνός 3 rapid, swift, sweeping, rushing; rash, hot.

κρανᾱός 3 rocky, stony.

κράνεια, κρανείη, ἡ cornel-tree. [wood.

κρανέϊνος 3 made of cornel-

κρᾱνίον, τό skull.

κράνος, τό helmet.

κρᾶσις, ἡ a mixing, blending; temperature.

κράσ-πεδον, τό border, edge; fringe.

κρᾶτα, τό = κάρα.

κραται-γύαλος 2 with strong breast-plates.

κραταιΐς, ἡ force, bulk.

κραταιός 3 strong, mighty.

κραταιόω to strengthen. — P. to become strong.

κραταί-πεδος 2 with hard ground.

κραται-ρῑνος 2 with a hard hide or shell.

κρατερός 3 = καρτερός.

κρατερό-φρων 2 stout-hearted.

κρατερ-ῶνυξ, υχος with strong hoofs or claws.

κρατευταί, οἱ forked frame of a spit.

κρατέω to be strong or mighty, to have power, be lord, rule; to conquer, subdue, prevail over; to obtain by force; to surpass; to hold fast, seize; to check, hinder.

κρᾱτήρ, ῆρος, ὁ mixing vessel, bowl, b sin.

κρᾱτηρίζω to pour out a libation. [excel.]

κρατιστεύω to be best, to κράτιστος 3 strongest, mightiest; most excellent, best; bravest; noblest.

κράτος, τό strength, might, power, force; violence; dominion, rule, superiority, ascendency, victory.

κρατύνω and M. to strengthen, fortify, secure; to rule, govern; to possess.

κρατύς, ὁ strong. mighty.

κραυγάζω, κραυγανάομαι = κράζω. [ing.]

κραυγή, ἡ crying, scream-

κρέας, ως, τό flesh, meat.

κρεῖον, τό dresser.

κρείσσων, κρείττων 2 stronger, mightier, better; braver; superior, surpassing, lord, master, victor; nobler; worse, more dangerous.

κρείων, οντος, ὁ, κρείουσα, ἡ lord, master, ruler; mistress.

κρεμάννῡμι to hang, hang up. — P. (κρέμαμαι) to be hung up or suspended, to be in suspense.

κρεμαστός 3 hung up, hanging. [bird.]

κρέξ, κρεκός, ἡ an unknown

κρεουργηδόν adv. cut up in butcher's fashion.

κρεο-φάγος 2 eating flesh.

κρέσσων 2 = κρείσσων.

κρήγυος 2 agreeable, delighting.

κρή-δεμνον, τό head-dress, veil; battlements; lid, cover.

κρῆθεν adv. from the head, from above.

κρημνός, ὁ steep precipice, slope, steep bank or edge.

κρημνώδης 2 precipitous, steep.

κρηναῖος 3 of a spring or fountain. [well.]

κρήνη, ἡ spring, fountain,

κρηπίς, ῖδος, ἡ shoe, boot; foundation, base; enclosing wall. [refuge.]

κρησφύγετον, τό place of

κρητήρ, ὁ = κρατήρ.

κρῖ, τό = κριθή.

κρίζω to creak, screech.

κρῑθή, ἡ barley.

κρίθινος 3 of barley.

κρίκος, ὁ ring, circle, bracelet.

κρῖμα, κρίμα, τό sentence, judgment; accusation, condemnation.

κρίνον, τό, κρίνος, τό lily.

κρίνω to separate, divide; to pick out, choose, prefer, approve; to judge, decide, explain, think, believe, accuse, bring to trial, examine, question; condemn. — *M.* to choose for oneself. — *P.* to be chosen, judged, or decided; to be accused, tried, or condemned; to contend, fight.

κρῑο-πρόσωπος 2 ram-faced. [ram.]

κρῑός, ὁ ram; battering-ram.

κρίσις, ἡ separation; discord, dispute; a choosing, deciding, judgment, sentence; trial, examination, law-suit, court of justice, condemnation, justice, punishment; issue, event.

κριτήριον, τό means for judging, test; court of justice; law-suit.

κριτής, οῦ, ὁ judge.

κριτικός 3 able to judge.

κριτός 3 chosen, picked out.

κροαίνω = κρούω.

κρόκη, ἡ woof, thread.

κροκόδειλος, ἡ lizard; crocodile. [robed.]

κροκό-πεπλος 2 saffron-robed.

κρόκος, ὁ saffron.

κροκύς, ύδος, ἡ flock of wool. [onion.]

κρόμμυον, κρόμυον, τό

κρόσσαι, αἱ battlements; steps. [cause to rattle.]

κροταλίζω to rattle; to

κρόταλον, τό rattle, castanet. [forehead, temple.]

κρόταφος, ὁ side of the

κροτέω to knock, strike; to clap the hands.

κροτητός 3 rattling.

κρότος, ὁ a clapping, applause; rattling noise.

κρουνός, ὁ spring, well.

κρούω to knock, strike; to beat; to clap. — *M.*πρύμναν κρούεσθαι to row back stern foremost.

κρύβδα, κρύβδην = κρύφα.

κρυερός 3 chilly; awful.

κρῡμός, ὁ frost; wintertime.

κρυόεις 3 = κρυερός.

κρύος, τό frost, ice.

κρυπτάδιος 3 = κρυπτός.

κρυπτή, ἡ vault, crypt.

κρυπτός 3 hidden, covered; secret.

κρύπτω to hide, cover, conceal; to keep secret; to be hidden, conceal oneself.

κρυσταλλίζω to shine like crystal. [crystal.]

κρύσταλλος, ὁ ice; rock-crystal.

κρύφα, κρυφῇ, κρυφηδόν *adv.* secretly. [κρυπτός]

κρυφαῖος 3, κρύφιος 3 =

κρωβύλος, ὁ tuft of hair; crest. [urn.]

κρωσσός, ὁ pitcher, jar,

κτάομαι *M.* to gain, get for oneself, acquire; *perf.* κέκτημαι to possess, have.

κτέαρ, ατος, τό = κτῆμα.

κτεατίζω = κτάομαι and κέκτημαι.

κτείνω to slay, kill, murder.

κτείς, κτενός, ὁ comb.

κτενίζω to comb.

κτέρας, τό, *pl.* κτέρεα, έων gifts for the dead, funeral. [funeral honours.]

κτερίζω, κτερεΐζω to pay

κτερίσματα, τά = κτέρεα.

κτῆμα, τό possession, property, goods, treasure.

κτηνηδόν adv. like beasts.

κτῆνος, τό possession, property; cattle, sheep.

κτήσιος 3 of one's property.

κτῆσις, ἡ a getting, an acquiring; possession, property, goods.

κτητός 3 gained, acquired.

κτήτωρ, ορος, ὁ owner.

κτίδεος 3 made of the skin of a fitchet or marten.

κτίζω to people, colonize; to found, establish, institute; to create.

κτίλος, ὁ ram.

κτιλόω to tame. — M. to win one's affections.

κτίννῦμι, κτιννύω = κτείνω.

κτίσις, ἡ, κτίσμα, τό a founding, foundation, establishing; creation; creature. [creator.]

κτίστης, ου, ὁ founder.

κτιστύς, ύος, ἡ = κτίσις.

κτυπέω to crash, ring, resound; to thunder.

κτύπος, ὁ crash, sound, noise, rattling clash; cries.

κύαθος, ὁ dipper, cup.

κυαμευτός 3 chosen by beans. [beans; election.]

κύαμος, ὁ bean; vote by)

κυάνεος 3 dark-blue; dark.

κυανό-πεζα, ἡ dark-footed.

κυανό-πρῳρος 2, -πρῴρειος 2 with dark prow.

κύανος, ὁ azure-stone, blue steel; smalt-blue.

κυανο-χαίτης, ου, -χαῖτα dark-haired.

κυαν-ῶπις, ιδος dark-eyed.

κυβεία, ἡ dice-playing; deceit.

κυβερνάω to be a steersman; to steer; to direct, guide, govern.

κυβέρνησις, ἡ a steering; governing.

κυβερνήτης, ου, κυβερνητήρ, ῆρος, ὁ steersman; governor.

κυβερνητικός 3 skilled in steering or governing.

κυβευτής, οῦ dice-player.

κυβευτικός 3 skilled in dicing.

κυβεύω to play at dice.

κυβιστάω to turn a somersault, to turn over.

κυβιστητήρ, ῆρος, ὁ mountebank; diver.

κύβος, ὁ cube.

κυδάζω to revile.

κυδαίνω to praise, glorify, honour, adorn.

κυδάλιμος 2 glorious.

κυδάνω = κυδαίνω; to boast.

κυδι-άνειρα, ἡ men-honouring. [boast.]

κυδιάω to be proud, to)

κύδιστος 3 most glorious, noblest.

κυδοιμέω to rave, rage; to drive in confusion.

κυδοιμός, ὁ tumult, confusion, uproar.

κῦδος, τό glory, fame, renown; pride; bliss, luck.

κυδρός 3 = κυδάλιμος.

κυέω, κυΐσκομαι P. to be pregnant.

κυκάω to stir up, mix, confound. — P. to get into confusion. [drink.]

κυκεών, ῶνος, ὁ mixed)

κυκλεύω to surround, beset.

κυκλέω to wheel along; to turn in a circle; to surround. — *intr.* and *M.* to form a circle; to move in a circle, to turn round.

κύκλιος 3 and 2, κυκλόεις 3 circular. [all around.]

κυκλόθεν *adv.* in a circle,

κύκλος, ὁ circle, circular body; circular motion; ring, wheel, disk, eye, shield; town-wall. [all around.]

κυκλόσε *adv.* in a circle,

κυκλο-τερής 2 circular.

κυκλόω to make round or circular; to turn in a circle; to encircle. — *M.* to form into a circle, to form a circle; to enclose.

κύκλωσις, ἡ an encircling, enclosing.

κύκνος, ὁ swan.

κυλίνδω, κυλινδέω to roll (on or along). — *P.* to be rolled; to roll along; to wallow.

κύλιξ, ικος, ἡ drinking-cup.

κύλισμα, τό, κυλισμός, ὁ a rolling; stirred-up dirt.

κυλίω = κυλίνδω. [bread.]

κυλλήστις, ιος, ὁ Egyptian

κυλλο-ποδίων, ονος crook-legged, halting.

κυλλός 3 crooked; maimed.

κῦμα, τό wave, billow, surge.

κυμαίνω and *P.* to swell or rise in waves.

κυματίας, ου surging; causing waves.

κυματο-αγής 2 breaking like waves. [beaten.]

κυματο-πλήξ, ῆγος wave-

κυματόομαι *P.* to rise in waves. [beach.]

κυματ-ωγή, ἡ strand,

κύμβαλον, τό cymbal.

κύμβαχος[1], ὁ crown of the helmet.

κύμβαχος[2] 2 head foremost.

κύμινδις, ιδος, ὁ night-hawk.

κύμινον, τό cumin.

κυνά-μυια, ἡ dog-fly.

κυνάριον, τό little dog.

κυνέη, κυνῆ, ἡ cap, bonnet; helmet. [less.]

κύνεος 3 like a dog, shame-

κυνέω to kiss.

κυν-ηγέσιον, τό chase, hunt; hunting expedition; pack of hounds; game. [sue.]

κυν-ηγετέω to chase, pur-

κυν-ηγέτης, ου, ὁ, κυνηγός, ὁ, ἡ huntsman, huntress.

κυν-ηγετικός 3 of hunting.

κυν-ηγία, ἡ = κυνηγέσιον.

κυνίδιον, τό little dog.

κυνικός 3 like a dog.

κυνίσκος, ὁ little dog. [ed.]

κυνο-κέφαλος 2 dog-head-

κυνό-μυια, ἡ = κυνάμυια.

κυνο-ραιστής, οῦ, ὁ dog-tick. [by dogs.]

κυνο-σπάρακτος 2 torn

κύντατος 3 most shameless.

κύντερος 3 more shameless.

κυν-ώπης, ου, κυν-ῶπις, ιδος dog-eyed.

κυπαρίσσινος 3 of cypress wood.

κυπάρισσος, ἡ cypress.

κύπειρον, τό, κύπειρος, ὁ cyperus.

κύπελλον, τό goblet.

κύπερος, ὁ = κύπειρος.

κύπτω to bend forward, stoop. [net, turban.]

κυρβασία, ἡ Persian bonnet; κύρβις, ὁ, ἡ movable pillar with inscriptions.

κὕρέω to hit or light upon, reach, meet with, arrive at; to gain, obtain; = τυγχάνω to happen, come to pass.

κὕριακός 3 belonging to a lord or master.

κὕριεύω to rule, be lord.

κὕριος 3 having power, ruling; valid, legal, entitled, capable: appointed, regular, authorized; principal; ὁ κ. lord, master, ruler, owner; ἡ κυρία mistress, lady; τὸ κύριον legal power; statute; appointed time.

κὕριότης, ητος, ἡ dominion; ruler.

κυρίσσω to butt, strike against. [prey.]

κύρμα, τό godsend, booty,]

κὕρος, τό power, authority; decision; ratification; validity.

κὕρόω and M. to make valid, confirm, ratify; to decide; to accomplish.

κύρτη, ἡ, κύρτος, ὁ fishing-basket.

κυρτός 3 curved, arched.

κυρτόω to curve, bend, arch.

κὕρω and M. = κὕρέω.

κύρωσις, ἡ = κὕρος. [der.]

κύστις, εως or ιδος, ἡ bladder.

κύτος, τό hollow, vessel, urn; skin; shield, cuirass.

κὕφός 3 bent, curved, stooping.

κυψέλη, ἡ chest, box.

κύω = κυέω.

κύων, κυνός. ὁ, ἡ dog, bitch; monster; dog-star; sea-dog.

κώ = πώ.

κῶας, τό fleece, sheep-skin.

κώδεια, ἡ head of a poppy.

κώδιον, τό = κῶας.

κώδων, ωνος, ὁ and ἡ bell; patrol; trumpet.

κώκῡμα, τό, κωκῡτός, ὁ a shrieking, wailing.

κωκύω to wail, lament; to bewail. [the knee.]

κώληψ, ηπος, ἡ hollow of]

κῶλον, τό limb, member; foot, leg, knee; part; story, side, wall.

κωλῡτής, οῦ, ὁ hinderer.

κωλῡτικός 3 hindering.

κωλύω to hinder, prevent, check, forbid.

κῶμα, τό deep sleep, trance.

κωμάζω to revel, to go in a festal procession, to celebrate a feast; to be wanton or playful. [a village.]

κωμ-άρχης, ου, ὁ head of]

κωμαστής, οῦ, ὁ reveller.

κώμη, ἡ village.

κωμήτης, ου, ὁ villager.

κωμικός 3 belonging to comedy, comic.

κωμό-πολις ἡ village-town, borough.

κῶμος, ὁ festal procession, revel, merry-making; band of revellers; feast, banquet.

κωμ-ῳδέω to ridicule.

κωμ-ῳδία, ἡ comedy.

κωμῳδ(ι)ο-ποιός ὁ comic poet. [poet.]

κωμ-ῳδός comic actor or]

κώνειον, τό hemlock.
κών-ωψ, ωπος, ὁ gnat.
κωπεύς, ὁ wood for oars.
κώπη, ἡ handle of an oar or sword or key; oar.
κωπήεις 3 with a handle.
κωπ-ήρης 2 furnished with oars.

κώρυκος, ὁ leather(n) bag.
κῶς, κώς = πῶς. πώς.
κωτίλλω to talk over, to wheedle.
κωφός 3 blunt, dumb, deaf and dumb, mute, speechless; dull, weak, stupid; insensate.

Λ

Λ, λ (λάμβδα, λάβδα) eleventh letter of the alphabet; as a numeral λ′ = 30.
λᾶας, ὁ stone; rock; crag.
λαβή, ἡ handle, haft, hilt, hold; weak side.
λαβρ-αγόρης, ου, ὁ bold prattler.   [boldly.]
λαβρεύομαι M. to talk]
λάβρος 2 rapid, furious, vehement, boisterous.
λαβύρινθος, ὁ labyrinth, maze.
λαγνεία, ἡ lust.
λαγός, ὁ = λαγῶς.
λαγχάνω to obtain by lot or fate; to draw lots; to be chosen by lot; to receive a share; to give a share.
λαγῶς, λαγώς, ῶ, λαγωός, ὁ hare.
λάδανον, τό = λήδανον.
λάζομαι = λαμβάνω.
λάθᾱ, ἡ = λήθη.
λᾱθι-κηδής 2 banishing care.   [sorrow.]
λᾱθί-πονος 2 forgetful of]
λάθρᾳ, λάθρᾱ adv. secretly, stealthily; without one's knowledge.
λαθραῖος 3 secret, stealthy.
λαῖγξ, ιγγος, ἡ pebble.

λαῖλαψ, απος, ἡ storm, hurricane.
λαιμός, ὁ throat, gullet.
λάϊνεος 3, λάϊνος 2 of stone.
λαιός 3 left (hand).
λαισήϊον, τό light shield.
λαῖτμα, τό depth, abyss.
λαῖφος, τό piece of cloth, sail; ragged garment.
λαιψηρός 3 swift, quick.
λᾱκέω = ληκέω = λάσκω.
λάκκος, ὁ hole, pit; cistern; pond.   [down.]
λακ-πάτητος 2 trodden]
λακτίζω to kick with the foot, trample (up)on; to move in convulsions.
λακτιστής, οῦ kicking, trampling.
λακωνίζω to imitate or side with the Laconians.
λακωνισμός, ὁ a siding with the Lacedæmonians.
λακωνιστής, οῦ imitating the Laconians.
λαλέω to talk, prate, chatter; to speak, teach, praise.
λάλημα, τό talk, prattling; prater.   [dialect.]
λαλιά, ἡ a talking, chat;]
λάλος 2 talkative.
λαμβάνω to take, seize,

grasp, catch, capture, obtain; to meet with, incur, suffer; to receive, take in; to choose, select; to take away, steal; to receive hospitably; to comprehend, understand, perceive; to come upon, overtake, find out, detect, convict. — M. to keep hold of, grasp, touch; to get possession of, win, gain, obtain.

λαμπαδη-δρομία, λαμπαδη-φορία, ἡ torch-race.

λαμπάδιον, τό small torch.

λαμπάς, άδος, ἡ torch; sun, light; lamp; torch-race; adj. lighted by torches.

λαμπετάω = λάμπω.

λαμπρός 3 bright, shining, beaming, brilliant; limpid; clear, sonorous, keen; fresh; manifest, evident; splendid, magnificent; noble.

λαμπρότης, ητος, ἡ brilliancy, splendour; glory, honour. [voice.]

λαμπρο-φωνία, ἡ clear **λαμπρό-φωνος** 2 clear-voiced.

λαμπρύνω to make bright, polish. — M. to be liberal.

λαμπτήρ, ῆρος, ὁ stand for torches; torch; beacon-light. [brilliant.]

λάμπω and M. to shine, be **λανθάνω** to escape a p.'s notice, to be hidden, unnoticed; to cause to forget. — M. to forget.

λάξ, adv. with the heel or foot. [in stone.]

λαξευτός 3 cut or hewn

λάξις, ιος, ἡ district.

λαός, ὁ people, crowd, host, army; pl. men, soldiers, fellows. [men.]

λᾱοσ-σόος 2 stirring the **λᾱο-φόρος** 2 = λεωφόρος.

λαπάρη, ἡ flank, loins.

λάπτω to lick, lap.

λάρναξ, ακος, ἡ receptacle; chest, urn, coffin.

λάρος, ὁ gull. [licious.]

λαρός 3 dainty, sweet, de-

λαρυγγίζω to shout with all one's lungs. [gullet.]

λάρυγξ, υγγος, ὁ throat,

λάσθη, ἡ mockery, insult.

λάσι-αύχην, ενος maned.

λάσιος 3 shaggy, woolly; grown with bushes.

λάσκω to crash, cry, ring, shriek; to speak loud, shout.

λᾱ-τομέω to hew stones.

λατρεία, ἡ, **λάτρευμα,** τό service, servitude, hired labour; worship.

λάτρις, ιος, ὁ servant, slave.

λαυκανίη, ἡ throat.

λαύρᾱ, ἡ lane, passage, defile.

λάφῡρον, τό booty, spoil.

λαφῡρο-πωλέω to sell booty.

λαφῡρο-πώλης, ου, ὁ seller of booty. [vour.]

λαφύσσω to swallow, de-

λαχανισμός, ὁ a gathering of vegetables. [getables.]

λάχανον, τό greens, ve-

λάχεια fem. level, flat.

λάχεσις, ἡ = λάχος.

λάχνη, ἡ wool; woolly hair; downy beard.

λαχνήεις 3 woolly; hairy.

λάχνος, ὁ = λάχνη.

λάχος, τό lot, share; section; fate.

λάω to seize, grasp; to wish.

λέαινα, ἡ lioness

λεαίνω to polish, smooth; to make agreeable; to bray or pound.

λέβης, ητος, ὁ kettle, caldron; basin; urn.

λεγεών, λεγιών, ῶνος, ὁ, ἡ legion.

λέγω[1] = λέχω to lay down or asleep. — M. to lie down to sleep.

λέγω[2] to pick, gather; to reckon among; to tell, relate, speak, say, declare, assert, promise; to call, name; to order, request; to recite, read. — M. to gather for oneself, to count up; to converse, discourse. — P. to be told, related, or said; ὁ λεγόμενος the so-called.

λεηλατέω to drive away booty, to plunder.

λεία, ἡ booty, plunder.

λεταίνω = λεαίνω.

λείβω to pour out; to pour a libation.

λεῖμμα, τό = λείφανον.

λειμών, ῶνος, ὁ meadow, pasture.

λειμώντος 3, λειμωνιάς, άδος, ἡ of a meadow.

λειμωνόθεν adv. from a meadow.   [chinned.]

λειο-γένειος 2 smooth-]

λεῖος 3 smooth, polished; level, flat; bald.   [ness.]

λειότης, ητος, ἡ smooth-]

λειπο-στρατία, ἡ, λειπο-στράτιον, τό desertion.

λειπο-ψῡχέω to swoon; to be dejected.

λειπο-ψῡχία, ἡ swoon.

λείπω to leave, leave remaining or behind; to abandon, desert; intr. to be gone; to fail, come short of. — M. to leave behind, bequeath. — P. and M. to be left, left behind, remain; to be inferior or weaker; to be abandoned; to be far from; to want, lack. [cate.]

λειριόεις 3 lily-like; deli-]

λεῖστός 3 = ληϊστός.

λειτουργέω to perform public duties; to bear the charges of public duties; to officiate.

λειτουργία, ἡ public service; expenditure for the state; divine service.

λείχω to lick.

λε.ψανον, τό remnant.

λεκτικός 3 eloquent.

λεκτός 3 picked out; said; to be spoken.

λέκτρον, τό couch, bed; bed-clothes; marriage-bed; marriage.

λελιημένος 3 longing for.

λελογισμένως adv. deliberately.

λέντιον, τό linen cloth.

λέξις, ἡ speech, mode of speech, style.

λεοντέη, λεοντῆ, ἡ lion's skin.   [ion, yoke.]

λέπαδνον, τό leather cush-]

λέπας, τό bare rock or hill.

λεπιδωτός 3 scaly, scaled.

λεπίς, ίδος, ἡ scale, shell.

λέπρᾱ, ἡ leprosy.

λεπρός 3 leprous.

λεπταλέος 3 fine, delicate.

λεπτό-γεως 2 with poor soil.

λεπτός 3 cleaned of the husks; thin, fine, slender, delicate, lean, narrow, small, weak; subtle, clever.

λεπτουργέω to do fine work.

λέπω to peel or bark.

λέσχη, ἡ town-hall; place of public resort; assembly; conversation, talk.

λευγαλέος 3 sad, wretched, miserable, pitiful; mischievous.

λευίτης, ου, ὁ Levite.

λευίτικός 3 Levitical.

λευκαίνω to make white.

λευκ-ανθής 2 white-blossoming, white.

λευκ-ανθίζω to be white.

λεύκ-ασπις, ιδος white-shielded.

λεύκη, ἡ white poplar; white leprosy.   [horses.)

λεύκ-ιππος 2 with white

λευκο-θώραξ, ᾱκος with white cuirass.

λευκό-λινον, τό white flax.

λευκό-πωλος 2 = λεύκ-ιππος.

λευκός 3 bright, brilliant, clear; white, pale.

λεύκ-οφρυς, υος with white eyebrows.   [white.)

λευκόω to whiten, paint)

λευκ-ώλενος 2 white-armed.   [wide.)

λευρός 3 smooth, level,)

λεύσσω to gaze, look (at), behold, see.

λευστήρ, ῆρος, ὁ one who stones, executioner.

λεύω to stone.   [grassy.)

λεχε-ποίης, ου meadowy,)

λέχος, τό couch, bed; bier; marriage-bed; marriage.

λέχοσδε adv. to bed.

λέχριος 3 slanting, oblique.

λέχω see λέγω[1].

λέων, οντος, ὁ lion.

λεωργός, ὁ offender.

λεώς, ώ, ὁ = λαός.

λεω-σφέτερος 2 one of their own people.

λεω-φόρος 2 frequented; high-way.

λήγω to cease, leave off; to abate, assuage; to keep back.

λήδανον, τό gum.

λήζω = λῄζω.

λήθη, ἡ a forgetting, forgetfulness.

λήθω = λανθάνω.

ληΐάς, άδος, ἡ captive.

ληΐ-βότειρα, ἡ crop-devouring.

λῄζω and M. to make plunder or spoil; to rob, ravage.

ληίη, ἡ = λεία.

λήϊον, τό cornfield, crop.

ληΐς, ίδος, ἡ = λεία.

λῄστήρ, ῆρος, ὁ robber, plunderer.   [booty.)

ληϊστός 3 to be seized as)

ληϊστύς, ύος, ἡ a plundering, robbing.   [booty.)

λῆϊτις, ιδος, ἡ dispenser of)

λήκυθος, ἡ oil-flask.

λῆμα, τό will, purpose; courage; arrogance, pride.

λῆμμα, τό income; profit, gain; gratification.

ληνός, ἡ, ὁ wine-press; trough. [share.]

λῆξις, ἡ allotment, lot,

ληρέω to talk idly; to be foolish or silly.

λήρημα, τό, λῆρος, ὁ idle talk, nonsense, frivolousness; swaggerer.

λησμοσύνη, ἡ = λήθη.

λῃστείᾶ, ἡ robbery, piracy, plundering expedition.

λῃστεύω = λῃΐζω. [bers.]

λῃστήριον, τό band of rob-

λῃστής, οῦ, ὁ robber, pirate, free-booter.

λῃστικός 3 inclined to rob, piratical. [receiving.]

λῆψις, ἡ a taking, seizing,

λιάζομαι P. to bend sideways; to withdraw, recede; to fall.

λίᾶν adv. very much; too much; καὶ λ. certainly, of course.

λιαρός 3 warm, tepid; soft.

λίβανος, ὁ frankincense (-tree). [censer.]

λιβανωτός, ὁ frankincense;

λιβανωτο-φόρος 2 bearing incense. [stream.]

λιβάς, άδος, ἡ drop; water;

λιβερτῖνος, ὁ freedman.

λίγα adv. of λιγύς.

λιγαίνω to cry aloud with clear voice.

λίγγω to sound, twang.

λίγδην adv. scrapingly.

λιγνύς, ύος, ἡ smoke.

λιγυ-πνείων, οντος shrill-blowing, whistling.

λιγυρός 3, λιγύς 3 shrill, clear, sharp, piercing, clear-toned. [voiced.]

λιγύ-φθογγος 2 clear-

λίζω = λίγγω.

λίην = λίαν.

λιθάζω to stone.

λίθαξ, ακος. λίθεος 2, λίθινος of stone, stony, rocky.

λιθίδιον, τό small stone.

λιθο-βολέω to stone.

λιθο-κόλλητος 2 inlaid with precious stones.

λιθό-λευστος 2 stoned to death.

λιθο-λόγος, ὁ mason.

λίθος, ὁ stone, marble.

λιθο-σπαδής 2 made by tearing out a stone.

λιθό-στρωτος 2 paved with stones.

λιθο-τομίᾶ, ἡ quarry.

λιθουργός 2 working in stone; stone-mason.

λιθο-φορέω to carry stones.

λικμάω to winnow; to scatter.

λικμητήρ, ῆρος, ὁ winnower.

λίκνον, τό basket; cradle.

λικνο-φόρος, ὁ basket-bearer.

λικριφίς adv. sideways.

λιλαίομαι to long for, desire, crave.

λῑμαίνω to hunger, starve.

λιμήν, ένος, ὁ harbour, haven, port, bay; refuge; gathering-place. [nant.]

λιμναῖος 3 marshy, stag-

λίμνη, ἡ lake, pool, pond; basin; swamp; sea.

λιμνώδης 2 like a lake.

λῑμο-κτονίᾶ, ἡ a hungering, fasting.

λῑμός, ὁ hunger; famine.

λίνεος, λινοῦς 3 of flax, linen. [linen cuirass.]

λίνον, τό flax, linen; thread; fishing-net, fishing-line; linen cloth; wick.

λίνος, ὁ song of Linos.

λῖπα adv. unctuously.

λῑπαρέω to persist, persevere; to entreat, beg earnestly.

λῑπαρής 2 persisting, persevering; entreating; liberal, lavishing.

λῑπαρίᾱ, ἡ perseverance.

λῑπαρο-κρήδεμνος 2 with bright head-band.

λῑπαρο-πλόκαμος 2 with shining locks.

λῑπαρός 3 oily, shining, fat, greasy; bright, brilliant; rich, blessed, copious, ample; comfortable, easy; splendid; fresh, gay.

λιπαρῶς adv. of λιπαρής and λιπαρός. [guents.]

λιπάω to shine with un-) λίπος, τό fat, oil.

λιπο-στρατίᾱ, ἡ = λειπο-στρατία.

λιπόω = λιπάω.

λῖς¹, ὁ lion.

λῖς² smooth. [cloth.]

λῖς³, λῑτός, ὁ linen, linen) λίσσομαι M. to beg, pray, entreat, beseech, implore.

λισσός 3 smooth. [prayer.]

λιστός 3 to be won by) λιστρεύω to dig round.

λίστρον, τό shovel; spade.

λιτανεύω = λίσσομαι.

λιτή, ἡ prayer, entreaty.

λίτομαι = λίσσομαι.

λιτότης, ητος, ἡ plainness, simplicity.

λίτρᾱ, ἡ pound.

λίτρον, τό soda. [greedy)

λίχνος, 3 and 2 lickerish;) λίψ, λιβός, ὁ south-west wind. [of the liver.)

λοβός, ὁ lobe of the ear or)

λογάδην adv. picked out.

λογάς, άδος gathered, picked.

λογίᾱ, ἡ collection.

λογίζομαι M. to count, reckon, calculate; to reckon among; to consider, reason, reflect; to conclude, infer, judge, think.

λογικός 3 rational, fit for reasoning. [markable.]

λόγιμος 3 considerable, re-)

λόγιος 3 eloquent; learned; λόγιον, τό oracle.

λογισμός, ὁ reckoning, computation, arithmetics; consideration, thought, reasoning, reflection; cause, conclusion, judgment; project; reason, insight.

λογιστής, οῦ, ὁ calculator, auditor, judge.

λογιστικός 3 skilled in calculating; arguing, sensible.

λογο-γράφος, ὁ historian, annalist; writer of speeches.

λογο-μαχέω to dispute about words.

λογο-μαχίᾱ, ἡ dispute about words.

λογο-ποιέω to invent words or news.

λογο-ποιός, ὁ historian;

writer of fables; inventor of stories.

λόγος, ὁ a saying, speaking, speech, mode of speaking; eloquence, discourse; conversation, talk; word, expression; assertion; principle, maxim; proverb; oracle; promise; order, command; proposal; condition, agreement; stipulation, decision; pretext; fable, news, story, report, legend; prose-writing, history, book, essay, oration; affair, incident; thought, reason, reckoning, computation, reflection, deliberation, account, consideration, opinion; cause, end; argument, demonstration; meaning, value; proportion; Christ.

λόγχη, ἡ spear-head, lance.

λοέω = λούω.

λοετρόν, τό = λουτρόν.

λοιβή, ἡ libation, drink-offering. [nicious.]

λοίγιος 2 destructive, per-

λοιγός, ὁ ruin, mischief, destruction, death.

λοιδορέω and *M.* to revile, abuse; to blame.

λοιδορία, ἡ a reviling, abuse, reproach.

λοίδορος 2 reviling, abusive. [lence.]

λοιμός, ὁ plague, pesti-

λοιμώδης 2 pestilential.

λοιπός 3 remaining, surviving, future.

λοισθήιος 2, **λοίσθιος** 3 and 2, **λοῖσθος** 2 left behind; last.

λεξός 3 slanting, oblique.

λεπός, ὁ husk, peel, bark.

λουτρόν, τό bath, bathing-place; ablution, baptism; libation.

λουτρο-χόος 2 pouring water for a bath.

λούω to wash, bathe. — *M.* to wash oneself. [hill.]

λοφιά, ὁ mane, bristles;

λόφος, ὁ neck, crest of a helmet, tuft of hair; ridge of a hill, hill.

λοχ-ᾱγέω to lead a λόχος.

λοχ-ᾱγίᾱ, ἡ office of a λοχαγός.

λοχ-ᾱγός, ὁ captain, leader of a λόχος.

λοχάω and *M.* to lie in wait *or* ambush; to set a trap for.

λοχείᾱ, ἡ child-birth; child.

λοχεῖος 3 of child-birth.

λοχεύω to bring forth. — *P.* to be born.

λοχ-ηγέω = λοχᾱγέω.

λοχίζω to arrange men in companies; = λοχάω.

λοχίτης, ου, ὁ soldier of the same company; fellow-soldier; life-guard.

λόχμη, ἡ lair, thicket.

λοχμώδης 2 overgrown with bushes.

λόχος, ὁ ambush, ambuscade; company of soldiers, band.

λόω = λούω.

λύγδην *adv.* with sobs.

λυγίζω to bend, twist. — *P.* to writhe.

λύγξ¹, λυγκός, ὁ lynx.

λύγξ², λυγγός, ἡ hiccough.

λύγος, ὁ willow-twig.

λύθρος 3 sad, mournful, miserable; mischievous; cowardly.

λύθρον, τό, λύθρος, ὁ gore, blood; filth.

λυκά-βᾱς, αντος, ὁ sun's course, year.

λυκέη, ἡ a wolf's skin.

λυκη-γενής 2 born from light.

λυκιο-εργής 2 of Lycian workmanship. [ing.]

λυκο-κτόνος 2 wolf-slay-

λύκος, ὁ wolf.

λῦμα, τό dirty water, filth; disgrace.

λῡμαίνομαι M. to disgrace, outrage; to maltreat; to destroy, spoil; to hurt.

λῡμαντής, οῦ, λῡμεών, ῶνος, ὁ destroyer, spoiler.

λῡμη, ἡ disgrace, outrage; maltreatment, mutilation; ruin.

λῡπέω to afflict, grieve, annoy, trouble. — P. to be grieved, sad or mournful.

λύπη, ἡ, λύπημα, τό sorrow, grief, pain. distress.

λῡπηρός, λῡπρός 3 sad, painful, wretched, distressed.

λύρᾱ, ἡ lyre.

λῦσι-μελής 2 limb-relaxing.

λῦσις, ἡ a loosing, release, ransoming, deliverance; dissolution, separation; departure; divorce.

λῡσι-τελέω to be useful or advantageous.

λῡσι-τελής 2 useful, advantageous.

λύσσα, ἡ rage, fury.

λυσσαίνω, λυσσάω to be raving mad, to rage; to be angry.

λυσσητήρ, ῆρος, λυσσώδης 2 raving. raging.

λῠτήριος 2 releasing.

λύτρον, τό ransom.

λυτρόω and M. to release on receipt of ransom; to redeem.

λύτρωσις, ἡ redemption.

λυτρωτής, οῦ, ὁ redeemer.

λυχνία, ἡ lamp-stand.

λυχνο-καΐη, ἡ feast of lamps.

λύχνος, ὁ light, lamp, torch.

λύω to loosen, untie, slacken, unbend; to set free, release, redeem; to dissolve, sever; to destroy; to abrogate, annul; to atone, amend; to profit; to be useful. — M. to loosen for oneself; to redeem, ransom, relieve, release.

λωβάομαι M., λωβεύω to act shamefully; to insult, maltreat, disgrace; to mutilate, hurt; to seduce.

λώβη, ἡ outrage, disgrace, shame; maltreatment, mutilation; ruin.

λωβητήρ, ῆρος, ὁ slanderer; destroyer; murderer.

λωβητός 3 ill-treated, outraged, insulted; insulting.

λωΐων 2, λωΐτερος 3 better, more profitable.

λώπη, ἡ jerkin, mantle.

λωπο-δυτέω to steal clothes.

λωπο-δύτης, ου, ὁ clothes-stealer, thief, rogue.

λῷστος 3 the best, dearest.

λωτόεις 3 rich in lotus.

λωτός, ὁ lotus: clover; lo-tus-tree and fruit; lily of the Nile.

λωτο-φάγος, ὁ lotus-eater.

λώφησις, ἡ cessation.

λώφων 2 = λωτων.

M

M, μ (μῦ) twelfth letter of the alphabet; as a numeral μ' = 40.

μᾶ Particle of affirmation and protestation.

μάγαδις, ιδος, ἡ string-instrument, harp.

μαγγάνευμα, τό = μαγεία.

μαγγανεύω to cheat, put a trick upon.

μαγειᾶ, ἡ magic, delusion, juggling tricks.

μαγειρική, ἡ cookery.

μάγειρος, ὁ cook.

μαγεύω to enchant, charm; to be a magician.

μαγίᾱ, ἡ = μαγεία.

μάγος, ὁ soothsayer, astrologer, magus: enchanter, wizard. [of the Magi.]

μαγο-φόνια, τά slaughter]

μάζα, μᾶζα, ἡ barley-bread.

μαζός, ὁ = μαστός.

μάθημα, τό; μάθησις, ἡ the act of learning; knowledge, learning, science, art, doctrine.

μαθητεύω to be a scholar; to teach, instruct. [ciple.]

μαθητής, οῦ, ὁ pupil, dis-]

μαθητός 3 to be learned.

μαθήτρια, ἡ female pupil.

μαῖα, ἡ good mother, foster-mother.

μαιμακτηριών, ῶνος, ὁ fifth Attic month (November).

μαιμάω to strive after, to be eager for; to rave.

μαινάς, άδος, ἡ raving; Mænad.

μαίνω to make mad. — P. to be mad, to rave, rage, to be furious or frenzied.

μαίομαι M. to strive, endeavour; to seek.

μάκαρ, αρος, ὁ (fem. μάκαιρα) blessed, happy, fortunate: rich.

μακαρίζω to call happy.

μακάριος 3 and 2 = μάκαρ. [cing happy.]

μακαρισμός, ὁ a pronoun-]

μακαριστός 3 to be pronounced happy, enviable; welcome.

μακεδνός 3 tall, slender.

μάκελλα, ἡ pick-axe, shovel.

μάκελλον, τό meat-market.

μάκιστος 3 = μήκιστος.

μακρ-αίων 2 long-lived, lasting. [with prolixity.]

μακρ-ηγορέω to speak]

μακρ-ημερίᾱ, ἡ season of the long days.

μακρό-βιος 2 long-lived.

μακρόθεν adv. from afar.

μακρο-θυμέω to be forbearing: to be patient.

μακρο-θυμίᾱ, ἡ forbearance, patience.

μακρο-λογέω to speak at length. [at length.]

μακρο-λογία a speaking

μακρός 3 long; tall, high, deep, far; long-lasting; tedious, prolix, circumstantial. [lived.]

μακρο-χρόνιος 2 long-

μάλα adv. much, very much, quite, wholly, particularly, exceedingly; certainly, verily.

μαλακία, ἡ softness, weakness; illness; slackness, cowardice.

μαλακίζομαι P. and M. to become weak, effeminate, lazy, cowardly, or timid; to be appeased.

μαλακός 3 soft, tender, sickly; mild, gentle; tender, delicate; effeminate, cowardly; careless, remiss; luxurious, wanton.

μαλάσσω to soften, appease. — P. to be softened by entreaties; to be relieved.

μαλερός 3 strong, mighty, terrible, vehement, raging; greedy.

μάλη, ἡ arm-pit.

μαλθακ- see μαλακ-.

μάλιστα adv. most, most strongly; especially, mostly; even, most certainly; by far; at most.

μᾶλλον adv. more, more strongly, rather, the more, yet, far; too much; by all means. [fleece.]

μαλλός, ὁ flock of wool,

μάμμη, ἡ grandmother.

μαμωνᾶς, ᾶ, ὁ mammon.

μάν = μήν. [mandrake.]

μανδραγόρᾱς, ου or ᾶ, ὁ

μανθάνω to learn, have learnt, know; to ask, inquire, hear, perceive; to understand. [enthusiasm.]

μανία, ἡ madness, frenzy;

μανικός 3 (μανίας, άδος, ἡ), μανιώδης 2 mad, frantic, raving; revelling.

μάννα, τό manna.

μᾱνός 3 thin, scanty, slack.

μαντεία, ἡ; μαντεῖον, τό, μάντευμα, τό gift of prophesying, divination, prophecy, oracle.

μαντεῖος 3 = μαντικός.

μαντευτός 3 foretold by an oracle.

μαντεύω and M. to prophesy, divine; to presage, forebode; to consult an oracle. [τεία, -τεῖον.]

μαντηίη, μαντήιον = μαν-

μαντικός 3 prophetic, prophesying; ἡ -ή art of divination.

μάντις, ὁ, ἡ soothsayer, diviner, seer, prophet.

μαντοσύνη, ἡ = μαντεία.

μάομαι = μαίομαι; to rush on, hasten.

μάραθον, τό fennel.

μαραίνω to undo, destroy, quench. — P. to die away, disappear.

μαρὰν ἀθά our Lord comes.

μαργαίνω to rage.

μαργαρίτης, ου, ὁ pearl.

μάργος 3 and 2 raving, mad, frantic; lustful.

μαρμαίρω to sparkle, glisten, gleam.

16*

μαρμάρεος 3, μαρμαρόεις, 3 sparkling, glistening.

μάρμαρος 2 sparkling; ὁ, ἡ stone, rock; marble.

μαρμαρυγή, ἡ dazzling brightness; trembling motion.

μάρναμαι = μάχομαι.

μάρπτω to grasp, seize, hold, touch, reach, clasp.

μάρσιπος, ὁ bag, pouch.

μαρτυρέω to be a witness, to bear witness; to agree to, confirm; to confess, praise. — P. to obtain a (good) testimony.

μαρτυρία, ἡ, μαρτύριον, τό witness, testimony, evidence, proof; sermon.

μαρτύρομαι M. to call to witness; to testify, confirm by oath, protest.

μάρτυρος, ὁ, ἡ, μάρτυς, υρος, ὁ, ἡ witness; martyr.

μασάομαι M. to chew.

μάσασθαι see ἐπιμαίομαι.

μασθός, ὁ = μαστός.

μάσσω and M. to knead, handle.

μάσσων 2 comp. of μακρός.

μάσταξ, ακος, ἡ mouth, cavity of the mouth; mouthful, morsel.

μαστεύω to seek, inquire after; to endeavour, strive.

μαστήρ, ῆρος, ὁ seeker, investigator.

μαστιγέω = μαστιγόω.

μαστιγίας, ου, ὁ one who is frequently whipped; good-for-nothing.

μαστιγο-φόρος, ὁ whipbearer, constable.

μαστιγόω, μαστίζω to whip, scourge.

μάστιξ, ῑγος. μάστις, ιος, ἡ whip, scourge; plague.

μαστίω = μαστιγόω.

μαστός, ὁ teat; breast, woman's breast; hill, knoll.

μασχαλίζω to mutilate.

μασχαλιστήρ, ῆρος, ὁ shoulder-strap.

ματάζω to act foolishly.

ματαιο-λογία, ἡ idle talk.

ματαιο-λόγος 2 talking idly.

μάταιος 3 and 2 idle, foolish, vain, inefficient; unmeaning, unfounded; thoughtless, wanton, untrue, wicked. [vanity.]

ματαιότης, ητος, ἡ folly,

ματαιόω to make foolish.

ματάω to miss, do in vain; to loiter, linger.

ματεύω = μαστεύω.

μάτηρ, μάτρός, ἡ = μήτηρ.

ματία, ἡ folly; vain attempt.

μαῦρος = ἀμαυρός.

μάχαιρα, ἡ large knife; dagger; sword.

μαχαιρο-φόρος 2 swordbearing.

μάχη, ἡ combat, fight, battle; battle-field; single combat; quarrel.

μαχήμων 2 = μάχιμος.

μαχητής, οῦ, ὁ fighter, warrior; warlike.

μαχητός 3 conquerable.

μάχιμος 3 and 2 warlike.

μαχλοσύνη, ἡ lust, lewdness.

μάχομαι M. to fight, make

war; to resist, withstand; to quarrel. dispute.

μάφ, μαφιδίως *adv.* rashly, thoughtlessly, at random; fruitlessly, falsely; indecorously.

μάω see μάομαι.

μέγαθος, τό see μέγεθος.

μεγά-θυμος 2 high-minded, magnanimous.

μεγαίρω to grudge, envy, refuse, forbid.

μεγα-κήτης 2 with huge sea-animals.

μεγαλ-αυχέω and *M.* to boast highly.

μεγαλεῖος 3 magnificent, splendid; haughty

μεγαλειότης, ητος, ἡ magnificence, majesty.

μεγαλ-ηγορέω to boast.

μεγαλ-ήτωρ, ορος high-minded, héroic; overweening. [proud.]

μεγαλίζομαι *P.* to be/

μεγαλο-πράγμων 2 forming great designs.

μεγαλο-πρέπεια, ἡ magnificence, splendour; love of splendour.

μεγαλο-πρεπής 2 magnificent, splendid; magnanimous, liberal; fond of pomp.

μεγαλο-φρονέω to be hopeful; to be proud.

μεγαλο-φροσύνη, ἡ greatness of mind; haughtiness.

μεγαλό-φρων 2 high-minded; haughty.

μεγαλο-φῡχίᾱ, ἡ magnanimity; boldness.

μεγαλύνω to make great or powerful; to praise. ex-

tol. — *M.* to be exalted; to boast. [praised.]

μεγαλ-ώνυμος 2 much/

μεγάλως, μεγαλωστί *adv.* of μέγας. [λειότης.]

μεγαλωσύνη, ἡ = μεγα-/

μέγαρον, τό chamber, hall, apartment for men or for women, bed-chamber; house, mansion; inner room of a temple, sanctuary.

μέγας, μεγάλη, μέγα, *comp.* μείζων 2. *sup.* μέγιστος 3 large, great, big, grand; spacious, long, high, wide; powerful, mighty, strong, violent; arrogant, proud; illustrious. *adv.* μεγάλως (μεγαλωστί), μέγα, μεγάλα much, very much, exceedingly.

μέγεθος, τό greatness, bulk, size; might, power, excellence; importance. [men.]

μεγιστάνες, οἱ the chief/

μέδιμνος, ὁ a dry measure containing 48 χοίνικες.

μέδω, μεδέω to think of, give heed to, attend to; to devise; to rule; ὁ μέδων ruler, guardian. [turn.]

μεθ-αιρέω to catch in/

μεθ-άλλομαι *M.* to leap upon; to rush after.

μεθ-αρμόζω to alter; to correct.

μέθ-εξις, ἡ a partaking.

μεθ-έπω and *M.* to follow after; to obey; to call upon, visit; to pursue: to drive on in pursuit of; to manage. [late.]

μεθ-ερμηνεύω to trans-/

μέθη, ἡ drunkenness.

μέθ-ημαι to sit among.

μεθ-ημερινός 3 happening by day; daily.

μεθ-ημοσύνη, ἡ carelessness, remissness.

μεθ-ήμων 2 careless, lazy.

μεθ-ίημι to let loose, let go; to release, set free; to forgive, pardon; to lay in, bring to; to send away; to abandon; to neglect; to permit, allow. — *intr.* to cease, slacken, be careless. — *M.* to loose oneself from, let go, abandon.

μεθ-ιστάνω, μεθ-ίστημι to transpose, place in another way; to substitute, change, remove. — *intr.* and *P.* to appear in a crowd; to withdraw, retire; to change one's place, to go over to another party, to revolt. — *M.* to send away, remove.

μεθό = μεθ' ὅ.

μεθ-οδεία, ἡ craft, trick.

μέθ-οδος, ἡ way of inquiring; method. [with.]

μεθ-ομιλέω to converse

μεθ-όριος 3 bordering on; τὰ μεθόρια border, frontier.

μεθ-ορμάομαι *P.* to rush after; to follow closely.

μεθ-ορμίζω to bring to another anchorage — *intr.* and *M.* to sail to another place.

μέθυ, υος, τό wine.

μεθύσκω to make drunk. — *P.* to get drunk.

μέθυσος 3 drunk(en).

μεθ-ύστερος 3 later.

μεθύω to be drunk; to be drenched.

μείγνῡμι = μίγνῡμι.

μειδάω, μειδιάω to smile.

μειζότερος, μείζων *comp.* of μέγας.

μεικτός 3 = μικτός.

μείλᾱς = μέλας.

μείλιγμα, τό sedative, means of appeasing; propitiation.

μείλινος 3 = μέλινος.

μείλιον, τό love-gift.

μειλίσσω to make mild, soothe, propitiate. — *M.* to extenuate.

μειλιχίη, ἡ mildness.

μειλίχιος 3, μείλιχος 2 mild, gentle, sweet, soft, kind, gracious, bland.

μειον-εκτέω to have too little, to be at a disadvantage.

μειόω to lessen; to degrade. — *P.* to decrease. — *M.* to be inferior.

μειράκιον, τό boy, lad, young man. [boyish.]

μειρακιώδης 2 youthful;/

μείρομαι to receive as one's share; *perf.* ἔμμορα to have one's share; εἵμαρται it is decreed by fate; εἱμαρμένη fate, destiny.

μείς, μηνός, ὁ month.

μείωμα, τό deficiency.

μείων 2 *comp.* of μικρός.

μελάγ-γαιος 2 with black soil.

μελαγ-χαίτης, ου black-haired. [bile.]

μελάγ-χολος 2 with black/

μελάγ-χροος 2, μελαγ-χροιής 2 black-skinned, swarthy.

μέλαθρον, τό rafters of a roof; roof; house.

μελαίνω to blacken, dye black. — *intr.* and *M.* to grow black.

μελάμ-φυλλος 2 with dark foliage. [black.]

μελάν-δετος 2 bound with)

μελανιά, ή dark cloud.

μελανό-χροος, -χρως, οος 2 = μελάγχροος. [water.]

μελάν-υδρος 2 with black)

μελάνω = μελαίνω.

μέλας, αινα, αν black; dark, dusky, gloomy; τό μέλαν black dye; ink.

μέλδομαι *M.* to melt out.

μελεδαίνω to care for, tend; to be anxious.

μελεδών, ῶνος, ή, μελε-δώνη, ή, μελεδήμα, τό care, sorrow.

μελεδωνός, ὁ, ή attendant, guardian, nurse.

μελεϊστί *adv.* limb by limb.

μέλεος 3 fruitless, vain; careless, foolish; miserable, wretched.

μελετάω to take care of, to care for; to study, to prosecute earnestly, to practise, exercise; to exert oneself; to project, plan; to study; to declaim.

μελέτη, ή, μελέτημα, τό care, attention; study, practice, exercise; employment; pursuit; exercise of speaking. [diligently.]

μελετηρός 3 practising)

μελέτωρ, ορος, ὁ guardian: avenger.

μέλημα, τό object of care.

μέλι, τος, τό honey.

μελί-γηρυς, υος sweet-sounding.

μελίη, ή ash-tree; lance.

μελι-ηδής 2 honey-sweet.

μελί-κρατος, -κρητος 2 mixed with honey.

μελίνη, ή millet.

μέλινος 3 ashen.

μέλισσα, ή bee; honey.

μελίσσιος 3 made by bees.

μελιτόεις 3 rich in honey; made of honey.

μελιτόω to mix with honey. [er.]

μελιττουργός, ὁ bee-keep-)

μελί-φρων 2 honey-sweet.

μέλλησις, ή a being about, intention; a threatening, impending; delay.

μελλητής, οῦ, ὁ delayer.

μελλό-γαμος 2, μελλό-νυμφος 2 betrothed, about to be wedded.

μέλλω to be about, to be going, to intend, purpose; μέλλων future; to be destined; to be likely, probable, or certain; to be meaning to do; to delay, hesitate, scruple.

μελο-ποιός, ὁ lyric poet.

μέλος, τό limb; song, strain, melody.

μέλπηθρον, τό delight, amusement; sport, toy.

μέλπω and *M.* to sing and dance; to celebrate, praise.

μέλω and *M.* to be an object of care, to be a care

to; **μέλει μοί, μέλομαί τινος** I care for, take care of, tend.

μελ-φδός 2 singing.

μέμαα perf. of μάομαι with pres. sense.

μέμβλεται from μέλω.

μεμβράνᾱ, ἡ parchment.

μεμελημένως adv. carefully.　　[(μεθίημι).)

μεμετιμένος = μεθειμένος)

μέμηλα perf. of μέλω with pres. sense.　[pres. sense.)

μέμονα perf. of μάομαι with)

μεμπτός 3 to be blamed, despicable; blaming.

μέμφομαι M. to blame, reproach, reject, find fault with, despise.　　[μαι.)

μεμφι-μοιρέω = μέμφο-)

μεμφί-μοιρος 2 discontented.　　[discontent.)

μέμφις, ἡ blame, reproach;)

μέν conj. indeed, rather, certainly; **μέν ... δέ** on the one hand ... on the other; as well as.

μενεαίνω to long for ardently, to desire; to be angry.

μενε-δήϊος 2, **μενε-πτό-λεμος** 2 steadfast, staunch, brave.　　[fast, patient.)

μενετός 3 lasting, stead-)

μενε-χάρμης, ου, μενέ-χαρμος 2 = μενε-δήϊος.

μενο-εικής 2 plentiful; satisfying, heart-pleasing;

μενοινάω, -έω to have a mind, to intend, purpose; to reflect.

μένος, τό desire, ardour, wish, purpose; anger;

courage, spirit, vigour; power, strength; violence.

μὲν οὖν conj. indeed, rather; yet.

μενοῦνγε conj. rather.

μεντᾶν = μέντοι ἄν.

μέντοι conj. indeed, rather, certainly, of course; yet, however, nevertheless.

μένω to abide, stay, stay behind, linger; to remain, continue; to stand one's ground; trans. to await, expect, wait for.

μερίζω to divide into parts, attribute. — M. to be at variance.

μέριμνα, ἡ care, trouble.

μεριμνάω to care, to be anxious or thoughtful.

μερίμνημα, τό = μέριμνα.

μερίς, ίδος, ἡ part, portion, share, party; class, company.

μερισμός, ὁ a dividing, distributing; separation.

μεριστής, οῦ, ὁ divider.

μέρμερος 2 startling, horrible, dreadful.

μερμηρίζω to be anxious or thoughtful, to ponder; to devise.

μέρμῑς, ῑθος, ἡ string, cord.

μέρος, τό part, portion, share, lot; class; turn; station, rank; piece, section; party; district, place.

μέροφ, οπος mortal; others: endowed with speech.

μεσαι-πόλιος 2 half-gray.

μεσάμβρίη, ἡ = μεσημβρία.

μέσ-αυλος = μέσσαυλος.

μεσεύω to be neutral.

μεσηγύ(ς) adv. in the middle, between; meanwhile.

μεσήεις 3 middling.

μεσ-ημβρία, ἡ midday, south. [southern.]

μεσ-ημβρινός 3 at noon;

μεσῑτεύω to be a mediator.

μεσό-γαια, -γεια, ἡ inland, midland.

μεσό-γαιος 2 interior.

μεσό-δμη, ἡ cross-beam, cross-plank with a hole for the mast.

μεσ-όμφαλος 2 from the centre of the earth, central.

μεσο-ποτάμιος 2 between two rivers.

μέσος 3 middle, in the middle; moderate, middling, indifferent; impartial, neutral. τὸ μέσον the middle, centre; space between; interval; difference; distance; middle number; moderation; impartiality, neutrality; public(ity). [wall.]

μεσό-τοιχον, τό partition-

μεσο-τομέω to cut through the middle. [mid-heaven.]

μεσ-ουράνημα, τό zenith,

μεσόω to be in the middle, to be half over. [middle.]

μέσσατος 3 quite in the

μέσσ-αυλος, ὁ. μέσσαυλον, τό inner court, farm, stable.

μεσσηγύ = μεσηγύ.

μεσσίας, ου, ὁ the Messiah.

μεσσο-παγής 2 driven in to the middle.

μέσσος 3 = μέσος. [sated.]

μεστός 3 full, filled up;

μεστόω to fill up.

μέσφα adv. = μέχρι till.

μετά adv. among them; besides: afterwards. — prp. with gen. among, between; with, together with; at; according to. — with dat. among, in company with. — with acc. into the middle (of); in quest or pursuit of, after, behind; next to, next after; according to.

μετα-βαίνω to pass to another place, to pass over or on.

μετα-βάλλω to turn over, to turn about; to change, alter; to exchange. — intr., M. and P. to be changed. undergo a change; to change one's mind, fall off to; to exchange, traffic; to change one's clothes; to turn oneself; to take on one's back.

μετά-βασις, ἡ a passing over, shifting.

μετα-βιβάζω to carry over or away; to alter.

μετα-βολή, ἡ exchange, traffic; change; mutability.

μετα-βουλεύω and M. to decree after; to change one's mind.

μετ-άγγελος, ὁ, ἡ messenger, go-between.

μετα-γειτνιών, ῶνος, ὁ second Attic month (August to September).

μετα-γιγνώσκω to change one's mind; to repeal; to repent. [σις, ἡ repentance.]

μετά-γνοια, μετά-γνω-

μετα-γράφω to alter something written. — M. to have something translated.

μετ-άγω to convey to another place; to march after.

μετα-δαίνυμαι *M.* to partake of a feast.

μετα-δήμιος 2 native; at home.   [share of.]

μετα-δίδωμι to give a)

μετα-δίωκτος 2 overtaken.

μετα-διώκω to pursue, overtake; to follow close upon.

μετα-δοκεῖ τινι one changes one's mind, one repents.   [per.)

μετα-δόρπιος 2 after sup-)

μετά-δοσις, ἡ the giving a share.   [ning after.)

μετα-δρομάδην *adv.* run-)

μετα-δρομή, ἡ pursuit.

μετά-δρομος 2 pursuing; punishing.   [tion; change.]

μετά-θεσις, ἡ transposi-)

μετα-θέω to run after.

μετα-ίζω to take one's seat beside.   [to set out.)

μετ-αίρω to carry away;)

μετ-αίσσω to rush after.

μετ-αιτέω to demand one's share.   [complice.)

μετ-αίτιος 2 accessory; ac-)

μετ-αίχμιον, τό space between two armies; disputed frontier.   [to call in.)

μετα-καλέω to call back;)

μετα-κιάθω to follow after; to pursue; to visit; to march over.

μετα-κινέω to remove. — *M.* to depart.   [changed.)

μετα-κίνητός 3 to be)

μετα-κίω = μετακιάθω.

μετα-κλαίω to weep afterwards.

μετα-κλίνομαι *P.* to turn to the other side.

μετα-λαγχάνω to get a share of.

μετα-λαμβάνω to get a share, partake; to take in exchange. — *M.* to claim to oneself, assume.

μετα-λήγω to leave off.

μετά-ληψις, ἡ a partaking; changing.

μετ-αλλαγή, ἡ change.

μετ-αλλάσσω to exchange; to alter; to undergo a change.

μεταλλάω to question, inquire, search after.

μέταλλον, τό pit, mine; quarry.   [breasts.)

μετα-μάζιος 2 between the)

μετα-μανθάνω to learn differently: to unlearn.

μετα-μέλεια, ἡ, μετά-μελος, ὁ change of mind, repentance.

μετα-μέλει μοι, μετα-μέλομαι *P.* I repent.

μετα-μίγνυμι, -μίσγω to mix among, confound.

μετα-μορφόω to transform.

μετα-μώνιος 2 idle, vain; useless.

μετ-αναγιγνώσκω to make one alter his mind.

μετ-ανάστασις, ἡ migration.   [derer, alien.)

μετανάστης, ου, ὁ wan-)

μετα-νίσσομαι to pass over.

μετ-ανίσταμαι *M.* to change one's abode, to emigrate.

μετα-νοέω to change one's mind; to repent.

μετά-νοια, ἡ = μετάγνοια.

μεταξύ *adv.* and *prp.* with *gen.* between; meanwhile; afterwards; during.

μετα-παύομαι to rest in the mean time.

μετα-παυσωλή, ἡ rest, repose between.

μετα-πείθω to persuade to another opinion.

μετα-πέμπω and *M.* to send for, summon; to recall.

μετα-πίπτω to undergo a change; to fall differently; to be altered.

μετα-ποιέω to alter. — *M.* to lay claim to.

μετα-πορεύομαι *P.* to go after, to avenge.

μετα-πρεπής 2 excellent.

μετα-πρέπω to be conspicuous or excellent.

μετα-πύργιον, τό wall between two towers. [form.]

μετα-ρρυθμίζω to trans-}

μετ-άρσιος 2 lifted up; high in the air; on the high sea.

μετ-αροιόω to lift up.

μετα-σεύομαι *M.* to rush after; to rush up to.

μετα-σπάω to draw to the other side.

μέτασσαι, αἱ lambs of middle age.

μετά-στασις, ἡ a changing of place, removal; banishment; migration; change of government, revolution.

μετα-στένω to bewail afterwards.

μετα-στοιχί *adv.* in a line one after another.

μετα-στρέφω to turn about or round, to change one's

course; to alter. — *intr.* and *P.* to turn oneself to, to regard.

μετά-σχεσις, ἡ a partaking.

μετα-σχηματίζω to transform, remodel; to refer or apply to.

μετα-τάσσω to arrange differently. — *M.* to change one's opinion.

μετα-τίθημι to place among; to place differently; to alter, change. — *M.* to change one's opinion, to retract; to fall off; to impute, ascribe.

μετα-τρέπομαι *M.* to turn oneself round; to regard.

μετα-τροπαλίζομαι *M.* to turn frequently round (*intr.*).

μετ-αυδάω to speak among or to others.

μετ-αυτίκα *adv.* forthwith.

μετ-αῦτις *adv.* afterwards.

μετα-φέρω to carry to another place, to transfer; to change, alter; to change by mistake.

μετά-φημι to speak among or to others; to accost.

μετα-φορέω = μεταφέρω.

μετα-φράζομαι *M.* to consider after. [of the back.]

μετά-φρενον, τό upper part}

μετα-φωνέω = μετάφημι.

μετα-χειρίζω and *M.* to have in one's hands, to handle, manage, treat; to administer, govern; to pursue, practise. [migrate.]

μετα-χωρέω to go away,}

μέτ-ειμι[1] (-εῖναι) to be among, between, or near;

μέτεστί μοί τινος I have a claim or share of.

μέτ-ειμι[2] (-ιέναι) to go between or among; to go away; to come up to; to go after, follow, pursue, avenge; to visit; to strive after; to practise, manage.

μετ-εῖπον see μετάφημι.

μετ-εκβαίνω to step over into.

μετ-εμβιβάζω to put on board another ship.

μετ-ενδύω to put other clothes on.   [others.]

μετ-εξ-έτεροι 3 some

μετ-έπειτα adv. afterwards, thereupon.   [(ιέναι).]

μετ-έρχομαι = μέτειμι

μετ-εύχομαι M. to change one's wish.

μετ-έχω to have a share of, partake (of), to enjoy with others.

μετ-εωρίζω to lift up, raise; to excite, buoy up, encourage. — P. to rise; to come to the high sea; to be excited.

μετ-έωρος 2 lifted up, raised on high, suspended in the air, aloft; on the high sea; being in suspense, anxious, excited; fluctuating, doubtful; τὸ μετέωρον the high sea; τὰ μετέωρα things on high, high places, heavenly bodies, phenomena of the sky.

μετ-ίσχω = μετέχω.

μετ-οικεσία, ἡ emigration; captivity.

μετ-οικέω to change one's abode; to be a μέτοικος.

μετ-οίκησις, μετ-οικία, ἡ a living with; change of abode, migration.

μετ-οικίζω to bring to another abode, to settle as colonists.

μετ-οίκιον, τό tax paid by a μέτοικος.

μέτ-οικος 2 living with; foreigner, alien suffered to settle at Athens.

μετ-οίχομαι M. to have gone through; to be in pursuit of, to go after.

μετ-οκλάζω to squat timidly.   [new name.]

μετ-ονομάζω to call by a

μετ-οπάζω to give to companion.

μετ-όπιν, μετ-όπισθεν adv. behind, backwards, from behind; after(wards).

μετ-οπωρινός 3 autumnal.

μετ-όπωρον, τό autumn.

μετ-ουσία, ἡ, μετοχή, ἡ a partaking, communion, share.

μετ-οχλίζω to remove out of the way by a lever or by force.   [partaker.]

μέτ-οχος 2 partaking;

μετρέω to measure; to pass over; to estimate, compute.

μέτρημα, τό measure.

μέτρησις, ἡ a measuring.

μετρητής, οῦ, ὁ a liquid measure = 9 gallons.

μετρητικός 3 belonging to measuring.

μετριάζω to be moderate.

μετριο - παθέω to be lenient.

μέτριος 3 moderate, within measure; ordinary, convenient, sufficient, tolerable; fair, just, temperate, simple, orderly, honest, modest; indifferent, little.

μετριότης, ητος, ἡ moderation, modesty; average measure.

μέτρον, τό measure, rule, standard; vessel for measuring; size, measured space; full measure; prime of life; metre.

μετ-ωπηδόν adv. in frontline. [head.]

μετ-ώπιος 2 on the fore-

μέτ-ωπον, τό forehead; front, fore part.

μέχρι adv. and prp. with gen. until, unto, as far as; within, during; as long as.

μή adv. not, that not.

μηδαμά, μηδαμῆ adv. not at all; nowhere; never.

μηδαμόθεν adv. from no place.

μηδαμός 3 = μηδείς.

μηδαμοῦ adv. nowhere; not at all.

μηδαμῶς = μηδαμά.

μηδέ adv. and not, but not; nor.

μηδ-είς, μηδε-μία, μηδ-έν no one, none, not even one; nothing. [at any time.]

μηδέ-ποτε adv. never, not

μηδέ-πω adv. not as yet.

μηδ-έτερος 3 neither of the two. [side.]

μηδετέρωσε adv. to neither

μηδίζω to side with the Persians.

μηδισμός, ὁ a siding with the Persians.

μήδομαι to devise, counsel, advise; to plot, contrive, decree.

μῆδος¹, τό thought, plan, scheme, counsel.

μῆδος², τό a man's yard.

μηθείς = μηδείς. [shriek.]

μηκάομαι M. to bleat; to

μηκάς, άδος bleating.

μηκ-έτι adv. no more, no longer.

μήκιστος 3 longest; tallest; greatest. [greatness.]

μῆκος, τό length; tallness;

μή-κοτε = μήποτε.

μηκύνω to lengthen, prolong, extend.

μήκων, ωνος, ἡ poppy; head of a poppy; poppy-juice.

μηλέα, ἡ apple-tree.

μήλειος 2 of a sheep.

μηλο-βοτήρ, ῆρος, ὁ shepherd. [sheep.]

μηλό - βοτος 2 grazed by

μῆλον¹, τό apple; tree-fruit.

μῆλον², τό sheep; goat.

μηλο-σφαγέω to kill sheep.

μηλ-οφ, οπος like apples, golden.

μηλωτή, ἡ a sheep's skin.

μήν adv. truly, verily, indeed; yet, however; οὐ μὴν ἀλλά not but.

μήν, μηνός, ὁ month, new moon.

μήνη, ἡ moon.

μηνιθμός, ὁ = μῆνις.

μήνῑμα, τό cause of anger.

μῆνις, ιος, ἡ anger, wrath.
μηνίω to be angry or wroth.
μηνο‑ειδής 2 crescent‑shaped.
μήνῡμα, τό information.
μηνῡτής, οῦ, ὁ informer, denouncer.
μήνῡτρον, τό reward for information.
μηνύω to make known, denounce, betray; to inform, announce. [ever.
μή‑ποτε adv. never; lest)
μή‑που adv. lest anywhere.
μή‑πω adv. not yet.
μή‑πως adv. lest anyhow.
μῆρα, τά, pl. of μηρός.
μήρινθος, ἡ cord, string.
μηρίον, τό, μηρός, ὁ thigh‑bone, thigh.
μηρύομαι M. to furl the sails. [causer.
μήστωρ, ωρος, ὁ counsellor;)
μή‑τε adv. and not; μήτε ... μήτε neither ... nor.
μήτηρ, μητρός, ἡ mother.
μητιάω and M. to meditate, consider; to devise, contrive, invent.
μητί‑ετα, ὁ adviser.
μητιόεις 3 ingenious.
μητίομαι = μητιάω.
μή‑τις, τι none, no one, nothing; lest any one, lest anything.
μῆτις, ιος and ιδος, ἡ counsel, wisdom; device, project. [(up)on no account.)
μή‑τοι adv. in no wise,)
μήτρᾱ, ἡ womb. [cide.)
μητρ‑αλοίᾱς, ᾱ, ὁ matri‑)
μητρόθεν adv. from the mother's side.

μητρο‑πάτωρ, ορος, ὁ one's mother's father.
μητρό‑πολις, ἡ mother‑city, mother‑country, mother‑state; capital.
μητρυιά, ἡ stepmother.
μητρῷος, μητρώϊος 3 of a mother, maternal.
μήτρως, ωος, ὁ maternal uncle.
μηχανάω and M. to make by art, to construct, devise, contrive, prepare.
μηχανή, ἡ, μηχάνημα, τό artificial implement, instrument, machine; engine of war; contrivance, artificial means, device, mode, way.
μηχανητικός 3, μηχανικός 3, μηχανόεις 3 ingenious, inventive, clever.
μηχανο‑ποιός, ὁ maker of war‑engines. [cunning.)
μηχανο‑ρράφος 2 crafty,)
μῆχος, τό = μηχανή.
μιαίνω to dye; to stain, soil, pollute.
μιαι‑φονέω to slay.
μιαι‑φόνος 2 blood‑stained; murderer.
μιαρίᾱ, ἡ wickedness.
μιαρός 3 stained, polluted; wicked.
μίασμα, τό, μιασμός, ὁ stain, defilement, pollution, abomination.
μιάστωρ, ορος, ὁ wicked person, defiler; avenger.
μιγάζομαι M. = μίγνυμαι.
μιγάς, άδος mixed, confused.
μίγδα adv. promiscuously.

μῖγμα, τό mixture.

μῖγνῡμι, μῖγνύω to mix, mix up, mingle, bring together. — *P.* and *M.* to be mingled or brought together; to meet with; to lie with.

μῑκρο-λογέομαι *M.* to be a pedant, to be given to trifles. [ness, pedantry.]

μῑκρο-λογία, ἡ minute-]

μῑκρο-λόγος 2 narrow-minded. pedantic; stingy.

μῑκρο-πολίτης, ου, ὁ citizen of a small town or state.

μῑκρός 3 small, little, short; petty, mean; poor, trivial; young.

μῑκρότης, ητος, ἡ smallness, littleness.

μῑκρο-φῠχία, ἡ meanness of mind. [minded.]

μῑκρό-φῡχος 2 narrow-]

μῑκτός 3 mixed.

μίλιον, τό Roman mile.

μιλτ-ηλιφής 2 painted red.

μιλτο-πάρῃος 2 red-cheeked. [nium.]

μίλτος, ἡ red chalk; mi-]

μιλτόω to paint red.

μῑμέομαι *M.* to imitate, copy; to represent.

μίμημα, τό, μίμησις, ἡ an imitating, imitation; copy.

μιμητικός 3 imitative.

μιμητός 3 worth to be imitated.

μιμνάζω to stay, remain.

μιμνήσκω, μιμνῄσκω to remind(of), put in mind(of), admonish. — *P.* to remember, recall to one's me-

mory; to mention; to be mindful of.

μίμνω = μένω. [player.]

μῖμος, ὁ imitator, actor,]

μίν him, her, it; himself.

μινύθω to diminish, lessen, weaken; to decrease, decay, perish.

μίνυνθα *adv.* a short time.

μινυνθάδιος 2 lasting a short time.

μινυρίζω and *M.* to whimper, whine. [lation.]

μῖξις, ἡ a mixing; copu-]

μῑξο-βάρβαρος 2 half barbarian half Greek.

μῑξο-πάρθενος 2 half maiden (half serpent).

μῑσ-ανθρωπίᾱ, ἡ manhatred.

μῑσ-άνθρωπος, ἡ manhater. [of glens.]

μισγ-άγκεια, ἡ meeting]

μίσγω = μίγνυμι.

μῑσέω to hate.

μίσημα, τό = μῖσος.

μῑσητός 3 hated; to be hated.

μισθ-αποδοσίᾱ, ἡ payment of wages, recompense.

μισθ-αποδότης, ου, ὁ recompenser. [pay.]

μισθ-αρνέω to serve for]

μισθ-αρνίᾱ, ἡ hired service. [τός.]

μίσθιος 3 and 2 = μισθω-]

μισθο-δοσίᾱ, ἡ payment of wages.

μισθο-δοτέω to pay wages.

μισθο-δότης, ου, ὁ payer of wages.

μισθός, ὁ wages, pay, hire, rent, salary; reward; punishment.

μισθο-φορά, ἡ receipt of wages; pay.

μισθο-φορέω to receive wages; to serve for hire.

μισθο-φορία, ἡ hired service.

μισθο-φόρος 2 serving for hire; mercenary, hireling.

μισθόω to let out for hire, farm out. — *P.* to be hired for pay. — *M.* to engage on hire, to farm.

μίσθωμα, τό stipulated pay, rent; hired dwelling.

μίσθωσις, ἡ a letting for hire; = μίσθωμα.

μισθωτός 3 hired, to be hired; mercenary, hireling. [mocracy.]

μισό-δημος 2 hating de-)

μισο-λογία, ἡ hatred of letters.

μισό-λογος 2 hating argument. [bad.)

μισο-πονηρέω to hate the)

μῖσος, τό hatred, enmity; hateful thing or person.

μισο-τύραννος 2 tyrant-hating.

μισό-χρηστος 2 hating the good. [pieces.)

μιστύλλω to cut into little)

μίτος, ἡ thread; web.

μίτρα, ἡ girdle; head-dress.

μιτρη-φόρος 2 wearing a μίτρα.

μιτώδης 2 thread-like.

μνᾶ, ᾶς, ἡ mine (= 100 drachms).

μνάομαι *M.* = μιμνήσκομαι; to covet, strive after; to woo, court.

μνεία, ἡ = μνήμη.

μνῆμα, τό, μνημεῖον, τό memorial, remembrance; monument; sepulchre.

μνήμη, ἡ memory, remembrance; faculty of memory; monument; mention, relation; renown.

μνημονεύω to remember, recollect; to mention.

μνημονικός 3 of good memory.

μνημοσύνη, ἡ = μνήμη.

μνημόσυνον, τό = μνῆμα.

μνήμων 2 mindful, remembering, unforgetting.

μνησι-κακέω to remember old wrongs, to be resentful.

μνηστεύω and *M.* to woo, court, seek in marriage. — *P.* to be betrothed.

μνηστήρ, ῆρος, ὁ wooer, suitor.

μνῆστις, ἡ = μνήμη.

μνηστός 3 wooed, wedded.

μνηστύς, ύος, ἡ a wooing, seeking in marriage.

μογέω to toil, labour; to suffer, be in distress.

μογι-λάλος 2 stammering.

μογερός 3 distressed, wretched.

μόγις *adv.* with toil, hardly.

μογοσ-τόκος 2 causing throes in child-birth.

μόδιος, ὁ a corn-measure.

μόθος, ὁ noise or throng of battle.

μοῖρα, ἡ part, portion, division; portion of land; party; share; the due, due reverence; rank; lot, destiny, fate; death. [fortune.)

μοιρη-γενής 2 favourite of)

μοιρίδιος 3 destined, fated.

μοιχ-άγρια, τά fine of one taken in adultery.

μοιχαλίς, ίδος, ἡ adulterous. [tery.]

μοιχάω to commit adultery.

μοιχείᾱ, ἡ adultery.

μοιχεύω to commit adultery, to seduce to adultery. [adultery.]

μοιχίδιος 3 begotten in

μοιχός, ὁ adulterer.

μολεῖν inf. aor. of βλώσκω

μόλιβος, ὁ = μόλυβδος.

μόλις adv. with difficulty, hardly. [beggar.]

μολοβρός, ὁ dirty fellow,

μολπή, ἡ song, dance, music; play, amusement.

μολύβδαινα, ἡ, μολυβδίς, ίδος, ἡ leaden bullet.

μόλυβδος, ὁ lead.

μολύνω to stain, sully.

μολυσμός, ὁ defilement, pollution.

μομφή, ἡ blame, complaint.

μον-αρχέω to be a monarch.

μον-αρχίᾱ, ἡ monarchy, sovereignty.

μόν-αρχος, ὁ monarch.

μονάς, άδος, ἡ a unit.

μοναχῇ, -ῇ adv. single, alone.

μονή, ἡ a staying; an abiding; sojourn, dwelling; tarrying.

μόνιμος 2 staying; steadfast, constant; faithful.

μονο-γενής 2 only child.

μονο-ειδής 2 of one kind, simple.

μονό-κροτος 2 with one bench of oars.

μονο-μαχέω to fight in single combat. [bat.]

μονο-μαχίᾱ, ἡ single com-

μονό-ξυλος 2 made of one piece of wood.

μόνος 3 alone, only; forsaken, left alone; adv. μόνως, μόνον only, merely.

μον-όφθαλμος 2 one-eyed.

μονόω to leave alone; to make single. — P. to be forsaken; to be taken apart.

μόρα, ἡ division of Spartan infantry. [tree.]

μορίᾱ, ἡ the sacred olive-

μόριμος 2 = μόρσιμος.

μόριον, τό part; division; limb. [spectre, phantom.]

μορμολύκειον, τό bugbear,

μορμολύττομαι M. to frighten (children).

μορμύρω to roar.

μορμώ, οῦς, μορμών, ὁ ος, ἡ bugbear, spectre.

μορόεις, 3 mulberry-like.

μόρος, ὁ fate, destiny, death.

μόρσιμος 2 destined, fatal.

μορύσσω to blacken, soil.

μορφή, ἡ form, shape, figure, appearance, fashion; image; beauty, grace.

μόρφνος 3 dark-coloured.

μορφόω to form, shape.

μόρφωσις, ἡ a shaping; form, semblance.

μόσσυν, υνος, ὁ wooden tower or house.

μόσχειος 2 of a calf.

μοσχο-ποιέω to make a calf.

μόσχος, ὁ shoot, sprout; descendant; calf, young bull.

μουν- see μον-.

μουνάξ *adv.* alone, singly.

μουνόθεν *adv.* = μουνάξ.

μουνό-λιθος 2 made of one stone.

μοῦνος 3 = μόνος. [one.]

μουνο-φυής 2 grown in|

μουνυχιών, ῶνος, ὁ tenth Attic month (April to May).

μουσικός 3 of the Muses, devoted to the Muses, musical; musician; (lyric) poet; scholar, man of letters; ἡ μουσική, τὰ μουσικά art of the Muses, music, song, poetry, dancing, arts, letters, accomplishments.

μουσο-ποιός 2 poet, singer.

μοχθέω to toil, to weary oneself, to be troubled or distressed, to suffer.

μόχθημα, τό, μοχθηρία, ἡ toil, hardship; wretchedness; badness, wickedness.

μοχθηρός 3 toilsome, miserable, wretched; bad, wicked, villainous.

μοχθίζω to suffer.

μόχθος, ὁ toil, hardship; distress, misery.

μοχλεύω, μοχλέω to move by a lever.

μοχλός, ὁ lever; bar; pole.

μῦ-γαλῆ, ἡ shrew-mouse.

μῦδαλέος 3 dripping, wet.

μῦδάω to be dripping or wet; to decay, rot.

μύδρος, ὁ red-hot metal; lump of metal.

μῦελόεις 3 full of marrow.

μῦελός, ὁ marrow; brain.

μυέω to initiate into the mysteries; to instruct.

μύζω, μυζέω to suck.

μῦθέομαι *M.* to speak, say, tell; to name, explain; to consider.

μῦθο-λογεύω, -λογέω to tell tales, fables, or legends; to converse fully.

μῦθο-λογικός 3 fabulist.

μῦθος, ὁ word, speech, public speech; narration, news, intelligence; conversation, talk; thought, project, plan; advice, order; report, tale, story; affair, occurrence.

μῦθώδης 2 legendary.

μυῖα, ἡ fly.

μῦκάομαι *M.* to bellow, low, bray; to roar.

μῦκηθμός, ὁ a bellowing.

μύκης, ητος, ὁ mushroom; end of a scabbard.

μυκτήρ, ῆρος, ὁ nostril; nose; snout.

μυκτηρίζω to mock.

μύλαξ, ακος millstone.

μύλη, ἡ mill. [ground.]

μυλή-φατος 2 bruised,]

μυλικός, μύλινος 3 λίθος millstone. [stone.]

μυλο-ειδής 2 like a mill-]

μύλος, ὁ = μύλη; μύλαξ.

μυλών, ῶνος, ὁ mill-house.

μύνη, ἡ pretext. [τήρ.]

μυξωτήρ, ῆρος, ὁ = μυκ-]

μῦριάκις *adv.* ten thousand times.

μῦρί-αρχης, ου, μῦρί-αρχος, ὁ commander of ten thousand men.

μῦριάς, άδος, ἡ myriad (10 000).

μυρίζω to anoint.

μυρίκη, ἡ tamarisk. [risk.
μυρίκινος 3 of the tama-]
μύριοι 3 ten thousand.
μῦριό-καρπος 2 with countless fruit.
μῦριό-λεκτος 2 said ten
thousand times.
μῦρίος 3 countless, num-
berless, immense, endless.
μῦριο-φόρος 2 ναῦς big
transport-ship.
μύρμηξ, ηκος, ὁ ant.
μύρομαι M. to flow; to
melt into tears.
μύρον, τό fragrant oil, unguent, balsam.
μυρρίνη, μυρσίνη, ἡ myrtle,
myrtle-twig.
μύρτον, τό myrtle-berry.
μῦς, μυός, ὁ mouse.
μυσαρός 3 foul, loathsome.
μύσος, τό abomination;
atrocity.   [mystery.
μυστήριον, τό secret rite,]
μύστης, ου, ὁ one initi-
tiated.   [cret.
μυστικός 3 mystical; se-]
μυχμός, ὁ a groaning, sighing.   [most corner.
μυχοίτατος 3 in the in-]

μυχόνδε adv. to the in-
terior.
μυχός, ὁ inmost corner,
interior, recess.
μύω to be shut or closed;
to cease; to shut the eyes.
μυών, ῶνος, ὁ knot of
muscles.   [sighted.
μυωπάζω to be short-]
μύ-ωψ[1], ωπος short-sighted.
μύωψ[2], ωπος, ὁ gad-fly;
goad, spur.   [din.
μῶλος, ὁ toil; battle, battle-]
μῶλυ, υος, τό a magic herb.
μώλ-ωψ, ωπος stripe, mark,
bruise.
μῶμαι = μάομαι.
μωμάομαι M., μωμεύω to
blame, revile.   [shame.
μῶμος, ὁ blame; disgrace,]
μῶν = μὴ οὖν is it not?
μῶνυξ, υχος soliped.
μωραίνω to be silly or
foolish; to make foolish.
— P. to become a fool; to
become insipid.
μωρία, ἡ folly.
μωρο-λογία, ἡ silly speech.
μωρός, μῶρος 3 foolish,
stupid; insipid, tasteless.

N

N, ν (νῦ) thirteenth letter of the
alphabet; as a numeral ν' = 50.
ναί adv. verily, truly, yes.
νᾱϊάς, άδος, ἡ water-nymph,
Naiad.
ναιετάω = ναίω.   [ship.
νάϊος 3 belonging to a]
νᾱῗς, ῗδος, ἡ = ναϊάς.
ναίχι = ναί.
ναίω[1] to dwell, abide, in-

habit; to settle one in. —
P. to be inhabited; to settle.
ναίω[2] = νάω.
νάκη, ἡ, νάκος, τό fleece.
νᾶμα, τό fountain, stream.
νᾱμέρτεια, ἡ = νημέρτεια.
νᾱός, ὁ temple.
ναπαῖος 3 of a wooded
vale.   [vale, dell, glen.
νάπη, ἡ, νάπος, τό wooded]

17*

νάρδος, ἡ nard; nard-oil.

ναρθηκο‑φόρος, ὁ staff-bearer, thyrsus-bearer.

νάρθηξ, ηκος, ὁ reed, cane, rod. [benumbed.]

ναρκάω to grow stiff or

νάρκισσος, ὁ narcissus, daffodil.

νᾱσιῶτις, ιδος = νησιῶτις.

νᾶσος, ἡ = νῆσος.

νάσσω to stamp down.

ναυ‑αγέω to be ship-wrecked.

ναυ‑αγίᾱ, ἡ shipwreck.

ναυ‑άγιον, τό (piece of a) wreck.

ναυ‑αγός 2 shipwrecked.

ναυ‑αρχέω to be a sea-captain or admiral.

ναυ‑αρχίᾱ, ἡ office of an admiral. [admiral.]

ναύ‑αρχος, ὁ sea-captain,

ναυ‑βάτης, ου, ὁ sailor, seaman; sea-soldier.

ναυηγέω etc. = ναυαγ‑.

ναυ‑κληρέω to be a ship-owner; to steer, govern.

ναυ‑κληρίᾱ, ἡ a seafaring, voyage. [captain.]

ναύ‑κληρος, ὁ shipowner,

ναύ‑κρᾱρος, ὁ captain; president of a division of citizens. [the sea.]

ναυ‑κρατέω to be lord of

ναυ‑κρατής 2, ναυ‑κρά‑τωρ, ορος shipowner; commanding the sea. [money.]

ναῦλον, τό fare, passage-

ναυ‑λοχέω to lie in a harbour, at anchor, or in wait.

ναύ‑λοχος 2 affording safe anchorage.

ναυ‑μαχέω to fight at sea.

ναυ‑μαχησείω to long for a sea-fight.

ναυ‑μαχίᾱ, ἡ battle at sea.

ναύ‑μαχος 2 suited to a sea-fight.

ναυ‑πηγέω to build ships.

ναυ‑πηγήσιμος 2 fit for shipbuilding.

ναυ‑πηγίᾱ, ἡ shipbuilding.

ναυ‑πηγός, ὁ shipbuilder.

ναῦς, νεώς, ἡ ship.

ναῦσθλον, τό = ναῦλον.

ναυσί‑κλειτος 2, ναυσί‑κλυτος 2 famous for ships.

ναυσι‑πέρᾱτος 2 to be crossed by ships.

ναυσί‑πορος 2 navigable.

ναύ‑σταθμον, τό, ναύ‑σταθμος, ὁ harbour, anchorage, naval station.

ναυ‑στολέω to convey by sea; to go by sea, to voyage.

ναύτης, ου, ὁ = ναυβάτης.

ναυτικός 3 of or for a ship; naval; seafaring; τὸ ναυ‑τικόν fleet, navy.

ναυτιλίᾱ, ἡ a seafaring, navigation, voyage.

ναυτίλλομαι to go by ship, to sail. [man.]

ναυτίλος, ὁ sailor, ship-

ναυτο‑δίκαι, οἱ judges in commercial law-suits.

νάω to flow (over).

νεάζω to be young or younger, to grow up.

νεακόνητος 2 newly or lately whetted.

νεαλής 2 young, fresh.

νεᾱνίᾱς, ου youthful; young man, youth.

νεᾱνιεύομαι M. to be youthful, vigorous, wanton, or boastful.

νεᾱνικός 3 youthful, fresh, vigorous; wanton, insolent; hasty.

νεᾱνίς, ιδος, ἡ girl, maiden, young woman.

νεᾱνίσκος, ὁ = νεανίας.

νεᾱρός 3 youthful, fresh; = νέος.   [extreme.

νέατος 3 last, uttermost,|

νεβρίζω to wear a fawn's skin.   [fawn.|

νεβρός, ὁ, ἡ young deer,|

νεη-γενής 2 new-born.

νε-ήκης 2, **νε-ηκονής** 2 = νεακόνητος.

νε-ήλατον, τό honey-cake.

νέ-ηλυς, υδος newly come

νεηνίης etc. = νεανίας.

νείαιρα and **νείατος** 3 = νέατος.

νεικέω, **νεικείω** to quarrel, dispute; to scold, revile, insult.

νεῖκος, τό quarrel, dispute; a scolding, blaming, reproach; cause of quarrel; dispute before a judge; battle, fight.   [tom.|

νειόθεν adv. from the bot-|

νειόθι adv. at the bottom.

νειός, ἡ new or fallow land.

νείφω, **νίφω** to snow.

νεκάς, άδος, ἡ heap of slain men.   [corpse.|

νεκρός 3 dead; dead body,|

νεκρόω to kill, to make dead.

νέκρωσις, ἡ a making dead; deadness.

νέκταρ, αρος, τό nectar.

νεκτάρεος 3 like nectar; divine.

νέκυια, ἡ sacrifice for the dead.   [of the dead.|

νεκυο-μαντήϊον, τό oracle|

νέκυς, υος = νεκρός.

νεμέθω M. to graze.

νεμεσάω to be indignant, angry, or wroth; to find fault with, to blame. — M. and P. to be indignant; to be ashamed.

νεμεσητός 3 causing indignation; awful.

νεμεσίζομαι M. = νεμεσάω.

νέμεσις, ἡ indignation, anger, resentment; vengeance, punishment; wrong; remorse; sense of honour.

νέμος, τό pasture; grove, wood.

νέμω to divide; to distribute, assign, allot, grant; to possess, enjoy; to inhabit; to manage, control; to esteem, consider; to drive to pasture; to graze; to consume. — M. to distribute among themselves; to occupy; to control, manage; to enjoy; to graze, feed; to consume; to spread.

νεο-άλωτος 2 newly caught.

νεο-αρδής 2 newly watered.

νεό-γαμος 2 newly wedded.

νεο-γῑλός 3, **νεο-γνός** 2 new-born.

νεο-δαμώδης, ους, ὁ new citizen, one newly enfranchised.

νεό-δαρτος 2 newly flayed.

νεόθεν adv. anew, of late.

νεο-θηλής 2 fresh-sprouting.

νεοίη, ἡ youthful spirit.

νεο-κατάστατος 2 newly settled. [founded.]

νεό-κτιστος 2 newly

νέομαι to go; to come; to go away; to return.

νεο-μηνία, ἡ = νουμηνία.

νεο-πενθής 2 fresh-mourning.

νεό-πλυτος 2 newly washed.

νεό-ποκος 2 newly shorn.

νεό-πριστος 2 newly sawn.

νεό-ρραντος 2 newly sprinkled.

νεό-ρρυτος 2 fresh-flowing.

νέ-ορτος 2 newly risen.

νέος 3 young, youthful, early; thoughtless; new, fresh; unheard of, strange, unexpected; νεώτερόν τι novation; revolution; news, bad things; adv. νέον newly, anew, afresh; lately, just now. [cleaned.]

νεό-σμηκτος 2 newly

νεο-σπάς, άδος newly plucked.

νεοσσεύω = νοσσεύω.

νεοσσιά, ἡ nest with young birds. [child.]

νεοσσός, ὁ a young one;

νεό-στροφος 2 newly twisted.

νεο-σφαγής 2 newly killed.

νεό-τευκτος 2, νεο-τευχής 2 newly made.

νεότης, ητος, ἡ youth, youthfulness; body of young men.

νεό-τομος 2 newly cut.

νεουργός = νεότευκτος.

νε-ούτατος 2 newly wounded.

νεό-φυτος 2 newly converted.

νεο-χάρακτος 2 newly imprinted.

νεοχμός 2 = νέος.

νεοχμόω = νεωτερίζω.

νέποδες, ων, οἱ children.

νέρθεν = ἔνερθεν.

νέρτερος 3 lower, nether; infernal.

νεῦμα, τό nod, sign.

νεῦμαι = νέομαι.

νευρά, ἡ, νεῦρον, τό sinew, tendon; cord; bow-string; cord of a sling; strength, vigour.

νευρο-σπαδής 2, νευρό-σπαστος 2 drawn back, driven from the bow-string.

νευστάζω, νεύω to nod, beckon, bow; to promise.

νεφέλη, ἡ cloud, darkness; multitude.

νεφελ-ηγερέτης, -έτα, ὁ cloud-gatherer.

νέφος, τό = νεφέλη.

νεφρῖτις, ιδος, ἡ disease in the kidneys.

νεφρός, ὁ kidney.

νέω¹ to swim.

νέω² to spin. [to load.]

νέω³ to heap up, pile up;

νέω⁴ = νέομαι.

νεω-κόρος, ὁ, ἡ sweeper in a temple, temple-servant.

νε-ώρης 2 new, young.

νεώριον, τό dock-yard.

νέωρος 3 = νεώρης.

νεώς, ώ, ὁ = ναός (also gen. of ναῦς).

νεώς-οικοι, οἱ ship's houses, docks. [cently.]

νεωστί adv. lately, re-

νεωτερίζω to make changes

or innovations; to revolutionize.

νεωτερικός 3 youthful.

νεωτερισμός, ὁ, νεωτεροποιΐα, ἡ innovation, revolution.

νεωτερο-ποιός 2 innovating, revolutionary.

νή *adv.* yea, truly.

νηγάτεος 3 newly made, splendid.

νήγρετος 2 unwaking, sleeping soundly.

νήδυια, τά bowels.

νήδυμος 2 sweet, refreshing.

νηδύς, ύος, ἡ belly; stomach; womb.

νηέω = νέω³ to heap up.

νήθω = νέω² to spin.

νηϊάς, ή = ναϊάς.

νήϊος 3 = νάϊος.

νηΐς, ιδος = ναΐς.

νῆϊς, ιδος not knowing.

νηΐτης, ου = νάϊος.

νη-κερδής 2 useless, without gain.

νηκουστέω to disobey.

νηλεής 2 pitiless; unpitied. [ιδος = νηλειτής.|

νηλειτής 2, *fem.* νηλεῖτις,|

νηλής 2 = νηλεής.

νηλίπους, ποδος barefooted.

νηλίτης 2, *fem.* νηλῖτις, ιδος guiltless.

νῆμα, τό thread, yarn.

νημερτής 2 infallible, unerring.

νηνεμία, ἡ calm.

νήνεμος 2 breezeless, calm.

νηός, ὁ = νεώς; = νηός νεώς (ναῦς). [row.|

νη-πενθής 2 soothing sor-|

νηπιάζω to be a child.

νηπιαχεύω to play like a child.

νηπίαχος 2 = νήπιος.

νηπιέη, ἡ childishness.

νήπιος 3 infant, childish, foolish, harmless; weak.

νή-ποινος 2 without recompense; unavenged.

νηπύτιος 3 = νήπιος.

νήριτος 2 numberless.

νησίδιον, τό, νησίον, τό, νησίς, ιδος, ἡ small island.

νησιώτης, ου, ὁ islander.

νησιῶτις, ιδος insular.

νῆσος, ἡ island; peninsula.

νῆσσα, ἡ duck.

νηστεία, ἡ a fasting.

νηστεύω to fast.

νῆστις, ιδος and ιος fasting.

νησύδριον, τό = νησίδιον.

νητός 3 heaped up.

νηῦς, ἡ = ναῦς.

νηυσι-πέρητος 2 = ναυσιπέρητος.

νηφάλιος 3 sober.

νήφω to be sober.

νήχω and *M.* to swim.

νίζω to wash; to wash off, clean; to atone. — *M.* to wash oneself.

νῑκάω to conquer, prevail; to be superior or better; to win in court; to be victorious, carry the day; to vanquish, overcome, surpass.

νίκη, ἡ victory, conquest.

νῑκητήριον, τό prize of victory. [victory.|

νῑκητικός 3 conducing to|

νῑκη-φόρος bringing victory; victorious.

νῖκος, τό = νίκη.

νέν = αὐτόν, -ήν, -ό him, her, it.   [basin.]

νιπτήρ, ῆρος, ὁ washing-/

νίπτω = νίζω.

νίσσομαι, νίσομαι to go (away); to return.

νιφάς, άδος, ἡ snow-flake; snow-storm; snowy.

νιφετός, ὁ shower of snow.

νιφόεις 3 snow-covered.

νιφο-στιβής 2 passing over snow.

νίφω = νείφω.

νοέω to perceive, remark, notice, see; to think, consider; to devise, contrive; to intend, have a mind.

νόημα, τό thought; purpose, design; understanding; mind.

νοήμων 2 sensible.

νοητός 3 intelligible. [ous.]

νόθος 3 illegitimate; spuri-/

νόμαιον, τό custom, usage.

νομ-άρχης, ου, ὁ chief of a district.

νομάς, άδος, ὁ, ἡ roaming, wondering on pasture-grounds; nomad.

νομεύς, ὁ herdsman; rib of a ship.   [tend a flock.]

νομεύω to drive afield; to/

νομή, ἡ pasture; field; grazing flock; division, distribution.

νομίζω to hold or acknowledge as a custom or usage; to be wont; to adopt as a law; to use; to think, believe, acknowledge, take for; to be persuaded, judge. — P. to be in esteem; to be customary.

νομικός 3 legal; learned in the law; scribe.

νόμιμος 2 customary; legal, lawful; honest, righteous; τὰ νόμιμα custom, usage, law.

νόμισις, ἡ usage.

νόμισμα, τό usage, institution; current coin, money.

νομο-διδάσκαλος, ὁ teacher of the law.

νομο-θεσία, ἡ legislation.

νομο-θετέω to give laws, ordain by law.

νομο-θέτης, ου, ὁ lawgiver.

νομο-θετικός 3 law-giving.

νομός, ὁ = νομή; dwelling, residence; district; region.

νόμος, ὁ custom, usage; law, ordinance, statute; principle, rule, maxim; tune, mode of singing; song, melody.

νομο-φύλαξ, ακος, ὁ guardian of the laws.

νόος, νοῦς, ὁ mind, understanding, reason; thought; insight; purpose, intention; meaning, sense.

νοσέω to be sick.

νοσηλείᾱ, ἡ, νόσημα, τό = νόσος.   [sickly.]

νοσηρός 3 unhealthy;/

νόσος, ἡ sickness, disease, plague; insanity, madness; evil, distress; defect.

νοσσεύω to hatch.

νοσσιά, ἡ etc. = νεοσσιά etc.

νοστέω to return, come home; to travel.

νόστιμος 2 belonging to a return; returning.

νόστος, ὁ return home; travel, journey.

νόσφι(ν) adv. far, remote, apart; with gen. far from, away from; without, besides.

νοσφίζω to remove, put or take away; to rob. — M. to withdraw, retire; to forsake, abandon; to embezzle.

νοσώδης 2 = νοσηρός.

νοτερός 3 wet, moist; southern.

νοτίη, ἡ moisture, rain.

νότιος 3 and 2 = νοτερός.

νοτίς, ίδος, ἡ = νοτίη.

νότος, ὁ south or southwest wind; the south.

νου-θεσία, ἡ = νουθέτησις.

νου-θετέω to bring to mind, to warn, admonish, reprimand, chastise.

νου-θέτημα, τό, **νου-θέτησις**, ἡ admonition, warning.

νου-θετικός 3 admonitory.

νου-μηνίᾱ, ἡ new moon, first of the month.

νουν-εχής 2 sensible.

νοῦς, ὁ = νόος.

νοῦσος, ἡ = νόσος.

νύ = νύν.

νυκτερευτικός 3 fit for hunting by night.

νυκτερεύω to pass the night; to watch by night.

νυκτερινός 3 nightly; northern.

νυκτερίς, ίδος, ἡ bat.

νύκτερος 2 = νυκτερινός.

νυκτο-θήρᾱς, ου, ὁ hunting by night.

νυκτο-μαχίᾱ, ἡ night-battle. [watch.]

νυκτο-φύλαξ, ὁ night-

νύκτωρ adv. by night.

νυμφεῖος 3 bridal, nuptial; τὸ νυμφεῖον bride-chamber; marriage. [bride.]

νύμφευμα, τό marriage;

νυμφεύω and M. to wed, marry; to be married.

νύμφη, ἡ bride; young wife; maiden; nymph.

νυμφίδιος, **νυμφικός** 3 bridal, nuptial.

νυμφίος, ὁ bridegroom; husband. [chamber.]

νυμφών, ῶνος, ὁ bride-

νῦν, **νῦνί** adv. now, just now, at present; then, thereupon; therefore.

νύν, **νύ** adv. now, then; therefore.

νύξ, νυκτός, ἡ night.

νυός, ἡ daughter-in-law.

νύσσα, ἡ turning-stone, pillar on the race-course; winning-post; lists. [wound.]

νύσσω to prick, pierce,

νυστάζω to nod; to fall asleep; to slumber.

νυχθ-ήμερον, τό a day and night.

νύχιος 3 = νυκτερινός.

νώ = νῶι.

νώδυνος 2 soothing pain.

νωθής 2, **νωθρός** 3 lazy, sluggish; stupid.

νῶι, **νώ** we two. [us two.]

νωίτερος 3 belonging to

νωλεμές, **νωλεμέως** adv. incessantly; steadfastly.

νωμάω to distribute, portion out; to move to and

fro, brandish, wield, ply;
to direct, guide, govern;
to consider, observe, perceive. [or fame.]

νώνυμ(ν)ος 2 without name

νῶροφ, οπος flashing.
νωτίζω to turn one's back.
νῶτον, τό; **νῶτος, ὁ** the back.
νωχελίη, ἡ laziness.

Ξ

Ξ, ξ (ξῖ) fourteenth letter of the alphabet; as a numeral ξ' = 60.
ξαίνω to scratch.
ξανθός 3 yellow; red-yellow.
ξειν- see ξεν-.
ξεν-αγέω to lead mercenary soldiers. [cenaries.]
ξεν-αγός, ὁ leader of mer-
ξεν-ηλασίᾱ, ἡ banishment of foreigners.
ξενίᾱ, ἡ hospitality; hospitable reception or entertainment; usurpation of civic rights.
ξενίζω to receive hospitably; to entertain; to be like a foreigner. — P. to be astonished.
ξενικός 3 foreign, of a stranger; mercenary.
ξένιος 3 and 2 hospitable; τὸ ξένιον a guest's gift.
ξένισις, ἡ hospitable entertainment. [ξενίζω.]
ξενο-δοκέω, -δοχέω =
ξενο-δόκος 2 entertaining guests. [or strangers.]
ξενο-κτονέω to slay guests
ξενο-λογέω to engage mercenaries.
ξένος 3 foreign, strange; unacquainted with. ὁ ξ. foreigner, stranger; mercenary; guest, friend; ἡ ξένη foreign country.

ξενό-στασις, ἡ lodging for strangers.
ξενοσύνη, ἡ = ξενίᾱ.
ξενο-τροφέω to maintain mercenary troops.
ξενόω = ξενίζω; to be abroad; to be (lodged as) a guest, to be entertained.
ξερός 3 = ξηρός.
ξέστης, ου, ὁ a measure; jar.
ξέω to scrape; to polish (by scraping); to carve.
ξηραίνω to parch up, dry up. — P. to become dry.
ξηρός 3 dry, parched; ἡ ξηρά dry land.
ξηρότης, ητος, ἡ dryness.
ξιφίδιον, τό dagger.
ξιφο-κτόνος 2 slaying with the sword.
ξίφος, τό sword.
ξόανον, τό carved image; wooden statue of a god.
ξυήλη, ἡ curved sword.
ξυλίζομαι M. to gather wood.
ξύλινος 3 wooden.
ξύλον, τό wood, timber; piece of wood; tree, beam; wooden ware; stick, cudgel; shaft; spear; bench; cross; wooden collar, pillory.
ξυλουργέω to work wood.
ξύλ-οχος, ὁ thicket.
ξύλωσις, ἡ wood-work.

ξυνήϊος 3 public, common.
ξυνός 3 = κοινός.
ξυρέω, ξυράω to shear, shave.
ξυρόν, τό razor.

ξυστόν, τό shaft; spear, lance; pole.
ξυστός 3 polished.
ξύω to scrape, smooth, polish.

O

O, ο (ὂ μικρόν) fifteenth letter of the alphabet; as a numeral ο′ = 70.

ὁ, ἡ, τό demonstrative Pronoun this; definite Article the.

ὄαρ, ὄαρος, ἡ consort; wife. [liarly.]

ὀαρίζω to converse fami-/

ὀαριστής, οῦ, ὁ confidential friend.

ὀαριστύς, ύος, ἡ friendly converse, intimacy; company.

ὀβελίσκος, ὁ small spit.

ὀβελός, ὁ spit; pointed pillar.

ὀβολός, ὁ obol (6th part of a drachm).

ὀβριμο-εργός forcible.

ὀβριμο-πάτρη, ἡ daughter of a mighty father.

ὄβριμος 2 strong, mighty.

ὀγδόατος 3 = ὄγδοος.

ὀγδοήκοντα eighty.

ὄγδοος 3 eighth.

ὀγδώκοντα = ὀγδοήκοντα.

ὀγκηρός 3 pompous.

ὄγκιον, τό chest for iron tools. [hook.]

ὄγκος¹, ὁ barb, grapple-/

ὄγκος², ὁ bulk, mass, heap, size, weight; molestation; dignity; importance, pride.

ὀγκόω to puff, swell. — P. to be swollen or proud.

ὀγμεύω to make furrows, to trace a straight line.

ὄγμος, ὁ furrow; swath.

ὄγχνη, ἡ pear-tree; pear.

ὁδαῖος 3 belonging to a way or journey; τὰ ὁδαῖα merchandise.

ὀδάξ adv. with the teeth.

ὅ-δε, ἥ-δε, τό-δε this, that.

ὁδεύω to go, travel, journey.

ὁδ-ηγέω to show the way, to guide.

ὁδ-ηγός, ὁ guide.

ὁδίτης, ου, ὁ traveller.

ὀδμή, ἡ scent, odour.

ὁδοι-πορέω = ὁδεύω.

ὁδοι-πορία, ἡ journey, way.

ὁδοι-πόριον, τό reward for a journey.

ὁδοι-πόρος, ὁ = ὁδίτης.

ὁδο-ποιέω to make a road.

ὁδός, ἡ way, street, road, path; journey, voyage, march, expedition; departure, return; way, means, manner, occasion, method.

ὀδός, ὁ threshold.

ὀδούς, ὄντος, ὁ tooth, tusk.

ὁδο-φύλαξ, ακος, ὁ watcher of the roads.

ὁδόω to lead the right way, to guide. — P. to succeed.

ὀδυνάω to cause pain. — P. to feel pain, suffer.

ὀδύνη, ἡ pain, grief.

ὀδυνηρός 3 painful.

ὀδυνή-φατος 2 killing pain.

ὀδυρμα, τό, ὀδυρμός, ὁ wailing, lamentation.

ὀδύρομαι M. to wail, lament; to bewail.

ὀδύσσομαι M. to be angry.

ὀδών, όντος, ὁ = ὀδούς.

ὀδωτός 3 practicable.

ὄζος, ὁ branch, twig; servant.

ὄζω to smell, savour.

ὅθεν adv. whence, from whom or which, wherefore.

ὅθι adv. where.

ὀθνεῖος 3 foreign, strange.

ὄθομαι to give or pay heed to, to regard, care for.

ὀθόνη, ἡ linen; linen garment; veil.

ὀθόνιον, τό linen bandage.

ὀθούνεκα = ὅτου ἕνεκα because.   [hair.)

ὄ-θριξ, ὄτριχος with like)

οἵ woe, oh!

οἵ adv. whither.

οἴαξ, ἄκος, ὁ handle of the rudder; helm; ring.

οἴγνῡμι, οἴγω to open.

οἶδα see εἴδω.

οἰδάω, -έω, -άνω to cause to swell. — intr. and P. to swell.

οἶδμα, τό a swelling, waves.

οἰέτης 2 of the same age.

ὀϊζῡρός 3 miserable, poor, wretched.

ὀϊζῡς, ύος, ἡ woe, misery.

ὀϊζόω to wail; to toil; to suffer.

οἰήϊον, τό = οἴαξ.

οἰηκίζω to steer, manage.

οἴησις, ἡ opinion.

οἶκα = ἔοικα.   [home.)

οἴκαδε adv. homeward(s),)

οἰκεῖος 3 belonging to a home, a household, or a family; cognate, akin; intimate, familiar; proper, one's own; private, personal; home(-grown), native; fit, suited.

οἰκειότης, ητος, ἡ relationship; friendship.

οἰκειόω to make one's own; to make a person one's friend. — P. to become an intimate friend (of).

οἰκείωσις, ἡ appropriation.

οἰκετεία, οἰκέτεια, ἡ the servants.

οἰκέτης, ου, ὁ member of the household; servant, slave.

οἰκετικός 3 of slaves.

οἰκεύς, ὁ = οἰκέτης.

οἰκέω to inhabit, occupy; to settle; to dwell, live; to manage, govern; to be situated; to be governed. — P. to be inhabited, situated; to be settled or governed; ἡ οἰκουμένη the civilized world.

οἰκήϊος, οἰκηϊόω = οἰκεῖος, οἰκειόω.

οἴκημα, τό dwelling, house; chamber; story; cage; prison; temple; workshop.

οἴκησις, ἡ an inhabiting; house, dwelling.

οἰκητήρ, ῆρος, ὁ, οἰκητής, οῦ, ὁ inhabitant.

οἰκητήριον, τό a dwelling.

οἰκητός 3 inhabited; habitable.   [κητήρ.)

οἰκήτωρ, ορος, ὁ = οἰ-)

οἰκίᾱ, ἡ = οἶκος.

οἰκιακός of a household; domestic.

οἰκίδιον, τό = οἰκίσκος.

οἰκίζω to build, establish, found; to settle, colonize, people; transplant. — M. to settle oneself; to dwell.

οἰκίον, τό = οἶκος.

οἴκισις, ἡ settlement, colonization.

οἰκίσκος, ὁ small house, hut.

οἰκιστήρ, ῆρος, οἰκιστής, οὗ, ὁ founder of a colony, settler. [ter of a house.]

οἰκο-δεσποτέω to be mas-

οἰκο-δεσπότης, ου, ὁ master of a house.

οἰκο-δομέω to build a house: to build; to found; to edify

οἰκο-δόμησις, ἡ, οἰκο-δόμημα, τό, οἰκο-δομίᾱ, ἡ, οἰκο-δομή, ἡ the act of building; building, edifice, house.

οἰκο-δόμος, ὁ architect.

οἴκοθεν adv. from one's house or home; from one's own means, of oneself; from the beginning.

οἴκοθι, οἴκοι adv. in the house, at home.

οἰκόνδε adv. = οἴκαδε.

οἰκο-νομέω to be a steward; to manage, order.

οἰκο-νομικός 3 of a household; economical.

οἰκο-νόμος, ὁ householder, steward.

οἰκό-πεδον, τό ruins of a house. [bitable.]

οἰκο-ποιός 2 making ha-

οἶκος, ὁ house, habitation, dwelling; chamber, hall; temple; camp, nest; household; household property; family, race; servants; home.

οἰκός, οἰκότως = εἰκός.

οἰκουμένη, ἡ see οἰκέω.

οἰκουρέω to keep or guard a house; to stay at home.

οἰκούρημα, τό, οἰκουρίᾱ, ἡ watch of a house; guard, protection. [housekeeping.]

οἰκούρια, τά wages for

οἰκουρός 2 keeping the house, domestic.

οἰκο-φθορέομαι P. to be ruined in one's household.

οἰκο-φθορίᾱ, ἡ loss of fortune.

οἰκτείρω, οἰκτίζω and M. to pity, to bewail.

οἰκτιρμός, ὁ = οἶκτος.

οἰκτίρμων 2 compassionate.

οἰκτίρω = οἰκτείρω.

οἴκτιστος 3 superl. of οἰκτρός. [compassion.]

οἶκτος, ὁ a wailing; pity,

οἰκτρός 3 pitiable, lamentable; mournful.

οἰκ-ωφελίη, ἡ thrift in household affairs.

οἶμα, τό attack, rage.

οἰμάω to attack violently.

οἴμη, ἡ heroic tale; song, lay.

οἴμοι int. woe to me!

οἶμος, ὁ way, road, course; strip of land. [wailing.]

οἰμωγή, ἡ lamentation,

οἰμώζω to wail, lament; to bewail. [full of wine.]

οἰνηρός 3 rich in vines;

οἰνίζομαι to procure wine.

οἰνο-βαρής 2, οἰνο-βα-
ρείων 3 drunk(en) with
wine.

οἰνό-πεδος 2 bearing vine;
τὸ -ον vineyard. [in wine.]

οἰνο-πληθής 2 abounding

οἰνο-ποτάζω to drink wine.

οἰνο-ποτήρ, ῆρος, ὁ, οἰνο-
πότης, ου, ὁ wine-drinker.

οἶνος, ὁ wine. [ness.]

οἰνο-φλυγία, ἡ drunken-

οἰνο-χοέω, -χοεύω to pour
out wine. [ing wine.]

οἰνο-χόη, ἡ cup for draw-

οἰνο-χόος, ὁ cup-bearer.

οἰνό-χυτος 2 of poured-
out wine.

οἶν-οψ, οπος = οἰνώψ.

οἰνών, ῶνος, ὁ wine-cellar.

οἰν-ώψ, ῶπος wine-coloured.

οἰο-βώτης feeding alone.

οἰό-ζωνος 3 single wan-
derer.

οἰόθεν adv. alone.

οἴομαι see οἴω.

οἰο-πόλος 2 lonely, soli-
tary. [tary.]

οἶος 3 alone, only, soli-

οἷος 3 of what manner or
kind; such as; οἷός τέ
εἰμι I am able, I can;
οἷον, οἷα adv. how, as,
like (as), just as, for instance.

οἰο-χίτων, ωνος dressed
in a tunic only.

οἰόω to leave alone.

ὄϊς, οἶς, οἰός, ὁ, ἡ sheep.

οἴσπη, ἡ unwashed wool.

οἰστέος 3 to be borne,
bearable.

δϊστεύω to shoot arrows.

δϊστός, οἰστός, ὁ arrow.

οἰστράω, -έω to goad,
sting; intr. to rage.

οἴστρημα, τό sting.

οἰστρο-πλήξ, ῆγος stung
to madness.

οἶστρος, ὁ gadfly; sting,
pain; madness.

οἰσύϊνος 3 made of wicker-
work. [death.]

οἶτος, ὁ lot, fate, ruin,

οἰχνέω, οἴχομαι M. to go,
come, fly; to go away; to
be gone, to be absent, lost,
or dead.

οἴω, ὀΐω, οἴομαι, ὀΐομαι
P. to suppose, fear, think,
believe; to intend, purpose,
mean.

οἰωνίζομαι M. to forebode,
prophesy. [divining.]

οἰωνιστής, οῦ auguring.

οἰωνο-θέτης, ου, ὁ, οἰωνο-
πόλος, ὁ augur, diviner.

οἰωνός, ὁ bird of prey; bird
of omen; omen, presage.

ὀκέλλω to run aground.

ὀκλάζω to bend the knees,
to bend, sink down.

ὀκνέω, -είω to shrink from,
scruple, hesitate, fear.

ὀκνηρός 3 shrinking, he-
sitating; fearful, troublesome.

ὄκνος, ὁ hesitation, un-
readiness, disinclination.

ὀκριάω to exasperate.

ὀκρίοεις 3 awful. [days.]

ὀκτα-ήμερος 2 for eight

ὀκτακισ-χίλιοι 3 eight
thousand.

ὀκτά-κνημος 2 with eight
spokes. [dred.]

ὀκτα-κόσιοι 3 eight hunὀκτώ eight.

ὀκτω-καί-δεκα eighteen.

ὀκτω-καὶ-δέκατος 3 the eighteenth.

ὀλβίζω to pronounce happy.

ὀλβιο-δαίμων 2 blessed by a god.

ὄλβιος 3 prosperous, happy, fortunate, blessed; rich.

ὄλβος, ὁ happiness, bliss; wealth, power.

ὀλέθριος 3 and 2 destructive; undone.

ὄλεθρος, ὁ destruction, ruin, loss; defeat; rogue, rascal.

ὀλέκω = ὄλλυμι.

ὀλετήρ, ῆρος, ὁ destroyer.

ὀλιγάκις adv. seldom.

ὀλιγ-ανθρωπία, ἡ scantiness of people.

ὀλιγ-αρχέομαι P. to live in an oligarchy.

ὀλιγ-αρχία, ἡ oligarchy, government by a few.

ὀλιγ-αρχικός 3 oligarchical. [parts.]

ὀλιγαχόθεν adv. from few

ὀλιγ-ηπελέω to be weak.

ὀλιγ-ηπελία, ἡ weakness.

ὀλιγο-γονία, ἡ scanty procreation. [ful.]

ὀλιγό-γονος 2 little fruit-

ὀλιγο-δρανέω = ὀλιγηπελέω. [little faith.]

ὀλιγό-πιστος 2 having

ὀλίγος 3 few, little; small, short, weak, indifferent; οἱ ὀλίγοι the few, aristocrats; ὀλίγον a little, little, a short time. [part.]

ὀλιγοστός 3 only a little

ὀλιγο-χρόνιος 2 and 3 of short duration.

ὀλιγό-ψῡχος 2 faint-hearted.

ὀλιγ-ωρέω to regard lightly, neglect.

ὀλιγ-ωρία, ἡ a regarding lightly, neglect.

ὀλίγ-ωρος 2 disregardful, neglecting.

ὀλίζων 2 lesser (ὀλίγος).

ὀλισθάνω to slip, slide.

ὀλισθηρός 3 slippery.

ὁλκάς, άδος, ἡ trading vessel.

ὁλκός, ὁ strap; lifting-engine, hauling-machine; track, trail.

ὄλλῡμι to destroy, ruin, kill; to lose; pf. ὄλωλα I am undone or ruined. — M. to perish, die, to be undone or lost.

ὅλμος, ὁ roller; mortar.

ὁλόεις 3 = ὁλοός.

ὀλοθρευτής, οῦ, ὁ destroyer.

ὀλοθρεύω = ὄλλυμι.

ὁλοός 3 = ὁλοός.

ὀλοί-τροχος, ὀλοί-τροχος, ὁ rolling stone, piece of rock.

ὁλο-καυτέω to bring a burnt-offering. [offering.]

ὁλο-καύτωμα, τό burnt-

ὁλο-κληρία, ἡ soundness, entireness. [fect.]

ὁλό-κληρος 2 entire, per-

ὀλολυγή, ἡ a loud crying, wailing, lamentation.

ὀλολύζω to cry aloud, to wail; to shout.

ὀλοό-τροχος, ὁ = ὀλοί-.

ὀλοός 3 destructive; hurtful, painful.

ὀλοό-φρων 2 meaning mischief, pernicious.

ὅλος 3 whole, complete, entire, all.

ὁλο-τελής 2 perfect.

ὀλοφυδνός 3 wailing, lamenting. miserable.

ὀλοφυρμός, ὁ lamentation.

ὀλοφύρομαι M. and P. to wail, lament; to feel pity or compassion.

ὀλόφυρσις, ἡ = ὀλοφυρμός.

ὀλοφώϊος 2 malicious. artful.

ὅλυνθος, ὁ winter fig.

ὄλυρα, ἡ spelt.

ὁμαδέω to make a noise.

ὅμαδος, ὁ noise, din; throng, crowd.

ὅμ-αιμος 2, ὁμ-αίμων 2 related by blood; brother; sister. [of arms, alliance.]

ὁμ-αιχμίᾱ, ἡ brotherhood

ὅμ-αιχμος, ὁ companion in arms. [level; average.]

ὁμαλής 2, ὁμαλός 3 even.

ὁμ-αρτέω to walk together; to follow; to meet.

ὁμαρτῆ, ὁμαρτήδην adv. together, jointly.

ὅμ-αυλος 2 united.

ὄμβριος 3 of rain, rainy.

ὄμβρος, ὁ water, moisture; rain, shower of rain or snow.

ὀμείρομαι to long for.

ὀμ-ευνέτις, ιδος, ἡ consort. [together.]

ὀμ-ηγερής 2 assembled

ὀμ-ηγυρίζομαι M. to call together.

ὀμ-ήγυρις, ἡ assembly.

ὀμ-ηλικίᾱ, ἡ equality of age: = ὁμῆλιξ.

ὀμ-ῆλιξ, ικος of the same age; comrade.

ὀμηρείᾱ, ἡ the giving a pledge.

ὀμηρέω to meet.

ὅμ-ηρος, ὁ, ὅμ-ηρον, τό pledge, security; hostage.

ὀμῑλαδόν adv. in crowds.

ὁμῑλέω to be together, to associate, converse, to be friends; to live with; to meet, encounter; to negotiate, to be engaged in.

ὁμίλημα, τό = ὁμιλία.

ὁμῑλητής, οῦ, ὁ friend; scholar.

ὁμῑλίᾱ, ἡ a living together, intercourse, company; conversation; instruction; assembly, meeting.

ὅμῑλος, ὁ crowd, throng of people, mob; troop of warriors; tumult of battle.

ὁμίχλη, ἡ, ὀμίχλη, ἡ mist, fog; cloud.

ὄμμα, τό eye, look; face; sight, image, spectacle.

ὀμματο-στερής 2 eyeless.

ὄμνῡμι, ὀμνύω to swear, affirm by oath; to swear by.

ὁμο-βώμιος 2 having one common altar.

ὁμο-γάστριος 2 of the same mother.

ὁμο-γενής 2 kindred.

ὁμό-γλωσσος 2 speaking the same language.

ὁμό-γνιος 2 protecting the same race. [one mind.]

ὁμο-γνωμονέω to be of

ὁμο-γνώμων 2 having the same mind.

ὁμο-δοξέω = ὁμογνωμονέω.

ὁμό-δουλος, ὁ, ἡ fellow-slave.

ὁμο-εθνής 2 of the same tribe. [character.]

ὁμο-ήθης 2 of the same] character.

ὁμόθεν adv. from the same place or origin.

ὁμο-θῡμαδόν adv. unanimously.

ὁμοιάζω to be like.

ὁμοίίος 3 = ὅμοιος.

ὁμοιο-παθής 2 being similarly affected.

ὅμοιος, ὅμοιος 3 like, similar, resembling; the same, of the same rank; equal citizen; equal; common, mutual; a match for; agreeing, convenient.

ὁμοιότης, ητος, ἡ likeness, resemblance.

ὁμοιό-τροπος 2 agreeing, similar.

ὁμοιόω to make (a)like, to liken, compare. — P. to be or become (a)like.

ὁμοίωμα, τό, ὁμοίωσις, ἡ likeness, image; a likening; simile.

ὁμο-κλέω, -κλάω to cry aloud; to cheer on; to upbraid.

ὁμο-κλή, ἡ loud cry, shout; command; menace.

ὁμο-κλητήρ, ῆρος, ἡ a cheerer on, encourager.

ὁμό-κλῑνος 2 neighbour at table.

ὁμο-λογέω to agree with; to grant, concede, allow, admit, confess; to promise; to assent (to), come to an agreement, make a treaty; ὁμολογεῖται it is allowed, granted. — M. to come to

an understanding or agreement.

ὁμο-λογία, ἡ, ὁμο-λόγημα, τό agreement; confession; assent; terms, treaty; capitulation.

ὁμο-λογουμένως adv. confessedly; agreeably to, conformably to. [mother.]

ὁμο-μήτριος 3 of the same] mother.

ὁμο-νοέω to be of one mind. [cord.]

ὁμό-νοια, ἡ unity, con-] cord.

ὁμο-πάτριος 2 of the same father. [same city.]

ὁμό-πτολις, εως of the] same city.

ὁμόργνῡμι to wipe off.

ὁμ-ορέω to border on.

ὅμ-ορος 2 bordering on.

ὁμο-ρροθέω to agree with.

ὁμός 3 common; one and the same; adv. ὁμῶς together; equally, alike.

ὁμό-σε adv. straight on; to the same place.

ὁμο-σῑτέω to eat together.

ὁμό-σῑτος 2 eating together. [alike.]

ὁμό-σκευος 2 equipped] alike.

ὁμό-σπλαγχνος 2 kindred; brother. [at table.]

ὁμό-σπονδος 2 companion] at table.

ὁμό-σπορος 2 kindred.

ὁμό-σπόρος 2 married to the same wife. [side.]

ὁμο-στιχάω to walk be-] side.

ὁμό-στολος 2 companion.

ὁμό-τεχνος 2 of the same craft or trade. [oured.]

ὁμό-τῑμος 2 equally hon-] oured.

ὁμο-τράπεζος 2 companion at table. [τροπος.]

ὁμό-τροπος 2 = ὁμοιό-] τροπος.

ὁμό-τροφος 2 brought up together.

ὁμοῦ adv. together, at the same place; at once; near.

ὁμ-ουρέω see ὁμορέω.

ὁμο-φρονέω to have the same mind.

ὁμο-φροσύνη, ἡ concord.

ὁμό-φρων 2 of one mind.

ὁμο-φυής 2 of the same nature.   [tribe.]

ὁμό-φῦλος 2 of the same

ὁμο-φωνέω to speak the same language.

ὁμό-φωνος 2 speaking the same language.

ὁμο-χροίη, ἡ skin.

ὁμό-ψηφος 2 having an equal vote; of one mind.

ὁμόω to unite.

ὀμφαλόεις 3 having a boss.

ὀμφαλός, ὁ navel; knob or boss of a shield; centre.

ὄμφαξ, ακος, ἡ unripe grape.   [speech; oracle.]

ὀμφή, ἡ (divine) voice;

ὁμ-ώνυμος 2 of the same name.

ὁμ-ωρόφιος 2 living under the same roof.

ὅμως adv. nevertheless, yet.

ὁμῶς adv. see ὁμός.

ὁμ-ωχέτης, ου worshipped together.

ὄναρ, τό dream, vision.

ὀνάριον, τό little ass.

ὄνᾶσις, ἡ = ὄνησις.

ὄνειαρ, ατος, τό help, assistance; refreshment; food, victuals.

ὀνείδειος 2 reproachful.

ὀνειδίζω to reproach, upbraid, blame.

ὄνειδος, τό, ὀνείδισμα, τό, ὀνειδισμός, ὁ reproach. blame; disgrace.

ὀνείρειος 3 of dreams.

ὄνειρον, τό = ὄνειρος.

ὀνειρο-πολέω to dream.

ὀνειρο-πόλος ὁ interpreter of dreams.

ὄνειρος, ὁ dream, vision.

ὀνεύω to haul up.

ὀνήσιμος 2 useful.

ὀνησί-πολις, εως benefiting the state.

ὄνησις, ἡ profit, help; bliss, delight.

ὄνθος, ὁ dung, dirt.

ὀνικός 3 μύλος upper millstone.

ὀνίνημι to benefit, help; to gratify, delight. — M. and P. to have profit, advantage, delight, or enjoyment.

ὄνομα, τό name, word, term; title; fame, report; pretence, pretext.

ὀνομάζω to name, call by name; to speak of; to pronounce, enumerate; to promise. — P. to be called.

ὀνομαίνω = ὀνομάζω.

ὀνομα-κλήδην = ἐξονομακλήδην.

ὀνομά-κλυτος 2 famous.

ὀνομαστί adv. by name.

ὀνομαστός 3 to be named; named, renowned.

ὄνος, ὁ, ἡ ass; windlass, crane: upper millstone.

ὀνοστός 3 blamable.

ὀνο-φορβός, ὁ ass-keeper.

ὄντως *adv.* really, actually, indeed. [claw, hoof.]

ὄνυξ, υχος, ὁ nail, talon,

ὄξος, τό vinegar.

ὀξυ-βελής 2 sharp-pointed.

ὀξύ-δερκής 2 sharp-sighted.

ὀξύ-θηκτος 2 sharp-edged.

ὀξύ-κώκῦτος 2 loudly bewailed.

ὀξυ-λαβέω to be quick.

ὀξύνω to sharpen; to provoke.

ὀξυόεις 3 sharp-pointed.

ὀξύς 3 sharp, keen, pointed; pungent; piercing, shrill, clear; quick, swift; passionate, fiery; bold; active; clever.

ὀξύτης, ητος, ἡ sharpness; quickness; hotness, passion.

ὀξύ-τονος 2 sharp-sounding, piercing.

ὀξύ-φωνος 2 with clear voice.

ὀξύ-χολος 2 given to anger.

ὀπᾱδέω to follow, accompany. [attendant.]

ὀπᾱδός, ὁ, ἡ companion,

ὀπάζω to give as a companion or follower; to add, attach; to pursue, press hard. — *M.* to take as a companion.

ὀπαῖον, τό hole in the roof (for the smoke).

ὅ-πᾱτρος 2 of the same father. [ὀπαδός.]

ὀπάων, ονος, ὀπέων =

ὀπή, ἡ hole, opening; cave.

ὅπη, ὅπῃ *adv.* where; whither; how, in what way.

ὀπηδέω = ὀπᾱδέω.

ὁ-πηνίκα *adv.* when; since.

ὀπίζομαι *M.* to care for, regard; to honour; to dread.

ὄπιθεν = ὄπισθεν.

ὀπῑπεύω to gaze at; to observe, watch.

ὄπις, ιδος, ἡ regard, respect; punishment, vengeance.

ὄπισθε(ν) *adv.* behind, after, hereafter; *prp.* with *gen.* behind.

ὀπίσθιος 3 hinder.

ὀπισθο - νόμος 2 grazing backwards. [guard.]

ὀπισθο-φύλακες, οἱ rear-

ὀπισθο-φυλακέω to guard the rear.

ὀπισθο-φυλακία, ἡ (command of the) rear.

ὀπίστατος 3 hindmost.

ὀπίσω *adv.* behind, backwards; in future; back; *prp.* with *gen.* after, behind.

ὀπλέω to make ready.

ὁπλή, ἡ hoof.

ὁπλίζω to prepare, equip, make ready, harness; to arm; to train. — *M.* to prepare for oneself. — *P.* and *M.* to get or be ready; to be going. [ing.]

ὅπλισις, ἡ equipment; arm-

ὁπλῑτ - ἀγωγός 2 leading the heavy-armed.

ὁπλῑτεύω to serve as a heavy-armed soldier.

ὁπλίτης, ου, ὁ heavy-armed (foot-)soldier.

ὁπλῑτικός 3 belonging to a ὁπλίτης. [oneself.]

ὅπλομαι to prepare for

ὁπλο-μαχία, ἡ art of using heavy arms, tactics.

18*

ὅπλον, τό toil, implement; furniture of a ship; arms, harness, armour, weapon; camp, quarter; = ὁπλῖται.

ὁπλότατος 3 youngest.

ὁπλότερος 3 younger, fresh. [try.]

ὁποδαπός 3 of what country.

ὁπόθεν adv. whence.

ὅποι adv. whither, thither where.

ὁποῖος 3 of what sort, kind, or quality.

ὀπός, ὁ juice of plants, especially: of the fig-tree.

ὁπόσε adv. = ὅποι.

ὁπόσος 3 as many, as many as; as large as.

ὁπότε, ὁπόταν adv. when, whensoever: because, since.

ὁπότερος 3 which of the two: one of the two.

ὁποτέρωθεν adv. from which of the two sides.

ὁποτέρωσε adv. to which of the two sides.

ὅπου adv. where; when; how; because, since.

ὀπταλέος 3 = ὀπτός.

ὀπτάνομαι to be seen.

ὀπτασίᾶ, ἡ sight, appearance.

ὀπτάω to roast; to bake.

ὀπτήρ, ῆρος, ὁ spy.

ὀπτός 3 roasted; baked.

ὀπυίω to marry, wed; to be married. — P. to become a wife. [sight]

ὀπωπή, ἡ sight; (faculty of)

ὀπώρᾱ, ἡ late summer and early autumn; fruit-time; tree-fruit.

ὀπωρίζω to gather fruit(s).

ὀπωρινός 3 of early autumn.

ὀπωρ-ώνης, ου, ὁ fruiterer.

ὅπως adv. how, in what manner; as, when, as soon as; that, in order to.

δρᾶμα, τό, δρᾶσις, ἡ sense of sight; sight; view.

ὁρᾱτός 3 visible.

ὁράω to see, to look; to have sight; to look to, to take heed (of), beware (of); to look at, behold, perceive, observe; to see again; to visit; to understand; conceive; to know. — P. to be seen, to appear, become visible.

ὀργάζω to knead; tan.

ὀργαίνω to make angry; to be angry.

ὄργανον, τό instrument, implement, tool.

ὀργάω to teem, swell; to be wanton; to long for.

ὀργή, ἡ impulse; feeling, disposition, temper; passion, eagerness; anger, wrath; punishment.

ὄργια, τά secret rites or worship, mysteries.

ὀργίζω to make angry. — P. to become angry.

ὀργίλος 3 given to anger.

ὀργυιά, ὀργυιά, ἡ fathom.

ὀρέγω, ὀρέγνῦμι and M. to reach, stretch out, extend; to hand, offer, give. — M. and P. to stretch oneself out; to reach to; to aim at, grasp at; to long for, desire. [ranging.]

ὀρει-βάτης, ου mountain-

ὀρεινός 3, ὄρειος 3 and 2

mountainous, hilly; living on the mountains, mountaineer.

ὀρεκτός 3 stretched out.

ὄρεξις, ἡ desire, longing.

ὀρέομαι to hasten.

ὀρεσί-τροφος 2 mountain-bred. [βάτης.]

ὀρεσσι-βάτης, ου = ὀρει-]

ὀρέστερος 3 = ὀρεινός.

ὀρεστιάς, άδος mountain-nymph.

ὀρεύς, ὁ mule.

ὀρεχθέω to pant, quiver.

ὀρέω = ὁράω.

ὀρεω-κόμος, ὁ muleteer.

ὄρθιος 3 and 2 straight up, rising upwards, upright, uphill, straight on, in a column or file; shrill, loud, clear.

ὀρθό-κραιρος 3 with straight horns; with upright beaks. [top.]

ὀρθό-κρανος 2 with high]

ὀρθο-ποδέω to walk or go straight. [steep.]

ὀρθό-πους, ποδος uphill,]

ὀρθός 3 straight, upright, erect; straight forward, in a straight line; unharmed, safe, prosperous; anxious, attentive, expecting; right, just, righteous, upright; true, exact, convenient, decent.

ὀρθότης, ητος, ἡ upright standing; rightness, right sense. [aright.]

ὀρθο-τομέω to handle]

ὀρθόω to set upright, raise; to erect, build; to maintain; to make straight; to im-

prove, repair; to extol, exalt; to bring to a happy end. — P. to stand or sit upright; to succeed, prosper, flourish; to be right or true.

ὀρθρίζω to rise early.

ὄρθριος 3, ὀρθρινός 3 early in the morning.

ὄρθρος, ὁ early morning, daybreak.

ὁρίζω to divide, confine, define, limit; to mark out by boundaries. — M. to mark out for oneself; to assign; to determine; to define (a word).

ὀρίνω = ὄρνυμι.

ὅριον, τό boundary, frontier; dock. [adjure.]

ὁρκίζω to make swear; to]

ὅρκιον, τό oath; pledge, surety; treaty, covenant; victim sacrificed at a treaty. [of oaths.]

ὅρκιος 2 sworn; guardian]

ὅρκος, ὁ oath; vow; sworn stipulation; form of oath; cojurer, witness.

ὁρκόω to make swear.

ὁρκ-ωμοσία, ἡ a swearing.

ὁρκ-ωμοτέω to take an oath.

ὁρκωτής, οῦ, ὁ one who administers an oath.

ὁρμαθός, ὁ row, chain; flight (of bats).

ὁρμαίνω = ὁρμάω to set in quick motion; to rouse, stir up; to consider, ponder, contrive, devise. — intr., M. and P. to start, set out, proceed, depart; to proceed or begin from; to hurry or rush on, make an attack; to be about, to be eager, to purpose; to begin.

ὁρμέω and *M.* to lie at anchor; to depend upon.

ὁρμή, ἡ assault, attack, onset; start, setting out, march; impulse, intention, eagerness.

ὅρμημα, τό passionate desire; attack. [place.]

ὁρμητήριον, τό starting-]

ὁρμίζω to bring into harbour, to anchor. — *M.* and *P.* to come to anchor, to lie at anchor, to reach the harbour.

ὅρμος[1], ὁ chain; necklace.

ὅρμος[2], ὁ anchorage, harbour.

ὄρνεον, τό bird.

ὀρνίθειος 2 of fowl.

ὀρνιθο-σκόπος 2 observing the flight of birds.

ὄρνις, ῑθος, ὁ, ἡ bird; fowl, cock, hen; bird of augury; augury, prophecy.

ὄρνῡμι, -ύω to stir (up), rouse, move; to incite, chase; to encourage, cheer on; to cause, excite. — *intr.* and *M.* to stir oneself, start up, arise; to be roused, excited, or troubled, to rush or hurry on, hasten; to rise to do, to begin.

ὁρο-θεσία, ἡ boundary.

ὀροθύνω to stir up, rouse.

ὄρομαι to watch, be on guard. [tain-range.]

ὄρος, τό mountain, moun-]

ὀρός, ὁ whey.

ὅρος, ὁ boundary, limit,

frontier; land-mark; standard; definition.

ὀροσάγγαι, οἱ benefactors of the king.

ὀρούω to start up or forward, to rush on, hasten.

ὀροφή, ἡ roof, ceiling.

ὄροφος, ὁ reed for thatching; roof. [twig.]

ὄρπηξ, ηκος, ἡ branch,]

ὀρρωδέω to be afraid, fear, dread.

ὀρρωδία, ἡ affright, fear.

ὀρσο-θύρη, ἡ back-door; others: raised door.

ὀρτάζω = ἑορτάζω.

ὀρτάλιχος, ὁ young bird, chicken.

ὀρτή, ἡ = ἑορτή.

ὄρτυξ, υγος, ὁ quail.

ὄρυγμα, τό pit, hole, trench; mine, tunnel.

ὀρυκτός 3 dug (out).

ὀρυμαγδός, ὁ noise, tumult, roaring. [(gazelle?).]

ὄρυς, υος, ὁ wild animal]

ὀρύσσω to dig, dig up; to cover with earth, bury; to dig through.

ὀρφανία, ἡ bereavement.

ὀρφανίζω to make orphan.

ὀρφανός 3 left orphan; destitute, bereft.

ὀρφανιστής, οῦ, ὁ guardian.

ὀρφναῖος 3 dark, dusky.

ὄρχαμος, ὁ leader, lord, master.

ὄρχατος, ὁ garden.

ὀρχέομαι *M.* to dance.

ὀρχηδόν *adv.* one after another.

ὀρχηθμός, ὁ, ὄρχημα, τό, ὄρχησις, ἡ dance, dancing.

ὀρχηστήρ, ῆρος, ὀρχηστής, οὖ, ὁ dancer.

ὀρχήστρᾱ, ἡ place for dancing; orchestra. [girl.]

ὀρχηστρίς, ίδος, ἡ dancing

ὀρχηστύς, ύος, ἡ = ὄρχησις.

ὄρχις, εως and ιος, ὁ testicle.

ὄρχος, ὁ row of vines.

ὅς, ἥ, ὅ relat. pron. who, which, that; demonstr. pron. this, that; he, she, it; possess. pron. his, her, one's own.

ὁσάκις adv. as many times as.

ὁσ-ημέραι adv. daily.

ὁσίᾱ, ἡ divine law; sacred duty.

ὅσιος 3 and 2 sanctioned by divine law or by the law of nature, sacred, approved by the gods; holy, pious; chaste, pure; atoning.

ὁσιότης, ητος, ἡ piety, religiousness.   [to atone.]

ὁσιόω to hallow; to purify;

ὀσμή, ἡ = ὀδμή.

ὅσος 3 as great as, how great, as much, far, long as.

ὅσ-περ, ἥ-περ, ὅ-περ who or which indeed.

ὄσπριον, τό pulse, legumes.

ὄσσα, ἡ rumour; voice.

ὁσσάκι = ὁσάκις.

ὁσσάτιος 3 = ὅσος.

ὄσσε, τώ the eyes.

ὄσσομαι M. to see; to see in one's mind; to forebode, foretell.

ὀστέϊνος 3 of bone, bony.

ὀστέον = ὀστοῦν, τό bone.

ὅσ-τις, ἥ-τις, ὅ τι whosoever; whichsoever; who, which, that.

ὀστρακίζω to banish by potsherds, ostracize.

ὀστρακισμός, ὁ banishment by potsherds, ostracism.

ὄστρακον, τό potsherd.

ὀσφραίνομαι to smell, to track by scent. [smelling.]

ὄσφρησις, ἡ (sense of)

ὀσφῦς, ύος, ἡ hip.

ὅτ-αν adv. whenever.

ὅτε adv. when, whenever; before that; since.

ὁτέ adv. sometimes.

ὅτι conj. that; because; with sup. of adj. as ... as possible.

ὅτλος, ὁ suffering, distress

ὄτοβος, ὁ noise, din, sound

ὀτοτοῖ int. ah! woe!

ὀτραλέος 3, ὀτηρός 3 nimble, quick.

ὅτριχες pl. of ὅθριξ.

ὀτρυντύς, ύος, ἡ encouragement.

ὀτρύνω to stir up, rouse, encourage, wake; to send; to speed. — M. to hasten.

οὐ, οὐκ, οὐχ not.

οὗ adv. where; when.

οὐά, οὐᾶ for shame!

οὐαί ah! woe!

οὖας, ατος, τό = οὖς.

οὐδαμᾶ, οὐδαμῇ, -ῆ adv. nowhere; to no place; never; in no way, not at all.

οὐδαμόθεν adv. from no place.

οὐδαμόθι = οὐδαμοῦ.

οὐδαμοῖ, οὐδαμόσε adv. to no place.   [δαμά.]

οὐδαμοῦ, οὐδαμῶς = οὐ-

οὖδας, εος, τό ground, surface of the earth.

οὐδέ *conj.* but not; and not; nor; not even.

οὐδείς, οὐδεμία, οὐδέν no one, none, nobody, nothing; good-for-nothing, worthless, powerless.

οὐδενόσ-ωρος 2 worth no notice.

οὐδέ-ποτε *adv.* never.

οὐδέ-πω *adv.* not yet; not at all.

οὐδε-πώποτε = οὐδέποτε.

οὐδέτερος 3 neither of the two. [of the two sides.]

οὐδετέρωσε *adv.* to neither

οὐδός¹, ὁ = ὁδός.

οὐδός², ἡ = ὁδός.

οὖθαρ, ατος, τό udder.

οὐθ-είς, οὐθ-έν = οὐδείς, οὐδέν.

οὐκ-έτι *adv.* no longer, no more, no further.

οὐκ-οῦν *adv.* not therefore? not then? is it not?; not therefore, so not; indeed not.

οὐκ-οῦν *adv.* is it not? not then?; therefore, accordingly.

οὐλαί, αἱ (bruised) barley for a sacrifice. [band.]

οὐλαμός, ὁ throng, tumult,

οὖλε hail to thee!

οὐλή, ἡ scar.

οὔλιος 3 pernicious.

οὐλό-θριξ, τριχος with curly hair. [headed.]

οὐλο-κάρηνος 2 curly-

οὐλόμενος 3 pernicious, destructive.

οὖλος¹ 3 whole, entire.

οὖλος² 3 woolly, fleecy, thick; matted.

οὖλος³ = οὔλιος.

οὐλό-χυται, αἱ = οὐλαί.

οὖν *adv.* indeed, really, certainly; therefore, accordingly, consequently.

οὔνεκα *conj.* wherefore; because. — *prp.* with *gen.* for, on account of.

οὔνομα etc. see ὄνομα.

οὔνομαι = ὄνομαι.

οὔ-περ *adv.* by no means.

οὔ-περ *adv.* just where.

οὔ-πη, οὔ-πη *adv.* nowhere; in no wise.

οὔ-ποθι *adv.* nowhere.

οὔ-ποτε *adv.* never.

οὔ-πω, οὐ-πώποτε not yet, never yet.

οὔ-πως *adv.* in no wise, not at all.

οὐρά, ἡ tail; after-part, rear, rear-rank. [rear.]

οὐρ-αγός, ὁ leader of the

οὐραῖος 3 of the tail.

οὐράνιος 3 heavenly, in or from heaven.

οὐρανίωνες, οἱ the heavenly gods. [ven.]

οὐρανόθεν *adv.* from hea-

οὐρανόθι *adv.* in heaven.

οὐρανο-μήκης 2 as high as heaven. [ment.]

οὐρανός, ὁ heaven; firma-

οὔρειος 3 = ὄρειος.

οὔρεσι-βώτης, ου feeding on the mountains. [guard.]

οὐρεύς, ὁ mule; watcher,

οὐρέω to make water.

οὐρία, ἡ fair wind.

οὐρίαχος, ὁ lowest end.

οὐρίζω¹ to sail with a fair wind.

οὐρίζω² = ὁρίζω.

οὔριος 3 fair, prosperous.

οὔρισμα, τό boundary line.

οὖρον[1], τό urine.

οὖρον[2], τό boundary, distance (of throwing), stretch.

οὖρος[1], ὁ fair wind; fair time.

οὖρος[2], ὁ watcher, guard.

οὖρος[3], ὁ = ὄρος.

οὐρός, ὁ trench, channel.

οὖς, ὠτός the ear; handle.

οὐσίᾱ, ἡ the being, essence, substance; property.

οὐτάζω, οὐτάω to hit, strike, wound, hurt.

οὔ-τε adv. and not; οὔτε ... οὔτε neither ... nor.

οὐτιδανός 3 worthless.

οὔ-τις, οὔ-τι no one, nobody, nothing.

οὔ-τοι adv. indeed not.

οὗτος, αὕτη, τοῦτο this, this one.

οὕτω, οὕτως, οὑτωσί adv. thus, in this way or manner, only so.

οὐχί adv. no, not.

ὀφειλέτης, ου, ὁ debtor.

ὀφείλημα, τό, ὀφειλή, ἡ debt.

ὀφείλω to owe, be indebted; ὀφειλόμενος 3 due, τὸ ὀφειλόμενον one's due, to be bound, to be under an obligation; ὤφελον I ought, o that I!

ὀφέλλω[1] = ὀφείλω.

ὀφέλλω[2] to increase, augment, strengthen; to promote, help.

ὄφελος, τό profit, advantage; usefulness.   [eyes.

ὀφθαλμίᾱ, ἡ disease of the

ὀφθαλμιάω to have bad eyes or a disease of the eyes.   [service.

ὀφθαλμο-δουλείᾱ, ἡ eye-

ὀφθαλμός, ὁ the eye; face; the dearest, choicest, best, help, delight.

ὄφις, ὁ serpent, snake.

ὀφλισκάνω to incur a debt or punishment, to lose one's cause, to be found guilty; to incur a charge.

ὄφρα conj. as long as, while; until; that, in order that; adv. some time.

ὀφρύη, ἡ = ὀφρύς.

ὀφρυόεις 3 hilly.

ὀφρῦς, ύος, ὁ eyebrow; forehead; pride, dignity; edge, brow of a hill.

ὄχα adv. by far.

ὄχανον, τό handle.   [canal.

ὀχετεύω to divert by a

ὀχετ-ηγός 2 drawing a canal.   [ditch.

ὀχετός, ὁ conduit, canal,

ὀχεύς, ὁ handle, band, strap; clasp; bolt.

ὀχεύω to cover.

ὀχέω to bear, endure. — P. and M. to be carried or borne; to drive, ride.

ὄχημα, τό carriage, chariot, vessel.

ὀχθέω to be vexed.

ὄχθη, ἡ, ὄχθος, ὁ height, hill; high bank of a river; edge.

ὀχλέω to move by a lever, to roll; to molest, trouble.

ὀχληρός 3 troublesome.

ὀχλίζω = ὀχλέω.

ὀχλικός 3 = ὀχλώδης.

ὀχλο-ποιέω to make a riot.
ὄχλος, ὁ molestation, disturbance, trouble; throng, crowd, the common people, mob. [common, turbulent.]
ὀχλώδης 2 like a mob,
ὀχμάζω to hold fast; to rein in.
ὄχος, ὁ receptacle, support; carriage, chariot. [tenable.]
ὀχυρός 3 firm, strong,
ὀχυρόω and *M.* to fortify.
ὀχύρωμα, τό fort, stronghold, fortress. [saying.]
ὄψ, ὀπός, ἡ voice; speech,
ὀψάριον, τό = ὄψον.
ὀψέ *adv.* long after; late, too late; in the evening.
ὀψείω to wish to see.
ὀψία, ἡ evening; afternoon.
ὀψί-γονος 2 late-born, afterborn.

ὀψίζω and *P.* to be (too) late. [tardy.]
ὄψιμος 2, ὄψιος 3 late,
ὄψις, ἡ faculty of sight, a seeing, viewing; sight, appearance; view, vision; perception; eye; face.
ὀψι-τέλεστος 2 of late fulfilment.
ὄψον, τό by-meat, anything eaten with bread; meat, fish, dainty food, sauce.
ὀψο-ποιέω and *M.* to dress or season meat.
ὀψο-ποιΐα, ἡ, ὀψο-ποιϊκή, ἡ cookery.
ὀψο-ποιός, ὁ cook.
ὀψο-φάγος 2 eater of meat; dainty feeder. [dainties.]
ὀψ-ωνέω to buy victuals or
ὀψ-ώνιον, τό = ὄψον; provisions; wages.

Π

Π, π (πῖ) sixteenth letter of the alphabet; as a numeral π' = 80.
πᾶ, πά = πῇ, πή.
πᾱγά, ἡ = πηγή.
παγετώδης 2 icy, chilly.
πάγη, ἡ snare; trap.
παγιδεύω to entrap.
παγίς, ίδος, ἡ = πάγη.
πάγ-κακος 2 utterly bad, nefarious.
πάγ-καλος 2 and 3 most beautiful or good.
πάγ-καρπος 2 rich in all sorts of fruit. [cealing.]
πάγ-κευθής 2 all-con-]
πάγ-κλαυτος 2 ever weeping, all tearful; all-lamented.

πάγ-κοινος 2 common to all. [rest to all.]
παγ-κοίτης, ου giving]
παγ-κόνιτος 2 quite covered with dust. [ful.]
παγ-κρατής 2 all-power-]
παγ-κρατιάζω to practise the παγκράτιον.
παγ-κρατιαστής, οῦ, ὁ wrestler and boxer.
παγ-κράτιον, τό combined wrestling and boxing.
πάγος, ὁ ice; frost; rock, peak, hill, crag.
παγ-χάλεπος 2 most difficult.
παγ-χάλκεος 2, πάγ-χαλκος 2 all-brazen.

πάγ-χρηστος 2 good for all things.

πάγ-χριστος 2 all-anointed.

παγ-χρύσεος 2 all golden.

πάγχυ *adv.* quite, wholly.

πάθη, ἡ, πάθημα, τό, πάθος, τό occurrence, accident; misfortune, suffering, loss; grief; passion, affection.

παιάν, ᾶνος, ὁ saviour, physician; pæan, choral song (of triumph). [pæan.]

παιᾱνίζω to chant the

παιγνιά, ἡ play, sport.

παιγνιήμων 2, παιγνιώδης 2 sportive, jocose.

παιδ-αγωγέω to lead, train, or educate boys.

παιδ-αγωγός, ὁ trainer of boys, tutor, master, teacher.

παιδάριον, τό little child, boy, or girl.

παιδείᾱ, ἡ education, teaching, training, discipline, correction; letters, knowledge, science; school.

παιδεῖος 2 = παιδικός.

παιδ-εραστέω to love boys.

παιδ-εραστής, οῦ, ὁ lover of boys. [boys.]

παιδ-εραστίᾱ, ἡ love of

παίδευμα, τό, παίδευσις, ἡ = παιδεία.

παιδευτής, οῦ, ὁ instructor, teacher, corrector.

παιδεύω to bring up, train, teach, instruct, educate; to accustom.

παιδίᾱ, ἡ = παιδεία.

παιδιά, ἡ child's play; sport, game.

παιδικός 3 belonging to

children, childish, young; τὰ παιδικά darling. [child.]

παιδιόθεν *adv.* from a

παιδίον, τό = παιδάριον.

παιδίσκη, ἡ girl, damsel, young female slave.

παιδίσκος, ὁ = παιδάριον.

παιδνός 3 and 2 = παιδικός.

παιδο-κτόνος 2 child-slaying. [children.]

παιδο-ποιέω to beget

παιδο-ποιΐᾱ, ἡ the begetting of children.

παιδο-ποιός 2 begetting children.

παιδο-τρίβης, ου, ὁ training-master for boys.

παιδο-τρόφος 2 rearing children.

παιδουργίᾱ, ἡ mother.

παιδο-φόνος 2 = παιδοκτόνος.

παίζω to sport, play, jest; to invent in jest.

παιήων, ονος, ὁ = παιάν.

παιπαλόεις 3 steep, rocky, cragged.

παῖς, παιδός, ὁ, ἡ child, -on, daughter, descendant; boy, girl, young man or woman; servant, slave.

παιφάσσω to quiver, to move like lightning.

παίω to strike, smite; to hit, wound; *intr.* to dash against.

παιών, ῶνος, ὁ = παιάν.

παιωνίζω = παιανίζω.

παιώνιος 3 healing, saving.

παιωνισμός, ὁ the chanting of the pæan. [stop.]

πᾱκτόω to close fast; to

παλάζω = πάλλω.

παλάθη, ἡ fruit-cake.

πάλαι *adv.* of old, formerly, before; just past.

παλαι-γενής 2 aged. [old.]

παλαιό-πλουτος 2 rich of]

παλαιός 3 old, aged; ancient; antiquated.

παλαιότης, ητος, ἡ age, antiquity.

παλαιόω to make old; to abrogate. — *P.* to become obsolete.

πάλαισμα, τό a wrestling; trick, artifice; struggle.

παλαισμοσύνη, ἡ art of wrestling.

παλαιστής, οῦ, ὁ wrestler.

παλαιστιαῖος 3 a palm long or broad. [legendary.]

παλαί-φατος 2 ancient,]

παλαίω to wrestle, struggle; to succumb.

παλάμη, ἡ palm; hand; power, force; device, method, means.

παλαμναῖος, ὁ murderer; avenger.   [defile.]

παλάσσω[1] to besprinkle,]

παλάσσω[2] = πάλλω.

παλέω = παλαίω.

πάλη, ἡ a wrestling, struggle.   [birth.]

παλιγ-γενεσία, ἡ new]

παλίγ-κοτος 2 relapsing; malignant.

παλιλ-λογέω to say again.

παλίλ-λογος 2 collected again.

παλιμ-πετές *adv.* back.

παλιμ-πλάζω to drive back.

πάλιν *adv.* back, backwards; reversely; again, once more.

παλιν-άγρετος 2 revocable.

παλιν-αυτόμολος, ὁ deserter for a second time.

παλιν-όρμενος 3, παλίν-ορσος 2 hastening back.

παλίν-τιτος 2 requited.

παλίν-τονος 2 elastic.

παλιν-τριβής 2 crafty, obdurate.   [back.]

παλίν-τροπος 2 turning]

παλιν-ῳδίᾱ, ἡ recantation.

παλιρ-ρόθιος 2 flowing back.   [back, ebb.]

παλίρ-ροια, ἡ a flowing]

παλίρ-ρυτος 2 flowing in requital.   [back.]

παλίσ-ουτος 2 rushing]

παλ-ίωξις, ἡ pursuit in turn.   [as a concubine.]

παλλακεύομαι *M.* to keep]

παλλακή, παλλακίς, ιδος, ἡ concubine.

πάλλω to swing, wield, whirl, brandish, shake. — *M.* to move quickly, quiver, tremble.

πάλος, ὁ lot.

παλτόν, τό dart, javelin.

παλτός 3 hurled.

παλύνω to strew, scatter; to besprinkle.

παμ-βῶτις, ιδος all-feeding.

πάμ-μαχος 2 all-conquering.   [θης 2 enormous.]

πάμ-μεγας 3, παμ-μεγέ-]

παμ-μέλᾱς 3 all black.

παμ-μήκης 2 of enormous length.   [month.]

πά''-μηνος 2 through every]

παμ-μήτωρ, ορος, ἡ true mother.

πάμ-μορος 2 quite unhappy.

πάμ - παν, παμ - πήδην
wholly, quite.

παμ-πληθεί *adv.* with the whole multitude. [πολυς.]

παμ - πληθής 2 = πάμ-

πάμ-πληκτος 2 beaten all over. [varied.]

παμ-ποίκιλος 2 quite

πάμ-πολις, εως prevailing in all cities. [very great.]

πάμ-πολυς 3 very much;]

πχμ-πόνηρος 2 utterly bad.

πάμ-πρωτος 3 the very first.

παμ-φαής 2 all-shining.

παμφαίνω, παμφανάω to shine brightly.

παμ-φεγγής 2 = παμφαής.

πάμ-φλεκτος 2 all-blazing.

παμ-φόρος 2 all-productive.

πάμ-φ̄χος 2 in full vigour.

πάν-αγρος 2 catching all.

παν-άθλιος 3 quite unhappy.

πᾶν-αιθος 2 all-blazing.

παν-αίολος 2 all-shining, variegated. [ήμερος.]

παν-άμερος 2 = παν-

παν-άμωμος 2 quite blameless.

παν-άπαλος 2 quite tender or young. [happy.]

παν-άποτμος 2 quite un-]

παν-άργυρος 2 all of silver.

πάν-αρχος 2 all-ruling.

παν-αφῆλιξ, ικος quite without one's early friends.

παν-αώριος 2 all-untimely.

παν-δαισία, ή complete banquet.

παν-δάκρῡτος 2 most lamented; all in tears.

παν-δαμάτωρ, ορος all-subduing.

παν-δημεί *adv.* with the whole people or force.

πάν-δημος 2, παν-δήμιος 2 of the whole people, public, universal; common.

πάν-δικος 2 quite just.

παν-δοκεύω to receive or entertain all.

παν-δοχεῖον, τό inn.

παν-δοχεύς, ὁ inn-keeper.

πάν-δυρτος 2 ever-lamenting.

παν-ηγυρίζω to keep or attend a festival.

παν-ήγυρις, ή public festival. [long.]

πάν-ημαρ *adv.* all day]

παν-ημέριος 3, παν-ήμερος 2 lasting the whole day, all day.

πάνθηρ, ηρος, ὁ panther.

παν-θ̄υμαδόν *adv.* in high wrath. [ped.]

πάν-θυτος 2 all-worship-]

παν-ῐμερος 2 all-desired.

παν-νύχιος 3 all night long. [festival, vigil.]

παν-νυχίς, ιδος, ή night-]

πάν-νυχος 2 = παννύχιος

παν-οικησία, παν-οικία *adv.* with the whole house.

παν-ομφαῖος 2 author of all oracles.

παν-οπλία, ή full armour.

πάν-ορμος 2 quite fit for landing.

παν-ουργέω to act wickedly.

παν-ούργημα, τό wickedness.

παν-ουργία, ή fraud, villany, knavery.

παν-οῦργος 2 crafty, cunning, villanous, knavish, wicked; knave, rogue, villain.

παν-όφιος 2 visible to all.

παν-σαγία, ἡ = πανοπλία.

παν-σέληνος 2 of the full moon.

πάν-σοφος 2 very wise.

παν-στρατιά, ἡ the whole army.

παν-συδίη, παν-συδί adv. with all speed, in a hurry.

πάν-συρτος 2 accumulated.

παντᾶ, παντᾶ = πάντη.

παντά-πᾶσιν adv. = πάνυ.

πάντ-αρχος 2 all-ruling.

πανταχῆ, πανταχῆ adv. everywhere, in every direction, in every way; wholly. [sides.]

πανταχόθεν adv. from all

πανταχοῖ, πανταχόσε adv. in all directions.

πανταχοῦ = πανταχῆ.

παν-τελής 2 all complete, entire. [ταχῆ.]

πάντη, πάντη adv. = παν-

πάν-τιμος 2 all-honoured.

παν-τλήμων 2 quite unhappy. [ing all.]

παντο-γήρως, ων enfeebl-

παντοδαπός 3 = παντοῖος.

πάντοθεν = πανταχόθεν.

παντοῖος 3 of all kinds, manifold. [mighty.]

παντο-κράτωρ, ορος all-

παντο-πόρος 2 versatile.

παντ-όπτης, ου all-seeing.

πάντοσε = πανταχόσε.

παντουργός 2 = πανοῦργος.

πάντως, πάνυ adv. wholly, entirely, altogether; at any rate; at least; very much; certainly, indeed.

παν-υπέρτατος 3 the very uppermost.

παν-ύστατος 3 last of all.

παν-ωλεθρία, ἡ utter ruin.

παν-ώλεθρος 2, παν-ώλης 2 utterly ruined, destroyed; all-destructive.

πάομαι M. to acquire; perf. to possess.

παπαῖ woe! ah!

παπάζω to call papa.

πάππας, ου, ὁ papa.

πάππος, ὁ grandfather.

παππῷος 3 of one's grandfather.

παπταίνω to look timidly or cautiously; to peer about.

πάρ = παρά.

παρά adv. near, beside, along. — prp. with gen. from beside; from alongside of, from; with dat. by the side of, beside, near, in the presence of; according to; with acc. along; beside; towards; during; beyond, except; against, in comparison with.

παρα-βαίνω to go by the side of; to go beyond, transgress; to pass over, omit, neglect.

παρα-βάλλω to throw beside, to put before; to put side by side, to compare; intr. to come near, approach; to pass over. — M. to expose oneself; to stake; to rival; to compare; to omit, neglect; to deceive, betray.

παρά-βασις, ἡ transgression, crime. [ραβάτης.]

παρα-βάσκω to be a πα-

παρα-βάτης, ου, ὁ warrior standing beside the charioteer; transgressor.

παρα-βατός to be transgressed. [one.]

παρα-βιάζομαι M. to urge

παρα-βλήδην adv. with a side stroke or indirect cut.

παρά-βλημα, τό screen, cover.

παρα-βλώσκω to assist.

παρα-βλώψ, ῶπος looking sideways. [help.]

παρα-βοηθέω to come to

παρα-βολεύομαι M. to stake, risk.

παρα-βολή, ἡ comparison, simile; proverb, parable; venture.

παρά-βολος 2 risking, reckless; perilous.

παρ-αγγελίά, ἡ announcement, proclamation; command, order; doctrine, teaching.

παρ-αγγέλλω to announce; to pass the watchword, to give the word of command; to exhort, encourage; to command, to summon.

παρ-άγγελμα, τό, παρ-άγγελσις, ἡ = παραγγελία.

παρα-γίγνομαι M. to be present or at hand; to arrive at, to happen; to assist, help.

παρα-γιγνώσκω to decide wrong, to err in one's judgment.

παρ-αγκάλισμα, τό embrace.

παρ-άγορος 2 consoling.

παρα-γράφω to write beside, add in writing.

παρα-γυμνόω to disclose, reveal.

παρ-άγω to lead beside, by, or past; to lead up or along, to introduce, to bring forward; to make march sideways; to delay, keep in suspense; to lead astray, mislead, deceive; intr. to pass by, on, or away.

παρ-αγωγή, ἡ passage along the coast; sliding motions of the oars; variety in speech; fallacy, misleading. [beside.]

παρα-δαρθάνω to sleep

παρά-δειγμα, τό pattern, model, example; warning.

παρα-δειγματίζω to expose to shame.

παρα-δείκνῡμι to show, exhibit, represent, assign.

παράδεισος, ὁ park; paradise.

παρα-δέχομαι M. to take or receive from; to charge oneself with; to admit, allow. [occupation.]

παρα-διατριβή, ἡ useless

παρα-δίδωμι to give over, consign, deliver, transmit; to entrust; to abandon, betray; to grant, allow.

παρά-δοξος 2 unexpected; incredible, marvellous; strange, startling.

παρά-δοσις, ἡ a handing

over, transmission, surrender; tradition.

παρα-δράω to serve.

παρα-δυναστεύω to rule beside one.

παρα-δύομαι M. to steal or creep in or past.

παρα-δωσείω to be ready to deliver up.

παρ-αείδω to sing to.

παρ-αείρομαι M. to hang down on one side.

παρα-ζηλόω to provoke to jealousy or anger.

παρα-θαλασσίδιος 2, παρα-θαλάσσιος 2 on the seaside.   [age.]

παρα-θαρσύνω to encourage.]

παρα-θέω to run beside or past; to outrun.

παρα-θεωρέω to compare; to overlook, despise.

παρα-θήκη, ἡ = παρακαταθήκη.

παραί = παρά.   [βάτης.]

παραι-βάτης = παραι-

παρ-αίνεσις, ἡ consolation, exhortation, advice, warning.

παρ-αινέω to exhort, counsel. warn, recommend.

παρ-αίρεσις, ἡ a taking away; lessening.

παρ-αιρέω to take away from; to lessen; to divert on. — M. to draw over to one's own side; to take away.   [band.]

παρ-αίρημα, τό strip,]

παρ-αίσιος 2 fatal, ominous.

παρ-αΐσσω to rush on past.

παρ-αιτέομαι M. to beg from, to obtain by entreaty,

to intercede, plead for; to avert by entreaty, beg off; to decline, reject.

παρ-αίτησις, ἡ an obtaining by prayer; deprecation.

παρ-αίτιος 2 = αἴτιος.

παραί-φασις, ἡ exhortation, encouragement.

παρ-αιωρέομαι P. to hang down on one side.

παρα-καθέζομαι M., παρα-κάθημαι, παρα-καθίζω and M. to sit down beside.

παρα-καθίστημι to put or place down beside.

παρα-καίομαι P. to be burnt beside.

παρα-καλέω to call to, summon, send for, call to aid; exhort, encourage, excite; to invite; to comfort.   [veil.]

παρα-καλύπτω to cover,]

παρα-καταβάλλω to throw down beside; to put on.

παρα-καταθήκη, ἡ deposit, trust, pledge.

παρα-καταλείπω to leave behind for protection.

παρα-καταλέχομαι to lie down beside.

παρα-καταπήγνῦμι to drive in beside.

παρα-κατατίθεμαι M. to give in trust, deposit.

παρα-κατέχω to keep back.

παρά-κειμαι to lie beside; to be ready, at hand.

παρα-κελεύομαι M. to exhort, encourage; to advise.

παρα-κέλευσις, ἡ, παρα-κελευσμός, ὁ an exhorting, cheering on.

παρα-κελευστός 3 summoned; helper. [venture.]

παρακινδύνευσις, ἡ risk,

παρα-κινδῡνεύω to venture, hazard, risk.

παρα-κῑνέω to move aside; *intr.* to be mad, beside oneself.

παρα-κίω to pass by.

παρα-κλήϊω to shut out.

παρά-κλησις, ἡ a calling to, summons; exhortation, imploring, comforting; encouraging. [aside.]

παρα-κλίδόν *adv.* turning

παρα-κλίνω to turn or bend aside; to open; *intr.* to slip away, escape.

παρ-ακμάζω to be faded or withered.

παρ-ακοή, ἡ disobedience.

παρα-κοίτης, ου, ὁ husband.

παρά-κοιτις, ἡ wife.

παρ-ακολουθέω to follow close; to attach oneself to; to understand.

παρα-κομιδή, ἡ a transporting, passage.

παρα-κομίζω to carry along or across, to convey. — *M.* to procure for oneself. — *P.* to sail beside or along.

παρ-ακούω to hear by the way; to hear wrong, misunderstand; to disobey.

παρα-κρεμάννῡμι to let hang down.

παρα-κρῑνομαι *P.* to be drawn up along.

παρα-κρούω and *M.* to strike beside; to strike

the scale of a balance; to cheat, deceive.

παρα-κτάομαι *M.* to acquire beside. [shore.]

παρ-άκτιος 3 on the sea-

παρα-κύπτω to stoop aside; to take a side glance at; to look at.

παρα-λαμβάνω to receive from another, to succeed to an office, to take possession of; to capture, seize; to light upon; to hear, learn; to take with one, to intercept; to invite.

παρα-λέγομαι to sail along.

παρα-λείπω to leave remaining; to leave unnoticed, to neglect.

παρα-λέχομαι *M.* to lie beside. [αλος.]

παρ-άλιος 2 and 3 = παρ-

παρ-αλλαγή, ἡ change, transfer; relief, relay.

παρ-αλλάξ *adv.* alternately; crosswise.

παρ-αλλάσσω to change, alter; to exchange; to pervert, seduce; to pass by; *intr.* to escape; to deviate, vary; to miss.

παρα-λογίζομαι *M.* to reckon wrong; to cheat.

παρά-λογος 2 unexpected; ὁ π. wrong reckoning, miscalculation; disappointment. [sea, maritime.]

πάρ-αλος 2 lying by the

παρα-λῡπέω to grieve, vex in surplus.

παρα-λυτικός 3 paralytic.

παρα-λύω to loosen from the side, to detach from;

to relieve, release, set free, dismiss: to affect with palsy, to enfeeble.

παρ-αμείβω to change, alter; to pass by; to exceed, surpass. — M. to change for oneself; to pass by, outrun. [less of.]

παρ-αμελέω to be heed-] παρα-μένω to stay beside, to stand fast, hold out; to survive. [for the legs.]

παρα-μηρίδια, τά armour]

παρα-μίγνῦμι to mix with.

παρα-μιμνήσκομαι M. to mention by the way.

παρα-μίμνω = παραμένω.

παρα-μίσγω = παραμίγνῦμι.

παρα-μόνιμος 2, παράμονος 2 steadfast, faithful.

παρα-μῦθέομαι M. to exhort, cheer, encourage; to advise; to console, soothe.

παρα-μῦθία, ἡ, παραμῦθιον, τό exhortation, persuasion; consolation, soothing. [beside.]

παρ-αναγιγνώσκω to read]

παρα-ναιετάω to dwell beside. [beside.]

παρα-νηνέω to heap up]

παρα-νήχομαι M. to swim by or along the coast.

παρ-ανίσχω to hold up beside.

παρά-νοια, ἡ madness.

παρα-νομέω to transgress the law, to offend.

παρα-νόμημα, τό, παρανομία, ἡ transgression, law-breaking. [wrong.]

παρα-νομίζω to judge]

παρά-νομος 2 contrary to law, unlawful; lawless, unjust.

παρά-νους 2 mad.

πάρ-αντα adv. sideways.

παρα-παίω to be mad or crazy.

παρά-πᾶν adv. on the whole, altogether.

παρ-απαφίσκω to befool.

παρα-πείθω to win by persuasion, to prevail upon; to seduce.

παρα-πέμπω to send by or along; to escort; to leave unnoticed, be heedless of; to convey, transport.

παρα-πέτασμα, τό curtain; veil.

παρα-πέτομαι M. to fly by.

παρα-πήγνῦμι to fix beside or near. — P. to be fixed to. [bitter.]

παρα-πικραίνω to em-]

παρα-πικρασμός, ὁ exasperation.

παρα-πίπτω to fall in with; to befal, happen, offer itself; to commit a fault, to err; to fall off.

παρα-πλάζω to make wander from the right way, to mislead. — P. to go astray.

παρα-πλέω to sail along or by; to sail up.

παρα-πλήξ, ῆγος, παράπληκτος 2 sloping; mad.

παρα-πλήσιος 3 and 2 nearly like, resembling, about equal.

παρά-πλους, ὁ a sailing beside or by; passage.

παρα-πλώω = παραπλέω.

παρα-πνέω to blow by the side. [terleit.

παρα-ποιέω to copy, coun-

παρα-πομπή, ἡ escort; transport supply.

παρα-πορεύομαι P. to go beside or past. [a river.

παρα-ποτάμιος 3 beside

παρα-πράσσω to do beside, to help in doing.

παρα-πρεσβεία, ἡ fraudulent embassy.

παρα-πρεσβεύω and M. to act fraudulently as an ambassador. [grasped.

παρ-άπτομαι P. to be

παρά-πτωμα, τό trespass, sin. [as a border.

παρα-ρράπτω to sow to

παρα-ρρέω to flow by or down; to slip from memory; to be lost or missing: to steal in.

παρα-ρρήγνῡμι to break, rend; intr. to burst.

παρα-ρρητός 3 to be persuaded.

παρα-ρρίπτω to throw aside; to run the risk.

παρά-ρρυμα, τό protecting cover.

παρ-αρτάω, -έω to prepare, make ready; to be ready. [mile.

παρασάγγης, ου, ὁ Persian

παρα-σάσσω to stuff or cram beside.

παρά-σημος 2 marked; stamped falsely, counterfeit, base.

παρα-σῑτέω to eat with one; to be a parasite.

παρα-σκευάζω to get rea-

dy, prepare, equip, provide, procure, furnish; to make, render; to make willing; to manage. — M. to prepare for oneself; to prepare oneself, get ready, prepared. [preparing.

παρα-σκευαστής, οῦ, ὁ

παρα-σκευαστικός 3 fit for procuring a thing.

παρα-σκευή, ἡ preparation, a getting ready, equipment, provision, furniture, pomp; force, power, armament; means, resources; scheme, plot, intrigue; Friday. [camp beside.

παρα-σκηνέω, -όω to en-

παρα-σκοπέω to look at.

παρα-σπάω and M. to draw aside or over; to detach from a party.

παρα-σπονδέω to act contrary to a treaty.

παρά-σπονδος 2 contrary to a treaty. faithless.

παρα-σταδόν adv. standing beside. [pl. portic.

παρα-στάς, άδος, ἡ pillar;

παρα-στατέω to stand by.

παρα-στάτης, ου, ὁ next man; comrade, compeer, helper. [sistant.

παρα-στάτις, ιδος, ἡ as-

παρα-στείχω to step by; to pass into.

παρα-στρατηγέω to outwit by stratagems.

παρα-σφάλλω to push off sideways.

παρα-σχίζω to make a cut beside. [side.

παρα-τανύω to spread be-

19*

παρά-ταξις, ἡ an arranging; army in array.

παρα-τάσσω to put beside others; to draw up in order of battle. — *M.* to meet in battle; to arrange one's men.

παρα-τείνω to stretch out beside; to stretch or draw out; to protract, prolong; to torture, put to the rack. — *intr.* and *P.* to run along; to be stretched; to be tortured.

παρα-τείχισμα, τό wall built beside.

παρα-τεκταίνομαι *M.* to transform; to falsify.

παρα-τηρέω and *M.* to watch, observe. [tion.]

παρα-τήρησις, ἡ observa-

παρα-τίθημι to place beside or before; to supply, provide; to compare; to declare, explain. — *M.* to set before oneself; to be provided with; to call in to aid; to deposit; to entrust; to stake, hazard.

παρα-τρέπω to turn aside, divert, mislead; to make one alter one's mind; to pervert, falsify.

παρα-τρέχω to run by or past; to outrun, run down; to escape; to run up to.

παρα-τρέω to start aside from fear.

παρα-τρίβω to rub beside.

παρα-τροπέω to turn aside. [τρέπω.]

παρα-τρωπάω = παρα-

παρα-τυγχάνω to be pre-

sent by chance, to happen; to offer itself; ὁ παρα-τυχών any chance person.

παρ-αυδάω to speak to, to console; to colour, palliate. [near.]

πάρ-αυλος 2 neighbouring,

παρ-αυτίκα = παραχρῆμα.

παρα-φαίνομαι *P.* to show oneself.

παρα-φέρω to bear or carry by or along; to bring forward, produce, serve up; to mention, allege; to carry away, avert, lead away, remove; *intr.* to differ.

παρα-φεύγω to flee by or past. [to; to persuade.]

παρά-φημι and *M.* to speak

παρα-φθάνω and *M.* to be beforehand, to overtake.

παρα-φορέω to present.

παρά-φορος 2 staggering.

παρά-φραγμα, τό breastwork; bulwark. [oneself.]

παρα-φρονέω to be beside

παρα-φρονία, ἡ, παρα-φροσύνη, ἡ madness.

παρα-φρόνιμος 2, παρά-φρων 2 mad.

παρα-φρυκτωρεύομαι *M.* to make fire-signals to the enemy. [take care.]

παρα-φυλάσσω to watch,

παρα-φύομαι *M.* to grow at the side.

παρα-χειμάζω to pass the winter. [tering.]

παρα-χειμασία, ἡ a win-

παρα-χέω to heap up beside; to pour in beside.

παρα-χόω to throw up beside.

παρα-χράομαι M. to depreciate, undervalue, disregard; to misuse.

παρα-χρῆμα adv. on the spot, instantly, at once, immediately, straightway.

παρα-χωρέω to go aside, to make room; to concede, grant, yield.

παρδαλέη, ἡ panther's skin.

παρδαλίς, ὁ, ἡ panther.

παρ-εγγυάω to hand on, recommend; to pass on the watchword or word of command; to exhort, encourage, command.

παρ-εγγύη, ἡ call, exhortation; watchword.

παρ-εδρεύω to sit beside.

πάρ-εδρος 2 sitting beside; companion at table; assessor, assistant.

παρ-έζομαι M. to sit beside. [piece.]

παρειά, ἡ cheek; cheek-

παρείᾱς, ου, ὁ serpent sacred to Æsculapius.

παρ-είκω to yield, give way; to permit, allow; παρείκει it is allowed or practicable. [έρχομαι.]

πάρ-ειμι[1] (-ιέναι) = παρ-

πάρ-ειμι[2] (-εῖναι) to be by, present, or near; to stand by, help, assist; to have arrived; to be extant, at hand, or possible; τὰ παρόντα present circumstances.

παρ-ειπεῖν see παράφημι.

παρ-ειρύω to draw along the side.

παρ-εισάγω to introduce secretly.

παρ-είσακτος 2 introduced secretly. [in besides.]

παρ-εισδέχομαι M. to take

παρ-εισδύομαι to come in secretly, to slip in.

παρ-εισφέρω to bring in beside.

παρ-έκ, παρ-έξ, πάρ-εξ adv. out beside, along, past, or beyond; senselessly, foolishly. — prp. with gen. outside, before, except; with acc. beyond, alongside of, without. [κειμαι.]

παρ-εκέσκετο see παρά-

παρεκ-προφεύγω to flee away from before.

παρ-εκτός adv. besides.

παρ-ελαύνω to drive by or along; intr. to drive, ride, march, sail, or run by, past, or along.

παρ-έλκω, -ελκύω to draw to the side; to delay. — M. to draw to oneself.

παρ-εμβάλλω to throw up (a wall).

παρ-εμβολή, ἡ a drawing up in battle-order; fort, camp, barracks.

παρ-ενθήκη, ἡ insertion, addition; digression.

παρ-ενοχλέω to trouble or annoy besides.

παρ-έξ see παρέκ.

παρ-εξάγω to delude.

παρ-έξειμι = παρεξέρχομαι. [stern of a ship.]

παρεξ-ειρεσία, ἡ prow or

παρ-εξελαύνω, -ελάω to drive out past; intr. to go, ride, or drive out past.

παρ-εξέρχομαι M. to go

out beside; to transgress, elude.

παρ-εξευρίσκω to find out besides. [side.]

παρ-εξίημι to let pass be-

παρ-επίδημος 2 immigrant, stranger. [close.]

παρ-έπομαι M. to follow

πάρ-εργον, τό by-work, by-matter, addition.

πάρ-εργος 2 secondary, subordinate, by the way.

παρ-έρχομαι M. to go by, beside, past, or beyond; to pass; to escape notice; to neglect, slight; to surpass, overreach, delude; to overtake, outrun; to come to, pass to; to come forward, make one's appearance.

πάρ-εσις, ἡ forgiveness.

παρ-έστιος 2 by the hearth, domestic.

παρ-ευθύνω to direct aside.

παρ-ευνάζομαι P. to sleep beside.

παρ-εύρεσις, ἡ pretext.

παρ-ευρίσκω to find out, invent.

παρ-έχω to hold in readiness; to offer, furnish, supply, afford; allow, grant; to cause, render; to show, exhibit, represent, produce. — M. to offer, supply, produce or display from one's own means or on one's own part.

παρ-ηβάω to grow old.

παρ-ηγορέω and M. to exhort, encourage.

παρ-ηγορία, ἡ exhortation; consolation.

παρήϊον, τό, παρηΐς, ΐδος, ἡ = παρειά.

παρ-ήκω to reach or extend to; to come forth.

πάρ-ημαι M. to sit by or beside; to be present or near.

παρ-ηορίαι, αἱ reins of the by-horse.

παρ-ήορος 2 by-horse; sprawling; silly.

παρθενεύω M. to remain a maiden.

παρθενίᾱ, ἡ maidenhead.

παρθένιος 3, παρθενικός 3 of a maiden, maidenly; son of an unmarried woman.

παρθεν-οπίπης, ου, ὁ one who looks at maidens.

παρθένος, ἡ maiden, virgin, young woman.

παρθενών, ῶνος, ὁ maiden's chamber; temple of Athena.

παρ-ιαύω to sleep beside.

παρ-ίζω to place beside; (and M.) to be seated beside.

παρ-ίημι to let fall at the side, to let by, past, or through; to relax, yield, give way; to remit, to let pass, allow, permit; to forgive, pardon; to neglect, abandon, refuse; to let in. — M. to beg to be excused; to beg off; to grant.

παρ-ιππεύω to ride along; to ride up to.

παρ-ισόω to make like. — M. to vie with.

παρ-ίστημι to place by, beside, near, or before; to present, offer; to bring to one's side, win over, persuade; to make ready; to explain, describe, prove; to cause. — *intr.* and *P.* to stand beside, by, or near, to be near, at hand, or present; to help, assist; to surrender, submit; to come to one's mind, to suggest itself.— *M.* to place at one's side; to produce; to win over, to overcome, subdue.   [to offer.⟩

παρ-ίσχω to keep ready;⟩

πάρ-οδος, ἡ way past, passage, passing by; entrance.

πάροιϑεν *adv.* before; with *gen.* in front of, in the presence of.

παρ-οικέω to dwell by or along; to be a neighbour or stranger.   [hood.⟩

παρ-οίκησις, ἡ neighbour-⟩

παρ-οικίᾱ, ἡ a dwelling abroad.   [near.⟩

παρ-οικίζομαι *P.* to settle⟩

παρ-οικοδομέω to build beside.   [foreigner.⟩

πάρ-οικος 2 neighbouring;⟩

παρ-οιμιᾱ, ἡ proverb; parable.   [to maltreat.⟩

παρ-οινέω to be drunken;⟩

παροίτερος 3 fore, front.

παρ-οίχομαι *M.* to have passed by.

παρ-οκωχή, ἡ = παροχή.

παρ-ολιγωρέω to be careless.

παρ-ομοιάζω to be like.

παρ-όμοιος 2 and 3 nearly like or equal.

παρ-οξυντικός 3 inciting.

παρ-οξύνω to sharpen, incite, spur on, irritate.

παρ-οξυσμός, ὁ an inciting, provoking.

παρ-οράω to look at, notice; to look past, overlook.   [anger.⟩

παρ-οργίζω to provoke to⟩

παρ-ορμάω to stir up, set in motion.

παρ-ορμίζω to bring to anchor beside.   [side.⟩

παρ-ορύσσω to dig be-⟩

πάρος *adv.* before, formerly, in front; *conj.* = πρίν before. — *prp.* with *gen.* before, rather than.

παρ-οτρύνω = παρορμάω.

παρ-ουσίᾱ, ἡ presence; arrival, return; assistance; right time.

παρ-οχή, ἡ a supplying, offering.   [dish.⟩

παρ-οψίς, ίδος, ἡ small⟩

παρ-ρησίᾱ, ἡ freedom of speech, licence of speech; courage.

παρρησιάζομαι to speak freely.   [φασις.⟩

πάρ-φασις, ἡ = παραι-⟩

παρ-ωϑέω to push aside, drive away, displace; to conceal.   [cornice.⟩

παρ-ωροφίς, ίδος, ἡ eaves,⟩

πᾶς, πᾶσα, πᾶν all, whole, entire; every; τὸ πᾶν, τὰ πάντα the whole, everything; the universe. [all.⟩

πᾶσι-μέλουσα, ἡ a care to⟩

πάσσαλος, ὁ peg.

πάσ-σοφος 2 = πάνσοφος.

πασ-συδί see πανσυδί.

πάσσω to sprinkle upon; to interweave.

πάσσων 2 *comp.* of παχύς

παστάς, άδος, ἡ porch, colonnade, portico; bridal
chamber; dining - room;
tomb. [Passover.]

πάσχα, τό the paschal lamb,

πάσχω to suffer, to be af-
fected·by; to be liable to.

παταγέω and M. to clatter,
make a noise.

πάταγος, ὁ noise, clattering,
chattering (of the teeth).

πατάσσω to beat, knock;
to kill. [consume.]

πατέομαι M. to eat, taste,

πατέω to tread, walk; to
tread on, trample on.

πατήρ, τρός, ὁ father; forefather, ancestor; founder.

πάτος, ὁ tread, path.

πάτρα, ἡ = πατρίς.

πατρ-αλοίας, ᾱ, -φας, ου,
ὁ parricide.

πατριά, ἡ descent, lineage;
people, tribe, family.

πατρι-άρχης, ου, ὁ pa-
triarch.

πατρικός 3, πάτριος 3
and 2 of one's father or
forefathers; hereditary, customary, native, national.

πατρίς, ίδος, ἡ one's country, fatherland, native city;
race. [countryman.]

πατριώτης, ου, ὁ fellow-

πατρόθεν adv. from the
father's side.

πατρο - κασίγνητος, ὁ fa-
ther's brother, uncle.

πατρο-κτόνος 2 parricidal.

πατρο-παράδοτος 2 handed
down from one's fathers.

πατροῦχος, ἡ sole heiress.

πατρο-φόνος 2, πατρο-

φονεύς, ὁ, πατρο-φόντης,
ου = πατροκτόνος.

πατρῷος 3, πατρώϊος 3
= πάτριος.

πάτρως, ωος, ὁ father's
brother, uncle.

παῦλα, ἡ rest, repose, pause,
end. [short.]

παῦρος 2 very little, small,

παυστήρ, ῆρος, ὁ, παυ-
στήριος 2 allaying; re-
liever.

παυσωλή, ἡ = παῦλα.

παύω to cause to cease,
to stop, bring to an end;
to check, hinder; to depose.
— P. and M. to come to an
end, leave off, cease, rest;
to be deposed.

παφλάζω to bubble, foam.

πάχετος 2, πάχιστος 3
see παχύς.

πάχνη, ἡ hoar-frost.

παχνόομαι P. to be frozen.

πάχος, τό thickness.

παχύνω to thicken, fatten;
to make dull.

παχύς 3 (πάσσων, παχίων,
πάχιστος) thick, fat, stout,
great, large; rich, wealthy;
stupid, dull.

παχύτης, ητος, ἡ = πάχος.

πεδάω to bind, fetter, check,
constrain; to entangle.

πέδη, ἡ fetter.

πεδιάς, άδος, ἡ level, even;
plain country. [boot.]

πέδῑλον, τό sandal; shoe;

πεδινός 3 even, level, flat.

πεδίον, τό a plain, field,
open country; πεδίονδε
adv. to the plain.

πέδον, τό ground, soil;

πέδονδε *adv.* to the ground; πεδόθεν *adv.* from the bottom of the heart.

πέζα, ἡ foot; end, top.

πεζ-έταιροι, οἱ foot-guards in Macedonia.

πεζεύω to go on foot; to travel by land.

πεζῇ *adv.* on foot; by land.

πεζικός 3 = πεζός.

πεζο-μαχέω to fight by land. [land.]

πεζο-μαχίᾱ, ἡ fight by/

πεζός 3 on foot; by land; ὁ π. walker; foot-soldier, infantry.

πειθ-αρχέω and *M.* to obey.

πειθός 3 persuasive.

πείθω to persuade, prevail upon, win over; to appease, propitiate, win by entreaty; to bribe; to cause, impel; to mislead, cheat. — *intr.* and *P.* to be won over or persuaded; to believe, trust, rely on; to listen to, obey, comply with, yield.

πειθώ, οῦς, ἡ persuasion, eloquence.

πείκω to pick, card.

πεῖνα, πείνη, ἡ hunger; famine. [famished.]

πεινάω to be hungry or/

πεῖρα, ἡ trial, attempt, proof; experience; enterprise; plot, design.

πειράζω = πειράω.

πειραίνω to tie to, fasten by a knot; to finish, complete.

πεῖραρ¹, ατος, τό end, farthest point; issue; instrument.

πεῖραρ², ατος, τό rope; snare.

πείρασις, ἡ, πειρασμός, ὁ temptation. [deal.]

πειρατήριον, τό trial, or-/

πειράω, -έω *M.* and *P.* to try, attempt, undertake; to make a trial (of), to test, experience, examine; to try one's skill; to try to persuade; to lead into temptation; to know by experience.

πειρητίζω = πειράω.

πείρινς, ινθος, ἡ wicker-basket in a carriage.

πείρω to pierce through, to spit; to stud with nails; to cleave, pass through.

πεῖσα, ἡ obedience.

πεῖσμα, τό rope, cable.

πεισμονή, ἡ = πειθώ.

πειστικός 3 = πειστήριος.

πέκω to comb, card.

πελαγίζω to form a sea.

πελάγιος 3 of or on the sea. [open sea.]

πέλαγος, τό the high sea,/

πελάζω to bring near. — *intr.* and *P.* to approach, draw near, to be brought near; to reach to, meet.

πέλανος, ὁ offering-cake.

πέλας *adv.* near; ὁ π. neighbour, fellow-man. — *prp.* with *gen.* near to.

πελάτης, ου, ὁ neighbour; day-labourer.

πελάω = πελάζω.

πέλεθρον, τό = πλέθρον.

πέλεια, πελειάς, άδος, ἡ rock-pigeon. [axe.]

πελεκάω to hew with an/

πελεκίζω to behead.

πέλεκκον, τό axe-handle.

πέλεκυς, εως, ὁ axe.

πελεμίζω to swing, shake; to make tremble. — P. to be shaken, to tremble; to flee trembling.

πελιτνός 3 livid, fallow.

πέλλα, ἡ milk-pail.

πέλομαι see πέλω.   [tast.

πελτάζω to serve as a peltast.

πελταστής, οῦ, ὁ a light-armed soldier, peltast.

πελταστικός 3 armed with a light shield.

πέλτη, ἡ light shield; shaft, spear.   [στής.

πελτο-φόρος 2 = πελτα-

πέλω and M. to be in motion; to go, come; to behave; to be; to become; to happen.

πέλωρ, τό monster.

πελώριος 3 and 2, πέλωρος 3 huge, immense.

πέμμα, τό cakes, baker's ware.

πεμπάζω and M. to count by fives.   [ber five.

πεμπάς, άδος, ἡ the num-

πεμπταῖος 3 in five days.

πέμπτος 3 the fifth.

πεμπτός 3 sent.

πέμπω to send, send away or home, dismiss; to send word; to throw, shoot; to escort, convoy, attend; to conduct a procession. — M. to send for.

πεμπ-ώβολον, τό five-pronged fork.

πέμψις, ἡ a sending.

πενέστης, ου, ὁ labourer; bondsman.

πένης, ητος poor, needy.

πενθερά, ἡ mother-in-law.

πενθερός, ὁ father-in-law.

πένθος, τό grief, sorrow; misfortune.

πενία, ἡ poverty, need.

πενιχρός 3 = πένης.

πένομαι to toil, work; to be poor; to prepare, be busy with.   [five drachms.

πεντα-δραχμος 2 worth

πεντα-έτης, -ετής 2, πεντα-έτηρος 2 five years old.

πέντ-αθλον, τό contest of the five exercises.

πέντ-αθλος, ὁ practising (or winning) the five exercises.

πεντάκις adv. five times.

πεντακισ-μύριοι 3 fifty thousand.

πεντακισ-χίλιοι 3 five thousand.   [dred.

πεντα-κόσιοι 3 five hun-

πεντακοσιο-μέδιμνος 2 reaping 500 μέδιμνοι.

πεντά-πηχυς, υ, εως of five cubits.

πεντα-πλάσιος 3 fivefold.

πεντά-πολις, ἡ union of five cities.

πεντά-στομος 2 with five mouths.   [in five parts.

πένταχα, πενταχοῦ adv.

πέντε five.   [drachms.

πεντε-δραχμιά, ἡ five

πεντε-καί-δεκα fifteen.

πεντε-καί-δεκατος 3 fifteenth.   [five talents.

πεντε-τάλαντος 2 worth

πεντ-ετηρίς, ίδος, ἡ space of five years; festival celebrated every five years.

πεντήκοντα fifty.

πεντηκοντήρ, ῆρος, ὁ leader of fifty men. [acres.]

πεντηκοντό-γυος 2 of fifty

πεντηκοντ-όργυιος 2 of fifty fathoms.

πεντηκόντ-ορος 2 ship with fifty oars.

πεντηκοντούτης 2 lasting fifty years. [κόσιοι.]

πεντηκόσιοι 3 = πεντα-

πεντηκοστός 3. fiftieth; ἡ -ή Pentecost.

πεντηκοστύς, ύος, ἡ division of fifty men.

πεντ-ήρης, ἡ quinquereme.

πεπαίνω to make ripe. — P. to be softened.

πέπλος, ὁ, πέπλωμα, τό garment, robe, cloak, long dress; curtain.

πεποίθησις, ἡ trust.

πέπων[1] 2 ripe; soft, gentle; weakling.

πέπων[2] 2 dear; friend.

πέρ enclitic particle much, very; even; however, at any rate.

πέρᾱ adv. beyond; farther; over; longer. — prp. with gen. beyond, more than. (comp. περαιτέρω still farther, beyond).

πέραθεν adv. from beyond.

περαίνω to bring to an end, finish, complete, accomplish. — P. to be accomplished.

περαῖος 3 being beyond.

περαιόω to carry across. — P. to pass over.

πέρᾱν adv. on the other side, across, beyond; over

against. — Prp. with gen. over against, beyond.

πέρας, ατος, τό end, extremity, issue, goal; accomplishment; adv. at last.

πέρᾱσις, ἡ end; passage from life.

πέρατος 3 last, extreme.

περᾱτός 3 to be passed over.

περάω to carry across; to sell beyond the sea; to pass through, traverse; intr. to come through, to penetrate, to come over, across, or beyond; to exceed.

πέργαμον, τό, πέργαμα, τά, περγαμός, ὁ castle, citadel. [tridge.]

πέρδιξ, ῑκος, ὁ and ἡ par-

πέρηθεν, πέρην = πέραθεν, πέραν.

πέρθω to destroy, ravage; to get by plunder.

περί adv. around, about; exceedingly. — Prp. with gen. around, about; on account of, for, for the sake of; above, beyond, more than; περὶ πολλοῦ of much consequence. — with dat. around, about; hard by, near; for, on account of. — with acc. about, around; near, by; in relation to, with regard to.

περι-αγγέλλω to announce around, to send a message round; to send round orders.

περι-άγνυμι, P. to be echoed all round.

περι-άγω and M. to lead (drive, or turn) round or about; intr. to go round.

περι-αιρετός 3 able to be taken off.

περι-αιρέω to take off all round; to pull down; to abrogate, to take away. — M. to take away from oneself; to strip off; to rob.

περι-αλγέω to feel heavy pain. [ingly.]

περί-αλλα adv. exceed-

περι-αμπέχω to put round about.

περι-άπτω to attach to, to fasten round; to inflict; to kindle round about.

περι-αστράπτω to flash all round.

περι-αυχένιος 2 running round the neck.

περι-βαίνω to go round; to sound round; to sit astride on; to protect, defend.

περι-βάλλω to throw round, about, or over; to put round, to embrace, surround; to invest, attribute, ascribe; to sail round, double; to surpass. — M. to throw round oneself, to put on; to aim at, take possession of; to put round oneself for defence; to encompass, surround, enclose.

περί-βλεπτος 2 gazed at or on; notable, famous.

περι-βλέπω and M. to look round about, to gaze on.

περι-βόητος 2 notorious, of good or evil fame; surrounded by noise.

περι-βόλαιον, τό, περι-βολή, ή, περί-βολος, ὁ wall, enclosure; circum-

ference, circuit, compass; curve; an aiming at; cover, garment, sheath, veil.

περι-βρύχιος 2 surging around.

περι-γίγνομαι to be superior, prevail (over), overcome; to result, proceed; to survive, escape, remain.

περι-γλαγής 2 full of milk.

περι-γνάμπτω to sail round, double.

περι-γραπτός 2 circumscribed, enclosed.

περι-γράφω to circumscribe; to define, determine.

περι-δεής 2 very timid or fearful.

περι-δείδω to fear very much. [repast.]

περί-δειπνον, τό funeral

περι-δέξιος 2 (equally) skilful with both hands.

περι-δέω to bind round.

περι-δίδομαι M. to wager, stake.

περι-δινέω to whirl round. — P. to spin round.

περι-δίω = περιδείδω.

περί-δρομος 2 running round, circular; standing detached. [round.]

περι-δρύπτω to scratch

περι-δύω to put off around.

περι-ειλέω to wrap round.

περι-ειλίσσω = περιελίσσω.

περί-ειμι[1] (-ιέναι) = περιέρχομαι.

περί-ειμι[2] (-εῖναι) to be around; to be superior, to surpass; to result, ensue; to remain, survive, be extant.

περι - είργω to enclose round, fence in, confine.

περι-σείρω to file, put together.

περι-έλασις, ἡ a driving round; way round.

περι-ελαύνω to drive or ride round; to push round; to press hard, distress.

περι-ελίσσω to wind or roll round. — M. to wind round oneself. [or about.]

περι-έλκω to drag round/

περι-έπω to be busy about, to attend to, take care of; to honour, treat (well).

περι - εργάζομαι M. to waste one's labour; to intermeddle.

περι-εργος 2 wasting one's labour; over-careful, over-officious, forward; petty, paltry; interfering.

περι-έργω = περισείργω.

περι-έρχομαι to go round or about, to execute a wheel; to take a round-about way; to travel about or through; to come round to; to come in turn; to elapse; to enclose, surround; to overreach, cheat.

περι-έσχατα, τά outside; circuit.

περι-έχω to hold around, encompass, embrace, surround; to surpass, be superior; to comprehend, hold. — M. to hold fast by, cling to, insist on, protect; to entreat earnestly; to strive after.

περι-ζώννῡμι to gird round.

περι-ηγέομαι M. to lead round.

περι-ήγησις, ἡ outline.

περι-ήκω to have come round; to have arrived at.

περι-ήλυσις, ἡ a coming round; revolution.

περι-ημεκτέω to be much aggrieved or disconcerted.

περι-ηχέω to sound all round.

περι-θεσις, ἡ a putting on.

περι-θέω to run round.

περί-θῡμος 2 very angry.

περι-ίζομαι M. to sit round about.

περι-ίστημι to place or set round; to bring to a certain state; to alter; intr. and M. to stand round about, encircle, surround; to turn out, be changed into, devolve upon; to avoid, shun.

περι-ίσχω to surpass.

περι-κάθαρμα, τό offscouring, offscum.

περι - κάθημαι M., περι-καθίζω to sit down round about; to beleaguer.

περι-καίω to set on fire round about.

περι-καλλής 2 very beautiful. [round.]

περι-καλύπτω to cover all/

περι-καταρρέω to fall down all round.

περί-κειμαι to lie round, to embrace; to be put round; to be clothed. [round.]

περι-κείρω to shear all/

περι-κεφαλαίᾱ, ἡ helmet.

περι-κήδομαι M. to be very anxious.

περί-κηλος 2 quite dry.

περι-κλείω, -κλήω, -κλητω and M. to shut in all round. [round.]

περι-κλύζω to wash all]

περι-κλυτός 3 far-famed, renowned.

περι-κομίζω to carry round. — P. to go round.

περι-κοπή, ἡ mutilation.

περι-κόπτω to cut off, mutilate; to waste, plunder.

περι-κρατής 2 mastering.

περι-κρύπτω to conceal wholly. [about.]

περι-κτείνω to kill round]

περι-κτίων, ονος, περι-κτίτης, ου, ὁ neighbour.

περι-κυκλόω, -έω to en-circle. [circling.]

περι-κύκλωσις, ἡ an en-]

περι-λαμβάνω to seize around, embrace; to sur-round; to comprehend.

περι-λάμπω to shine round about. [περικλυτός.]

περι-λεσχήνευτος 2 =]

περι-λιμνάζω to surround with a marsh.

περί-λοιπος 2 left remain-ing [ful.]

περι-λῦπος 2 very sorrow-]

περι-μαιμάω to search thoroughly.

περι-μάρναμαι to fight for or round about.

περι-μάχητος 2 fought for; much desired. [around.]

περι-μάχομαι M. to fight]

περι-μένω to wait, wait for.

περί-μετρος 2 exceedingly large, immense; τὸ περί-μετρον circumference.

περι-μήκης 2, -μήκετος 2 very long or high.

περι-μηχανάομαι M. to devise cunningly. [round.]

περι-ναιετάω to dwell]

περι-ναιέτης, ου, ὁ neigh-bour. [up round.]

περι-νέω, -νηέω to heap]

περί-νεως, ω, ὁ passenger.

περί-νοια, ἡ overwiseness.

πέριξ adv. and prp. with gen. or acc. round about, all round.

περί-ξεστος 3 polished all round. [round.]

περι-ξυρέω to shear all]

περί-οδος, ἡ a going round, way round, circuit, circum-ference; periodical return; cycle; period; circuitous way. [περίοικος.]

περι-οικίς, ίδος, fem. of]

περι-οικοδομέω to build round about, to enclose.

περί-οικος 2 dwelling round about, neighbouring; free inhabitant in Laconia.

περι-οπτέος 3 to be regard-ed, overlooked, or suffered.

περι-οράω to look around for, wait for; to overlook, neglect; to suffer, allow. — M. to wait for; to be anxious (about); to avoid, shun

περι-οργής 2 very wrathful.

περί-ορθρον, τό dawn.

περι-ορμέω, -ορμίζομαι M. to anchor round.

περι-ορύσσω to dig round.

περι-ουσία, ἡ overplus, residue; abundance, plenty; advantage; superiority.

περι-ούσιος 2 exceeding, excellent.

περι-οχή, ἡ contents.
περι-πατέω to walk about; to lead a life.
περί-πατος, ὁ walk, a walking about; colonnade, hall.
περι-πείρω to pierce or bore through.
περι-πέλομαι M. to move round, revolve; to surround.
περι-πέμπω to send round or about.
περι-πετής 2 falling round, clasping, embracing; piercing; falling in with; reversed.   [(a)round.]
περι-πέτομαι M. to fly
περι-πευκής very sharp.
περι-πήγνυμαι P. to grow stiff round.
περι-πίμπλημι to fill full.
περι-πίμπρημι to set on fire round about.
περι-πίπτω to fall around, upon, or into; to incur; to fall in with, to meet.
περι-πλανάομαι P. to roam about.
περι-πλέκω to twist round about. — P. to fold oneself round, to cling to.
περι-πλευμονίᾱ, ἡ inflammation of the lungs.
περι-πλέω to sail about; to sail round, double.
περι-πλέως 2, περι-πλήθης 2 quite full; populous.
περίπλοος, -πλους, ὁ a sailing round, circumnavigation.
περι-πλώω = περιπλέω.
περι-ποιέω to make to remain over and above; to save, preserve, protect; to

procure. — M. to save for oneself; to acquire.
περι-ποίησις, ἡ a saving; an acquiring; possession.
περιπόλ-αρχος, ὁ commander of the boundary-watch.   [or about.]
περι-πολέω to go round
περιπόλιον, τό fort, garrison.
περί-πολος, ὁ, ἡ patrol; boundary-guard; attendant.
περι-ποτάομαι M. = περι-πέτομαι.
περι-πρό adv. advancing (or pushing forward) round about. [poured out round.]
περι-προχέομαι P. to be
περι-πτύσσω and M. to enfold, enwrap; to surround.
περι-πτυχής 2 enfolding; fallen round.   [cident.]
περί-πτωμα, τό chance, in-
περι-ρραίνω to besprinkle round.   [water vessel.]
περι-ρραντήριον, τό holy-
περι-ρρέω to flow round; to fall down; to flow abundantly.
περι-ρρήγνῡμι to break off round. — P. to be broken or parted all round.
περι-ρρηδής 2 stumbling or reeling over. [round.]
περι-ρροή, ἡ a flowing
περί-ρροος 2, -ρρυτος 2 surrounded with water, sea-girt.
περι-σθενέω to be overpotent.   [rigid.]
περι-σκελής 2 very hard,
περι-σκέπτομαι M. to look round; to consider well.

περί-σκεπτος 2 protected around. [σκέπτομαι.]

περι-σκοπέω = περι-σκέπτω

περι-σπάω to draw off from around.—M. to be distracted.

περι-σπερχέω to become alarmed or excited.

περι-σπερχής 2 hasty.

περι-σσαίνω to wag the tail round one.

περισσεία, ἡ = περίσσευμα.

περι-σσείομαι P. to wave or float about.

περίσσευμα, τό abundance, plenty; remnant.

περισσεύω to be over and above; to be too many for; to have more than enough; to grow, excel; to shower upon, enrich.

περισσός 3 above measure, more than enough; extraordinary, unusual, strange, monstrous; excellent; superfluous, excessive; useless; exaggerated; remaining, over; odd (numbers). τὸ περισσόν surplus, residue.

περισσότης, ητος, ἡ oddness (of numbers).

περι-σταδόν adv. standing round about.

περι-σταυρόω to palisade around. — M. to fortify oneself with a palisade.

περι-στείχω to step around.

περι-στέλλω to dress, manage, perform round; to take care of, protect; to clothe and bury a corpse; to cover, wrap in.

περι-στεναχίζομαι M. to resound around.

περι-στένω to cram full all around.

περιστερά, ἡ pigeon, dove.

περι-στεφανόω to surround with a crown.

περι-στεφής 2 crowned round. [φανόω.]

περι-στέφω = περιστεφανόω

περι-στίζω to stick round with; to place round in a row.

περι-στοιχίζω and M. to net in, surround with snares.

περι-στρατοπεδεύω and M. to encamp about, beleaguer.

περι-στρέφω to whirl or spin round. — P. to be turned round.

περι-στρωφάομαι M. to go round. [all round.]

περί-στῦλος 2 with pillars

περι-σῦλάω to rob entirely.

περι-σφύριον, τό anklet.

περι-σχίζω to cleave all round. — P. to be split or divided. [death.]

περι-σῴζω to save from

περι-τάμνω = -τέμνω.

περι-τείνω to stretch all round.

περι-τειχίζω to wall all round, fortify; to beleaguer.

περι-τείχισις, ἡ, περι-τείχισμα, τό, περι-τειχισμός, ὁ a walling round, circumvallation, blockade.

περι-τέλλομαι M. to run round, revolve.

περι-τέμνω to cut round, to cut off, to intercept; to rob. — M. to rob. — P. to be cut off.

περι-τέχνησις, ἡ cunning.

περι-τίθημι to put or place round about; to put on; to confer upon, invest with. — M. to put round oneself.

περι-τίλλω to pluck round.

περι-τομή, ἡ circumcision.

περι-τρέπω to turn round about or upside down, destroy. *intr.* and *P.* to go round. [deal round about.)

περι-τρέφομαι *P.* to con-)

περι-τρέχω to run round; to run round about; to run through, to discuss.

περι-τρέω, περι-τρομέομαι *M.* to tremble round about.

περι-τροπέω = περιτρέπω.

περι-τροπή, ἡ total change, revolution.

περι-τρόχαλος 2, περί-τροχος 2 round.

περι-τυγχάνω to fall in with, meet by chance, encounter, light upon.

περι-υβρίζω to insult wantonly, to ill-treat.

περι-φαίνομαι *P.* to be visible all round. [ledge.)

περι-φάνεια, ἡ full know-)

περι-φανής 2, περι-φαντος 2 seen all round, manifest; famous, excellent.

περι-φέρω to carry round or about; to move or drive round in a circle; to carry or bring to; to divulge; to endure. — *P.* to move round, revolve; to wander about.

περι-φεύγω to flee from.

περι-φλεύω to burn all round. [fied.)

περι-φοβος 2 much terri-)

περι-φορά, ἡ a carrying round; revolution, circuit.

περι-φορητός 3 carried round.

περι-φραδής 2 very thoughtful, cautious.

περι-φράζομαι *M.* to consider carefully.

περι-φρονέω to despise.

περι-φρουρέω to guard on all sides.

περί-φρων 2 = περιφραδής.

περι-φύομαι *M.* to grow all round; to cling to.

περι-χαρής 2 highly rejoiced, exceedingly glad.

περι-χέω to pour round about, over, or upon. — *P.* to surround, be spread all round. [over.)

περι-χρῡσόω to gild all)

περι-χώομαι *M.* to be in high wrath.

περι-χωρέω to go round; to pass over to.

περί-χωρος 2 surrounding, neighbouring.

περί-ψημα, τό an offscouring, offscum. [all round.)

περι-ψῑλόω to make bald)

περι-ώδυνος 2 very painful.

περι-ωθέω to thrust about; to expel; to vex.

περι-ωπή, ἡ circumspection, look-out, caution.

περι-ώσιος 2 immense.

περκνός 3 dark-coloured.

πέρνημι to sell.

περονάω to pierce. — *M.* to pin with a brooch.

περόνη, περονίς, ίδος, ἡ brooch, clasp. [boast.)

περπερεύομαι to brag,)

περσίζω to imitate the Persians.

περσιστί *adv.* in the Persian language, in Persian.

πέρυσι *adv.* last year.

περυσινός 3 of last year.

περ-φερέες, οἱ escorters.

πέσημα, τό a falling.

πεσσείᾱ, ἡ game at draughts.

πεσσεύω to play at draughts.

πεσσός, ὁ game at draughts, and stone for it.

πέσσω to make soft or ripe; to boil, cook; to digest.

πέταλον, τό leaf; tablet.

πετάννῡμι to spread out, unfold. [= πτηνός.]

πετεεινός 3, **πετεηνός** 3

πέτομαι *M.* to fly, dart, rush; to escape.

πέτρᾱ, ἡ rock, crag; stone.

πετραῖος 3, **πετρήεις** 3, **πετρήρης** 2, **πέτρινος** 3 rocky; living among the rocks.

πετρο-βολίᾱ, ἡ a stoning.

πετρο-βόλος 2 throwing stones.

πέτρος, ὁ = πέτρα.

πετρώδης 2 = πετραῖος.

πεύθομαι *M.* = πυνθάνομαι. [prudent.]

πευκάλιμος 3 sensible,)

πευκεδανός 3 bitter, destructive.

πεύκη, ἡ fir; torch.

πευκήεις 3, **πεύκινος** 3 of fir-wood.

πῆ, **πῇ** *adv.* which way? where? how? why?

πή, **πή** *adv.* anyway; somewhere; somehow.

πήγανον, τό rue. [fleeced.]

πηγεσί-μαλλος 2 thick-)

πηγή, ἡ spring, well, source; fount.

πήγνῡμι to stick, fix, make firm, plant; to harden, to cause to congeal or freeze. *intr.* and *P.* to be fixed, stiff, or frozen, to congeal.

πηγός 3 strong, stout.

πηγυλίς, ίδος icy.

πηδάλιον, τό rudder.

πηδάω to spring, leap, dart, rush, fly; to throb.

πήδημα, τό a leaping.

πηδόν, τό blade of an oar.

πηκτίς, ίδος, ἡ Lydian harp.

πηκτός fixed in; compact.

πήληξ, ηκος, ἡ helmet.

πηλίκος 3 how great, much, or old? [doll.]

πήλινος 3 of clay; earthen)

πηλός, ὁ clay, loam; mud.

πηλώδης 2 like clay; muddy.

πῆμα, τό a suffering; misery, harm.

πημαίνω to make suffer, to hurt, grieve, ruin, injure.

πημονή, ἡ = πῆμα. [time?)

πηνίκα *adv.* at what day-)

πηνίον, τό shuttle.

πηός, ὁ related by marriage.

πήρᾱ, ἡ wallet. [blind.]

πηρός 3 maimed, lame;)

πηρόω to maim, lame.

πηχυαῖος 3, **πήχυιος** 3 a cubit long.

πῆχυς, εως, ὁ fore-arm; cubit; middle of a bow; side of a lyre.

πιάζω = πιέζω.

πιαίνω to fatten.

πῑαρ, τό fat, tallow.

πίδαξ, ακος, ἡ spring, fountain.

πιδήεις 3 rich in springs.

πιεζέω, πιέζω to press, squeeze; to apprehend, arrest; to trouble.

πίειρα fem. of πίων.

πιθανο-λογία, ἡ gift of persuasion.

πιθανός 3 persuading, persuasive, winning; plausible, credible, likely; obedient, true.

πιθέω to obey.

πίθηκος, ὁ ape.

πιθηκο-φαγέω to eat ape's flesh. [vessel.]

πίθος, ὁ tub, cask; earthen}

πικραίνω to make bitter. — P. to grow angry.

πικρία, ἡ bitterness; irritation, malice. [married.]

πικρό-γαμος 2 unhappily}

πικρός 3 piercing, keen; sharp, bitter; harsh, cruel, severe, stern; morose; repugnant, odious, hateful.

πικρότης, ητος, ἡ = πικρία.

πίλναμαι to approach.

πῖλος, ὁ felt; felt-hat; felt-covering; felt-cuirass.

πιμελή, ἡ fat.

πιμπλάνω, πίμπλημι to fill (up). — P. to be or become full, to be filled or satisfied.

πίμπρημι = πρήθω.

πινάκιον, τό, πίναξ, ακος, ὁ board; treacher; plate; table; tablet; map; painting; drawing.

πίνος, ὁ dirt, filth.

πινύσκω to make prudent.

πινυτή, ἡ prudence.

πινυτός 3 prudent, wise.

πίνω to drink.

πλότης, ητος, ἡ fatness.

πιπράσκω, πιπρήσκω to sell; to betray.

πίπτω to fall, fall down; to be thrown down; to fail, err, sin; to rush upon, attack; to sink down; to be killed; to turn out, happen.

πῖσος, τό meadow.

πίσσα, ἡ pitch. [lief.]

πιστευτικός deserving be-}

πιστεύω to believe, trust in, put faith in, confide in; to entrust, to give one credit for. — P. to be believed or trusted.

πιστικός 3 = πιθανός.

πίστις, ἡ trust, faith, belief; faithfulness, honesty; credit, trust, security, assurance, pledge of faith, warrant, oath; treaty; hostage; argument, proof.

πιστός 3 faithful, trusty; sure, trustworthy, credible; believing, relying on; τὸ πιστόν = πίστις.

πιστότης, ητος, ἡ faithfulness.

πιστόω to make faithful or trustworthy. — P. to have confidence, to trust in; to pledge oneself. — M. to give one another pledges; to bind one by oaths.

πίσυνος 2 confiding in.

πίσυρες, α four. [τάννυμι.]

πιτνάω, πίτνημι = πε-}

πίτνω = πίπτω.

πίτυρα, τά bran.

20*

πίτυς, υος, ἡ pine-tree.

πιφαύσκω and M. to let appear; to show, make known, declare.

πίων, πῖον, πίονος fat, plump; fertile; rich, wealthy; plentiful.

πλᾱγά, ἡ = πληγή.

πλάγιος 3 slanting, sideways; τὸ πλάγιον side, flank.

πλαγκτός 3 wandering, roaming; mad, insane; striking. [ing.]

πλαγκτοσύνη, ἡ a wander-]

πλάζω to strike; to beat back; to drive away, out of the course; to mislead. — P. to wander, go astray; to glance off.

πλάθω to approach.

πλαίσιον, τό square.

πλακοῦς, οῦντος, ὁ cake.

πλανάω, -έω to lead astray; to deceive. — P. to go astray, wander; to wander in mind, be at a loss.

πλάνη, ἡ, πλάνημα, τό a wandering, going astray; error; perverseness.

πλάνης, ητος, πλανήτης, ου wandering, roaming; vagabond.

πλάνησις, ἡ = πλάνη.

πλάνος 2 wandering, deceiving; vagabond.

πλάξ, ακός, ἡ table, plain; table-land, flat land.

πλάσμα, τό image, figure, plastic work, imagery; fiction, forgery.

πλάσσω to form, mould, shape, fabricate; to forge.

— M. to invent for oneself; to feign. [sculptor.]

πλάστης, ου, ὁ modeller;]

πλαστός 3 formed, moulded; forged, invented.

πλάτανος, πλατάνιστος, ἡ plane-tree.

πλατεῖα, ἡ street.

πλάτη, ἡ blade of an oar, oar; ship.

πλάτος, τό breadth; plain.

πλατύνω to make broad, widen. [broad.]

πλατύς[1] 3 flat, level; wide,]

πλατύς[2] 3 salt, brackish.

πλέγμα, τό plaited work.

πλεθριαῖος 3 of the size of a plethron.

πλέθρον, τό a measure of length (100 feet); square measure, acre.

πλεῖος 3 = πλέως.

πλειστάκις adv. most times.

πλεκτός 3 plaited, twisted.

πλέκω to plait, twist; to devise, contrive.

πλεονάζω to be more than enough; to claim too much, to presume on; to grow, increase; to exaggerate.

πλεονάκις adv. more frequently.

πλεον-εκτέω to have more, to claim more, be greedy; to be superior, gain some advantage, overreach.

πλεονέκτημα, τό = πλεονεξία.

πλεον-έκτης, ου, πλεονεκτικός 3 greedy, grasping; selfish.

πλεον-εξία, ἡ advantage, gain; superiority; greediness, grasping temper, arrogance.

πλέος 3 = πλέως or πλήρης.

πλεύμων, ονος, ὁ = πνεύμων.

πλευρά, ἡ rib; side; flank.

πλευρο-κοπέω to smite or break the ribs.

πλευρόν, τό = πλευρά.

πλέω to sail, go by sea; to swim.

πλέως, ᾱ, ων = πλήρης.

πληγή, ἡ, πλῆγμα, τό blow, stroke; wound; a drubbing; shock.

πλῆθος, τό mass, throng, crowd; the greater part, multitude; the people, mob; army; democracy; size, length, magnitude.

πληθύνω to make full, increase; intr. = πληθύω.

πληθύς ύος, ἡ = πλῆθος.

πληθύω and P., πλήθω to be or become full, to abound, spread, swell. [satiety.

πληθώρη, ἡ abundance;

πλήκτης, ου, ὁ a striker; an abuser. [scuffle.

πληκτίζομαι M. to fight,

πλῆκτρον, τό plectrum (instrument for striking the lyre); punting-pole.

πλημ-μέλεια, ἡ mistake, fault; offence. [fend.

πλημ-μελέω to err; to of-

πλημ-μελής 2 making a false note; erring; offending.

πλημμυρίς, ἡ, πλημυρίς, ίδος, ἡ flood.

πλήμνη, ἡ nave of a wheel.

πλήν adv. and prp. with gen. more than; except; besides, however.

πλήξ-ιππος 2 driving or working horses.

πλήρης 2 full, filled with; well provided; satisfied, satiated; complete.

πληρο-φορέω to fill up, to fulfil; to assure, persuade fully.

πληρο-φορίᾱ, ἡ fulness; full conviction.

πληρόω to make full, fill; to man; to complete, supply; to satiate; to perform.

πλήρωμα, τό, πλήρωσις, ἡ a filling up; manning; complement; crew, equipment; satiety, fulness; whole sum.

πλησιάζω to approach; to converse, associate with.

πλησίος 3 near, close by; ὁ πλ. neighbour, fellow-man; adv. πλησίον near, hard by.

πλησιό-χωρος 2 neighbouring; neighbour.

πλησ-ίστιος 2 swelling the sails. [pletion.

πλησμονή, ἡ satiety, re-

πλήσσω to strike, smite, beat, hit; to wound; to strike back, drive away; to frighten, trouble. — M. to beat oneself.

πλινθεύω to make into bricks; to make bricks; to build of bricks.

πλινθηδόν, adv. in the shape of bricks.

πλίνθινος 3 of bricks.

πλινθίον, τό small brick.

πλίνθος, ἡ brick.

πλίσσομαι M. to stride.

πλοῖον, τό ship, vessel.

πλόκαμος, ὁ, πλόκος, ὁ braid, lock of hair.

πλόος, πλοῦς, ὁ voyage; time or wind for sailing.

πλούσιος 3 rich, wealthy; noble.

πλουτέω to be rich.

πλουτίζω to enrich.

πλουτο-κρατία, ἡ government of the wealthy.

πλοῦτος, ὁ wealth, riches; treasure, plenty; power.

πλοχμός, ὁ = πλόκαμος.

πλυνός, ὁ washing-pit.

Πλυντήρια, τά washing-festival.

πλύνω to wash, cleanse.

πλωΐζω to sail on the sea.

πλώΐμος 2, πλώσιμος 2, πλωτός 3 navigable; seaworthy; floating.

πλώω = πλέω.

πνείω = πνέω.

πνεῦμα, τό wind, air; breath; life, spirit, mind; inspiration; ghost, spiritual being, Holy Ghost. [divine.]

πνευματικός 3 spiritual;]

πνεύμων, ονος, ὁ the lungs.

πνέω to blow, breathe; to exhale, smell; to pant. — P. to be prudent or wise; to be souled.

πνῑγηρός 3 stifling, hot.

πνῖγος, τό stifling heat.

πνῖγω to stifle, choke, throttle; to stew. — P. to be drowned.

πνικτός 3 stifled, strangled.

πνοή, πνοιή, ἡ = πνεῦμα.

πόα, ἡ grass, fodder; meadow; summer.

ποδ-αβρός 2 tender-footed.

ποδ-αγός, ὁ guide.

ποδα-νιπτήρ, ῆρος, ὁ basin for washing the feet.

ποδά-νιπτρον, τό water for washing the feet.

ποδ-απός 3 of what country?

ποδ-άρκης 2 swift-footed.

ποδεών, ῶνος, ὁ end, extremity.

ποδ-ηγός 2 = ποδαγός.

ποδ-ηνεκής 2 reaching to the feet. [wind.]

ποδ-ήνεμος 2 swift as the]

ποδ-ήρης 2 = ποδηνεκής.

ποδίζω to bind the feet (of).

ποδ-ώκεια, ἡ swiftness of foot.

ποδ-ώκης 2 quick of foot.

ποθεινός 3 longed for, desired.

πόθεν adv. whence? from what place? why? how? where?

ποθέν adv. from anywhere.

ποθέω to long for, desire; to miss.

ποθή, ἡ = πόθος.

πόθι, ποθί = ποῦ, πού.

πόθος, ὁ desire, longing for; regret; want.

ποί, ποῖ = πῇ, πή.

ποία, ἡ = πόα.

ποιέω to make, do, produce, bring about, effect, cause; to perform, build, accomplish, execute; to create, beget; to compose, write, represent in poetry; to be active. — M. to make for oneself; to hold, reckon, esteem.

ποίη, ἡ = πόα. [grass.]

ποιήεις 3 grassy, rich in]

ποίημα, τό work, piece of workmanship; instrument; poem, book.

ποίησις, ἡ a making, creating; poetry, poem.

ποιητής, οῦ, ὁ maker, creator; poet.

ποιητικός 3 capable of making, productive; poetical. [well made.]

ποιητός 3 made, fabricated;)

ποιη-φαγέω to eat grass.

ποικιλίᾱ, ἡ a being party-coloured or variegated; embroidery.

ποικίλλω to variegate, colour; to embroider; to work artificially; to be captious.

ποίκιλμα, τό = ποικιλία.

ποικιλο-μήτης, ου full of various devices.

ποικίλος 3 party-coloured, pied, dappled, worked in various colours; changeful, various, varying, variegated; intricate, ambiguous; cunning.

ποικιλό-στολος 2 with variegated robe. [riddles.]

ποικιλ-ῳδός 2 singing)

ποιμαίνω to be a shepherd; to keep or feed a flock; to guide, govern; to tend. — P. to graze. [ruler.]

ποιμήν, ένος, ὁ shepherd;)

ποίμνη, ἡ flock, herd.

ποιμνήϊος 3 of a flock or herd.

ποίμνιον, τό = ποίμνη.

ποινή, ἡ ransom, wergild; requital, vengeance; penalty, punishment. [punishing.]

ποίνιμος 2 avenging,)

ποῖος 3 of what nature? of what kind?

ποιπνύω to pant, gasp; to hasten, bustle.

ποιώδης 2 = ποιήεις.

πόκος, ὁ shorn-off wool, fleece, tuft of wool.

πολεμαρχεῖον, τό residence of a polemarch. [march.]

πολεμαρχέω to be a pole-)

πολεμ-αρχίᾱ, ἡ office of a polemarch.

πολέμ-αρχος, ὁ leader in war, polemarch.

πολεμέω to make war; to wage war with.

πολεμήϊος 3 = πολεμικός.

πολεμησείω to wish for war.

πολεμίζω = πολεμέω.

πολεμικός 3, πολέμιος 3 of or for war, warlike, hostile; ὁ π. enemy, adversary; ἡ πολεμική art of war; τὸ πολεμικόν signal for battle; τὰ πολεμικά, πολέμια matters of war, hostilities.

πολεμιστής, οῦ, ὁ warrior.

πολεμόνδε adv. to the war.

πολεμο-ποιέω to cause war.

πόλεμος, ὁ war, fight, battle.

πολεμόω to make hostile. — M. to make one an enemy. — P. to be made an enemy.

πολεύω to turn up; to wander about. [the city.]

πολιάς, άδος, ἡ guardian of)

πολίζω to found, build a city.

πολιήτης, ου, ὁ = πολίτης.

πόλιν-δε adv. to the city.

πολιο-κρόταφος 2 with gray hair on the temples.

πολιορκέω to besiege, beleaguer; to harrass, vex.

πολιορκίᾱ, ἡ siege.

πολιός 3 gray, white.

πολιοῦχος 2 town-protecting.

πόλις, ἡ city, town; citadel; country, state, republic; body of citizens.

πόλισμα, τό = πόλις.

πολῑτ-άρχης, ου, ὁ ruler of the city or state.

πολῑτείᾱ, ἡ, πολίτευμα, τό right of a citizen, citizenship; life of a citizen; government, administration; policy, constitution; democracy; commonwealth.

πολῑτεύω to be a citizen, live in a free state, to have a certain form of government; to administer public affairs — M. and P. to govern, administer; to be a statesman; = Akt. — P. to be governed.

πολίτης, ου, ὁ citizen; fellow-citizen.

πολῑτικός 3 of or for a citizen; constitutional, civil, politic, public; ὁ. π. statesman; ἡ -ή science of politics. [tizen.]

πολῖτις, ιδος, ἡ female ci-)

πολίχνη, ἡ small town.

πολλάκις adv. many times, often.

πολλα-πλάσιος 3, πολλα-πλασίων 2 many times as many. [many ways.]

πολλαχῇ, -ῆ adv. often;)

πολλαχόθεν adv. from many places. [sides.]

πολλαχόσε adv. to many)

πολλαχοῦ = πολλαχῇ.

πολλός 2 = πολύς.

πολλοστός 3 little, slight.

πόλος, ὁ axis, pole; firmament; sundial.

πολύ-αινος 2 much-praised.

πολύ-ᾱϊξ, ῑκος impetuous.

πολυ-ανδρέω to be populous. [soming.]

πολυ-ανθής 2 much-blos-)

πολυ-ανθρωπίᾱ, ἡ multitude of people.

πολύ-ανθρωπος 2 populous. [silver.]

πολύ-άργυρος 2 rich in)

πολυ-άρητος 2 much prayed for.

πολυ-αρκής 2 sufficient.

πολυ-άρματος 2 with many chariots. [flocks.]

πολύ-αρνι (dat.) with many)

πολυ-αρχίᾱ, ἡ polyarchy, government of many.

πολυ-βενθής 2 very deep.

πολύ-βουλος 2 rich in counsel. [cattle.]

πολυ-βούτης, ου rich in)

πολυ-γηθής 2 very glad.

πολύ-γλωσσος 2 with many tongues; slanderous.

πολυ-γονίᾱ, ἡ prolificacy.

πολύ-γονος 2 prolific.

πολυ-δαίδαλος 2 very skilful.

πολυ-δάκρυος, -δάκρῡτος, πολύδακρυς 2 much-wept; much-weeping.

πολυ-δειράς, άδος with many summits. [trees.]

πολύ-δενδρος 2 with many)

πολύ-δεσμος 2 with many bands.

πολυ-δίφιος 2 waterless.

πολύ-δωρος 2 well-dowered.

πολυ-ειδής 2 of many shapes. [sired.]

πολύ-ευκτος 2 much de-]

πολύ-ζηλος 2 much beloved; full of envy.

πολύ-ζυγος 2 with many benches. [in crowds.]

πολυ-ηγερής 2 assembled]

πολυ-ήρατος 2 lovely.

πολυ-ηχής 2 much resounding.

πολυ-θαρσής 2 very bold.

πολυ-θρύλητος 2 much spoken of, notorious.

πολύ-θυτος 2 with many sacrifices. [knowledge.]

πολυ-ιδρείη, ἡ extensive]

πολύ-ιδρις, ιος rich in knowledge, knowing much.

πολύ-ιππος 2 rich in horses.

πολυ-καγκής 3 very dry or parched.

πολυ-καρπία, ἡ rich crop.

πολύ-καρπος 2 rich in fruit. [ning.]

πολυ-κέρδεια, ἡ much cun-]

πολυ-κερδής 2 crafty.

πολύ-κερως, ων of many horned beasts.

πολύ-κεστος 2 richly embroidered. [ful.]

πολυ-κηδής 2 very sorrow-]

πολυ-κλήῑς, ῑδος, -κλῇῑς, ῑδος with many oars.

πολύ-κληρος 2 with large inheritance.

πολυ-κλητος 2 called from many sides. [washed.]

πολύ-κλυστος 2 much]

πολύ-κμητος 2 wrought with much toil.

πολύ-κνημος - with many glens. [many.]

πολύ-κοινος 2 common to]

πολυ-κοιρανίᾱ, ἡ rule of many. [thy.]

πολυ-κτήμων 2 very weal-]

πολύ-κωπος 2 with many oars. [cornfields.]

πολύ-λήῑος 2 with many]

πολύ-λλιστος 2 much implored. [ing.]

πολυ-λογίᾱ, ἡ much speak-]

πολυ-λόγος 2 talkative.

πολυ-μαθής 2 knowing much. [ways.]

πολυ-μερῶς adv. in many]

πολυ-μηκάς, άδος muchbleating.

πολύ-μηλος 2 rich in flocks.

πολύ-μητις, ιος of many counsels. [tiveness.]

πολυ-μηχανίᾱ, ἡ inven-]

πολυ-μήχανος 2 inventive.

πολύ-μνηστος 2 much wooed. [toil.]

πολύ-μοχθος 2 with much]

πολύ-μῦθος 2 talkative.

πολύ-ξενος 2 very hospitable; visited by many.

πολύ-ξεστος 2 much polished.

πολύ-οινος 2 rich in wine.

πολυ-οφίᾱ, ἡ abundance of meat or food. [cunning.]

πολυ-παίπαλος 2 crafty,]

πολυ-πάμων 2 wealthy; much suffering. [perience.]

πολυ-πειρίᾱ, ἡ much ex-]

πολυ-πενθής 2 very mournful. [many springs.]

πολυ-πῐδαξ, ακος with]

πολύ-πικρος 2 very bitter or keen.

πολύ-πλαγκτος 2, πολυπλάνητος much-wandering. [intricate.]

πολύ-πλοκος 2 tangled,]

πολύ-ποίκιλος 2 much-variegated. [painful.]

πολύ-πονος 2 laborious,]

πολύ-πους, -ποδος many-footed; sea-polypus.

πολυ-πραγμονέω to be very busy; to be meddlesome or officious; to intrigue.

πολυ-πραγμοσύνη, ἡ a being busy with many things; a meddling, over-curiousness; quarrelsomeness.

πολυ-πράγμων 2 busy with many things; meddling, officious, curious; quarrelsome. [sheep.]

πολυ πρόβατος 2 rich in]

πολύ-πτυχος 2 with many valleys.

πολύ-πῠρος 2 rich in wheat.

πολύ-ρραφος 2 much-stitched.

πολύ-ρρην, ηνος, -ρρηνος 2 rich in flocks. [ing.]

πολύ-ρρυτος 2 much-flow-]

πολύς, πολλή, πολύ much, many, frequent; large, ample, spacious, long; heavy, strong, mighty; οἱ πολλοί the majority, the many. — Adv. πολύ, πολλά much, very; often; far, by far; very much. — Comp. πλείων, πλέων 2 more, more numerous; larger, stronger; οἱ πλείονες the greater part,

majority; the democrats; τὸ πλέον to greater part, advantage, profit. — Superl. πλεῖστος 3 most, very much, οἱ πλεῖστοι the greatest number.

πολυ-σαρκία, ἡ fleshiness.

πολυ-σῑτία, ἡ abundance of corn.

πολύ-σκαρθμος 2 much-springing, swift. [spread.]

πολυ-σπερής 2 widely]

πολυ-σπλαγχνος 2 very compassionate. [grapes.]

πολυ-στάφυλος 2 rich in]

πολυ-στεφής 2 with many wreaths. [ing.]

πολύ-στονος 2 much sigh-]

πολύ-σχιστος 2 much-split.

πολυ-τέλεια, ἡ great expense, sumptuousness.

πολυ-τελής 2 costly, expensive, sumptuous.

πολυ-τίμητος, πολύ-τῑμος, πολύ-τῑτος 2 much valued, costly.

πολύ-τλᾱς, αντος, πολυτλήμων 2 much-enduring, persevering.

πολύ-τλητος 2 unfortunate.

πολυ-τρήρων 2 with many doves. [porous.]

πολύ-τρητος 2 full of holes.]

πολυ-τροπία, ἡ versatility.

πολύ-τροπος 2 versatile, ingenious; crafty; manifold; much wandering.

πολυ-φάρμακος 2 knowing many drugs.

πολύ-φημος 2 with many voices; much talked of.

πολύ-φθορος 2 full of destruction.

πολύ-φλοισβος 2 loud-roaring. [many.]

πολύ-φορβος nourishing]

πολυ-φροσύνη, ἡ great understanding. [ingenious.]

πολύ-φρων 2 very wise,]

πολύ-χαλκος 2 rich in copper. [handed.]

πολύ-χειρ, ειρος many-]

πολυ-χειρίᾱ, ἡ plenty of hands. [long.]

πολύ-χρόνιος 2 lasting]

πολύ-χρῡσος 2 rich in gold.

πολυ-ψηφίᾱ, ἡ majority of votes.

πολυ-ψῆφις, ιδος with many pebbles. [names; famous.]

πολυ-ώνυμος 2 with many]

πολυ-ωπός 2 close-meshed.

πόμα, τό drink.

πομπαῖος 3 escorting.

πομπεία, ἡ jeering, buffoonery.

πομπεύς, ὁ = πομπός.

πομπεύω to conduct, escort, attend; to lead a procession; to jeer.

πομπή, ἡ a sending, an escorting, conduct, escort; a sending home; solemn procession; intervention.

πόμπιμος 2 = πομπαῖος; sent.

πομπός, ὁ, ἡ one who escorts, guide; messenger.

πονέω and M. to toil, work hard, to be busy; to be worn out, to suffer, be distressed, feel pain; trans. to work at, perform zealously; to gain by toil.

πονηρίᾱ, ἡ badness, wickedness

πονηρός 3 bad, wicked, villanous; useless, ill, distressed, painful, dangerous.

πόνος, ὁ toil, drudgery, hard work, hardship: battle; distress, pain, suffering, grief, misery; result of labour, work.

ποντίζω to plunge into the sea. [lord of the sea.]

πόντιος 3 of or in the sea;]

ποντόθεν adv. from the sea.

πόντονδε adv. into the sea.

ποντο-πορεύω, -έω to pass over the sea.

ποντο-πόρος 2 sea-faring.

πόντος, ὁ open sea.

πόποι int. ah! woe! shame!

πόρδαλις = πάρδαλις.

πορείᾱ, ἡ journey, march, way, expedition; a walking, gait; manner of life.

πορεῖν aor. (of πόρω) to bring, give, offer, bestow, grant; πέπρωται it has been fated, or allotted.

πορεύω to bring, carry, convey, furnish. — P. to be carried; to go, walk, march, travel; to pass over, traverse. [plunder.]

πορθέω to destroy, waste,]

πορθμεῖον, τό ferry, ford; passenger's fare.

πορθμεύς, ὁ ferryman.

πορθμεύω to carry or ferry over; intr. and P. to be carried over. [strait; ferry.]

πορθμός, ὁ passage; ford,]

πορίζω to bring, conduct, convey; to furnish, provide, supply; to contrive, fabricate. — M. to get for oneself, procure; to provide from one's own means.

πόριμος 2 rich in resources; inventive.

πόρις = πόρτις.

πορισμός, ὁ means of acquiring.

ποριστής, οῦ, ὁ provider, purveyor; adviser. [cure.]

ποριστικός 3 able to procure.

πόρκης, ου, ὁ ring, ferrule.

πορνεία, ἡ fornication; idolatry.

πορνεύω and M. to fornicate.

πόρνη, ἡ harlot.

πόρνος, ὁ fornicator.

πόρος, ὁ passage; ford, strait, bridge, thoroughfare, way for ships; sea, river; means of achieving, resource, income, revenue.

πόρπαξ, ᾱκος, ὁ handle.

πόρπη, ἡ pin, clasp, brooch.

πόρρω, adv. and prp. with gen. forwards, onwards, further; far off, afar; before, in future; far towards; far from; far into.

πόρρωθεν adv. from afar; from long ago.

πορσαίνω, πορσύνω to make ready, provide, procure; to offer, present, give.

πόρσω = πόρρω.

πόρταξ, ακος, ἡ, πόρτις, ἡ heifer, calf.

πορφύρα, ἡ purple, purplefish; purple cloth.

πορφύρεος, -οῦς 3 purple, purple-coloured; dark-red, bloody; bright, shining.

πορφυρεύς, ὁ fisher for purple-fish; purple-dyer.

πορφυρό-πωλις, ιδος, ἡ dealer in purple.

πορφύρω to wave, heave, be agitated.

ποσάκις adv. how often?

πόσε adv. whither?

πόσις[1], ἡ a drinking; drink; drinking-bout.

πόσις[2], ὁ husband.

πόσος 3 how much? how great?

ποσσ-ῆμαρ, adv. how many days? [the feet.]

ποσσί-κροτος 2 beaten by

πόστος 3 which of a number? [unheard of it.]

ποταίνιος 2 new, fresh;

ποτάμιος 3 of or on a river.

ποταμόνδε adv. into the river. [canal.]

ποταμός, ὁ river, stream;

ποταμο-φόρητος 2 carried away by a river.

ποτάομαι P. to fly, flit.

ποταπός 3 = ποδαπός.

πότε adv. when?

ποτέ adv. at any time, once; sometimes; perhaps.

ποτέομαι = πέτομαι.

πότερος 3 which of the two? either of the two; πότερον... ἤ whether... or.

ποτέρωθι adv. on which of two sides? [two ways?]

ποτέρως adv. in which of

ποτέρωσε adv. to which of two sides?

ποτή, ἡ a flying, flight.

ποτήριον, τό drinking-cup.

ποτής, ῆτος, ἡ drink.

ποτητός 3 winged; τὸ π. bird.

ποτί = πρός.

ποτι-βάλλω = προσβάλλω.

ποτίζω to give to drink; to water. [sweet.]

πότιμος 2 fit to drink;

πότμος, ὁ lot, destiny, fate; misfortune; death.

πότνα, πότνια, ἡ mistress; revered, august.

ποτόν, τό drink, beverage; liquid, water. [ing-bout.]

πότος, ὁ a drinking; drink-

ποτός 3 for drinking.

ποττώς = ποτὶ τώς, πρὸς τούς. [manner?]

ποῦ adv. where? in what

πού adv. anywhere; at any time; perhaps.

πουλυ-βότειρα, ἡ nourishing many.

πουλύ-πους = πολύπους.

πουλύς, ὁ = πολύς.

πούς, ποδός, ὁ foot, hoof, talon; lower corner of a sail, tightening rope; gait, course; race; foot (as a measure).

πρᾶγμα, τό, **πρᾶξις**, ἡ a doing, deed, execution, transaction; action; fact, occurrence; matter, circumstance; business, task, enterprise; affair, object; condition; difficulty, annoyance, intrigue; reality; public or private affairs, state-affairs, public business, government, politics; matter of consequence; effect, issue, success, profit.

πρᾱγματείᾱ, ἡ employment, business; pursuit, diligent study, diligence; written work, history.

πρᾱγματεύομαι M. and P.

to be busy, pursue a business; to take in hand, to carry on; to execute, accomplish, work out.

πρᾶγος, τό = πρᾶγμα.

πραιτώριον, τό hall of the praetor or governor; encampment of the imperial body-guard.

πρᾱκτικός 3 fit for action or business; active, busy, able, energetic.

πρᾱκτωρ, ορος, ὁ doer, worker; tradesman; tax-collector; beadle; avenger.

πρᾱνής 2 bent forward, head-foremost; down-hill, steep.

πρᾶξις, ἡ = πρᾶγμα.

πρᾷος, πρᾶος, πραεῖα, πρᾷον, πρᾶον soft, mild; gentle, kind, even-tempered; regardless of.

πρᾳότης, ητος, ἡ meekness, mildness, gentleness, patience.

πραπίς, ίδος, ἡ midriff, diaphragm; mind, heart.

πρασιά, ἡ bed in a garden.

πράσιμος 2 for sale.

πρᾶσις, ἡ sale.

πράσσω to pass through; to effect, achieve, do, work; to win, gain; to manage, practise, administer, transact; to mind, intend; to demand, exact (money). — intr. to be in a certain state or condition; to fare. — M. to do or exact for oneself, to earn (money).

πρᾱτός 3 sold.

πραΰνω to soften, soothe.

πραϋ-πάθεια, πραϋτης, ητος. ἡ = πραότης.

πραϋς 3 = πρᾶος.

πρέμνον, τό butt-end of a tree, trunk, stump.

πρεπόντως adv. fitly, decently, beseemingly.

πρέπω to be conspicuous, distinguished, or seen, to be manifest; to resemble; πρέπει it is fitting, it suits or becomes. [decent, proper.]

πρεπώδης 2 beseeming,)

πρέσβα, ἡ aged; august.

πρεσβεία, ἡ primogeniture; embassy.

πρεσβεῖον, τό privilege; gift of honour.

πρέσβευσις, ἡ = πρεσβεία.

πρεσβευτής, οῦ, ὁ ambassador.

πρεσβεύω to be older or the eldest; to take precedence, be superior, rule over; to be an ambassador; to send ambassadors; to honour, revere, worship; to mediate as an ambassador. — M. to send ambassadors; to be an ambassador.

πρεσβυ-γένεια, ἡ the being first-born.

πρεσβυ-γενής 2 first-born.

πρέσβυς, ὁ old; old man; revered, honoured, mighty; οἱ πρεσβύτεροι elders, chiefs, ancestors; οἱ πρέσβεις ambassadors. [of elders.]

πρεσβυτέριον, τό council)

πρεσβύτης, ου, ὁ = πρέσβυς.

πρεσβῦτις, ιδος, ἡ old woman.

πρῆγμα etc. see πρᾶγμα.

πρήθω to sparkle; to blow out; to swell out; to kindle, burn.

πρηκτήρ = πράκτωρ.

πρηνής = πρανής.

πρῆξις = πρᾶξις.

πρῆσις = πρᾶσις.

πρήσσω = πράσσω.

πρηστήρ, ῆρος, ὁ flash of lightning. [place.]

πρητήριον, τό trading-)

πρήθυνω, πρηϋς = πρα...

πρίασθαι to buy, purchase.

πρίζω = πρίω.

πρίν adv. before, formerly, first, sooner; ὁ πρίν ancient, preceding. Conj. before that.

πριστός 3 sawn.

πρίω to saw, saw up or asunder; to seize with the teeth, hold fast.

πρίων, ονος, ὁ saw.

πρό adv. and prp. with gen. before, in front; beforehand, sooner; outside; in defence of, in favour of, for; instead of, in lieu of; in comparison to. [summons.]

προ-άγγελσις, ἡ early)

προ-αγορεύω to tell beforehand, prophesy, forewarn; to publish, proclaim publicly; to ordain in advance, order, command.

προ-άγω to lead on or forward; to carry forward, bring on; to induce, persuade; to promote, advance; to go on, advance, proceed, lead the way.

προ-άγων, ῶνος, ὁ preliminary contest; introduction.

προ - αγωνίζομαι *M.* to fight before.

προ-αδικέω to wrong first.

προ-αιδέομαι *P.* to be indebted to or under obligations to one for a favour.

προ-αίρεσις, ἡ free choice; purpose; plan, mode; party, sect.

προ-αιρέω to bring forward; to prefer. — *M.* to choose for oneself, prefer; to intend, purpose

προ - αισθάνομαι *M.* to perceive before, to know beforehand. [beforehand.]

προ-αιτιάομαι *M.* to accuse)

προ-ακούω to hear before.

προ-αλής 2 abrupt. [fore.]

προ-αμαρτάνω to sin be-)

προ-αμύνομαι *M.* to defend oneself beforehand.

προ-αναβαίνω to go up before. [to sea before.]

προ-ανάγομαι *M.* to put)

προ - αναισιμόω, προ-αναλίσκω to spend or use up before.

προ-αναχώρησις, ἡ a going away before. [fore.]

προ-απαντάω to meet be-)

προ-απέρχομαι to depart first. [fore.]

προ-αποθνήσκω to die be-)

προ-απόλλυμι to destroy before. — *P.* to perish before.

προ - αποπέμπω, προ-α-ποστέλλω to send away first or before.

προ-αποτρέπομαι *M.* to desist before. [show first.]

προ-αποφαίνομαι *M.* to)

προ-αποχωρέω to go away before. [first.]

προ-αρπάζω to snatch up)

προ-άστειον, -άστιον, τό suburb, environs.

προ-αύλιον, τό vestibule.

προ-αφικνέομαι *M.* to arrive first or before.

προ-αφίσταμαι *M.* to revolt or fall off before.

προ-βαίνω to step forward, advance, make progress, to go on; to elapse; to grow older; to go before, be superior (to).

προ-,άλλω to throw before, down, or away; to put forward, propose, oppose; to stake, pledge, venture. — *M.* to put before oneself, to hold before oneself as a defence; to use a pretence, allege; to throw away, abandon; to propose for election; to surpass.

πρό-βασις, ἡ cattle.

προβατικός 3 of or for sheep.

προβάτιον, τό little sheep.

πρό-βατον, τό cattle; flock, sheep.

προ-βιβάζω to bring forward; to lead on; to incite beforehand. [vide for.]

προ-βλέπομαι *M.* to pro-)

πρό-βλημα, τό projection, cape: guard, defence, shelter, bulwark; armour, spear; excuse, pretext; problem.

προ-βλής, ῆτος projecting; foreland.

πρό-βλητος 2 thrown away.

προ-βλώσκω to come forth (from), go out of.

προ-βοάω to shout before, cry out.

προ-βόλαιος, ὁ spear.

προ-βολή, ἡ, πρό-βολος, ὁ = πρόβλημα; a putting forward (of arms), defence, attack; preliminary impeachment.

προ-βοσκός, ὁ herdsman.

προ-βούλευμα, τό preliminary decree.

προ-βουλεύω to consult, consider before; to form a preliminary decree; to provide for. — M. to consider first.

πρό-βουλος, ὁ preliminary counsellor.   [before.]

προ-βωθέω to come to aid.

προ-γενής 2 born before, old, ancient, aged.

προ-γίγνομαι M. to be born before; to happen before; to come forward, appear.

προ-γιγνώσκω to know or learn beforehand; to decide beforehand.   [ledge.]

πρό-γνωσις, ἡ foreknow-

πρό-γονος 2 born before, elder; ancestor, forefather.

προ-γράφω to write before; to write in public.

προ-δαῆναι to know before.

προ-δείδω to fear beforehand.

προ-δείκνυμι to show forth, point out; to point before one; to publish beforehand.

προ-δειμαίνω to fear beforehand.   [signifier.]

προ-δέκτωρ, ορος, ὁ pre-

πρό-δηλος 2 manifest, known to all.

προ-δηλόω to show future things.

προ-διαβαίνω to go across before.   [beforehand.]

προ-διαβάλλω to slander.

προ-διαγιγνώσκω to consider before.

προ-διαφθείρω to destroy or ruin beforehand.

προ-διδάσκω to teach beforehand.

προ-δίδωμι to give or pay in advance; to give up, betray, forsake, abandon; intr. to flee, turn traitor; to fail.

προ-διηγέομαι M. to relate beforehand.

πρό-δικος, ὁ advocate, guardian.   [ther.]

προ-διώκω to pursue fur-

προ-δοκεῖ, pf. προεδόχαται it was resolved before.

προ-δοκή, ἡ (shooting-) stand, ambush.

πρό-δομος, ὁ fore-house.

προ-δοσιά, ἡ treachery.

προ-δότης, ου, ὁ traitor; runaway.

προ-δοτικός 3 traitorous.

πρό-δοτος 2 betrayed, abandoned.   [ward.]

προ-δρομή, ἡ a running for-

πρό-δρομος 2 running before, forerunner: scout, vanguard; skirmisher.

προ-εδρίᾱ, ἡ presidency, precedence; first place.

πρό-εδρος, ὁ president.

προ-εέργω to obstruct by stepping in the way.

προ-εθίζω to accustom beforehand.   [ἔρχομαι.]

πρό-ειμι¹ (-ιέναι) = προπρό-ειμι² (-εῖναι) to be before.

προ-είπον see προαγορεύω.

προ-εισάγω to bring in before. [fore.]

προ-εκθέω to run out before.

προ-εκκομίζω to carry out before. [ney in advance.]

προ-εκλέγω to collect mo-

προ-εκφόβησις, ἡ an intimidating beforehand.

προ-ελαύνω intr. and P. to ride forward, advance.

προ-ελπίζω to hope before.

προ-εμβάλλω to make an inroad, attack before.

προ-ενάρχομαι to begin before. [aloud.]

προ-εννέπω to pronounce

προ-ενοίκησις, ἡ a dwelling in before.

προ-εξαγγέλλω to announce beforehand. [first.]

προ-εξάγω to bring out

προ-εξᾴσσω, -ᾴσσω to rush out before.

προ-εξανίστημι intr. and M. to rise before others or too soon; to start first.

προ-εξέδρᾱ, ἡ high seat.

προ-έξειμι, προ-εξέρχομαι to go out before.

προ-εξορμάω to start before.

προ-επαγγέλλω and M. to promise before. [fore.]

προ-επαινέω to praise before.

προ-επανασείω to menace before. [first.]

προ-επιχειρέω to attack

προ-εργάζομαι M. to do or work before; to earn before.

προ-ερέσσω to row forward. [forward.]

προ-ερύω to draw on or

προ-έρχομαι to go forth, on, or forward, advance; to appear in public; to pass; to proceed, start; to go first.

προ-ετικός 3 prodigal.

προ-ετοιμάζω to prepare.

προ-ευαγγελίζομαι M. to bring glad tidings beforehand.

προ-έχω to hold before; to have before; to know beforehand; to have in preference to. intr. to project, jut out; to be before, be the first, superior, eminent; οὐ προέχει it is not better. — M. to hold before oneself, hold out as a pretext; to offer.

προ-ηγεμών, όνος, ὁ guide.

προ-ηγέομαι M. to go before or forward, lead the way; to be the leader.

προ-ηγητής, οῦ, ὁ = προηγεμών. [others.]

προ-ηγορέω to speak for

προ-ήκης 2 pointed in front.

προ-ήκω to have advanced; to be the first or superior.

προ-θέλυμνος 2 having several layers; from the root.

πρό-θεσις, ἡ exhibition, show; purpose, design.

προ-θέσμιος 3 appointed, fixed before; ἡ προθεσμίᾱ term, period, limitation.

προ-θέω¹ to run forward.

προ-θέω² = -τίθημι.

προ-θνήσκω to die before.

προ-ϑρῴσκω to leap forward.

προ-ϑῡμέομαι P. to be willing, ready, eager, or zealous; to desire, endeavour.

προ-ϑῡμίᾱ, ἡ willingness, readiness; zeal, wish, desire; good will.

πρό-ϑῡμος 2 ready, willing; eager, earnest, zealous; well-disposed.

πρό-ϑυρον, τό front door; space before a door; porch, entry. [before.]

προ-ϑύω and M. to sacrifice

προ-ΐάλλω, προ-ΐάπτω to send forth. [first seat.]

προ-ΐζομαι M. to take the

προ-ΐημι to send before, on, or forward; to dismiss, let go; to forsake, abandon, throw away; to deliver over; to allow. — M. to utter, pronounce; to devote oneself (to); to offer, present; to entrust; to allow, suffer; to abandon, throw away, neglect.

προ-ΐκτης, ου, ὁ beggar.

προΐξ, προίξ, προικός, ἡ gift, present: dower: adv. προῖκα, προικός freely, without return.

προ-ΐστημι to place before or in front. — intr. and P. to place oneself before, to stand before; to be opposed to; to protect, guard; to approach, entreat; to be at the head (of), to be set over, be the chief, manage, govern; to place before oneself; to prefer.

προ-ΐσχω = προέχω.

πρόκα adv. at once, suddenly.

προ-κάϑημαι M. to sit before; to protect, defend.

προ-καϑίζω and M. to sit down before, in front, or in public.

προ-καϑίστημι, pf. and M. to be placed before.

προ-καϑοράω to view beforehand.

προ-καίω to burn before.

προ-καλέω, προ-καλίζω to call forth. — M. to challenge; to summon, incite, invite; to offer, propose; to cause, effect.

προ-καλινδέομαι = προκυλίνδομαι.

προ-κάλυμμα, τό curtain, covering; screen; pretext.

προ-καλύπτω to hang before as a covering. — M. to veil or screen oneself; to pretend.

προ-κάμνω to toil before; to grow weary beforehand; to work for another.

προ-καταγγέλλω to announce beforehand.

προ-καταγιγνώσκω to accuse or condemn beforehand. [fore.]

προ-κατακαίω to burn be-

προ-καταλαμβάνω to seize or occupy beforehand, anticipate; to prevent.

προ-καταλέγω to describe beforehand.

προ-καταλύω to break up or annul before.

προ-καταρτίζω to make ready before.

προ-κατάρχομαι *M.* to begin first. [before.]

προ-καταφεύγω to escape beforehand, before, or first;

προ-κατέχω to occupy or take possession of before.

προ-κατηγορέω to accuse beforehand.

προ-κατηγορίᾱ, ἡ previous accusation.

πρό-κειμαι *M.* to lie before; to lie exposed; to jut out; to be set before or in front of; to be proposed.

προ-κήδομαι *M.* to take care of.

προ-κηραίνω to be anxious.

προ-κηρύσσω to proclaim publicly.

προ-κινδῡνεύω to run the first risk; to fight as a champion; to defend.

προ-κῑνέω to move forward.

προ-κλαίω to weep beforehand or aloud.

πρό-κλησις, ἡ challenge; summons, proposal.

προ-κλίνω to lean forward.

πρό-κλυτος 2 far-famed.

προ-κομίζω to bring forward. [growth.]

προ-κοπή, ἡ progress,

προ-κόπτω to promote; *intr.* and *P.* to advance, thrive.

πρό-κρῐμα, τό preference.

προ-κρίνω to choose before, prefer; to judge, decide. — *P.* to be preferred or thought superior. [in rows.]

πρό-κροσσος 2 and 3 ranged

προ-κυλίνδομαι, **-δέομαι** *M.* to be rolled forward; to prostrate oneself.

προ-λαμβάνω to take (away) beforehand, before, or first; to obtain first, anticipate; to claim before, prefer; to apprehend, surprise.

προ-λέγω to foretell, prophesy; to tell publicly, proclaim; to choose before.

προ-λείπω to leave, forsake; to omit. — *intr.* to cease, disappear.

προ-λεσχηνεύομαι *M.* to discuss orally before.

προ-λεύσσω to see at a distance, foresee.

προ-λοχίζω to lay an ambush before, to beset with an ambush.

προ-μανθάνω to learn before; to continue learning.

προ-μαντείᾱ, ἡ precedence in consulting an oracle.

πρό-μαντις, ὁ, ἡ prophetic; prophet, priest.

προ-μαρτύρομαι *M.* to witness beforehand.

προ-μαχέω, **προ-μαχίζω** and *M.*, **προ-μάχομαι** to fight in front or as a champion. [part; bulwark.]

προ-μαχεών, ῶνος, ὁ ram-

πρό-μαχος fighting before or in front; fighting for.

προ-μελετάω to practise beforehand. [ful before.]

προ-μεριμνάω to be care-

προ-μετωπίδιον, τό skin of the forehead; front-piece.

προμήθεια, ἡ foresight; care.

προμηθέομαι *P.* to consider or take care (of) beforehand.

προ-μηθής 2 cautious, caring.

προμηθία, ἡ = προμήθεια.

προ-μηνύω to inform beforehand. [beforehand.]

προ-μίγνῠμαι P. to lie with]

προ-μνάομαι M. to woo for another; to advise; to presage.

προ-μνηστῖνοι 3 one by one.

προ-μνήστρια, -μνηστρίς, ίδος, ἡ match-maker.

προ-μολεῖν see προβλώσκω.

πρόμος, ὁ foremost, leader, prince; champion.

πρό-νᾱος 2 = προνήϊος.

προ-ναυμαχέω to fight at sea for. [ground.]

προ-νέμομαι M. to gain]

προ-νήϊος 3 before a temple; ὁ πρ. vestibule.

προ-νηστεύω to fast beforehand. [forehand.]

προ-νῑκάω to conquer be-]

προ-νοέω and P. to perceive beforehand, to presage; to consider, care, or think beforehand; to provide.

προ-νοητικός 3 provident, cautious.

πρό-νοια, ἡ foresight, forethought; providence; purpose, intention; care.

προ-νομή, ἡ a foraging.

πρό-νοος, πρό-νους 2 cautious, prudent. [fawn.]

πρόξ, προκός, ἡ hind-calf,]

πρό-ξεινος, ὁ = πρόξενος.

προ-ξενέω to be a public guest; to be a protector or patron; to negotiate, manage, procure; to recommend.

προ-ξενία, ἡ the being a πρόξενος.

πρό-ξενος, ὁ, ἡ public guest or host, agent of a foreign state; patron.

προ-ξυγγίγνομαι M. to meet with beforehand.

πρό-οδος, ἡ a going on, advance.

πρό-οιδα to know before.

προ-οιμιάζομαι M. to make a preamble.

προ-οίμιον, τό prelude, preamble, preface, introduction; hymn; false show.

προ-όμνῠμι to swear before.

προ-ομολογέω to agree beforehand. [manifest.]

πρό-οπτος 2 seen from afar,]

προ-οράω to look forward; to see before or from afar; to foresee; to provide for, consider beforehand; to take care, be cautious.

προ-ορίζω to determine beforehand.

προ-ορμάω and P. to start forward or in advance.

προ-ορμίζω to moor in front.

προ-οφείλω to owe from a former time. — P. to be in arrear. [ing.]

πρό-οψις, ἡ a previous see-]

πρό-παππος, ὁ great-grandfather.

προ-παραβάλλομαι M. to put in rows beforehand.

προ-παρασκευάζω to make ready beforehand.

προ-παρέχω to offer before. — M. to provide oneself before.

προ-πάροιθεν *adv.* and *prp.* with *gen.* in front of, before, forward(s); along.

πρό-πᾶς, ᾱσα, ᾱν all; altogether.

προ-πάσχω to suffer before.

προ-πάτωρ, ορος, ὁ forefather, ancestor.

πρό-πειρα, ἡ previous trial.

προ-πέμπω to send before, in advance, on, or forth; to afford, offer; to send away, dismiss; to conduct, escort; to pursue. [impetuosity.]

προ-πέτεια, ἡ rashness,

προ-πετής 2 falling forward(s); prostrate; ready; rash, prone, hasty.

προ-πηλακίζω to cover with mud; to maltreat, abuse, reproach.

προ-πηλακισμός, ὁ insult.

προ-πίνω to drink to; to give or trifle away.

προ-πίπτω, -πίτνω to fall forward; to rush forward; to prostrate oneself.

προ-πλέω to sail before.

πρό-πλοος, -πλους 2 sailing before.

προ-ποδίζω to step forward.

προ-ποιέω to do beforehand; to prepare.

προ-πολεμέω to fight for.

πρό-πολος, ὁ, ἡ servant in a temple, priest, priestess.

προ-πομπός, ὁ, ἡ conductor.

προ-πονέω to work beforehand; to work or toil for. — *M.* to suffer on.

πρό-πονος, ὁ previous toil.

προ-πορεύομαι *P.* to go forward.

προ-πρηνής 2 bent forward; lying on one's face.

προπρο-κυλίνδομαι to roll on and on or to and fro.

προ-πύλαιον, πρό-πυλον, τό entry, porch, vestibule.

προ-πυνθάνομαι to learn or hear before.

προ-ρέω to flow forward.

πρό-ρρησις, ἡ previous announcement; order.

πρό-ρρητος 2 foretold, ordered. [radical.]

πρό-ρριζος 2 by the roots;

πρός *adv.* besides, over and above. — *Prep.* with *gen.* from, from forth, from the side of; on the side of, against, towards; on the part of, in presence of, before; with a *passive verb* = ὑπό; according to; suiting. — with *dat.* at, on, near, hard by, in presence of; in addition to, besides. — with *acc.* towards, to, upon; against, in answer to; in regard to; according to; in proportion to; in comparison of. [the Sabbath.]

προ-σάββατον, τό eve of

προσ-αγορεύω to address, accost, greet; to call by name; to speak, utter.

προσ-άγω to bring on; to lead on, induce; to add, supply, introduce; *intr.* to advance, approach. — *M.* to attach to oneself, win over; to induce.

προσ-αγωγή, ἡ a bringing on; admission, access; solemn procession.

προσ-αγωγός 2 attractive.

προσ-ᾴδω to sing to; to agree, consent.

προσ-αιρέομαι M. to choose in addition to.

προσ-αΐσσω to rush to.

προσ-αιτέω to ask besides; to beg of. [sides.]

προσ-ακούω to hear be-]

προσ-αλείφω to smear upon. [come to aid.]

προσ-αμύνω to defend,]

προσ-αναβαίνω to mount besides. [besides.]

προσ-αναγκάζω to force]

προσ-αναιρέομαι M. to undertake besides.

προσ-αναισιμόω, προσ-αναλίσκω to spend or consume besides.

προσ-αναπληρόω to fill up by addition.

προσ-ανατίθεμαι M. to take on oneself in addition; to consult with; to un-bosom oneself.

προσ-άνειμι to go up to.

προσ-ανειπεῖν to announce besides.

προσ-ανέχω to approach.

προσ-άντης 2 up-hill, steep; arduous, adverse, hostile.

προσ-απαγγέλλω to re-port besides.

προσ-απειλέω to threaten besides.

προσ-αποβάλλω to lose besides. [nounce besides.]

προσ-απογράφω to de-]

προσ-αποδείκνῡμι to prove besides.

προσ-απόλλῡμι, -ύω to destroy or kill besides. —

intr. and M. to perish be-sides. [off besides.]

προσ-αποστέλλω to send]

προσ-άπτω to attach or fasten to; to add, attri-bute, grant; intr. to be added. — M. to touch, lay hold on. [fit to.]

προσ-αραρίσκω to join,]

προσ-αρκέω to lend aid; to grant, afford.

προσ-αρμόζω to attach, fit to. [join to.]

προσ-αρτάω to fasten,]

προ-σάττω to equip be-forehand. [by name.]

προσ-αυδάω to accost, call]

προσ-αύω to burn partly.

προσ-αφικνέομαι M. to arrive besides.

προσ-αφίστημι to cause to revolt besides.

προσ-βαίνω to go towards, up, or to: to come near, to step on: to attack.

προσ-βάλλω to throw to or upon; to apply to, affix; to add, assign; to thrust, hit, shine upon; to offer, pre-sent. — intr. and M. to throw oneself upon; to ap-proach, attack; to come to land; to strike against; to contribute. [cent.]

πρόσ-βασις, ἡ access, as-]

προσ-βατός 3 accessible.

προσ-βιάζομαι P. to be pressed towards.

προσ-βιβάζω to bring or convey to.

προσ-βλέπω to look at or on.

προσ-βοάομαι M. to call to oneself.

προσ-βοηθέω to come to aid.

προσ-βολή, ἡ a throwing upon; a coming on, attack, assault; landing; harbour.

προσ-βωθέω = -βοηθέω.

προσ-γελάω to smile upon.

προσ-γίγνομαι M. to come to; attach oneself to; to be present; to arrive; to happen to.   [writing.]

προσ-γράφω to add in]

προσ-δανείζω to lend in addition.

πρόσ-δεγμα, τό reception.

προσ-δεῖ there is still wanting.

προσ-δέομαι P. to want besides; to beg, ask besides.

προσ-δέρχομαι P. to look at; to look around.

προσ-δέχομαι M. to receive, accept; to admit; to wait for, expect; to suppose.

προσ-δέω¹ to tie to.

προσ-δέω² see προσ-δεῖ, -δέομαι.   [besides.]

προσ-δηλέομαι M. to ruin]

προσ-διαλέγομαι P. to converse with besides.

προσ-διαφθείρω to destroy besides.   [sides.]

προσ-δίδωμι to give be-]

προσ-δοκάω = -δέχομαι.

προσ-δοκέω to seem besides.   [anticipation.]

προσ-δοκίᾱ, ἡ expectation,]

προσ-δόκιμος 2 expected.

προσ-εάω to let approach.

προσ-εγγίζω to approach.

προσ-εγγράφω to inscribe besides

προσ-εδρείᾱ, ἡ blockade, siege.

προσ-εδρεύω to sit near; to adhere, keep to.

πρόσ-εδρος 2 enclosing.

προσ-εικάζω to make like, to liken.

προσ-είκελος 3 resembling.

προσ-ειλέω to press against.

πρόσ-ειμι¹ = προσέρχομαι.

πρόσ-ειμι² (-εῖναι) to be near, by, or at; to be added or attached; to be there, belong to.

προ-σείω to hold out.

προσ-εκβάλλω to expel besides.

προσ-εκτικός 3 attentive.

προσ-ελαύνω to drive or ride towards.   [upon.]

προσ-εμβαίνω to trample]

προσ-εμπικραίνομαι P. to be angry all the more.

προσ-εμφερής 2 resembling.   [greet.]

προσ-εννέπω to accost,]

προσ-εξαιρέομαι M. to select for oneself besides.

προσ-έοικα to resemble, be like; to be fit.

προσ-επεξευρίσκω to invent besides

προσ-επικτάομαι M. to acquire besides. [join in.]

προσ-επιλαμβάνω M. to]

προσ-επιστέλλω to charge besides.

προσ-εργάζομαι M. to effect or acquire besides.

προσ-ερεύγομαι M. to vomit forth against.

προσ-έρπω to creep on, approach.

προσ-έρχομαι *M.* to go or come up, to, or forward, to approach; to mount; to visit; to advance, attack; to come in (of money).

προσ-ερωτάω to question besides.

προσ-εταιρίζομαι *M.* to take as a comrade.

προσ-εταιριστός 3 taken as a comrade.

προσ-έτι *adv.* besides.

προσ-ευρίσκω to find besides. [of prayer.]

προσ-ευχή, ἡ prayer; place [close to.]

προσ-εύχομαι *M.* to pray to or for.

προσ-εχής 2 adjoining,

προσ-έχω to hold to, bring to, direct to; to bring to land; πρ. τινί (τὸν νοῦν) to turn one's mind or attention to, to attend, give heed to; to devote oneself to, to be attached to; to have besides. — *M.* to attach oneself to, cling to; to be implicated in.

προσ-ζημιόω to punish into the bargain. [greet.]

προσ-ηγορέω to accost,

προσ-ηγορία, ἡ an addressing; a naming, title.

προσ-ήγορος 2 accosting, imploring; accosted.

προσ-ήκω to have arrived, be near; to reach to; to concern, affect. **προσήκει** it belongs to or concerns; it befits or beseems.

προσ-ήκων 3 belonging to; befitting, seemly; related, akin.

προσ-ηλόω to nail to.

προσ-ήλυτος, ὁ a new comer, stranger, proselyte.

πρόσ-ημαι to sit close to.

προ-σημαίνω to announce before, to order.

προσ-ηνής 2 kind, gentle; suitable.

προσ-θᾱκέω to sit beside.

πρόσθεν *adv.* (and *prp.* with *gen.*) in front of, before, to the front, forwards, further; in defence of; formerly, of old; ὁ πρ. front man; τὸ πρ., τὰ πρ. the front, vanguard, place in front; day before.

πρόσ-θεσις, ἡ an adding; a putting on.

προσ-θέω to run to.

προσ-θήκη, ἡ addition, supplement, appendix; assistance.

προσ-θιγγάνω to touch.

πρόσθιος 3 the foremost.

προσ-ιζάνω, -ίζω to sit on or by.

προσ-ίημι to admit. — *M.* to suffer to approach; to admit, allow, approve, accept.

προσ-ίκελος 2 = προσείκελος.

προσ-ιππεύω to ride up to.

προσ-ίστημι to place near. *intr.* and *M.* to stand near or beside; to arrive at; to enter one's mind.

προσ-ίσχω = προσέχω.

προσ-καθέζομαι, -κάθημαι, -καθίζω to sit near or beside; to besiege; to keep to; to be hard upon one.

πρόσ-καιρος 2 transitory.

προσ-καλέω to call to or

on, summon. — *M.* to call to aid; to call into court.

προσ-καρτερέω to persevere still longer; to adhere to.

προσ-καταλείπω to leave behind; to lose besides.

προσ-κατηγορέω to accuse besides.

πρόσ-κειμαι to lie near or upon; to be joined with, involved in, added, or imposed; to belong to; to be attached or devoted to; to be hard upon one.

προ-σκέπτομαι *M.* = προσκοπέω.

προσ-κεφάλαιον, τό pillow.   [allied to.]

προσ-κηδής 2 affectionate;

προσ-κηρūκεύομαι *M.* to send a herald to.

προσ-κληρόομαι *P.* to be associated with.

πρόσ-κλησις, ή citation, summons.

προσ-κλίνω to lean against. — *P.* to attach oneself to.

πρόσ-κλισις, ή inclination.

προσ-κνάομαι *M.* to rub oneself against.

προσ-κολλάω to glue to. — *P.* to cleave to.

προσ-κομίζω to carry, convey to.

πρόσ-κομμα, τό stumble; offence, fault; scandal.

προ-σκοπέω and *M.* to see or consider beforehand; to provide against.

προ-σκοπή, ή a spying beforehand.   [κομμα.]

προσ-κοπή, ή = πρόσ-

προσ-κόπτω to stumble; to take offence.

προσ-κρούω to strike against; to offend; to take offence.

προσ-κτάομαι *M.* to gain or acquire besides.

προσ-κυλίω to roll to.

προσ-κυνέω to prostrate oneself before; to worship.

προσ-κυνητής, οὗ, ὁ worshipper.

προσ-κύρω to befal, meet with.   [rower.]

πρόσ-κωπος 2 rowing;

προσ-λαλέω to speak to.

προσ-λαμβάνω and *M.* to take hold of; to take with one or to oneself; to receive besides or in addition; to win besides.   [or on.]

προσ-λεύσσω to look at

προσ-λέχομαι *M.* to lie near.

πρόσ-ληψις, ή reception.

προσ-λογίζομαι *M.* to reckon in addition to.

προσ-μάσσω to knead to.

προσ-μάχομαι *M.* to assail.

προσ-μένω to abide, remain; to wait for.

προσ-μεταπέμπομαι *M.* to send for besides.

προσ-μίγνūμι, -ύω to mix to; to join to; *intr.* to unite oneself to; to approach, arrive at, land; to meet in battle.   [assault.]

πρόσ-μιξις, ή approach,

προσ-μίσγω = -μίγνūμι.

προσ-μισθόομαι to hire besides.

προσ-ναυπηγέω to build still more ships.

προσ-νέμω and *M.* to attribute; to devote, assign.

προσ-νέω to swim towards.

προσ-νίσσομαι *M.* to go to, come near.

προσ-νωμάω to move to.

πρόσ-οδος, ἡ an approaching, advance, attack; public appearance; solemn procession; path; income, revenue; return, profit.

πρόσ-οιδα to know besides.

προσ-οικέω to dwell by or near. [in addition.]

προσ-οικοδομέω to build/

πρόσ-οικος 2 dwelling near to; neighbour.

προσ-ολοφύρομαι *M.* to complain to.

προσ-ομιλέω to converse with; to busy oneself with

προσ-όμνῡμι to swear in addition.

προσ-ομολογέω to concede, grant, or agree to besides; to surrender.

προσ-όμουρος 2 neighbouring. [at, behold.]

προσ-οράω and *M.* to look/

προσ-ορέγομαι *P.* to entreat earnestly.

προσ-ορμίζω to anchor near. — *P.* and *M.* to put to shore.

προσ-όρμισις, ἡ a landing.

πρόσ-ορος, -ουρος 2 adjoining; neighbour.

προσ-ουδίζω to dash to the earth.

προσ-οφείλω,-οφλισκάνω to owe besides; to incur or deserve besides. [dignant.]

προσ-οχθίζω to be in-/

προσ-όφιος 2 visible.

πρόσ-οψις, ἡ sight; view; appearance. [or jest with.]

προσ-παίζω to sport, play,/

προσ-παίω to knock at, to strike against. [in besides.]

προσ-παρακαλέω to call/

προσ-παρασκευάζω to prepare besides. [besides.]

προσ-παρέχω to furnish/

προσ-πασσαλεύω to nail to. [sides.]

προσ-πάσχω to suffer be-/

πρόσ-πεινος 2 very hungry.

προσ-πελάζω to bring near (to). — *intr.* and *P.* to approach.

προσ-πέμπω to send to.

προσ-περιβάλλω to put around besides. — *M.* to seek to obtain still more.

προσ-περονάω to fix to.

προσ-πέτομαι *M.* to fly, rush to. [πυνθάνομαι.]

προσ-πεύθομαι *M.* = προσ-/

προσ-πήγνῡμι to fix to.

προσ-πίλναμαι *M.* = προσπελάζω.

προσ-πίπτω to fall against or upon; to run up to; to attack, assault; to attach oneself to; to fall in with, encounter; to happen, occur; to fall down before one, supplicate.

προσ-πίτνω = προσπίπτω.

προσ-πλάζω to strike against.

προσ-πλάσσω to form upon.

προσ-πλέω to sail against.

προσ-πληρόω to fill up, complete; to man besides.

προσ-πλωτός 3 navigable.

προσ-πλώω = -πλέω.

προσ-ποιέω to add to. — M. to add to oneself; to take to oneself, pretend, lay claim to; to appropriate, arrogate; to feign. allege.

προσ-ποίησις, ἡ acquisition, addition; claim, pretence.

προσ-πολεμέω to make war against.

προσ-πολεμόομαι M. to make an enemy of one.

προσ-πολέομαι to come near. [vant, attendant.]

πρόσ-πολος 2 serving; ser-)

προσ-πορεύομαι P. to go near. [besides.]

προσ-πορίζω to procure)

προσ-πταίω to strike against; to stumble; to fail, suffer defeat or loss.

προσ-πτύσσω M. to fold oneself close to, to cling close round; to entreat, solicit; to embrace, treat kindly; greet.

προσ-πυνθάνομαι M. to inquire besides.

προσ-ρέω to flow up to.

προσ-ρήγνῡμι to dash against.

πρόσ-ρησις, ἡ an addressing; a naming.

πρόσσοθεν adv. forwards.

προσ-σταυρόω = προ-σταυρόω. [wards.]

προσ-στείχω to step to-)

προσ-στέλλω to fit to; προσεσταλμένος tight; plain, modest.

προσ-συμβάλλομαι M. to contribute to besides.

πρόσσω = πόρρω.

πρόσ-ταγμα, τό, πρόσ-ταξις, ἡ command, order.

προσ-ταλαιπωρέω to suffer or persist still longer.

προ-στασίᾱ, ἡ a leading, governing, presidency; administration.

προσ-τάσσω to place to or beside; to assign, appoint, ascribe; to array; to order, ordain, enjoin. [στασία.]

προ-στατεία, ἡ = προ-)

προ-στατεύω, -έω to be at the head (of), govern; to manage; to be forthcoming.

προ-στατήριος 3 protecting.

προ-στάτης, ου, ὁ front man; protector, defender, patron; leader, chief, ruler, head; suppliant. [tectress.]

προ-στάτις, ιδος, ἡ pro-)

προ-σταυρόω to palisade in front. [within a wall.]

προσ-τειχίζω to include)

προ-στείχω to go forward, advance. [spend besides.]

προσ-τελέω to pay or)

προ-στέλλω to send forward. — P. to go forward.

προ-στερνίδιον, τό breastplate of horses. [fast to.]

προσ-τήκω intr. to stick)

προσ-τίθημι to put to, upon, or in front; to enjoin, command, impose; to attribute, impute, deliver, procure, apply to; to add; join to. — M. to associate oneself, join; to agree to; to take to oneself; to add for oneself. [plicate.]

προσ-τρέπω and M. to sup-)

προσ-τρέχω to run to.

προσ-τρόπαιος 2 suppliant.

προσ-τροπή, ἡ entreaty, prayer. [τρόπαιος.]

πρόσ-τροπος 2 = προσ-

προσ-τυγχάνω to meet with by chance; to obtain.

προ-στῷον, τό corridor.

προ-συγγίγνομαι = προ-ξυγγ. [mix first.]

προ-συμμίσγω to inter-

προ-συνοικέω to dwell together before. [tional food.]

προσ-φάγιον, τό addi-

πρόσφατος 2 fresh, new.

προσ-φερής 2 resembling; serviceable.

προσ-φέρω to bring or carry to, upon, or near, to set before one; to offer, furnish, provide; to add, increase; to apply to. — M. and P. to approach, to come near; to converse; to rush against, attack; to deal with, treat; to behave oneself; to take to oneself, eat; to give besides. [to.]

πρόσ-φημι and M. to speak

προσ-φθέγγομαι M. to speak to, address.

πρόσ-φθεγκτος 2 addressed. [salutation.]

προσ-φθεγμα, τό address,

προσ-φιλής 2 dear, beloved; pleasing; kind, friendly. [larly to.]

προσ-φοιτάω to go regu-

προσ-φορά, ἡ gift, present, offering; addition, increase.

προσ-φορέω = προσφέρω.

προσ-φυής 2 growing upon; natural; fitted.

προσ-φύω intr. and M. to grow upon; to cling to.

προσ-φωνέω to call in; to address, greet.

προσ-φώνημα, τό address, salutation.

πρό-σχημα, τό outward show, ornament; pretence, screen, pretext.

προσ-χόω to heap up besides; to choke up with earth, throw earth against; to form by alluvion.

προσ-χράομαι M. to employ besides.

προσ-χρῄζω, -χρῄζω to require or desire besides.

πρόσ-χυσις, ἡ a sprinkling.

προσ-χωρέω to approach; to be like; to accede, consent, agree to; to yield, surrender. [neighbour.]

πρόσ-χωρος 2 adjoining;

πρόσ-χωσις, ἡ a heaping up, mound; alluvion.

προσ-ψαύω to touch.

πρόσω = πόρρω.

πρόσωθεν adv. from afar.

προσωπο-ληπτέω to be a respector of persons.

προσωπο-λήπτης, ου, ὁ respector of persons.

προσωπο-ληψία, ἡ respect of persons.

πρόσ-ωπον, τό face, countenance, mien; look, appearance, figure; mask; person. [sist.]

προσ-ωφελέω to help, as-

προσ-ωφέλησις, ἡ assistance, help. [beforehand.]

προ-ταλαιπωρέω to suffer

προ-ταμιεῖον, τό ante-room of a magazine.

προ-τάμνω = -τέμνω.

προ-ταρβέω to fear beforehand. [forehand.]

προ-ταριχεύω to salt be-

προ-τάσσω to place in front; to determine beforehand.

προ-τείνω to stretch out or forth, put forward; to offer, expose; to pretend, promise, feign. — M. to claim, demand; to pretend.

προ-τείχισμα, τό outwork.

προ-τελέω to pay in advance.

προ-τεμένισμα, τό place in front of a sacred ground.

προ-τέμνω to cut beforehand; to cut off in front.

προτεραῖος 3 on the day before.

προτερέω to be before, in front, or beforehand.

πρότερος 3 before, forward, in front; sooner, earlier; former, older; higher, superior; adv. πρότερον formerly, before, sooner; προτέρω further, forward. [beforehand.]

προ-τεύχω to make or do

προτί = πρός.

προ-τίθημι to place before, prefer; to set out, propose, expose, put forth, present; to fix; to permit, allow; to impose, lay to one's charge; to exhibit, show, publish, ordain; to bring under discussion. — M. to put before oneself;

to put forth on one's own part; to pretend, feign; to purpose; to put out publicly, proclaim, announce; to prefer, to offer.

προ-τιμάω and M. to honour more or above, to prefer, distinguish. — P. to be preferred in honour.

προ-τίμησις, ἡ preference.

προτι-μυθέομαι M. to speak to.

προ-τιμωρέω to help beforehand. — M. to revenge oneself before.

προτι-όσσομαι to look at; to presage.

προ-τίω = προ-τιμάω.

πρό-τμησις, ἡ belly.

προ-τολμάω to venture before. [stay-sail.]

πρό-τονος, ὁ rope of the

προ-τρεπτικός 3 admonishing, persuasive.

προ-τρέπω to turn or urge forward; to impel, exhort, persuade, compel. — M. to turn oneself to, to devote oneself to; to exhort.

προ-τρέχω to run forward; to outrun. [before.]

πρό-τριτα adv. three days

προ-τροπάδην adv. turned forward(s), headlong.

προ-τύπτω to burst forward.

προὐννέπω = προεννέπω.

προὐξεφίεμαι to enjoin beforehand.

προ-ὑπάρχω to be beforehand, begin with; to exist before.

προῦπτος 2 = πρόοπτος.

προυσελέω to maltreat.

προ-φαίνω to show forth, bring to light, display; to predict, foreshow, promise. — *P.* to appear from afar, to come to light; to appear before.

πρό-φαντος 2 foreshown, foretold.

προ-φασίζομαι *M.* to use a pretence, allege, prevaricate.

πρό-φασις, ἡ pretence, pretext, evasion, excuse; cause, motive; prediction.

προ-φερής 2 preferred, excellent; older.

προ-φέρω to bring to, before, or forward; to produce; to declare, proclaim; to present, propose; to object, reproach; *intr.* to surpass, exceed, be beforehand.

προ-φεύγω to flee forward(s); to escape.

προφητεία, ἡ prophecy.

προφητεύω to be a prophet or interpreter of oracles; to prophesy.

προ-φήτης, ου, ὁ prophet, interpreter of oracles, seer, foreteller.

προφητικός 3 prophetic.

προφῆτις, ιδος, ἡ prophetess. [hand.]

προ-φθάνω to be before-

προ-φράζω to foretell; to say openly.

πρόφρασσα *fem.* of πρόφρων.

πρό-φρων 2 kindly, willing; hearty; earnest.

προ-φυλακή, ἡ guard in front, out-post.

προ-φυλακίς, ιδος, ἡ guardship.   [vanced guard.]

προ-φύλαξ, ακος, ὁ ad-

προ-φυλάσσω to keep guard before or in front, to be on guard. — *M.* to guard oneself, ward off. [before.]

προ-φύω *intr.* to be born

προ-φυτεύω to beget.

προ-φωνέω to proclaim publicly.

προ-χειρίζομαι *M.* to take into one's hand, to choose, appoint, decree; to make ready. — *P.* to be arranged or ready before.

πρό-χειρος 2 at hand, ready; easily procured; common; cheap. [before.]

προ-χειροτονέω to choose

προ-χέω to pour forth or out. — *P.* to be poured out, to stream forth.

πρόχνυ *adv.* kneeling; precipitously.

προ-χοή, ἡ a pouring out; mouth of a river.

πρό-χοος, -χους, ὁ pitcher, jug.

προ-χρίω to smear before.

πρό-χυσις, ἡ a pouring or spreading out; alluvion.

προ-χωρέω to go forward, advance; to make progress, succeed. [push forward.]

προ-ωθέω to thrust or

προ-ωλής 2 wholly ruined.

πρυλέες, έων, οἱ foot-soldiers, champions. [poop.]

πρύμνα, πρύμνη, ἡ stern,

πρύμνη-θεν *adv.* from the stern.   [a ship's stern.]

πρυμνήσια, τά ropes from

προμνός 3 hindmost, endmost. [mountain.]

πρυμν-ώρεια, ἡ foot of a]

πρυτανεία, ἡ presidency, office of a Prytanis; chief command of the day.

πρυτανεῖον, τό town-hall, hall of the Prytanes.

πρυτανεύω to be a Prytanis; to manage, administer.

πρύτανις, ὁ Prytanis, president, ruler, chairman, master.

πρῴ = πρωΐ. [see πρώιος.]

πρῳαίτερος, πρῳαίτατος]

πρῴην adv. lately, just now; the day before yesterday.

πρωθ-ήβης, ου, fem. πρωθ-ήβη in the first bloom of youth. [too early.]

πρωΐ adv. early in the day;]

πρωιζά = πρῴην.

πρώιμος 2, πρωινός 3, πρώιος 3 early, early in the day. [height.]

πρών, πρῶνος, ὁ foreland;]

πρῷρα, ἡ fore-part of a ship. [front.]

πρῷρᾱ-θεν adv. from the]

πρῳρεύς, ὁ look-out man in a ship. [first rank.]

πρωτεῖον, τό first prize;]

πρωτεύω to be the first, have precedence.

πρώτιστος 3 first of all.

πρωτό-γονος 2 first-born; high-born.

πρωτο-καθεδρίᾱ, πρωτο-κλισίᾱ, ἡ first seat.

πρωτο-παγής 2 newly built.

πρωτό-πλοος, -πλους 2

sailing for the first time; sailing foremost.

πρῶτος 3 first, foremost, earliest, highest, noblest; τὰ πρῶτα the first prize or rank, highest degree, chief part.

πρωτο-στάτης, ου, ὁ front-rank man; file-leader; chief. [right.]

πρωτο-τόκια, τά birth-]

πρωτο-τόκος 2 giving birth for the first time.

πρωτό-τοκος 2 first-born.

πταίρω = πτάρνυμαι.

πταῖσμα, τό stumble, false step; accident, failure, defeat.

πταίω to stumble (against); to fail, make a mistake, undergo a mishap.

πτᾱνός 3 = πτηνός.

πταρμός, ὁ a sneezing.

πτάρνυμαι to sneeze.

πτελέᾱ, ἡ elm-tree.

πτέρνα, ἡ heel; ham.

πτερόεις 3 feathered, winged.

πτερόν, τό feather, wing; soaring, flight; augury, omen; anything like wings.

πτερόω to feather.

πτερύγιον, τό little wing; pinnacle.

πτέρυξ, υγος, ἡ = πτερόν.

πτερωτός 2 = πτερόεις.

πτηνός 3 feathered, winged; fledged; fleeting, swift; coy, bashful.

πτήσσω intr. to crouch, cower; to be frightened, to tremble; to flee; trans. to frighten, alarm, terrify.

πτίλον, τό feather; wing.
πτίσσω to husk; to pound.
πτοέω, πτοιέω = πτήσσω.
πτόησις, πτοίησις, ἡ fear; passion.
πτολεμίζω etc. = πολ.
πτολι-πόρθιος, πτολί-πορθος, ὁ destroyer of cities.
πτόρθος, ὁ shoot, branch.
πτύγμα, τό a folding, fold.
πτυκτός 3 folded.
πτύξ, πτυχός fold; layer, plate; cleft; dell.
πτύον, τό winnowing-shovel.
πτύρω to frighten, scare.
πτύσμα, τό spittle.
πτύσσω to fold, double up. — M. to be bent.
πτυχή, ἡ = πτύξ.
πτύω to spit, spit out.
πτωκάς, άδος, ἡ = πτώξ.
πτῶμα, τό fall, ruin, disaster; corpse.   [hare.]
πτώξ, πτωκός shy; ὁ, ἡ
πτῶσις, ἡ = πτῶμα.
πτωσκάζω, πτώσσω = πτήσσω.   [beggary.]
πτωχεία, ἡ a begging,
πτωχεύω to be a beggar, to be poor.
πτωχός 3 beggarly, beggar.
πῡγ-αργος, ὁ white-rump.
πυγή, ἡ rump, buttocks.
πυγμαῖος 3 of the size of a fist; pigmy.
πυγ-μαχέω = πυκτεύω.
πυγ-μαχίη, ἡ a boxing.
πυγ-μάχος, ὁ = πύκτης.
πυγμή, ἡ fist; a boxing.
πυγούσιος 3 one cubit long.
πυγών, όνος, ἡ elbow · cubit.

πύελος, ἡ bathing-tub; trough; coffin.
πυθμήν, ένος, ὁ bottom, stand, base, foundation, root.   [P. to rot, decay.]
πύθω to cause to rot. —
πύθων, ωνος ventriloquist.
πύκα adv. thickly; frequently; wisely.
πυκάζω to make thick or close; to press together, shut up; to cover thick, shelter; intr. to enwrap oneself.   [cautious.]
πυκι-μήδης 2 sensible,
πυκινός 3 = πυκνός.
πυκνί dat. of πνύξ.
πυκνό-πτερος 2 thick-feathered.
πυκνός 3 thick, close, compact, well-guarded; crowded; frequent; strong, well made, great, mighty; careful, cautious, discreet.
πυκνό-στικτος 2 thick-spotted.
πυκνότης, ητος, ἡ thickness, closeness, compactness; crowd.
πυκτεύω to be a boxer.
πύκτης, ου, ὁ boxer.   [ing.]
πυκτικός 3 skilled in box-
πυλ-αγόρᾱς, ου, πυλ-άγορος, ὁ orator at the Amphictyonic council.
πυλ-αγορέω to be a πυλαγόρας.   [keeper.]
πυλ-άρτης, ου, ὁ gate-
πυλα-ωρός, ὁ = πυλωρός.
πύλη, ἡ gate, door, entrance, inlet; mountain-pass.
πυλίς, ίδος, ὁ little gate.

πύλος, ὁ gateway.

πυλ-ουρός, ὁ = πυλωρός.

πυλόω to · enclose with gates. [vestibule.]

πυλών, ῶνος, ὁ porch;

πυλ-ωρός, ὁ, ἡ gate-keeper; guard.

πύματος 3 uttermost, last.

πυνθάνομαι M. to inquire, ask; to hear, learn; to understand, know.

πύξ adv. with the fist.

πύξινος 3 of boxwood.

πῦρ, πυρός, τό fire; lightning; fire-sign; fever-heat; blaze.

πυρά, ἡ place where fire is kindled, funeral-pile, burial-place.

πυρ-άγρα, ἡ a pair of fire-tongs. [hot.]

πυρ-ακτέω to make red-

πῡραμίς, ίδος, ἡ pyramid.

πυργηδόν adv. in masses.

πυργο-μαχέω to assail a tower.

πύργος, ὁ tower, towered wall; castle, fortress, bulwark; division or column of soldiers.

πυργόω M. to furnish with towers; to raise on high.

πυργώδης 2 like a tower.

πύργωμα, τό = πύργος.

πῦρεῖα, τά contrivance to light a fire.

πυρέσσω to have a fever.

πυρετός, ὁ fever-heat.

πυρή, ἡ = πυρά.

πῡρήν, ῆνος, ὁ stone of a fruit. [φόρος.]

πυρη-φόρος 2 = πυρο-

πυρία, ἡ vapour-bath.

πυρι-ήκης 2 pointed in the fire. [the fire.]

πυρί-καυστος 2 burnt in

πύρινος[1] 3 of wheat.

πύρινος[2] 3 fiery.

πυρι-φλεγής 2 blazing with fire.

πυρ-καϊά, ἡ stake, funeral-pile; conflagration; stump of an olive-tree.

πύρνον, τό wheaten bread.

πῡρός, ὁ wheat.

πῡρο-φόρος 2 wheat-bearing.

πυρόω to burn, waste with fire. [breathing.]

πύρ-πνοος, -πνους 2 fire-

πυρ-πολέω to keep up a fire; to waste with fire.

πυρράζω to be fiery-red.

πυρρίχη, ἡ war-dance.

πυρρός 3 fire-coloured, red.

πυρσεύω to make fire-signs. [con.]

πυρσός[1], ὁ fire-brand; bea-

πυρσός[2] 3 = πυρρός.

πυρ-φόρος 2 fire-bearing; torch-bearing. [tion.]

πύρωσις, ἡ fire, conflagra-

πύστις, ἡ an inquiring, asking; question, trial; report.

πώ adv. yet, ever, anyhow.

πώγων, ωνος, ὁ beard.

πωλέομαι M. to frequent, wander about.

πωλέω to sell. [horses.]

πωλικός 3 drawn by (young)

πωλο-δαμνέω to break young horses. [foal.]

πῶλος, ὁ a young one;

πῶμα[1], τό cover, lid.

πῶμα[2], τό drink, potion.

πώ-ποτε *adv.* ever yet.

πώρινος 3 made of tuff-stone.

πῶρος, ὁ tuff-stone.

πωρόω to petrify, harden, obdurate.

πώρωσις, ἡ a hardening, callousness.

πῶς *adv.* how? in what way or manner? how much!

πωτάομαι = πέτομαι.

πῶυ, εος, τό flock of sheep.

P

P, ρ (ῥῶ) seventeenth letter of the alphabet; as a numeral ρ´ = 100.

ῥά, ῥ´ = ἄρα.   [Rabbi.]

ῥαββί, ῥαββεί master,]

ῥαββουνί = ῥαββί.

ῥαβδίζω to cudgel, flog.

ῥαβδο-νομέω to be an umpire.   [staff.]

ῥάβδος, ἡ rod, stick, wand,]

ῥαβδ-οῦχος, ὁ staff-bearer; umpire; lictor.

ῥαδινάκη, ἡ petroleum.

ῥαδινός 3 slender, tender; swift.

ῥάδιος 3 easy; ready, willing, complaisant; heedless, reckless.

ῥαδιούργημα,τό,ῥαδιουργίᾱ, ἡ recklessness; laziness, indolence; wickedness, roguery.   [grain.]

ῥαθάμιγξ, ιγγος, ἡ drop:]

ῥᾳ-θυμέω to be reckless or idle.

ῥᾳ-θυμίᾱ, ἡ thoughtlessness, carelessness; laziness; easiness; pastime.

ῥά-θυμος 2 light-minded, careless; lazy; pleasure-seeking.   [cover.]

ῥᾴζω to grow easy, re-]

ῥαίνω to sprinkle, besprinkle.

ῥαιστήρ, ῆρος, ὁ hammer.

ῥαίω to smash, shiver, shatter. — *P.* to be shattered; to burst; to be maltreated.

ῥακά worthless fellow.

ῥάκος, τό rag, tatter; patch.

ῥαντίζω to sprinkle; to cleanse.

ῥαντισμός, ὁ a sprinkling.

ῥαπίζω to cudgel, whip, box on the ear.   [cheek.]

ῥάπισμα, τό slap on the]

ῥαπτός 3 sewed, stitched.

ῥάπτω to sew, stitch (together); to contrive, plot.

ῥαστώνη, ἡ easiness, facility; readiness, cessation; relief, rest, ease; laziness.

ῥαφή, ἡ seam.

ῥαφίς, ίδος, ἡ needle.

ῥαχίᾱ, ἡ surf, surge, breakers; coast.

ῥαχίζω to cut in pieces.

ῥάχις, ἡ back: backbone.

ῥαψ-ῳδέω to recite poems.

ῥαψ-ῳδός, ὁ singing, reciting; reciter of poems.

ῥέγκω, ῥέγχω to snort.

ῥέδη, ἡ wagon.

ῥέεθρον, τό = ῥεῖθρον.

ῥέζω to do, act, work, make, effect, accomplish; to sacrifice.

ῥέθος, τό limb; face.

ῥεῖα adv. easily, lightly.

ῥεῖθρον, τό river, stream; bed of a river.

ῥέπω to incline downwards; to preponderate, prevail; to incline towards.

ῥεῦμα, τό flow, stream, river, flood; a bleeding; volcanic eruption.

ῥέω and P. to flow, stream, run, gush; to fall or drop off, melt away.

ῥῆγμα, τό a breaking, fracture; downfall.

ῥηγμίν, ῖνος, ἡ = ῥαχία.

ῥήγνῡμι to break, break in pieces, rend, smash; to let break loose. [coverlet.]

ῥῆγος, τό carpet, blanket,

ῥηΐδιος 3 = ῥᾴδιος.

ῥηκτός 3 to be broken or rent.

ῥῆμα, τό word, saying, phrase; sentence, speech; thing.

ῥηξ-ηνορίη, ἡ a breaking through ranks of warriors.

ῥηξ-ήνωρ, ορος breaking through ranks of warriors.

ῥῆσις, ἡ a saying, speaking, mode of speech; = ῥῆμα.

ῥήσσω to tear, rend, break; to beat with the feet, dance.

ῥητήρ, ῆρος = ῥήτωρ.

ῥητορεύω to be a public speaker. [rhetorical.]

ῥητορικός 3 oratorical,

ῥητός 3 said, spoken, settled, determined, concerted; to be told.

ῥήτρα, ἡ speech; agree-

ment, treaty; maxim, law, statute.

ῥήτωρ, ορος, ὁ orator, public speaker; statesman; politician; rhetorician.

ῥῑγεδανός 3 causing shudder.

ῥῑγέω to shudder with cold, to be chill; to shudder at, shrink from.

ῥίγιον, ῥίγιστος see ῥῖγος.

ῥῖγος, τό frost, cold; comp. ῥίγιον worse, more horribly; sup. ῥίγιστος.

ῥῑγόω to be cold or chill.

ῥίζα, ἡ root; stem, origin; family.

ῥιζόω to let strike root; to plant. — P. to be firmly rooted.

ῥίμφα adv. lightly, swiftly.

ῥιμφ-άρματος 2 with a swift chariot.

ῥῑνόν, τό, ῥῑνός, ἡ skin, hide, leather; shield.

ῥῑνο-τόρος 2 piercing shields.

ῥίον, τό peak, promontory.

ῥῑπή, ἡ throw, flight, swing; rushing motion; impetus.

ῥῑπίζω to blow up a flame.

ῥῖπος, τό reed mat, wicker hurdle.

ῥῑπτάζω to throw to and fro.

ῥίπτω, ῥῑπτέω to throw, cast, or hurl down, out, away, forth, or to and fro.

ῥίς, ῥῑνός, ἡ nose; pl. nostrils.

ῥίψ, ῥῑπός, ἡ wand, rod; reed, bulrush; mat, hurdle.

ῥῑψο-κίνδῡνος 2 foolhardy.

ῥοδανός 3 waving.

ῥοδο-δάκτυλος 2 rosy-fingered.

ῥοδόεις 3 of roses.

ῥόδον, τό rose.

ῥοή, ἡ = ῥόος. [murmur.]

ῥοθέω to roar, rush, buzz,

ῥόθιος 2 roaring, rushing.

ῥόθος, ὁ a roaring, rushing noise.

ῥοιά, ἡ pomegranate-tree.

ῥοιβδέω to swallow down.

ῥοῖβδος, ὁ a roaring, hissing, whizzing.

ῥοιζέω to whistle, whizz.

ῥοιζηδόν adv. with a rushing noise.

ῥοῖζος, ὁ = ῥοῖβδος.

ῥομφαίᾱ, ἡ large sword.

ῥόος, ὁ stream, current; flood, wave.

ῥόπαλον, τό club, stick, cudgel, mace; knocker of a door.

ῥοπή, ἡ inclination downwards, turn of the scale; turning-point, crisis, decision, result; weight, momentum, push, impetus.

ῥόπτρον, τό = ῥόπαλον.

ῥοῦς, ὁ = ῥόος. [down.]

ῥοφέω to sip; to swallow

ῥοχθέω to roar.

ῥοώδης 2 flowing, surging.

ῥύαξ, ἄκος, ὁ stream that bursts forth; stream of lava. [undantly.]

ῥυδόν adv. in streams; ab-

ῥυθμίζω to bring into proportion; to order, arrange; to govern, educate.

ῥυθμός, ὁ measure, rhythm; proportion, harmony, symmetry; form, shape.

ῥῦμα, τό string of a bow; bow-shot; protection, deliverance.

ῥύμη, ἡ swing, impetus; attack, force; street.

ῥῡμός, ὁ pole of a carriage.

ῥύομαι M. to save, deliver, protect, redeem; to cure, heal; to shield, cover; to check, hold back.

ῥύπα, τά, pl. of ὁ ῥύπος.

ῥυπαίνω, ῥυπαρεύω to sully.

ῥυπαρίᾱ, ἡ dirt; sordidness.

ῥυπαρός 3 dirty.

ῥυπάω, -όω to be dirty; to dirty.

ῥύπος, ὁ dirt, filth.

ῥύσιον, τό booty, prey; pledge, restitution, amends.

ῥῡσί-πολις, ὁ, ἡ saving the city. [course.]

ῥύσις, ἡ stream, river,

ῥυσός 3 wrinkled.

ῥυστάζω to drag to and fro, to maltreat.

ῥυσταχτύς, ύος, ἡ ill-treatment.

ῥυτήρ[1], ῆρος, ὁ one who draws a bow, archer; rope, thong; rein. [fender.]

ῥυτήρ[2], ῆρος, ὁ saver, de-

ῥυτίς, ίδος, ἡ wrinkle; stain, taint.

ῥυτόν, τό drinking-horn.

ῥυτός[1] 3 dragged along.

ῥυτός[2] 3 flowing.

ῥωγαλέος 3 rent, ragged.

ῥωμαλέος 3 strong, mighty.

ῥώμη, ἡ strength, force, might; army; energy.

ῥώννυμι to strengthen, con-

firm. — *P.* to exert one-self; to be resolved. — *pf.*
ἐρρῶσθαι to be ·strong, vigorous; ἔρρωσο farewell.
ῥώξ, ῥωγός, ἡ chink, fissure, narrow passage.

ῥώομαι *M.* to move swiftly, to rush on; to dance.
ῥωπήιον, τό = ῥώψ.
ῥωχμός, ὁ = ῥώξ.
ῥώψ, ῥωπός, ἡ shrub, bush, underwood.

Σ

Σ, σ, ς (σίγμα) eighteenth letter of the alphabet; as a numeral σ′ = 200.
σαβαχθανί thou hast forsaken me.
σαβαώθ hosts, armies.
σαββατισμός, ὁ the keeping of the Sabbath. [week.]
σάββατον, τό sabbath; *pl.*]
σάγαρις, ἡ double-axe, battle-axe.
σαγηνεύω to catch in a net.
σαγήνη, ἡ drag-net.
σαθρός 3 rotten, decayed, unsound, sick, perishable.
σαίνω to wag the tail; fawn, wheedle, caress; to shake.
σαίρω to sweep clean.
σακεσ-παλος 2 brandishing a shield. [bearer.]
σακεσ-φόρος 2 shield-]
σακίον, τό small bag.
σακκέω to strain, filter.
σάκκος, σάκος, ὁ bag, sack; sack-cloth; mourning-dress.
σάκος, τό large shield.
σαλεύω to swing, shake; to incite. — *intr.* and *P.* to totter, move to and fro, toss, roll.
σάλος, ὁ tottering, rolling, surging; surge; disquiet.

σαλπιγκτής, οῦ, ὁ = σαλ-πικτής. [trumpet-signal.]
σάλπιγξ, ιγγος, ἡ trumpet;]
σαλπίζω to sound the trumpet, to give a trumpet-signal.
σαλπικτής, σαλπιστής, οῦ, ὁ trumpeter. [sandal.]
σάνδαλον, σανδάλιον, τό]
σανδαράκινος 3 minium-coloured. [catalogue.]
σανίδιον, τό writing-tablet,]
σανίς, ίδος, ἡ board, plank; wooden frame-work; writing-tablet; fold of a door; pole; pillory.
σάος = σῶς.
σαό-φρων 2 = σώφρων.
σαόω = σῴζω.
σαπρός 3 rotten, decayed; putrid; worthless.
σαργάνη, ἡ wickerwork; basket. [castic.]
σαρδάνιος 3 scornful, sar-]
σάρδιον, τό, σάρδιος, ὁ carnelian, sardoin. [nyx.]
σαρδ-όνυξ, υχος, ὁ sardo-]
σαρκίζω to strip off the flesh.
σαρκικός 3, σάρκινος 3 of flesh, fleshy; fleshly, carnal, sensual.
σαρκο-φάγος 2 eating flesh; limestone coffin.
σαρκώδης 2 fleshy.

σάρξ, σαρκός, ἡ flesh, piece of flesh; body.

σαρόω to sweep clean.

σατᾶν, σατανᾶς, ᾶ, ὁ satan, devil.

σάτον, τό a corn-measure.

σατραπείᾱ, ἡ satrapy.

σατραπεύω to be a satrap.

σατράπης, ου, ὁ satrap, Persian governor.

σάττω to fill, stuff, cram; to load; to equip.

σαύρᾱ, ἡ, σαῦρος, ὁ lizard.

σαυρωτήρ, ῆρος, ὁ butt-end of a spear.

σάφα, σαφέως see σαφής.

σαφηνής, σαφής 2 clear, plain, manifest; distinct; true, certain, real.

σαφηνίζω to make clear or plain; to announce.

σάω to strain, sift.

σβέννῡμι to quench, put out, quell. — intr. and P. to be quenched, go out, die.

σβεστήριος 3 fit for quenching.

σεβάζομαι M. = σέβω.

σέβας, τό awe, reverence, worship, respect; astonishment; wonder; majesty; pride, glory. [or worship.)

σέβασμα, τό object of awe)

σεβαστός 3 venerable, awful, august.

σέβω and P. to feel awe, fear, shame, or respect; to honour, revere, worship; to wonder.

σειρά, ἡ rope, string, chain.

σειραῖος 3, σειρη-φόρος 2 fastened by a rope; near horse.

σειρός, ὁ = σιρός.

σεισ-άχθεια, ἡ a shaking off of burdens.

σεισμός, ὁ earthquake.

σείω to shake, brandish; σείει there is an earthquake. — M. and P. to be shaken, to move to and fro.

σέλας, τό brightness, light, beam; fire, flame.

σεληναῖος 3 moon-lit.

σελήνη, ἡ moon, moonshine.

σεληνιάζομαι to be lunatic.

σέλῑνον, τό parsley.

σέλμα, τό rowing-bench; deck.

σεμίδᾱλις, ἡ finest wheaten flour.

σεμνο-λόγος, ὁ speaking solemnly. [seer.)

σεμνό-μαντις, ὁ reverend)

σεμνός 3 august, sacred, solemn, dignified, holy; majestic, noble, stately; grave, honest; haughty, arrogant; pompous.

σεμνότης, ητος, ἡ solemnity, dignity, majesty; pomposity.

σεμνόω, σεμνύνω to dignify, make solemn, pompous, or stately; to magnify, amplify. — M. to boast, be proud.

σεύω to put in quick motion; to drive or chase away; to bring forth; to throw, hurl, shake. — M. and P. to rush, run, start, dart or spout forth; to strive (for), desire.

σηκάζω to pen, coop up.

σηχο-κόρος, ὁ stableman.

σηχός, ὁ pen, fold, enclosure, stable; sacred precinct, shrine; enclosed trunk of an olive-tree.

σῆμα, τό sign, mark, token; omen; trace; signal, word of command; image, seal, written character, device, emblem; mound, tomb.

σημαίνω to signify, mark, seal; to give a sign or signal, to command, rule; to show a sign, point out, announce, prove. — M. to mark for oneself, note down; to infer, conclude.

σημαντρίς, ίδος, ἡ sealed earth.

σήμαντρον, τό seal.

σημάντωρ, ορος, ὁ leader, commander; messenger.

σημεῖον, τό = σῆμα.

σημειόω to mark. — M. to mark for oneself.

σήμερον adv. to-day.

σηπεδών, όνος, ἡ putrefaction.

σήπω to make rotten. — intr. and P. to rot, decay.

σῆραγξ, αγγος, ἡ cleft, hollow.

σηρικός 3 silken.

σής, σεός, σητός, ὁ moth.

σησάμινος 3 made of sesame.

σήσαμον, τό sesame.

σητό-βρωτος 2 moth-eaten.

σθεναρός 3 strong, mighty.

σθένος, τό strength, might; courage; power, force; army.

σθενόω to strengthen.

σθένω to be strong or mighty; to rule, have power; to be able.

σιαγών, όνος, ἡ jaw-bone.

σίαλον, τό spittle.

σίαλος 2 fat; fat hog.

σῖγα adv. silently; secretly.

σιγάζω to silence. [tering.]

σῖγαλόεις 3 shining, glit-

σιγάω to be silent, keep silence; to conceal. [quiet.]

σιγή, ἡ silence, stillness,

σιγηλός 3 silent, still, mute.

σίγλος, ὁ shekel.

σιγύννης, ου, ὁ javelin; retail-dealer.

σιδηρεία, ἡ a working in iron.

σιδήρεος 3, σιδήρεος 3 of iron or steel; hard, unfeeling. [weapon.]

σιδήριον, τό iron tool or

σιδηρο-βρώς, ῶτος iron-eating, whetting. [iron.]

σιδηρό-δετος 2 clad with

σιδηρο-κμής, ῆτος slain by the sword.

σίδηρος, ὁ iron, steel; iron tool, sword, knife, sickle, axe; ironmonger's shop.

σιδηροῦς 3 = σιδήρεος.

σιδηρο-φορέω and M. to wear arms. [with iron.]

σιδηρόω to overlay or cover

σίζω to hiss.

σικάριος, ὁ assassin.

σίκερα, τό strong drink.

σιλλικύπριον, τό wonder-tree (ricinus).

σίλφιον, τό a kind of plant.

σιμικίνθιον, τό apron.

σιμός 3 flat-nosed, flat; up-hill. [waste.]

σινα-μωρέω to damage,

σινά-μωρος 2 hurtful.

σίναπι, ιδος, εως, τό mustard.

σινδών, όνος, ή fine linen; linen cloth or shirt.

σινέομαι = σίνομαι.

σινιάζω to sift, winnow.

σίνομαι to damage, hurt; to rob, plunder, ravage.

σίνος, τό damage, harm; mischief. [cious.

σίντης, ου robbing, rapa-

σιός, ὁ = θεός.

σιρός, ὁ pit, hole.

σισύρᾱ, σίσυρνα, ἡ rough or furred coat.

σῖτα, τά pl. of σῖτος. [corn.

σῐτ-αγωγός 2 conveying

σιτευτός 3 fatted.

σιτεύω, σιτέω to feed, fatten. — P. to be fed, to eat.

σῖτ-ηγός = σιταγωγός.

σιτηρέσιον, τό food, provisions; pay for maintenance.

σίτησις, ἡ a feeding; public maintenance.

σιτίζω = σιτεύω.

σίτιον, τό = σῖτος.

σιτιστός = σιτευτός.

σῖτο-δεία, ἡ want of food, dearth.

σῖτο-δοτέω to deal out corn. — P. to be furnished with corn. [sions.

σῖτο-μέτριον, τό provi-

σῖτο-νόμος 2 dealing out food. [food; baker.

σῖτο-ποιός 2 preparing

σῖτο-πομπία, ἡ transport of corn. [merchant.

σῖτο-πώλης, ου, ὁ corn-

σῖτος, ὁ wheat, corn; flour, bread; food, provisions.

σῖτο-φάγος 2 eating bread.

σῖτο-φόρος 2 conveying provisions.

σῖτο-φύλακες, οἱ corn-inspectors. [corn.

σῑτ-ώνης, ου, ὁ buyer of

σιφλόω to maim; to hurt.

σιωπάω = σιγάω.

σιωπή, ἡ = σιγή.

σκάζω to halt, limp.

σκαιός 3 left, on the left hand or side; western; awkward, clumsy, silly; unlucky.

σκαιοσύνη, σκαιότης, ητος, ἡ awkwardness, stupidity; coarseness.

σκαίρω to bound, dance.

σκάλλω to dig, hoe.

σκαλμός, ὁ thole of an oar.

σκανδαλίζω to give offence, scandalize. — P. to take offence. [scandal.

σκάνδαλον, τό offence.

σκαπτός 3 dug.

σκάπτω to dig, hoe.

σκάφη, ἡ, σκάφος, τό hollow vessel, trough, tub; ship. boat, canoe.

σκαφίς, ίδος, ἡ tub, bowl.

σκεδάννῡμι to scatter, disperse, spread abroad. — P. and M. to be scattered, to be spread about.

σκέδασις, ἡ a scattering.

σκέλλω to dry up, parch. — intr. and P. to be parched.

σκέλος, τό leg.

σκέμμα, τό = σκέψις.

σκεπάζω = σκεπάω.

σκέπαρνον, τό carpenter's axe.

σκέπας, αος, τό = σκέπη.

σκέπασμα, τό a covering; shelter; dress.

σκεπάω to cover; to shelter, protect. [protection.]

σκέπη, ἡ covering; shelter;

σκέπτομαι M. = σκοπέω.

σκευ-αγωγέω to secure one's goods.

σκευάζω to prepare, make ready, make; to provide, equip; to dress up.

σκευή, ἡ, **σκεῦος**, τό dress, attire; ornament; equipment; disguise; vessel, implement, tool; pl. utensils, tools, baggage; tacklings, riggings. [gage.]

σκευο-φορέω to carry bag-]

σκευο-φόρος 2 carrying baggage; carrier, porter, baggage-boy.

σκευ-ωρέομαι M. to contrive cunningly.

σκέψις, ἡ an examining, observation, consideration.

σκηνάω, -έω, -όω to dwell in a tent; to dwell, live, be encamped. — M. to dwell; to build for oneself.

σκηνή, ἡ, **σκήνημα**, τό tent, hut, house; tabernacle, temple; stage, theatre; arbour, bower; banquet.

σκηνίδιον, τό small tent.

σκηνο-πηγία, ἡ feast of the tabernacles.

σκηνο-ποιός, ὁ tent-maker.

σκῆνος, τό = σκηνή.

σκηνο-φύλαξ, ακος, ὁ guard of tents.

σκηνόω = σκηνάω.

σκήνωμα, τό = σκηνή.

σκηπάνιον, τό = σκῆπτρον.

σκηπτός, ὁ storm, gale; thunderbolt.

σκηπτοῦχος 2 bearing a staff or sceptre.

σκῆπτρον, τό staff, stick; sceptre; kingly power.

σκήπτω to prop; to hurl, let fall upon; intr. to fall upon or down. — M. and P. to support oneself; to pretend, allege as an excuse.

σκηρίπτομαι M. to support oneself, to lean against.

σκῆψις, ἡ pretence, excuse, reason.

σκιά, ἡ shadow, shade, darkness; outline; ghost, phantom, spectre.

σκιᾱ-γραφία, ἡ outline; phantom. [cover, veil.]

σκιάζω to overshadow; to]

σκιᾱ-μαχέω to fight in the shade; to fight with a shadow.

σκιᾱ-τροφέω to rear in the shade or at home. — intr. and P. to be reared in the shade or effeminately.

σκιάω = σκιάζω.

σκίδνημι = σκεδάννυμι.

σκιερός 3 shady, shaded.

σκίμ-πους, ποδος, ὁ couch, low bed.

σκιο-ειδής 2 shadowy.

σκιόεις 3 = σκιερός.

σκίπων, ωνος, ὁ staff.

σκιρτάω to bound, leap.

σκληρο-καρδία, ἡ hardness of heart.

σκληρός 3 dry, hard, harsh, rough, inflexible; stiff, tough; stern, stubborn; cruel, unyielding.

σκληρότης, ητος, ἡ hardness, stubbornness.

σκληρο-τράχηλος 2 stiff-necked.

σκληρύνω to harden.

σκολιόν, σκόλιον, τό drinking-song.

σκολιός 3 crooked, bent, slanting; tortuous, unjust.

σκόλοφ, οπος, ὁ pale, stake; thorn.

σκόπελος, ὁ rock, crag.

σκοπέω and M. to look at, about, or out, to behold, survey, view; to consider, regard, observe; to spy out; to examine, inquire (into), ascertain; to pay regard to, to heed.

σκοπή, σκοπιά, ἡ a spying, looking out, watch; watch-tower, look-out.

σκοπιάζω and M. to keep watch, spy.

σκοπός, ὁ spy; guardian, watcher; mark, aim; object, scope.

σκόροδον, τό garlic.

σκορπίζω to scatter.

σκορπίος, ὁ scorpion.

σκοταῖος 3, σκοτεινός 3 dark, shady; in the dark; blind; secret.

σκοτία, ἡ = σκότος.

σκοτίζω to make dark.

σκότιος 3 and 2 = σκοταῖος.

σκοτο-μήνιος 2 moonless.

σκότος, ὁ and τό darkness, gloom; night; blindness; swoon; nether world; place of concealment; derangement of mind; unclearness.

σκοτόω to make dark.

σκοτώδης 2 dark.

σκύβαλον, τό dirt, filth.

σκυδμαίνω, σκύζομαι to be angry or wroth.

σκυθρωπάζω to look angry or sullen.

σκυθρ-ωπός 2 angry-looking, sullen.

σκύλαξ, ακος, ὁ, ἡ young dog, whelp.

σκύλευμα, τό = σκῦλον.

σκυλεύω to spoil a slain enemy; to rob. [to annoy.]

σκύλλω to rend, mangle;]

σκῦλον, σκύλον, τό spoils; booty, prey. [whelp.]

σκύμνος, ὁ young animal,]

σκυτάλη, ἡ stick, staff; letter-staff, despatch, message. [staff.]

σκυταλίς, ίδος, ἡ small]

σκύταλον, τό = σκυτάλη.

σκῦτεύς, ὁ shoemaker, saddler. [maker.]

σκυτεύω to be a shoe-]

σκύτινος, σκύτινος 3 leathern.

σκῦτος, τό hide, leather.

σκῦτο-τομεῖον, τό shoemaker's shop.

σκυτο-τόμος, ὁ = σκυτεύς.

σκύφος, ὁ cup, beaker.

σκωληκό-βρωτος 2 worm-eaten.

σκώληξ, ηκος, ὁ worm.

σκῶλος, ὁ pointed pale.

σκῶμμα, τό jest, joke.

σκώπτω to jest; to jeer, mock.

σκώφ, ωπός, ὁ owl.

σμαράγδινος 3 of emerald.

σμάραγδος, ἡ emerald.

σμαραγέω to sound hollow, to resound; to crash.

σμάω to rub or wipe off. — M. to wipe off; to smear oneself.

σμερδαλέος 3, σμερδνός 3 terrible, awful.

σμῆνος, τό swarm of bees, bee-hive; crowd.

σμήχω to rub off.

σμιχρός 3 = μικρός.

σμυγερός 3 toilsome.

σμύρνα, ἡ myrrh.

σμυρνίζω to season with myrrh.   [smoulder:\

σμύχω to burn, make\
σμῶδιξ, ιγγος, ἡ weal, bloody stripe.   [μαι.\

σοέομαι, σοῦμαι = σεύο-\
σολοικίζω to speak in-correctly.

σόλοικος 2 speaking in-correctly; boorish.

σόλος, ὁ iron disc.

σόος = σῶς.

σορός, ἡ urn; coffin.

σός, σή, σόν thy, thine.

σουδάριον, τό handkerchief.

σοφίᾱ, ἡ cleverness, skill; prudence; craft; knowledge; wisdom; philosophy.

σοφίζω to make wise, in-struct, teach. — M. to devise, contrive shrewdly.

σόφισμα, τό device, cunning contrivance, craft, trick, artifice, deceit.

σοφιστής, οῦ, ὁ crafty man, artist, master; pru-dent man, philosopher; teacher of wisdom or elo-quence; sophist, sham-philosopher.

σοφιστικός 3 sophistical.

σοφός 3 clever, skilful; prudent; cunning; learned; wise.

σόω = σῴζω.

σπαδίζω to draw off.

σπάθη, ἡ spattle; broad sword.

σπάκα = κύνα. [want of.\

σπανίζω and P. to be in\

σπάνιος 3 needy; scarce, scanty; rare.

σπανιότης, ητος, σπάνις, ἡ need, scarcity.

σπανιστός 3 = σπάνιος.

σπανο-σῑτίᾱ, ἡ want of food.   [off; torn body.\

σπάραγμα, τό piece torn\

σπαραγμός, ὁ convulsion.

σπαράσσω and M. to tear, rend in pieces. [cloth.\

σπάργανον, τό swaddling-\

σπαργανόω to swaddle.

σπαργάω to teem, be full.

σπάρτον, τό rope, cable.

σπαρτός 3 scattered, sown.

σπάσμα, τό, σπασμός, ὁ convulsion.   [ously.\

σπαταλάω to live luxuri-\

σπάω to draw, pull, drag; to tear, rend; to drain.

σπεῖος, τό = σπέος.

σπεῖρα, ἡ twisted fold; coil, net; body of soldiers.

σπειρίον, τό light gar-ment.

σπεῖρον, τό wrapper, gar-ment, shroud; sail.

σπείρω to sow, engender; to scatter, spread. — P. to be scattered.

σπεκουλάτωρ, ορος, ὁ guard; executioner.

σπένδω to pour out a drink-offering. — *M.* to make a treaty or truce, conclude a peace; to stipulate by treaty.

σπέος, τό cave, grot.

σπέρμα, τό seed, germ; race, family; descent, origin; issue, offspring.

σπερμο-λόγος, ὁ babbler.

σπέρχω to drive or press on. *intr.* and *P.* to haste, hurry; to be hot or angry.

σπεύδω = σπουδάζω.

σπήλαιον, τό cave. [wide.]

σπιδής 2 far-stretched,

σπιθάμη, ἡ span (a measure).

σπιλάς¹, άδος, ἡ crag, rock.

σπιλάς², άδος, ἡ, σπίλος, ὁ, σπίλος, ὁ lime-floor; stain, blemish. [nate.]

σπιλόω to stain, contami-

σπινθήρ, ῆρος, ὁ spark.

σπλαγχνίζομαι *P.* to have compassion or pity.

σπλάγχνον, τό inward parts, bowels; heart, inward nature.

σπλήν, ηνός, ὁ milt.

σπογγίζω to wipe with a sponge.

σπόγγος, ὁ sponge.

σποδιά, ἡ, σποδός, ὁ ashes; heap of ashes; dust.

σπολάς, άδος, ἡ leather bodkin; jerkin.

σπονδ-αρχίαι, αἱ right of beginning a libation.

σπονδή, ἡ drink-offering, libation; *plur.* treaty of peace, truce, covenant.

σπορά, ἡ = σπόρος.

σποράδην *adv.* of σποράς.

σποράς, άδος scattered, detached.

σπορητός, ὁ = σπόρος.

σπόριμος 2 sown; fit for sowing.

σπόρος, ὁ a sowing; seed; birth, descent; produce, crop, offspring.

σπουδάζω *intr.* to make haste, to be zealous, busy, or earnest. — *trans.* to do hastily or earnestly, pursue zealously.

σπουδαιο-λογέομαι *M.* to speak on serious objects.

σπουδαῖος 3 hasty, swift; earnest, zealous; busy, serious; honest, good, grave; excellent, esteemed, costly; serviceable, weighty.

σπουδή, ἡ haste, speed; zeal, earnestness, seriousness, regard, pains, trouble, rivalry.

σπυρίς, ίδος, ἡ basket.

σταγών, όνος, ἡ drop.

στάδιον, τό stadium (a measure of length); racecourse.

στάδιος 3 standing, standing fast; ἡ σταδίᾱ close fight. [drop, destil, drip.]

στάζω *trans.* and *intr.* to measure out, calculate; to estimate, judge.

σταθμάω and *M.* to measure out, calculate; to estimate, judge.

στάθμη, ἡ chalk-line, rule.

σταθμός, ὁ standing-place; stable, fold, dwelling, quarters; resting-place, station, stage, day's march; standing-post, door-post; balance, weight.

σταῖς, σταιτός, τό wheaten dough.

σταίτινος 3 of dough.

στάλαγμα, τό drop.

σταμίς, ῖνος, ὁ pillar, rib of a ship.

στάμνος, ὁ, ἡ jar, pot.

στασιάζω to rise in rebellion, revolt, to quarrel, dispute; to be divided into factions.

στασιασμός, ὁ = στάσις.

στασιαστής, οῦ, ὁ = στασιώτης. [σιώδης.]

στασιαστικός 3 = στασιασμός.

στάσιμος 2 standing.

στάσις, ἡ a standing; position, station, condition; standing-place; a rising, revolt, sedition, party-strife; discord, quarrel; party, faction.

στασιώδης 2 seditious; divided into factions.

στασιώτης, ου, ὁ partisan; insurgent. [ώδης.]

στασιωτικός 3 = στασιασμός.

στατήρ, ῆρος, ὁ stater, a gold or silver coin.

στατός 3 standing, placed.

σταυρός, ὁ palisade; cross.

σταυρόω to palisade; to crucify.

σταύρωμα, τό, σταύρωσις, ἡ palisade, stockade.

σταφυλή, ἡ bunch of grapes.

στάχυς, υος, ὁ ear of corn.

στέαρ, ατος, τό fat, tallow; fish-oil.

στεγάζω = στέγω.

στεγανός 3 covering; tight; covered, roofed. [the house.]

στέγ-αρχος, ὁ master of

στέγασμα, τό, στέγη, ἡ covering, roof; ceiling; shelter, house, dwelling.

στεγνός 3 covering, sheltering; covered.

στέγος, τό = στέγη.

στέγω to cover, shelter; to protect, keep off; to contain, hold; to conceal, hide, keep secret; to bear, endure.

στείβω to tread; to tread on; to tread under food.

στειλειή, ἡ, στειλειόν, τό handle.

στεινο- etc. see στενο-.

στειπτός 3 trodden on.

στεῖρα, ἡ stem, cut-water.

στεῖρος 3 barren.

στείχω to walk, step, go, march; to approach; to go away.

στέλεχος, τό stump, trunk.

στέλλω to arrange; to make ready, equip; to furnish, fit out, clothe, adorn; to invite, fetch, summon; to send, despatch. — intr. and P. to equip oneself, make oneself ready; to start, set off, depart; to go, come, travel. — M. to put on (one's clothes), to send for; to retire from, avoid.

στέμμα, τό fillet, wreath, chaplet; olive-branch.

στέναγμα, τό, στεναγμός, ὁ = στόνος.

στενάζω = στένω.

στενακτός 3 to be sighed for; sighing.

στεναχίζω and M. στενάχω and M. = στένω. [στ. defile.]

στενό-πορος 2 narrow; τὰ

στενός 3 narrow, strait; scanty; τὸ στενόν, τὰ στενά strait, narrows; limited means, embarrassment.

στενότης, ητος, ἡ narrowness, straitness.

στενο-χωρέω to straiten; to be straitened. — *P.* to be distressed.

στενο-χωρίᾱ, ἡ narrowness; defile; distress, anguish.

στένω¹ to make narrow. — *P.* to be compressed; to be crammed or full.

στένω² to sigh, moan, groan; to sound, ring; *trans.* to bemoan, bewail, lament.

στεν-ωπός 2 narrow; ὁ στ. narrow way, strait.

στέργημα, τό love-charm.

στέργω to love, like, be fond of; to be pleased with; to be content or satisfied; to pray.

στερεός 3 stiff, stark, solid; strong; stubborn, constant; cruel, unrelenting.

στερεό-φρων 2 stubborn.

στερεόω to make firm or strong.

στερέω to deprive, bereave. — *P.* to be deprived (of), to lose.   [mament.]

στερέωμα, τό firmness; fir-

στέρησις, ἡ privation, loss.

στερίσκω = στερέω.

στέριφος 3 = στερεός; = στεῖρος.   [loved.]

στερκτός 3 beloved, to be

στέρνον, τό breast; heart.

στερνοῦχος 2 far-stretched.

στέρομαι *P.* to be deprived.

στεροπή, ἡ flash of lightning; glare.

στεροπ-ηγερέτα, ὁ sender of lightning.

στέροφ, οπος flashing, dazzling.

στερρός 3 = στερεός.

στεῦμαι to make gestures; to take on as if, show signs as if; to promise, threaten.

στεφάνη, ἡ = στέφανος.

στεφανη-φορέω to wear a wreath.

στεφανη-φόρος 2, στεφανίτης, ου wearing a wreath, crowned, wreathed; giving a wreath as prize.

στέφανος, ὁ circlet, crown, wreath; circle, ring; crown of victory, prize, reward.

στεφανόω to encircle, surround, put round as a crown; to crown, wreath, adorn, distinguish, reward. — *M.* to crown oneself.

στεφάνωμα, τό, στέφος, τό = στέφανος.

στέφω = στεφανόω.

στῆθος, τό breast; heart, feelings; understanding.

στήκω to stand.

στήλη, ἡ pillar, post; boundary-post; upright stone.

στηλίτης, ου inscribed on a pillar as infamous.

στήμων, ονος, ὁ warp in the loom; thread.

στηριγμός, ὁ prop, support, firmness.

στηρίζω to set fast, prop, confirm. — *intr.* and *M.* to stand fast; to lean against; to have a footing.

στιβαρός 3 compact, stout, sturdy.

στιβάς, άδος, ἡ bed of straw, litter; tuft of leaves.

στιβέω to search through.

στίβη, ἡ rime, hoar-frost.

στίβος, ὁ path, footstep, track, trail.

στείβω = στείβω. [matiser.]

στιγεύς, ὁ brander, stig-

στίγμα, τό prick, point; brandmark, blemish, stain.

στιγματίᾱς, ου, ὁ one who has been branded.

στιγμή, ἡ = στίγμα.

στίζω to prick, sting; to tattoo; to brand.

στικτός 3 spotted.

στίλβω to shine, glitter.

στιλπνός 3 glittering.

στίξ, στιχός, ἡ = στίχος.

στῖφος, τό dense crowd, column of warriors.

στιχάομαι M. to march in rows.

στίχος, ὁ row, line; battle-array; line of writing, verse.

στλεγγίς, ίδος, ἡ scraper; comb.

στοά, ἡ colonnade, portico.

στοιβάς, άδος, ἡ = στιβάς.

στοιχεῖον, τό first principle, element, primary matter; elements of knowledge; letter of the alphabet.

στοιχέω = στιχάομαι.

στοῖχος, ὁ = στίχος.

στολάς, άδος, ἡ = σπολάς.

στολή, ἡ dress, garment, clothing; equipment; state-dress.

στόλος, ὁ equipment, sending, expedition, journey;

army, fleet, armament; troop, people; ship's beak.

στόμα, τό mouth; tongue, speech, language, words; face; outlet; chasm, cleft; point, edge; front.

στόμ-αργος 2 talkative, obtrusive in speech.

στόμ-αχος, ὁ throat; stomach; mouth. [bridle-bit.]

στόμιον, τό mouth, opening;

στομόω to stop the mouth; to prepare an attack.

στόμωσις, ἡ a sharpening; sharp speech.

στοναχέω = στένω.

στοναχή, ἡ = στόνος.

στοναχίζω = στεναχίζω.

στονόεις 3 roaring; moaning; mournful.

στόνος, ὁ a roaring, sighing, groaning.

στόρνῡμι to spread out, stretch out; to cover with blankets; to spread smooth, to level; to calm; to strew over.

στοχάζομαι M. to aim at, shoot at, look at; to hit the mark; to guess, conjecture.

στοχαστικός 3 sagacious.

στόχος, ὁ aim, guess.

στράπτω to lighten.

στρατάομαι P. to be encamped.

στρατ-άρχης, ου, ὁ general.

στρατείᾱ, ἡ expedition, campaign; army; military service.

στράτευμα, τό expedition; army; camp; soldiers.

στρατεύω and M. to serve

as a soldier; to take the field, march, fight.

στρατηγέω to be a general; to command, lead, manage.

στρατήγημα, τό stratagem, strategy.

στρατηγίᾱ, ἡ office of a general, command; strategy.

στρατηγιάω to wish to be general.

στρατηγικός 3 fit for a general, skilled in command. [tent.]

στρατήγιον, τό general's

στρατηγίς, ίδος, ἡ of a general.

στρατ-ηγός, ὁ general, leader, commander of an army; admiral; governor; consul; a military magistrate at Athens.

στρατηλασίη, ἡ = στρατεία.

στρατ-ηλατέω = στρατηγέω. [στρατηγός.]

στρατ-ηλάτης, ου, ὁ =

στρατιά, ἡ army, force; band, company; campaign.

στράτιος 3 military, warlike.

στρατιώτης, ου, ὁ soldier, warrior, mercenary.

στρατιωτικός 3 of or for soldiers; fit for military service.

στρτιῶτις, ιδος, fem. (ναῦς) troop-ship.

στρατο-λογέω to levy an army. [τάομαι.]

στρατόομαι P. = στρα-

στρατοπεδ-άρχης, ου, ὁ commander of the imperial guard.

στρατοπεδείᾱ, στρατοπέ-

δευσις, ἡ an encamping; station; encamped army.

στρατοπεδεύομαι M. to encamp; to lie at anchor.

στρατό-πεδον, τό encampment, camp; army; fleet.

στρατός, ὁ camp; army, body of soldiers; people.

στρεβλόω to twist, distort; to sprain, wrench; to rack, torture.

στρέμμα, τό sprain.

στρεπτός 3 twisted, plaited; pliant, flexible; ὁ στ. neckchain; cracknel.

στρεπτο-φόρος 2 wearing a necklace. [hausted.]

στρεύγομαι P. to be ex-

στρεφο-δῑνέομαι P. to be whirled or giddy.

στρέφω to twist, turn, bend; to turn about, wheel round, alter, twist back, sprain. — intr. and P. to be twisted, twist oneself, turn oneself (round about, to and fro); to turn back, flee; to roam about; to attach oneself (to); to be changed; to evade.

στρηνιάω to be wanton.

στρῆνος, τό vigour; wantonness.

στρογγύλος 3 round(ed); στρογγύλη ναῦς merchantship.

στρόμβος, ὁ whirl-gig.

στρουθίον, τό, στρουθός, ὁ sparrow; ostrich. [eddy.]

στροφάλιγξ, ιγγος.ἡ whirl,

στροφάς, άδος whirling.

στροφο-δῑνέομαι P. = στρεφοδ.

στρόφος, ὁ rope, cord, band.

στρυφνός 3 sour; morose.

στρῶμα, τό = στρωμνή.

στρωματό-δεσμον, τό sack for packing beds in.

στρωμνή, ἡ couch, bed; mattress; bedding.

στρώννῡμι = στόρνυμι.

στρωτός 3 spread.

στρωφάω to turn, spin. — P. to roam about; to stay, dwell.

στυγερός = στυγνός.

στυγέω to hate, abhor, detest; to fear; to make horrid.

στυγητός 3 abominated.

στύγιος 3 Stygian.

στυγνάζω to be sad or gloomy.

στυγνός 3 hated, abominated; horrible, terrible; gloomy, morose, sad; mournful, miserable.

στῦλος, ὁ pillar, prop.

στυππεῖον, τό tow.

στυπτηρία, ἡ alum.

στυράκιον, τό, στύραξ[1], ακος, ὁ end of a spearshaft.   [tree.]

στύραξ[2], ακος, ὁ, ἡ storax.

στυφελίζω to thrust, push; to shake; to drive; to beat; to maltreat.

στυφελός 3 and 2 close, dense, solid, rough, harsh.

σύ thou.   [herd of swine.]

σύ-βόσιον, -βόσσιον, τό

σύ-βώτης, ου, ὁ swineherd.

συγ-γένεια, ἡ relationship; kinsfolk, family.

συγ-γενής 2 born with one, inborn; connected by birth, related; kinsman; resembling, natural.

συγ-γενίς, ίδος, ἡ fem. of συγγενής.   [together.]

συγ-γηράσκω to grow old

συγ-γίγνομαι M. to come together, meet; to converse with; to come to assist; to live with.

συγ-γιγνώσκω to concur in opinion, agree, consent; to acknowledge, concede, yield; to know with; to excuse, pardon. — M. to grant, allow, yield.

σύγ-γνοια, ἡ, συγ-γνώμη, ἡ, συγ-γνωμοσύνη, ἡ pardon, forgiveness, excuse; permission.

συγ-γνώμων 2 forgiving, indulgent, allowing; pardonable.

σύγ-γονος 2 = συγγενής.

σύγ-γραμμα, ὁ written paper, essay; (prose-)book.

συγ-γραφεύς, ὁ writer, author; historian; prose-writer; writer of laws and statutes

συγ-γραφή, ἡ a writing down = σύγγραμμα.

συγ-γραφικῶς adv. exactly.

συγ-γράφω to write or note down; to describe, compose; to write history; to draw up a contract or resolution.

συγ-γυμνάζομαι P. to train oneself together.

συγ-καθαιρέω to pull down or overthrow together.   [together.]

συγ-καθαρμόζω to inter

συγ-καθέζομαι P., συγκάθημαι to sit with.

συγ-καθίζω and *M.* to sit together; to place together.

συγ-καθίημι to let down; *intr.* to stoop, condescend.

συγ-καθίστημι to establish together or with.

συγ-κακοπαθέω, συγ-κακουχέομαι *P.* to suffer together.

συγ-καλέω to call together, summon. — *M.* to call to oneself. [veil completely.]

συγ-καλύπτω to cover,

συγ-κάμνω to work, labour, or suffer together or with.

συγ-κάμπτω to bend together. [down together.]

συγ-καταβαίνω to go

συγ-κατάγω to lead down with. [together.]

συγ-καταδιώκω to pursue

συγ-καταδουλόω and *M.* to subdue together.

συγ-καταζεύγνῡμι to entangle. [jointly.]

συγ-καταθάπτω to bury

συγ-κατάθεσις, ἡ agreement. [gether.]

συγ-καταίθω to burn to-

συγ-κάταινος 2 agreeing.

συγ-κατακαίω, -κάω to burn at once. [down with.]

συγ-κατάκειμαι *M.* to lie

συγ-κατακλείω, -κληίω to shut in together.

συγ-κατακτάομαι *M.* to acquire together.

συγ-κατακτείνω to slay together.

συγ-καταλαμβάνω to seize or capture together.

συγ-καταλείπω to leave behind together.

συγ-καταλύω to overthrow jointly.

συγ-κατανέμομαι *M.* to possess in company.

συγ-καταπράττω and *M.* to effect together.

συγ-κατασκεδάννῡμι to pour over at once.

συγ-κατασκευάζω to make ready or prepare together.

συγ-καταστρέφομαι *M.* to help in subduing.

συγ-κατατίθεμαι *M.* to lay down at the same time; to consent to.

συγ-καταψηφίζω to choose in addition. — *M.* to condemn together.

συγ-κατεργάζομαι *M.* to accomplish together; to help in procuring; to assist.

συγ-κατέρχομαι to return together. [for together.]

συγ-κατεύχομαι *M.* to pray

συγ-κατηγορέω to accuse together. [together.]

συγ-κατοικέω to dwell

συγ-κατοικίζω to colonize jointly; to help in restoring.

σύγ-κειμαι to lie with, be together; to be composed or agreed (upon).

συγ-κελεύω to join in bidding. [or to the ground.]

συγ-κεντέω to stab down

συγ-κεράννῡμι to mix or blend together.

συγ-κεφαλαιόω to sum up.

συγ-κινδῡνεύω to be partners in danger.

συγ-κῑνέω to raise up.

σύγ-κλεισις, ἡ a shutting up; tightness.

συγ-κλείω, -κλήω, συγ-κλείω to shut up, enclose, compress; to encompass, surround; to close, shut. — intr. and M. to be joined, concentrated, united, or shut in.

συγ-κληρονόμος, ὁ co-heir.

σύγ-κληρος 2 assigned by the same lot.

συγ-κληρόω to assign by the same lot.

σύγ-κλητος 2 called together; ἡ σ. senate.

συγ-κλίνομαι P. to lie with.

συγ-κλονέω to confound.

σύγ-κλυς, υδος flocked together. [or sleep with.]

συγ-κοιμάομαι P. to lie)

συγ-κοινόομαι M. to make common with, give a share.

συγ-κοινωνέω to get a share.

συγ-κοινωνός 2 partaking.

συγ-κομιδή, ἡ a bringing together, gathering in; concourse.

συγ-κομίζω to bring together, gather in; to afford together; to bury together. — M. to gather in for oneself, to procure for oneself; to send for.

συγ-κόπτω to beat together; to knock to pieces; to beat soundly, slay.

σύγ-κρασις, ἡ a mixing together, blending.

συγ-κρίνω to put together; to compare; to judge.

συγ-κροτέω to beat, strike, or hammer together; to drill, train well.

συγ-κρούω to strike together; to set at variance, make enemies; — intr. to collide.

συγ-κρύπτω to help in hiding; to conceal completely.

συγ-κτάομαι M. to acquire jointly, to help to acquire.

συγ-κτίζω to found together. [founder.]

συγ-κτίστης, ου, ὁ fellow-)

συγ-κυβεύω to play at dice with.

συγ-κύπτω to bend forward or stoop so as to meet; to draw nearer; to conspire; to be bent or curved.

συγ-κυρέω and M. to encounter, meet; to happen, come to pass. [chance.]

συγ-κυρία, ἡ coincidence,)

συγ-χαίρω to rejoice with.

συγ-χέω to pour together, mix by pouring, mingle; to confound, trouble, disturb; to frustrate, spoil, break up.

σύγ-χορευτής, οῦ, ὁ partner in a dance.

συγ-χόω to cover over with earth; to demolish.

συγ-χράομαι M. to have intercourse with.

συγ-χύννω = συγχέω.

σύγ-χυσις, ἡ a mixing, confounding; disturbing; overthrow, revolt.

συγ-χώννυμι = συγχόω.

συγ-χωρέω to go together; to agree, accede, assent to; to give way, yield, acquiesce in, concede; συγχωρεῖ it is allowed or possible.

23*

σύειος 3 of swine.

συ-ζάω to live with or together.

συ-ζεύγνῡμι to yoke together, couple, unite.

συ-ζητέω to debate.

συ-ζήτησις, ἡ disputation.

συ-ζητητής, οῦ, ὁ disputer.

συ-ζυγίᾱ, ἡ union; pair.

σύ-ζυγος 2 yoked together; consort, mate.

συ-ζωοποιέω to quicken at the same time.

σῡκάμῑνος, ἡ, σῦκο-μορέᾱ, ἡ fig-mulberry.

σῡκῆ, σῡκέη, ἡ fig-tree.

σῦκον, τό fig.

σῡκο-φαντέω to be a false accuser, slanderer or extorter.

σῡκο-φάντης, ου, ὁ fig-informer, false accuser, slanderer, extorter.

σῡκο-φαντίᾱ, ἡ false accusation, slander.

σῡλ-αγωγέω to carry off as booty.

σῡλάω, σῡλεύω to take away; to strip off, despoil, pillage, plunder.

σύλη, ἡ = σῦλον pl.

συλ-λαβή, ἡ syllable.

συλ-λαλέω to talk with.

συλ-λαμβάνω M. to put or bring together; to collect; to comprehend; to take away, carry away; to lay hold of, seize, arrest; to receive; to perceive, understand; to take part (in), assist, help.

συλ-λέγω to collect, gather, call together, levy (an army).

— P. to assemble, meet. M. to collect for oneself.

συλ-λήβδην, adv. taken together, in short.

συλ-λήπτρια, ἡ, -λήπτωρ, ορος, ὁ partner, assistant.

σύλ-ληψις, ἡ a seizing, comprehension.

συλ-λογή, ἡ a gathering, collecting, assembly, concourse; a levying of soldiers.

συλ-λογίζομαι M.to reckon, consider, think, reflect; to infer, conclude.

σύλ-λογος, ὁ = συλλογή.

συλ-λοχίτης, ου, ὁ soldier of the same company.

συλ-λῡπέομαι P. to feel compassion.

συλ-λύω to help in loosing.

σῦλον, τό seizure of a cargo; privateering.

σῶμα, τό = θῶμα.

συμ-βαίνω to go or come together, meet; to agree, make an agreement, make friends, reconcile; to suit, fit, correspond, be like; to coincide, happen, fall out, come to pass, turn out, result, succeed. συμ-βαίνει it happens, it is possible.

συμ-βάλλω and M. to throw together, bring together, unite, mix, join closely; to engage in, begin; to set together, incite; to compare, compute, guess; to interpret, understand; to come together, meet, join, encounter, fight. — M. to agree, make a treaty; to συμβασείω to wish to make a treaty.

contribute, furnish, be useful; to put forth, produce, offer; to judge, consider.

συμ-βασείω to wish to make a treaty.

συμ-βασιλεύω to reign jointly. [ment.]

σύμ-βασις, ἡ treaty, agree-/

συμ-βατήριος 2, συμβατικός 3 tending to agreement, conciliatory.

συμ-βιάζω to oppress all together.

συμ-βιβάζω to bring or put together; to reconcile; to compare, contrast; to guess; to perceive; to prove; to teach.

συμ-βιόω to live with.

συμ-βοάω to cry aloud or shout together with; to call to.

συμ-βοήθεια, ἡ joint aid

συμ-βοηθέω to render joint aid.

συμβόλαιος 3 stipulated. τὸ συμβόλαιον intercourse; bargain; contract; debenture; debt, money lent; symptom, token.

συμ-βολή, ἡ a meeting; encountering, engagement, battle; joint, end, joining; contribution.

σύμ-βολον, τό treaty (of commerce); mark, sign, token, signal, symbol; ticket, badge.

συμ-βουλεύω to advise, counsel; to propose. — M. to take counsel with, deliberate, consult.

συμ-βουλή, -βουλίᾱ, ἡ,

συμ-βούλιον, τό advice, counsel, consultation; senate, council.

συμ-βούλομαι P. to wish too, agree. [counsellor.]

σύμ-βουλος, ὁ, ἡ adviser,/

συμ-μαθητής, οῦ, ὁ schoolfellow, fellow-disciple.

συμ-μανθάνω to learn together; aor. to be used to.

συμ-μάρπτω to grasp together.

συμ-μαρτυρέω and M. to bear witness with, corroborate. [ness.]

σύμ-μαρτυς, υρος, ὁ wit-/

συμ-μαχέω to fight jointly, to be allied in war; to help.

συμ-μαχίᾱ, ἡ alliance in war; allies; assistance.

συμ-μαχικός 3 of or for alliance; τὸ συμμαχικόν auxiliaries, allied forces; treaty of alliance; treasury of allies.

συμ-μαχίς, ίδος, fem. of σύμμαχος; allied state; body of allics. [μαχέω.]

συμ-μάχομαι M. = συμ-/

σύμ-μαχος 2 allied, fighting jointly; ally; assistant, helper.

συμ-μένω to stay together; to abide, continue.

συμ-μερίζομαι M. συμμετέχω, συμ-μετίσχω to receive a share along with.

συμ-μέτοχος 2 partaking in jointly.

συμ-μετρέω and M. to measure, compute, measure out. — P. to be commensurate, correspond.

συμ-μέτρησις, ἡ admeasurement. [symmetry.]

συμ-μετρίᾱ, ἡ proportion,

σύμ-μετρος 3 measured with, commensurate with, in due proportion, symmetrical, fitting, fitted.

συμ-μητιάομαι M. to take counsel with.

συμ-μιγής 2 = σύμμικτος, adv. σύμμιγα along with.

συμ-μίγνυμι to mix with, mingle with; to unite; to communicate to.— intr. and P. to be mingled, blended, or united; to have intercourse; to converse with; to encounter, engage in battle, come to blows; to befall.

σύμ-μικτος 2 intermingled, promiscuous, confounded; common. [imitator.]

συμ-μῑμητής, οῦ, ὁ fellow-

σύμ-μιξις, ἡ a mixing together; marriage.

συμ-μίσγω = -μίγνυμι.

συμ-μορίᾱ, ἡ class of taxpayers; division of the fleet.

σύμ-μορος 2 paying taxes along with.

συμ-μορφίζω to form alike

σύμ-μορφος 2 of like shape.

συμ-μορφόω = συμμορφίζω.

συμ-παθέω to feel with, sympathize. [nate.]

συμ-παθής 2 compassio-

συμ-παίζω to play with.

συμ-παίω to beat or strike together or against one another.

συμ-παραγίγνομαι M. to arrive at the same time, be present, assist.

συμ-παραθέω to run along with.

συμ-παρακαλέω to call upon, invite, comfort, or exhort at the same time.

συμ-παρακομίζω to conduct (together).

συμ-παραλαμβάνω to take along with. [along with.]

συμ-παραμένω to stay

συμ-παρασκευάζω to join in preparing, to make ready or provide jointly. [helper.]

συμ-παραστάτης, ου, ὁ

συμ-παρατάσσομαι M. to be drawn up in battle-array with, to fight along with.

συμ-πάρειμι[1] (-ιέναι) to go along at the same time.

συμ-πάρειμι[2] (-εῖναι) to be present with or at the same time. [along with.]

συμ-παρέχω to present

συμ-παρίσταμαι M. to stand beside one at the same time.

σύμ-πᾱς, ᾱσα, ᾱν all together, all at once; the whole, in sum.

συμ-πάσχω to suffer with, sympathize. [suading.]

συμ-πείθω to join in per-

συμ-πέμπω to send along with; to join in a procession.

συμ-περαίνω and M. to finish along with; to achieve entirely.

συμ-περιλαμβάνω to comprehend together with.

συμ-περιπατέω to walk to and fro with. [congeal.]

συμ-πήγνῡμι to fasten; to

σύμ-πηκτος 2 compact.

συμ-πιέζω to press together.

συμ-πίνω to drink with.

συμ-πίπτω to fall down; to fall in with, meet with; to come to blows; to coincide; to happen, come to pass; to fall into.

συμ-πλαταγέω to clap together.

συμ-πλέκω to plait together. — P. to be plaited or entangled; to come to close quarters.

συμ-πλέω to sail together.

σύμ-πλεως, ων quite full.

συμ-πληϑύω -πληρόω to fill or man completely; to complete.

σύμ-πλοος, -πλους, ὁ, ἡ fellow-passenger, comrade.

συμ-πνέω to be of the same mind.

συμ-πνίγω to choke up.

συμ-ποδίζω to fetter (the feet); to entangle.

συμ-πολεμέω to make war along with.   [jointly.

συμ-πολιορκέω to besiege

συμ-πολῑτεύω and M. to live in the same state, be a fellow-citizen.

συμ-πονέω to partake in work or misery.

συμ-πορεύομαι P. to go or travel together.   [ther.

συμ-πορίζω to bring toge-

συμποσί-αρχος, ὁ president of a drinking-party.

συμ-πόσιον, τό drinking-bout, entertainment; banquet.   [drinker, guest.

συμ-πότης, ου, ὁ fellow-

συμ-πράκτωρ, ορος. ὁ helper, assistant.

συμ-πράσσω to help in doing, assist. — M. to join in avenging.

συμ-πρεσβεύω and M. to be a fellow-ambassador.

σύμ-πρεσβυς, εως, ὁ fellow-ambassador.

συμ-πρεσβύτερος, ὁ fellow-elder.   [ὠνέομαι.)

συμ-πρίασθαι, aor. of συν-

συμ-προϑῡμέομαι P. to have equal zeal or eagerness.

συμ-προπέμπω to join in escorting.   [ther.)

συμ-πτύσσω to fold toge-

σύμ-πτωμα, τό chance; accident, misfortune.

συμ-φερόντως adv. profitably.

συμ-φερτός 3 united.

συμ-φέρω to bring together, collect; to contribute; to bear jointly. — intr. to be useful, profitable, advantageous, or expedient; συμφέρει it is profitable; it happens; to agree with; to assist, be serviceable. — P. to come together; to agree together, assent to; to converse with, have intercourse with; to encounter; to happen, come to pass.

συμ-φεύγω to flee along with; to be a fellow-exile.

σύμ-φημι to assent, say yes, approve; to promise.

συμ-φιλέω to join in loving.

συμ-φιλονῑκέω to take sides.   [frightening.)

συμ-φοβέω to join in

συμ-φοιτάω to go regularly to together.

συμ-φοιτητής, οῦ, ὁ schoolfellow.

συμ-φορά, ἡ event, chance, good luck; misfortune, disaster, calamity; defeat; success, result. [camp.]

συμ-φορεύς, ὁ aide-de-

συμ-φορέω = συμφέρω.

σύμ-φορος 2 useful, profitable, favourable; convenient.

συμ-φρ δμων 2 counsellor.

συμ-φράζομαι to take counsel with; to consider.

συμ-φράσσω to press together.

σύμ-φρουρος 2 protecting.

συμ-φυγάς, άδος, ὁ fellowexile. [watchman.]

συμ-φύλαξ, ακος, ὁ fellow-

συμ-φυλάσσω to watch together. [same tribe.]

συμ-φῡλέτης, ου, ὁ of the

συμ-φύρω to knead or mix together.

συμ-φυτεύω to plant in together; to contrive together.

σύμ-φυτος 2 grown together; innate, cognate.

συμ-φύω to let grow together. — intr. and P. to grow together or into one.

συμ-φωνέω to agree in sound, be in unison; to make an agreement.

συμ-φώνησις, ἡ, συμφωνίᾱ, ἡ harmony; music.

σύμ-φωνος 2 harmonious, agreeing in sound; concordant.

συμ-ψάω to sweep away.

συμ-ψηφίζω to reckon together. — M. to vote with.

σύμ-ψῡχος 2 unanimous.

σύν, ξύν adv. together, at once. — prp. with dat. with, in company with, together with, in connexion with; in accordance with; furnished with, by means of; under the command of.

συν-άγγελος, ὁ fellowmessenger.

συν-αγείρω to gather together, assemble, collect.

συν-άγνῡμι to break in or to pieces, shiver.

συν-αγορεύω to agree to, join in recommending.

συν-άγω to lead or bring together, collect, assemble; to summon, admit; to contract, draw together, straiten. — P. to be assembled; to be admitted. [cruiter.]

συν-αγωγεύς, ὁ uniter; re-

συν-αγωγή, ἡ a collecting, gathering, uniting; place of meeting, synagogue; preparation.

συν-αγωνίζομαι M. to contend along with; to assist, help.

συν-αγωνιστής, οῦ, ὁ fellow-combatant; helper.

συν-άδελφος 2 having brother or sister. [wrong.]

συν-αδικέω to join in doing

συν-άδω to accord with.

συν-αείρω[1] = συναίρω.

συν-αείρω[2] to yoke together.

συν-αθλέω = συναγωνίζομαι.

συν-αθροίζω to gather together. [blood.]

σύν-αιμος 2 related by

συν-αινέω to join in approving; to assent, agree.

συν-αίνυμαι to take together.

συν-αιρέω to seize together, comprise, comprehend; to seize wholly; to snatch away, destroy; to help in taking.

συν-αίρω and M. to raise or lift up together. — M. to undertake jointly.

συν-αίτιος 2 and 3 accessory, accomplice. [captive.]

συν-αιχμάλωτος, ὅ fellow-

συν-αιωρέομαι to be held in suspense with.

συν-ακολουθέω to follow along with. [same time.]

συν-ακούω to hear at the

συν-αλγέω to suffer pain with; to feel pity.

συν-αλίζω to assemble. — P. to come together.

συν-αλλαγή, ἡ change, interchange; intercourse, conversation; reconciliation, intervention; lot, vicissitude.

συν-αλλάσσω to associate; to reconcile, settle; intr. to have intercourse or to deal with. — P. to be united or reconciled.

συν-αμφότερος 3 both together; both in the same manner. [along with.]

συν-αναβαίνω to go up

συν-αναγκάζω to enforce at the same time.

συν-αναιρέω to destroy at the same time.

συν-ανάκειμαι to recline at table with.

συν-αναλίσκω to spend or waste along with.

συν-αναμίγνυμαι P. to have intercourse with.

συν-αναπαύομαι M. to refresh oneself together with.

συν-αναπείθω to join in persuading. [exacting.]

συν-αναπράσσω to join in

συν-αναχωρέω to go back together.

συν-ανίστημι to help in restoring; intr. and M. to rise together.

συν-αντάω and M. to meet with; to happen.

συν-άντησις, ἡ a meeting.

συν-αντιάζω = συναντάω.

συν-αντιλαμβάνομαι M. to lay hold of along with, to help.

συν-άντομαι = -αντάω.

συν-αορέω to be joined to.

συν-άορος 2 united, linked with; consort.

συν-απάγω to lead away with.

συν-άπας 3 = σύμπας.

συν-άπειμι (-ιέναι) to go away with.

συν-αποβαίνω to disembark along with.

συν-αποθνήσκω to die together with.

συν-απολαμβάνω to receive at once.

συν-απόλλυμι to destroy, lose together. — M. to perish together.

συν-απονεύω to bend away according to.

συν-αποπέμπω, συν-αποστέλλω to send away together.

συν-άπτω and *M.* to tie or join together, unite. — *intr.* to join, attach oneself (to), to partake in; to border on; to take counsel together; to come to blows.

συν-αράσσω to strike together, dash to pieces.

συν-αρέσκει μοί τι it pleases me too.

συν-αρμόζω and *M.* to fit together, to join; to agree together.

συν-αρμολογέομαι to be joined exactly.

συν-αρμόττω = -αρμόζω.

συν-αρπάζω to seize abruptly; to snatch or carry away.

συν-αρτάω to knit together. — *P. pf.* to be caught by.

συν-άρχω to rule jointly with, be a colleague.

συν-ασπιδόω to keep the shields close together.

συν-ασπιστής, οῦ, ὁ fellow-soldier.

συν-αυδάω to agree to.

σύν-αυλος 2 dwelling together.

συν-αυξάνω, -αύξω to let grow or increase together. — *P.* to grow larger together.

συν-αφαιρέω and *M.* to assist in delivering.

συν-αφίστημι to make revolt together. — *intr* and *M.* to revolt along with.

συν-άχθομαι *P.* to mourn with. [with.]

συν-δαΐζω to kill together)

συν-δακρύω to weep with.

συν-δειπνέω to dine together.

σύν-δειπνον, τό banquet.

σύν-δειπνος 2 dining together. [fetter; bundle.]

σύν-δεσμος, ὁ band, union;)

συν-δεσμώτης, ου, ὁ fellow-prisoner. [ther.]

σύν-δετος 2 bound toge-)

συν-δέω to bind together, fetter; to join, unite.

συν-διαβάλλω to slander or accuse jointly; to cross over together. [over with.]

συν-διαβιβάζω to carry)

συν-διαγιγνώσκω to decide jointly. [together.]

συν-διαιτάομαι *P.* to live)

συν-διακινδυνεύω to incur danger jointly.

συν-διαλύω to break up or abolish jointly.

συν-διαπεραίνω to help in finishing.

συν-διαπολεμέω to join in making war to the end.

συν-διαπράσσω to effect together — *M.* to help in negotiating.

συν-διασκέπτομαι *M.*, συν-διασκοπέω to examine together with.

συν-διασῴζω to help in preserving.

συν-διαταλαιπωρέω to endure hardship with.

συν-διατελέω to continue with. [time with.]

συν-διατρίβω to pass one's)

συν-διαφέρω and *M.* to bear with to the end.

συν-διαχειρίζω to manage jointly.

συν-διέξειμι (-ιέναι) to go through along with.

συν-δικάζω to assist in judging. [vocate.]

συν-δικέω to act as an advocate.

σύν-δικος 2 helping · in court; advocate; attorney; assistant.

συν-διώκω to help in pursuing. [to me too.]

συν-δοκεῖ μοι it seems good

συν-δοκιμάζω to test along with.

συν-δοξάζω to join in approving of or in extolling.

συν-δούλη, ἡ, **σύν-δουλος**, ὁ, ἡ fellow-slave.

συν-δράω to do together.

συν-δρομή, ἡ concourse.

σύν-δυο two and two, two together.

σύν-εγγυς *adv.* quite near.

συν-εδρία, ἡ, -έδριον, τό a sitting together or in council; senate; senate-house.

σύν-εδρος 2 sitting together; sitting in council.

συν-εθέλω to wish likewise.

συν-εθίζω to accustom. — *P.* to become used to.

συν-είδησις, ἡ joint knowledge; consciousness; conscience.

συν-ειλέω to press or bind together. [χομαι.]

σύν-ειμι[1] (-ιέναι) = συνέρ-

σύν-ειμι[2] (-εῖναι) to be or live together, to be joined.

united, or associated; to have intercourse (with); to assist.

συν-είργω to shut in together; to enclose or bind together, gird; to unite.

συν-είρω to string together; to unite. [with.]

συν-εισάγω to bring in

συν-εισβάλλω to invade together. [together.]

συν-εισέρχομαι to go in

συν-εισπίπτω to fall into along with; to invade together. [together.]

συν-εισπλέω to sail into

συν-εισφέρω to join in contributing. [gether.]

συν-εκβαίνω to go up to-

συν-εκβάλλω to cast out together. [bringing out.]

συν-εκβιβάζω to help in

συν-έκδημος, ὁ travelling companion.

συν-εκδίδωμι to help in portioning out.

συν-εκδύομαι *M.* to put off clothes together.

συν-εκκομίζω to help in burying. [cutting off.]

συν-εκκόπτω to help in

συν-εκλεκτός 3 chosen along with.

συν-εκπέμπω to assist in sending out or escorting.

συν-εκπίνω to drink off together.

συν-εκπίπτω to fall out; to be thrown out together.

συν-εκπλέω, -πλώω to sail out together.

συν-εκπορίζω to help in procuring.

συν-εχπράσσομαι *M.* to help in avenging.

συν-εχσῴζω to help in preserving.

συν-εχτρέφω to rear up jointly. [funeral.]

συν-εχφέρω to attend a

συν-ελαύνω to drive or bring together; to clench (the teeth); to exhort. — *intr.* to meet in quarrel.

συν-ελευθερόω to help in freeing.

συν-εμβάλλω to join in making an inroad.

συν-έμπορος, ὁ fellow-traveller, companion.

συν-εξαιρέω to help in destroying or capturing.

συν-εξαχούω to hear exactly with one.

συν-εξαμαρτάνω to err or commit a fault along with.

συν-εξαπατάω to deceive or cheat along with.

συν-έξειμι (-ιέναι) = συν-εξέρχομαι to go out together.

συν-εξορμάω to help to urge on.

συν-εοχμός, ὁ junction.

συν-επάγω to help in leading against or in inciting.

συν-επαινέω to join in praising; to approve, recommend.

συν-έπαινος 2 approving.

συν-επαιτιάομαι *M.* to accuse together.

συν-επαχολουθέω to follow along with.

συν-επαμύνω to help in warding off.

συν-επανίσταμαι *M.* to join in a revolt.

συν-έπειμι (-ιέναι) to join in attacking.

συν-επελαφρύνω to help in relieving.

συν-επεύχομαι *M.* to join in a prayer or vow.

συν-επιβουλεύω to plot against jointly.

συν-επιλαμβάνω and *M.* to support, assist.

συν-επιμαρτυρέω to bear witness along with.

συν-επιμελέομαι *P.* to join in taking care of.

συν-επισχέπτομαι *M.* and συν-επισχοπέω to examine along with.

συν-επισπάομαι *M.* to draw to oneself; to win for oneself. [speeding.]

συν-επισπεύδω to join in

συν-επίσταμαι *P.* to know along with.

συν-επιστρατεύω to make war together with.

συν-επισχύω to help in assisting.

συν-επιτελέω to join in accomplishing.

συν-επιτίθεμαι *M.* to join in attacking.

συν-επιτρίβω to destroy together. [close upon.]

συν-έπομαι *M.* to follow

συν-επόμνῡμι to swear at the same time.

συν-εργάζομαι *M.* to work together. [ἔργον.]

συν-εργάτης, ου, ὁ = σύν-

συν-εργέω to help in work.

σύν-εργος, συν-εργός 2

helping in work, cooperating.

συν-έργω = -είργω.

συν-έρδω to work together.

συν-ερείδω to fasten, bind, or press together.

συν-έριθος, ό, ή fellow-worker.

συν-έρχομαι M. to go together or with; to meet; to make an appointment or an agreement; to encounter, meet in battle; to have intercourse (with); to come in (money), be gathered. [with.]

συν-εσθίω to eat together]

σύν-εσις, ή a joining; understanding, intelligence.

συν-εστιάομαι P. to feast together.

συν-εστίη, ή banquet.

συν-έστιος, ή sharing one's hearth, inmate.

συν-εστώ, οῦς, ό a being together. [friend.]

συν-έταιρος, ό companion.

συν-ετός 3 intelligent, sensible, sagacious; intelligible. [in happiness with.]

συν-ευδαιμονέω to share]

συν-ευδοκέω to be pleased with, agree to, consent (to).

συν-εύδω, συν-ευνάζομαι P. to sleep with.

σύν-ευνος, ό, ή bedfellow.

συν-ευ-πάσχω to be benefited with.

συν-ευπορέω to join in providing or assisting.

συν-εύχομαι M. to pray together. [together.]

συν-ευωχέομαι P. to feast]

συν-εφάπτομαι M. to lay hold of together.

συν-εφέλκω to draw after along with. [together.]

συν-εφέπομαι M. to follow]

συν-εφίστημι intr. and M. to superintend together; to rise together with.

συν-έχεια, ή perseverance.

συν-εχής 2 holding together, continuous, unbroken; contiguous, adjacent; frequent, unceasing.

συν-έχθω to hate along with.

συν-έχω to hold or keep together; to contain, comprise; to constrain, compress, vex. — intr. and P. to be joined or united; to be affected by; to be busy.

συν-ηγορέω to be an advocate.

συν-ήγορος 2 advocate, interceder; agreeing with.

συν-ήδομαι P. to rejoice with; to congratulate.

συν-ήθεια, ή intercourse; habit, usage.

συν-ήθης 2 familiar, intimate; of like mind and habits; costumary, habitual.

συν-ήκω to come together.

συν-ηλικιώτης, ου, ό of equal age. [day with.]

συν-ημερεύω to pass the]

συν-ημοσύνη, ή agreement.

συν-ήορος 2 = συναορος.

συν-ηρετέω to be a friend to. [vered.]

συν-ηρεφής 2 thickly co-]

σύν-θακος 2 sitting with.

συν-θάπτω to help to bury.

συν-θεάομαι M. to view or behold together.

συν-θεσίη, ἡ = συνθήκη.

σύν-θεσις, ἡ composition, combination.

σύν-θετος 2 compound, combined, complex; settled; agreed upon. [to succeed.]

συν-θέω to run along with;]

συν-θήκη, ἡ = σύνθεσις; agreement, treaty, covenant, peace; commandment, order.

σύν-θημα, τό = συνθήκη; preconcerted signal, token; watch-word. [hunter.]

συν-θηρατής, οῦ. ὁ fellow-)

συν-θηράω, -εύω to hunt or catch together. [της.]

σύν-θηρος, ὁ = συνθηρα-)

συν-θλάω to crush, shatter.

συν-θλίβω to press together.

συν-θνήσκω to die with.

συν-θρύπτω to break in or to pieces.

συν-θύω to sacrifice with.

συν-ίζω to sit together.

συν-ίημι to seat or bring together; to perceive, hear; to understand, know exactly. — M. to come to an agreement; to perceive.

συν-ίππαρχος, ὁ joint commander of horse.

συν-ιστάνω, συν-ιστάω, συν-ίστημι to place, bring. or set together, to unite; to bring together in dispute or battle; to introduce or recommend to; to compose, create, found, cause; to prove, show. — M. to put

together, to produce or create for oneself. — intr. and M. to come or stand together; to league together, conspire; to encounter, meet in battle, be engaged or implicated in; to be composed; to begin; to be combined; to stand fast; to continue, live, exist; to stand still, make a halt.

συν-ίστωρ, ορος 2 knowing together with.

συν-ίσχω = συνέχω.

συν-ναίω to dwell together.

συν-νάσσω to cram together.

συν-ναυβάτης, ου, συν-ναύτης, ου. ὁ shipmate.

συν-ναυμαχέω to fight at sea along with.

συν-ναυστολέω to go in the same ship.

συν-νεύω to nod assent.

συν-νέω, -νηέω to heap up together. [tory.]

συν-νῖκάω to join in vic-)

συν-νοέω and M. to consider, reflect ([up]on).

σύν-νοια, ἡ meditation; trouble.

σύν-νομος 2 feeding together; companion, friend, consort, mate.

σύν-νους 2 meditating, thoughtful. [with.]

συν-οδεύω to travel along)

συν-οδίᾱ, ἡ company of travellers. [traveller.]

συν-οδοιπόρος, ὁ fellow-)

σύν-οδος, ἡ assembly, meeting, company; council; encounter, attack, battle.

σύν-οιδα to know together with; to know thoroughly; to be conscious.

συν-οικέω to dwell or live together; to wed; *trans.* to inhabit together.

συν-οίκημα, τό a dwelling together; cohabitant.

συν-οίκησις, ἡ, συν-οικίᾱ, ἡ cohabitation; marriage; house let out to tenants.

συν-οίκια, τά festival of union.

συν-οικίζω to make dwell together, to join in one state, concentrate; to people, colonize; to give to wife.

συν-οίκισις, ἡ a joining in one state; colony.

συν-οικοδομέω to build together; to build jointly.

σύν-οικος 2 dwelling or living together; house-mate, companion.

συν-ολολύζω to scream or shout together. [with.]

συν-ομιλέω to converse]

συν-όμνῡμι to swear along with or together; to join in conspiracy.

συν-ομολογέω and *M.* to agree with or to; to concede, promise; to make a treaty.

συν-ομορέω to border on.

συν-οράω to see together or at once.

συν-οργίζομαι *P.* to grow angry along with.

συν-ορίνω to stir up, excite; to rush on against each other. [anchor together.]

συν-ορμίζω to bring to]

σύν-ορος, -ουρος 2 bordering on.

συν-ουσίᾱ, ἡ a being or living together, intercourse; society, party; conversation; banquet.

συν-ουσιαστής, οῦ, ὁ companion, friend, disciple.

συν-οφρυόομαι *M.* to frown.

συν-οχή, ἡ connection, meeting; straitness; anguish.

σύν-οψις, ἡ survey.

σύν-ταγμα, τό. σύν-ταξις, ἡ a putting together in order; order, arrangement; array of battle; body of troops, contingent; contribution, tax, rate, pay.

συν-ταράσσω to stir up together; to disturb utterly, trouble, disquiet, confound, vex. — *P.* to be drawn into confusion.

συν-τάσσω to put together in order; to put in array; to arrange, organize, systematize; to command, ordain; to assign. — *P.* to collect one's thoughts. — *M.* to put in order for oneself; to draw up in a line.

συν-ταχύνω to hasten (*trans.* and *intr.*).

συν-τείνω to stretch, strain, exert; to direct to; *intr.* to tend towards.

συν-τειχίζω to help in fortification.

συν-τεκμαίρομαι *M.* to infer from, conjecture, estimate.

συν-τεχνοποιέω to breed children with.

συν-τεκταίνομαι *M.* to help in building or framing.

συν-τέλεια, ἡ joint payment or contribution; union of tax-payers; completion, end.

συν-τελέω to accomplish or complete together, bring quite to an end; to pay joint taxes, contribute; to belong to a certain class.

συν-τελής 2 paying joint taxes; tributary to.

συν-τέμνω to cut down; to cut short, abridge, curtail; to make a short cut; to rush on to.

συν-τήκω to melt together. — *intr.* and *P.* to melt away, fade, disappear.

συν-τηρέω to help in preserving, watching, or protecting.

συν-τίθημι to put or place together, compose, construct; to contrive, devise; to unite, comprehend, sum up. — *M.* to put together for oneself; to perceive, observe, hear; to agree on, concert, make a treaty or covenant; to set in order.

συν-τῑμάω to honour along with. [in many places.]

συν-τιτρώσκω to wound]

σύν-τομος 2 cut short, abridged, shortened, concise, brief.

σύν-τονος 2 stretched, strait, intense; earnest; vehement.

συν-τράπεζος, ὁ companion at table. [three.]

σύν-τρεις, -τρια three and]

συν-τρέφω to rear up together.

συν-τρέχω to run together or along with; to come together, assemble; to rush together, encounter; to agree; to meet.

συν-τρίβω to rub together; to crush, shiver; to wear away, undo.

σύν-τριμμα, τό destruction.

σύν-τροφος 2 reared up together; foster-brother; living with; familiar, common; natural.

συν-τυγχάνω to meet with, fall in with; ὁ συντυχών any one; to happen, come to pass; chance

συν-τυχία, ἡ incident, occurrence, chance; accident; happy event.

συν-υποκρίνομαι to simulate along with.

συν-υπουργέω to join in assisting. [gether.]

συν-υφαίνω to contrive to-]

συν-ωδίνω to be in travail or labour together.

συν-ῳδός 2 = σύμφωνος.

συν-ωθέω to thrust together. [political club.]

συν-ωμοσία, ἡ conspiracy;]

συν-ωμότης, ου, ὁ fellow-conspirator. [by oath.]

σύν-ωμοτος 2 confirmed]

συν-ωνέομαι *M.* to buy together; to take into one's pay. [team; pair.]

συν-ωρίς, ίδος, ἡ double]

συν-ωφελέω to join in helping, to be of use.

σῦριγξ, ιγγος, ἡ shepherd's

pipe; spear-case; wheel-box; blood-vessel.

συρμαίᾱ, ἡ purging oil; radish.

συρμαΐζω to purge.

συρ-ράπτω to sew or stitch together.

συρ-ράσσω to clash together; to rush on.

συρ-ρέω to flow together; to come together.

συρ-ρήγνῡμι to break in pieces; *intr.* to rush or run together; to clash together; to break down, fall in or to pieces. — *P.* to be broken.

συρφετός, ὁ offscum, rubbish; mob, crowd.

σύρω to drag, draw, trail.

σῦς, συός, ὁ, ἡ swine, pig; boar.

συ-σκευάζω to pack up; to make ready, prepare; to contrive. — *M.* to pack up, to get ready for marching off; to prepare, equip, contrive for oneself; to win over. [in devising.]

συ-σκευωρέομαι *M.* to help/

συ-σκηνέω, -όω to live in the same tent; to dine with. [gether.]

συ-σκηνίᾱ, ἡ a dining to-/

σύ-σκηνος, ὁ comrade.

συ-σκιάζω to overshadow or cover thickly.

σύ-σκιος 2 shady. [jointly.]

συ-σκοπέω to observe/

συ-σκοτάζει it grows dark.

συ-σπαράσσω to dishevel or distort utterly.

συ-σπάω to draw together.

συ-σπειράω to press to-

gether; to form in close order.

συ-σπεύδω, συ-σπουδάζω to join in speeding, to be busy with.

σύσ-σημος 2 concerted.

συσ-σῑτέω to dine together.

συσ-σίτιον, τό common meal.

σύσ-σῑτος, ὁ mess-mate.

συσ-σῴζω to help to save.

σύσ-σωμος 2 belonging to the same body. [combat.]

συ-σταδόν *adv.* in near/

συ-στασιάζω to join in sedition, be factious.

συ-στασιαστής, οῦ, ὁ, συ-στασιώτης, ου, ὁ partisan; fellow-rioter.

σύ-στασις, ἡ association, arrangement; a standing together, union, meeting; hardness, rigour; riot; conspiracy; close combat, conflict; emotion. [tory.]

συ-στατικός 3 commenda-/

συ-σταυρόω to crucify along with.

συ-στέλλω to draw together, contract; to abridge, condense, lessen, shorten; to put together; to wrap; to humble. — *P.* to restrict oneself.

συ-στενάζω to sigh with.

σύ-στημα, τό composition.

συ-στοιχέω to correspond to. [paign.]

συ-στρατείᾱ, ἡ joint cam-/

συ-στρατεύω and *M.* to join in an expedition, to serve along with. [mander.]

συ-στράτηγος, ὁ joint com-/

συ-στρατιώτης, ου, ὁ fellow-soldier.

συ-στρατοπεδεύομαι M. to encamp along with.

συ-στρέφω to twist together; to combine, contract, compress. — P. to form one body or crowd; to conspire.

συ-στροφή, ἡ body of men, crowd; revolt, plot.

συ-σχηματίζομαι M. to accommodate oneself to.

σύφε(ι)ός, ὁ pig-sty.

σύ-φορβός, ὁ swineherd.

συχνός 3 frequent, often; numerous, copious; long; far.   [derer; sword.]

σφαγεύς, ὁ butcher, mur-

σφαγή, ἡ slaughter, butchery; sacrifice; murder; wound; throat.

σφαγιάζω = σφάττω. [fice.]

σφάγιον, τό victim; sacri-

σφάγιος 3 killing.

σφαδάζω to struggle in convulsions.

σφάζω = σφάττω.

σφαῖρα, ἡ ball; globe.

σφαιρηδόν adv. like a ball.

σφαιρο-ειδής 2 ball-like.

σφακελίζω to become gangrenous.

σφάκελος, ὁ gangrene.

σφαλερός 3 slippery, smooth; precarious, fallacious, delusive; perilous.

σφάλλω to make fall or stumble; to destroy, ruin, undo; to baffle, disconcert. — P. and M. to totter, stagger, reel, fall, perish; to be defeated, disappointed, or baffled; to be unsuccessful; to fail; be deceived; to err, transgress.

σφάλμα, τό stumble, fall; failure, disaster, defeat; trespass; blunder.

σφαραγέομαι M. to be full to bursting; to hiss.

σφάττω to slaughter, kill, slay; to sacrifice.   [ger.]

σφεδανός 3 vehement, ea-

σφεῖς, σφέα they.

σφέλας, τό footstool.

σφενδονάω to sling.

σφενδόνη, ἡ sling; hoop of a ring; stone of the sling.

σφενδονήτης, ου, ὁ slinger.

σφενδονητική, ἡ art of slinging.   [priate.]

σφετερίζομαι to appro-

σφέτερος 3 their (own).

σφηκόω to pinch in at the waist; to bind tight.

σφήξ, σφηκός, ὁ wasp.

σφοδρός 3 vehement, violent; impetuous, eager, zealous; mighty. — adv.

σφόδρα, σφοδρῶς very much, vehemently.   [tuosity.]

σφοδρότης, ητος, ἡ impe-

σφονδύλιος, ὁ vertebra; vertebral column.

σφραγίζω to seal up, shut up; to confirm; to mark, sign.

σφραγίς, ῖδος, ἡ seal; signet-ring; sign, token; authorization.

σφράγισμα, τό seal.

σφρηγίς = σφραγίς.

σφῦρα, ἡ hammer.

σφυρ-ήλατος 2 beaten out with the hammer.

σφυρίς, ίδος, ἡ little basket.
σφυρόν, τό ankle.
σφωέ both of them; *gen.* and *dat.* σφωίν.
σφῶι, σφώ both of you; *gen.* and *dat.* σφῶιν, σφῷν.
σφωίτερος 3 belonging to you two. [(a vein).]
σχάζω to slit; to cut open|
σχεδία, ἡ raft, float; boat; pontoon-bridge.
σχεδίην *adv.* near, in close combat. [near.]
σχεδόθεν *adv.* from nigh,|
σχεδόν *adv.* near, nigh, close; impending, at hand; nearly, almost, pretty well.
σχέσις, ἡ = σχῆμα.
σχετλιάζω to wail. [tion.]
σχετλιασμός, ὁ indigna-|
σχέτλιος 3 bold; insolent; wicked; cruel, savage; shocking, horrid; miserable, wretched; strange, astonishing.
σχῆμα, τό a bearing, mien, behaviour; figure, form, shape, outward appearance; constitution, nature; dress; manner, fashion; stateliness, dignity.
σχηματίζω to form, fashion, shape, dress; to adorn. — *M.* to pretend. [dancing.]
σχημάτιον, τό figure in|
σχίζα, ἡ cleft piece of wood. [parate.]
σχίζω to split, cleave, se-|
σχῖνος, ἡ mastich-tree.
σχίσις, ἡ division; by-road.
σχίσμα, τό division, schism.
σχιστός 3 parted, divided.
σχοινίον, τό rope, cord.

σχοῖνος, ὁ rush, reed; thicket of rushes; rope, cord, cable; measuring-line.
σχοινο-τενής 2 straight.
σχολάζω to be at leisure, have spare time; to have leisure *or* time for; to devote oneself to; to linger, delay.
σχολαῖος 3 at leisure; slow.
σχολαιότης, ητος, ἡ slowness.
σχολή, ἡ leisure, spare time, rest, ease; peace; work of leisure, disputation, discussion; school; delay, slowness; idleness. — *adv.* σχολῇ at leisure, slowly; hardly, scarcely.
σώζω, σῴζω to save, keep safe, preserve, protect, spare, bring back safe and sound; to observe, keep secret; to remember. — *M.* to keep *or* save for oneself.
σωκέω to be able.
σῶκος 2 strong.
σωλήν, ῆνος, ὁ pipe.
σῶμα, τό body; dead body, corpse; person, individual; slave; life, existence; sensual pleasures; main point.
σωμ-ασκέω to train one's body. [cise.]
σωμ-ασκία, ἡ bodily exer-|
σωματικός 3, σωματο-ειδής 2 bodily.
σῶος 3 = σῶς. [heap with.]
σωρεύω to heap up; to|
σωρός, ὁ heap.
σῶς, σῶν safe and sound, healthy, entire; sure.
σῶστρον, τό reward for

24*

saving one's life, for bringing back a runaway slave.

σωτήρ, ῆρος, ὁ, **σώτειρα**, ἡ saviour, preserver, deliverer.

σωτηρία, ἡ a saving, deliverance, means of preserving; safe existence; well-being, ease.

σωτήριος 2 saving, delivering; saved; τὰ -α = σωτηρία, offering for preservation.

σωφρονέω to be sensible, reasonable, discreet, or moderate.

σωφρονίζω to bring to reason, to make wise; to admonish; to correct, chastise.

σωφρονισμός, ὁ a warning; = σωφροσύνη.

σωφρονιστής, οῦ, ὁ chastiser, censor.

σωφροσύνη, ἡ prudence, moderation, discretion; self-control; chastity, decent behaviour.

σώφρων 2 sensible, discreet, prudent; moderate, temperate, sober; modest.

σώω = σώζω.

T

T, τ (ταῦ) nineteenth letter of the alphabet; as a numeral τ´ = 300.

ταβέρνα, ἡ inn.

τᾰγεία, ἡ command, rule.

τᾰγεύω to command, rule.

τάγμα, τό body of soldiers, division; command.

τᾰγός, ὁ commander, ruler; chief of a confederacy.

ταινία, ἡ riband; fillet.

ταινιόω to adorn with a head-band.

τακτικός 3 fit for arranging or for tactics.

τακτός 3 ordered, arranged, fixed.

τάκω = τήκω.

ταλα-εργός 2 able to work.

ταλαιπωρέω to suffer hardship or distress, to do hard work, to toil, drudge.

ταλαιπωρία, ἡ hardship, hard work, distress; affliction, suffering.

ταλαί-πωρος 2 toilsome, wretched, miserable.

ταλαί-φρων 2, **ταλαι-κάρδιος** 2 wretched; bold, daring.

ταλαντιαῖος 3 worth a talent; weighing a talent.

τάλαντον, τό, *pl.* pair of scales; talent.

ταλα-πείριος 2 suffering much, severely tried by fate.   [pain, miserable.]

ταλα-πενθής 2 enduring/ τό λαρος, ὁ basket.

τάλᾱς, **τάλαινα**, **τάλᾰν** enduring, patient, suffering, wretched; audacious.

ταλασία, ἡ wool-spinning.

ταλασιουργέω to spin wool.

ταλασί-φρων 2 = ταλαί-φρων.

ταλαύρῑνος 2 shield-bearing.   [φρων.]

ταλά-φρων 2 = ταλαί-]

ταλιθά girl, maiden.

τᾶλις, ιδος, ἡ maiden.

ταμεῖον, τό = ταμιεῖον.

ταμεσί-χρως, οος cutting the skin. [housewife.]

ταμία, ἡ housekeeper,

ταμίας, ου, ὁ housekeeper, dispenser, steward; treasurer.

ταμιεῖον, τό storehouse; treasury; chamber.

ταμιεύω and M. to be a housekeeper, steward, or manager; to manage.

τάμνω = τέμνω.

τάν, τᾶν thou; ὦ τᾶν my good friend!

τανα-ήκης 2 with a long point or edge. [long.]

ταναός 3 and 2 stretched,

ταναύ-πους, ποδος stretching the feet, long-striding.

τανηλεγής 2 grieving much (others: stretching at full length). [down.]

τανταλόω to swing, hurl

τανύ-γλωσσος 2 long-tongued. [long point.]

τανυ-γλώχιν, ῑνος with

τανυ-ήκης 2 = ταναήκης.

τανῦν = τὰ νῦν. [robe.]

τανύ-πεπλος 2 with long

τανύ-πους = ταναύπους.

τανυ-πτέρυξ, υγος, ταναυσί-πτερος 2 with out-stretched wing. [ing.]

τανυστύς, ύος, ἡ a stretch-

τανύ-φλοιος 2 with thin bark. [leaves.]

τανύφυλλος 2 with long

τανύω = τείνω.

ταξιαρχέω to be a taxiarch.

ταξι-άρχης, ου, ταξί-

άρχος, ὁ taxiarch, commander of a division; captain.

τάξις, ἡ an arranging, putting in order, disposition; order, arrangement; class, post, rank, office, duty; military arrangement, line of soldiers, battle-array, order of battle; body of troops, division of an army, band, company.

ταπεινός 3 low, level; small, narrow; trifling, insignificant, poor; humble, lowly; humiliated, downcast, mean.

ταπεινότης, ητος, ἡ lowness; lowliness, weakness; baseness, poorness; dejection, humiliation; humility.

ταπεινο-φροσύνη, ἡ humility, meekness.

ταπεινό-φρων 2 humble.

ταπεινόω to make low; to humble, bring down.

ταπείνωσις, ἡ = ταπεινότης. [ίδος, ἡ carpet.]

τάπης, ητος, ὁ, ταπίς,

ταράσσω to stir up, disturb, trouble, confound; to rouse alarm, agitate, raise up; perf. τέτρηχα to be in uproar or confusion.

ταραχή, ἡ, τάραχος, ὁ disorder, confusion, tumult, noise, uproar, sedition.

ταραχώδης 2 confused, troubled, disordered, fickle, angry; troubling.

ταρβαλέος 3 frightened.

ταρβέω to be afraid or alarmed.

τάρβος, τό, ταρβοσύνη, ἡ fear, fright, awe.

ταρίχευσις, ἡ an embalming. [balmer.]

ταρίχευτής, οῦ, ὁ embalm-

ταρῑχεύω to preserve by smoking or salting; to embalm. [salting fish.]

ταρῑχήϊαι, αἱ places for

τάρῑχος, ὁ, τό salted meat; mummy.

ταρσός, ταρρός, ὁ frame of wicker-work; crate; mat of reeds; gabion; blade or flat of the foot; oar.

ταρταρόω to hurl into Tartarus.

τάρφος, τό thicket.

ταρφύς 3 thick, frequent, numerous.

ταρχύω to bury, inter.

τάσσω to arrange, put in order; to draw up in line or in order of battle; to post, station, appoint; to assign to a class; to order, command, give instructions; to fix, settle. — M. to order, arrange for oneself; to agree upon among themselves; to bind oneself to paying by instalments.

ταύρειος 3 of oxen or cows; of bullock's hide.

ταυρηδόν adv. like a bull, staringly.

ταυρο-κτονέω to kill bulls.

ταυρο-κτόνος 2 bull-slaying. [ing bulls.]

ταυρο-πόλος 3 and 2 hunt-

ταῦρος, ὁ bull, ox.

ταυρο-σφάγος 2 bull-slaughtering.

ταύτῃ adv. on this side, here; hither; in this way or manner.

τάφε, ταφεῖν see τέθηπα.

ταφεύς, ὁ burier.

ταφή, ἡ = τάφος¹.

τάφιος 3 of a burial.

τάφος¹, ὁ burial; grave, tomb; funeral-feast.

τάφος², τό astonishment.

ταφρεία, ἡ the making a ditch.

ταφρεύω to make a ditch.

τάφρος, ἡ ditch, trench.

τάχα adv. quickly, soon; perhaps.

ταχινός 3 quick, swift.

τάχος, τό quickness, swiftness, speed. [quickly.]

ταχυ-άλωτος 2 captured

ταχυ-ναυτέω to sail fast.

ταχύνω to hasten, make quick, be quick.

ταχύ-πωλος 2 with swift horses. [moving.]

ταχύ-ρρωστος 2 swift-

ταχύς 3 swift, quick, fast, fleet. — adv. ταχέως, ταχύ quickly, soon; at once; perhaps.

ταχυτής, ῆτος, ἡ = τάχος.

ταώς, ώ, ταῶς, ῶ, ὁ pea-

τέ enclit. part. and. [cock.]

τέγγω to wet, moisten; to shed. — P. to be poured (forth), to be softened.

τέγεος 2 roofed. [room.]

τέγος, τό roof; chamber,

τέθηπα perf. aor. ἔταφον to be amazed or astonished; to wonder at.

τεθριππο - βάτης, ου, ὁ driving in a four-horse chariot.

τέθρ-ιππον, τό team of four horses, four-in-hand.

τεθριππο-τροφέω to keep a four-horse chariot.

τεθριππο-τρόφος 2 keeping a four-horse chariot.

τεῖν = σοί, dat. of σύ.

τείνω to stretch, strain, extend, draw tight; to stretch out, lay prostrate, lengthen; intr. to tend to, aim at, strive; to extend to; to refer or belong to. — P. to be stretched tight; to rush, run with full speed; to be spread. — M. to stretch oneself or for oneself.

τεῖος adv. = τέως. [star.]

τεῖρος, τό constellation,

τείρω to rub: to rub away, wear out; to distress.

τειχεσι - πλήτης, ου, ὁ stormer of walls.

τειχέω, τειχίζω to build a wall or fort; to fortify, to wall in; to build.

τειχ-ήρης 2 besieged.

τειχιόεις 3 walled.

τειχίον, τό wall.

τείχισις, ἡ the building a wall; fortress.

τείχισμα, τό = τεῖχος.

τειχισμός, ὁ = τείχισις.

τειχο-μαχέω to attack the walls. [walls.]

τειχο-μαχία, ἡ attack of

τειχο-ποιός, ὁ officer of the board of works.

τεῖχος, τό wall; fortification, fortress, castle.

τειχο - σκοπιά, ἡ review from the walls.

τειχο-φύλαξ, ακος, ὁ guard of the walls.

τειχύδριον, τό small fortified place.

τείως = τέως.

τεκμαίρομαι M. to know from certain signs, to infer, conclude, judge; to decree, ordain, appoint, show by a sign.

τέκμαρ[1], τό end, goal, mark, boundary; just cause.

τέκμαρ[2], τεκμήριον, τό sign, token, mark; proof, demonstration.

τεκμηριόω to prove.

τέκμωρ, τό = τέκμαρ[1] and [2].

τεκνίον, τό little child.

τεκνο - γονέω to bear children.

τεκνο-γονία, ἡ a child-bearing. [dren.]

τεκνόεις 3 rich in chil-

τεκν - ολέτειρα, ἡ bereft of children. [one.]

τέκνον, τό child; a young

τεκνο-ποιέομαι M. to beget children.

τεκνο-ποιία, ἡ the begetting or bearing of children.

τεκνο - ποιός 2 begetting or bearing children.

τεκνο - τροφέω to rear children.

τεκνόω and M. to beget or bear children. [ποιία.]

τέκνωσις, ἡ = τεκνο-

τέκος, τό = τέκνον.

τεκταίνομαι M. to make, build, frame, construct; to contrive, devise.

τεκτονικός 3 belonging to the art of building; carpenter, builder.

τεκτοσύνη, ἡ carpentry.

τέκτων, ονος, ὁ carpenter, joiner, builder; master workman.

τελαμών, ῶνος, ὁ strap for supporting a thing; baldrick, shoulder-belt; surgeon's bandage.

τελέθω to be there; to come forth; to become.

τέλειος 3 and 2 complete, finished, fulfilled, accomplished; perfect, entire, full-grown, full in number; spotless; definite, fixed; accomplishing, able to do.

τελειότης, ητος, ἡ perfection, full growth.

τελειόω to make perfect or successful.

τελείω = τελέω.

τελείωσις, ἡ completion; perfection.

τελειωτής, οῦ, ὁ finisher.

τελεό-μηνος 2 with full months.

τέλεος = τέλειος.

τελεσ-φορέω to bring (or come) to ripeness.

τελεσ-φόρος 2 bringing to an end, accomplishing; brought to an end, complete, fulfilled.

τελετή, ἡ initiation, celebration; pl. mysteries.

τελευταῖος 3 last, highest, extreme.

τελευτάω to complete, accomplish, finish, fulfil; intr. to end, come to an

end, die, be fulfilled; part. τελευτῶν at last.

τελευτή, ἡ end, death; issue, event; success; accomplishment.

τελέω to end, bring to an end, complete, finish, perform, execute, fulfil; to pay one's dues or taxes, to spend money; to pay; to consecrate, initiate (in the mysteries). — intr. and P. to be fulfilled, to come to an end, turn out.

τελήεις 3 perfect, complete; promising success.

τέλλω to accomplish. — intr. and P. to rise, arise.

τέλμα, τό pool; mortar, clay.

τέλος, τό end, issue; death; term, fulfilment, accomplishment; complete state, result, event; highest or ideal station, full power, magistrate, government (τὰ τέλη); tax, duty, toll; cost, expense; present, offering; initiation, celebration, mysteries; body of soldiers, division, squadron. [end.]

τέλοσ-δε adv. towards the

τέλσον, τό boundary.

τελ-ώνης, ου, ὁ toll-gatherer; publican.

τελ-ώνιον, τό toll-house.

τεμάχιον, τό, τέμαχος, τό slice, morsel.

τεμένιος 3 belonging to sacred land.

τέμενος, τό piece of land cut off for a certain purpose, crown-estate; sacred land, precincts of a temple.

τέμνω to cut, hew; to use the knife; to cut up, slaughter, sacrifice; to wound; to carve; to cut off or down, to sever; to lay waste; to fell trees; to cut or draw a line.

τέμω = τέμνω.

τέναγος, τό shallow water; swamp.

τένων, οντος, ὁ sinew; tendon (of the nape).

τέρας, α(τ)ος, τό sign, omen, prodigy; wonder, monster.

τερα-σκόπος, τερατο-σκόπος, ὁ soothsayer.

τερατώδης 2 marvellous, prodigious.

τερεβίνθινος 3 of the turpentine-tree.

τέρετρον, τό gimlet.

τέρην, εινα, εν, gen. ενος smooth, soft, delicate.

τέρμα, τό end, boundary; goal, mark.   [bordered.]

τερμιόεις 3 tasselled; long-

τέρμιος 3 last, extreme.

τερπι-κέραυνος 2 delighting in thunder.   [sant.]

τερπνός 3 delightful, plea-

τέρπω to refresh; to cheer, delight, please.

τερπωλή, ἡ = τέρψις.

τερσαίνω, τέρσω to wipe up, dry up. — P. to become dry.

τερψί-μβροτος 2 pleasing the heart of man.

τέρψις, ἡ enjoyment, delight.   [four oxen.]

τεσσαρα-βοιός 2 worth

τεσσαράκοντα forty.

τεσσαρακοντα-ετής 2 forty years old.

τεσσαρακοστός 3 fortieth.

τέσσαρες, α four.

τεσσαρα-καί-δεκα fourteen.   [fourteenth.]

τεσσαρεσ-καί-δέκατος 3

τεσσεραχοντ-όργυιος 2 of forty fathoms.

τέσσερες = τέσσαρες.

τεταγών taking, seizing.

τεταρταῖος 3 on the fourth day.   [fourth part.]

τεταρτη-μόριον, τό the

τέταρτος 3 fourth.

τετίημαι to be grieved; τετιηώς grieved.

τετμεῖν aor. to arrive at, overtake.   [four acres.]

τετρά-γυος 2 as large as

τετράγωνο-πρόσωπος 2 square-faced.

τετρά-γωνος 2 with four angles, square; perfect, complete.   [soldiers.]

τετράδιος, τό body of four

τετρα-έτης 2 four years old.

τετρα-θέλυμνος 2 of four layers.   [perforate.]

τετραίνω to bore through,

τετράκις adv. four times.

τετρακισ-μύριοι 3 forty thousand.   [thousand.]

τετρακισ-χίλιοι 3 four

τετρακόσιοι 3 four hundred.   [wheeled.]

τετρά-κυκλος 2 four-

τετρά-μετρος 2 consisting of four metres or eight feet.   [months.]

τετρά-μηνος 2 lasting four

τετρα-μοιρία, ἡ fourfold pay.

τετρ-άορος 2 drawn by four horses.

τετρα-πάλαιστος 2 of four handbreadths. [cubits.]

τετρά-πηχυς, υ of four]

τετρα-πλάσιος 3, τετρα-πλοῦς 3 fourfold. [cities.]

τετρά-πολις, εως of four]

τετρά-πους, πουν four-footed. [trärch.]

τετρ-αρχέω to be a te-]

τετρ-άρχης, ου, ὁ one of four princes.

τετράς, άδος, ἡ the number four; fourth day.

τετρα-φάληρος 2, τετρά-φαλος 2 with four ridges or bosses.

τετρά-φῦλος 2 divided into four tribes.

τέτραχα, τετραχῇ, τε-τραχθά adv. fourfold, in four parts. [stories.]

τετρ-ώροφος 2 with four]

τέττα dear father.

τέττιξ, ῑγος, ὁ grass-hopper; hair pin. [τοῦ (τινός).]

τευ = τοῦ (τίνος); τευ =]

τεῦχος, τό tool, implement, utensil; armour, arms; ship's implements; vessel, urn.

τεύχω to make, build, construct, work, form; to cause, create.

τέφρά, ἡ ashes.

τεφρόω to reduce to ashes.

τεχνάζω, τεχνάω and M. to devise, work, make by art; to execute skilfully; to use tricks, to devise cunningly. [artifice, trick.]

τέχνασμα, τό work of art;]

τέχνη, ἡ art, skill, craft, trade, science; artifice, cunning, trick; work of art.

τεχνήεις 3 made by art, ingenious.

τέχνημα, τό work of art; tool; artifice, trick; cunning person.

τεχνικός 3 artistic, skilful.

τεχνίτης, ου, ὁ artist, craftsman, expert; workman, master; deceiver.

τέως adv. so long, meanwhile; hitherto, till now; ere this; for a time.

τῆ adv. there! take!

τῇ adv. here, there, thither; in this way; where; how, as.

τῇδε adv. here, there; in this way; therefore.

τήθη, ἡ grandmother.

τῆθος, τό oyster. [tion.]

τηκεδών, όνος, ἡ consump-]

τήκω to melt; to make pine, consume. — intr. and P. to melt; to pine away; to vanish, decay.

τηλ-αυγής 2 far-shining.

τῆλε = τηλοῦ.

τηλεδαπός 3 coming from afar, foreign, distant.

τηλεθάω to bloom, flourish.

τηλε-κλειτός 3, τελε-κλυτός far-famed.

τηλέ-πορος 2 far, distant.

τηλε-φανής 2 seen or heard from afar.

τηλίκος 3, τηλικόσδε 3, τηλικοῦτος 3 so great; so much; so old or young.

τηλόθεν adv. from afar.

τηλόθι = τηλοῦ.

τηλόσε adv. to a distance.

τηλοῦ *adv.* far away, at a distance.

τηλύγετος 3 youthful, late-born; spoiled child.

τηλ-ωπός 2 seen or heard from afar, far off. [tend.)

τημελέω to take care of,)

τήμερον *adv.* to-day.

τῆμος *adv.* at that time, then; thereupon.

τηνίκα, τηνικάδε, τηνικαῦτα = τῆμος.

τῆος = τέως.

τῇπερ *adv.* in which way.

τηρέω to watch, observe, take care of, guard; to keep, preserve; to keep in prison.

τήρησις, ἡ a watching, guarding, preserving; prison. [to be in want.)

τητάω to deprive. — *P.*)

τηΰσιος 3 useless, vain.

τιάρα, ἡ, τιάρης, ου, ὁ tiara, turban.

τιᾰρο-ειδής 2 like a tiara.

τιέω *see* τετίημαι.

τίη *adv.* why?

τιθαιβώσσω to make a nest, to make honey.

τιθασεύω to tame, make tractable.

τιθασός 2 tamed, tame.

τίθημι to put, place, set, lay; to inter; to ordain, establish, order, fix; to reckon, count; to estimate, esteem, consider; to suppose; to make, cause, create, effect, appoint. — *M.* ὅπλα τίθεσθαι to put on arms, to fight; to take up one's quarters, to bivouac; to lay down one's arms, to surrender. [foster.)

τιθηνέομαι to tend, nurse,)

τιθήνη, ἡ nurse. [beget.)

τίκτω to bring forth, bear,)

τίλλω to pluck, pull, tear. — *M.* to mourn, bewail.

τίλων, ωνος, ὁ a kind of fish.

τῑμά-ορος = τιμωρός.

τῑμάω to estimate; to judge, condemn; to esteem, honour, respect, revere, value, cherish, love; to reward, honour with; to estimate the amount of punishment.

τῑμή, ἡ estimate, valuation, census; price, worth; penalty, punishment, damages, reward; honour, esteem, distinction; place of honour, dignity, magistracy, privilege.

τῑμήεις 3 = τίμιος.

τίμημα, τό valuation, estimate; census, rate of assessment; property; penalty, fine.

τίμιος 3 valued, esteemed, honoured; costly, precious.

τῑμιότης, ητος, ἡ worth, value, preciousness.

τῑμωρέω and *M.* to avenge, revenge; to help, succour; to punish, chastise.

τῑμωρητήρ, ῆρος, ὁ helper, avenger.

τῑμώρημα, τό, τῑμωρίᾱ, ἡ vengeance, punishment; help, aid, succour. [ing.)

τῑμωρός 2 avenging, help-)

τινάσσω and *M.* to swing, shake; to disturb, upset.

τίνομαι *M.* = τίνομαι.

τίνω (ῑ or ῐ) to pay; to pay a penalty or debt; to reward; to atone. — *M.* to avenge, punish, make suffer, take vengeance.

τίπτε *adv.* why then?

τίς, τί, *gen.* τίνος, who? which? what? τί why? wherefore? how?

τὶς, τὶ, *gen.* τινός, any one, some one, a certain; anything, something; many a one, each, every one; *pl.* many, several.

τίσις, ἡ payment; penalty, punishment, atonement, retribution, reward; vengeance.

τιταίνω to stretch, spread out, extend, draw, strain. — *M.* to stretch oneself or for oneself, exert oneself.

τίτθη, ἡ nurse.

τίτλος, ὁ superscription.

τιτός 3 requited.

τιτράω, τίτρημι = τετραίνω.

τιτρώσκω to pierce; to wound, hurt; to overpower.

τιτύσκομαι to make ready, prepare; t aim at; to intend, design.

τίω = τιμάω.

τλάμων 2, τλήμων 2 enduring, persevering, steadfast, bold; suffering, wretched.

τλῆναι to suffer, endure, bear; to dare, risk.

τλητός 3 suffering, patient; pliant; endurable.

τμήγω to cut, hew. — *P.* to be severed or dispersed.

τμήδην *adv.* by cutting, scratching.

τμῆμα, τό, τμῆσις, ἡ cut, incision; section; piece.

τμητός 3 cut, hewn.

τόθι *adv.* there.

τοί¹ = οἱ, οἵ; = σοί.

τοί² *adv.* in truth, certainly, verily.

τοι-γάρ, τοιγαρ-οῦν, τοι-γάρ-τοι *adv.* so then, therefore, accordingly; therefore indeed.

τοί-νυν *adv.* yet, so then, therefore; further, moreover.

τοῖος 3, τοιόσ-δε 3, τοι-οῦτος 3 of such kind or quality, quite such.

τοιουτό-τροπος 2 of such kind. [side of a ship.]

τοῖχος, ὁ wall of a house;

τοιχωρυχέω to be a housebreaker, burglar.

τοιχ-ώρυχος, ὁ housebreaker, burglar, thief.

τοκάς, άδος, ἡ one who has brought forth.

τοκεύς, ὁ begetter; *pl.* parents.

τόκος, ὁ a bringing forth, birth; offspring, child, son; descent; use-money, interest. [daring; venture.]

τόλμα, ἡ courage, boldness,

τολμάω to bear, endure, undergo; to take heart, to dare.

τολμήεις 3, τολμηρός 3 enduring, steadfast; bold; daring.

τόλμημα, τό adventure, enterprise.

τολμητής, οῦ, ὁ bold or foolhardy man.

τολμητός 3 ventured, to be ventured.

τολυπεύω to devise, invent; to toil through.

τομάω to need cutting.

τομή, ἡ a cutting, hewing; cut, stroke; hewn surface or corner; stump of a tree, end of a beam.

τομός 3 cutting, sharp.

τόνος, ὁ rope, cord; chord; a stretching, tension; tone, note; metre.

τοξάζομαι M. = τοξεύω.

τόξ-αρχος, ὁ captain of the archers.

τόξευμα, τό missile, arrow, bolt; body of archers; bowshot.

τοξευτής, οῦ, ὁ = τοξότης.

τοξευτός 3 struck by an arrow.

τοξεύω to shoot with the bow, to strike with an arrow; to aim at; to hit.

τοξικός 3 belonging to archery. [arrow; archery.[

τόξον, τό bow; missile,[

τοξοσύνη, ἡ archery.

τοξότης, ου, ὁ bowman, archer; policeman.

τοξο-φόρος 2 bearing a bow; archer.

τοπάζιον, τό topaz.

τοπάζω to guess, divine.

τόπος, ὁ place, spot; passage in a book; region, district; space, locality; position, rank, opportunity.

τορεύω to enchase, engrave.

τορέω to bore through.

τόρμος, ὁ hole.

τορνεύω to turn on a lathe.

τόρνος, ὁ compasses.

τορνόω to make round.

τόρος 3 piercing, shrill; clear, distinct, sharp.

τόσος 3, **τοσόσδε** 3, **τοσοῦτος** 3 so great, so wide, so long, so much, so little, so strong.

τοσσάκι adv. so often.

τόσσος 3 = τόσος.

τότε adv. then, at that time; formerly; just then.

τοτέ adv. at times, now and then.

το-τηνίκα adv. then.

τοτοτοῖ woe!

τοὔνεκα adv. therefore.

τόφρα adv. so long, till then, meanwhile.

τραγ-έλαφος, ὁ goat-stag, antelope.

τραγήματα, τά sweetmeats.

τραγικός 3 tragic; majestic, pompous.

τράγος, ὁ he-goat.

τραγο-σκελής 2 goat-footed.

τραγ-ῳδέω to declaim pathetically.

τραγ-ῳδία, ἡ tragedy.

τραγ-ῳδός, ὁ tragic poet or actor.

τρᾱνής 2 clear, distinct.

τράπεζα, ἡ table; dining-table, board; dinner, meal; money-changer's table; shop. [to a table.[

τραπεζεύς, έως belonging[

τραπεζίτης, ου, ὁ money-changer, banker.

τραπέω to tread grapes.

τραυλός 3 stammering.

τραῦμα, τό wound, hurt; loss, defeat. [man.]

τραυματίας, ου, ὁ wounded]

τραυματίζω to wound.

τραφερός 3 firm, dry (land) [to expose to view.]

τραχηλίζω to lay bare;]

τράχηλος, ὁ neck, throat.

τραχύνω to make rough or rugged. [harsh, angry.]

τραχύς 3 rough, rugged;]

τραχύτης, ητος, ἡ roughness, ruggedness; hardness.

τρεῖς, τρία three.

τρέμω to tremble, quiver.

τρέπω to turn, turn round, away or about; to divert, alter, change, direct; to turn to flight; to hinder, prevent. — intr., P. and M. to turn oneself; to be changed.

τρέφω to make solid, congeal, curdle; to feed, nourish, rear, bring up, nurse, tend; intr. to become solid, grow up. — P. to be fed; to grow (up); to live; to be brought up.

τρέχω to run.

τρέω to tremble, quiver; to fear; to flee.

τρῆμα, τό hole, aperture.

τρήρων, ωνος timid, shy.

τρητός 3 bored through.

τρηχύς 3 = τραχύς.

τρ.αινα, ἡ trident.

τριᾰκάς, άδος, ἡ the number thirty. [thirty days.]

τριακονθ-ήμερος 2 of]

τριάκοντα thirty.

τριάκοντα-έτης 2, τριᾰ-

χοντα - έτις, ιδος, fem. lasting thirty years.

τριᾰκοντ-αρχία, ἡ rule of thirty men. [κονθήμερος.]

τριάκοντ-ήμερος 2 = τριᾰ-]

τριᾰκόντ - ορος, ἡ vessel with thirty oars.

τριᾰκοντούτης, fem. τρι-ᾱκοντοῦτις, ιδος = τρι-ᾱκονταέτης.

τριᾰκόσιοι 3 three hundred.

τριᾰκοστός 3 thirtieth.

τριάς, άδος, ἡ the number three, triad.

τρῖβή, ἡ a rubbing, wearing away, spending; a practising, practice, skill; delay, evasion; pastime.

τρί-βολος 2 three-pointed; thistle. [= τριβή.]

τρίβος, ὁ, ἡ path, road;]

τρῖβω to rub, thrash, grind, pound, bruise; to wear away, spend, consume; to damage, weaken, waste; to delay, tarry. — P. to be busied with.

τρίβων, ωνος, ὁ worn cloak; adj. practised, versed, or skilled. [pearls.]

τρί-γληνος 2 with three]

τρι-γλώχῑν, ῑνος three-forked. [ration.]

τρι-γονία, ἡ third gene-]

τρί-γωνον, τό triangle.

τρί-δουλος, ὁ thrice a slave.

τρι-έλικτος 2 thrice wound.

τρι-ετηρίς, ιδος, ἡ triennial festival. [ennial.]

τρι-έτης, -ετής 2 tri-]

τρι-ετία, ἡ space of three years.

τρίζω to chirp, twitter, squeak, crack.

τριηκάς etc. see τριακάς etc.

τριηραρχέω to be captain of a trireme; to fit out a trireme.

τριηρ-αρχία, ἡ the fitting out of a trireme.

τριηραρχικός 3 belonging to a τριηραρχία.

τριήρ-αρχος, ὁ trierarch: commander of a trireme; one who has to fit out a trireme.

τριηρ-αύλης, ου, ὁ flute-player of a trireme.

τριήρης, ους, ἡ trireme, ship with three banks of oars.

τριηρίτης, ου, ὁ serving on board a trireme.

τρι-κάρηνος 2, τρί-κρᾱνος 2 three-headed.

τρί-λιστος 2 thrice prayed for. [tres.]

τρί-μετρος 2 of three me-/
τρί-μηνος 2 lasting three months.

τρι-μοιρία, ἡ triple pay.

τριξός = τρισσός.

τρί-οδος, ἡ the meeting of three roads.

τρι-πάλαιστος 2 three hands broad. [long.]

τρί-πηχυς, υ three cubits/
τρί-πλαξ, ακος threefold.

τρι-πλάσιος 3 thrice as great or as much.

τρί-πλεθρος 2 three ple-thra long. [triple.]

τρι-πλοῦς 3 threefold,/
τρι-πόλιστος 2, τρί-πολος 2 thrice ploughed; much talked of.

τρίπος, ὁ, τρί-πους, ποδος, ὁ three-footed; tripod.

τρί-πτυχος 2 of three layers; threefold.

τρίς adv. thrice.

τρισ-άθλιος 3 thrice-un-happy. [pleased.]

τρισ-άσμενος 3 thrice-/
τρισ-καί-δεκα thirteen.

τρισκαιδεκα-στάσιος 2 of thirteen times the weight.

τρισ-καί-δέκατος 3 thir-teenth. [blessed.]

τρίσ-μακαρ, αρος thrice/
τρισ-μόριοι 3 thirty thou-sand. [poured.]

τρί-σπονδος 2 thrice-/
τρισσός 3 threefold.

τρί-στεγος 2 with three stories. [rows.]

τρί-στοιχος 2 in three/
τρισ-χίλιοι 2 three thou-sand. [the third part.]

τριτ-αγωνιστέω to act/
τριτ-αγωνιστής, οῦ, ὁ player who acts the third part. [on the third day.]

τριταῖος 3 in three days;/
τρίτατος 3 = τρίτος.

τριτη-μόριος 3 forming a third part. [third part.]

τριτη-μορίς, ίδος. ἡ the/
τρίτος 3 third.

τρι-φάσιος 3 threefold, three. [clover.]

τρί-φυλλον, τό trefoil,/
τρί-φῦλος 2 consisting of three tribes.

τρίχα adv. in three parts.

τριχά-ῑκες, οἱ in three tribes. [τρίχα.]

τριχῆ, τριχῇ, τριχθά =/
τρίχινος 3 of hair.

τρι-χοίνικος 2 holding three χοίνικες.

τριχοῦ *adv.* in three places.

τρίχωμα, τό growth of hair.

τρῖψις, ἡ a rubbing, touching; resistance, elasticity.

τρι-ώβολον, τό three-obol piece. [stories.

τρι-ώροφος 2 of three

τρομέω and *M.* to tremble, quiver; to fear.

τρόμος, ὁ a trembling; fear.

τροπαῖον, τρόπαιον, τό sign of victory, trophy.

τροπαῖος, τρόπαιος 3 giving victory.

τροπέω to turn.

τροπή, ἡ a turning, turn; solstice; flight; defeat; victory; change.

τρόπις, ἡ ship's keel.

τρόπος, ὁ turn, direction; manner, way, fashion, custom, mode of life; character, temper. [for oars.

τροπός, ὁ leathern thong

τροπο-φορέω to bear with one's manners. [πός.

τροπωτήρ, ῆρος. ὁ = τρο-

τροφεῖα, τά reward for rearing, wages of a nurse; food, sustenance.

τροφεύς, ὁ = τροφός.

τροφέω = τρέφω.

τροφή, ἡ food, nourishment; maintenance; rearing, nursing; means or mode of living; offspring, brood.

τρόφιμος 2 nourished, reared up; foster-child.

τρόφις, ι, τροφόεις 3 well-fed.

τροφός, ὁ, ἡ feeder, nurse.

τροφο-φορέω to bear like a nurse.

τροχάζω to run along.

τροχ-ηλάτης, ου, ὁ charioteer. [wheels.

τροχ-ήλατος 2 moved on

τροχιά, ἡ track; way.

τροχίλος, ὁ plover.

τροχο-ειδής 2 circular.

τροχός, ὁ wheel, potter's wheel, disc; wheel of torture. [tion.

τρόχος, ὁ course, revolu-

τρύβλιον, τό cup. bowl.

τρυγάω to gather in.

τρύγητος, ὁ the gathering of fruits, harvest. [dove.

τρυγών, όνος, ἡ turtle-

τρύζω to coo; to mutter.

τρύμαλιά, ἡ hole or eye of the needle. [refuse.

τρύξ, υγός. ἡ must; dregs,

τρύπανον, τό borer, gimlet.

τρυπάω to bore, pierce through.

τρύπημα, τό hole.

τρυσ-άνωρ, ορος harrassing men.

τρυ-φάλεια, ἡ helmet.

τρυφάω to live delicately or in luxury, be effeminate or licentious; to be insolent or haughty.

τρυφερός 3 delicate, effeminate, luxurious.

τρυφή, ἡ delicacy, luxury; pride, insolence.

τρύφος, τό piece, morsel, fragment.

τρῡχόω, τρύχω to wear out, consume, waste; to vex, distress, afflict. [haust.

τρύω to wear out, exτρωγλο-δύτης, ου, ὁ dwelling in caves.

τρώγω to gnaw, chew, eat.

τρώκτης, ου, ὁ knave, cheat.

τρῶμα etc. see τραῦμα.

τρωπάω to change. — M. to turn oneself.

τρωτός 3 vulnerable.

τρωχάω to run.

τρώω = τιτρώσκω.

τύ = σύ.

τυγχάνω to hit (a mark), to hit upon; to fall in with, meet; to reach, gain, get, gain one's end. — intr. to happen, be at a place; to come to pass, fall out, occur by chance. [axe.]

τύκος, ὁ hammer; battle-

τυκτός 3 made, well-made, wrought by art, artificial; made ready.

τῦλος, ὁ, τύλη, ἡ a swelling, hard swelling, callosity; nail, peg.

τυλόω to knob with iron.

τύμβευμα, τό = τύμβος.

τυμβεύω to bury; intr. to be buried.

τυμβ-ήρης 2 buried; tomb-like. [grave.]

τύμβος, ὁ mound; tomb,

τυμβο-χοέω to throw up a mound over a grave.

τυμβο-χόη, ἡ the throwing up a mound.

τυμβό-χωστος 2 thrown up into a mound. [a stick.]

τυμπανίζω to beat with

τυμπανίστρια, ἡ a woman that beats a drum.

τύμπανον, τό drum.

τύνη = σύ.

τυπή, ἡ = τύπος.

τυπικός 3 typical.

τύπος, ὁ stroke, blow; impress, stamp, mark; figure, image, statue; outline, sketch, model, type; system, character. [model.]

τυπόω to stamp, form,

τύπτω to strike, beat, smite, hit; to wound. — M. to mourn for. [urn.]

τύπωμα, τό figure; vessel,

τυραννεύω, -έω to be a tyrant or absolute ruler. — P. to be ruled with absolute power.

τυραννικός 3 fit for a τύραννος, royal, princely; tyrannical.

τυραννίς, ίδος, ἡ absolute power, monarchy, royalty.

τύραννος, ὁ absolute monarch, sovereign, lord, master; tyrant; adj. princely, imperious, despotic.

τυρβάζομαι M. to be concerned; to be in disorder.

τύρβη, ἡ crowd, disorder.

τυρός, ὁ cheese. [castle.]

τύρσις, εως, ιος, ἡ tower,

τυτθός 2 small, young; adv. τυτθόν a little.

τυφλός 3 blind; dull; unseen, dim, invisible, secret. [blind or dull.]

τυφλόω to blind, make

τῦφος, ὁ smoke, mist; conceit, vanity.

τυφόω to make dull or foolish.

τύφω to raise smoke, make a cloud. — P. to smoke.

τῡφῶς, ῶ, τῡφῶν, ῶνος, ὁ hurricane. [wind.]

τῡφωνικός 3 like a whirl-

τύχη, ἡ chance; fortune, luck, hap; accident.

τῷ adv. therefore, then, in this wise or case.

τωθάζω to scoff at.

τώς, τῶς adv. so, thus.

τωὐτό = ταὐτό.

Y

Υ, υ (ὖ ψιλόν) twentieth letter of the alphabet; as a numeral υ' = 400.

ὕαινα, ἡ hyena.

ὑακίνθινος 3 dark-blue.

ὑάκινθος, ὁ, ἡ hyacinth; jacinth (sapphire).

ὑάλινος 3 of glass.

ὕαλος, ὁ crystal; glass.

ὑβ-βάλλω = ὑποβάλλω.

ὑβρίζω to be or become wanton, insolent, licentious, or extravagant; to outrage, insult, affront, maltreat.

ὕβρις, ἡ, ὕβρισμα, τό wantonness, insolence, licentiousness; violence, outrage, insult.

ὑβριστής, οῦ, ὁ wanton, insolent, licentious, or wicked man.

ὑβριστικός 3 given to wantonness or insolence; luxurious, wicked, violent.

ὑγιαίνω to be or become sound or healthy; to be sound of mind; to be wholesome.

ὑγίεια, ἡ health, soundness.

ὑγιεινός 3, ὑγιηρός 3, ὑγιής 2 healthy, sound; wholesome; sound in mind, true, genuine.

ὑγρός 3 wet, moist, liquid, flowing; pliant, supple; languid, languishing.

ὑγρότης, ητος, ἡ wetness, moisture; suppleness.

ὑδατο-τρεφής 2 growing in or by the water.

ὑδατώδης 2 watery.

ὕδρᾱ, ἡ water-serpent.

ὑδραίνω to wet; to wash.

ὑδρεία, ἡ a fetching water.

ὑδρεύω to draw or fetch water.

ὑδρήϊον, τό = ὑδρία.

ὑδρηλός 3 watered, moist.

ὑδρίᾱ, ἡ water-pot, bucket; urn.

ὑδρο-ποτέω to drink water.

ὑδρο-πότης, ου, ὁ water-drinker.

ὕδρος, ὁ = ὕδρα.

ὑδρο-φορέω to carry water.

ὑδρο-φόρος 2 carrying water; water-carrier.

ὑδρωπικός 2 dropsical.

ὕδωρ, ατος, τό water, rain, sweat; water of the water-clock.

ὕελος, ὁ = ὕαλος.

ὑέτιος 3 bringing rain.

ὑετός, ὁ rain.

ὕθλος, ὁ fun, buffoonery.

ὕδιον, τό little pig.

υἱδοῦς, οῦ, ὁ grandson.

ὑϊκός 3 swinish. [a son.]

υἱο-θεσίᾱ, ἡ adoption as

υἱός, ὁ son, grandson.
υἱωνός, ὁ grandson.
ὑλαγμός, ὁ a barking.
ὁλάεις 3 = ὑλήεις. [ing.]
ὑλακό-μωρος 2 ever bark-
ὑλακτέω, ὑλάω and M. to bark, howl; to bark at.
ὕλη, ἡ wood, forest, woodland; timber; fuel; brushwood; matter, stuff, raw material; ballast; stock, plenty.
ὑλήεις 3 wooded.
ὑλο-τόμος 2 woodcutter.
ὑλώδης 2 woody.
ὑμεῖς you.
ὑμέναιος, ὁ wedding-song; wedding; Hymen, the god of marriage.
ὑμέτερος 3 your, yours.
ὑμνέω to sing; to praise; to keep talking about a thing.
ὕμνος, ὁ song, hymn; melody.
ὑμός 3 = ὑμέτερος.
ὑπ-αγκάλισμα, τό embrace; wife.
ὑπ-άγω to lead or bring under; to yoke; to summon before a court; to draw from under; to seduce, deceive; intr. to withdraw, retire slowly or secretly; to advance, go on slowly. — M. to bring under one's power; to draw to oneself. [down; retreat.]
ὑπ-αγωγή, ἡ a leading.
ὑπ-αείδω to accompany with the voice.
ὑπαί = ὑπό.
ὑπ-αιδέομαι P. to have awe or respect.

ὕπαιθα adv. out under; escaping to one side.
ὑπ-αίθρειος, -αίθριος, ὕπ-αιθρος 2 in the open air.
ὑπ-αίθω to set on fire.
ὑπ-αΐσσω to dart from under; to rush on.
ὑπ-αισχύνομαι P. to feel somewhat ashamed.
ὑπ-αίτιος 2 accused, guilty, responsible.
ὑπ-ακοή, ἡ obedience.
ὑπ-ακούω to listen, hearken; to answer; to obey, submit to; to appear in court.
ὑπ-αλείφω to anoint, besmear.
ὑπ-αλεύομαι M., ὑπ-αλύσκω to avoid, escape.
ὑπ-άλυξις, ἡ an escaping.
ὑπ-αναλίσκω to spend gradually. [degrees.]
ὑπ-αναχωρέω to retire by.
ὕπ-ανδρος 2 subject to a man, married. [stand up.]
ὑπ-ανίσταμαι M. to rise,.
ὑπ-αντάω to go to meet, to meet. [meet.]
ὑπ-άντησις, ἡ a going to.
ὑπ-αντιάζω = ὑπαντάω.
ὑπ-απειλέω to threaten indirectly.
ὑπ-άπειμι (-ιέναι) to go away secretly.
ὕπαρ, τό reality; adv. really; in a waking state. [good.]
ὕπ-αρξις, ἡ subsistence,.
ὑπ-αρχή, ἡ the beginning.
ὕπ-αρχος, ὁ vice-commander; governor.
ὑπ-άρχω to begin, to be the first; to lie under; to

come into being, arise; to exist, be ready, at hand; to belong to, fall to; to be possible, sufficient, or useful; ὑπάρχων extant, present; τὰ ὑπάρχοντα property, means, present circumstances; ὑπάρχει it is possible or in one's power.

ὑπ-ασπίδιος 2 covered by a shield.

ὑπ-ασπιστής, οῦ, ὁ shield-bearer; life-guardsman.

ὑπ-άσσω = ὑπαΐσσω.

ὑπ-άτοπος 2 somewhat absurd. [consul.]

ὕπατος 3 highest; last;

ὕπ-αυλος 2 under cover of a house or tent.

ὑπ-άφρων 2 somewhat silly.

ὕπεαρ, ατος, τό cobbler's awl.

ὑπ-έγγυος 2 responsible.

ὑπ-εικάθω, -είκω to retire, withdraw, escape; to yield, give way, obey, submit to.

ὕπ-ειμι[1] (-εῖναι) to be or lie under or underneath; to lie at the bottom; to be at hand.

ὕπ-ειμι[2] (-ιέναι) to come on secretly; to retire gradually.

ὑπείρ = ὑπέρ.

ὑπ-είσας part. aor. of ὑφέζω.

ὑπ-εισδύομαι M. to steal in.

ὑπ-έκ, ὑπ-έξ adv. and prp. with gen. out from under or from beneath.

ὑπ-εκδύομαι M. to slip out of, escape, steal out.

ὑπ-έκκειμαι to be brought secretly into a safe place.

ὑπ-εκκομίζω to carry away secretly.

ὑπ-εκπέμπω to send away or escort secretly.

ὑπ-εκπροθέω to run out before; to outrun.

ὑπ-εκπρολύω to put out, unyoke (horses).

ὑπ-εκπρορέω to flow forth from under.

ὑπ-εκπροφεύγω to escape secretly. [under.]

ὑπ-εκσαόω to save from

ὑπ-εκτίθεμαι M. to remove secretly; to carry away safely.

ὑπ-εκτρέπω to turn secretly. — M. to avoid.

ὑπ-εκτρέχω to run away, escape; to run beyond.

ὑπ-εκφέρω to carry away secretly; to remove a little; intr. to run away; to have the start. [cretly.]

ὑπ-εκφεύγω to escape se-

ὑπ-εκχωρέω to retire secretly, withdraw.

ὑπ-ελαύνω to ride up to.

ὑπ-εναντίος 3 opposite; hostile; adversary.

ὑπ-ενδίδωμι to give way a little.

ὑπ-ένερθεν adv. and prp. with gen. underneath; beneath; in the nether world.

ὑπ-εξάγω to lead or carry out secretly; intr. to retire secretly.

ὑπ-εξαιρέω and M. to take away, remove by stealth; to take out privily.

ὑπ-εξαλέομαι M. to escape.

ὑπ-εξανάγομαι *P.* to put to sea secretly.

ὑπ-εξαναδύομαι *M.* to come up from under gradually.

ὑπ-έξειμι = ὑπεξέρχομαι.

ὑπ-εξειρύω to draw out from under.

ὑπ-εξελαύνω to drive away secretly; *intr.* to march away secretly.

ὑπ-εξέρχομαι to go away secretly or slowly; to withdraw, emigrate.

ὑπ-εξέχω to withdraw secretly, escape.

ὑπ-εξίσταμαι *M.* to stand up; to give way (to), avoid, shun; to desist.

ὑπέρ *prp.* with *gen.* over; above; across; beyond; for, in behalf of, in defence of, for the sake of, because of, by reason of; in the name of. [yards.]

ὑπέρα, ἡ brace of the

ὑπερ-αγαπάω to love exceedingly. [hard.]

ὑπερ-αής 2 blowing very

ὑπερ-αίρω to surpass, outdo. — *intr.* and *M.* to rise above.

ὑπερ-αιωρέομαι *P.* to be suspended over, project over; to come off a place at sea.

ὑπέρ-ακμος 2 over-ripe.

ὑπερ-άκριος 2 over the heights. [exceedingly.]

ὑπερ-αλγέω to be grieved

ὑπερ-αλγής 2 grieving exceedingly.

ὑπερ-άλλομαι *M.* to leap over.

ὑπερ-ανατείνω to stretch over.

ὑπερ-άνω *adv.* above on high. [for.]

ὑπερ-αποθνῄσκω to die

ὑπερ-απολογέομαι *M.* to speak for, defend.

ὑπερ-αρρωδέω to fear excessively.

ὑπερ-αυξάνω *intr.* to grow excessively. [proud.]

ὑπερ-αυχέω to be over-

ὑπέρ-αυχος 2 over-proud.

ὑπερ-άχθομαι *P.* to be vexed or grieved beyond measure.

ὑπερ-βαίνω to step over; to transgress, trespass, offend; to pass over, take no notice of; to go beyond.

ὑπερβαλλόντως *adv.* exceedingly, beyond measure.

ὑπερ-βάλλω to throw over or beyond, to throw farther; to exceed the right measure, to overflow, surpass, outdo, excel, exaggerate, overrun; to go beyond, pass over, cross, traverse, double. — *M.* to surpass, excel, exceed; to put off, delay.

ὑπερ-βασία, ἡ transgression, trespass, offence; wantonness.

ὑπερ-βατός 3 to be passed over; transposed. [whelm.]

ὑπερ-βιάζομαι *M.* to over-

ὑπέρ-βιος 2 overwhelming; overweening, excessive; passionate, wanton.

ὑπερ-βολή, ἡ a passing over, passage, mountain-pass, height; excess, highest degree; preeminence, preponderance; delay, putting off. [heavy.]

ὑπερ-βριθής 2 exceedingly]

ὑπερ-δεής 2 much inferior in number.

ὑπερ-δείδω, ὑπερ-δειμαίνω to fear exceedingly.

ὑπερ-δέξιος 2 situated above one.

ὑπερ-δικέω to plead for.

ὑπέρ-δικος 2 most just.

ὑπ-ερείδω to prop, support. [down.]

ὑπ-ερείπω aor. to fall]

ὑπερ-έκεινα adv. beyond.

ὑπερ-εκπερισσοῦ, -ῶς adv. more than superabundantly.

ὑπερ-εκπλήσσομαι P. to be frightened or astonished excessively.

ὑπερ-εκτείνω to stretch beyond measure.

ὑπερ-εκχύνομαι P. to overflow. [intercession for.]

ὑπερ-εντυγχάνω to make]

ὑπερ-επαινέω to praise exceedingly. [from below.]

ὑπ-ερέπτω to take away]

ὑπερ-έρχομαι to go beyond.

ὑπερ-εσθίω to eat immoderately. [well.]

ὑπέρ-ευ adv. exceedingly]

ὑπερ-εχθαίρω to hate exceedingly.

ὑπερ-έχω to hold over; intr. to rise above, be above, stand out; to be superior or more powerful, to excel.

ὑπερ-ήδομαι P. to rejoice exceedingly. [half.]

ὑπερ-ήμισυς, υ more than]

ὑπερ-ηνορέων, οντος overbearing, overmanly.

ὑπερηφανέω to be proud or overweening.

ὑπερηφανία, ἡ arrogance, haughtiness.

ὑπερή-φανος 2 excellent, splendid; arrogant, overweening.

ὑπερ-θαλασσίδιος 2 above the sea. [exceedingly.]

ὑπερ-θαυμάζω to wonder]

ὑπέρθεν adv. from above; above; over; beyond.

ὑπερ-θρῴσκω to leap over.

ὑπέρ-θῡμος 2 high-spirited; generous.

ὑπερ-θύριον, ὑπέρ-θυρον, τό lintel.

ὑπερ-ίημι to throw beyond. [hurriedly.]

ὑπερ-ικταίνομαι to run]

ὑπερ-ίσταμαι M. to stand over, to protect.

ὑπερ-ίστωρ, ορος knowing but too well.

ὑπερ-ίσχω = ὑπερέχω.

ὑπερ-κάθημαι M. to sit over or above; to lie in wait.

ὑπερ-καταβαίνω to step down over.

ὑπέρ-κειμαι M. to lie over or beyond. [wanton.]

ὑπέρ-κοπος 2 overbearing.]

ὑπερ-κτάομαι M. to acquire through one's own fault.

ὑπερ-κύδας, αντος triumphant.

ὑπερ-λίαν adv. beyond all measure.

ὑπερ-λῡπέομαι *P.* to be grieved beyond measure.

ὑπερ-μαχέω, -μάχομαι to fight for.

ὑπερ-μεγέθης, -μεγάθης 2 exceedingly large.

ὑπερ-μεθύσκομαι *P.* to be excessively drunk.

ὑπερ-μενέων, οντος, ὑπερμενής 2 high-spirited; excessively mighty.

ὑπερ-μήκης 2 exceedingly long or mighty.

ὑπερ-μῑσέω to hate excessively.

ὑπέρ-μορον *adv.* beyond destiny. [far.]

ὑπερ-νῑκάω to surpass by

ὑπερ-νοέω to think on still more. [south wind.]

ὑπερ-νότιος 2 beyond the

ὑπέρ-ογκος 2 of excessive size or bulk; overgrown; overweening. [or beyond.]

ὑπερ-οικέω to dwell above

ὑπέρ-οικος 2 dwelling above or beyond.

ὕπερον, τό pestle, club.

ὑπερ-οπλία, ἡ presumption, defiance.

ὑπερ-οπλίζομαι *M.* to despise wantonly.

ὑπέρ-οπλος 2 overweening, arrogant. [disdainful.]

ὑπερ-όπτης, ου despiser;

ὑπερ-οπτικός 3, ὑπέροπτος 2 haughty, overweening, proud, disdainful.

ὑπερ-οράω to look over, survey; to overlook, disregard, slight, despise, disdain; to let pass, indulge.

ὑπερ-όριος 3 and 2 outlandish, foreign.

ὑπερ-οχή, ἡ superiority, excess; preeminence, excellence.

ὑπέρ-οχος 2 prominent; distinguished. [disdain.]

ὑπερ-οφία, ἡ haughtiness;

ὑπερ-περισσεύω to become excessively abundant.

ὑπερ-περισσῶς *adv.* beyond all measure. [over.]

ὑπερ-πέτομαι *M.* to fly

ὑπερ-πίμπλημι to overfill.

ὑπερ-πίπτω to be gone by, to elapse.

ὑπερ-πλεονάζω to be superabundant.

ὑπέρ-πολυς 3 overmuch.

ὑπερ-πονέω to toil exceedingly; to endure for another.

ὑπερ-πόντιος 2 beyond the sea; across the sea.

ὑπέρτατος 3 uppermost, highest.

ὑπερ-τείνω to stretch over; to extend beyond; *intr.* to project beyond. [the mark.]

ὑπερ-τελής 2 going beyond

ὑπερ-τέλλω to rise over.

ὑπερτερία, ἡ upper frame of a carriage.

ὑπέρτερος 3 upper, higher; superior, better, more excellent, stronger; further, more.

ὑπερ-τίθημι and *M.* to commit, entrust; to delay, put off. [ceedingly.]

ὑπερ-τῑμάω to honour ex-

ὑπερ-τρέχω to outrun; to surpass; to pass over.

ὑπ-έρυϑρος 2 somewhat red. [high.]

ὑπερ-ύψηλος 2 exceedingly

ὑπερ-υψόω to exalt exceedingly. [pear above.]

ὑπερ-φαίνομαι P. to ap-

ὑπερ-φέρω to carry over; intr. to project; to excel; be superior.

ὑπερ-φίαλος 2 overbearing, arrogant, excessive, over-powerful. [ceedingly.]

ὑπερ-φιλέω to love ex-

ὑπερ-φρονέω to be haughty or overproud; to disdain.

ὑπέρ-φρων 2 high-minded; arrogant.

ὑπερ-φυής 2 immense, excessive, enormous, extraordinary; strange.

ὑπερ-φύομαι M. to surpass. [ceedingly.]

ὑπερ-χαίρω to rejoice ex-

ὑπερ-χλίω, -χλιδάω to be arrogant or proud.

ὑπ-έρχομαι M. to go or come under, to creep into; to come up, advance slowly; to deceive; to fawn, flatter.

ὑπερῴα, ἡ palate. [back]

ὑπ-ερωέω to go or shrink

ὑπερῷον, ὑπερῷον, τό upper story, upper room.

ὑπερῳόϑεν adv. from the upper story. [question.]

ὑπ-ερωτάω to insert a

ὑπ-εύϑῠνος 2 liable to give account, responsible.

ὑπ-έχω to hold under, put under, hold out; to lend, grant, afford, allow; to take upon oneself, submit to, suffer.

ὑπ-ήκοος 2 obedient, subject.

ὑπ-ημύω to bend the head.

ὑπ-ήνεμος 2 sheltered from the wind.

ὑπήνη, ἡ beard.

ὑπηνήτης, ου bearded.

ὑπ-ηοῖος 3 about dawn, early.

ὑπ-ηρεσία, ἡ rower's service; crew, sailors; service.

ὑπ-ηρέσιον, τό cushion on a rower's bench.

ὑπ-ηρετέω to serve, do service; to aid, obey, comply with; to gratify, afford.

ὑπ-ηρέτημα, τό service, assistance.

ὑπ-ηρέτης, ου, ὁ rower, sailor; servant; assistant; porter; aide-de-camp, inferior officer. [ing.]

ὑπ-ηρετικός 3 fit for serv-

ὑπ-ίλλω to draw in the tail; to check, restrain.

ὑπ-ισχνέομαι M., ὑπ-ίσχομαι to promise; to engage, betroth; to assure, assert.

ὕπνος, ὁ sleep, sleepiness.

ὑπνόω, ὑπνώω intr. and P. to sleep.

ὑπό adv. and prp. with gen. under; from under; by; through, by reason of, because of, in consequence of; with. — with dat. under; by force of, under one's power, subject to. — with acc. towards and under; towards; about, near upon; about the time of; behind; in the power of.

ὑπό - βαθρον, τό prop; rocking frame of a cradle.

ὑπο-βαίνω to go under or down, stand under.

ὑπο-βάλλω to throw or put under; to rejoin, retort; to suggest, contrive. — M. substitute; to invent, forge.

ὑπο-βλέπω and M. to look askance, scornfully, suspiciously, or angrily; to glance at.

ὑπο-βλήδην adv. replying interruptingly.

ὑπό-βλητος 2, ὑπο-βολιμαῖος 3 substituted, spurious, counterfeit.

ὑπο-βρύχιος 3, ὑπό-βρυξ, υχος under water.

ὑπό-γαιος 2 subterraneous.

ὑπο-γίγνομαι to be born after. [secretary.]

ὑπο-γραμματεύς, ὁ under-

ὑπο-γραμματεύω to be an under-secretary. [model.]

ὑπο-γραμμός, ὁ pattern,

ὑπο-γραφή, ἡ subscription; outline, sketch, design.

ὑπο-γράφω to subscribe, write under; to sketch out, delineate.

ὑπό-γυος 2 close at hand.

ὑπο-δαίω to set on fire under. [mit.]

ὑπο-δάμναμαι P. to sub-

ὑπο-δεής 2 feeble, weak; inferior; insignificant.

ὑπό-δειγμα, τό sign; model, pattern, example.

ὑπο-δείδω, ὑπο-δειμαίνω to fear a little. to shrink from.

ὑπο-δείκνυμι to show secretly; to delineate; to give to understand, to suggest, intimate; to show, prove.

ὑπο-δέμω to build under.

ὑπο-δεξίη, ἡ hospitality.

ὑπο-δέξιος 3 receiving, capacious, ample.

ὑπό-δεσις, ἡ a binding under; sandal, shoe.

ὑπο-δέχομαι M. to receive, welcome, entertain; to endure, bear; to become pregnant; to undertake, promise, admit, allow; to border upon.

ὑπο-δέω to bind under; to put on shoes.

ὑπό-δημα, τό sandal, shoe.

ὑπό-δικος 2 subject to trial. [servant.]

ὑπο-δμώς, ῶος, ὁ under-

ὑπο-δοχή, ἡ reception, entertainment; supposition, opinion. [ly.]

ὑπό-δρα adv. looking stern-

ὑπο-δράω to wait on.

ὑπο-δρηστήρ, ῆρος, ὁ waiter, servant.

ὑπο-δύνω, ὑπο-δύομαι M. to slip or slide under or into, to dive under; to put on under; to put on shoes; to steal into; to come on, emerge from; to undertake, undergo; to insinuate oneself. [priestess.]

ὑπο-ζάκορος, ἡ under-

ὑπο-ζεύγνυμι to yoke under. — P. to take on oneself.

ὑπο-ζύγιος 2 put under

the yoke; τὸ ὑποζύγιον beast of burden.

ὑπο-ζώννῡμι to gird under, undergird. [little.]

ὑπο-θερμαίνω to heat a

ὑπό-θερμος 2 somewhat hot; passionate.

ὑπό-θεσις, ἡ foundation; supposition; question, subject of discussion; argumentation, principle, summary; design, proposal.

ὑπο-θήκη, ἡ, ὑπο-θημοσύνη, ἡ hint, advice, warning. [make a noise.]

ὑπο-θορυβέω to begin to

ὑπο-θωπεύω to flatter.

ὑπο-θωρήσσομαι M. to arm oneself secretly.

ὑπο-κάθημαι M., ὑποκαθίζομαι M. to sit down at; to lie in ambush.

ὑπο-καίω to burn from below. [der.]

ὑπο-κάμπτω to bend un-

ὑπο-καταβαίνω to go down by degrees.

ὑπο-κατακλίνομαι P. to submit. [neath.]

ὑπο-κάτω adv. below, be-

ὑπό-κειμαι to lie under, below, or at the bottom; to be put under the eyes; to be laid down, taken for granted, or settled; to be subject to; to submit; to be proposed; to be at hand.

ὑπο-κηρύσσομαι M. to have a thing proclaimed.

ὑπο-κῑνέω to move gently; to incite a little; *intr.* to move a little.

ὑπο-κλαίω to weep at.

ὑπο-κλέπτομαι P. to be defrauded. [under.]

ὑπο-κλίνομαι P. to lie

ὑπο-κλονέομαι P. to press on in wild flight.

ὑπο-κλοπέομαι M. to be hidden. [secretly.]

ὑπο-κνίζομαι to be tickled

ὑπο-κορίζομαι M. to extenuate, palliate; to disparage.

ὑπο-κρητηρίδιον, τό base of a mixing vessel.

ὑπο-κρίνομαι M. to answer; to interpret; to play a part, be a player; to feign, dissemble.

ὑπό-κρῐσις, ἡ answer; hypocrisy.

ὑπο-κρῐτής, οῦ, ὁ actor; hypocrite. [secret.]

ὑπο-κρύπτω to hide, keep

ὑπό-κυκλος 2 running upon wheels. [pregnant.]

ὑπο-κύομαι to become

ὑπο-κύπτω to stoop or bend under; to submit.

ὑπό-κωφος 2 rather deaf.

ὑπο-λαμβάνω to take from below; to take on one's back; to receive, accept; to take up; to answer, rejoin; to take up, fight with; to think, suppose, conceive, understand; to follow close; to draw away, entice.

ὑπο-λάμπω to shine from beneath; to shine into.

ὑπο-λέγω to say or name after; to suggest; to say beforehand; to mean.

ὑπό-λειμμα, τό remnant.

ὑπο-λείπω to leave re-

maining, leave behind. —
P. to be inferior.

ὑπο-λευκαίνομαι *P.* to become white underneath.

ὑπο-λήνιον, τό tub of a
wine-press, press-tub.

ὑπό-ληψις, ἡ answer, reply;
objection; opinion.

ὑπ-ολίζων 2 somewhat
smaller.

ὑπο-λιμπάνω = ὑπολείπω.

ὑπο-λογίζομαι *M.* to take
into account.

ὑπό-λογος, ὁ a taking into
account; *adj.* taken into
account.

ὑπό-λοιπος left remaining
or behind. [captain.]

ὑπο-λόχᾱγος, ὁ under-

ὑπο-λύω to loosen from
below; to untie; to slacken
gradually. — *M.* to untie
one's shoes; to free from
secretly.

ὑπο-μαλακίζομαι *P.* to become a little cowardly.

ὑπό-μαργος 2 a little mad.

ὑπο-μείων 2 somewhat in-
ferior, subordinate.

ὑπο-μένω to stay behind;
to abide, await; to sur-
vive; to endure; to wait
for; to stand one's ground;
to undertake; to resist.

ὑπο-μίγνυμι to come near
or approach secretly.

ὑπο-μιμνήσκω to remind;
to mention. — *P.* to re-
member, recollect.

ὑπο-μνάομαι *M.* to woo or
court secretly.

ὑπό-μνημα, τό, ὑπό-μνη-
σις, ἡ remembrance; re-

minding, mention, admoni-
tion; memorial, memoir.

ὑπ-όμνῡμαι *M.* to take an
oath to stay legal pro-
ceedings.

ὑπο-μονή, ἡ perseverance,
patience; endurance.

ὑπο-νείφω to snow a
little.

ὑπο-νήϊος 2 lying at the
foot of mount Neion.

ὑπο-νοέω to suspect; to
conjecture, guess.

ὑπό-νοια, ἡ suspicion; conjecture, guess, opinion.

ὑπο-νομηδόν *adv.* by un-
derground channels.

ὑπό-νομος, ὁ underground
passage, mine.

ὑπο-νοστέω to go down,
decrease, fall. [der.]

ὑπο-πάσσω to strew un-

ὑπό-πεμπτος 2 sent se-
cretly. [cretly.]

ὑπο-πέμπω to send se-

ὑπο-περκάζω to become
dark-coloured by degrees.

ὑπο-πετάννῡμι to spread
out under. [neath.]

ὑπό-πετρος 2 stony be-

ὑπο-πιάζω to oppress.

ὑπο-πίμπλημι to fill by
degrees. [much.]

ὑπο-πίνω to drink rather

ὑπο-πίπτω to fall down,
prostrate oneself; to get
under. [Mount Placos.]

ὑπο-πλάκιος 3 under

ὑπό-πλεος 2 rather full.

ὑπο-πλέω to sail along
under.

ὑπο-πνέω to blow gently.

ὑπο-πόδιον, τό footstool.

ὑπο-ποιέω to cause secretly. — M. to win cunningly.

ὑπό-πτερος 2 winged, feathered.

ὑπ-οπτεύω to be suspicious, to suspect; to divine, conjecture.

ὑπ-όπτης, ου, ὁ suspicious.

ὑπο-πτήσσω to crouch or cower down; to hide oneself from fear; to be shy or abashed.

ὕπ-οπτος 2 suspected, critical; suspicious, fearing.

ὑπ-όρνῡμι to stir up, rouse gradually. — intr. and M. to rise.

ὑπο-ρρήγνῡμαι P. to break or open from beneath.

ὑπό-ρρηνος 2 suckling a lamb.   [undermine.]

ὑπ-ορύσσω to dig under,|

ὑπο-σημαίνω to order by a signal.

ὑπο-σκελίζω to trip one up.

ὑπο-σπανίζομαι to suffer want a little.

ὑπο-σπάω to draw away from under.

ὑπό-σπονδος 2 under a truce, by way of a treaty.

ὑπο-σσείω to move below.

ὑπο-στάθμη, ἡ sediment.

ὑπό-στασις, ἡ foundation; substance, matter, reality, real nature; confidence.

ὑπο-σταχύομαι M. to grow up, thrive.

ὑπό-στεγος 2 under a roof; entering a house.

ὑπο-στέλλω to draw or take down; to keep back.

— M. to shrink back from, conceal, dissemble.

ὑπο-στένω, -στενάζω, -στεναχίζω to sigh or moan; to ring.

ὑπο-στολή, ἡ despondency.

ὑπο-στόρνῡμι to spread out under.   [under-captain.]

ὑπο-στρατηγέω to be an|

ὑπο-στράτηγος, ὁ subordinate commander.

ὑπο-στρέφω to turn round about or back. — intr. and P. to wheel round, turn and flee; to return; to take care of; to evade, elude.

ὑπο-στροφή, ἡ a turning round; retreat; return; flight.   [στόρνῡμι.]

ὑπο-στρώννῡμι = ὑπο-|

ὑπό-σχεσις, ὑπο-σχεσίη, ἡ promise.

ὑπο-ταγή, ἡ subordination.

ὑπο-τανύω to spread out under.

ὑπο-ταράσσω to trouble a little, to perplex.

ὑπο-ταρβέω to fear.

ὑπο-ταρτάριος 2 living below in Tartarus.

ὑπο-τάττω to place or arrange under; to subject. — P. to obey.

ὑπο-τείνω to stretch under; to hold out, suggest hopes; to cause; to strain, sharpen, highten.

ὑπο-τειχίζω to build a cross-wall.

ὑπο-τείχισις, ἡ, ὑπο-τείχισμα, τό cross-wall.

ὑπο-τελέω to pay off; to pay tribute.

ὑπο-τελής 2 tributary.

ὑπο-τέμνω and M. to cut away below; to cut off, intercept; to thwart.

ὑπο-τίθημι to put or place under; to delay, keep in suspense; to substitute; to pawn, mortgage; to suppose, suggest, admonish, promise. — M. to lay down as a principle or rule; to propose to oneself; to intend, purpose; to suggest, advise.

ὑπο-τοπέω, -εύω and M. to suspect.

ὑπο-τρέμω to tremble in the knees; to shrink from.

ὑπο-τρέχω to run (in) under; to sail by or past; to ingratiate oneself.

ὑπο-τρέω, ὑπο-τρομέω to tremble; to shrink back.

ὑπό-τρομος 2 trembling with fear.

ὑπό-τροπος 2 returning.

ὑπο-τύπτω to strike or push down; to dip down.

ὑπο-τύπωσις, ἡ outline; model.

ὕπ-ουλος 2 festering inwardly; rotten underneath; illusory.　　　　[ven.

ὑπ-ουράνιος 2 under heaven.

ὑπ-ουργέω to serve, be helpful; to perform, afford.

ὑπούργημα, τό, ὑπ-ουργίᾱ, ἡ service rendered, complaisance.　[helpful.

ὑπ-ουργός 2 serviceable.

ὑπο-φαίνω to show from under, to bring to light, show a little. — intr. and

P. to come in sight, be seen a little. [for light.

ὑπό-φαυσις, ἡ an opening.

ὑπο-φείδομαι M. to forbear, be regardful.

ὑπο-φέρω to carry away, save, rescue; to carry downwards; to hold out, proffer; to pretend; to endure, suffer. — P. to sail down stream; to be seduced or misled.　　　　　[cretly.

ὑπο-φεύγω to escape secretly.

ὑπο-φήτης, ου, ὁ interpreter, prophet.

ὑπο-φθάνω and M. to be beforehand.

ὑπο-φθέγγομαι M. to speak gently.　　　　　[envy.

ὑπο-φθονέω to feel secret envy.

ὑπό-φθονος 2 with secret envy.

ὑπο-φορά, ἡ pretence, objection.　　　　　[dually.

ὑπο-χάζομαι to retire gradually.

ὑπό-χειρ, χειρός, ὑπο-χείριος 2 under the hand, at hand; under one's power, subject.

ὑπο-χέω to pour, strew, or spread under; to administer to.　　　[under.

ὑπ-οχλέομαι to be rolled.

ὕπ-οχος 2 subject, dependent, subdued.

ὑπο-χρίω to besmear under or a little.

ὑπο-χωρέω to withdraw, retire, recoil; to advance slowly.

ὑπό-φαμμος 2 sandy.

ὑπ-οφία, ἡ suspicion, jealousy.

ὑπ-όφιος 2 suspected, despised.

ὑπτιάζω to bend back.

ὕπτιος 3 bent back; on one's back; turned up, inverted; level, flat.

ὑπ-ωμοσίᾱ, ἡ oath taken to stop proceedings at law.

ὑπ-ώπια, τά face.

ὑπ-ωπιάζω to vex, annoy.

ὑπ-ώρεια, ἡ foot or slope of a mountain.

ὑπ-ωρόφιος 2 and 3 under the roof. [pig.]

ὗς, ὑός, ὁ, ἡ swine, sow.

ὑσμίνη, ἡ battle, combat.

ὕσσωπος, ἡ hyssop.

ὕστατος 3 last, utmost, extreme.

ὑστέρᾱ, ἡ womb.

ὑστεραῖος 3 following, later, next.

ὑστερέω to be behind, late, or later; to come too late; to miss, fail; to be in want of; to come short of, be inferior; to delay, be wanting. — P. to be in want.

ὑστέρημα, τό, ὑστέρησις, ἡ a coming short, deficiency, want.

ὑστερίζω = ὑστερέω.

ὕστερος 3 the latter; coming after, following, later; younger; too late; inferior, weaker; ὕστερον adv. afterwards, later, in future. [ing after.]

ὑστερο-φθόρος 2 destroy-

ὗς-τριξ, ιχος, ὁ, ἡ hedgehog, porcupine.

ὑφαίνω to weave; to contrive, devise.

ὑφ-αιρέω to take away from under; to draw away, seduce; to withhold. — M. to purloin, abstract; to make away with.

ὕφ-αλος 2 submarine.

ὑφάντης, ου, ὁ weaver.

ὑφαντικός 3 skilled in weaving.

ὑφαντός 3 woven.

ὑφ-άπτω to set on fire from underneath. [rob.]

ὑφ-αρπάζω to filch away,

ὕφασμα, τό texture, web.

ὑφάω = ὑφαίνω.

ὑφ-ειμένως adv. dejectedly.

ὑφ-έλκω to draw away under. [cretly.]

ὑφ-έρπω to creep on se-

ὑφ-ηγέομαι M. to lead the way, to guide; to advance slowly. [guiding.]

ὑφ-ήγησις, ἡ a leading,

ὑφ-ηγητήρ, ῆρος, ὑφ-ηγητής, οῦ, ὁ guide.

ὑφ-ηνίοχος, ὁ charioteer.

ὑφ-ίημι to send down; to put under; to lower; to admit, submit. — intr. and M. to yield, abate, slacken; despond; to creep or steal in.

ὑφ-ίστημι to place under; to place secretly. — intr. and M. to stand under; to post oneself secretly; to stand one's ground; to resist; to take upon oneself, to engage in; to promise.

ὑφ-οράω and M. to look askance or with suspicion.

ὑ-φορβός, ὁ swineherd.

ὑφ-ορμίζομαι M. to come to anchor.

ὕφ-υδρος 2 under water.

ὑφ-αγόρᾱς, ου boasting.

ὑφ-ερεφής 2 with high roof.

ὑψηλός 3 high, lofty, steep; proud, stately. [minded.]

ὑψηλο-φρονέω to be high-

ὑφ-ηρεφής = ὑφερεφής.

ὑφ-ηχής 2 neighing with raised head.

ὕψι adv. high, on high; ὕψιστος 3 highest.

ὑψί-βατος 2 high-legged.

ὑψί-βρεμέτης, ου high-thundering.

ὑψί-ζυγος 2 ruling on high. [topped.]

ὑψί-κάρηνος 2 high-

ὑψί-κέρως, ων with high horns. [liage.]

ὑψί-κομος 2 with high fo-

ὑψί-κομπος 2 boastful.

ὑψι-πετήεις 3, -πέτης, ου flying on high.

ὑψι-πέτηλος 2 with high foliage.

ὑψί-πολις, ι eminent in one's city.

ὑψί-πους, ποδος walking on high.

ὑψί-πυλος 2 with high gates. [towers.]

ὑψί-πυργος 2 with lofty

ὕψιστος 3 see ὕψι.

ὑψόθεν adv. from on high; on high.

ὑψόθι adv. on high.

ὑψ-όροφος 2 = ὑφερεφής.

ὕψος, τό height, top; sublimity.

ὑψόσε adv. upwards.

ὑψοῦ = ὕψι.

ὑψόω to heighten, raise.

ὕψωμα, τό height, elevation.

ὕω to water, wet; to let rain; to rain. — P. to be rained on; to rain.

Φ

Φ, φ (φῖ) twenty-first letter of the alphabet; as a numeral φ' = 500. [νός.]

φαάντατος 3 sup. of φαει-

φαγέδαινα, ἡ eating ulcer.

φαγεῖν aor. of ἐσθίω.

φάγος, ὁ glutton.

φαέθων 3, φαεινός 3 shining, beaming.

φαείνω to shine; to illuminate. — P. to become visible.

φαεινός 3 = φαεινός.

φαεσί-μβροτος 2 shining on mortals.

φαιδιμόεις 3, φαίδιμος 2 shining, brilliant; illustrious; famous, glorious.

φαιδρός 3 beaming, gay.

φαιδρόω, φαιδρῡνω to cheer up, gladden.

φαινόλης, ου, ὁ cloak.

φαίνω to bring to light, make visible, show, make clear or audible; to display, exhibit, explain; to announce, denounce, make known; to promise, grant; intr. to give light, shine. — P. to come to light, appear, to shine forth; to be conspicuous; to make one's appearance; to be denounced.

φάκελος, ὁ bundle.

φαλαγγηδόν *adv.* in rows.

φαλάγγιον, τό spider.

φάλαγξ, αγγος, ἡ round piece of wood, trunk; spider; line of battle, order of battle, phalanx, body of soldiers, compact mass.

φαλακρόομαι *P.* to become bald.

φαλακρός 3 bald.

φάλαρον, τό brazen boss; cheek-piece of horses.

φαληριάω to become white with foam.

φαλλός, ὁ wooden pole; membrum virile, penis.

φάλος, ὁ fore-piece, ridge or crown of a helmet.

φανερός 3 or 2 visible, manifest, conspicuous; public; known, famous.

φανερόω to make visible, manifest, or known. — *P.* to become known or famous.

φανέρωσις, ἡ manifestation.   [torch.\

φἄνός 3 = φαεινός; ὁ φ.\

φαντάζομαι *P.* to appear, show oneself.

φαντασίᾱ, ἡ appearance; display, show; splendour; imagination.

φάντασμα, τό appearance; apparition, phantom, vision, spectre.

φάος, ους, τό light, daylight, sunlight; lamp of life; eye-sight; lamp, torch; life, deliverance, happiness; darling.

φάραγξ, αγγος, ἡ ravine, cleft, chasm.

φαρέτρᾱ, ἡ, φαρετρεών, ῶνος, ὁ quiver.

φαρμακείᾱ, ἡ the use of drugs or spells; poisoning, witchcraft; medicine.

φαρμακεύς, ὁ poisoner, sorcerer.   [or poisons.\
φαρμακεύω to use drugs\

φάρμακον, τό drug, medicine, remedy; poison, enchanted potion; dye, colour.

φαρμακο-ποσίᾱ, ἡ the drinking of medicine or poison.

φαρμακός, ὁ = φαρμακεύς.

φαρμάσσω = φαρμακεύω; to enchant, bewitch; to temper, harden.

φάρος, φάρος, τό web, cloth; sheet; sail; cloak.

φάρσος, τό part, portion, division. [throat; chasm.\

φάρυγξ, υγγος, ὔγος, ἡ\
φάσγανον, τό knife, sword.

φάσις, ἡ information, assertion.

φάσκω = φημί.

φάσμα, τό = φάντασμα.

φάσσα, ἡ wood-pigeon.

φασσο-φόνος 2 pigeon-killing.   [betroth.\
φατίζω to say, speak; to\

φάτις, ἡ = φήμη.

φάτνη, ἡ manger. crib.

φαυλίζω to depreciate, slight.

φαῦλος 3 and 2 bad; slight, trifling; useless, mean, common, worthless; vulgar; insignificant, simple, plain; careless, evil, male-volent. [ness; badness.]

φαυλότης, ητος, ἡ mean-}

φάω to shine.

φέβομαι to flee; to shun.

φέγγος, τό light, splendour.

φείδομαι M. to keep clear or aloof, turn away from; to spare, use sparingly.

φειδώ, οῦς, όος, ἡ, φειδωλή, ἡ a sparing; thrift.

φειδωλός 3 sparing, thrifty.

φελόνης, ου, ὁ = φαινόλης.

φενακίζω to cheat, deceive.

φενάκισμός, ὁ imposture.

φένω to slay, murder.

φέρβω to feed, nourish.

φερ-έγγυος 2 giving surety or bail; trusty, competent.

φερέ-οικος 2 carrying one's house with one.

φέριστος, φέρτατος 3 best, bravest, most excellent.

φερνή, ἡ dowry.

φέρτε = φέρετε.

φέρτρον, τό bier, litter.

φέρω to bear, carry, bear along; to suffer, endure; χαλεπῶς or βαρέως φέρειν to bear impatiently; take a thing amiss; to fetch, bring, present; to occasion, cause; to pay; to bring forth, produce; to carry away (booty), rob, gain, win; to lead to, to stretch, aim at, refer to, tend to; to have in one's mouth. — P. to be carried or borne on or along; to move quickly, to hasten, run,

fly. — M. to carry away for oneself; to bring with one; to win, gain.

φεῦ int. ah! alas! woe! oh!

φεύγω to flee, take flight, run away; to flee before one; to shun, shrink from, fear; to be banished; to be an exile; to be accused or prosecuted.

φευκτός 3 to be avoided.

φεῦξις, ἡ = φυγή.

φή, φῆ adv. just as.

φήγινος 3 oaken.

φηγός, ἡ a species of oak.

φήμη, ἡ speech, talk; report, rumour; legend; saying, word; voice; prophetic voice, omen.

φημί to say, speak, tell; to call by name; to answer; to think, believe, imagine, fancy; to assert, say yes; οὔ φημι to say no, deny, forbid. — M. = Act. to think oneself.

φημίζω to speak out; to divulge a report.

φῆμις, ἡ = φήμη.

φήνη, ἡ sea-eagle.

φήρ, φηρός, ὁ monster.

φθάνω to come or reach before or beforehand, be sooner or first.

φθαρτός 3 corruptible.

φθέγγομαι M. to raise one's voice, to cry aloud, to sound; to call, speak; to murmur.

φθέγμα, τό = φθογγή.

φθείρ, ρός, ὁ louse.

φθειρο-τραγέω to eat fir-cones.

φθείρω to destroy, ruin; to corrupt, spoil, waste; to kill; to seduce. — *P.* to perish, be lost or cast away.

φθινάς, άδος consuming, wasting.

φθιν-οπωρινός 3 late in autumn. [tumn.]

φθιν-όπωρον, τό late au-)

φθινύθω, φθίνω to decay, wane, pine away, perish; *trans.* to consume, waste, destroy.

φθῑσ-ήνωρ, ορος, **φθῑσί-μβροτος** 2 man-destroying.

φθίσις, ή decline; consumption.

φθιτός 3 decayed, dead.

φθίω = φθίνω.

φθογγή, ή, **φθόγγος,** ὁ voice; cry, sound; speech.

φθονερός 3 envious.

φθονέω to envy, be jealous, grudge, bear ill-will; to refuse.

φθόνησις, ή, **φθόνος,** ὁ envy, grudge, jealousy, ill-will; denial.

φθορά, ή, **φθόρος,** ὁ corruption, decay, destruction; death; transitoriness.

φιάλη, ή cup, bowl, vessel, urn.

φιδίτιον, τό common Spartan meal; hall for those meals.

φιλ-άγαθος 2 loving goodness. [love.]

φιλ-αδελφία, ή brotherly)

φιλ-άδελφος 2 brotherly, sisterly.

φιλ-αίτιος 2 fond of blaming, censorious.

φίλ-ανδρος 2 loving one's husband.

φιλ-ανθρωπία, ή love for mankind, benevolence, charity, humanity.

φιλ-άνθρωπος 2 benevolent, humane, kind.

φιλ-απεχθημοσύνη, ή quarrelsomeness, malignity.

φιλ-απεχθήμων 2 quarrelsome. [travelling.]

φιλ-απόδημος 2 fond of)

φιλ-αργυρία, ή covetousness. [money, covetous.]

φιλ-άργυρος 2 fond of)

φίλ-αρχος 2 fond of rule.

φίλ-αυλος 2 fond of the flute.

φίλ-αυτος 2 self-loving.

φιλ-έλλην, ηνος, ὁ fond of the Greeks.

φιλ-έταιρος 2 loving one's comrades.

φιλέω to love; to receive hospitably, to entertain; to court; to kiss; to be fond of; to be wont.

φίλη, ή friend, mistress.

φιλ-ήδονος 2 fond of pleasure. [ing.]

φιλ-ήκοος 3 fond of hear-)

φίλημα, τό kiss. [oar.]

φιλ-ήρετμος 2 loving the)

φιλία, ή love, affection; friendship. [tionate.]

φιλικός 3 friendly, affec-)

φίλιος 3 of a friend, friendly; kindly. [Philip.]

φιλιππίζω to side with)

φιλιππισμός, ὁ a siding with Philip.

φίλ-ιππος 2 fond of horses.

φιλίτιον, τό friendly meal.

φιλογυμναστέω to be fond of bodily exercise.

φιλο-γυμναστία, ἡ love for bodily exercise.

φιλο-δέσποτος 2 loving one's master.

φιλο-δικέω to be fond of lawsuits. [suits.

φιλό-δικος 2 fond of law-/

φιλό-δωρος 2 fond of giving. [mals.

φιλό-ζῳος 2 fond of ani-/

φιλό-θεος 2 loving God.

φιλό-θηρος 2 fond of hunting.

φιλ-οικτίρμων 2, φιλ-οίκτιστος 2 compassionate; fond of complaining.

φιλ-οικτος 2 piteous; fond of lamenting. [beautiful.

φιλο-καλέω to love the/

φιλό-καλος 2 loving the beautiful. [of gain.

φιλο-κερδέω to be greedy/

φιλο-κερδής 2 greedy of gain. [mocking.

φιλο-κέρτομος 2 fond of/

φιλο-κίνδῡνος 2 fond of danger, bold. [gain.

φιλο-κτέανος 2 fond of/

φιλό-λογος 2 fond of words or learning; scholar.

φιλο-λοίδορος 2 slanderous.

φιλο-μαθής 2 loving knowledge. [smiling.

φιλο-μμειδής 2 sweet-/

φιλό-μουσος 2 fond of the Muses. [blaming.

φιλό-μωμος 2 fond of/

φιλο-νεικέω, φιλο-νικέω to be fond of dispute; to be ambitious or obstinate; to quarrel.

φιλο-νῑκία, ἡ rivalry; ambition, jealousy; obstinacy.

φιλό-νῑκος 2 contentious, rivalling; fond of strife; obstinate.

φιλο-ξενία, ἡ hospitality.

φιλό-ξενος 2 hospitable.

φιλο-παίγμων 2 fond of sport, sportive, gay.

φιλο-πόλεμος 2 fond of war, warlike.

φιλό-πολις, ιδος loving one's city, patriotic.

φιλο-πονέω to love work, be diligent.

φιλό-πονος 2 diligent, industrious. [drinking.

φιλο-ποσία, ἡ love of/

φιλο-πρᾱγμοσύνη, ἡ activity, fussiness, officiousness.

φιλο-πράγμων 2 busy, officious, meddlesome.

φιλο-πρωτεύω to strive to be the first. [πόλεμος.

φιλο-πτόλεμος = φιλο-/

φίλος 2 loved, beloved, dear, pleasing; loving, friendly, fond; ὁ φίλος friend, companion; husband; lover; kinsman. [jesting.

φιλο-σκώμμων 2 fond of/

φιλο-σοφέω to love wisdom or knowledge, to be a philosopher, seek after knowledge; to inquire into, study.

φιλο-σοφία, ἡ love of wisdom or knowledge, scientific or systematic study, philosophy; investigation, research.

φιλό-σοφος 2 fond of knowledge, loving wisdom, scientific, literary, learned; ὁ φ. philosopher. [tenderly.]

φιλό-στοργος 2 loving

φιλο-στρατιώτης, ου, ὁ soldier's friend.

φιλο-σώματος 2 loving one's body. [children.]

φιλό-τεκνος 2 fond of

φιλο-τεχνέω to love arts, to be ingenious.

φιλότης, ητος, ἡ love, friendship; hospitality.

φιλοτήσιος 3 of love or friendship, friendly.

φιλο-τῑμέομαι P. to love honour or distinction; to take a pride in, make it one's boast; to endeavour earnestly.

φιλο-τῑμία, ἡ love of honour or distinction; ambition, emulation, point of honour; liberality, ostentation.

φιλό-τῑμος 2 loving honour or distinction; ostentatious; emulous.

φιλο-φρονέομαι M. and P. to be affectionate, show kindness, be benevolent or well disposed; to greet.

φιλο-φροσύνη, ἡ friendliness, love, benevolence.

φιλό-φρων 2 friendly, kindly, affectionate.

φιλο-χρήματος 2 fond of money, covetous.

φιλό-χρηστος 2 righteous, honest.

φιλο-χωρέω to be fond of a certain place. [ing.]

φιλο-ψευδής 2 fond of ly-

φιλό-ψογος 2 fond of blaming. [one's life.]

φιλο-ψῡχέω to be fond of

φιλο-ψῡχία, ἡ love of life.

φίλτρον, τό love-charm, spell; enticement.

φιλύρα, ἡ lime-tree.

φῑμόω to muzzle, gag. — P. to be silent.

φῑτρός, ὁ trunk of a tree.

φῑτύω to engender, beget.

φλαυρίζω, φλαῦρος see φαυλίζω, φαῦλος. [badly.]

φλαυρουργός 2 working

φλεγέθω = φλέγω.

φλέγμα, τό flame, fire, heat; phlegm.

φλεγμαίνω to be inflamed.

φλεγμονή, ἡ heat, inflammation.

φλέγω to set on fire; to burn, scorch; to inflame, torment. — intr. and P. to shine, flame, blaze, flash; be inflamed.

φλέψ, φλεβός, ἡ vein.

φλῑβω to rub, press.

φλῑή, ἡ door-post.

φλόγεος 3 flaming, blazing.

φλογίζω to burn up. — P. to blaze.

φλογιστός 3 burnt.

φλόγωσις, ἡ = φλεγμονή.

φλόϊνος 3 of rushes or reed.

φλοιός, ὁ bark, bast.

φλοῖσβος, ὁ roaring noise; battle-din. [blaze.]

φλόξ, φλογός, ἡ fire, flame

φλόος, φλοῦς, ὁ rush, reed

φλυᾱρέω to talk nonsense, speak idly; to slander.

φλυᾱρία, ἡ idle talk; nonsense.

φλύαρος 2 talking idly, prattling. tule.|

φλύκταινα, ἡ blister; pus-|

φοβερός 3 frightful, terrible; fearful, afraid.

φοβέω to terrify, put to flight. — *P.* to be frightened, be put to flight, to flee; to fear, be alarmed or afraid; to feel awe.

φόβη, ἡ hair, mane.

φόβημα, τό terror.

φοβητός 3, φόβητρον, τό frightful. [terror; awe.|

φόβος, ὁ flight; fear, fright,|

φοιβό-λαμπτος 2 seized or inspired by Phœbus.

φοῖβος 3 bright; pure.

φοινήεις 3 blood-red.

φοινίκεος 3 purple, crimson.

φοινικήιος 3 of the palm-tree. [garment.|

φοινικίς, ίδος, ἡ purple|

φοινικιστής, οῦ, ὁ wearer of purple.

φοινικόεις 3 = φοινίκεος.

φοινικο-πάρῃος 2 red-cheeked.

φοῖνιξ, ικος purple-red, crimson; ὁ φ. purple dye; ὁ, ἡ φ. date-palm, date; phœnix (a fabulous bird); lyre.

φοίνιος 3, φοινός 3 blood-red; bloody; blood-thirsty.

φοινίσσω to redden.

φοιτάς, άδος, ἡ strolling woman.

φοιτάω to go to and fro or up and down; to hasten; to roam wildly about; to go regularly, to frequent; to (go to) visit; to come in, be imported.

φοίτησις, ἡ a going to and fro.

φολκός 3 crook-legged.

φονάω to be blood-thirsty.

φονεύς, ὁ, ἡ murderer.

φονεύω to murder, slay.

φονή, ἡ = φόνος.

φονικός 3, φόνιος 3, φονός 3 murderous; bloody; relating to murder or blood.

φόνος, ὁ murder, slaughter, massacre; dagger; deadly wound; blood shed in murder; place of murder.

φοξός 3 with a pointed head.

φορά, ἡ a carrying, bearing; payment; fertility; load, burden; tax, tribute; fruit, crop; quick motion, rush, onset. [lent motion.|

φοράδην *adv.* with a vio-|

φορβάς, άδος nourishing.

φορβή, ἡ food, fodder, victuals.

φορεύς, ὁ bearer.

φορέω = φέρω. [ment.|

φόρημα, τό burden; orna-|

φορμηδόν *adv.* crosswise; in layers. [lute.|

φόρμιγξ, ιγγος, ἡ lyre;|

φορμίζω to play on the lyre. [corn-measure.|

φορμός, ὁ basket; mat;|

φόρον, τό the Forum.

φόρος, ὁ tribute; income, revenue.

φορός 2 favourable.

φορτ-ηγέω to carry loads.

φορτ-ηγικός 3 carrying loads.

φορτίζω to load.

φορτικός 3 carrying loads;

burdensome; importune; vulgar; abject.

φορτίον, τό load, burden; freight; baggage.

φορτίς, ίδος, ἡ ship of burden.

φόρτος, ὁ = φορτίον.

φορτο-φορέω to carry loads.

φορύνω, **φορύσσω** to stain, defile.

φόως, τό = φῶς.

φραγέλλιον, τό scourge.

φραγελλόω to scourge.

φράγμα, τό, **φραγμός**, ὁ a fencing in; fence, hedge, enclosure, wall, partition; stoppage.

φραδής 2, **φράδμων** 2 prudent, cunning.

φράζω to make clear; to show; to pronounce, declare, tell, utter; to beckon; to promise; to order, advise. — M. and P. to think, believe, consider; to perceive, remark, notice; to understand; to purpose, contrive.

φράσσω to fence in, fortify, block up, defend, protect. — M. to fence or fortify for oneself.   [a clan.]

φράτηρ, ερος, ὁ member of∫

φρατρία, ἡ tribe, clan.

φρέαρ, ατος, τό well, water-tank.   [duit; mine.]

φρεᾱτία, ἡ reservoir, con-∫

φρεν-απατάω to deceive.

φρεν-απάτης, ου, ὁ deceiver.   [prudent.]

φρεν-ήρης 2 sound of mind,∫

φρενο-βλαβής 2 crazy, mad.

φρενόθεν adv. away from one's mind.

φρενο-μόρως adv. in mind.

φρενόω to make wise, inform, teach.

φρήν, φρενός, ἡ midriff; breast; soul, mind, heart; sense, understanding, reason.

φρήτρη, ἡ = φρατρία.

φρίκη, ἡ a shuddering; ripple or ruffling of the sea; awe, fear.   [rible.]

φρῑκώδης 2 awful, hor-∫

φρῑμάσσομαι M. to snort.

φρῖξ, φρῑκός, ἡ = φρίκη.

φρίσσω to be ruffled; to bristle; to shudder, shiver, feel a chill.

φροιμιάζομαι = προοιμιάζομαι.

φροίμιον, τό = προοίμιον.

φρονέω to think, be sound in mind, be wise; to understand, consider, know; to be minded or disposed; to mean, intend, purpose.

φρόνημα, τό, **φρόνησις**, ἡ mind, will; thought, insight; purpose; high spirit, pride, arrogance.

φρόνιμος 2 in one's senses; prudent, sensible, wise.

φρόνις, ιος, ἡ practical wisdom.

φροντίζω to think, consider, reflect; to give heed to, care about, be thoughtful.

φροντίς, ίδος, ἡ thought, care, heed; reflection; anxiety; concern.

φροντιστής, οῦ, ὁ thinker.

φροντιστικῶς *adv.* carefully. [gone, departed.]

φροῦδος 3 gone away;

φρουρά, ἡ watch, guard; watchfulness; prison; garrison; levy, conscription.

φρουρ-αρχία, ἡ commandership in a fortress.

φρούρ-αρχος, ὁ commander of a garrison.

φρουρέω to watch, keep guard, to serve as a garrison; to watch, guard, keep; to observe, beware of.

φρούρημα, τό watch, guard.

φρουρικός 3 belonging to a watch or garrison.

φρούριον, τό watch-post, fort; garrison.

φρουρίς, ίδος, ἡ guard-ship.

φρουρός, ὁ watcher, guard.

φρύαγμα, τό a snorting, neighing. [neigh.]

φρυάσσω and *M.* to snort,]

φρυγανισμός, ὁ a collecting of wood.

φρύγανον, τό dry wood, fire-wood.

φρύγω to roast; to parch.

φρυκτός 3 roasted; ὁ φ. firebrand; signal-fire.

φρυκτωρέω to give signals by fire.

φρυκτωρός, ὁ one who watches signal-fires.

φύγαδε *adv.* to flight.

φυγαδεύω to chase, banish.

φυγαδικός 3 for an exile.

φυγάς, άδος fugitive, banished, exile; deserter.

φυγγάνω = φεύγω.

φυγή, ἡ flight, escape, banishment; place of refuge.

φυγο-πτόλεμος 2 shunning war.

φύζα, ἡ flight; terror.

φυζανικός 3 flying, cowardly.

φυή, ἡ growth, stature.

φῦκιόεις 3 rich in sea-weed. [paint.]

φῦκος, τό sea-weed; red]

φυκτός 3 to be escaped.

φυλακή, ἡ a watching, keeping guard; night-watch; watch, guard; watchfulness, caution; watch-post, life-guard, garrison; prison. [prison.]

φυλακίζω to throw into]

φυλακός, ὁ, φυλακτήρ, ῆρος, ὁ = φύλαξ.

φυλακτήριον, τό watch-post, fort; preservation; amulet. [for preserving.]

φυλακτικός 3 cautious, fit]

φύλαξ, ακος, ὁ, ἡ watcher, guard; sentinel; keeper.

φύλ-αρχος, ὁ chief of a tribe; commander of cavalry.

φυλάσσω to watch; to keep guard; to serve as a garrison; to be on one's guard, to take heed; *trans.* to watch, guard, keep, secure, preserve, protect; to observe. — *M.* to keep guard; to keep, bear in memory; to take heed; to shun, avoid.

φῦλή, ἡ tribe, clan; people; division of soldiers.

φυλίη, ἡ wild olive-tree (buckthorn?).

φυλλάς, άδος, ἡ heap of leaves; foliage, leafy bushes.

φύλλον, τό leaf; *pl.* foliage.

φῦλο-κρινέω to distinguish races.

φῦλον, τό race, family; tribe, people, nation; troop; kind, sex.

φύλοπις, ιδος, ἡ din of battle; battle, strife.

φῦμα, τό tumour, ulcer.

φύξηλις, ιδος = φυζανικός.

φύξιμος 2 able to flee; τὸ φ-ον place of refuge.

φύξις, ιος, ἡ = φυγή.

φύραμα, τό dough.

φυράω to mix up, knead.

φύρω to mix, mix up, mingle, knead; to confound; to wet.

φῦσα, ἡ pair of bellows.

φῡσάω to blow, puff, snort; to puff up, blow up, make swell. [pipe.

φῡσητήρ, ῆρος, ὁ blow-

φῡσιάω = φυσάω.

φῡσί-ζοος 2 life-giving.

φῡσικός 3 belonging to nature; produced by nature, natural, inborn.

φῡσιόω = φυσιάω.

φῦσις, ἡ birth, origin; nature, inborn quality, natural parts; temper, disposition; stature; sex; natural order; creative power; the universe; creature.

φῡσίωσις, ἡ vanity, pride.

φῡταλίη, ἡ orchard, vineyard.

φῡτάλμιος 2 producing; from one's birth.

φῡτείᾱ, ἡ plantation; plant.

φύτευμα, τό = φυτόν.

φύτευσις, ἡ a planting.

φῠτεύω to plant; to beget; to produce.

φῠτόν, τό plant, tree; creature; child. [father.

φῠτο-σπόρος, ὁ begetter,

φυτουργός 2 begetting.

φύω to produce, beget, bring forth, make to grow; to get, gain. — *intr.* and *P.* to grow, spring up, come into being, be born or produced; to be by nature; to fall to one by nature.

φώκη, ἡ seal, sea-dog.

φωλεός, ὁ hole, den.

φων-ασκέω to practise one's voice. [the voice.

φων-ασκία, ἡ practise of

φωνέω to speak loud, raise one's voice, sound, cry, call, speak, pronounce; to address; to invite, bid.

φωνή, ἡ voice, sound, tone, cry, speech, language, dialect, word. [speech.

φωνήεις 3 gifted with

φώνημα, τό = φωνή.

φώρ, φωρός, ὁ thief.

φωράω to detect a thief, trace, discover.

φωριαμός, ἡ chest, trunk.

φώς, φωτός, ὁ man; husband; hero.

φῶς, φωτός, τό = φάος.

φωστήρ, ῆρος, ὁ luminary, star; splendour.

φως-φόρος 2 bringing light; morning-star.

φωτεινός 3 bright, lighted.

φωτίζω to give light, bring to light. [ing.

φωτισμός, ὁ an enlighten-

X

X, χ (χῖ) twenty-second letter of the alphabet; as a numeral χ' = 600.

χάζω to cause to retire from; to bereave. — *M.* to give way, retire, retreat (from), desist.

χαίνω to yawn, gape; to gasp for; to utter.

χαίρω to rejoice, be glad, delighted, or pleased; to like, be wont, delight in. χαῖρε, χαίρετε hail! welcome! farewell! χαίρειν ἐᾶν to bid farewell or welcome; to set at nought.

χαίτη, ἡ long hair; mane.

χάλαζα, ἡ hail.

χᾱλ-αργός 2 swift-footed.

χαλαρός 3 slackened, languid.

χαλάω to loosen, slacken, unstring, let fall, let loose, let go, give up; to leave off, cease; to become slack; to gape; to give way, yield; to come to rest.

χαλεπαίνω to be hard, bad, severe, harsh, grievous, angry, or embittered. — *P.* to be treated severely.

χαλεπός 3 hard, severe, grievous, difficult, troublesome, dangerous; rough, rugged, disagreeable; bitter, harsh, cruel, angry, morose. — *adv.* χαλεπῶς with difficulty, hardly, scarcely; severely, harshly, angrily; ill.

χαλεπότης, ητος, ἡ difficulty, trouble; hardship, severity, harshness.

χαλέπτω to oppress.

χαλῑν-αγωγέω to curb, restrain.

χαλῑνός, ὁ bridle, rein.

χαλῑνόω to bridle (a horse).

χάλιξ, ικος, ὁ, ἡ gravel; mortar, cement.

χαλι-φρονέω to be silly.

χαλι-φροσύνη, ἡ thoughtlessness. [silly.]

χαλί-φρων 2 thoughtless,]

χάλκ-ασπις, ιδος with brazen shield.

χαλκεία, ἡ art of a smith.

χαλκεῖον, τό forge, smithy; copper vessel.

χάλκειος 3, **χάλκεος** 3, **χαλκοῦς** 3 of copper or bronze, brazen.

χαλκεό-φωνος 2 with a voice of brass. [smith.]

χαλκεύς, ὁ smith; gold-]

χαλκευτικός 3 skilled in smithing. [smith.]

χαλκεύω to forge, be a]

χαλκεών, ῶνος, ὁ smithy.

χαλκηδών, όνος, ὁ calcedony. [headed with brass.]

χαλκ-ήρης 3 covered or]

χαλκί-οικος 2 with a brazen temple.

χαλκίον, τό copper vessel.

χαλκίς, ιδος, ἡ nighthawk. [brass.]

χαλκο-βαρής 2 heavy with]

χαλκο-βατής 2 with brazen base.

χαλκο-βόης 2 with a voice of brass.

χαλκο-γλώχῖν, ῖνος with points of brass.

χαλκό-δετος 2 brass-bound.

χαλκο-θώρᾱξ, ᾱκος with a brazen breastplate.

χαλκο-κνήμῑς, ῑδος with greaves of brass.

χαλκο-κορυστής, οῦ armed with brass.   [gold.]

χαλκο-λίβανον, τό half-

χαλκο-πάρηος 2 with cheeks of brass.

χαλκο-πλευρος 2 with sides of brass. [of brass.]

χαλκό-πληκτος 2 forged]

χαλκό-πους brazen-footed.

χαλκό-πυλος 2 with gates of brass.

χαλκός, ὁ copper; bronze; brass; brazen vessel; copper coin; brazen arms.

χαλκό-στομος 2 with brazen mouth.   [smith.]

χαλκο-τύπος, ὁ copper-

χαλκο-χίτων, ωνος brazen-coated.

χάλκωμα, τό brazen vessel.

χάλυψ, υβος, ὁ steel.

χαμάδις, χαμᾶζε adv. to the ground.

χαμᾶθεν adv. from the ground.   [or earth.]

χαμαί adv. on the ground]

χαμαι-εύνας, άδος, χαμαι-εύνης, ου sleeping on the ground.   [footstool.]

χαμαί-ζηλος 2 low; ὁ]

χαμαι-κοίτης, ου = χαμαι-εύνης.   [χαμᾶθεν.]

χαμαῖθεν, χαμόθεν =]

χάμψαι, οἱ crocodiles.

χανδάνω to hold, contain.

χανδόν adv. greedily.

χάος, ους, τό chaos.

χαρά, ἡ joy, delight, pleasure; darling.

χάραγμα, τό bite; mark, stamp, character.

χαράδρᾱ, ἡ rent, cleft, ravine, gully; bed of a mountain-stream; torrent.

χαραδριός, ὁ plover.

χαραδρόω to tear up into clefts.

χαρακτήρ, ῆρος, ὁ stamp, mark; characteristic trait, character; token.

χαράκωμα, τό palisaded fort, wall.

χάραξ, ακος, ὁ, ἡ pointed stake, pole; pale; palisade, fortified camp.

χαράσσω to point, sharpen; to scratch; to notch; to exasperate, irritate.

χαρίεις 3 graceful, lovely, charming, pleasing, pretty; elegant, accomplished, refined, witty; welcome, dear.

χαριεντίζομαι M. to jest.

χαρίζομαι M. to show favour or kindness; to gratify, indulge; to offer willingly, give freely; to offer; to abandon; to pardon; to be pleasing, agreeable, or acceptable.

χάρις, ιτος, ἡ joy, pleasure; grace, loveliness; favour, kindness, goodwill; boon; gratitude, thanks; respect; the being beloved. — χάριν τινός in favour of, for the sake of.

χάρισμα, τό gift of grace, free gift.

χαριτόω to show favour.

χάρμα, τό, χαρμονή, ἡ = χαρά. [bat; battle.

χάρμη, ἡ desire for com-

χαρμόσυνος 3 joyful.

χαρ-οπός 3 glad-eyed; bright-eyed.

χάρτης, ου, ὁ leaf of paper.

χαρτός 3 delightful.

χάσκω to yawn, gape.

χάσμα, τό cleft, chasm.

χασμάομαι M. to gape wide, to stand gaping.

χατέω, χατίζω to want; to desire, long, wish.

χαυλι-όδων, οντος, ὁ with projecting teeth.

χειά, ἡ hole. [rim.

χεῖλος, τό lip; edge, brim,

χεῖμα, τό = χειμών.

χειμάδιον, τό = χειμασία.

χειμάζω, χειμαίνω trans. to expose to a storm or to the winter; to trouble, af- flict; intr. to be stormy; to pass the winter. — P. to suffer from a storm.

χειμά-ρροος, -ρρους 2 swollen in winter; torrent, mountain-stream. [ters.

χειμασία, ἡ winter-quar-

χειμερίζω = χειμάζω.

χειμερινός 3, χειμέριος 2 and 3 wintry; stormy.

χειμών, ῶνος, ὁ winter; frost, cold; storm, tempest; distress, suffering.

χείρ, χειρός, ἡ hand, fist; arm; side; close fight; present time; nearness; deed, bravery, might, pow-

er, violence; handwriting; grappling-hook; body of men, band.

χειρ-αγωγέω to lead by the hand. [the hand.

χειρ-αγωγός 2 leading by

χειρ-απτάζω to handle.

χειρῐδωτός 2 sleeved.

χείριος 3 in the power of one.

χειρίς, ῐδος, ἡ glove, sleeve; money-bag.

χείριστος 3 see χέρης.

χειρό-γραφον, τό a hand- writing, bond.

χειρο-δάϊκτος 2 mangled by the hand.

χειρό-δεικτος 2 pointed out by the hand, manifest.

χειρο-ήθης 2 accustomed to the hand, manageable.

χειρό-μακτρον, τό towel, napkin.

χειρο-νομέω to gesticulate.

χειρόομαι M. to master, subdue. — P. to be sub- dued. [as a hand.

χειρο-πληθής 2 as large

χειρο-ποιέομαι M. to do with one's own hands.

χειρο-ποίητος 2 made by hand.

χειρότερος 3 = χείρων.

χειρο-τέχνης, ου artisan, mechanic; artist.

χειρο-τονέω to stretch one's hand; to give one's vote, to vote for, elect.

χειρο-τονία, ἡ a voting by show of hands, election.

χειρουργέω to do with the hands, execute.

χειρούργημα, τό, χειρουργίᾱ, ἡ manual labour; craft. [subduing.]

χείρωμα, τό a mastering,

χείρων see χέρης.

χειρῶναξ, ακτος, ὁ artisan, mechanic.

χειρωναξίᾱ, ἡ handicraft.

χελῑδών, όνος, ἡ swallow.

χελώνη, ἡ tortoise; penthouse.

χέραδος, τό gravel, shingle.

χερειότερος 3, χερείων 2 = χείρων (χέρης).

χέρης, ηος, ειος mean, little; weak; bad. — comp.

χείρων 2 less, weaker, worse, inferior. — sup.

χείριστος 3 worst, lowest.

χερμάδιον, τό field-stone.

χερνῆτις, ιδος, ἡ workwoman. [basin.]

χέρνιβον, τό wash(ing)-

χερνίπτομαι M. to wash one's hands; to sprinkle with holy water.

χέρ-νιψ, ιβος, ἡ water for washing; holy water.

χερο - πληκτος 2 struck with the hand.

χερρό - νησος, χερσό - νησος, ἡ peninsula.

χερσαῖος 3 living on dry land. [insular.]

χερσονησο-ειδής 2 pen-

χέρσος 2 dry; firm; barren, destitute; ἡ χ. mainland, continent.

χεῦμα, τό what is poured; vessel for pouring.

χέω to pour, pour out, shed; to cause to rain or snow; to throw up (earth); to scatter, shower; to let

fall. — P. to be poured out or thrown up, stream forth, to be spread around. — M. to pour for oneself.

χηλευτός 3 plaited.

χηλή, ἡ hoof, talon, claw; break-water.

χηλός, ἡ chest, box.

χήν, χηνός, ὁ, ἡ goose.

χην-αλώπηξ, εκος, ὁ foxgoose.

χήνεος 3 of a goose.

χήρᾱ, ἡ widow.

χηραμός, ὁ cleft, hole.

χηρεύω to be destitute, bereft, or widowed.

χῆρος 3 destitute, bereft; widowed.

χηρόω to make destitute or desolate; to unpeople; to bereave of a husband; to

χηρωστής, οῦ, ὁ collateral relation.

χήτει adv. (dat. of χῆτος) from want or need of.

χθαμαλός 3 low, on the ground. [day.]

χθές (ἐχθές) adv. yester-

χθιζός 3 of yesterday.

χθόνιος 3 and 2 earthly; native, indigene; of the nether world. [the earth.]

χθονο-στιβής 2 treading

χθών, χθονός, ἡ soil, ground, earth; country.

χιλί - αρχος, χιλί - άρχης, ου, ὁ commander of a thousand men.

χῑλιάς, άδος, ἡ the number one thousand.

χῑλι-ετής 2 a thousand years old.

χῑλιοι 3 a thousand.

χῑλιοστός 3 thousandth.

χῑλός, ὁ grass, green fodder; pasture.

χῑλόω to feed with grass.

χίμαιρα, ἡ she-goat.

χιονίζω to snow upon.

χιονό-κτυπος 2 beaten by snow.

χιτών, ῶνος, ὁ under-garment, frock, tunic; coat of mail, coat, jerkin.

χιτωνίσκος, ὁ short coat.

χιών, όνος, ἡ snow.

χλαῖνα, ἡ mantle, cloak; carpet. [ing of cloaks.]

χλαμυδουργία, ἡ the mak-

χλαμύς, ύδος, ἡ upper garment, cloak; military cloak.

χλανίδιον, τό small cloak.

χλανιδο-ποιΐα, ἡ the making of fine upper garments.

χλανίς, ίδος, ἡ state-garment. [to mock.]

χλευάζω to joke, jest;

χλευασμός, ὁ mockery, scoffing.

χλῑαρός 3 lukewarm.

χλιδάω to pride oneself; to be luxurious.

χλιδή, ἡ delicacy, luxury; finery, beauty; wantonness.

χλόη, ἡ young verdure; tender shoot.

χλούνης, ου, ὁ wild boar.

χλωρηΐς, ίδος pale green.

χλωρός 3 light green, yellow; pale; green, fresh, vigorous. [grey beard.]

χνοάζω to get a downy or

χνόη, ἡ box of a wheel; axle.

χνόος, ὁ foam, crust.

χόανος, ὁ crucible.

χοή, ἡ a pouring; libation.

χοϊκός 3 of earth or clay.

χοῖνιξ, ικος, ἡ a corn-measure; daily bread; fetter, shackle.

χοιράς, άδος, ἡ rock, cliff.

χοίρειος 3, χοίρεος 3 of swine.

χοῖρος, ὁ pig, swine.

χολάδες, ων, αἱ bowels.

χολάω to be bilious or angry. [wrath.]

χολή, ἡ, χόλος, ὁ gall, bile;

χολόω to make angry. — P. and M. to become angry.

χολωτός 3 angry.

χόνδρος, ὁ grain, corn, morsel.

χορδή, ἡ gut; chord, string.

χορευτής, οῦ, ὁ choral dancer.

χορεύω and M to form a chorus; to dance in a chorus; to dance; to celebrate with a choral dance.

χορ-ηγέω to lead a chorus; to pay the expenses for a chorus.

χορ-ηγία, ἡ office of a χορηγός; equipment; means, wealth.

χορ-ηγός, ὁ leader of a chorus; one who defrays the costs for bringing out a chorus. [chorus.]

χορο-ποιός 2 arranging a

χορός, ὁ dancing-place; dance in a ring, choral dance; chorus, choir.

χορτάζω to feed, fatten.

χόρτασμα, τό food, fodder.

χόρτος, ὁ fence, enclosure, cattle-farm; pasture; fodder, food.

χοῦς, *gen.* χοός, ὁ rubbish, sand; a liquid measure.

χόω to throw up, heap up (earth); dam up, fill up.

χραίνω to besmear, soil, pollute.

χραισμέω to help, aid; to defend. [to befal.]

χραύω to scratch, wound;]

χράω[1] to desire, demand.

χράω[2] to lend, supply (*M.* to borrow); to give oracle, pronounce. — *P.* to be pronounced as an oracle. — *M.* to consult an oracle.

χράομαι *M.* to want, long for; to use; to be possessed of; to have dealings with, converse with; to treat, practise.

χρείᾱ, ἡ use, advantage; intercourse; service, business, office; need, necessity; want, poverty; desire.

χρεῖος, τό = χρέος.

χρεμετίζω to neigh.

χρέος, τό = χρεία; debt; amends, damages; trespass; the due. [want, need.]

χρεώ, οῦς, ἡ necessity;]

χρέως, τό = χρέος.

χρεωφειλέτης, ου, ὁ debtor.

χρή it is necessary, it must, it is right or proper; it is fated; there is need.

χρῄζω to want, need; to desire, wish, long for; to prophesy.

χρῄσκομαι = χράομαι.

χρῆμα, τό a thing, matter, business; piece, copy; fact; enterprise; amount, money. *pl.* goods, money, power.

χρηματίζω to do business; to transact state business; to negotiate, debate, consult, answer; to bear a name or title. — *M.* to negotiate; to make money, transact business.

χρηματισμός, ὁ transaction of business; divine answer; a doing business; money-making, gain.

χρηματιστής, οῦ, ὁ tradesman, man of business.

χρηματιστικός 3 fitted for money-making; portending gain.

χρήσιμος 3 and 2 useful, serviceable, profitable; honest; made use of.

χρῆσις, ἡ = χρεία.

χρησμο-λόγος 2 giving or interpreting oracles.

χρησμός, ὁ oracular response. [phesying; want.]

χρησμοσύνη, ἡ art of pro-]

χρησμ-ῳδέω to prophesy.

χρησμ-ῳδίᾱ, ἡ prophecy.

χρησμ-ῳδός 2 prophesying.

χρηστεύομαι *M.* to be kind.

χρηστηριάζομαι *M.* to consult an oracle.

χρηστήριος 3 prophetic; τό χρηστήριον oracle; victim, sacrifice.

χρηστο-λογίᾱ, ἡ flowery or dissembling speech.

χρηστός 3 useful, serviceable, beneficial; honest, righteous, good, brave; kind.

χρηστότης, ητος, ἡ honesty, goodness.

χρῖμα, τό unguent.

χρίμπτω to touch the surface, to scratch. — *P.* to come near.

χρῖσμα, τό = χρῖμα.

χρῑστός 3 anointed.

χρίω to besmear, anoint, colour; to sting, prick.

χρόα, χροιά, ἡ = χρώς.

χρόμαδος, ὁ a gnashing.

χρονίζω to spend time; to tarry.

χρόνιος 3 and 2 for a long time, lasting long; after a long time, late.

χρόνος, ὁ time, duration; period; term.

χρονο-τριβέω = χρονίζω.

χρῡσ-άμπυξ, υχος with a golden frontlet.

χρῡσ-άορος 2 with a golden sword. [ing.]

χρῡσ-αυγής 2 gold-gleam-]

χρύσεια, τά gold mine.

χρύσεος, χρυσοῦς 3 golden, gilt; gold-coloured; precious; blessed, lovely.

χρῡσ-ηλάκατος 2 with a golden arrow or spindle.

χρῡσ-ήλατος 2 beaten out of gold. [gold.]

χρῡσ-ήνιος with reins of]

χρύσιον, τό = χρυσός.

χρῡσῖτις, ιδος auriferous.

χρῡσο-δακτύλιος 2 with gold rings. [gold.]

χρῡσό-δετος 2 bound with]

χρῡσο-ειδής 2 like gold.

χρῡσό-θρονος 2 on a throne of gold.

χρῡσό-κομος 2 golden-haired.

χρῡσό-λιθος, ὁ topaz.

χρῡσο-μίτρης, ου with a head-band of gold.

χρῡσό-παστος 2 embroidered with gold.

χρῡσο-πέδῑλος 2 with sandals of gold. [prase.]

χρῡσό-πρασος, ὁ chryso-]

χρῡσό-πτερος 2 with wings of gold. [a golden staff.]

χρῡσό-ρραπις, ιδος with]

χρῡσό-ρρυτος 2 flowing with gold.

χρῡσός, ὁ gold; gold vessel; gold coin. [with gold.]

χρῡσό-στροφος 2 twisted]

χρῡσο-φορέω to wear gold.

χρῡσο-φόρος 2 wearing gold. [ing gold.]

χρῡσο-φύλαξ, αχος watch-]

χρῡσο-χάλῑνος 2 with a golden bridle.

χρῡσο-χόος, ὁ goldsmith.

χρῡσόω to gild. [stain.]

χρώζω to touch; besmear,]

χρῶμα, τό colour; complexion; embellishment; paint. [flesh; complexion.]

χρώς, χρωτός, ὁ skin; body;]

χύσις, ἡ a pouring; heap.

χυτλόομαι *M.* to bathe and anoint oneself.

χυτός 3 poured out; heaped up; melted.

χύτρα, ἡ. χυτρίς, ιδος, ἡ, χύτρος, ὁ pot, jug.

χωλεύω to be lame, to halt.

χωλός 3 lame, halting; maimed. [tomb.]

χῶμα, τό mound; dam;]

χώννῡμι = χόω.

χώομαι *M.* to be wroth or angry.

χώρα, ἡ space, room, place; dwelling-place; locality; station, post-station; district, region, territory, country, land; field, farm, estate.

χωρέω to give way, withdraw, retire; to go forward, start, come, go; to succeed; to hold, contain, have room for.

χωρίζω to part; to sever, separate. — *P.* to be divided; to be at variance; to go away.

χωρίον, τό = χώρα.

χωρίς *adv.* and *prp.* with *gen.* separately, asunder, apart, alone; differently, otherwise; except; far from, without.

χωρισμός, ἡ separation.

χωρίτης, ου, ὁ countryman, peasant.

χωριτικός 3 rustic, boorish.

χῶρος¹, ὁ = χώρα.

χῶρος², ὁ north-east wind.

χῶσις, ἡ a heaping up, raising a mound.

Ψ

Ψ, ψ (ψῖ) twenty-third letter of the alphabet; as a numeral ψ´ = 700.

φακάς, άδος, ἡ drizzling rain.

φάλλω to pull, pluck; to play the lyre with the fingers; to sing, praise.

φαλμός, ὁ a playing on the lyre; song, psalm.

φαλτήριον, τό stringed instrument.

φάλτρια, ἡ lute-player.

φάμμινος 3 sandy.

φάμμος, ἡ sand; heap of sand; down, strand.

φαμμώδης 2 sandy.

φάρ, φαρός, ὁ starling.

φαύω to touch; to affect.

φάω to rub, crumble.

φέγω to blame.

φεδνός 3 thin, spare; bald.

φεκάς, άδος, ἡ = φακάς.

φέλιον, τό bracelet; ring.

φελιο-φόρος 2 wearing bracelets.

φελλίζομαι *M.* to stammer.

φευδ-άγγελος, ὁ false messenger. [brother.]

φευδ-άδελφος, ὁ false]

φευδ-απόστολος, ὁ false apostle. [bush.]

φευδ-ενέδρα, ἡ sham am-]

φευδής 2 lying, false; fictitious, sham.

φευδο-διδάσκαλος, ὁ false teacher. [herald.]

φευδο-κῆρυξ, ῦκος, ὁ false]

φευδο-λόγος 2 lying.

φευδό-μαντις, ὁ, ἡ lying prophet(ess).

φευδο-μαρτυρέω to bear false witness.

φευδο-μαρτυρίᾱ, ἡ false witness. [ing witness.]

φευδό-μαρτυς, υρος, ὁ ly-]

φευδο-πάρθενος, ἡ pretended maid.

φευδο-προφήτης, ου, ὁ false prophet.

φευδ-όρκιος 2 perjured.

φεῦδος, τό lie, falsehood, untruth.

φευδο-στομέω to tell lies.

φευδό-φημος 2 telling lies.

φευδό-χρῑστος, ὁ a false Christ.

φεύδω to represent as a lie; to give one the lie; to cheat, defraud. — *P.* to be cheated or deceived; to be false. — *M.* to lie, cheat, feign; to belie, falsify.

φευδ-ώνυμος 2 falsely named.

φεῦσμα, τό = ψεῦδος.

φευστέω to lie.

φεύστης, ου, ὁ liar, cheat.

φήγμα, τό gold-dust.

φηλ-αφάω to grope one's way; to feel, touch.

φήν, φηνός, ὁ gall-insect.

φήρ = φάρ. [to vote.]

φηφῐδο-φόρος 2 entitled

φηφίζω to count, reckon; to put to the vote; to decide. — *M.* to give one's vote with a pebble; to vote for, resolve, decide; to adjudge.

φηφίς, ῖδος, ἡ pebble.

φήφισμα, τό vote, decree; proposition. [votes.]

φηφο-ποιός 2 falsifying

φῆφος, ἡ small stone, pebble; counting-stone; counter; accounts; voting-stone; vote; resolution, decree, election; sentence.

φήχω to rub down; to curry.

φιάς, άδος, ἡ drop.

φιθυρίζω to whisper, mutter. [ing, slander.]

φιθυρισμός, ὁ a whisper-

φιθυριστής, οῦ, ὁ whisperer, slanderer.

φιθυρός 3 whispering.

φῑλός 3 bare, naked; bald; stript of; treeless; uncovered, unarmed; without heavy armour; simple, plain; οἱ φιλοί light troops.

φῑλόω to make bare or bald; to strip of, deprive (of).

φιμύθιον, τό, φίμυθος, ὁ white lead.

φιμυθιόω to paint with white lead.

φιχίον, τό crumb, morsel.

φόγος, ὁ blame, reproach.

φολόεις 3 smoky, sooty.

φοφέω to make a noise; to ring.

φόφος, ὁ noise, sound; idle talk.

φῦθος, τό = ψεῦδος.

φῡχ-αγωγέω to lead souls to the nether world; to lead, win, or entertain souls.

φῡχεινός 3 = ψυχρός.

φῡχή, ἡ breath, spirit; life; living being, person; soul of man, heart, spirit; desire, appetite; courage; departed soul, ghost.

φυχικός 3 living, mental; animal, natural.

φῦχος, τό cold, frost; winter.

φῦχρός 3 cool, cold, chill; unfeeling, heartless; spiritless; vain, fruitless; unreal; frigid.

φῡχρότης, ητος, ἡ coldness.

φύχω to breathe, blow; to cool, refresh.

φωμίζω to eat; to feed.

φωμίον, τό, φωμός, ὁ bit, morsel.

φώρᾱ, ἡ itch, scab.

φώχω to rub (to powder).

Ω

Ω, ω (ὦ μέγα) twenty-fourth letter of the alphabet; **as a** numeral ω' = 800.

ὦ, ὤ o! ah!

ὧδε *adv.* thus, so, in this wise; so very; so much; hither; here.

ᾠδεῖον, τό house of songs.

ᾠδή, ἡ song, lay, poem.

ᾠδί = ὧδε.

ὠδίν or **ὠδίς,** ῖνος, ἡ pains of child-birth, labour-pains; birth.

ὠδίνω to be in labour or travail; to be in pains, to suffer; to toil, work painfully.

ᾠδός, ὁ = ἀοιδός.

ὠθέω, ὠθίζω to thrust, push, force away; to thrust back or into, to push on. — *M.* to hurry on; to push from oneself. — *P.* to struggle, be in dispute.

ὠθισμός, ὁ a thrusting, pushing, struggling; battle.

ὦκα *adv.* of ὠκύς.

ὠκεανός, ὁ ocean.

ὠκύ-αλος 2 sailing fast.

ὠκυ-βόλος 2 quick-hitting.

ὠκύ-μορος 2 dying early; bringing early death.

ὠκυ-πέτης, ου swift-flying.

ὠκύ-πορος 2 swift-passing.

ὠκύ-πους, ποδος swift-footed.

ὠκύ-πτερος 2 swift-winged.

ὠκύ-ρ(ρ)οος 2 swift-flowing.

ὠκύς 3 swift, quick.

ὠκυ-τόκος 2 causing quick birth, fertilizing.

ὠλένη, ἡ elbow, lower arm.

ὠλεσί-καρπος 2 losing its fruit.

ὦλλος = ὁ ἄλλος.

ὦλξ, ὠλκός, ἡ furrow.

ὠμ-ηστής, οῦ eating raw flesh; savage, brutal.

ὠμο-βόειος, -βόεος, -βόϊνος 3 of raw oxhide.

ὠμο-γέρων, οντος, ὁ fresh old man. [pieces of flesh.]

ὠμο-θετέω to put on raw)

ὠμό-θυμος 2 brutal.

ὤμοι woe is me.

ὠμο-κρατής 2 strong-shouldered. [arm.]

ὦμος, ὁ shoulder, upper)

ὠμός 3 raw, undressed, unripe; rude, cruel, brutal, savage.

ὠμότης, ητος, ἡ rawness; cruelty. [flesh.]

ὠμο-φάγος 2 eating raw)

ὠμό-φρων 2 savage-minded.

ὦν = οὖν.

ὦνα = ὦ ἄνα(ξ).

ὠνέομαι *M.* to buy, purchase; to farm; to offer to buy.

ὠνή, ἡ = ὦνος.

ὠνητός 3 bought, hired; to be bought.

ὤνιος 2 and 3 to be bought, for sale; τὰ ὤνια market-wares.

ὦνος, ὁ a buying, purchase, barter; price.

ᾠόν, τό egg.

ὧρ, ἡ = ὄαρ.

ὥρα, ἡ care, concern, regard.

ὥρα, ἡ limited time or period; season; spring and summer; fruit(s), produce; climate, weather; year; time of day; hour; moment; prime of life, youth; right time.

ὡραῖος 3, ὥριος 3 suitable to the season, ripe; youthful, blooming, mature; ἡ ὡραία season for gathering fruit(s); τὰ ὡραῖα fruit(s) of the season.

ὠρύομαι M. to howl, low, roar, shout.

ὥς, ὧς adv. thus, so, in this way: καὶ ὥς nevertheless; οὐδ' ὥς not even so; in this case; for instance; therefore.

ὡς[1] adv. as, just as; with sup. as...possible; with part. by reason of, for the sake of. — conj. = ὅτι; = ὥστε; = ὅπως; = ὅτε; = ἐπειδή.

ὡς[2] prp. with acc. = πρός.

ὡσαννά hosanna (save now!). [the same manner.]

ὡσαύτως adv. just so, in

ὡσεί adv. as if, as though; just as; about.

ὥσπερ adv. even as, just as; as soon as; for instance.

ὥστε adv. as, like, as, just as. — conj. therefore, so that, so as, on condition that.

ὠτακουστέω to listen anxiously.

ὠτάριον, τό, ὠτίον, τό ear.

ὠτειλή, ἡ wound; sear.

ὠτίς, ίδος, ἡ bustard.

ὠτώεις 3 with ears or handles.

ὠφέλεια, ἡ help, assistance; profit, advantage.

ὠφελέω to help, aid, assist, benefit. — P. to be helped, derive profit.

ὠφέλημα, τό = ὠφέλεια.

ὠφελήσιμος 2 = ὠφέλιμος.

ὠφέλησις, ὠφελίᾱ, ἡ = ὠφέλεια.

ὠφέλιμος 2 useful, serviceable, profitable.

ὠχράω to turn pale.

ὠχρός 3 pale.

ὦχρος, ὁ paleness.

ὤψ, ὠπός, ἡ eye; face; countenance.